Lecture Notes in Computer Science 13557

More information about this series at https://link.springer.com/bookseries/558

Jesica de Armas · Helena Ramalhinho ·
Stefan Voß (Eds.)

Computational Logistics

13th International Conference, ICCL 2022
Barcelona, Spain, September 21–23, 2022
Proceedings

Springer

Editors
Jesica de Armas
Universitat Pompeu Fabra
Barcelona, Spain

Helena Ramalhinho
Universitat Pompeu Fabra
Barcelona, Spain

Stefan Voß
Universität Hamburg
Hamburg, Germany

ISSN 0302-9743 ISSN 1611-3349 (electronic)
Lecture Notes in Computer Science
ISBN 978-3-031-16578-8 ISBN 978-3-031-16579-5 (eBook)
https://doi.org/10.1007/978-3-031-16579-5

This Springer imprint is published by the registered company Springer Nature Switzerland AG
The registered company address is: Gewerbestrasse 11, 6330 Cham, Switzerland

Preface

The increasing availability of information, together with current complex logistics operations have led to the need of better optimization proposals. Recently, important efforts and initiatives from all sides of optimization have been undertaken to improve logistics operations with sophisticated algorithms and information systems. This resulted in advances in several logistics sectors, such as maritime shipping, urban logistics, warehousing, production and supply chain management. Computational logistics, as the driver between decision making and operations, has become a key component for economic and industrial growth.

Computational logistics covers the management of logistic activities and tasks by the combined use of computational technologies, advanced decision support and optimization techniques. It is applied in several areas such as the flow and storage of goods and services, as well as the flow of related information. In this context, modeling and algorithmic approaches are developed, verified, and applied for planning and execution complex logistics tasks, including identification of the most efficient routing plans and schedules to transport passengers or distribute goods. The models and algorithms are integrated with computing technologies, not only for getting satisfactory results in reasonable times, but also exploiting interactivity with the decision maker through visual interfaces, and for extracting knowledge from data to improve future decision making. This promotes the joint effort of practitioners and scholars for better understanding and solving the logistics problems at hand.

The International Conference on Computational Logistics (ICCL) is a forum where recent advances in the computational logistics research area are presented and discussed. This volume offers a selection of 32 peer-reviewed papers out of 64 contributions submitted to the 13th ICCL edition, held at the University Pompeu Fabra, Barcelona, Spain, during September 21–23, 2022. The papers show various directions of importance in computational logistics, classified into five topic areas reflecting the interest of researchers and practitioners in this field. The papers in this volume are grouped according to the following parts:

1. **Maritime and Port Logistics**
   Maritime and port logistics are the backbone of global supply chains and international trade. The performance and functioning of its related activities are remarkably influenced by the quality of its planning and management. In ICCL 2022, the contributions that fall into this category relate to, among others, berth allocation, bulk logistics, crane scheduling, and various real-world maritime applications.
2. **Vehicle Routing and Urban Logistics**
   Vehicle Routing is a well-known family of optimization problems that constitutes an important part of real-world transport and logistics activities. Due to the many specific real-world features, there is a strong necessity of modeling and developing efficient solution approaches that permit advancements in this area. Additionally, the progress in urban transport as well as the development of cities and other

regions require current systems to be adapted and updated to cope with changes that involve new transportation means, such as drones, integrated planning, and intermodal transport. The papers in this category relate to a diverse range of topics, such as waste collection, school bus routing, green routing, drone-assisted delivery, long-haul transportation, and last mile delivery, among others.

3. **Warehousing and Location**
   Warehousing is an important piece of the supply chain and logistics puzzle. Warehousing and inventory storage affect everything from sourcing raw materials and, efficiently managing inventory, to getting orders delivered to customers on time. Though the principles of warehousing have not changed much over the years, warehousing solutions have evolved. In the same vein, the location of warehouses impact on all other logistics operations. Contributions considering cross-docking, block stacking, palletizing, warehouse layouts, energy savings and facility location fall into this category.
4. **Supply Chain and Production Management**
   The management of supply chains and production covers different relevant logistics operations. The works included in this category pursue the efficient organization and management of the diverse resources and operations involved. Thus, the papers that appear in this category relate to a range of topics concerning distribution, workforce management, lot sizing, production scheduling, risk tolerance, freight costs, information sharing and collaboration, and other supply chain-related topics.

The ICCL 2022 was the 13th edition of this conference series, following the earlier ones held in Shanghai, China (2010, 2012), Hamburg, Germany (2011), Copenhagen Denmark (2013), Valparaiso, Chile (2014), Delft, The Netherlands (2015), Lisbon, Portugal (2016), Southampton, UK (2017), Salerno, Italy (2018), Barranquilla, Colombia (2019) and Enschede, The Netherlands (2020, 2021). The editors thank all the authors for their contributions as well as the program committee and reviewers for their invaluable support and feedback. We trust that the present volume supports the continued advances within computational logistics and inspires all participants and readers to its fullest extent.

November 2022

Jesica de Armas
Helena Ramalhinho
Stefan Voß

Organization

Program Committee

Tolga Bektas	University of Liverpool, UK
Francesco Carrabs	University of Salerno, Italy
Raffaele Cerulli	University of Salerno, Italy
Alysson M. Costa	University of Melbourne, Australia
Joachim R. Daduna	Berlin School of Economics and Law, Germany
Adriana Daza	Universidad del Norte, Colombia
Jesica de Armas (Chair)	Universitat Pompeu Fabra, Spain
René De Koster	Erasmus University Rotterdam, Germany
Elena Fernández	Universitat Politècnica de Catalunya, Spain
Jian Gang Jin	Shanghai Jiao Tong University, China
Maria Isabel Gomes	Universidade Nova de Lisboa, Portugal
Rosa Gonzalez Ramirez	Universidad de Los Andes, Chile
Hans-Dietrich Haasis	University of Bremen, Germany
Alessandro Hill	California Polytechnic State University, USA
Patrick Hirsch	BOKU, Vienna
Raka Jovanovic	Qatar Environment and Energy Research Institute, Qatar
Ioannis Lagoudis	University of Piraeus, Greece
Manuel Laguna	University of Colorado Boulder, USA
Eduardo Lalla-Ruiz	University of Twente, The Netherlands
Janny Leung	University of Macau, China
Pedro Martins	Polytechnic Institute of Coimbra, Portugal
Frank Meisel	University of Kiel, Germany
Gonzalo Mejía	Universidad de La Sabana, Colombia
Martijn Mes	University of Twente, The Netherlands
Dario Pacino	Technical University of Denmark, Denmark
Julia Pahl	University of Southern Denmark, Denmark
Luciana Pessoa	PUC-Rio, Brazil
Carlos Quintero	Universidad de La Sabana, Colombia
Markus Rabe	TU Dortmund, Germany
Helena Ramalhinho (Chair)	Universitat Pompeu Fabra, Spain
Rosephine Rakotonirainy	University of Cape Town, South Africa
Daniel Riera	Universitat Oberta de Catalunya, Spain
Jessica Rodriguez-Pereira	Universitat Pompeu Fabra, Spain
Dirk Sackmann	HS Merseburg, Germany
Juan J. Salazar González	Universidad de La Laguna, Spain

Frederik Schulte	Delft University of Technology, The Netherlands
Douglas Smith	University of Missouri - St. Louis, USA
Anand Subramanian	Universidade Federal da Paraíba, Brazil
Shunji Tanaka	Kyoto University, Japan
Kevin Tierney	Bielefeld University, Germany
Stefan Voß (Chair)	University of Hamburg, Germany

Additional Reviewers

Alan Dávila de León
Ping He
Fabio Luiz Usberti
Xiaohuan Lyu
José Eduardo Pécora Jr.
Orivalde Soares da Silva Junior
Xinyu Tang
Bruno Vieira

Contents

Maritime and Port Logistics

Hybrid Berth Allocation for Bulk Ports with Unavailability and Stock Level Constraints

Xiaohuan Lyu(✉) and Frederik Schulte(✉)

Department of Maritime and Transport Technology, Delft University of Technology, Mekelweg 2, 2628 CD Delft, The Netherlands
{X.Lyu-1,F.Schulte}@tudelft.nl

Abstract. Berth allocation is fundamental to port-related operations in maritime shipping. Port managers have to deal with the increasing demands either by expanding the terminals or by improving efficiency to maintain competitiveness. Port expansion is a long-term project, and it requires much capital investment. Thus, the question of how to enhance the efficiency of berth allocation has received much research interest. Research on the Berth Allocation Problem (BAP) in container ports is quite advanced. However, only limited research focuses on BAP in bulk ports, although some similarities exist. Contributing to Operations Research approaches on the BAP, this paper develops a hybrid BAP mixed-integer optimization model dedicated to bulk ports. In addition to considering the handling characteristics of bulk ports, we also incorporate more practical factors such as unavailability and stock levels. The objective of the proposed model is to minimize the demurrage fee for all vessels under consideration of unavailability and stock constraints. We use the commercial software CPLEX to obtain the optimal solutions for a set of distinct instances, explicitly considering the situation of multiple cargo types on one vessel, which provides a better fit for the loading or discharging operations in real-world bulk ports. This is the first study to our knowledge that dedicates itself to the BAP in bulk ports and considers unavailability and stock constraints simultaneously. Our solutions can provide timely and effective decision support to bulk port managers.

Keywords: Berth Allocation Problem · Bulk ports · Unavailability · Stock levels · Optimization · Mixed-integer program

1 Introduction

Over the past decades, the tonnage of bulk cargo carried by sea shipping has increased sharply. Based on [21], in 2020, the international dry bulk trade and tanker trade was 8.085 billion tons, accounting for 75.9% of the world's total

Supported by the scholarship from China Scholarship Council (CSC) under the Grant CSC 202107720039.

J. de Armas et al. (Eds.): ICCL 2022, LNCS 13557, pp. 3–15, 2022.
https://doi.org/10.1007/978-3-031-16579-5_1

cargo load. The ever-growing demand makes efficient loading or discharging of vessels a great challenge, and it has generated many research interests recently. Generally, the Berth Allocation Problem (BAP) is concerned with the optimal decisions on assigning a berthing position and berthing time to the calling vessels. Operation Research (OR) methods and techniques contribute significantly to the BAP in container ports and provide strong managerial support for port managers [23] and [22]. However, research dedicated to BAP in bulk ports has received relatively little attention.

Although the BAPs in bulk ports are similar to those in container ports, some unique characteristics differentiate them. A significant difference is that the bulk vessels can only be allocated to the berthing position where the installed handling equipment can serve the cargo type on the vessel. In other words, berth assignments at bulk ports are more restrictive than container ports. [24] establish innovative models and solution algorithms specifically for BAP in bulk ports, which highlights the specific features of bulk port operations, that is, the cargo type of vessels and the equipped handling facilities of berths. Furthermore, the cargo type restricts the berthing position and influences the service starting and completion time. For instance, specific cargo can be discharged from the vessel only when its storage places can accommodate the corresponding quantity. [2] model stock level constraints but not consider the time-variant property of the stock that is changing with the loading or discharging process. Besides, [10] and [19] stress that the unavailability of berths frequently appears in practice because of extreme weather or maintenance requirements. However, few studies have focused on the BAP model for bulk ports with stock level restrictions, let alone combing it with unavailability considerations.

This paper presents a Mixed-Integer Programming (MIP) model for the hybrid BAP in bulk ports, which explicitly considers the constraint of time-variant stock level and practical unavailability. We use the commercial software CPLEX to obtain solutions for a set of instances, and the results show the effectiveness of the proposed model.

2 Related Work

Operational problems related to BAP have been widely investigated within the context of container ports. For more details, we recommend readers to refer to [3] and [4].

The layout of the terminals is generally categorized as discrete, continuous, and hybrid. As shown in Fig. 1, in the continuous BAP, the calling vessels can berth at any position along the quay line. In the discrete BAP, the quay line is separated into different berths, and the calling vessels can only occupy at most one berth. Obviously, the continuous case can better use the quay, but it also increases calculation complexity. While the hybrid BAP allows the continuous case and the discrete case to happen simultaneously; thus, it is more flexible. In Table 1, we list the related work on BAP in bulk ports. We group them according to four feature categories: objective, type, method, and practical

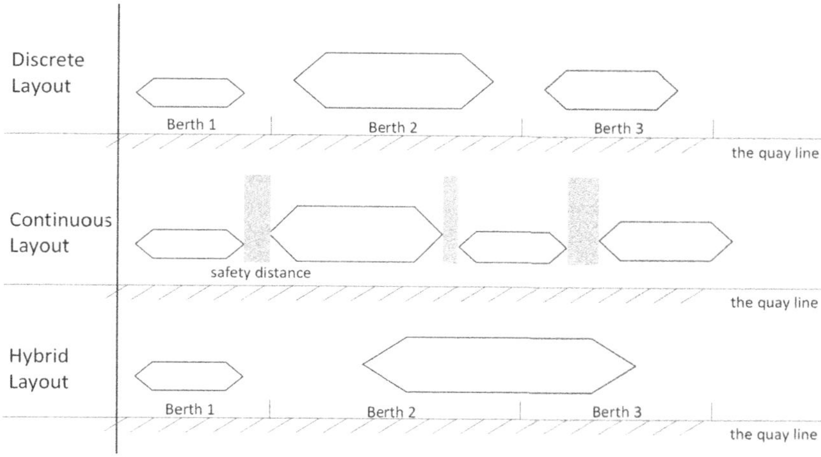

Fig. 1. Three types of the berthing layout.

considerations. Two different main objectives are identified: time-based and cost-based. Type refers to three layouts as illustrated in Fig. 1. The solution method can be divided into heuristics or exact algorithms. The practical considerations include the integrated problem, stock level, night operation permission, specific cargo type, unavailability, and tidal constraints.

Some studies focus on the optimization of individual berth allocation. [25] model and solve the hybrid BAP in bulk ports to minimize the duration time of all vessels. In bulk ports, specialized equipment is required to handle specific types of cargo; for instance, liquid bulk is generally discharged using pipelines installed at only certain sections along the quay. Thus, the BAP model for bulk ports has to incorporate the cargo type on the vessel and the handling equipment fixed on the berths. The authors propose an exact solution based on generalized set partitioning and a heuristic method based on squeaky wheel optimization to obtain near-optimal solutions for the large problem size. Some practical factors that can influence the decision-making process of berth allocation have been considered in the literature. [8] and [6] address the continuous BAP considering the constraints of tides which can influence the departure time of full loaded vessels. Since the stock level of the specific cargo type must be kept in some range for safety consideration, the decision to load or discharge vessels should also consider stock level. [2] propose an integer linear programming model based on discrete BAP, which considers not only tidal effects but also the stock level. A Simulated Annealing-based (SA) algorithm is designed to find reasonable solutions for difficult instances. [9] propose a continuous BAP model with the objective to maximize the daily throughput of the terminal and, at the same time, minimize the delay of ships' departure. In fact, all the studies mentioned above aim to minimize the berthed time of vessels. [19] present a discrete BAP with the objective to minimize the costs (demurrage) incurred. The maintenance of the berth, another practical factor, is also considered in the model, which means that some berths cannot receive vessels at a particular time.

The other operational problems are often interrelated to the decisions of berth allocation; thus, there are some papers studying integrated BAP. [14] and [15] study the integrated problem of berth allocation and handling equipment assignment, but they are focused on container transshipment terminals. [17] address the integrated berth allocation with handling equipment assignment. [18] develop a Decision Support System (DSS) for the port authority to make decisions on berth and ship unloader assignment to minimize the waiting time, operating time, and ships priority deviation. [5] integrate the BAP with yard management by considering constraints of the storage position in berth allocation operation. Real bulk port data is used to validate the model, and the results show that the model can work with up to 40 vessels within reasonable computational time. [20] discuss how to combine the berth and yard assignment to be a single large-scale optimization problem with the objective to minimize the total service time for all vessels berthing at the port. A branch-and-price algorithm is proposed to solve the integrated problems. [12] propose a novel machine learning-based system to coordinate the berthing and yard activities. Based on that, they also insert vessel-specific buffer time to increase the robustness of the results in response to disruption [13]. [26] establish a systematical planning model from berth allocation to yard storage in dry bulk terminals. They also incorporate the tidal time windows in the modal to increase the applicability of the proposed method in real-world terminals. Following the trend of sharing economy, some scholars have seen the potential of collaboration among terminals within one port [16]. [7] consider the continuous BAP and [10] study the discrete BAP for multiple continuous quays in bulk terminals.

3 Model Formulation

This section first describes the berth allocation process in bulk ports and then introduces the relevant notations. Next, it develops a Mixed-Integer Programming (MIP) model and the linearized formulation.

3.1 Problem Description

Figure 2 shows an illustrative example of the process for berth allocation in bulk ports. In this context, we consider a set of vessels $N = \{1, 2, \ldots, |N|\}$ that will call at the port within the planning horizon $T = \{0, 1, \ldots, |T|\}$. We discrete the quay into a set of berths $M = \{1, 2, \ldots, |M|\}$. The berth features (e.g., length, draft, and installed equipment) limit the vessels they can serve. We define M_i to represent the set of berths that vessel i can be served. In practice, the stock level of each cargo type has to be satisfied during loading or discharging operations. For example, the vessel cannot be discharged if the terminal's stock level of the corresponding cargo carried by some vessels would exceed the capacity,

Table 1. An overview related to the literature on the BAP in bulk ports

Reference	Objective		Type			Method		Practical considerations					
	Time	Cost	D	C	H	ES	HS	I	S	N	M	U	T
Perez and Jin [17]	✓		✓			✓		✓					
Ernst et al. [8]	✓			✓		✓							✓
Lassoued and Elloumi [11]	✓		✓			✓							
Barros et al. [2]	✓		✓				✓		✓				✓
Umang et al. [25]	✓				✓	✓	✓				✓		
Robenek et al. [20]	✓		✓			✓		✓					
Pratap et al. [18]	✓	✓	✓				✓	✓					
Hu et al. [9]	✓			✓			✓						
Unsal and Oguz [26]	✓		✓			✓		✓					
Peng et al. [16]	✓	✓	✓			✓	✓	✓					
Cheimanoff et al. [6]	✓			✓			✓						✓
Ribeiro et al. [19]		✓	✓				✓					✓	
Cheimanoff et al. [7]	✓			✓			✓	✓					✓
Krimi et al. [10]		✓		✓			✓	✓				✓	
Andrade and Menezes [1]	✓	✓	✓				✓	✓					
Bouzekri et al. [5]		✓			✓	✓		✓				✓	
de Leon et al. [12]	✓		✓				✓						
de Leon et al. [13]	✓		✓				✓				✓		
This paper		✓			✓	✓			✓	✓	✓	✓	

Type: D (Discrete), C (Continuous), H(Hybrid)
Method ES (Exact Solution), HS (Heuristic Solution)
Feature: I (Integrated with other problems), S (Stock level), N (Night operation permission), M (Multiple cargo types on one vessel), U (Unavailability), T (Tide)

even though the berth is idle. These vessels can only wait until there is sufficient capacity. Determined by the length of the vessels and berths, we allow one vessel to occupy two berths simultaneously. Some unavailability constraints may arise due to weather conditions or facility breakdown; for instance, cranes must undergo planned maintenance in order to stay in a good performance. To sum up, the hybrid BAP model for bulk ports in this paper incorporates the following points:

(1) One vessel is allowed to occupy two berths under the setting of the hybrid layout.
(2) The unavailability time window of each berth is considered, which can be caused by weather conditions, maintenance requirements, or other stochastic factors.
(3) Each vessel has the earliest and the latest service time. This time window is related to the expected arrival time and the priority of the vessel.
(4) The stock level of each cargo type changes with the loading or discharging process, and the stock level of the corresponding cargo type should be within the range of deadstock and capacity.

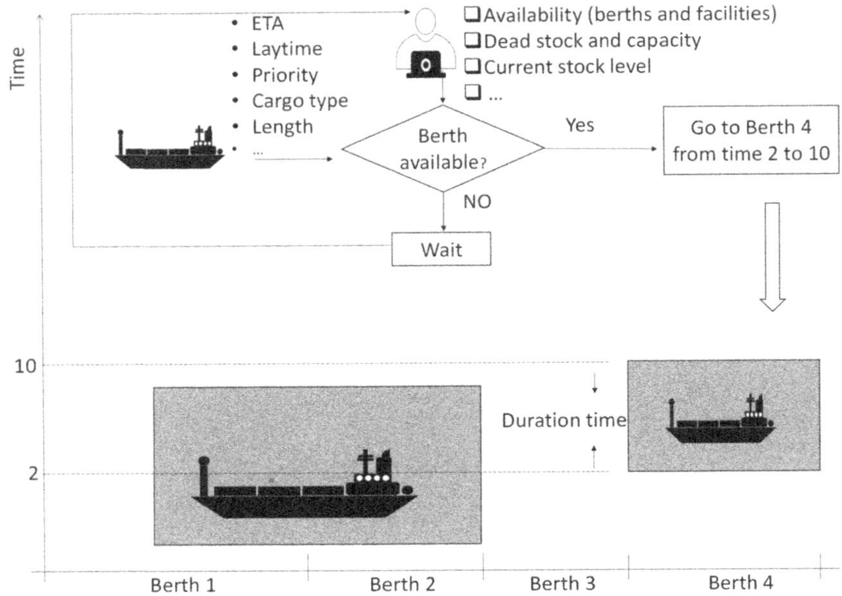

Fig. 2. The berth allocation process in bulk ports

3.2 Notation

Sets

- N: Set of all vessels, $N = \{0, 1, \cdots, |N|\}$;
- M: Set of berths, $M = \{0, 1, \cdots, |M|\}$;
- M_i : Set of berths that can serve vessel i determined by cargo types;
- T: Set of time periods, $T = \{0, 1, \cdots, |T|\}$;
- Θ: Set of product types, $\Theta = \{0, 1, \cdots, |\Theta|\}$;

Parameters

- l_i: the length of vessel i;
- $r_{i\theta}$: rate of operation of vessel i on cargo type θ;
- $q_{i\theta}$: quantity of cargoes on vessel i for cargo type θ;
- t_i: expected arrival time of vessel i;
- h_i: processing time of vessel i;
- g_i: laytime of vessel i;
- c_i: hourly demurrage cost of vessel i;
- $[\alpha_i, \beta_i]$: start time window for vessel i (α_i is related to arrival time of vessel, and β_i is related to priority and roud-trip duration)
- $w_{l\theta}$: dead inventory level of cargo type θ;
- $w_{h\theta}$: capacity of the inventory level of cargo type θ;
- $w_{0\theta}$: current inventory level of cargo type θ at the start of planning horizon;
- b_k: the position of berth k;

- L_k: the maximum length of berth k;
- $[s_k, e_k]$: berth k is available to serve vessels from time s_k to e_k;

Decision Variables

- x_{ik}: equal to 1 if berth k is the start section of vessel i, and 0 otherwise;
- y_{ijk}: equal to 1 if vessel i and vessel j are both assigned to berth k and vessel i is processed before vessel j, and 0 otherwise;
- st_i: the starting time of vessel i;
- z_{ik}: equal to 1 if vessel i is berthed at k and $k+1$, and 0 otherwise, $k \in [0, 1, \ldots, |M|-1]$;
- γ_{it}: equal to 1 if vessel i is berthed at time t, and 0 otherwise;
- ξ_{it}^{θ}: equal to 1 if cargo type θ of vessel i are operated at time t, and 0 otherwise;

3.3 Model

With the notation defined above, we propose the formulation of the hybrid BAP in bulk ports with unavailability and stock constraints, which specifically considers the situation of multiple cargo types on one vessel.

$$min \quad z = \sum_{i \in N} c_i (ct_i - t_i - g_i)^+ \tag{1}$$

Subject to:

$$\sum_{k \in M_i} x_{ik} = 1 + \sum_{k \in M \setminus \{|M|\}} z_{ik} \quad \forall i \in N \tag{2}$$

$$st_i \geq t_i \quad \forall i \in N \tag{3}$$

$$st_i \leq \gamma_{it} * t + M(1 - \gamma_{it}) \quad \forall i \in N, t \in T \tag{4}$$

$$st_i + h_i \geq \gamma_{it} * (t+1) \quad \forall i \in N, t \in T \tag{5}$$

$$\sum_{t \in T} \gamma_{it} \geq h_i \quad \forall i \in N \tag{6}$$

$$ct_i \geq st_i + h_i \quad \forall i \in N \tag{7}$$

$$\sum_{i \in N} st_j \geq ct_i - M(1 - y_{ijk}) \quad \forall i \in N, j \in N, i \neq j, k \in M \tag{8}$$

$$y_{ijk} + y_{jik} \leq 0.5(x_{ik} + x_{jk}) \quad \forall i \in N, j \in N, i \neq j, k \in M \tag{9}$$

$$y_{ijk} + y_{jik} \geq x_{ik} + x_{jk} - 1 \quad \forall i \in N, j \in N, i \neq j, k \in M \tag{10}$$

$$x_{ik} + x_{i,k+1} \geq 2 z_{ik} \quad \forall i \in N, k \in M \setminus \{|M|\} \tag{11}$$

$$\sum_{k \in M \setminus \{|M|\}} z_{ik} \leq 1 \quad \forall i \in N \tag{12}$$

$$l_i x_{ik} \leq \sum_{k \in M} L_k x_{ik} \quad \forall i \in N, k \in M \tag{13}$$

$$\sum_{\theta \in \Theta} \xi_{it}^{\theta} = \gamma_{it} \quad \forall i \in N, t \in T \tag{14}$$

$$\gamma_{i\theta} * \sum_{t \in T} \xi_{it}^{\theta} \geq q_{i\theta} \quad \forall i \in N, \theta \in \Theta \tag{15}$$

$$w_{l\theta} \leq w_{0\theta} + \sum_{i \in N} \sum_{m=0}^{m=t} \gamma_{i\theta} * \xi_{it}^{\theta} \leq w_{h\theta} \quad \forall t \in T, \theta \in \Theta \tag{16}$$

$$x_{ik} * s_k \leq st_i \leq x_{ik} * (e_k - h_i) \quad \forall i \in N, k \in M \tag{17}$$

$$\alpha_i \leq st_i \leq \beta_i \quad \forall i \in N \tag{18}$$

$$x_{ik} \in \{0, 1\} \quad \forall i \in N, k \in M \tag{19}$$

$$y_{ijk} \in \{0, 1\} \quad \forall i \in N, j \in N, i \neq j, k \in M \tag{20}$$

$$\xi_{it}^{\theta} \in \{0, 1\} \quad \forall i \in N, t \in T, \theta \in \Theta \tag{21}$$

$$z_{ik} \in \{0, 1\} \quad \forall i \in N, k \in M \backslash \{|M|\} \tag{22}$$

$$\gamma_{it} \in \{0, 1\} \quad \forall i \in N, t \in T \tag{23}$$

The objective function (1) is to minimize the demurrage fee of all vessels. Constraint (2) ensures each vessel i occupies at least one berth. Constraint (3)–(7) restrict the completion time and the start time of Vessel i. Constraints (8)–(10) are no overlapping restriction for vessels that be served at the same berth. Constraints (11)–(13) allow vessels to occupy two berths. Constraints (14)–(16) ensure that the current inventory during the loading or discharging of vessels can satisfy the requirement of stock of specific cargo type. Some practical factors which restrict the starting time and completion time of vessels are considered in this model. Constraint (17) represents the available time window of berths. Constraint (18) is the available time window of vessels. Constraints (19)–(23) specify the range of decision variables. The objective function (1) is nonlinear. Thus, they need to be linearized by defining an additional decision variable $\mu_i = (ct_i - t_i - g_i)^+$. The related additional constraints are defined as follows:

$$\mu_i \geq 0 \quad \forall i \in N \tag{24}$$

$$\mu_i \geq ct_i - ti - g_i \quad \forall i \in N \tag{25}$$

Therefore, the model can be reformulated as a mixed-integer linear program as follows:

$$min \quad z = \sum_{i \in N} c_i \mu_i \tag{26}$$

Subject to Constraints (2)–(25).

4 Numerical Experiments

In this section, the MIP model proposed in Sect. 3.3 is tested using the CPLEX solver with the computational limit of 600 s. All tests are running on an Intel

Core i5 (1.7 GHz) processor and use the version of CPLEX 12.8.0 under the C++ environment. We introduce the instance generation first and then analyze the model's performance under four different scenarios.

4.1 Generation of Instances

We generate 12 instance sizes with different $|M|$ and $|N|$ as well as the consideration of unavailability and multiple cargo types within the time horizon of one week, as shown in Table 2. The unavailability can be incurred by maintenance requirements for facilities, extreme weather, or other unforeseen factors. The length of vessels and berths are generated following a uniform distribution of $[80, 180]$ and $[120, 160]$. The other detailed attributes related to the vessel are generated randomly, including arrival time, processing time, laytime, demurrage, night operation permission, and the cargo tonnage and type they carried.

Table 2. Information about the generated instances

Instance	$\|N\|$	$\|M\|$	Unavailability	Multiple cargo types
I1	6	3	No	Single
I2	6	3	Yes	Single
I3	12	3	No	Single
I4	12	3	Yes	Single
I5	18	3	No	Single
I6	18	3	Yes	Single
I7	6	5	No	Multiple
I8	6	5	Yes	Multiple
I9	12	5	No	Multiple
I10	12	5	Yes	Multiple
I11	18	5	No	Multiple
I12	18	5	Yes	Multiple

4.2 Results Analysis and Discussion

As highlighted in Sect. 2, the night berthing permission is considered in our model; thus, for those vessels that cannot be operated during the night (assumed from 1 am to 6 am), the following constraints (27) and (28) are added:

$$\begin{aligned} & st_i - \gamma_{iq} * t - M(1 - \gamma_{iq}) < 0 \\ & \forall i \in N, q \in [p * 24 + 1, p * 24 + 5], p \in [0, 31], t = p * 24 + 1 \end{aligned} \tag{27}$$

$$\begin{aligned} & ct_i \geq \gamma_{iq} * t \\ & \forall i \in N, q \in [p * 24 + 1, p * 24 + 5], p \in [0, 31], t = p * 24 + 5 \end{aligned} \tag{28}$$

Table 3 shows the result of the expected demurrage fee and the computational time. The proposed MIP model can find the optimal solutions for all 12 instances by applying CPLEX, with up to 18 vessels and 5 berths. In Fig. 3, we compare the demurrage fee in four scenarios which differentiate in whether consider multiple cargo types and unavailability or not. We find that berths' unavailability can always significantly increase the demurrage fee, especially when the berths are busy. However, the multiple cargo types on the same vessel have no significant impact when the port is idle, but it will obviously increase demurrage fees when the port is busy.

Table 3. Computational results for the proposed MIP model

Instance	Obj ($)	Time (s)	Instance	Obj ($)	Time (s)
I1	4347.00	1.64	I7	4036.50	2.28
I2	7762.50	1.27	I8	4657.50	0.80
I3	4968.00	11.36	I9	3283.15	2.50
I4	5267.00	19.17	I10	4621.50	4.89
I5	7464.00	179.38	I11	6110.00	24.34
I6	8393.50	240.02	I12	29330.00	306.67

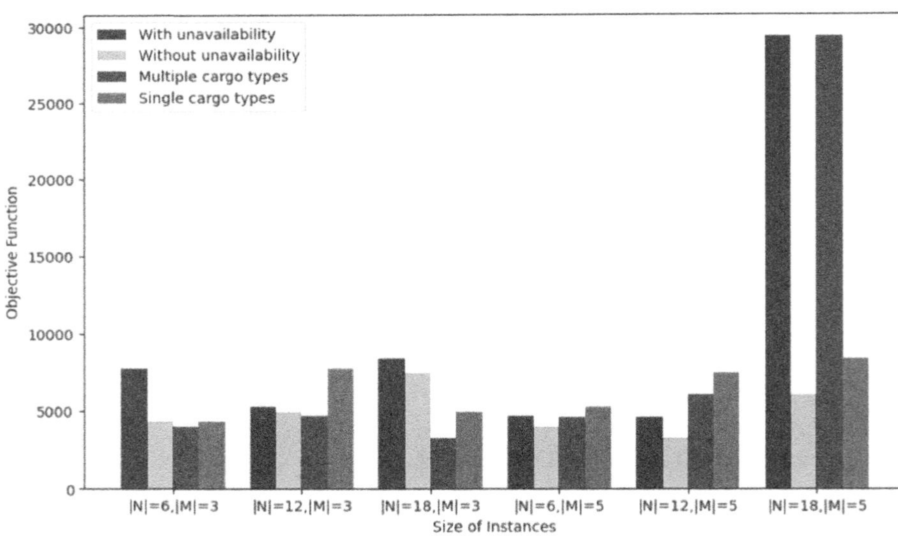

Fig. 3. The comparison of demurrage fee under four different scenarios

4.3 Managerial Insights and Policy Implications

This paper proposes a hybrid BAP model for bulk port managers to decide when and where to operate on the calling vessels considering the constraints of the unavailability of facilities and the stock level. With the experimental results in Sect. 4.2, the following implications are provided for the bulk port managers:

(1) In practice, unavailability of berths happens frequently, caused by many practical factors, such as extreme weather and facility maintenance. The BAP model, which ignores the unavailability, does not work in many practical applications and even makes the port into trouble. In addition, the unavailability of berths can significantly influence the berth allocation plan and further impact the total demurrage fee. Thus, the bulk port managers should consider the unavailability when making decisions on berthing plans.
(2) Constraints (27) and (28) are for satisfying the requirement of individual vessels on night berthing permissions and thus improve the customer service level of the ports.
(3) Whether to consider stock level constraints largely depends on the actual situation of the ports. When the storage is approaching capacity, it is necessary to consider the stock level limitation in berth allocation. Otherwise, the vessel must wait until there is enough storage space, which can also make the ports into trouble.

5 Conclusions

Prior work on mathematical models and algorithms has solved the basic BAP in bulk ports. In [24], for instance, the author reports the specific features of berth operations in bulk ports that distinguish them from container ports. However, these studies have either ignored some practical constraints (e.g., unavailability of berths and storage) or have not considered the multiple cargo types on one vessel, which can make it hard to apply those approaches under real-world conditions. In this work, we propose a hybrid BAP model for bulk ports with unavailability and stock level constraints, and we consider the case of multiple cargo types on one vessel specifically. We show the effectiveness of the proposed model by conducting numerical experiments on a set of distinct instances. The hybrid BAP extends earlier work of [25], providing a better fit for the loading or discharging operations in real-world bulk ports. The commercial software CPLEX can obtain optimal solutions with up to 18 vessels within 600 s. Most notably, this is the first study to our knowledge that dedicates itself to the BAP in bulk ports and considers unavailability and stock constraints simultaneously. Our solutions provide timely and effective decision support to port managers. However, our model can not solve large-scale instances by CPLEX within a reasonable computing time. Future work should therefore develop some algorithms for larger instances.

References

1. de Andrade, J.L.M., Menezes, G.C.: An integrated planning, scheduling, yard allocation and berth allocation problem in bulk ports: model and heuristics. In: Mes, M., Lalla-Ruiz, E., Voß, S. (eds.) ICCL 2021. LNCS, vol. 13004, pp. 3–20. Springer, Cham (2021). https://doi.org/10.1007/978-3-030-87672-2_1

2. Barros, V.H., Costa, T.S., Oliveira, A.C., Lorena, L.A.: Model and heuristic for berth allocation in tidal bulk ports with stock level constraints. Comput. Ind. Eng. **60**(4), 606–613 (2011)
3. Bierwirth, C., Meisel, F.: A survey of berth allocation and quay crane scheduling problems in container terminals. Eur. J. Oper. Res. **202**(3), 615–627 (2010)
4. Bierwirth, C., Meisel, F.: A follow-up survey of berth allocation and quay crane scheduling problems in container terminals. Eur. J. Oper. Res. **244**(3), 675–689 (2015)
5. Bouzekri, H., Alpan, G., Giard, V.: A dynamic hybrid berth allocation problem with routing constraints in bulk ports. In: Lalic, B., Majstorovic, V., Marjanovic, U., von Cieminski, G., Romero, D. (eds.) APMS 2020. IAICT, vol. 591, pp. 250–258. Springer, Cham (2020). https://doi.org/10.1007/978-3-030-57993-7_29
6. Cheimanoff, N., Fontane, F., Kitri, M.N., Tchernev, N.: A reduced vns based approach for the dynamic continuous berth allocation problem in bulk terminals with tidal constraints. Expert Syst. Appl. **168**, 114215 (2021)
7. Cheimanoff, N., Fontane, F., Kitri, M.N., Tchernev, N.: Exact and heuristic methods for the berth allocation problem with multiple continuous quays in tidal bulk terminals. Expert Syst. Appl. **201**, 117141 (2022)
8. Ernst, A.T., Oğuz, C., Singh, G., Taherkhani, G.: Mathematical models for the berth allocation problem in dry bulk terminals. J. Sched. **20**(5), 459–473 (2017). https://doi.org/10.1007/s10951-017-0510-8
9. Xiaona, H., Wei, Y., Junliang, H., Zhicheng, B.: Study on bulk terminal berth allocation based on heuristic algorithm. In: Du, Z. (ed.) Modern Computer Science and Applications. Advances in Intelligent Systems and Computing, vol. 191, pp. 413–419. Springer, Heidelberg (2013). https://doi.org/10.1007/978-3-642-33030-8_67
10. Krimi, I., Todosijević, R., Benmansour, R., Ratli, M., El Cadi, A.A., Aloullal, A.: Modelling and solving the multi-quays berth allocation and crane assignment problem with availability constraints. J. Glob. Optim. **78**(2), 349–373 (2020). https://doi.org/10.1007/s10898-020-00884-1
11. Lassoued, R., Elloumi, A.: The discrete and dynamic berth allocation problem in bulk port. In: 2019 6th International Conference on Control, Decision and Information Technologies (CoDIT), pp. 1976–1980. IEEE (2019)
12. de León, A.D., Lalla-Ruiz, E., Melián-Batista, B., Moreno-Vega, J.M.: A machine learning-based system for berth scheduling at bulk terminals. Expert Syst. Appl. **87**, 170–182 (2017)
13. de León, A.D., Lalla-Ruiz, E., Melián-Batista, B., Moreno-Vega, J.M.: A simulation-optimization framework for enhancing robustness in bulk berth scheduling. Eng. Appl. Artif. Intell. **103**, 104276 (2021)
14. Lyu, X., Jin, J.G., Hu, H.: Berth allocation recovery for container transshipment terminals. Marit. Policy Manag. **47**(4), 558–574 (2020)
15. Lyu, X., Negenborn, R.R., Shi, X., Schulte, F.: A collaborative berth planning approach for disruption recovery. IEEE Open J. Intell. Transp. Syst. **3**, 153–164 (2022)
16. Peng, J., Zhou, Z., Li, R.: A collaborative berth allocation problem with multiple ports based on genetic algorithm. J. Coast. Res. **73**(10073), 290–297 (2015)
17. Perez, D., Jin, J.G.: Integrated dedicated berth allocation and specialised handling equipment assignment in bulk ports. Int. J. Shipping Transp. Logist. **12**(6), 543–562 (2020)

18. Pratap, S., Nayak, A., Kumar, A., Cheikhrouhou, N., Tiwari, M.K.: An integrated decision support system for berth and ship unloader allocation in bulk material handling port. Comput. Ind. Eng. **106**, 386–399 (2017)
19. Ribeiro, G.M., Mauri, G.R., de Castro Beluco, S., Lorena, L.A.N., Laporte, G.: Berth allocation in an ore terminal with demurrage, despatch and maintenance. Comput. Ind. Eng. **96**, 8–15 (2016)
20. Robenek, T., Umang, N., Bierlaire, M., Ropke, S.: A branch-and-price algorithm to solve the integrated berth allocation and yard assignment problem in bulk ports. Eur. J. Oper. Res. **235**(2), 399–411 (2014)
21. Sirimanne, S.N., et al.: Review of maritime transport 2021. In: United Nations Conference on Trade and Development, Geneva, Switzerland (2019)
22. Stahlbock, R., Voß, S.: Operations research at container terminals: a literature update. OR Spectr. **30**(1), 1–52 (2008)
23. Steenken, D., Voß, S., Stahlbock, R.: Container terminal operation and operations research-a classification and literature review. OR Spectr. **26**(1), 3–49 (2004)
24. Umang, N.: From container terminals to bulk ports: models and algorithms for integrated planning and robust scheduling. Ph.D. thesis, Ph.D. thesis. École Polytechnique Fédérale de Lausanne (2014)
25. Umang, N., Bierlaire, M., Vacca, I.: Exact and heuristic methods to solve the berth allocation problem in bulk ports. Transp. Res. Part E: Logist. Transp. Rev. **54**, 14–31 (2013)
26. Unsal, O., Oguz, C.: An exact algorithm for integrated planning of operations in dry bulk terminals. Transp. Res. Part E: Logist. Transp. Rev. **126**, 103–121 (2019)

A Self-adaptive Hybrid Search Technique with Its Application to the Quadratic Semi-assignment and Berth Allocation Problems

Mehrdad Amirghasemi[1(✉)], Marcella Bernardo Papini[1], and Stefan Voß[2]

[1] SMART Infrastructure Facility, Faculty of Engineering and Information Sciences, University of Wollongong, Wollongong, Australia
{mehrdad,marcella}@uow.edu.au

[2] Institute of Information Systems, University of Hamburg, Von-Melle-Park 5, 20146 Hamburg, Germany
stefan.voss@hamburg.de

Abstract. Both the quadratic semi-assignment problem and the berth allocation problem are about assigning items (vessels) to sets (berths) and have various applications from floor layout planning to schedule synchronization in public transit networks and maritime logistics. In this paper, a hybrid, modular solution strategy, in which an adaptive improvement technique is embedded into a genetic algorithm, is proposed and has been applied to both problems. For the purpose of self-adaptivity, all important parameters of the procedure are embedded in the employed genomes and evolve while the procedure is executed. In addition to the hybrid strategy, a simple branch and bound brute force method is implemented to find the optimal solution for small instances. Computational experiments show that the presented procedure finds the optimal solution for randomly generated 20×5 instances in less than a millisecond. These instances are the largest QSAP instances for which we could find optimal solutions within several hours' time.

Keywords: Quadratic semi-assignment · Berth allocation · Genetic algorithm · Metaheuristics · Maritime logistics

1 Introduction

The Quadratic Semi-Assignment Problem (QSAP) can be considered to be a generalization of the quadratic assignment problem (QAP). Whereas in the QAP, a one-to-one mapping between n *items* and n *locations* is required, in the QSAP, m *items* are to be assigned to n *sets*. Whilst some sets can have more than one item assigned to them, other sets can have no items allocated to them.

Sincere thanks to Harriet Simpson-Southward for her diligent proofreading of the manuscript.

J. de Armas et al. (Eds.): ICCL 2022, LNCS 13557, pp. 16–30, 2022.
https://doi.org/10.1007/978-3-031-16579-5_2

Berth allocation problems can also be considered to be an assignment problem, similar to the QSAP, in the sense that a number of vessels arriving at a container terminal are to be allocated to available berthing spaces, with the objective of minimizing the total service time. Inspired by the fact that a feasible solution for both problems can be represented by a single vector, showing the set (berth) that each item (vessel) is allocated to, we propose a self-adaptive hybrid strategy which can be utilized to tackle both problems. The proposed strategy is modular and has been adopted to solve randomly generated instances of both the QSAP and a basic formulation of the Dynamic Berth Allocation Problem (DBAP).

The proposed strategy consists of six components, namely; (i) an integration of best-improvement and regret-based construction methods, (ii) an integration of regret-based and ranked-based crossover operators, (iii) a local search technique, (iv) a perturbation mechanism, (v) a facilitating hash-based method for having quick access to the worst solution in the pool to replace it, and (vi) a self-adaptive module managing the interaction of other components. For the purpose of self-adaptivity, all important parameters of the procedure are embedded in the employed genomes and evolve while the procedure is executed. Due to this self-adaptive feature, and the fact that evolutionary operations like refreshment and crossover operations crossbreed the parameters, the procedure has been termed the Self-Adaptive Crossbreed Algorithm (SACA).

The rest of this paper is organized as follows. In Sect. 2, the problem formulation for both the QSAP and the DBAP is provided. The related work is outlined in Sect. 3 and Sect. 4 describes the SACA. Computational experiments are in Sect. 5, and Sect. 6 presents the concluding remarks.

2 Problem Formulation

Basic formulations for both the QSAP and the DBAP, with an emphasis on their similarities, are discussed in this section. The QSAP, based on the generalised formulation originally presented in [12], can be defined as follows. There are m items that are to be allocated to n sets. With i and j showing the items, and h and k showing the sets to which these two items are assigned, respectively, the cost component C_{ijhk} shows the cost of such allocations. The QSAP is formulated as follows.

$$\text{Minimize} \qquad Z = \sum_{i=1}^{m} \sum_{h=1}^{n} \sum_{j=1}^{m} \sum_{k=1}^{n} C_{ihjk} \times X_{ih} \times X_{jk}$$

Subject to:

$$\sum_{h=1}^{n} X_{ih} = 1 \quad \forall i = 1, \ldots, m$$

$$X_{ih} \in \{0, 1\} \quad \forall i = 1, \ldots, m \quad \forall h = 1, \ldots, n$$

In this formulation, $X_{ih} = 1$, if and only if item i is allocated to set h, and the first constraint ensures that each item is allocated to at most one set. It should be noted that the QSAP can be seen as the problem of synchronizing schedules in a public transit network. In effect, assuming cost C_{ijhk} is incurred for allocating schedule h to route i, and schedule k to route j, the objective is to allocate routes to schedules that will result in the lowest total cost [11,12].

The DBAP, as presented in [15], is similarly defined as follows. There are m vessels arriving at a container terminal at times A_i. They are to be allocated to n berthing points, each becoming available at the time S_j. The handling time of vessel i at berth j is shown with T_{ij}. Furthermore, each vessel can be allocated to exactly one berth, and the service time of a vessel at a berth cannot be interrupted. Whilst several alternative DBAP formulations have been proposed in the literature [9,10,18], the original mixed integer formulation of [15], wherein the end of berth availability times are not considered, is used here. Nevertheless, with small modifications, the SACA will be able to solve alternative variations of the DBAP.

As can be seen, solutions to both the QSAP and the DBAP can be encoded in a vector $v = (v_1, v_2, \ldots, v_m)$, where v_i shows the set (berth) that item (vessel) i is allocated to. Hence, the objective is to find a vector v^*, which minimizes the total allocation cost (service time). It should be noted, however, that distinct modules of the SACA are responsible for the objective function calculation of the QSAP and the DBAP.

3 Related Work

In this section, the related metaheuristics and practical applications of both the QSAP and the Berth Allocation Problem (BAP), with a focus on evolutionary and self-adaptive techniques, are briefly surveyed.

The QSAP has several practical applications in scheduling, clustering, and partitioning problems. These applications of the QSAP in real-life problems are discussed in [17,23,25], and [8]. For instance, in [25], the problem of reconstructing neuronal structures in over-segmented electron microscopy images is addressed. The neuronal image reconstruction problem was formulated as a QSAP with a quadratic function that calculates whether pairs of segments should be placed in the same cluster or in distinct clusters.

In [23], the problem of improving transfer quality in public mass transit networks is formulated as a QSAP. The problem consists of performing small changes to the public transit timetables to optimize transfer possibilities in the overall network. The authors solved the problem to optimality using CPLEX on small instances formulated based on real data from the Westpfalz Verkehrsverbund, Germany. In [17], the routing of ambulances in a dynamic disaster environment was studied, where there can be uncertainty in the number of casualties involved and their locations. This problem involves the selection of a path for each ambulance, which was modelled as a QSAP. The authors solved the path selection problem using a Tabu Search (TS), where the initial solution was calculated by a simple regret heuristic.

Finally, a small-scale faculty-wide examination timetabling problem is modelled as a QSAP in [8]. To solve the students' examination scheduling problem, the authors introduced a simulated annealing with a local search procedure that included six operators. The proposed solution approach was applied to a data set created based on real data from the Faculty of Economics and Management at the Otto-von-Guericke-University Magdeburg, Germany.

To the best of our knowledge, there are two studies that have focused on metaheuristics for the QSAP. In [12], three improvement procedures for a TS algorithm is investigated and the results are compared with a simulated annealing method in terms of solution quality and computation time. In [22] a polynomial algorithm, which finds an approximate solution for the QSAP, and computes an estimate for the accuracy of the resulting solution, is introduced. The authors conducted a computational experiment to analyse the errors, find posterior accuracy estimates, and evaluate the proposed polynomial algorithm complexity. While [13] focuses more on modeling and problem description aspects, a local search is proposed, too.

It is worth mentioning that, in the absence of further metaheuristic approaches for the QSAP, a large number of self-adaptive and decomposition-based heuristics have recently been proposed for the QAP in [2,3], and [26]. Furthermore, a generic parallel evolutionary framework with an application to the QAP, as well as the job-shop and flowshop scheduling problems, has been reported in [1]. Having described related methods to the QSAP, the metaheuristics applied to the DBAP are reviewed next.

The BAP is used to solve the problem of allocating and scheduling incoming container vessels to berthing positions at minimum total weighted turnaround time of the vessels [19]. The BAP can be studied from either a static or a dynamic point of view, giving rise to the Static BAP (SBAP) and Dynamic BAP (DBAP). The difference between these two BAP classes is that, in the latter, the ships arrive while work is in progress [15]. In the former, the ships are already in the port when the berths become available. In this study, the DBAP, wherein the quay is viewed as a discrete set of berthing locations, is considered. It is worth noting that a comprehensive survey of berth allocation and quay crane scheduling problems can be found in [6]. A modeling approach for a real-world berth allocation problem using the QSAP is described in [13]. While this approach has been used in practice, the fact that this idea was widely ignored in academia also stimulates further studies to shed light on these different concepts. The idea to use a quadratic term in the objective reflects, among others, the interaction of positioning vessels at different berths and considering the movement of transshipment containers from one vessel into the yard and then to another vessel for further transport.

For solving the DBAP in the public berth system, Genetic Algorithm (GA)-based heuristics, which employed only two different types of chromosome representations, were proposed in [21]. To validate the proposed heuristic, the authors evaluated it against a Lagrangian relaxation-based heuristic on randomly generated DBAP instances. The GA solutions performed well on small- and large-size instances. A GA-based heuristic was also developed in [4] to solve the DBAP. To validate the model, computational experiments were performed on data retrieved from the 2020 report on the port authority of Algeciras, Spain.

In [5], two GA-based metaheuristics that included an approximated dynamic programming method as a local search procedure, were introduced. The proposed metaheuristics were evaluated against two versions of the GA without a local search procedure: a standard GA and a standard memetic algorithm (MA). The computational results showed that incorporating a local search procedure in the MA yielded better solutions. The BAP is also solved by means of an optimization-based GA (OBGA) heuristic in [24]. In the OBGA, an optimization step was embedded right after the genetic operations were completed and before the next generation selection step. The OBGA was compared with a GA heuristic without an optimization component. The former outperformed the latter with regards to objective function variance and minimum values, especially as the problem size increased. The BAP was solved by applying a hybrid heuristic that combined a TS metaheuristic with a path relinking procedure in [20]. The proposed TS was based on the one of [10], with an additional neighbourhood structure to guide the search. To validate the proposed hybrid heuristic, its solutions were evaluated against those obtained in [10] and by the exact resolution of the mathematical model set partitioning problem introduced in [7]. The computational experiments showed that the proposed hybrid heuristic outperformed the algorithm proposed in [10] and found the optimal solution for some of the instances.

In [14], a multi-objective GA is introduced to solve the BAP, with the objective of prioritizing daytime workloads and reducing delayed and nighttime workloads. In the computational experiments, the authors tested four sets of algorithmic parameters, namely crossover and mutation probabilities, elite ratio, and the priority assessment window.

The key contribution of our study is the introduction of a generalised, modular and self-adaptive approach that can solve complex semi-assignment problems in maritime logistics. As the berth allocation is one of the most complex port tasks with the highest impacts on final costs, finding a generalized solution approach that can be easily tailored to perform well on multiple (harder) variations of the berth allocation and quay crane assignment [16] problems, is of high importance.

4 The SACA

As stated, the SACA has six main components. In this section, a general description of the SACA is presented first and then its pseudocode is presented in Algorithm 1. Following this, all of its components are described in detail.

As is seen in Algorithm 1, following general initializations in line 1, the SACA fills a solution pool via utilising construction and local search modules in lines 2 to 5. Next, in each iteration of the while loop starting at line 6, a solution is extracted from the pool and based on the encoded parameters in the solution, one of the REFRESH, CROSSOVER, or PERTURB actions is performed.

```
Data: poolSize, timeLimit
Result: The best found solution
Perform initialization;
/* fill the solution pool for the first time                */
for i ← 1 to poolSize do
    s ← ConstructSolution();
    s ← LocalSearch(s);
    Add s to the solution pool p;
while A termination criterion is not met do
    x_w ← GetPoolWorstSolution(p);
    Take a solution, x_1, from p, using roulette-wheel selection;
    Based on the embedded parameters in x_1 choose an Action;
    switch Action do
        case REFRESH                    /* Generate a fresh solution */
            x_2 ← ConstructSolution() ;
            x_2 ← LocalSearch(x_2) ;
            if Cost (x_2) < Cost (x_w) then
                Update the pool by replacing x_w with x_2;
            break;
        case CROSSOVER                  /* Apply one of the crossover */
            Take another solution, x_2, from p, using roulette-wheel
            selection;
            x_3 ← DoCrossover(x_1, x_2);
            x_3 ← LocalSearch(x_3);
            if Cost (x_3) < Cost (x_w) then
                Update the pool by replacing x_w with x_2;
            break;
        case PERTURB                    /* Augmented local search */
            x_2 ← Perturb(x_1);
            x_2 ← LocalSearch(x_2) ;
            if Cost (x_2) < Cost (x_w) then
                Update the pool by replacing x_w with x_2;
            break;
Return the best solution found;
```

Algorithm 1: The Self-Adaptive Crossbreed Algorithm (SACA)

While in the REFRESH action, a brand new solution is generated, CROSSOVER and PERTURB operators apply problem-specific crossover and perturbation modifications on solution(s) selected from the pool. It should be noted that in all three actions, a local search is applied to the output solution and the final solution only enters the pool if it has a higher quality than the worst solution in the pool.

Following an overall description of the SACA, in the following subsections, first the solution encoding is explained and, next the six modules of the SACA are described in detail.

4.1 Solution Encoding

The SACA represents a solution genome in two parts, as shown in Fig. 1. Whereas the first part of the genome shows the encoded solution, v, indicating the assigned set to each item, the second part is about governing the procedure and the way in which the procedure should improve the genome. With this in mind, parameters inside the genome allow the algorithm to execute itself in a self-adaptive manner.

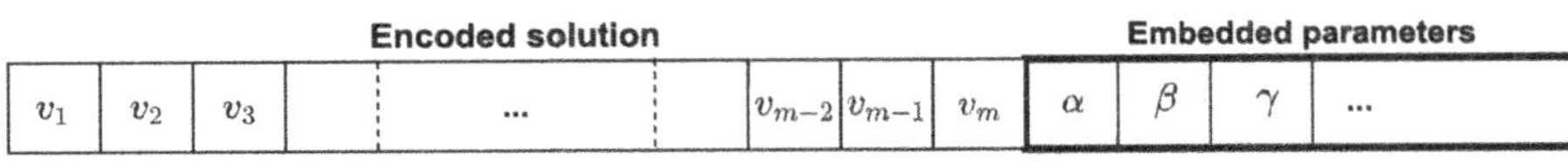

Fig. 1. The genome representation in the SACA

There are seven guiding pieces of information in each genome. The first piece determines the chance that the regret-based method is used in each step of the construction method [12]. Since either the local best-improvement or regret-based method can be used in each step of the construction method, one minus this value will show the chance of using the best-improvement method.

The second piece shows the number of perturbations required. The larger this number is, the more the initial solution for which local search is supposed to occur becomes distinct from the corresponding solution. The third piece shows the chance of applying the second crossover. It is worth noting that if it has been decided that a crossover should occur and the first does not, the second should.

Once a solution is selected from the pool, one of three specific actions, guided by the next three pieces, are performed. In effect, the fourth piece shows the probability that this solution is replaced with a refreshed solution generated by the construction method. The fifth piece shows the chance of an augmented local search occurring. By augmented local search we mean a local search that follows a perturbation. The term augmented is used to distinguish this local search from the ordinary local search employed. After all, a local search automatically occurs after each crossover as well as after the application of the construction method. An augmented local search, however, is aimed at rectifying a perturbed solution. Finally, for each solution selected, if neither a refreshment nor an augmented local search occur, a crossover operation occurs. Hence, the sixth piece indicates the chance of applying a crossover operator with respect to an augmented local search and refreshment.

Since in the first crossover operation, a percentage of genes are uniformly fixed to the two parents and the rest are fixed one by one to a parent which provides a better gene with respect to a regret-based criterion (see Sect. 4.3), the sixth piece shows the initial percentage of genes fixed to the two parents.

4.2 The Integration of a Best-Improvement and a Regret-Based Construction Method

The employed construction method has two operating modes, based on the input parameter, *isRegretBased*, as shown in Algorithm 2. In effect, after allocating the very first item to a set with the minimum aggregate cost to all other sets, it will iterate over all items in the while loop starting at line 8. In the case that the *isRegretBased* is true, the procedure selects the item with the highest *regret*, and assigns its minimum set to it. The regret value for an item is simply defined as the difference between the best and second best set allocation for an item [11].

In the case that *isRegretBased* is false, the best-improvement method is applied by simply selecting the item with minimum partial cost, and assigning the minimal set to it. It is worth noting that ties are broken randomly throughout this procedure.

4.3 The Integration of Regret-Based and Ranked-Based Crossover Operators

Similarly, the crossover operator has two operating modes, based on the input parameter. In a regret-based crossover, a percentage, say 80%, of items are fixed in the parent and offspring solutions. For the remaining 20%, the procedure selects the item with highest *regret* and assigns its minimum set to it. A ranked-based crossover, however, simply iterates over all items in parent solutions and incrementally constructs the offspring solution by selecting the items from the parent which incur the partial minimal cost.

4.4 The Local Search

Generally, a local search uses a neighborhood for each solution, which in some sense includes close solutions to that solution. An improving solution among such a neighborhood is selected, if possible. The improved solution replaces the current solution and the process of creating its neighbors and finding an improved solution to once again replace the current solution continues. Termination occurs when the current solution cannot be improved by any of its neighbors. To make the local search less intensive with respect to execution time, the neighborhood in the QSAP, in line with some other algorithms in the literature, have all been considered as solutions which have only one different allocation pair (item-set) in comparison to the current solution.

The local search fills the initial pool and occasionally generates some solutions for replacing the current solution. It also avoids unnecessary calculations by only performing updating calculations when required.

4.5 The Perturbation Method

The perturbation method needs the number of perturbations which have to be performed. Assuming k perturbations are required, k random items swap their

```
Data: isRegretBased
Result: The newly created solution
Initialize candidate items list, L as an empty list;
forall the items i do
    π_i ← null;
    Add i to L ;
(i_0, s_0) ← Item and set with minimum aggregate cost to all other sets ;
π_{i_0} ← s_0;
Remove i_0 from L ;
while L is not empty do
    i* ← null;
    s* ← null ;
    forall the items in L do
        if isRegretBased then
            i* ← the item with max regret across all sets ;
            s* ← the set with min partial cost for i* ;
        else
            i* ← the item with min cost across all sets ;
            s* ← the set with min partial cost for i* ;
    π_{i_*} ← s_*;
    Remove i_* from L ;
Return π ;
```

Algorithm 2: The solution construction method used in the SACA

sets with each other. When k = 4, for example, the first and second items first swap their sets, then the second and third items do so, and then the third and fourth items. Finally, the first and fourth items swap their sets. The larger the value of k, the more changes that occur to the solution which is supposed to go under local search. A small number for k causes the local search to easily reverse those changes and reach the original solution wastefully. On the other hand, selecting a large number for k is similar to creating a new solution using the construction method. Since this piece, like several other pieces, have been embedded in the genome, the procedure tries to adaptively find the value of k.

4.6 The Facilitating Heap-Based Module

The facilitating heap-based module is used for having quick access to the worst solution in the pool. As an efficient implementation of a priority queue, in the employed heap, the highest priority element is always kept at the root of a complete binary tree. Since the heap is not a sorted structure, it is most suited for cases in which we only need to update the maximum (minimum) element of the list based on adding a new item to the list or removing the item with maximum (minimum) value from the list.

In our procedure, the reason for needing to have quick access to such a solution with maximum value is that any new solution that has a cost smaller than the solution with the highest cost should replace it in the pool. In effect, after filling the initial pool, every genome created by either the construction method, the augmented local search, or crossover operations needs to be compared with the worst solution in the pool and replaced if the new genome has a higher quality than the worst solution.

4.7 The Managing Self-adaptive Module

The managing self-adaptive module manages the interaction of other components with the use of adaptive pieces embedded in the genome. It decides whether (i) an augmented local search, (ii) refreshment by the use of the construction method or (iii) crossover operators are required. In the first case, it initially performs the necessary perturbation and then executes a local search. In the second case, it replaces the current genome with a fresh genome generated by the construction method. In the third case, it selects another genome from the pool and manages to perform one of the two crossover operators on the two genomes available. In this case, deciding which crossover operator to select depends on the piece embedded in the genome showing the probability of using the first crossover. Upon creating a solution, if its quality is better than that of the worst solution in the pool, the worst solution in the pool is replaced with the generated solution.

5 Computational Experiments

The SACA has been implemented in C++ and experiments have been performed using an Intel Xeon 4.0 GHz processor on Amazon Web Services cloud and a total of 30 and 50 randomly generated instances for the QSAP and the DBAP, respectively. These instances contain 15 to 50 items (vessels) and 5 to 10 sets (berths). The SACA has been run 10 times on each instance with a new seed. In addition, the optimal solution is also computed via an effective branch and bound method. The optimal value (OPT), the time to reach the optimal solution (T_{OPT}), the best and average deviation percentage from the optimal solution ($(S-OPT)/OPT*100$) and the best and average times, in seconds, are reported in Tables 1 and 2.

As can be seen in Table 1, while the SACA finds the optimal solution for 20×5 QSAP instances within milliseconds, the branch and bound method takes around 23 h (84382.8 s) to find the optimal solution for an instance of the same size.

Similarly, the SACA performs well in finding optimal solutions for the DBAP instances, as shown in Table 2. It should be noted that the branch and bound, compared to the QSAP, performs faster when applied to the DBAP. This could be due to the fact that the DBAP is not only quicker in objective function computation, but also the fact that the QSAP is relatively computationally harder due to the larger input size.

It is worth mentioning that the success of the SACA in finding optimal solutions for both the DBAP and the QSAP has several practical implications. For instance, the SACA could further be extended and customized for application to alternative variations of the berth allocation problem, as well as integrated with other problems regarding container terminals, such as quay crane assignment problems [16].

6 Concluding Remarks

We revisited the quadratic semi-assignment problem and proposed a hybrid search technique. The procedure proved to be efficient in finding optimal solutions for small instances. Also, computational experiments could indicate that different modules of the SACA, to different degrees, are all effective and synergetically contribute to solution quality. In terms of practical and managerial implications, different assignment and scheduling problems arising at container terminals [6], and their integration problems [16], could be solved much more efficiently using the modular and self-adaptive features of the SACA. In effect, the SACA should be seen as a viable approach for reaching high quality solutions with low computational cost.

The QSAP had been used for quite some time for berth allocation in a real-world setting. While academia had successfully investigated different directions, the use of the QSAP is not ruled out and additional studies may prove its suitability even more. Using the QSAP in public transport settings was documented to some extent while other applications still led a niche existence. Our approach is a first attempt to reopen the QSAP as a modeling and solution attempt towards berth allocation. (We should note that the same argument holds for using the resource-constrained project scheduling problem and this might be another possible direction for future research).

The future direction for improving the procedures is twofold. First, in the QSAP formulation, instead of using the same-size square matrix in each cell of item-to-item matrices, matrices with different sizes should be employed. In this case, the only restriction is that matrices sitting in the same row should have the same number of columns and matrices sitting in the same column should have the same number of rows. In this case, the procedure can not only handle assigning items to sets but it can cope with situations in which each item has its own separate fixed options from which one can be selected. Such a procedure can handle the optimal assignment of different strategies to different decision makers in cases where each decision maker has their own set of decisions. It is worth noting that such a possible formulation suits system equilibrium rather than user equilibrium.

Second, parallel computing can be employed to improve efficiency. In such computing, several execution of processes can be carried out simultaneously. Without dividing the problem into smaller ones for solving each at the same time, each execution of the process can solve the same large problem with different parameters and communicate with other execution processes the best solution

Table 1. Comparison of average percent deviation from the optimal solution (OPT) for randomly generated the QSAP instances

Problem	n	m	OPT	T_{OPT}(s)	%DEV_{best}	T_{best}(s)	%DEV_{avg}	T_{max}(s)
qsap15x5-01	15	5	292	50.14	0.000	0.000	0.000	10
qsap15x5-02	15	5	315	50.14	0.000	0.000	0.000	10
qsap15x5-03	15	5	294	50.14	0.000	0.000	0.000	10
qsap15x5-04	15	5	295	50.14	0.000	0.000	0.000	10
qsap15x5-05	15	5	287	50.14	0.000	0.000	0.000	10
qsap15x5-06	15	5	285	50.14	0.000	0.000	0.000	10
qsap15x5-07	15	5	305	50.14	0.000	0.001	0.000	10
qsap15x5-08	15	5	305	50.14	0.000	0.000	0.000	10
qsap15x5-09	15	5	305	50.14	0.000	0.000	0.000	10
qsap15x5-10	15	5	299	50.14	0.000	0.000	0.000	10
qsap15x7-01	15	7	275	3107.62	0.000	0.001	0.000	10
qsap15x7-02	15	7	283	3107.62	0.000	0.001	0.071	10
qsap15x7-03	15	7	273	3107.62	0.000	0.001	1.026	10
qsap15x7-04	15	7	282	3107.62	0.000	0.000	0.000	10
qsap15x7-05	15	7	288	3107.62	0.000	0.001	0.000	10
qsap15x7-06	15	7	271	3107.62	0.000	0.004	5.535	10
qsap15x7-07	15	7	266	3107.62	0.000	0.019	0.000	10
qsap15x7-08	15	7	295	3107.62	0.000	0.000	0.000	10
qsap15x7-09	15	7	273	3107.62	0.000	0.001	0.586	10
qsap15x7-10	15	7	275	3107.62	0.000	0.001	0.000	10
qsap20x5-01	20	5	575	84382.80	0.000	0.000	0.000	10
qsap20x5-02	20	5	573	84382.80	0.000	0.002	0.000	10
qsap20x5-03	20	5	592	84382.80	0.000	0.000	0.000	10
qsap20x5-04	20	5	590	84382.80	0.000	0.002	1.068	10
qsap20x5-05	20	5	588	84382.80	0.000	0.002	0.000	10
qsap20x5-06	20	5	591	84382.80	0.000	0.000	0.000	10
qsap20x5-07	20	5	588	84382.80	0.000	0.001	0.000	10
qsap20x5-08	20	5	541	84382.80	0.000	0.000	0.000	10
qsap20x5-09	20	5	600	84382.80	0.000	0.000	0.000	10
qsap20x5-10	20	5	579	84382.80	0.000	0.002	0.000	10

encountered [1]. Such a parallel computing method is easy to program and can exploit multiple cores existing in the majority of current personal computers, and cloud-based virtual machines. This easy-to-implement parallelism could keep the entire hardware busy, adding to the SACA potential efficiency.

Table 2. Comparison of average percent deviation from the optimal solution (OPT) for randomly generated DBAP instances

Problem	n	m	OPT	T_{OPT}(s)	%DEV_{best}	T_{best}(s)	%DEV_{avg}	T_{max}(s)
bap15x5-01	15	5	47	<0.01	0.000	0.000	0.000	5
bap15x5-02	15	5	357	<0.01	0.000	0.000	0.000	5
bap15x5-03	15	5	78	<0.01	0.000	0.000	0.000	5
bap15x5-04	15	5	155	<0.01	0.000	0.000	0.000	5
bap15x5-05	15	5	86	<0.01	0.000	0.000	0.000	5
bap15x5-06	15	5	166	<0.01	0.000	0.000	0.000	5
bap15x5-07	15	5	137	<0.01	0.000	0.000	0.000	5
bap15x5-08	15	5	196	<0.01	0.000	0.000	0.000	5
bap15x5-09	15	5	143	<0.01	0.000	0.000	0.000	5
bap15x5-10	15	5	50	<0.01	0.000	0.000	0.000	5
bap15x7-01	15	7	208	<0.01	0.000	0.000	0.000	5
bap15x7-02	15	7	164	<0.01	0.000	0.000	0.000	5
bap15x7-03	15	7	68	<0.01	0.000	0.000	0.000	5
bap15x7-04	15	7	169	<0.01	0.000	0.000	0.000	5
bap15x7-05	15	7	31	<0.01	0.000	0.000	0.000	5
bap15x7-06	15	7	42	<0.01	0.000	0.000	0.000	5
bap15x7-07	15	7	53	<0.01	0.000	0.000	0.000	5
bap15x7-08	15	7	66	<0.01	0.000	0.000	0.000	5
bap15x7-09	15	7	102	<0.01	0.000	0.000	0.000	5
bap15x7-10	15	7	52	<0.01	0.000	0.000	0.000	5
bap20x5-01	20	5	49	<0.1	0.000	0.000	0.000	5
bap20x5-02	20	5	60	<0.1	0.000	0.000	0.000	5
bap20x5-03	20	5	409	<0.1	0.000	0.000	0.000	5
bap20x5-04	20	5	282	<0.1	0.000	0.000	0.000	5
bap20x5-05	20	5	142	<0.1	0.000	0.000	0.000	5
bap20x5-06	20	5	173	<0.1	0.000	0.000	0.000	5
bap20x5-07	20	5	196	<0.1	0.000	0.000	0.000	5
bap20x5-08	20	5	137	<0.1	0.000	0.000	0.000	5
bap20x5-09	20	5	125	<0.1	0.000	0.000	0.000	5
bap20x5-10	20	5	300	<0.1	0.000	0.000	0.000	5
bap40x10-01	40	10	99	<30	0.000	0.000	0.000	5
bap40x10-02	40	10	94	<30	0.000	0.000	0.000	5
bap40x10-03	40	10	162	<30	0.000	0.000	0.000	5
bap40x10-04	40	10	90	<30	0.000	0.000	0.000	5
bap40x10-05	40	10	176	<30	0.000	0.000	0.000	5
bap40x10-06	40	10	117	<30	0.000	0.000	0.000	5
bap40x10-07	40	10	69	<30	0.000	0.000	0.000	5
bap40x10-08	40	10	348	<30	0.000	0.000	0.000	5
bap40x10-09	40	10	247	<30	0.000	0.000	0.000	5
bap40x10-10	40	10	268	<30	0.000	0.000	0.000	5
bap50x10-01	50	10	282	>150	0.000	0.001	0.000	5
bap50x10-02	50	10	145	>150	0.000	0.000	0.000	5
bap50x10-03	50	10	203	>150	0.000	0.000	0.000	5
bap50x10-04	50	10	73	>150	0.000	0.000	0.000	5
bap50x10-05	50	10	80	>150	0.000	0.000	0.000	5
bap50x10-06	50	10	191	>150	0.000	0.000	0.000	5
bap50x10-07	50	10	301	>150	0.000	0.000	0.000	5
bap50x10-08	50	10	188	>150	0.000	0.000	0.000	5
bap50x10-09	50	10	337	>150	0.000	0.000	0.000	5
bap50x10-10	50	10	125	>150	0.000	0.000	0.000	5

References

1. Amirghasemi, M.: An effective parallel evolutionary metaheuristic with its application to three optimization problems. Appl. Intell. 1–23 (2022). https://doi.org/10.1007/s10489-022-03599-w
2. Amirghasemi, M., Zamani, R.: An effective structural iterative refinement technique for solving the quadratic assignment problem. In: Cerulli, R., Raiconi, A., Voß, S. (eds.) ICCL 2018. LNCS, vol. 11184, pp. 446–460. Springer, Cham (2018). https://doi.org/10.1007/978-3-030-00898-7_30
3. Amirghasemi, M., Zamani, R.: Developing an effective decomposition-based procedure for solving the quadratic assignment problem. In: Paternina-Arboleda, C., Voß, S. (eds.) ICCL 2019. LNCS, vol. 11756, pp. 297–316. Springer, Cham (2019). https://doi.org/10.1007/978-3-030-31140-7_19
4. Arango, C., Cortés, P., Escudero, A., Onieva, L.: Genetic algorithm for the dynamic berth allocation problem in real time. In: Yang, X.S., Cui, Z., Xiao, R., Gandomi, A.H., Karamanoglu, M. (eds.) Swarm Intelligence and Bio-Inspired Computation, pp. 367–383. Elsevier, Oxford (2013). https://doi.org/10.1016/B978-0-12-405163-8.00017-X
5. Bacalhau, E.T., Casacio, L., de Azevedo, A.T.: New hybrid genetic algorithms to solve dynamic berth allocation problem. Expert Syst. Appl. **167**, 114198 (2021). https://doi.org/10.1016/j.eswa.2020.114198
6. Bierwirth, C., Meisel, F.: A survey of berth allocation and quay crane scheduling problems in container terminals. Eur. J. Oper. Res. **202**(3), 615–627 (2010). https://doi.org/10.1016/j.ejor.2009.05.031
7. Buhrkal, K., Zuglian, S., Ropke, S., Larsen, J., Lusby, R.: Models for the discrete berth allocation problem: a computational comparison. Transp. Res. Part E: Logist. Transp. Rev. **47**(4), 461–473 (2011). https://doi.org/10.1016/j.tre.2010.11.016
8. Bullnheimer, B.: An examination scheduling model to maximize students' study time. In: Burke, E., Carter, M. (eds.) PATAT 1997. LNCS, vol. 1408, pp. 78–91. Springer, Heidelberg (1998). https://doi.org/10.1007/BFb0055882
9. Christensen, C., Holst, C.: Berth allocation in container terminals. Master's thesis, Department of Informatics and Mathematical Modelling, Technical University of Denmark (2008)
10. Cordeau, J.F., Laporte, G., Legato, P., Moccia, L.: Models and tabu search heuristics for the berth-allocation problem. Transp. Sci. **39**(4), 526–538 (2005). https://doi.org/10.1287/trsc.1050.0120
11. Domschke, W.: Schedule synchronization for public transit networks. Oper. Res. Spektr. **11**(1), 17–24 (1989)
12. Domschke, W., Forst, P., Voß, S.: Tabu search techniques for the quadratic semi-assignment problem. In: Fandel, G., Gulledge, T., Jones, A. (eds.) New Directions for Operations Research in Manufacturing, pp. 389–405. Springer, Heidelberg (1992). https://doi.org/10.1007/978-3-642-77537-6_23
13. Hoffarth, L., Voß, S.: Liegeplatzdisposition auf einem container terminal—Ansätze zur Entwicklung eines entscheidungsunterstützenden systems. In: Operations Research Proceedings 1993. ORP, vol. 1993, pp. 89–95. Springer, Heidelberg (1994). https://doi.org/10.1007/978-3-642-78910-6_28
14. Hu, Z.H.: Multi-objective genetic algorithm for berth allocation problem considering daytime preference. Comput. Industr. Eng. **89**, 2–14 (2015). https://doi.org/10.1016/j.cie.2015.04.035

15. Imai, A., Nishimura, E., Papadimitriou, S.: The dynamic berth allocation problem for a container port. Transp. Res. Part B: Methodol. **35**(4), 401–417 (2001). https://doi.org/10.1016/S0191-2615(99)00057-0
16. Iris, C., Pacino, D., Ropke, S.: Improved formulations and an adaptive large neighborhood search heuristic for the integrated berth allocation and quay crane assignment problem. Transp. Res. Part E: Logist. Transp. Rev. **105**, 123–147 (2017). https://doi.org/10.1016/j.tre.2017.06.013
17. Jotshi, A., Batta, R.: Finding robust paths for routing ambulances in a dynamic disaster environment. In: Proceedings of the IIE Annual Conference, pp. 1–6 (2004)
18. Kramer, A., Lalla-Ruiz, E., Iori, M., Voß, S.: Novel formulations and modeling enhancements for the dynamic berth allocation problem. Eur. J. Oper. Res. **278**(1), 170–185 (2019). https://doi.org/10.1016/j.ejor.2019.03.036
19. Lalla-Ruiz, E., Voß, S.: Improving solver performance through redundancy. J. Syst. Sci. Syst. Eng. **25**(3), 303–325 (2016). https://doi.org/10.1007/s11518-016-5301-9
20. Lalla-Ruiz, E., Melian-Batista, B., Moreno-Vega, J.M.: Artificial intelligence hybrid heuristic based on tabu search for the dynamic berth allocation problem. Eng. Appl. Artif. Intell. **25**(6), 1132–1141 (2012). https://doi.org/10.1016/j.engappai.2012.06.001
21. Nishimura, E., Imai, A., Papadimitriou, S.: Berth allocation planning in the public berth system by genetic algorithms. Eur. J. Oper. Res. **131**(2), 282–292 (2001). https://doi.org/10.1016/S0377-2217(00)00128-4
22. Panyukov, A.V., Shangin, R.E.: Algorithm for the discrete Weber's problem with an accuracy estimate. Autom. Remote. Control. **77**(7), 1208–1215 (2016). https://doi.org/10.1134/S0005117916070079
23. Schröder, M., Solchenbach, I.: Optimization of transfer quality in regional public transit. Technical report 84, Fraunhofer (ITWM) (2006)
24. Theofanis, S., Boile, M., Golias, M.: An optimization based genetic algorithm heuristic for the berth allocation problem. In: 2007 IEEE Congress on Evolutionary Computation, pp. 4439–4445 (2007). https://doi.org/10.1109/CEC.2007.4425052
25. Vitaladevuni, S.N., Basri, R.: Co-clustering of image segments using convex optimization applied to EM neuronal reconstruction. In: 2010 IEEE Computer Society Conference on Computer Vision and Pattern Recognition, pp. 2203–2210 (2010). https://doi.org/10.1109/CVPR.2010.5539901
26. Zamani, R., Amirghasemi, M.: A self-adaptive nature-inspired procedure for solving the quadratic assignment problem. In: Khosravy, M., Gupta, N., Patel, N., Senjyu, T. (eds.) Frontier Applications of Nature Inspired Computation. STNC, pp. 119–147. Springer, Singapore (2020). https://doi.org/10.1007/978-981-15-2133-1_6

The Multi-port Continuous Berth Allocation Problem with Speed Optimization

Bernardo Martin-Iradi(✉), Dario Pacino, and Stefan Ropke

DTU Management, Technical University of Denmark,
Akademivej Building 358, 2800 Kgs., Lyngby, Denmark
{bmair,darpa,ropke}@dtu.dk
https://www.man.dtu.dk/

Abstract. We study the multi-port continuous berth allocation problem with speed optimization. This problem integrates vessel scheduling with berth allocation at multiple terminals in a collaborative setting. We propose a graph-based formulation and a branch-and-price method to solve the problem. The results show that the branch-and-price procedure outperforms the baseline solver. In our computational study, we highlight the trade-off between solution quality and computational complexity, as a function of the segment length used to model a continuous quay.

Keywords: Transportation · Maritime logistics · Container terminal · Exact methods

1 Introduction

The liner shipping industry is one of the major forms of international freight transportation. Seaborne trade and container throughput has continued growing steadily until 2019 and, despite the COVID-19 disruption in 2020, maritime trade recovered and is projected to expand by 4.3 % in 2021. The world fleet is also growing, not only in number of ships (more than 3 % in 2021), but also in size (the carrying capacity of mega-vessels rose from 6 to almost 40 per cent in the last 10 years) [1]. To accommodate the growing trade volume, ports and their container terminals need to either expand their capacity or improve the efficiency of their operations. Whereas the former usually requires a costly investment and in some cases it is not physically possible, the latter can be explored by means of operations research.

One of the key logistical operations in a container terminal is the berth allocation [2]. This operation is mathematically modeled as the berth allocation problem (BAP), where the aim is to assign berthing positions to incoming ships. The BAP is NP-hard [3] and has been extensively studied in the literature [4].

Most BAP studies consider either a discrete or a continuous quay. In the discrete variant, the quay is discretized into a set of berthing positions which can

J. de Armas et al. (Eds.): ICCL 2022, LNCS 13557, pp. 31–43, 2022.
https://doi.org/10.1007/978-3-031-16579-5_3

only serve one ship at a time. In the continuous version, ships can berth at any point within the quay as long as they respect a safety distance from other ships. The literature studies on the continuous BAP have approached the modeling part in different ways. Some studies use a continuous variable to define the berthing position of the ship [5,6], whereas other studies divide the quay into segments of short length (e.g., 10 m) and allow ships to occupy multiple consecutive segments based on their length [7,8]. In practice, the position of the quayside bollards can restrict the berthing positions for the ships, strengthening the latter modeling approach. We observe that a solution to the discrete BAP is feasible for the continuous BAP but it is not guaranteed that a solution to the continuous BAP is feasible for the discrete version of the problem. As a result, the continuous BAP provides a better or equal solution than the continuous one, but it is normally harder to solve. Our study follows the second modeling approach and investigates this trade-off between solution quality and computational complexity.

The main cost driver for a liner shipping company (i.e., carrier) is fuel consumption. The relation between fuel consumption and the vessel's sailing speed is non-linear, which translates in the fuel consumption growing significantly at higher speeds. Therefore, optimizing the sailing speed is one of the main priorities for carriers. The mathematical problem that studies this operation is known as the vessel scheduling problem (VSP) and has been actively researched in the last two decades [9]. The VSP aims at defining the sailing speeds between consecutive ports (i.e., voyage leg) to optimize fuel consumption while guaranteeing a service frequency on the route.

The optimization of the BAP and VSP have helped significantly improve the efficiency of operations for terminal operators and carriers, but can potentially lead to logistics issues in practice. On one hand, berth allocation is myopic as most container terminals plan their berth independently from other terminals. This is motivated by the competitive environment and reticence to share information. As a result, if one of the terminals faces a congestion, delayed vessels can propagate the delay to the next ports in their routes, leading to higher operational costs for both carriers and terminals [10]. On the other hand, the VSP is mainly studied from the carriers' perspective, and does not explicitly account for the berth allocation at the terminals. Overseeing the berth assignments can potentially result in longer turnaround times for vessels.

Recently, efforts have been made to address these issues by exploring collaborative schemes that take advantage of information sharing. In [11] we see the first effort to integrate the BAP and VSP into the multi-port berth allocation problem with speed optimization (MBAP), which aims at planning the berth allocation of multiple terminals simultaneously while also optimizing the sailing speed of the ships. The MBAP relies in a high level of collaboration, and recent studies show that these types of collaborative problems can be mutually beneficial to both the carriers and terminal operations [12,13].

To the best of our knowledge, the MBAP has only been studied considering a strictly discrete quay. The contributions of this paper are three-fold: (i) we present two mathematical formulations for the MBAP with a continuous quay based on a graph representation of the problem, (ii) we define a new set of benchmark instances based on real port data, and (iii) we propose an efficient exact method for the problem and demonstrate its performance over state-of-the-art commercial solvers.

2 Problem Formulation

In this section, we present two graph-based formulations for the MBAP with a continuous quay. We follow the modeling approach of diving the quay into

Table 1. Notation for the MIP formulation of the continuous MBAP

Sets and parameters	
N	Set of ships
P	Set of ports
T_p	Set of operational time instants at port $p \in P$
S	Set of speeds
L_p	Length of quay in port $p \in P$
$P_i \subseteq P$	Set of ports planned to be visited by ship $i \in N$ sorted in visiting order
$C_i. = \{1, ..., c\}$	Number of port calls for ship $i \in N$, one for each port visit
$\rho(c)$	The port $p \in P$ corresponding to port visit number $c \in C_i$ for ship $i \in N$
$\sigma(p)$	The port visit $c \in C_i$ corresponding to port $p \in P_i$ for ship $i \in N$
$x_0^{i,c}$	The ideal berthing position for ship $i \in N$ at port visit $c \in C_i$ measured at the leftmost position of the ship
$h_0^{i,c}$	Handling time at the ideal berthing position for ship $i \in N$ at port visit $c \in C_i$
EST_i^c	The expected start time of berthing for ship $i \in N$ at port visit $c \in C_i$
EFT_i^c	The expected finish time of berthing for ship $i \in N$ at port visit $c \in C_i$
LFT_i^c	The latest finish time of berthing for ship $i \in N$ at port visit $c \in C_i$
β	The relative increase in handling time per unit of distance
$\Delta^{p,p'}$	Distance between ports $p, p' \in P$
Θ_s	Travel time per unit of distance at speed $s \in S$
Γ_s^i	Fuel consumption per unit of distance at speed $s \in S$ fro ship $i \in N$
l_i	Length of ship $i \in N$
F	Fuel cost in USD per tonne
H	Cost of handling time in USD per hour
D_i	Cost of delay time in USD per hour for ship $i \in N$
I_i	Cost of waiting time in USD per hour for ship $i \in N$

segments of small size as in [8], where ships can occupy multiple segments simultaneously based on their length. Table 1 summarizes the notation of the problem.

It is general practice, especially on the discrete version of the BAP, to define a different handling time depending on the berthing position. For the study of a continuous quay, we follow the method presented in [8] where deviations from a preferred berthing position are penalized using a deviation factor $\beta \geq 0$ (relative increase in handling time per unit of distance, i.e., meters). Given the minimum handling time $h_0^{i,c}$ at the preferred berthing position, and the actual deviation from the chosen position Δb (measured in meters). The handling time at a given position b is computed as follows:

$$h_i^c(b) = (1 + \beta \Delta b) h_0^{i,c} \tag{1}$$

where $\Delta b = |b - x_0^{i,c}|$.

2.1 Network-Flow Formulation

Let $G = (O, A)$ be a directed graph formed by the sets of nodes O and arcs A. Additionally, we define the subset of arcs $A^k \subseteq A$ which denote the arcs available for a given ship $k \in N$.

We denote B_p to the set of quay segments of Φ meters for port $p \in P$. We define a node n for each port $p \in P$, berthing position $b \in B_p$, and time instant $t \in T_p$ Therefore, visiting a node can be interpreted as berthing at position b (left-most position) of port p at time instant t. Let $h_i^{c,b}$ be the handling time of ship i at port visit c and berthing position $b \in B_p$ and let $b_0^{i,c}$ be the berthing segment including position $x_0^{i,c}$.

$$h_i^{c,b} = (1 + \beta \Phi |b - b_0^{i,c}|) h_0^{i,c} \tag{2}$$

Equation 2 defines the computation of $h_i^{c,b}$ and it is adapted from Eq. 1. Since each node refers to a single position b, we can pre-compute the handling time related to each node. The cost of a node $c_{p,b,t}^i$ for ship i is defined in Eq. 3

$$c_{p,b,t}^i = H(h_i^{c,b}) + D_i(d_i^c) \tag{3}$$

where the delay d_i^c of ship i at port visit c is given as $d_i^c = \max(0, t + h_i^{c,b} - EFT_i^c)$.

Given the sequence of ports to visit by each ship, arcs are added to connect nodes of consecutive ports that correspond to feasible berths given the range of feasible sailing speeds. We add an arc between (p, b, t) and (p', b', t') for ship i if the ports are consecutive in the ships route $(p, p' \in P_i, p \prec p')$, and if the time difference allows to sail at a feasible speed $(t + h_i^{\sigma(p),b} + \Delta^{p,p'} \Theta_{MAX} \leq t')$ where Θ_{MAX} is the fastest feasible speed. Note that there is, at most, one arc between any pair of nodes. This arc corresponds to the speed level providing the lowest waiting time at the next port while still arriving on time. We do not allow the possibility of sailing faster to arrive to the same berthing time, as it does not provide any benefit and it only incurs in both higher waiting and fuel costs.

Additionally, the time instants of the nodes need to satisfy the time windows $EST_i^c \geq t$ and $t' + h_i^{\sigma p',b'} \leq LFT_i^c$, and the left-most berthing position should consider the length of the ship $b + l_i^{\Phi} \leq B_p$ where l_i^{Φ} is the number of berthing segments that ship $i \in N$ occupies given a segment of length Φ. The cost c_a^i of an arc $a = ((p,b,t),(p',b',t'))$ for ship i is defined in Eq. 4

$$c_a^i = I_i(t' - (t + h_i^{\sigma(p),b} + \Delta^{p,p'}\Theta_s)) + F(\Delta^{p,p'}\Gamma_s^i) \tag{4}$$

where $s \in S$ is the speed level associated with the arc.

Within the node set, we include $o, d \in O$ as artificial source and sink nodes respectively. Artificial source arcs are added for each ship connecting the source node with all the nodes of the first port in the route. In the same way, we add artificial sink nodes for each ship connecting the nodes from the last port in the route with the sink node. Let $\delta_k^+(u)$ be the set of nodes that can be reached by following a single outgoing arc $a \in A^k$ from node $u \in O$ for ship $k \in N$. Likewise, let $\delta_k^-(u)$ be the set of nodes that can be reached by following a single incoming arc $a \in A^k$ from node $u \in O$ for ship $k \in N$. We use the notation $[x;y]$ to define an interval between x and y where y is included and $[x;y)$ where y is not.

For each ship $n \in N$, port $p \in P$, berthing position $b \in B_p$ and operating time instant $t \in T_p$, we define the set $C(n,p,b,t) \subseteq O$ that denote the graph nodes for ship n whose berthing period covers time t and whose berthing position covers segment b (i.e. nodes that are *in conflict* with any ship berthing at time t and position b).

An example is depicted in Fig. 1 and the expression can be stated as follows:

$$C(n,p,b,t) := \left\{ v = (p,b',t') \in O \middle| b' \in \left(\max(b - l_n^{\Phi}, 0); b \right], t' \in \left(\max(t - h_n^{\sigma(p),b'}, 0); t \right] \right\}$$

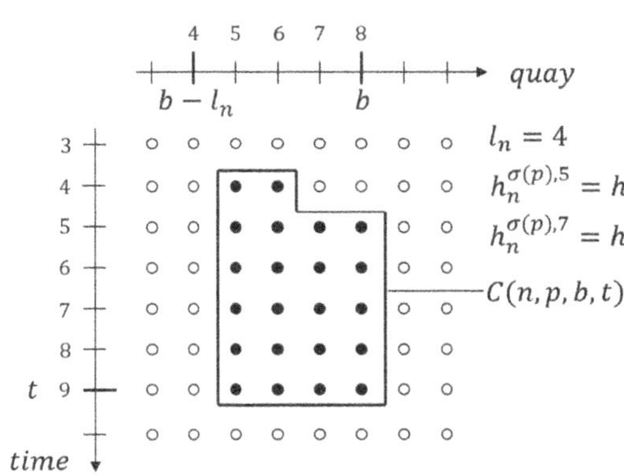

Fig. 1. An example of the set $C(n,p,b,t)$.

Finally, let $x_{i,j}^k$ be a binary variable deciding if arc $(i,j) \in A^k$ is selected for ship $k \in N$ and let $c_{i,j}^k$ be the weight associated to the same arc. For simplicity, we add the cost of node i in the cost of the arc (i, j) to merge the node and arc costs $c_{i,j}^k = c_i^k + c_{i,j}^k$.

$$\min \sum_{k \in N} \sum_{(i,j) \in A^k} c_{i,j}^k x_{i,j}^k \tag{5}$$

$$\sum_{j \in \delta_k^+(o)} x_{o,j}^k = 1 \quad \forall k \in N \tag{6}$$

$$\sum_{i \in \delta_k^-(d)} x_{i,d}^k = 1 \quad \forall k \in N \tag{7}$$

$$\sum_{i \in \delta_k^-(j)} x_{i,j}^k - \sum_{i \in \delta_k^+(j)} x_{j,i}^k = 0 \quad \forall j \in O \backslash \{o, d\}, k \in N \tag{8}$$

$$\sum_{k \in N} \sum_{i \in C(k,p,b,t)} \sum_{j \in \delta_k^+(i)} x_{i,j}^k \leq 1 \quad \forall p \in P, b \in B_p, t \in T_p \tag{9}$$

$$x_{i,j}^k \in \{0, 1\} \quad \forall (i, j) \in A, k \in N \tag{10}$$

The objective function (5) minimizes the cost of the selected arcs as in [13] which is the weighted sum of operational costs, namely, waiting time cost, handling time cost, delay time cost and fuel consumption cost. Constraints (6) and (7) ensure that, for each ship, only one arc leaves from the source node and arrives to the sink node respectively. Constraints (8) enforce flow conservation ensuring that for each node, except the source and sink ones, there are as many incoming as outgoing arcs. Constraints (9) avoid overlapping of ships in time and space by ensuring that each berthing position is occupied by at most one ship at each time instant. Finally, constraints (10) define the binary property of the variable.

2.2 Set Partitioning Formulation

Only the set of constraints (9) is not independent between ships. We, therefore, exploit the structure of the formulation and apply Dantzig-Wolfe decomposition [14] and transform the network-flow formulation into a set partitioning problem (SPP) formulation where constraint (9) is handled in the master problem and each variable (i.e., column) refers to a whole feasible schedule of a ship along its route. According to [15], the pure binary nature of the variables of the network flow formulation allows us to impose binary conditions on the variables of the new master problem.

$$\min \sum_{j \in \Omega} c_j \lambda_j \tag{11}$$

$$\sum_{j \in \Omega} A_j^i \lambda_j = 1 \quad \forall i \in N \tag{12}$$

$$\sum_{j \in \Omega} B_j^{p,b,t} \lambda_j \leqslant 1 \quad \forall p \in P, b \in B_p, t \in T_p \tag{13}$$

$$\lambda_j \in \{0,1\} \quad \forall j \in \Omega \tag{14}$$

The set of all columns is comprised in Ω and the decision variable λ_j is set to 1 if column $j \in \Omega$ is chosen as part of the solution and 0 otherwise. We denote c_j as the cost related to column $j \in \Omega$. In order to replicate the objective of the MIP formulation, this cost consists of the idleness, handling cost, delay and bunker consumption cost of the ship denoted by the column. Let A_j^i be a parameter that is equal to 1 if column $j \in \Omega$ corresponds to ship $i \in N$ and 0 otherwise. Likewise, let $Q_j^{p,b,t}$ be a parameter that is equal to 1 if the ship of column $j \in \Omega$ is occupying position $b \in B_p$ at time instant $t \in T_p$ at port $p \in P$ and 0 otherwise.

The objective function (11) minimizes the cost c_j of the columns which corresponds to the same weighted sum as the objective function of the network-flow formulation. Constraints (12) ensure that one column is selected for each ship. Constraints (13) guarantee that each berthing segment of each port is covered by at most one ship at any time instant. Finally, constraints (14) set the binary property of the decision variables.

3 Solution Method

To solve (11)–(14), we present a *branch-and-price* method. We notice that the number of possible paths for each ship in the network is prohibitively large even for small size instances. Therefore, we opt for exploring delayed column generation methods. Notice that, by decoupling the pricing problem into N independent sub-problems, each of them results in a single shortest path problem. Given the directed and acyclic nature of the network, the problem can be solved using efficient label setting algorithms.

At each iteration, we solve the master problem with a restricted set of columns and obtain the dual solution. With that solution, we solve each of the pricing problems, and if a solution with a negative reduced cost is found, we add the corresponding new column to the master problem. We keep iterating until no more negative reduced costs are found.

3.1 Branching

Completing the column generation procedure gives us the optimal solution for the linear relaxation of the problem, which does not guarantee the solution to be integer. To achieve integer optimality, we need to embed column generation in a *branch-and-bound* procedure. This whole process is also known as *branch-and-price*, where column generation is performed at each node in the *branch-and-bound* tree.

A poor branching strategy can lead to exploring an excessively large or unbalanced tree and therefore, slow convergence. This is the case when branching on the path variables of the set partitioning formulation or arc variables from the network-flow formulation. Moreover, branching in these variables can impose additional restrictions in the pricing problem.

We propose branching on a set of nodes that aims to create a balanced partition. Given a fractional solution, we start by grouping the berthing times and positions per ship and port visit. For each ship and port visit, we compute the average and variance of their solution berthing times and positions. This results in $2 \cdot |N| \cdot |C_i|$ candidates, and we select the case with the highest variance to branch on. As an example, we assume that the case with the highest variance is the berthing position of ship A at visit B, with an average berthing position X. Then, our branching strategy enforces ship A to berth to the left or right of position X at visit B. This branching strategy guarantees at least one candidate and aims to provide a balanced branch-and-bound tree.

3.2 Computing Bounds

For some of the largest instances, even solving the root node with column generation can be computationally expensive. If the time limit is reached and the column generation procedure has not converged, we can derive a valid lower bound. In our case, given the convexity constraints of the master problem that ensure the solution to contain one column per ship, our valid lower bound can be computed as indicated in Eq. 15. Let z^* be the solution to the master problem at the last iteration and $\bar{c}_j$ the minimum reduced cost of pricing problem of ship $j \in N$, if negative, otherwise zero.

$$z^{LB} = z^* + \sum_{j \in N} \bar{c}_j \tag{15}$$

Once a percentage of the total time limit has reached and if the branch-and price procedure has not converged, we solve the original integer version of the problem with all the column generated in the branch-and-bound tree. This allows to obtain an initial upper bound or tighten the current one.

4 Results

In this section we perform a computational comparison between the proposed method applied to the set partitioning formulation, and a baseline commercial solver applied to the network-flow formulation.

4.1 Instance Generation

The benchmark instances provided by [11,13] are defined for the discrete case of the MBAP and are not rich enough to capture the aspects of the new variant of the problem. For this reason, we propose a new set of instances for the continuous MBAP.

We consider three different ship types: (i) feeder or small (l_n :$\leq$ 200 m), (ii) medium (l_n: 201–300 m), and large (l_n :$>$ 300 m). Larger vessels have a larger dead-weight and load capacity which implies a higher fuel consumption in general. Therefore, we define a different speed-fuel consumption relation Γ_s^i for each ship type, as well a different minimum handling time $h_0^{i,c}$ at each of the port visits.

All instances consider 3 terminals located in 3 of the main ports in northern Europe: (i) Rotterdam APMT ($L_1 = 1600$ m), (ii) Bremerhaven NTB ($L_2 = 1800$ m), and (iii) Hamburg EGH ($L_3 = 2100$ m).

The duration of the ships' time windows (i.e., $EST_i^c, EFT_i^c, LFT_i^c$) is based on historical port call data.

We define six different ship patterns based on real port data, each having a given type of ship and visiting either 2 or 3 ports in different orders. The set N of ships for a given instance is sampled from the ship patterns.

Parameters such as the ideal berthing position for the ships or the position and duration of external ships $\bar{N}$ are selected at random. We assume that the entire quay is available for berthing, unless an external ship is occupying it. The distance between ports is computed based on the actual sea distance of the maritime routes. Finally, we consider a set of 10 different speed levels, ranging uniformly between 17–21.5 knots.

To generate the entire set of instances, we use 3 parameter values: (i) number of ships to optimize, (ii) number of external ships per port, and (iii) the length of the quay segments. Table 2 indicates the values used for each parameter. For each combination of number of ships to optimize and number of external ships, we generate three instances, each with a different randomized seed. Then, for each instance, we divide the quay into segments of different length, resulting in a final set comprising 432 instances.

Table 2. Parameter values used to generate the instance set.

Number of ships to optimize	Number of external ships per port	Segment length (m)
4–15	3–5	10, 20, 50, 100

4.2 Comparison of Exact Methods

We set an algorithm time limit of 1 h. In the case of the branch-and-price method, we allocate 90 % of the time limit for the standard branch-and-price procedure and 10 % to solve the integer problem with all the columns generated. The model is entirely written in *Julia* [16] and using *CPLEX v. 12.10* as the solver on a single thread. It has been tested in a Xeon Gold 6226R with 64 GB of memory.

The results are summarized in Table 3, where we compare the branch-and-price method with the network-flow formulation solved by CPLEX. The instances have been grouped per number of ships to optimize, and the segment size. Each row comprises 9 instances. We compute the number of instances solved to optimality, the average computational time, and the optimality gap. We also compute the improvement in objective value with regards to the instances with a coarser segment length.

From the results in Table 3, we observe that the proposed branch-and-price method performs better than commercial solvers on the network-flow formulation. In the case of CPLEX, it is able to solve a few instances faster than the branch-and-price method, but we noticed that for instances with highly dense graphs (see Table 4), CPLEX runs out of memory when building the model. The average computational time in these cases corresponds to the runs of instances where CPLEX was not interrupted due to memory issues. On the contrary, branch-and-price finds a feasible upper bound for all instances within the time limit. We can observe that the impact in the solution quality of having a shorter segment length is significant. The operational costs can be reduced in more than 7% in some cases with a segment of 10 m instead of 100 m. However, this improvement comes at the expense of higher computational needs. From a practical perspective, solving the problem with a more coarse segment length could be useful when quick solutions are needed, for instance, when facing a disruption and needing to re-plan or when testing multiple scenarios.

Table 5 shows the average results grouped by segment length. Dividing the quay in segments of 100 m allows the method to solve all the instances, while for segments of 10 m, we can solve 74% of the instances maintaining a tight optimality gap. Moreover, halving the segment length from 100 to 50 m helps saving more than 2% in operational costs with an average run time of less than 5 min. Regarding individual operational costs, we observe that using shorter segments allows to achieve significant savings in waiting time and delay. The savings in handling time are lower but still positive. However, we notice that the fuel consumption costs increase marginally with shorter segments, suggesting that for most instances ships already sail at the slowest speed. Therefore, we can argue that, although using shorter segments does not necessarily translate into fuel savings, it helps to save in overall operational costs, by using the resources at the terminal more efficiently. As suggested in [13], the total savings arising from this collaborative problem could be distributed efficiently among the participating carriers and terminal operators, resulting in cost savings for all players and incentivizing further collaboration.

Table 3. Computational results for the set of instances grouped by number of ships to optimize and the length of the quay segments. "*" indicates that all instances reached the memory limit.

Instance		Branch-and-price				CPLEX		
Number of ships	Segment length (m)	Optimal instances (out of 9)	Optimality gap (%)	Time (s)	Objective improve-ment (%)	Optimal instances (out of 9)	Optimality gap (%)	Time (s)
4	10	9	0.00	114.0	−1.94	0	*	*
4	20	9	0.00	30.4	−1.63	6	0.00	512.5
4	50	9	0.00	19.7	−1.10	9	0.00	74.5
4	100	9	0.00	17.0	–	9	0.00	7.9
5	10	9	0.00	43.9	−1.98	0	*	*
5	20	9	0.00	24.1	−1.82	2	0.00	336.3
5	50	9	0.00	15.2	−0.93	9	0.00	119.3
5	100	9	0.00	13.8	–	9	0.00	13.2
6	10	9	0.00	76.3	−1.33	0	*	*
6	20	9	0.00	25.8	−1.13	4	0.00	1447.4
6	50	9	0.00	18.2	−0.83	9	0.00	128.7
6	100	9	0.00	16.3	–	9	0.00	13.1
7	10	9	0.00	282.4	−1.44	0	*	*
7	20	9	0.00	233.3	−1.29	0	*	*
7	50	9	0.00	80.9	−0.78	9	0.00	289.3
7	100	9	0.00	25.6	–	9	0.00	30.1
8	10	9	0.00	63.3	−2.06	0	*	*
8	20	9	0.00	20.6	−1.72	0	*	*
8	50	9	0.00	28.6	−0.57	9	0.00	311.4
8	100	9	0.00	17.7	–	9	0.00	32.8
9	10	7	0.21	994.0	−7.89	0	*	*
9	20	7	0.10	886.0	−7.46	0	*	*
9	50	8	0.00	571.2	−6.74	8	0.00	495.3
9	100	9	0.00	217.7	–	8	0.00	48.6
10	10	6	0.21	1160.8	−6.31	0	*	*
10	20	7	0.07	860.9	−5.94	0	*	*
10	50	9	0.00	137.6	−1.73	9	0.00	585.1
10	100	9	0.00	38.2	–	9	0.00	58.0
11	10	7	0.12	1225.3	−6.70	0	*	*
11	20	9	0.00	787.9	−6.26	0	*	*
11	50	9	0.00	186.1	−1.29	9	0.00	919.2
11	100	9	0.00	42.8	–	9	0.00	84.4
12	10	6	0.15	1480.8	−5.68	0	*	*
12	20	6	0.30	1189.8	−4.88	0	*	*
12	50	9	0.00	278.8	−4.13	8	0.04	1328.5
12	100	9	0.00	123.1	–	8	0.00	117.8
13	10	7	0.14	1131.9	−2.78	0	*	*
13	20	7	0.04	1150.2	−2.27	0	*	*
13	50	9	0.00	373.6	−1.41	6	0.18	1268.3
13	100	9	0.00	75.9	–	8	0.00	105.5
14	10	2	1.17	2974.9	−2.05	0	*	*
14	20	2	0.27	2595.2	−1.84	0	*	*
14	50	9	0.00	428.6	−1.22	6	0.00	1501.7
14	100	9	0.00	155.0	–	6	0.00	172.2
15	10	0	1.69	3365.4	−2.41	0	*	*
15	20	2	0.82	2606.4	−2.26	0	*	*
15	50	9	0.08	1115.1	−2.17	6	0.62	2064.8
15	100	9	0.00	534.9	–	6	0.13	583.9

Table 4. Average network sizes across instances with different quay segment lengths.

Segment length (m)	Average number of nodes	Average number of arcs
100	13,483	327,392
50	26,963	1,240,023
20	67,227	7,336,565
10	134,808	25,981,650

Table 5. Average operational cost savings compared to a segment length of 100 m.

Segment length (m)	Optimal instances (%)	Optimality gap (%)	Time (s)	Waiting cost (%)	Delay cost (%)	Handling cost (%)	Fuel cost (%)	Total (%)
10	74.1	0.46	1076.1	−9.12	−12.46	−0.87	0.45	**−3.84**
20	78.7	0.19	867.6	−6.81	−10.29	−0.70	0.51	**−3.48**
50	99.1	0.01	271.1	−5.13	−8.93	−0.62	0.19	**−2.08**
100	100.0	–	106.5	–	–	–	–	–

5 Conclusion

In this paper, we have studied a logistical problem that aims at simultaneously optimize the vessel scheduling and their berthing assignment in their port visits. We have modeled the continuous quay version of the problem as a network-flow formulation which we have re-formulated into a a set partitioning formulation. Decoupling the pricing problems per ship, allows to compute new columns by solving a shortest path problem. The results highlight the better performance of the proposed branch-and-price method compared to baseline solvers. Moreover, we show that using shorter quay segments can lead to a better use of the terminal resources and provide savings for carriers and terminal operators.

A natural next step for future work would be to study a different modeling approach for the continuous MBAP using a continuous variable to define the berthing position. Another aspect that deserves attention is the scalability of the method where exploring approaches to reduce the size of the graphs can help solving larger instances. Also, further research on possible valid inequalities could help fasten the algorithm. Moreover, we could explore ways to embed exact methods, such as the one presented, with heuristic procedures. This type of matheuristic could provide high quality solutions in shorter computational times.

References

1. UNCTAD: Review of maritime transport 2021 UNCTAD. https://unctad.org/system/files/official-document/rmt2021_en_0.pdf. Accessed 7 May 2022
2. Steenken, D., Voß, S., Stahlbock, R.: Container terminal operation and operations research - a classification and literature review. OR Spectr. **26**(1), 3–49 (2004)

3. Lim, A.: The berth planning problem. Oper. Res. Lett. **22**(2–3), 105–110 (1998)
4. Bierwirth, C., Meisel, F.: A follow-up survey of berth allocation and quay crane scheduling problems in container terminals. Eur. J. Oper. Res. **244**(3), 675–689 (2015)
5. Kim, K.H., Moon, K.C.: Berth scheduling by simulated annealing. Transp. Res. Part B: Methodol. **37**(2), 541–560 (2003)
6. Lyu, X., Negenborn, R.R., Shi, X., Schulte, F.: A collaborative berth planning approach for disruption recovery. IEEE Open J. Intell. Transp. Syst. **3**, 153–164 (2022)
7. Imai, A., Sun, X., Nishimura, E., Papadimitriou, S.: Berth allocation in a container port: using a continuous location space approach. Transp. Res. Part B: Methodol. **39**(3), 199–221 (2005)
8. Meisel, F., Bierwirth, C.: Heuristics for the integration of crane productivity in the berth allocation problem. Transp. Res. Part E: Logist. Transp. Rev. **45**(1), 196–209 (2009)
9. Dulebenets, M.A., Pasha, J., Abioye, O.F., Kavoosi, M.: Vessel scheduling in liner shipping: a critical literature review and future research needs. Flex. Serv. Manuf. J. **33**(1), 43–106 (2019). https://doi.org/10.1007/s10696-019-09367-2
10. Notteboom, T.E., Vernimmen, B.: The effect of high fuel costs on liner service configuration in container shipping. J. Transp. Geogr. **17**(5), 325–337 (2009)
11. Venturini, G., Iris, C., Kontovas, C., Larsen, A.: The multi-port berth allocation problem with speed optimization and emission considerations. Transp. Res. Part D: Transp. Environ. **54**, 142–159 (2017)
12. Dulebenets, M.A.: Minimizing the total liner shipping route service costs via application of an efficient collaborative agreement. IEEE Trans. Intell. Transp. Syst. **20**(1), 123–136 (2019)
13. Martin-Iradi, B., Pacino, D., Ropke, S.: The multiport berth allocation problem with speed optimization: exact methods and a cooperative game analysis. Transp. Sci. **56**(4), 972–999 (2022)
14. Dantzig, G.B., Wolfe, P.: Decomposition principle for linear-programs. Oper. Res. **8**(1), 101–111 (1960)
15. Jans, R.: Classification of Dantzig-Wolfe reformulations for binary mixed integer programming problems. Eur. J. Oper. Res. **204**(2), 251–254 (2010)
16. Bezanson, J., Edelman, A., Karpinski, S., Shah, V.B.: Julia: a fresh approach to numerical computing. SIAM Rev. **59**(1), 65–98 (2017)

Optimization of a Ship-Based Logistics System for Carbon Capture and Storage

Anders Bennæs[1], Martin Skogset[1], Tormod Svorkdal[1], Kjetil Fagerholt[1], Lisa Herlicka[2], Frank Meisel[2(✉)], and Wilfried Rickels[3]

[1] Department of Industrial Economics and Technology Management, Norwegian University of Science and Technology, Trondheim, Norway
kjetil.fagerholt@ntnu.no

[2] Faculty of Business, Economics and Social Science, Christian-Albrechts-University Kiel, Kiel, Germany
{lisa.herlicka,meisel}@bwl.uni-kiel.de

[3] Kiel Institute for the World Economy, Kiel, Germany
wilfried.rickels@ifw-kiel.de

Abstract. Carbon Capture and Storage (CCS) is the process of capturing CO_2 before it enters the atmosphere, transporting it, and then storing the CO_2 in a permanent underground storage site. CCS is projected to play an important role for compliance with the temperature degree goals set by the Paris Agreement, and with this in mind, we study the so-called Ship-Based CCS Logistics Problem (SCLP). The SCLP deals with designing a cost-effective ship-based logistics system to ensure that CO_2 captured from emission sources in the hinterland of loading ports is transported to unloading ports nearby the final storage sites. As part of this, one needs to determine the intermediate storage capacities at the loading ports, ship fleet size and mix, fleet deployment and sailing speeds along each chosen route. To solve the SCLP, we propose a new mixed integer programming model, where candidate ship routes are generated as input. We use our optimization model to analyze three future supply scenarios based on estimations of the volume of captured CO_2 from emission sources in mainland Europe that is brought via ports of Antwerp, Dunkirk, Rotterdam and Wilhelmshaven to Norwegian storage sites. Our computational results show that the logistics cost per tonne of CO_2 will be around 10 Euros in low volume scenarios and drop to about 8 Euros in high demand scenarios due to economies of scale. In the considered high demand scenario for the year 2050 about 100 ships are required that perform several thousand round trips per year within the considered port network.

Keywords: Carbon capture and storage · Maritime logistics system · Optimization · Case study

1 Introduction

Under the Paris Agreement in 2015, almost 200 countries pledged to limit global warming to well below 2 °C relative to preindustrial levels with the aim to keep

J. de Armas et al. (Eds.): ICCL 2022, LNCS 13557, pp. 44–59, 2022.
https://doi.org/10.1007/978-3-031-16579-5_4

warming even at 1.5 °C [22]. To reach this goal, global CO_2 emissions need to reach net-zero in the early 2050s [13]. Carbon Capture and Storage (CCS) might be a central technology for reaching these goals, as it can be applied to many industries. CCS is the process of capturing CO_2 before it enters the atmosphere, transporting it, and then injecting it in a permanent underground storage site. The International Energy Agency (IEA) has found that to achieve the goals of the Paris Agreement, nearly 15% of the cumulative emission reduction has to come from CCS till 2070 [14].

There are only two operating CCS projects in Europe today, namely on the offshore natural gas fields Sleipner and Snøhvit, both located in the coastal waters of Norway. In the early 2000s CCS was widely supported as a CO_2 mitigation option and Europe had more than 30 announced demonstration projects in the power and industry sector. However, all these projects were later cancelled, probably due to the public and private focus on short-term recovery after the global financial crisis. Recently a new wave of CCS projects has emerged. On a global scale, there are today 135 commercially intended CCS projects [10]. Out of these, only 27 are operational and most are in the early development phase, and there is a clear need for more research to make the CCS projects commercially viable [11].

With this in mind, we study the Ship-Based CCS Logistics Problem (SCLP). The SCLP deals with designing a cost-effective ship-based logistics system to ensure that CO_2 captured from emission sources in the hinterland of loading ports is transported to a set of unloading ports, from where it can be transported to the final storage sites. A source of inspiration for this is the Norwegian Northern Lights Project, which considers the transportation and storage part of the Norwegian full-scale CCS project known as *Longship*. Longship is designed for capturing CO_2 from industrial sources in the Oslo-fjord region and shipping liquefied CO_2 to an onshore terminal placed in Kollsnes on the Norwegian west coast. From there, the liquefied CO_2 is transported in offshore pipelines to a storage site under the seabed in the North Sea for permanent storage. Longship considers the CCS processes at two Norwegian industrial emission sources, however the Northern Lights Project aims at offering transportation and storage of CO_2 as a service for other European emission sources as well. Therefore, we consider in this paper the transportation of CO_2 captured in northern Europe, i.e., mainly in Germany and France.

The research on ship-based CCS logistics is relatively sparse. In the early IPCC CCS report [12], both pipeline and ship transportation of CO_2 were considered feasible. Aspelund et al. [2] present a study on technical solutions for ship-based transportation of CO_2, while Roussanaly et al. [19] use a CCS value chain simulation tool to benchmark offshore pipelines and shipping to an offshore site in a base case for a range of distances and capacities. Kjärstadt et al. [15] investigate CO_2 transport options and associated costs for CO_2 sources in Scandinavia. Both costs for ship and offshore pipeline transportation are calculated as a function of volume and distance. The recent in-depth cost estimation study [20] investigates the impact of the choice of CO_2 shipping conditions of 7 bar/−46 °C (low pressure) and 15 bar/−25 °C (medium pressure). They do an analysis for yearly volumes of up to 20 megatonnes (MTPA) and transportation distances up to 2000 km as in [19] and [21]. The analysis includes key elements in the ship-based CO_2 transport chain, where cost estimates are determined for liquefaction, intermediate storage, shipping, and reconditioning.

While cost assessments have been the most common approach for analyzing ship-based CCS, there has been a development in more recent times where optimization models also have been used. Nam et al. [16] formulate a mixed integer programming (MIP) model for the design of a ship-based offshore CCS system in Korea. They divide the optimization problem into two subproblems: a CO_2 liquefaction plant location problem and an offshore CO_2 transportation problem. The liquefaction plant location problem is solved first and aims at minimizing the annual capital and operating cost by choosing an optimal number and locations for the liquefaction plants serving different CO_2 sources. The results from the CO_2 liquefaction plant location problem are used as input in the subsequent transportation problem, whereby multiple liquefaction plants are summarized into one site as origin for the transportation problem and a fixed intermediate storage capacity is considered. The goal of the transportation problem is to determine the optimal fleet size and mix of ships, fleet deployment and route service frequency for the transportation of the CO_2 from the liquefaction plants to the offshore storage sites. System-wide supply chain optimization is focused in [6]. This work presents a MIP model to determine the optimal design of a European supply chain for CCS. The model comprises offshore and onshore pipelines and shipping to and from existing docks as transportation options and includes emissions from European industrial emission sources such as steel industries, cement plants and refineries. By determining cost-optimal transportation capacities and modes for different capture scenarios, one ship type with a capacity of 10 000 tonnes and an average speed of 14 km per hour are assumed. The recent study from Bjerketvedt et al. [3] takes a more operational approach than the previously described models and investigates the impact of operational fluctuations and uncertainties on the design and expected cost of ship-based CO_2 transport. The model is a two-stage stochastic programming model for a single-source, single-sink CCS chain. As for our problem, [3] makes investment decisions on the capacities of liquefaction, storage and reconditioning. However, the ship size is given and the model is based on only one ship operating. The ship's sailing time is considered uncertain due to changing weather conditions.

In this paper we extend the current literature on using optimization models to solve and analyze the SCLP. More specifically, our contributions are as follows. First, we propose a new MIP model for the SCLP. Second, we use the MIP on a real case where we study future capture scenarios from mainland Europe with the Northern Lights storage infrastructure in Kollsnes, Norway, as the chosen storage site. The case study is in alignment with the ambition of Northern Lights, which is to offer flexible transportation and storage infrastructure for CO_2 across national borders. Analyzing the SCLP in this context gives valuable insights into both operational and investment costs of a ship-based CCS logistics system for different volumes of CO_2. It can thus be used as a tool in decision-making regarding the choice of transportation technologies for CCS projects in the future.

The outline of this paper is as follows. Section 2 provides a formal definition of the Ship-based CCS Logistics Problem (SCLP), while the proposed MIP model for the SCLP is provided in Sect. 3. Section 4 presents our case study and analyses, while concluding remarks are given in Sect. 5.

2 Problem Definition

In this section, we provide a formal definition of the Ship-based CCS Logistics Problem (SCLP). The SCLP is the strategic planning problem of designing a cost-effective ship-based transportation network for captured CO_2 that is intermediately stored at a given set of loading ports and brought from there to a set of unloading ports nearby the final storage locations.

Accordingly, we categorize each port in the SCLP as either loading or unloading port. Each loading port has an associated estimated supply of pressurized CO_2 that has been captured and transported through pipelines from the various emission sources in its surroundings and hinterland. A given set of candidate ship types is available for the seaborne transportation from the loading to the unloading ports, each with a specific tank design pressure (low or medium pressure), capacity, fuel consumption function and cost structure. Each ship type has a given sailing speed range and the fuel consumption depends on the chosen speed. There is also a given service time for loading and unloading a ship at a port.

Before being transported, the CO_2 must be liquefied and stored at the loading ports. For this purpose, each port has a liquefaction unit and an intermediate storage facility that needs to be selected among a set of candidate storage types. The liquefaction unit has a cost structure dependent on the inlet pressure and the storage tank design pressure. The storage types differ in capacities, costs and tank design pressure (low or medium pressure). The same type of storage is needed at the unloading ports. When a ship arrives at an unloading port, the CO_2 is unloaded to this intermediate storage. Before being injected into the geological storage site, CO_2 must be pressurized and reconditioned to make it suitable for pipeline transportation. For this purpose, each unloading port has a reconditioning unit with a given cost. The loading and unloading port facilities, namely the storage as well as liquefaction (loading ports) or reconditioning units (unloading ports), have different designs and capacities for the different pressure configurations. These have to be compatible with the CO_2 pressure configuration and capacity of the chosen ships.

The goal of the SCLP is to minimize the total costs related to the ship-based logistics system over a representative planning period (e.g., a year). The costs can be divided into five parts. The first part is the cost of the chosen fleet of ships, which consists of hiring and sailing costs. The hiring costs are the chartering costs of the ship fleet and include the crew costs. The sailing costs relate to the fuel consumption of the ships, which depend on the chosen sailing speed. The second cost element is the storage cost, consisting of both investment and operating costs. The last three cost elements are the costs for liquefaction, reconditioning and loading/unloading, in which all three have associated investment and operating costs dependent on the CO_2 throughput of their respective ports.

The SCLP includes decisions at the strategic, tactical and operational level. At the strategic level, there are decisions about fleet size and mix (i.e., number of each candidate ship type), the capacity and type of the storage, liquefaction and reconditioning facilities, including what pressure configurations to use at each port. The tactical decisions include the deployment of the ships in the chosen fleet, i.e., the number of times over the given planning horizon each ship type should sail a given route, and the amount of CO_2 transported between the ports along the routes. Finally, since the sailing speed of the ships heavily influence the fuel consumption, and hence the operating costs, we also include the operational decisions about the sailing speeds along the routes. These decisions must be made while ensuring that all supply of CO_2 in a loading port is transported, and the storage capacities at the ports are not violated at any time. We combine these three levels of decision making into one holistic model to get a best possible estimate of the total cost for the considered CCS supply chain. For this purpose, the strategic investment and fleet decisions are complemented by tactical and operational decisions of the transportation by ship to make sure that all relevant cost of the resulting system are entirely included into the evaluation.

We make certain simplifications and practical assumptions to ensure that the SCLP model is tractable yet useful. First of all, we assume a constant steady-state supply of CO_2 at the loading ports. Since the CO_2 is captured at multiple sources, we believe this is a reasonable assumption due to the law of great numbers and because industry will provide a rather constant outflow of CO_2. We assume that the CO_2 is arriving at the loading ports in a pressurized state through pipelines, which heavily reduces the total transportation cost due to lower liquefaction costs. We consider this also to be a fair assumption, as pipelines are the most used mode of onshore transportation for large CO_2 volumes [10]. We also assume that the unloading ports always have sufficient capacity to receive, store and recondition the CO_2 when a ship arrives. Finally, to prevent interactions among different routes and to contribute to operational feasibility, we assume that a given loading port will be serviced by only one outgoing route that is operated by only one selected ship type.

3 Mathematical Model

In Sect. 3.1 we present our modeling approach and introduce the notation, before the mathematical model is presented in Sect. 3.2. The complete notation used for the model is shown in Table 1, whereas the subsequent section concentrates on describing the most relevant notation only.

3.1 Modeling Approach and Notation

The modeling is done with a strategic perspective, where decisions focus on fleet size and mix as well as on the selection of intermediate storage capacities. The tactical and operational modeling of the ship-based transportation follows [4] and [5], where we pre-generate all feasible sailing routes as input to the model, leaving the model with the decision of choosing on which routes among this set of candidate routes to deploy the ships. A route in our model is a cycle that includes a given subset of ports that are visited in the sequence that yields the shortest path possible for visiting these ports. We consider cyclic routes as ships will travel those routes consecutively several times within the planning horizon, from which they have to return to their starting point after visiting the last port in the route. The set of all candidate routes is denoted $\mathcal{R}$, while the set of routes that visit port i is denoted $\mathcal{R}_i^N$. Furthermore, the model handles the situation where each ship type only can operate a subset of the routes. This is defined through the set $\mathcal{R}_v$, which includes all routes that are feasible for ships of type v. The ports that are part of route r are defined by the set $\mathcal{N}_r$, while the sets $\mathcal{N}_r^L$ and $\mathcal{N}_r^U$ consist of the loading and unloading ports in route r, respectively.

Before ship transport, the CO_2 is pressurized. Since several candidate pressure states are feasible due to different available technologies, $\mathcal{P}$ defines the set of candidate pressures for CO_2 during ship transport (e.g., low and medium pressure). Furthermore, while the set $\mathcal{V}$ includes all ship types that are available, the set $\mathcal{V}_p$ is the set of ship types that operate at pressure state p.

Furthermore, a ship's fuel consumption as a function of sailing speed typically is non-linear and convex [18]. We follow the modeling approach of [1] where we define a number of discrete sailing speed options, defined by the set $\mathcal{S}$, and approximate the fuel consumption, as well as the sailing time and costs, based on linear combinations of these.

The model includes four types of decisions, i.e., 1) the fleet size and mix of ships, 2) the capacities of the storages, 3) deployment of the ships (including speed selection) and 4) the quantities loaded onto and unloaded from ships at different ports. The four types of decisions are related to four types of variables. The first decision is determined by the variable u_{vr}, which is the number of ships of type v that sail route r. The second decision variable is y_{ipb}, a binary variable taking the value 1 if storage capacity b with pressure state p is chosen at port i, 0 otherwise. The third decision relates to x_{vrs}, which is the number of times route r is sailed by ship type v at speed s. The fourth decision is handled by q_{ipvr}, which denotes the total quantity transferred between ships of ship type v and port i at a pressure state p on all round trips of a route r. To handle the assumption that each loading port only can be included in one chosen route, the binary variable a_{vr} is 1 if ships of ship type v sail route r, 0 otherwise. The last variable h_{ip} is the number of times storage with pressure p in port i is visited. An auxiliary variable z_{ipb} is used for linking h_{ip} and y_{ipb}.

Table 1. Notation used in this study.

Sets	
$\mathcal{N}^U$	Set of unloading ports
$\mathcal{N}^L$	Set of loading ports
$\mathcal{N}$	Set of ports, $\mathcal{N} = \mathcal{N}^L \cup \mathcal{N}^U$
$\mathcal{R}$	Set of candidate routes
$\mathcal{N}_r^L$	Set of loading ports in route r, $\mathcal{N}_r^L \subseteq \mathcal{N}^L$
$\mathcal{N}_r^U$	Set of unloading ports in route r, $\mathcal{N}_r^U \subseteq \mathcal{N}^U$
$\mathcal{N}_r$	Set of ports in route r, $\mathcal{N}_r = \mathcal{N}_r^L \cup \mathcal{N}_r^U$
$\mathcal{V}$	Set of ship types
$\mathcal{R}_v$	Set of candidate routes for a ship type v. $\mathcal{R}_v \subseteq \mathcal{R}$
$\mathcal{R}_i^N$	Set of candidate routes that include port i, $\mathcal{R}_i^N \subseteq \mathcal{R}$
$\mathcal{R}_{iv}$	Set of candidate routes that visit port i and are feasible for ship type v, $\mathcal{R}_{iv} = \mathcal{R}_i^N \cap \mathcal{R}_v$
$\mathcal{B}_i$	Set of candidate storage capacities for port i
$\mathcal{S}$	Set of sailing speed options for ships
$\mathcal{P}$	Set of optional pressure states to store and transport CO_2
$\mathcal{V}_p$	Set of ship types that operate with pressure p, $\mathcal{V}_p \subseteq \mathcal{V}$
Parameters	
C_{vrs}^T	Cost of sailing route r for ship type v at speed option s
C_v^H	Cost of hiring a ship of type v in the planning horizon
C_p^L	Fixed and variable costs per tonne liquefied CO_2 in pressure state p
C_p^R	Fixed and variable costs per tonne reconditioned CO_2 in pressure state p
C^{LU}	Fixed and variable costs per tonne CO_2 loaded and unloaded to/from ships
C_{ipb}^B	Fixed costs of storage capacity b with pressure p at port i
K_v^V	Capacity of ship type v (tonnes of CO_2)
K_b^B	Capacity of storage option b (tonnes of CO_2)
P^B	Minimum storage capacity as the proportion of loading/unloading quantity per visit in a port
S_i	Total CO_2 supplied at port i during the planning horizon (tonnes CO_2)
T_{vrs}	Time to complete one round trip of route r by a ship of ship type v at speed s
$\overline{T}$	Length of the planning horizon (days)
M_{vrs}^X	Minimum number of round trips needed for a ship of type v to transport all the supply on route r when sailing at speed s
M_{ip}^H	Number of visits needed if the ship with the least amount of storage capacity needs to handle all the supply from port i with pressure p
Variables	
u_{vr}	Number of ships of ship type v sailing route r during the planning horizon
y_{ipb}	Binary variable; 1 if storage capacity b with pressure state p is used at port i, 0 otherwise
x_{vrs}	Number of times route r is sailed by ship type v at speed s
q_{ipvr}	Total quantity transferred between ships of ship type v and a storage with pressure p at port i on all round trips of route r
a_{vr}	Binary variable; 1 if ship type v sails route r, 0 otherwise
h_{ip}	Number of times the storage with pressure p in port i is visited
z_{ipb}	Auxiliary variable that links h_{ip} and y_{ipb}, such that z_{ipb} is equal to h_{ip} if storage capacity b with pressure type p is chosen in port i, and 0 otherwise

3.2 Model Formulation

Using the notation introduced in Sect. 3.1, we can formulate the mathematical model for the SCLP as follows.

The objective of the model is to minimize the total costs of the ship-based logistics system. The objective function consists of five parts that are summed up. The first part is the ship costs given by (1), where the first term calculates the total sailing costs, while the latter is the total hiring costs for the selected ships. Thereafter, the investment costs of the selected storages are presented in (2). Finally, costs related to liquefaction, reconditioning, and loading and unloading are presented in (3), (4) and (5), respectively.

$$\min \rightarrow w = \sum_{v \in \mathcal{V}} \sum_{r \in \mathcal{R}_v} \sum_{s \in \mathcal{S}_v} C^T_{vrs} x_{vrs} + \sum_{v \in \mathcal{V}} \sum_{r \in \mathcal{R}_v} C^H_v u_{vr} \tag{1}$$

$$+ \sum_{i \in \mathcal{N}} \sum_{b \in \mathcal{B}_i} \sum_{p \in \mathcal{P}} C^B_{ipb} y_{ipb} \tag{2}$$

$$+ \sum_{i \in \mathcal{N}^L} \sum_{p \in \mathcal{P}} \sum_{v \in \mathcal{V}_p} \sum_{r \in \mathcal{R}_{iv}} C^L_p q_{ipvr} \tag{3}$$

$$+ \sum_{i \in \mathcal{N}^U} \sum_{p \in \mathcal{P}} \sum_{v \in \mathcal{V}_p} \sum_{r \in \mathcal{R}_{iv}} C^R_p q_{ipvr} \tag{4}$$

$$+ \sum_{i \in \mathcal{N}} \sum_{p \in \mathcal{P}} \sum_{v \in \mathcal{V}_p} \sum_{r \in \mathcal{R}_{iv}} C^{LU} q_{ipvr} \tag{5}$$

The model needs to secure feasible and consistent transportation of CO_2 between the loading and unloading ports, which is ensured by Constraints (6)–(8). Constraints (6) make sure that the quantity loaded is equal to the quantity unloaded at the ports in each route. Furthermore, ships cannot carry more CO_2 than their capacities, which is ensured by Constraints (7). Finally, Constraints (8) make sure that there is a sufficient number of ships of each ship type available to sail the routes at the chosen sailing speeds.

$$\sum_{i \in \mathcal{N}^L_r} q_{ipvr} - \sum_{i \in \mathcal{N}^U_r} q_{ipvr} = 0 \qquad p \in \mathcal{P}, v \in \mathcal{V}_p, r \in \mathcal{R}_v \tag{6}$$

$$K^V_v \sum_{s \in \mathcal{S}} x_{vrs} - \sum_{i \in \mathcal{N}^L_r} q_{ipvr} \geq 0 \qquad p \in \mathcal{P}, v \in \mathcal{V}_p, r \in \mathcal{R}_v \tag{7}$$

$$\sum_{s \in \mathcal{S}} T_{vrs} x_{vrs} - \overline{T} u_{vr} \leq 0 \qquad v \in \mathcal{V}, r \in \mathcal{R}_v \tag{8}$$

Constraints (9) state that the total amount of CO_2 supplied from a loading port during the planning horizon must be shipped. In Constraints (10), the number of times each storage at a port is visited, represented by variable h_{ip}, is calculated. Constraints (11) ensure that at most one storage facility can be built for each pressure state in a port. Constraints (12) make sure that each port gets a sufficient storage capacity for each pressure state, where the chosen capacity must be at least P^B times the average amount loaded or unloaded per ship visit at the given port.

$$\sum_{p \in \mathcal{P}} \sum_{v \in \mathcal{V}_p} \sum_{r \in \mathcal{R}_{iv}} q_{ipvr} \geq S_i \qquad i \in \mathcal{N}^L \tag{9}$$

$$\sum_{v \in \mathcal{V}_p} \sum_{r \in \mathcal{R}_{iv}} \sum_{s \in \mathcal{S}} x_{vrs} = h_{ip} \qquad i \in \mathcal{N}, p \in \mathcal{P} \tag{10}$$

$$\sum_{b \in \mathcal{B}_i} y_{ipb} \leq 1 \qquad i \in \mathcal{N}, p \in \mathcal{P} \tag{11}$$

$$\sum_{b \in \mathcal{B}_i} K_b^B z_{ipb} - P^B \sum_{v \in \mathcal{V}} \sum_{r \in \mathcal{R}_{iv}} q_{ipvr} \geq 0 \qquad i \in \mathcal{N}, p \in \mathcal{P} \tag{12}$$

Constraints (13)–(15) relate z, y and h variables with each other. From these constraints, $z_{ipb} = h_{ip}$ if storage capacity b with pressure type p is chosen in port i (i.e., if $y_{ipb} = 1$), and $z_{ipb} = 0$ otherwise.

$$z_{ipb} \leq M_{ip}^H y_{ipb} \qquad i \in \mathcal{N}, p \in \mathcal{P}, b \in \mathcal{B}_i \tag{13}$$

$$z_{ipb} \leq h_{ip} \qquad i \in \mathcal{N}, p \in \mathcal{P}, b \in \mathcal{B}_i \tag{14}$$

$$z_{ipb} \geq h_{ip} - M_{ip}^H (1 - y_{ipb}) \qquad i \in \mathcal{N}, p \in \mathcal{P}, b \in \mathcal{B}_i \tag{15}$$

Constraints (16)–(18) restrict the possible combination of routes in the solution. Constraints (16) ensure that a_{vr} becomes 1 if a route is sailed, while the next constraints make sure a_{vr} is 0 if the corresponding route is not sailed. A storage in a port can only be visited in one selected route sailed by one ship type, which is ensured by Constraints (18). The variable domains are presented in Constraints (19)–(25). Note that variables x_{vrs} and h_{ip} are defined as continuous variables even though they represent a number of round trips or visits, respectively. This is due to the strategic-tactical perspective of the SCLP where those numbers take relatively high values due to the long time horizon and, thus, do not have to be integer.

$$x_{vrs} \leq M_{vrs}^X a_{vr} \qquad v \in \mathcal{V}, r \in \mathcal{R}_v, s \in \mathcal{S} \tag{16}$$

$$a_{vr} \leq u_{vr} \qquad v \in \mathcal{V}, r \in \mathcal{R}_v \tag{17}$$

$$\sum_{v \in \mathcal{V}_p} \sum_{r \in \mathcal{R}_{iv}} a_{vr} \leq 1 \qquad i \in \mathcal{N}^L, p \in \mathcal{P} \tag{18}$$

$$u_{vr} \in \mathbb{Z}^+ \qquad v \in \mathcal{V}, r \in \mathcal{R}_v \tag{19}$$

$$y_{ipb} \in \{0, 1\} \qquad i \in \mathcal{N}, p \in \mathcal{P}, b \in \mathcal{B}_i \tag{20}$$

$$x_{vrs} \geq 0 \qquad v \in \mathcal{V}, r \in \mathcal{R}_v, s \in \mathcal{S} \tag{21}$$

$$q_{ipvr} \geq 0 \qquad i \in \mathcal{N}, p \in \mathcal{P}, v \in \mathcal{V}_p, r \in \mathcal{R}_{iv} \tag{22}$$

$$a_{vr} \in \{0, 1\} \qquad v \in \mathcal{V}, r \in \mathcal{R}_v \tag{23}$$

$$h_{ip} \geq 0 \qquad i \in \mathcal{N}, p \in \mathcal{P} \tag{24}$$

$$z_{ipb} \geq 0 \qquad i \in \mathcal{N}, p \in \mathcal{P}, b \in \mathcal{B}_i \tag{25}$$

4 Computational Study

In the following, we introduce our case study in Sect. 4.1 and present the results in Sect. 4.2.

4.1 Case Study and Input Data

The case study is prepared in order to explore the possibilities of connecting CO_2 emission sources in the European mainland to storage sites located in the North Sea. We use a representative planning horizon of one year (365 days). The case study and the calculation of its input parameters are described in more detail in the following.

Supply Scenarios and Ports: We use the supply scenarios from [17], which estimate the future supply of CO_2 of Germany, and allocate it to the ports Antwerp, Rotterdam and Wilhelmshaven. We also add the supply scenario from [9], which includes supply from Dunkirk. The supplies in each port for the years 2025, 2030 and 2050 are presented in Table 2. It should be noted that since the 2020 scenario estimated in [17] is currently not achieved, we denote the 2020 estimations as our 2025 scenario, which is one year after the Northern Lights project is planned to start its operations. Obviously, it is right now very difficult to establish realistic scenarios for future CO_2 supply volumes as using CCS technology is just in its beginning. In the end, even though we associate the identified volumes to particular years, it is of less relevance for our study when these volumes are actually achieved. Instead, our three scenarios serve the purpose of reflecting an initial situation, a ramp-up situation, and a mature situation. In what years these volumes are actually achieved is probably more a question of political regulations and technology adoption by industry. Finally, we consider one unloading port in our case study. This is Kollsnes, close to Bergen, Norway, which is the unloading port of the Northern Lights project.

Ship Types, Costs and Sailing Times: We define a set of candidate ship types to choose among. Each ship type is defined by a combination of a pressure state and a capacity. The relevant pressure states are defined based on [20], where the alternatives are 7 bar (low pressure) and 15 bar (medium pressure). Current CO_2 shipping technology is based on ships with medium pressure tanks.

Table 2. CO_2 supply scenarios, in megatonnes per annum (MTPA) [9,17]

Loading ports	2025	2030	2050
Antwerp	0.0	8.7	45.5
Dunkirk	3.0	5.0	10.0
Rotterdam	3.95	50.3	261.3
Wilhelmshaven	1.35	14.3	72.4
Total	8.3	78.3	389.2

However, there is ongoing research into the development of low pressure ships, and since we look at future supply scenarios, we include low pressure ships in the case study too. The feasible capacities for ships of each pressure state are also based on the analysis of [20]. For the low pressure state ships, we define 13 candidate ship types with capacities in the range from 2.5 to 50 kilotonnes (kt). As emphasized in [20], the medium pressure ships have a capacity limitation of 10 kt, so we define four candidate medium pressure ship types in the range from 2.5 to 10 kt.

For each candidate ship type, we estimate the hiring costs over the planning horizon. The hiring costs consist of two components: CAPEX (i.e., the cost of acquiring or chartering the ship) and OPEX (e.g., cost of the crew and maintenance). These cost estimates are based on [7] and [20]. We also estimate the sailing costs of the different ship types. These are dependent on the ships' fuel consumption, which again depends on the chosen speed, which we, based on [20], assume can be selected within the range of 10 to 16 knots for all ship types. For speed, we consider the three speed options of 10, 14 and 16 knots, where 14 knots is the design speed. The cost of fuel is set to 325 Euros per tonne [3].

The round trip times for the pre-generated candidate routes are generated based on sailing distance, ship speed and time spent in ports for loading and unloading, and is represented by the parameter T_{vrs}. For calculating the parameter, we assume that loading and unloading per port visit takes 12 h each, like in [3] and [20].

Storage Capacities and Costs: The storage alternatives are chosen so that they are aligned with the capacity alternatives for the candidate ship types. Thereby, we follow [3] who argue that the storage should have about 20% more capacity than the ship tanks to handle unforeseen events. Therefore, the set of storage alternatives corresponds to the ship capacities, where each value is multiplied by the parameter P^B, which is set to 1.2.

The storage costs are calculated based on the storage capacity and the pressure state. As for the ship hiring costs, the storage costs are subject to two components, namely a depreciated share of the investment costs (CAPEX) and some fixed OPEX. The investment costs are proportional with storage capacity and are set to 478 and 800 Euros per tonne of capacity for 7 bar and 15 bar, respectively [20]. The yearly fixed OPEX is set to 6% of the construction costs.

The liquefaction costs at the loading ports are calculated based on the throughput of CO_2. The throughput affects the required capacity of the liquefaction facility, which in turn affects the construction costs. As for ships and storages, the liquefaction facility construction cost represents a depreciated share of the investment costs and the OPEX is set as a share of the initial construction costs. The construction cost is estimated as a function of yearly liquefaction capacity. To estimate the construction costs, we use 15 and 13 Euros per tonne CO_2 of yearly liquefaction capacity for 7 bar and 15 bar, respectively [20]. Note that with these numbers, we assume that the CO_2 is pressurized when it arrives at the liquefaction facility, which is the case when the CO_2 comes from inland emitters in pipelines. Conversely, if the input CO_2 is at atmospheric pressure, which could be the case if the carbon capture takes place close to the liquefaction, the costs will be higher as there are more extensive requirements due to more pressurizing. The second part of the fixed costs is the yearly fixed OPEX, which is set to 6% of the investment costs [20]. As the liquefaction process is energy-intensive, there are also some variable costs [20]. These costs are subject to the consumption and unit price of electricity. The electricity consumption is 20 kWh and 11.25 kWh per tonne of CO_2 for liquefaction into 7 and 15 bar pressure, respectively, while the price of electricity is assumed to be 0.08 Euros per kWh.

The calculation of the reconditioning costs at the unloading ports is similar as for the liquefaction at the loading ports, including facility investment costs, OPEX and variable costs. Furthermore, the cost of reconditioning is very similar for low and medium incoming CO_2 pressure [7], thus we calculate the reconditioning cost independent of pressure. Based on the work by [3], the investment cost is set to 9 Euros per tonne of yearly CO_2 reconditioning capacity. Moreover, the OPEX is 4.6% of the investment costs and the variable cost is 0.41 Euros per tonne of reconditioned CO_2.

The costs of loading and unloading facilities in the ports are subject to investment costs and fixed OPEX. The investment cost is assumed linearly dependent on yearly throughput, given by 2.33 Euros per tonne CO_2. The fixed operational costs are set to 2% of the investment costs [20].

4.2 Results

Here, we present and compare the results for the 2025, 2030 and 2050 supply scenarios. To solve the model in Sect. 3, we use Gurobi (v. 9.1.2) on an Apple M1 processor. All scenario cases were solved to optimality in a matter of seconds.

The key performance measure that we are interested in is the cost per tonne of CO_2 for the downstream supply chain from the loading port to the final storage site. This measure is computed by taking the total cost of a solution as computed by the objective function components (1)–(5) and dividing this value by the total CO_2-supply in a scenario. As such, the cost involve ship costs, investments in storage sites, as well as cost for liquefaction, reconditioning, and loading and unloading. The resulting costs per tonne of CO_2 are shown in Table 3. These cost are 9.57, 8.23 and 7.99 Euros for the 2025, 2030 and 2050 scenario, respectively. They show that there are significant economies-of-scale when setting up a ship-based CCS logistics system given that the total CO_2 supply in the three scenarios

Table 3. Cost per tonne of CO_2 in different scenarios.

Scenario	Cost per tonne
2025	9.57
2030	8.23
2050	7.99

Table 4. Computational results for three demand scenarios.

Loading ports in route	Supply (Mt)	Ship capacity (kt)	# Ships	# Round trips	Avg. speed (kts)
2025 scenario					
Antwerp	–	–	–	–	–
Dunkirk	3.00	45	1	66.67	10.96
Rotterdam	3.95	50	1	79.00	12.29
Wilhelmshaven	1.35	15	1	91.48	12.46
2030 scenario					
Antwerp	8.7	45	3	193.00	10.00
Dunkirk	5.0	40	2	125.00	10.00
Rotterdam	50.3	50	15	1006.00	10.00
Wilhelmshaven	14.3	45	4	317.78	10.12
2050 scenario					
Antwerp	45.5	50	14	910.00	10.11
Dunkirk	10.0	50	3	200.00	10.96
Rotterdam	261.3	50	76	5226.00	10.07
Wilhelmshaven	72.4	50	18	1448.00	10.35

increases from 8.3 megatonnes (MTPA) per year in 2025, via 78.3 in 2030, to as high as 389.2 in 2050.

It should be noted that these costs do not constitute the full CCS-CO_2 cost since we do not consider the capturing at the emission sources, which constitutes the CCS supply chain's largest cost component, and the pipeline transportation from these to the loading ports. The price of emitting one tonne of CO_2 within the European Emission Trading System (ETS) is around 80 Euros per December 2021 and increasing [8]. The viability of the ship-based CCS logistics system will be based on the total supply chain costs. [6] estimate the costs for transporting the CO_2, including the inland transportation costs, to be between 6% and 18% of the total supply chain costs.

Table 4 provides more details of the optimal solutions for the 2025, 2030 and 2050 scenarios, respectively. These include information about the chosen ship types (in terms of capacity classes) and number of ships that are used to serve the different loading ports, as well as the number of round trips and chosen sailing speeds. It can be noted that all ship types selected in the optimal solutions and referred to in the tables are low pressure ships.

When setting up such a ship-based logistics system, several trade-offs must be considered. One consideration is whether to sail many round trips with smaller ships or to sail fewer rounds with higher capacity ships. If smaller ships are chosen, the ports will be visited more frequently, which allows also for smaller storage capacities (and costs). Despite this, it can be noted from the results in Table 4 that larger ships with capacities of 45 or 50 kt are preferred almost everywhere. This shows that there are economies-of-scale also with regard to the ship transportation. The exception is the ship type servicing Wilhelmshaven in the 2025 scenario, which has a capacity of only 15 kt. This is due to the low volumes in the given port in that scenario. We also observe that substantial ship fleets are required in the 2030 and 2050 scenarios. Especially in the high demand scenario of 2050, a fleet of 111 CCS-ships is required that perform in total 7784 round trips per year. The latter comes along with a very large number of port calls. For example, as all round trips involve the single unloading port Kollsnes, an average of 21 ship calls per day has to be handled at that port. Under the assumed port stay time of 12 h per visit, at least 10 ships have to be served in parallel throughout the whole year. Establishing the corresponding port infrastructure is surely a challenge.

Another trade-off is whether to choose low sailing speeds, which results in reduced fuel costs but a need for more ships, or whether to increase the sailing speeds, which will have the opposite effect. Based on the results from Table 4, we see that the chosen sailing speeds in most cases are close to its lower limit of 10 knots. This indicates that it is more important to reduce the fuel costs by reducing the sailing speed than having as few ships as possible. In a practical setting, this also gives a fleet with extra capacity which provides robustness and flexibility towards unforeseen events, e.g., where a ship breaks down or when the sailing times increase due to bad weather.

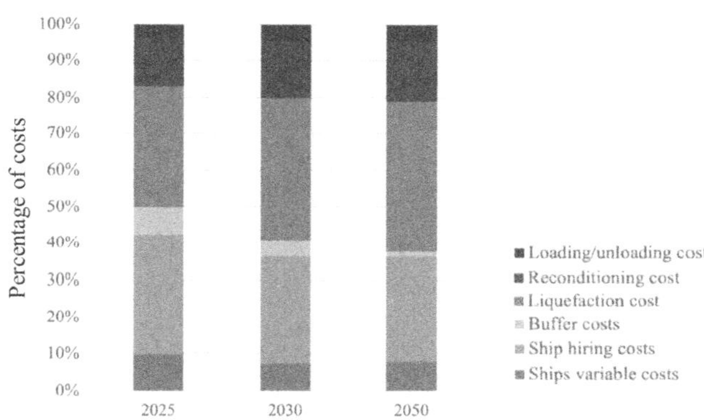

Fig. 1. Composition of costs for the three scenarios.

Figure 1 shows a break down of the total costs of the different solutions. We see that the cost of liquefaction of the CO_2 at the loading ports constitutes a share of 35–40% of the total costs (before the ship hiring costs at around 30%). Since the liquefaction costs heavily depend on the electricity price, we have performed a sensitivity analysis with regard to this. This analysis shows that an increase in electricity costs of 70% results in an increase of the total costs of the ship-based CCS logistics system by around 12% for the 2025 scenario and 14% for the 2030 and 2050 scenarios.

5 Concluding Remarks

To reach the Paris Agreement's two-degree goal, Carbon Capture and Storage (CCS) can play a central role. For this, we have studied the Ship-Based CCS

Logistics Problem (SCLP), which determines a cost-effective ship-based logistics system to ensure that CO_2 captured from emission sources in the hinterland of loading ports is transported to a set of unloading ports, from where it can be brought to final storage sites. As part of this, we determine the intermediate storage capacities at loading ports, ship fleet size and mix, fleet deployment and sailing speeds along each route. The problem is solved by formulating a mixed integer programming (MIP) model, where candidate routes are pre-generated as input.

We tested the model on three future supply scenarios based on estimations of the volume of captured CO_2 from emission sources in the hinterland of the ports of Antwerp, Dunkirk, Rotterdam, and Wilhelmshaven in the years 2025, 2030, and 2050, while Kollsnes is the only unloading port. The results show that there are significant economies-of-scale, as the transportation costs decrease with increased volumes. The cost per tonne of transported CO_2 is 9.57 Euros in the 2025 scenario with a total supply of 8.3 MTPA, 8.23 Euros in the 2030 scenario with a total supply of 78.3 MTPA, and 7.99 Euros in the 2050 scenario with a total supply of 389.2 MTPA. We also identified that a fleet of more than 100 CCS-ships is required in the 2050 scenario. These ships conduct almost 8000 round trips per year such that the involved ports have to establish infrastructure for handling up to 20 ships per day. Putting this into relation to the alternative of connecting mainland Europe and Norway by pipelines is subject of future research. Further topics of future research are the transition from one scenario to the next through a multi-period problem formulation and the handling of uncertainty especially for the very volatile input parameters like CO_2 supply volumes or shipping cost rates.

References

1. Andersson, H., Fagerholt, K., Hobbesland, K.: Integrated maritime fleet deployment and speed optimization: case study from RoRo shipping. Comput. Oper. Res. **55**, 233–240 (2015)
2. Aspelund, A., Mølnvik, M., De Koeijer, G.: Ship transport of CO_2: technical solutions and analysis of costs, energy utilization, exergy efficiency and CO_2 emissions. Chem. Eng. Res. Des. **84**(9), 847–855 (2006)
3. Bjerketvedt, V.S., Tomasgard, A., Roussanaly, S.: Optimal design and cost of ship-based CO_2 transport under uncertainties and fluctuations. Int. J. Greenhouse Gas Control **103**, 103190 (2020)
4. Chandra, S., Christiansen, M., Fagerholt, K.: Analysing the modal shift from road-based to coastal shipping-based distribution – a case study of outbound automotive logistics in India. Maritime Policy Manag. **47**(2), 273–286 (2020)
5. Dong, B., Christiansen, M., Fagerholt, K., Chandra, S.: Design of a sustainable maritime multi-modal distribution network – case study from automotive logistics. Transp. Res. Part E: Logist. Transp. Rev. **143**, 102086 (2020)
6. d'Amore, F., Romano, M.C., Bezzo, F.: Optimal design of European supply chains for carbon capture and storage from industrial emission sources including pipe and ship transport. Int. J. Greenhouse Gas Control **109**, 103372 (2021)

7. Element Energy: Shipping CO_2 - UK cost estimation study (2018). www.gov.uk/government/publications/shipping-carbon-dioxide-co2-uk-cost-estimation-study. Accessed 26 Apr 2022
8. Ember Climate: Daily carbon prices (2021). https://ember-climate.org/data/carbon-price-viewer/. Accessed 26 Apr 2022
9. European Commission: Candidate PCI projects in cross-border carbon dioxide (CO_2) transport networks (2021). https://energy.ec.europa.eu/system/files/2021-04/detailed_information_regarding_the_candidate_projects_in_co2_network_0.pdf. Accessed 26 Apr 2022
10. Global CCS Institute: Global status of CCS 2021 (2021). www.globalccsinstitute.com/wp-content/uploads/2021/10/2021-Global-Status-of-CCS-Global-CCS-Institute-Oct-21.pdf. Accessed 26 Apr 2022
11. Holz, F., et al.: A 2050 perspective on the role for carbon capture and storage in the European power system and industry sector. Energy Econ. **104**, 105631 (2021)
12. Intergovernmental Panel on Climate Change (IPCC): IPCC Special Report on Carbon Dioxide Capture and Storage (2005). https://www.ipcc.ch/site/assets/uploads/2018/03/srccs_wholereport-1.pdf. Accessed 26 Apr 2022
13. Intergovernmental Panel on Climate Change (IPCC): Climate change 2022, mitigation of climate change: summary for policy makers (2021). https://report.ipcc.ch/ar6wg3/pdf/IPCC_AR6_WGIII_SummaryForPolicymakers.pdf. Accessed 26 Apr 2022
14. International Energy Agency (IEA): CCUS in Clean Energy Transitions (2020). www.iea.org/reports/ccus-in-clean-energy-transitions. Accessed 26 Apr 2022
15. Kjärstad, J., Skagestad, R., Eldrup, N.H., Johnsson, F.: Ship transport - a low cost and low risk CO_2 transport option in the Nordic countries. Int. J. Greenhouse Gas Control **54**, 168–184 (2016)
16. Nam, H., Lee, T., Lee, J., Lee, J., Chung, H.: Design of carrier-based offshore CCS system: plant location and fleet assignment. Int. J. Greenhouse Gas Control **12**, 220–230 (2013)
17. Neele, F., Koenen, M., Seebregts, A., van Deurzen, J., Kerssemakers, K., Mastenbroek, M.: Report on possible development of CCS infrastructure in Germany (2011). www.co2europipe.eu/. Accessed 27 Apr 2022
18. Ronen, D.: The effect of oil price on containership speed and fleet size. J. Oper. Res. Soc. **62**(1), 211–216 (2011)
19. Roussanaly, S., Brunsvold, A.L., Hognes, E.S.: Benchmarking of CO_2 transport technologies: part II - offshore pipeline and shipping to an offshore site. Int. J. Greenhouse Gas Control **28**, 283–299 (2014)
20. Roussanaly, S., Deng, H., Skaugen, G., Gundersen, T.: At what pressure shall CO_2 be transported by ship? An in-depth cost comparison of 7 and 15 barge shipping. Energies **14**(18), 5635 (2021)
21. Roussanaly, S., Jakobsen, O.J.P., Hognes, E.H., Brunsvold, A.L.: Benchmarking of CO_2 transport technologies: part I - onshore pipeline and shipping between two onshore areas. Int. J. Greenhouse Gas Control **19**, 584–594 (2013)
22. United Nations: Report of the conference of the parties on its twenty-first session, held in Paris from 30 November to 13 December 2015 (2015). https://unfccc.int/resource/docs/2015/cop21/eng/10a01.pdf. Accessed 26 Apr 2022

A Linear Time Algorithm for Optimal Quay Crane Scheduling

Mathias Offerlin Herup, Gustav Christian Wichmann Thiesgaard(✉), Jaike van Twiller, and Rune Møller Jensen

IT University of Copenhagen, Rued Langgaards Vej 7, 2300 Copenhagen, Denmark
{ofhe,gthi,jaiv,rmj}@itu.dk

Abstract. This paper studies the Quay Crane Scheduling Problem (QCSP). The QCSP determines how a number of quay cranes should be scheduled in order to service a vessel with minimum makespan. Previous work considers the QCSP to be a combinatorially hard problem. For that reason, the focus has been on developing efficient heuristics. Our study shows, however, that the QCSP is tractable in the realistic setting, where quay cranes can share the workload of bays. We introduce a novel linear time algorithm that solves the QCSP and prove its correctness.

Keywords: Quay crane scheduling · Container terminals · Computational complexity

1 Introduction

In 2020 the global export of merchandise amounted to US$ 17.6 trillion [12] of which maritime transportation and container shipping accounted for roughly 80% [10]. Due to the significant size of the industry, there is a constant need for improvement, as even minor optimizations may yield massive economic results. That being said, container shipping is a complex industry consisting of several individual parties monitoring a number of sub-processes of their own.

Two central players are the container terminals and the carriers. The terminals act as links between land and sea, while the carriers transport containers between terminals. The key interface between them are quay cranes that load and discharge containers to vessels. Both terminals and carriers benefit from a minimum makespan of quay cranes operating a vessel [6].

The Quay Crane Scheduling Problem (QCSP) explores how a number of quay cranes should be assigned and organized in order to service a vessel such that a minimum makespan of the quay cranes is achieved. Quay cranes must adhere to several ordering and separation constraints. Due to these constraints, the

This research is sponsored in part by the Danish Maritime Fund under grant no. 2021-069.

M. O. Herup and G. C. W. Thiesgaard—These authors contributed equally to this work.

J. de Armas et al. (Eds.): ICCL 2022, LNCS 13557, pp. 60–73, 2022.
https://doi.org/10.1007/978-3-031-16579-5_5

QCSP has been considered a hard combinatorial optimization problem since its introduction by Daganzo [3]. In 2006, Lee et al. [8] proved a specific version of the problem called the QCSNIP to be *NP*-complete. Due to this complexity result, the use of heuristic algorithms in subsequent work has been widely justified as computing an optimal schedule would be too time consuming in practice, e.g., [1,11].

In contrast to the QCSP, however, the QCSNIP assumes that a bay at most can be serviced by a single quay crane throughout the whole schedule. This is an unrealistic assumption. It is common practice of terminals to have several quay cranes operating a bay during a schedule. They are merely restricted from operating a bay or a pair of adjacent bays simultaneously [6].

In this paper, we show that the QCSP is tractable in the realistic setting, where quay cranes can share the workload of bays. We introduce an algorithm that solves the QCSP to optimality in linear time and prove its correctness. Our results imply that it may be possible to formulate tractable and optimal quay crane scheduling algorithms that model all aspects of the real problem including variable separation distances, quay crane performance dependency on lift type, and time to move quay cranes between bays.

The remainder of the paper is organized as follows. Section 2 provides a brief introduction to the terminal domain. Section 3 reviews the existing literature relevant to the scope of this paper. Section 4 defines the QCSP. Section 5 discusses the validity of the QCSNIP model and corresponding proof as proposed by Lee et al. Furthermore, a linear time algorithm guaranteeing optimal solutions is proposed and its correctness is mathematically proven.

2 Container Terminals

Container terminals interact with carriers through service contracts. The contracts may include a berthing time window, a guaranteed number of crane moves to be processed during the port stay, and various handling fees. However, service contracts do not specify the number of quay cranes assigned to work on a given vessel, i.e., it is up to the terminal to decide the quay crane schedule as long as it ensures the guaranteed number of containers moved in the given berthing time window. As port fees are based on the time a vessel spends in a port, it is in a carrier's best interest to minimize this stay. In addition to a lower port fee, a shorter stay would enable a vessel to catch up on delays or sail at lower speeds, ultimately resulting in higher profits. Terminals also benefit from minimizing port stays since the resulting high utilization of equipment assets results in cost-efficient services [6].

A container terminal serves as a hub for shipment of containers. Containers are either transported to the terminal from the sea side on vessels or from the land side on trucks and trains. When containers are intermediately stored at the terminal, they are stored in the yard. The yard is an area designated to store containers in an organized manner. Containers are transported as needed from the yard to the quay when a vessel is being loaded and vice versa when

Fig. 1. A container terminal as seen from above (photo: Tom Fisk, 2019).

containers are being discharged from the vessel. Figure 1 shows a typical terminal organization.

A container vessel is a large ship specifically made for transporting containers. The layout of a vessel is split into bays, which are spaces on the ship that can store containers. Containers are discharged and loaded onto a vessel using quay cranes as illustrated in Fig. 2. All quay cranes of a berth section are mounted on a single track of rails which runs along the wharf. As quay cranes are all mounted on the same track, they can freely move to each side but are unable to pass each other. Moreover, quay cranes are wider than vessel bays meaning that two, and in rare cases three, adjacent bays cannot be operated by two quay cranes simultaneously.

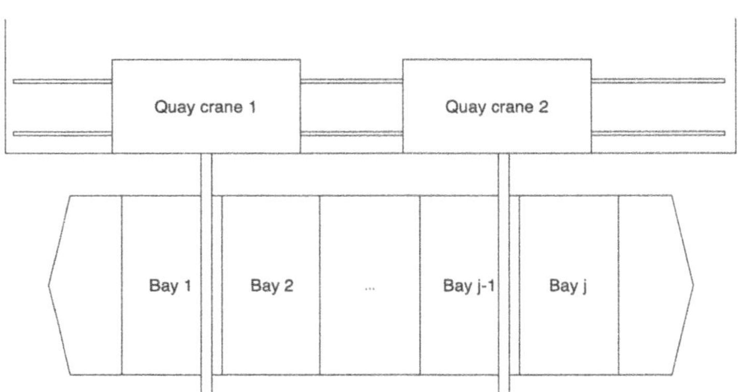

Fig. 2. A vessel being serviced by quay cranes.

There exists a plethora of techniques and equipment that enable quay cranes to load and discharge several containers at a time, e.g., twin-lifting, quad-lifting, and dual cycling. The move productivity of the quay cranes depends on the lift type and the skills of the human crane operator as well as the stowage condition of the vessel. If quay cranes must move over high stacks, it slows them down. In addition to moving containers, the quay cranes also spend time changing position between bays, known as *crane sets*. Normally this takes a few minutes, but if a quay crane passes the accommodation section, it must lift its arm possibly adding half an hour to the operation [6].

Quay crane scheduling is the problem of managing the movement of quay cranes, such that they operate as efficiently as possible. Part of this problem is determining the number of quay cranes to assign to a vessel based on the minimum number of crane moves defined in the service contract. Once this number is determined, a schedule is produced. The schedule describes where quay cranes should be positioned, which containers to load and discharge and when to execute these operations. The objective of the schedule is to process the vessel as fast as possible while using as few resources as possible. Producing an optimal schedule is considered a complex problem as there, as previously mentioned, are several real life limitations that restrict the movement and operation of quay cranes [6].

3 Literature Review

The scope of this paper is limited to the quay crane scheduling problem (QCSP) and its various formulations in previous literature [2]. The QCSP was first introduced by Daganzo [3]. The paper focuses on the general problem of processing all arriving ships while minimizing delays. Exact and approximate solutions are presented without considering operational constraints such as non-interference and non-neighbouring constraints; constraints which prevents quay cranes from passing each other on the same quay track and working on two adjacent bays at the same time respectively.

Hereafter, Kim and Park [7] introduce non-neighbouring constraints, non-interference constraints, precedence constraints, i.e., some operations precede others and task-separation constraints, i.e., some tasks cannot be done simultaneously. The study formulates a mixed-integer programming model and proposes a branch-and-bound ($B\&B$) method in order to find an optimal solution. Additionally, a GRASP metaheuristic is proposed to overcome the computational difficulty of the $B\&B$ method.

Subsequently, a paper stimulated by the work of Kim and Park [7] was written by Lee et al. [8] in which a concise mathematical model for the quay crane scheduling with non-interference constraints problem (QCSNIP) is formulated. However, for unclear reasons, Lee et al. omit the non-neighbouring constraint introduced by Kim and Park and imposes that the workload of a bay cannot be split between quay cranes. Moreover, they analyse the computational complexity of the problem and provide a proof of NP-completeness. In addition, the paper proposes a genetic algorithm that provides efficient performance and near-optimal solutions.

Hereafter, Moccia et al. [9] observed that Kim and Park's solutions [7] do not guarantee non-interference for every instance. Following this, they introduce travel time of quay cranes and propose a revised mixed-integer programming model along with a branch-and-cut algorithm ($B\&C$) to handle inputs with large solution spaces. A compact mathematical formulation of this model was subsequently proposed by Sammarra et al. [11].

Eventually, Bierwirth and Meisel [1] found that the revised model proposed by Sammarra et al. [11] may also obtain solutions that violate non-interference constraints, which is resolved in their study by the introduction of temporal distance constraints between tasks. Consequently, optimality of the solution would in some cases not be preserved. A heuristic that applies a $B\&B$ algorithm for searching a subset of above average quality, unidirectional schedules is proposed. Using the benchmark suite from Kim and Park [7], the heuristic found the best known solution in every problem instance and computational effort was cut down to a fraction of other methods proposed in previous work.

Subsequently, Fan et al. [4] introduce a key performance indicator called *Crane Intensity* (*CI*). *CI* indicates how well the workload is distributed among quay cranes with regards to minimum idle and movement time, and is thus argued to be an indicator of the quality of a quay crane schedule.

4 Problem Definition

This section defines the QCSP that is the scope of this paper. The QCSP is restricted by the following constraints.

1. Quay cranes move on the same track and thus cannot pass each other (*non-interference*).
2. Only one quay crane can work on a given bay at a time.
3. Quay cranes cannot work on two adjacent bays simultaneously (*non-neighbour-ing constraint*).

In addition to these constraints, we assume that time is discretized into equally sized time steps. In each time step a crane can make exactly one move, i.e., either loading a container to a bay or discharging a container from a bay. We further assume that it takes no time to move cranes between bays. Under these assumptions, an instance of the QCSP is defined by the following parameters.

B Total number of bays
C Total number of available quay cranes
m_j Total number of containers to be moved in bay j ($1 \leq j \leq B$).

A solution to a QCSP is referred to as a *schedule*. A schedule defines for each time step which bay each crane is assigned to. A schedule is feasible if the constraints of the QCSP are satisfied and the crane assignment allows all moves of each bay to be processed. The total number of time steps of a schedule is referred to as its *makespan* MS. A schedule for an instance of the QCSP is optimal if it is feasible and no other feasible schedule for the instance has a smaller MS. As an example, Fig. 3 shows a feasible and optimal schedule for a QCSP instance with $B = 7$, $C = 3$, and the total number of containers to be moved for each bay as shown in the figure, i.e., $m_1 = 2$, $m_2 = 5$, etc.

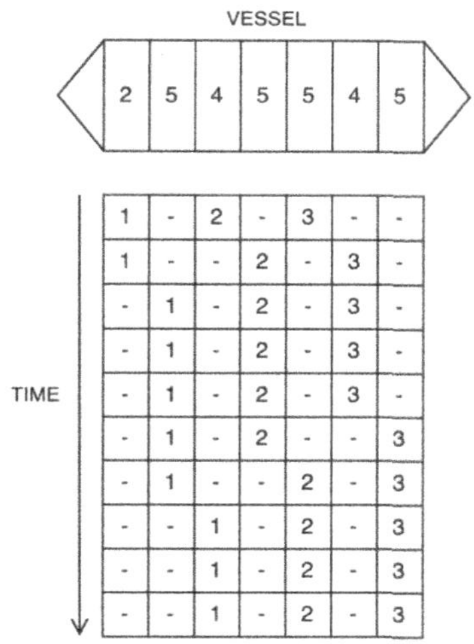

Fig. 3. An example of a feasible schedule of a QCSP instance.

5 Problem Complexity

Since its introduction by Daganzo [3], the QCSP has been considered a hard combinatorial problem. Lee et al. show that a special decision version of the QCSP, called the quay crane scheduling with non-interference constraints problem (QCSNIP), is NP-complete. The QCSNIP is restricted by the following constraints.

1. Quay cranes move on the same track and thus cannot pass each other (*non-interference*).
2. Only one quay crane can work on a hold[1] at a time until it completes the hold.
3. Compared with processing time of a hold by a quay crane, travel time of a quay crane between two holds is small and hence it is ignored.

Lee et al. prove that the QCSNIP is NP-complete by reducing the set partitioning problem to it. The decision version of the set partitioning problem is defined as

[1] A hold is the part of a bay, which is under deck. In this context, a hold can be considered equivalent to a bay.

follows [5]; given a finite set of H positive integers, $S = \{s_1, s_2, ..., s_H\}$, where the sum of all elements is equal to D; can S be partitioned into two disjoint subsets S_1 and S_2, such that $\sum_{s_i \in S_1} = \sum_{s_i \in S_2} = D/2$?

Lee et al. translate this problem into the QCSNIP by defining a hold for each element in S and some auxiliary holds. The set partitioning problem then becomes to find a schedule for two cranes, where the cranes work on subsets of the holds corresponding to S_1 and S_2. The proof is innovative and to our knowledge correct. Our main concern is that the QCSNIP substantially differs from the QCSP such that the complexity result of the QCSNIP cannot be transferred to the QCSP. In other words, the NP-completeness of the QCSNIP does not prove NP-hardness of the QCSP.

The most important limitation is that the QCSNIP assumes that *only one quay crane can work on a hold at a time until it completes the hold*, i.e., assumption 2. By constraining the workload of any bay to be processed to completion by one crane and one crane only, it is possible to let a bay of a vessel correspond to an element of a set in the set partitioning problem. However, this is not a realistic assumption. Several quay cranes often share the workload in a single bay, but cannot do so at the same point in time [6,13]. Without this restriction, Lee et al.'s reduction of the set partitioning problem to the QCSNIP is invalid.

Lee et al. also omit the non-neighbouring constraint, which ensures that a pair of cranes will not simultaneously work on any pair of adjacent bays. However, the removal of this constraint may not necessarily invalidate the reduction, as it may be possible to add "separation" bays to their reduction without invalidating it. Since the QCSP allows the workload of a bay to be split between quay cranes, Lee et al.'s NP-completeness proof does not apply to a decision version of the QCSP. In fact, below we show that the QCSP is tractable.

In the remainder of this section, we introduce the CreateSchedule algorithm that can solve the QCSP to optimality in time that is linear in $MS \times C$.

5.1 Makespan Lower Bounds

We first define lower bounds of the makespan MS as a function of the number of cranes C assigned to the vessel.

The lower limit to MS is defined as the largest sum of moves of any two adjacent bays, as only one bay of these adjacent bays can be processed by a single crane at any given time. We refer to this pair of bays as the long crane, LC, and the number of moves in the pair, m_{LC}, is defined in Eq. (1).

$$m_{LC} = max(m_j + m_{j+1}) \quad 1 \leq j < B. \tag{1}$$

To achieve an optimal schedule with *MS* equal to m_{LC}, a sufficient amount of quay cranes is required such that (*i*) a single quay crane can always operate the *LC* at all times and (*ii*) all other bays are completed in a number of moves less than or equal to m_{LC}. This means that the sum of all moves of the vessel M divided by the number of quay cranes needed, C_n, must be smaller than or equal to m_{LC} in order to optimally complete the vessel, as shown in Eq. (2).

$$\frac{M}{C_n} \leq m_{LC}, \tag{2}$$

Equation (2) can be rewritten into Eq. (3).

$$\frac{M}{m_{LC}} \leq C_n. \tag{3}$$

The number of quay cranes that can efficiently work in parallel on a given vessel is referred to as crane intensity, *CI* and is defined in Eq. (4).

$$CI = \frac{M}{m_{LC}}. \tag{4}$$

Thus, as shown in Eq. (5), if a sufficient number quay of cranes, C, are available for the processing of a given vessel ($CI \leq C$) the lowest possible makespan will be defined by m_{LC}.

$$\textit{If } CI \leq C, \textit{ then } MS = m_{LC}. \tag{5}$$

On the other hand, if an insufficient number of quay cranes are available for the processing of a given vessel (i.e., $CI > C$), the lowest possible makespan is defined by the ceiling of the total number of moves of the vessel divided by the number of available cranes as shown in Eq. (6).

$$\textit{If } CI > C, \textit{ then } MS = \left\lceil \frac{M}{C} \right\rceil. \tag{6}$$

5.2 The CreateSchedule Algorithm

Next, we define a linear time scheduling algorithm for the QCSP called CreateSchedule. It returns schedules that achieve the lower bounds of the makespan defined above and for that reason is optimal. The pseudocode of CreateSchedule is shown below. It returns a table of size $B \times MS$ containing positions of all cranes to all points in time.

```
1  function CreateSchedule(C, B, [m_1, m_2...m_B])
2      returns: table of size B × MS containing positions of cranes
3               to all points of time.
4      inputs: C, the number of available cranes
5              B, the number of bays of the vessel
6              [m_1, m_2...m_B], list containing amount of moves of each bay
7
8      if CI ≤ C then
9          MS ← m_LC
10     else
11         MS ← ⌈M/C⌉
12
13     schedule ← empty table of size B × MS
14     k ← 1
15     for i = 1 to C
16         for j = 1 to MS
17             while m_k = 0
18                 k ← k + 1
19             schedule[k][j] ← i
20             m_k ← m_k − 1
21     return schedule
```

The algorithm assumes that cranes and bays are sorted in an increasing numerical order from left to right as illustrated in Fig. 2. Initially, it calculates MS (line 8–11) in relation to CI as described in Sect. 5.1. Following this, every crane is assigned a workload equal to the calculated MS. Through *first iteration* of the inner and outer for-loop (line 15–20), the first crane with $i = 1$ is initially assigned a single move in the leftmost non-empty bay of the vessel. The remaining iterations of the inner for-loop (line 16–20) assigns crane 1 a workload equal to MS, such that it will be assigned as many moves as possible in the subsequent, non-empty bays. Note that the algorithm will confirm if a bay is empty in order to continue with non-empty bays (line 17–18). Any further iterations of the outer for-loop will assign any subsequent cranes, which will initially be assigned the bay where the previous crane finished. Hereafter, the process of assigning moves to quay crane is continued in an identical fashion, such that the crane can process at most MS moves.

In relation hereto, as M might not be divisible by MS, it may not be possible to assign every crane a workload equal to this. As a result, the last iteration of the outer-loop, corresponding to the last crane, might not execute MS iterations of the inner loop. As there might not be enough moves left in the vessel, this results in this crane having a smaller workload than MS.

The time complexity of CreateSchedule is dependent on the calculated makespan MS, which can be calculated in constant time. When assigning cranes to bays, MS defines the amount of iterations of the inner loop (line 16–20). In addition, the amount of cranes C define the number of iterations of the outer loop (line 15–20). By extension, the time complexity of CreateSchedule is $O(C \times MS)$.

Example

Given a vessel with $M = 30$, $C = 3$ and $MS = 10$, all cranes are assigned a workload of 10 moves. Crane 1 is assigned the leftmost non-empty bay of the vessel, i.e., bay 1 as shown in Fig. 4.

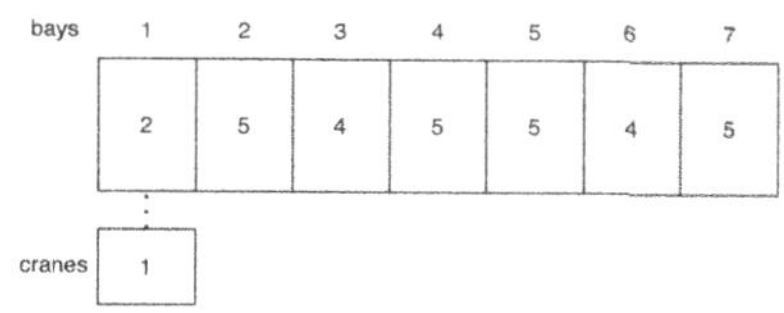

Fig. 4. Crane 1, assigned bay 1.

Hereafter, crane 1 is assigned workload from non-empty bays until it reaches its capacity at bay 3 as shown in Fig. 5.

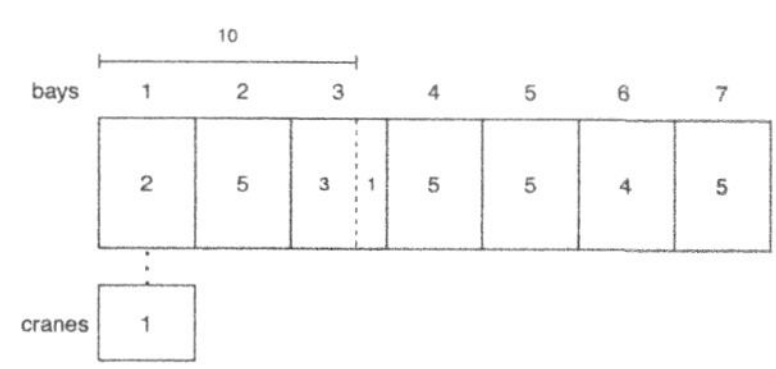

Fig. 5. Crane 1 starts in bay 1 and finishes in bay 3.

The subsequent crane 2 is initially assigned to bay 3 as crane 1 will not complete it entirely. Crane 2 has its workload assigned in the subsequent, non-empty bays until it reaches its capacity at bay 5. The following crane 3 is initially assigned bay 5, as crane 2 will not complete it entirely. Crane 3 has its workload assigned in the subsequent, non-empty bays until it reaches its capacity at bay 7 as shown in Fig. 6.

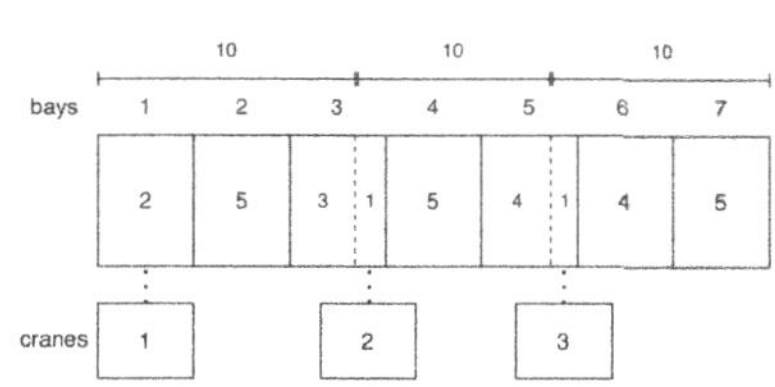

Fig. 6. All cranes are assigned.

Thus, all bays of the vessel are completed, resulting in a complete schedule as presented in Fig. 7.

INPUT:

C = 3

VESSEL:	2	5	4	5	5	4	5

OUTPUT:

t_1	1	-	2	-	3	-	-
t_2	1	-	-	2	-	3	-
t_3	-	1	-	2	-	3	-
t_4	-	1	-	2	-	3	-
t_5	-	1	-	2	-	3	-
t_6	-	1	-	2	-	-	3
t_7	-	1	-	-	2	-	3
t_8	-	-	1	-	2	-	3
t_9	-	-	1	-	2	-	3
t_{10}	-	-	1	-	2	-	3

Fig. 7. An example of a schedule.

5.3 Correctness Proof

CREATESCHEDULE does not explicitly prevent interference of cranes, which potentially leads to the constraints of the problem being broken. In other words, it remains to prove that the algorithm's assignment of cranes and workload does not violate non-interference and non-neighbouring constraints.

Proposition 1. *A schedule produced by* CREATESCHEDULE *does not violate the non-interference and non-neighbouring constraints of the QCSP.*

Proof. For two arbitrary adjacent cranes $i-1$ and i, it holds that their workload will only overlap in a single bay j. If crane $i-1$ is attending bay $j-1$, the bay to the left of bay j, then crane i is not allowed to attend bay j. Let the moves in bay j processed by crane i be represented by m_j^i. We have that m_j^i must be less than or equal to the sum of moves processed by crane $i-1$ from its starting bay s_{i-1} to bay $j-2$ as shown in Eq. (7). As a consequence, crane $i-1$ and i will not violate non-interference and non-neighbouring constraints.

$$m_j^i \leq \sum_{k=s_{i-1}}^{j-2} m_k^{i-1} \tag{7}$$

The moves processed by crane i in bay j are equal to the sum of moves in the pair m_{j-1} and m_j subtracted by the number of moves processed by crane $i-1$ in the pair, m_{j-1}^{i-1} and m_j^{i-1}, as shown in Eq. (8).

$$m_j^i = (m_{j-1} + m_j) - (m_{j-1}^{i-1} + m_j^{i-1}) \tag{8}$$

Considering Eq. (8) above, let us define the two different cases of *MS*.

First, consider the case where *MS* is defined by m_{LC} (line 8–9). The work processed by a crane $i-1$ before arriving at the pair of bays, $j-1$ and j, is defined in Eq. (9), and is equal to the total capacity of a crane, m_{LC} subtracted by the moves to be processed in the pair, by crane $i-1$.

$$\sum_{k=s_{i-1}}^{j-2} m_k^{i-1} = m_{LC} - (m_{j-1}^{i-1} + m_j^{i-1}) \tag{9}$$

When substituting Eq. (8) and (9) into Eq. (7), we get Eq. (10) that can be rewritten into Eq. (11).

$$(m_{j-1} + m_j) - (m_{j-1}^{i-1} + m_j^{i-1}) \leq m_{LC} - (m_{j-1}^{i-1} + m_j^{i-1}) \tag{10}$$

$$(m_{j-1} + m_j) \leq m_{LC} \tag{11}$$

Equation (11) is true by the definition of LC as there cannot exist any pair of bays of which the sum of moves exceed m_{LC}.

Second, consider the case where *MS* is defined by $\lceil \frac{M}{C} \rceil$ (line 10–11). The work processed by a crane $i-1$ before arriving at the pair of bays, $j-1$ and j, is defined by Eq. (12), and is equal to $\lceil \frac{M}{C} \rceil$ subtracted by the moves to be processed in the pair, by crane $i-1$.

$$\sum_{k=s_{i-1}}^{j-2} m_k^{i-1} = \left\lceil \frac{M}{C} \right\rceil - (m_{j-1}^{i-1} + m_j^{i-1}) \tag{12}$$

When substituting Eq. (8) and (12) into Eq. (7), we get Eq. (13) that can be rewritten into Eq. (14).

$$(m_{j-1} + m_j) - (m_{j-1}^{i-1} + m_j^{i-1}) \leq \left\lceil \frac{M}{C} \right\rceil - (m_{j-1}^{i-1} + m_j^{i-1}) \tag{13}$$

$$(m_{j-1} + m_j) \leq \left\lceil \frac{M}{C} \right\rceil \tag{14}$$

Equation (14) is true by the definition of *CI*. If we have fewer cranes than the crane intensity suggests, then splitting M over all cranes would result in the average workload of all cranes, i.e., $\lceil \frac{M}{C} \rceil$, being greater than m_{LC}.

Thus, given any vessel and any number of cranes, the non-interference and non-neighbouring constraints of the QCSP are satisfied by CREATESCHEDULE. ■

5.4 Extensions of the QCSP

The QCSP is more realistic than the QCSNIP, but as described in Sect. 2, real quay crane scheduling problems must take into account that time is spent moving between bays and that the productivity of cranes depends on the lift type. It is an open question whether these extensions of the QCSP makes it NP-hard. However, we do not see any obvious reasons that it should be the case.

Another issue is the operational scope of the QCSP. It does not consider in which order containers are picked from the yard of the terminal and brought to the quay cranes. From the terminal's point of view, this an important aspect of scheduling quay cranes as the schedule depends on where the containers are stored in the yard.

From the carriers point of view, on the other hand, the QCSP makes perfect sense. Recall that the relation between terminals and carriers is contractual. Typically, the terminal guarantees a total number of moves within a given time window [6]. In a situation, where the terminal fails to finish the vessel within the agreed time window, the carrier wants to be able to assess whether a makespan exists within this time window. The QCSP can answer this question, and it is perfectly fine for the carrier to ignore how the containers are handled on the yard as this is the terminal's problem. For that reason, modern stowage tools used by carriers include heuristics that are able to compute so-called *crane splits*. These crane splits corresponds to solutions of the QCSP [6].

6 Conclusion

In this paper, we show that the QCSP is tractable in the realistic setting, where quay cranes can share the workload of bays. This is done by proposing a linear time algorithm that finds optimal solutions to the QCSP and providing a proof of its correctness. Our findings imply that it may be possible to formulate tractable and optimal quay crane scheduling algorithms that model additional aspects of the real problem including variable separation distances, quay crane performance dependency on lift type, time to move quay cranes between bays, and varying processing time of containers.

Directions of future work include extending the QCSP with travel time of quay cranes, relaxing the single move per unit of time assumptions, processing time for various types of containers, and incorporating handling priority of cargo.

References

1. Bierwirth, C., Meisel, F.: A fast heuristic for quay crane scheduling with interference constraints. J. Sched. **12**(4), 345–360 (2009)
2. Bierwirth, C., Meisel, F.: A follow-up survey of berth allocation and quay crane scheduling problems in container terminals. Eur. J. Oper. Res. **244**(3), 675–689 (2015)
3. Daganzo, C.F.: The crane scheduling problem. Transp. Res. Part B: Methodol. **23**(3), 159–175 (1989)
4. Fan, L., Low, M.Y.H., Ying, H.S., Jing, H.W., Min, Z., Aye, W.C.: Stowage planning of large containership with tradeoff between crane workload balance and ship stability. In: World Congress on Engineering 2012, 4–6 July 2012, London, UK, vol. 2182, pp. 1537–1543. International Association of Engineers (2010)
5. Garey, M.R., Johnson, D.S.: Computers and Intractability, vol. 174. Freeman, San Francisco (1979)

6. Jensen, R.M., Pacino, D., Ajspur, M.L., Vesterdal, C.: Container Vessel Stowage Planning. Weilbach, Copenhagen (2018)
7. Kim, K.H., Park, Y.M.: A crane scheduling method for port container terminals. Eur. J. Oper. Res. **156**(3), 752–768 (2004)
8. Lee, D.H., Wang, H.Q., Miao, L.: Quay crane scheduling with non-interference constraints in port container terminals. Transp. Res. Part E: Logist. Transp. Rev. **44**(1), 124–135 (2008)
9. Moccia, L., Cordeau, J.F., Gaudioso, M., Laporte, G.: A branch-and-cut algorithm for the quay crane scheduling problem in a container terminal. Naval Res. Logist. (NRL) **53**(1), 45–59 (2006)
10. Psaraftis, H.N.: The future of maritime transport. In: Encyclopedia of Transportation. Elsevier (2020)
11. Sammarra, M., Cordeau, J.F., Laporte, G., Monaco, M.F.: A tabu search heuristic for the quay crane scheduling problem. J. Sched. **10**(4), 327–336 (2007)
12. Sirimanne, S.N., et al.: Review of maritime transport 2020. In: United Nations Conference on Trade and Development (2020)
13. Stahlbock, R., Voß, S.: Operations research at container terminals: a literature update. OR Spectr. **30**(1), 1–52 (2008)

Impact of Rubber-Tired Gantry Crane Dimension on Container Terminal Productivity

Marvin Kastner(✉) and Carlos Jahn

Hamburg University of Technology, Hamburg, Germany
marvin.kastner@tuhh.de

Abstract. When a Container Terminal (CT) is being newly planned or re-designed, the yard equipment must be selected before the yard layout can be planned. Commonly, Rubber-Tired Gantry cranes (RTGs) are selected for stacking the laden containers in the yard. These are available in different dimensions, typically designed to span over yard blocks between five to nine containers wide. The lift heights usually support four, five, or six containers that are stacked on top of each other. But what are the implications of the selected RTG dimension on the yard productivity? In a step-by-step analysis, the stacking density and yard productivity are estimated for the different RTG dimensions. The yard area of the CT MSC Valencia serves as an example and reference. It is shown that the stacking density ranges from 233 to 320 Twenty-foot Ground Slot (TGS) per hectare (ha) and from 853 to 1744 Twenty-foot Equivalent Unit (TEU) per ha. When the simplistic rule of one RTG per yard block is applied, with increasing RTG spans the yard productivity decreases from 360 to 240 moves per hour. An analysis of operational data indicates that the crane cycle times differ slightly but are less relevant in daily operations. It is concluded that RTG deployment strategies (avoiding idling times) should be further investigated considering a range of commonly purchased RTG dimensions. Furthermore, the impact of higher container stacks on the number of reshuffles needs to be revisited in this context.

Keywords: Container yard layout · Equipment selection · Maritime logistics

1 Introduction

In global supply chains, more than 80% of the traded volumes are transported by sea [24]. Thus, shipping companies, port authorities, and terminal operators play an integral role in interconnecting the global economy. An estimated 60% of maritime trade by weight is classified as bulk, while an estimated 20% is containerized trade, which allows for the standardized transport of, e.g., processed products and manufactured goods [24]. The necessary infrastructure is created, maintained, and updated by port construction projects, such as greenfield projects (i.e., creating a single new terminal or a whole new port), modernization projects (e.g., repairing the existing infrastructure), and expansion

J. de Armas et al. (Eds.): ICCL 2022, LNCS 13557, pp. 74–88, 2022.
https://doi.org/10.1007/978-3-031-16579-5_6

projects (e.g., adding berths, deepening existing berths, or adding yard area) (cf., e.g., [21]). These infrastructure projects are planned and executed by port planners [9]. Each change in the port and terminal infrastructure sets the ground for future economic growth and affects the position of the port as a whole and the terminals in particular in the global supply chains. CT operators can position themselves differently in the market in terms of costs, reliability, speed, and flexibility of the container handling processes [25]. However, the CT operators are constrained by the terminal infrastructure that, once constructed, can only be changed at high cost. This is both true for equipment operating on rails (cf. [9]) and tires (cf. [17]). To ensure the longevity of the terminal infrastructure, the pavement is reinforced at places of heavy-duty operations, e.g., RTGs only operate on RTG runway beams that are constructed to sustain the weight of the RTG [17]. Thus, the stacking equipment must be selected (but not necessarily procured) before the infrastructure construction work commences.

Most commonly, RTGs are used for stacking the containers in the yard [26]. The required investment is lower than for Rail-Mounted Gantry cranes (RMGs) because no rails are needed and the weight of the equipment is lower, requiring less reinforcement for the pavement [2]. At the same time, they achieve a higher stacking density than reach stackers or straddle carriers [2]. RTGs come in different dimensions. While the overall weight of the RTG determines how much the pavement requires reinforcement, the RTG span dictates the gap between the two RTG runway beams. But which RTG spans and which RTG lift heights are most commonly procured and, therefore, deserve special attention? In Table 1, the latest purchase data from [28] is displayed. When in the original data the span was provided in meters, the following rule of conversion was used:

$$s = 6.2m + 2.9m \cdot r \tag{1}$$

Here, s denotes the RTG span in meters, and r denotes the number of TGSs in one bay. The two constant measurements are based on [15]. For example, when comparing the weights of the RTGs which lift 1-over-5[1] with the models lifting 1-over-6, a difference of approximately 10t can be identified, with a total weight ranging between 64.8t for the 5+1[2] wide 1-over-5 high RTGs up to 82.3t for the 7+1 wide 1-over-6 high RTG [13]. Thus, the implications for construction are imminent – heavier equipment requires better reinforced pavements. Yet the question remains why one should opt for a certain RTG dimension. What are the driving factors for choosing a specific RTG span and lift height? In this publication, the consequences of the RTG span and lift height on the productivity of the CT are examined analytically. In Sect. 2, the first general concepts of yard layout planning are introduced. Then, in Sect. 3, the applied methods are introduced and explained. The results and insights are discussed in Sect. 4. Last, the conclusions are drawn in Sect. 5.

[1] 1-over-5 means that the containers can be stacked five containers high without blocking the RTG to lift another container over such a stack.

[2] 5+1 stands for a yard block 5 containers wide and an additional transfer lane, compare also Fig. 1.

Table 1. The number of RTGs delivered in 2021 or planned to be delivered in the next two years as of November 2021 [28]

	Lift height				
	1-over-3	1-over-4	1-over-5	1-over-6	Total
Span					
<20 m	-	-	10	-	10
5+1	5	-	-	-	5
6+1	-	17	342	201	560
7+1	-	8	102	89	199
8+1	-	4	13	12	29
8+2	-	6	-	-	6
9+1	-	-	10	5	15
10+1	-	-	-	2	2
Total	5	35	477	309	826

2 Theoretical Background

In the process of choosing the stacking equipment for the yard, the stacking density plays a major role [2,3,7]. A high stacking density is reached if more container stacks are placed in the yard, typically measured in TGS/ha. The yard capacity also takes the stacking height into account, leading to the second stacking density metric of TEU/ha (e.g., [2]). The stacking density directly impacts how fast a container can be retrieved from a stack: The more TGSs are available, the lower the mean stacking height is for a set quantity of containers. The lower the mean stacking height is, the less likely it is that reshuffling becomes necessary, minimizing the average time of retrieving containers [12].

When planning a port, first the annual throughput at the seaside of the CT is determined; based on the figures, the required yard throughput is calculated (expressed as TEU p.a.) [27]. The yard capacity (expressed in TEU) is interrelated with the required annual yard throughput, as the demand and supply approaches show.

In the demand approach, the required yard area is calculated for a given stacking equipment and expected annual container volumes and dwell times while considering a certain peak factor, e.g., for minor supply chain disturbances [3]. Such an approach is helpful when the overall yard area is not fixed yet, e.g., because different plots of land are available or because the overall CT area can be expanded into the sea or harbor basin by means of backfilling.

A second approach is the supply approach; here, the maximum annual container volume achievable with a given number of TGSs is determined based on the expected container dwell times, the mean stacking height, and a peak factor [3]. This approach is useful when a plot of land has already been assigned, the size is constrained (e.g., by a small harbor basin), and now the actual yard layout needs to be decided on – a question that also includes the selection of the yard equipment.

While performing the calculations for the yard capacity, the actual stacking density of the stacking equipment needs to be considered. Here, the RTG dimensions do make a difference in the calculation. The lift height of the RTG must support the assumed mean stacking height and limits the maximum height of the container stacks at the terminal. The span of the RTG determines how many TGSs can be placed side-by-side. In Fig. 1, the block design for an RTG yard and the typical RTG movements are depicted. Every yard block consists of the container stacking area organized into bays and rows, a transfer lane below the portal for the yard trucks, two RTG lanes (the ones which are especially reinforced), and a bypass lane. The RTG gantries on the RTG lane to reach the different bays, then it trolleys between the different rows (this both moves the operator cabin and the spreader within the portal), and finally it hoists and lowers the spreader either with or without a container. The two RTG lanes, the transfer lane, and the bypass lane are fixed in size and constitute the traffic area of the yard block. Thus, the more container rows an RTG spans, the larger the ratio of TGSs to the traffic area becomes, leading to a higher stacking density. This claim is further examined and quantified in the remainder of this paper.

In the back-to-back design, two yard blocks share a bypass lane, and every second yard block is mirrored along the x-axis. In Fig. 2, a simplified example yard layout is depicted. The road network is colored in dark gray, and each yard block colored in slate gray is provided with an identifier following the naming convention from [23]. The spare area is colored in light gray.

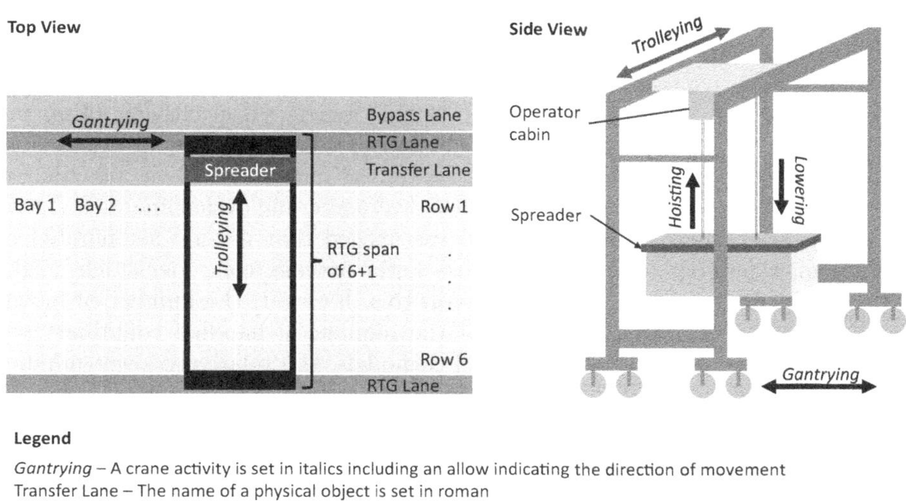

Fig. 1. The yard block structure and the RTG activities therein.

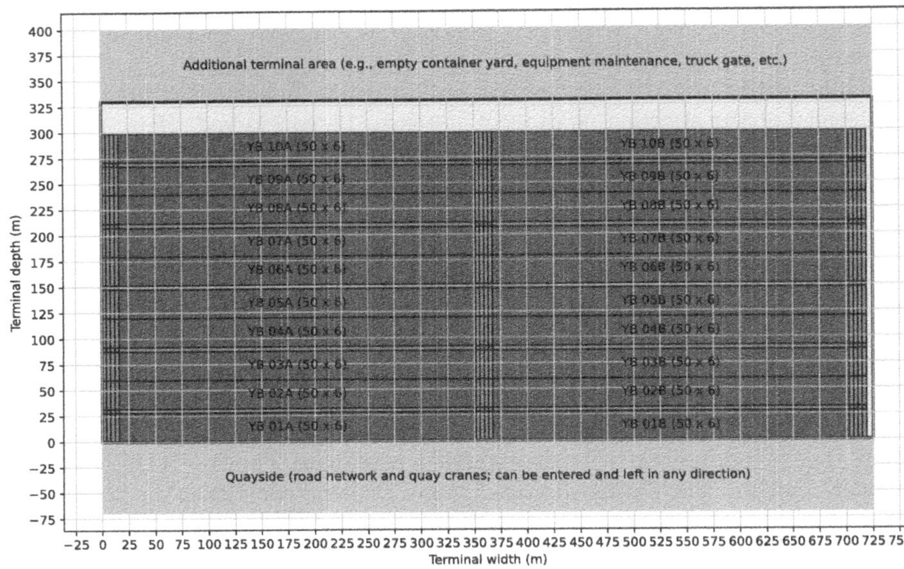

Fig. 2. In a back-to-back RTG layout, two blocks facing each other share a bypass lane.

Yet yard capacity is not everything – yard productivity is of similar importance. This term describes how fast containers can be stored in and retrieved from the yard. Given the assumption that sufficient equipment is available for horizontal transportation, the yard productivity can be simplified as the sum of the productivity of all stacking cranes. Crane productivity is typically measured in productive container moves per hour [7,27]. Reshuffles are considered unproductive and are thus not counted in this metric. Alternatively, often the cycle times of stacking equipment are reported, e.g., measured in minutes or seconds [1,27]. When double cycles[3] are rare, the number of moves per hour is approximated by dividing one hour by the average crane cycle time.

At the beginning of this section, it was argued that given a set number of containers, a number of TGSs leads to a lower average container stack height and thus fewer reshuffles. To capitalize on this, however, the number of moves per hour must not increase notably. If the number of handled containers per hour goes down notably with larger RTG models, the relatively lower number of unproductive moves might not create the expected positive impact.

Yard productivity is influenced by many factors, and there is no straightforward approach to determine the expected moves per hour based only on the layout information discussed so far. A major advantage of RTGs is that they can be transferred between yard blocks, allowing great flexibility during peaks

[3] A double cycle occurs when within one crane cycle both a truck-to-stack and a stack-to-truck task are executed, also see [27].

time [16]. This is especially true for the diesel models and partly for their electrified counterparts [4]. Thus, at each yard block either no, one, or several RTGs operate. The number of RTGs per yard block is limited by work safety concerns, e.g., at most two RTGs per yard block are reported for a case in Hong Kong [16]. Since all RTGs at a terminal are of the same size and run on the same runway beams, they cannot bypass each other, leading to interference issues well known and scientifically studied for RMG twin systems (e.g., [11]). Thus, with an increasing number of RTGs in the same yard block, the productivity of the equipment will eventually decrease. Moreover, transferring an RTG between two yard blocks takes time; 10–15 min are plausible figures here [16]. During the transfer, the road network is blocked, leading to longer cycle times for horizontal transport. To avoid these problems of crane interference and transferring RTGs between blocks, it is assumed that one RTG operates in one yard block. This assumption is also close to the current operations at the chosen example, CT MSC Valencia. They own 25 RTGs and have 22 yard blocks [23]. Given that assumption, the number of yard blocks gains importance. The wider RTG spans lead to fewer yard blocks for the same given yard depth, decreasing the number of RTGs operated on the same plot of land. If the productivity of each RTG is fixed at 15 moves per hour independently from its dimension (cf., e.g., [19]), the yard productivity decreases accordingly. Following the assumption that each Ship-To-Shore gantry crane (STS crane) accomplishes 30 moves per hour (cf. [19]), there should be two RTGs for each STS crane. Due to the complexity of equipment coordination in real operations, a ratio of 2.5 RTGs per STS crane is rather advisable [20]. At a yard depth of 330 m, for the 9+1 spanning RTG, only 16 yard blocks fit into the given plot of land, resulting in an average yard productivity of $16 \cdot 15 = 240$ moves per hour. This corresponds to the seaside productivity of eight STS crane; based on the assumption of 2.5 RTGs per STS crane, only 6.4 of them can reach appropriate productivity levels. For the same yard depth, a 5+1 wide RTG-based yard achieves $24 \cdot 15 = 360$ moves per hour, corresponding to the productivity of 12 or 9.6 STS crane, respectively. This means that with wider RTGs, the yard capacity increases but the yard productivity decreases, potentially throttling the seaside productivity.

But is the lower number of RTGs the only negative impact on yard productivity? As the equipment is larger, the speed of container handling might be affected. The producers indicate that the speed of the motors for gantrying, hoisting, trolleying, and lowering is identical, irrespective of the dimension [13,15]. With larger RTG dimensions, however, the overall path a container is trolleyed is longer. This raises the question of whether these longer distances notably impact the crane cycle times and thus the crane productivity. This line of argument is pursued further in the following.

3 Method

First, in Sect. 3.1, it is explained how the impact of the RTG dimension on the stacking density and yard capacity is estimated. Afterwards, in Sect. 3.2, the yard productivity is approximated.

3.1 Method to Estimate Stacking Density

For each RTG dimension, the stacking density is calculated for a fixed plot of land. This follows the perspective of the supply approach [3], with the difference that the number of TGSs is varied with each layout alternative. The terminal layout of MSC Terminal Valencia is used for reference [23]. This fixes the yard area and provides the opportunity to validate the estimated stacking densities for the commonly used RTG dimensions. Based on freely available satellite imagery [5,8], the sizes of layout objects are taken. In Table 2, the generalized lengths and widths used for further analysis are presented (also cf. [3]). It is assumed that 10 of the RTG lanes are used for laden containers and that the remaining lanes are used for empty containers which are handled by empty container handlers (see especially the year 2019 at [8]). These are thus out of scope for the further analysis. In addition, the reference layout is slightly simplified by dropping reefer racks and assuming a static yard block length. The yard area is determined by the yard depth and yard width and amounts to 24 ha of the total 38 ha [23]. To compare the differences in number of TGSs fitting into the area, alternative yard layouts based on the different RTG spans are constructed as follows:

Table 2. The assumed sizes of layout objects

Abbreviation	Measurement name	Length
TGS_w	width of TGS	2.438m
TGS_l	length of TGS	6.058m
sd_{TGS}	Safety distance for each TGS	0.3m
l_t	Truck lane width	4.0m
$l_{RTG/trucks}$	RTG lane width incl. safety distance to trucks	2.5m
$l_{RTG/RTG}$	RTG lane width incl. safety distance to other RTG	5.0m
y_d	Yard depth	330.0m
y_w	Yard width	725.0m
yb_l	Yard block length	335.0m
yb_w	Yard block width	50 TGS

1. Determine the yard block width for the number of r rows (cf. Fig. 1):

$$yb_w(r) = l_{RTG/trucks} + l_{RTG/RTG} + l_t + (TGS_w + sd_{TGS}) \cdot r$$

2. For the back-to-back design (cf. Fig. 2), start with a yard block of the width $yb_w(r)$ and then a bypass lane with a width of l_t.
3. Afterwards, place two yard blocks and a bypass lane of the same dimensions alternately until the yard depth y_d is used up.
4. If the last yard block is not adjacent to a bypass lane, then drop it.

This one-dimensional sequence of layout objects is then expanded into the second dimension by starting with four truck lanes, then the first one-dimensional sequence, another four truck lanes, then the same one-dimensional sequence, and the last four truck lanes After the construction of the two-dimensional layout, the number of positioned yard blocks (n_{yb}) is counted. Then, the number of TGS in the yard is derived:

$$n_{TGS} = n_{yb} \cdot r \cdot yb_w$$

This constructive algorithm is executed for the RTG dimensions of 5+1 up to 9+1. An example of a layout created according to these instructions is depicted in Fig. 2. Recently sold RTGs with spans of less than 20 m vary in actual dimensions and cannot be easily grouped; RTGs with spans of 8+2 and 10+1 account for less than 1% of total data and are thus ignored. The yard depth is slightly varied to check for the sensitivity of the solution.

Given the number of TGS, the stacking density of the example terminal is calculated. Now the heights of the container stacks come into play. The static capacity is calculated by multiplying the number of TGS by the maximum stacking height. This static capacity, however, does not take into account that RTGs need to reshuffle within a bay and thus require some empty buffer slots, all because RTGs do not gantry with containers [14]. The operational capacity for each bay is thus its static capacity minus the lift height plus 1, e.g., for a 7+1 wide and 1-over-5 high RTG, the static capacity is 35 and the operational capacity is 31 (also see [14]). Hence, the maximum average stacking height based on the operational capacity not only changes with the lift height of the RTG but also with the number of rows in a bay. In this step, the maximum stacking density based on the operational capacity for the lift heights of 1-over-4, 1-over-5, and 1-over-6 is calculated.

3.2 Method to Estimate Yard Productivity

In the scope of this analysis, yard productivity is defined by the sum of the productivity of all RTGs operating in the yard. We are especially interested in the maximum yard productivity, i.e., how many moves per hour the RTGs can achieve during a peak situation when they never need to wait for the next stacking task. For the sake of simplicity, it is assumed that each RTG operates independently. It is examined how long the crane cycle time of a larger RTG lasts. For that purpose, operational data of RTGs spanning over six container rows are examined and the influence of the RTG dimension on the time consumption is estimated. The data is taken from [1] and re-interpreted in that regard. RTGs perform three different types of stacking tasks [1]:

1. They move a container from a truck to a stack,
2. They move a container from a stack to a truck, and
3. They move a container from a stack to another stack.

In [1], the authors concentrated on the state of the spreader, including waiting times that appear in daily operations. For further analysis, several states of spreaders are summarized, leading to five remaining groups. For each group, the presented average data of all RTG models are summarized in boxplots. First, the RTG moves to its next task by gantrying and trolleying (referred to as *Moving Empty* by the original authors). Second, the RTG waits with an empty spreader (*Waiting Empty*). Then, the container is picked up (*Approaching Container*, *Waiting for Lifting*, *Lifting Container*, and *Catching Container*). Afterwards, the RTG trolleys to the right stack or the transfer lane (*Moving with Container*). Last, the container is placed at its destination and the spreader is hoisted again (*Waiting with Container*, *Approaching Landing*, *Waiting for Landing*, *Place Container*, and *Lift Empty*). This comparison of time consumption differentiates between the span-dependent and span-independent parts of the container handling process. In a second analysis, the trolleying data from [1] is analyzed. It is checked how much time on average it takes to trolley the spreader to its target position. The trolleyed distances are converted to TGS based on Eq. 1.

4 Results and Discussion

In Sect. 4.1, it is shown how the different RTG spans lead to different stacking densities. Later, in Sect. 4.2, the impact of the RTG dimension and the lower number of RTGs on the yard productivity is estimated.

4.1 Estimated Stacking Density

In Fig. 3, the stacking density for each RTG span is depicted. It is shown that the number of TGS/ha varies notably between the different block widths, ranging from 233 TGS/ha for an RTG span of 5+1 and a yard depth of 325 m up to 320 TGS/ha for an RTG span of 9+1 and a yard depth of 310 m. For a given block width, a jigsaw pattern appears. With increasing yard depth, the stacking density decreases until another yard block fits into the given area and a small peak appears (see Fig. 3). In rare cases, the RTG span does not have an impact at all, e.g., for the yard depth of 330 m and the yard block width of five or six TGS. In most cases, however, the stacking density increases with the increasing RTG span. The area utilization approximately increases by 16 TGS/ha with every additional row under the RTG span. The figures for the 5+1 and 6+1 wide RTGs are comparable to previously reported results [3], indicating that the measurements and the constructive algorithm are valid.

In Fig. 4, the maximum operational capacity is depicted. For each block width, the yard depth most advantageous to the specific RTG span is selected (cf. previous paragraph). When comparing the block widths of five and nine, the yard capacity increases by 48% on average. When comparing the stacking height of four with that of six, the yard capacity increases by 38% on average, thus leading to less capacity at the price of a higher chance of reshuffling. These results show that considering the RTG dimensions adds some complexity to estimating the stacking density.

Previously, a yard capacity of approximately 1000 TEU/ha has been reported for RTGs [2, 22]. For this estimate, however, only block widths of up to eight container rows and a stacking height of four have been considered [2]. The maximum of 1,744 TEU/ha clearly surpasses the value and is also larger than the stacking density of some of the RMG-based yard layouts [2]. This clearly indicates that the choice of stacking equipment cannot be made solely based on the stacking density. Instead, additional considerations, such as cost structures or opportunities for automation, need to be taken into account [7, 10, 25].

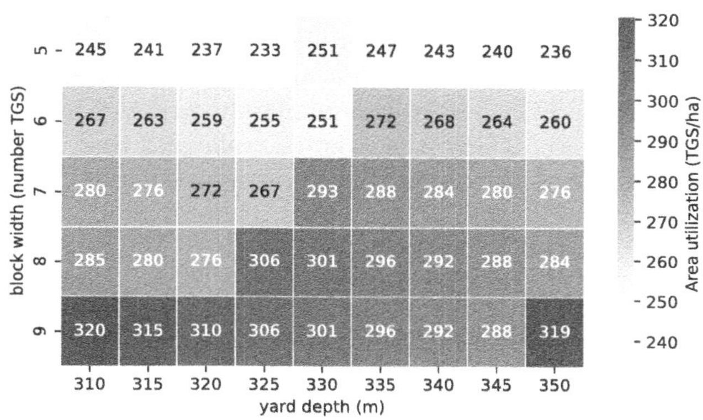

Fig. 3. With increasing yard block width, the area utilization increases for each variation of the yard depth.

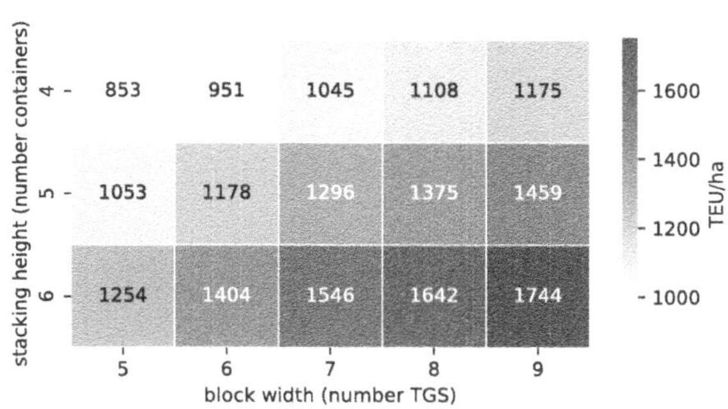

Fig. 4. The yard capacity increases with the stacking height and block width

4.2 Estimated Yard Productivity

The results of the operational data regarding crane cycle times are depicted in Fig. 5. The RTG spends approximately 60 s on average to move to the target location, possibly including gantrying. Then, approximately 60 s are spent waiting. This time varies largely between the different RTGs, indicating that this might change with the workload and/or the operational planning. Each of the next three tasks takes approximately 30 s on average: The container is first picked up, then trolleyed to its final destination, and only then is the spreader lowered. Finally, the container is placed at its target position. Including the waiting times, the total duration of a cycle amounts to 225 s, or 16 moves per hour. When the time consumed in the state of *Waiting Empty* is dropped, a theoretical cycle time of 155 s and 23 moves per hour on average are achievable. Such an average cycle time is not only theoretically possible but is also backed up by previous reports: When RTGs are switched on, they idle for one third of the time [18].

In Fig. 6, the trolleying times are shown. The arithmetic mean for the trolleying distance of one TGS lies at approximately 24 s and increases with the number of TGSs. For six TGSs, the average trolleying time amounts to 39 s. The ditched line indicates the data-fitted linear regression line for the following formula:

$$t_{avg}(d) = 21.44s + 3.1s \cdot d \tag{2}$$

Here, $t_{avg}(d)$ describes the arithmetic mean time consumed for trolleying a container over the distance d, which is measured in TGS. When using this formula to extrapolate the average time for trolleying nine TGS, this results in 49 s, just 10 s more than for six TGS. When it is assumed that all stacks are used at the same frequency, for the 9+1 wide RTG, two thirds of the trolleyed distances are the same as for the 6+1 spanning model, and only the remaining three TGS require slightly longer trolleying times, leading to average trolleying times of only five seconds more when moving a container. In comparison with the examined waiting times of the previous paragraph, this seems negligible. Thus, the impact of the RTG dimension on the crane cycle time and crane productivity is existent but minor in nature.

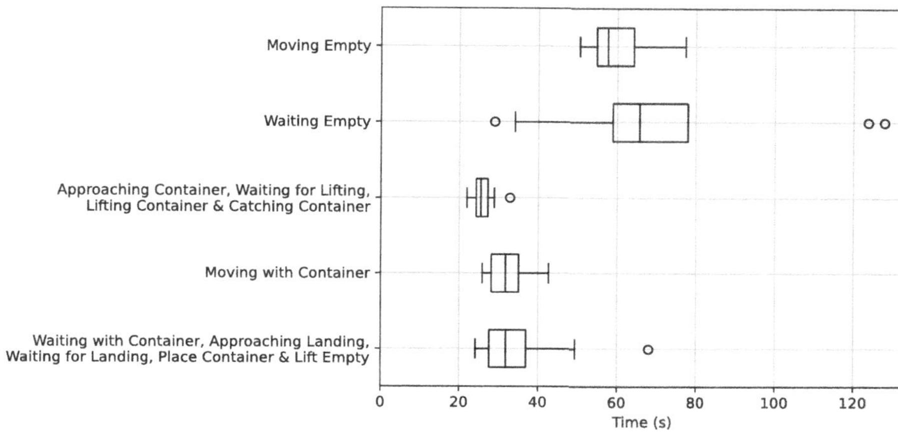

Fig. 5. Consumed times for RTG activities based on [1]

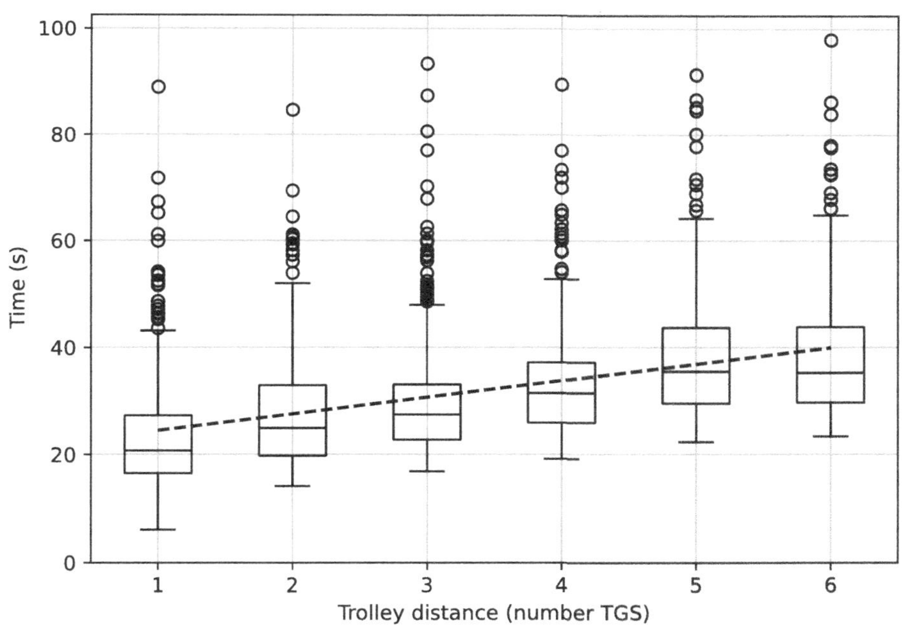

Fig. 6. Consumed times for trolleying based on [1]

5 Conclusion and Outlook

The dimensions of the recently purchased RTGs differ notably. In this paper, two analyses have been performed to estimate the impact of these dimensions on the yard productivity at CTs. In the first step, alternative layouts have been designed and evaluated regarding the stacking density. The results have been partially validated with previously reported figures and show that the stacking density increases tremendously with larger RTG dimensions. The increase from 233 to 320 TGS/ha leads to a lower average stacking height and thus less expected reshuffles given the same container throughput. With the decrease of reshuffles, the percentage of productive moves per hour are expected to increase for each RTG.

The exact increase depends on further assumptions regarding the interchangeability of containers; e.g., while loading a vessel, containers destined for that vessel that share the same port of destination and weight class are exchangeable [6,14]. Further work to examine the impact of different stacking heights on yard productivity based on realistic operational data considering container groups seems promising.

In the second step, the crane productivity of a single RTG has been calculated and the importance of its dimension is evaluated. Under the assumption of identical velocities for each movement independent of the RTG dimension, the longer trolleying distances for wider RTGs are negligible for the cycle times. Under the second assumption that one RTG operates in only one yard block, wider RTG spans lead to a lower number of yard blocks and thus less RTGs operating at the same time. The lower number of RTGs decreases the yard productivity significantly.

If a certain yard productivity is required that is higher than what can be reached with one RTG per yard block, several RTGs need to operate in the same yard block. This leads to known operational issues related to safety distances and crane interference. Whenever the flexibility of RTGs to switch blocks is capitalized on, the reassignment of RTGs between yard blocks adds operational complexity. Further work to examine these operational issues while considering several RTG dimensions is considered fruitful.

In Sect. 4.2, the line of argument was based on operational data of RTGs spanning over six TGSs. The time consumption data of trolleying the container have been extrapolated to an RTG spanning over nine TGSs (see Eq. 2). This indicated a difference of only approximately three seconds per TGS and was thus considered to be negligible. While the velocities indicated by the equipment producers might be identical for all RTG dimensions, practitioners have mentioned that larger RTGs tend to be less sturdy, potentially leading to longer crane cycle times. Actual operational data from RTGs of all kinds of dimensions are required to further back up these claims.

Acknowledgement. We thank Anil Chandrashekar for his assistance in extracting the data from [28] and [1] for further analysis and the anonymous reviewers for their valuable feedback.

References

1. Aulanko, S., Tervo, K.: Modeling and analysis of harbor crane work efficiency using work cycle recognition. In: 2010 IEEE/ASME International Conference on Advanced Intelligent Mechatronics, pp. 61–66. IEEE (2010)
2. Brinkmann, B.: Operations systems of container terminals: a compendious overview. In: Böse, J. (ed.) Handbook of Terminal Planning. Operations Research/Computer Science Interfaces Series, vol. 49, pp. 25–39. Springer, New York (2011). https://doi.org/10.1007/978-1-4419-8408-1_2
3. Chu, C., Huang, W.: Determining container terminal capacity on the basis of an adopted yard handling system. Transp. Rev. **25**(2), 181–199 (2005)
4. Conductix-Wampfler: E-RTG - RTG electrification (2012). https://www.conductix.de/sites/default/files/downloads/KAT0000-0004-E_E-RTG_RTG_Electrification.pdf
5. Google: Google Earth (2022). https://earth.google.com/web/@39.4410269,-0.32191601,-0.83023994a,1453.2929603d,35y,0h,0t,0r
6. Güven, C., Türsel Eliiyi, D.: Modelling and optimisation of online container stacking with operational constraints. Maritime Policy Manag. **46**(2), 201–216 (2019)
7. Huang, W.C., Chu, C.Y.: A selection model for in-terminal container handling systems. J. Mar. Sci. Technol. **12**(3), 4 (2004)
8. Institut Cartogràfic Valencià: Visor de cartografia (2022). https://visor.gva.es/visor/?extension=729457,4368623,731203,4369510&nivelZoom=17&capasids=Imagen;
9. Kaptein, R., Jacob, A., Alamir, R.: Translating automated container terminal operations into terminal infrastructure design. In: Jain, P., Stahlman, W.S. (eds.) Ports 2019: Papers from Sessions of the 15th Triennial International Conference, Reston, VA, pp. 644–652. American Society of Civil Engineers (2019). https://doi.org/10.1061/9780784482629.062
10. Kastner, M., Lange, A.-K., Jahn, C.: Expansion planning at container terminals. In: Freitag, M., Haasis, H.-D., Kotzab, H., Pannek, J. (eds.) LDIC 2020. LNL, pp. 114–123. Springer, Cham (2020). https://doi.org/10.1007/978-3-030-44783-0_11
11. Kemme, N.: State-of-the-art yard crane scheduling and stacking. In: Böse, J.W. (ed.) Handbook of Terminal Planning. ORSIS, pp. 383–413. Springer, Cham (2020). https://doi.org/10.1007/978-3-030-39990-0_17
12. Kim, K.H.: Evaluation of the number of rehandles in container yards. Comput. Ind. Eng. **32**(4), 701–711 (1997). https://doi.org/10.1016/S0360-8352(97)00024-7. New Advances in Analysis of Manufacturing Systems
13. Konecranes: Konecranes RTG: Vom Erfinder des modernen RTG-Krans (2021). https://www.konecranes.com/sites/default/files/2021-10/Konecranes%20RTG%20Typical%20Tech%20Spec%20DE_V3.pdf
14. Lee, B.K., Kim, K.H.: Comparison and evaluation of various cycle-time models for yard cranes in container terminals. Int. J. Prod. Econ. **126**(2), 350–360 (2010)
15. Liebherr: Technical description rubber tyre gantry crane (2020). https://www.liebherr.com/shared/media/maritime-cranes/downloads-and-brochures/brochures/lcc/liebherr-rtg-cranes-technical-description.pdf
16. Linn, R., Liu, J., Wan, Y., Zhang, C., Murty, K.G.: Rubber tired gantry crane deployment for container yard operation. Comput. Ind. Eng. **45**(3), 429–442 (2003)
17. Ospina, C.E., Kumar, V.K., Puente, J.: Design of container yard at Port of Balboa. In: Ports 2010: Building on the Past, Respecting the Future, pp. 912–921. American Society of Civil Engineers (2010)

18. Papaioannou, V., Pietrosanti, S., Holderbaum, W., Becerra, V.M., Mayer, R.: Analysis of energy usage for RTG cranes. Energy **125**, 337–344 (2017)
19. Petering, M.E.: Effect of block width and storage yard layout on marine container terminal performance. Transp. Res. Part E: Logist. Trans. Rev. **45**(4), 591–610 (2009)
20. Sha, M., Notteboom, T., Zhang, T., Zhou, X., Qin, T.: Simulation model to determine ratios between quay, yard and intra-terminal transfer equipment in an integrated container handling system. J. Int. Logist. Trade **19**(1), 1–18 (2021)
21. Ship Technology: Port construction projects. https://www.ship-technology.com/port-construction-projects/. Accessed 03 May 2022
22. Stahlbock, R., Voß, S.: Operations research at container terminals: a literature update. OR Spectr. **30**(1), 1–52 (2008)
23. Terminal Investment Limited (TIL): Infraestructuras (2022). https://www.msctv.es/en/about-us/infrastructures/
24. UNCTAD: Review of Maritime Transport 2021. United Nations Publications, New York, USA (2021)
25. Wang, P., Mileski, J.P., Zeng, Q.: Alignments between strategic content and process structure: the case of container terminal service process automation. Maritime Econ. Logist. **21**(4), 543–558 (2019). https://doi.org/10.1057/s41278-017-0070-z
26. Wiese, J., Kliewer, N., Suhl, L.: A survey of container terminal characteristics and equipment types. Working Paper 0901, DS & OR Lab, University of Paderborn (2009). https://wiwi.uni-paderborn.de/fileadmin/dep3ls5/Publikationen/A_Survey_of_Container_Terminal_Characteristics_and_Equipment_Types.pdf
27. Wiese, J., Suhl, L., Kliewer, N.: Planning container terminal layouts considering equipment types and storage block design. In: Böse, J. (ed.) Handbook of Terminal Planning. Operations Research/Computer Science Interfaces Series, vol. 49, pp. 219–245. Springer, New York (2011). https://doi.org/10.1007/978-1-4419-8408-1_12
28. WorldCargo news: Yard crane market stays steady. WorldCargo news (2021). https://flickread.com/edition/html/free/61c475d21af0b

Vehicle Routing and Urban Logistics

Fleet Size Control in First-Mile Ride-Sharing Problems

Jinwen Ye[1(✉)], Giovanni Pantuso[1], and David Pisinger[2]

[1] University of Copenhagen, 2100 Copenhagen, Denmark
{j.y,gp}@math.ku.dk
[2] Technical University of Denmark, 2800 Lyngby, Denmark
pisinger@man.dtu.dk

Abstract. The first-mile problem, which refers to the design of transport services that connect passengers to their nearby transit station, has attracted growing attention in recent years. In this paper we consider *first-mile ride-sharing* services and study the problem of optimally determining the fleet size and assigning vehicles to transport requests. We formulate the problem as a mixed-integer program and present a number of numerical experiments based on a small-scale system to analyse different configurations of the service, namely with and without fleet control (FC). Result shows that a configuration with FC is superior in terms of profits while service rates can be higher in a configuration without FC, depending on the revenue-sharing mechanism.

Keywords: Fleet control · First-mile · Ride-sharing

1 Introduction

As the size of urban areas and population increase, and with them road congestion and air pollution [1], ride-sharing services emerged as more sustainable urban transportation solution, linked to e.g., a reduction in the number of private cars on the road, emissions and road congestion [2]. Particularly, first-mile ride-sharing services, that is transportation services that connect passengers to their nearby transit station using shared vehicles, have attracted growing attention. According to the NYC taxicab data [3], there were 3 122 731 taxi trips to the Pennsylvania Station in New York City in 2017 that is, on average 8 555 taxis traveled to this station every day. However, 70.1% of these trips had only one passenger on board [4]. This leaves significant potential for the development of shared trips to transit stations.

In this article we study the problem of dimensioning a first-mile ride-sharing fleet and optimizing the process of order dispatching, which means assigning transport requests to vehicles. The problem of dimensioning shared fleets has recently been studied in a number of articles. In [5,7,9] the focus is on so-called *ride-hailing* services, where each vehicle satisfies one request at a time (i.e., rides are not shared). In this paper, we focus on *ride-sharing* services, where

J. de Armas et al. (Eds.): ICCL 2022, LNCS 13557, pp. 91–104, 2022.
https://doi.org/10.1007/978-3-031-16579-5_7

each vehicle satisfies multiple requests simultaneously. In [6] the size of a fleet of autonomous vehicles is determined. The autonomous vehicles are integrated into a transit network, and run according to predefined patterns. On the contrary, in our case, vehicles do not run according to predefined patters, but react to the arrival of requests. In [8] the focus is on ride-sharing services. The authors develop a method to determine how many vehicles are needed and where they should be located in order to service all the requests. The method is designed for offline use based on historical demand. In this article, we focus on online optimization and do not require vehicles to be placed at pre-determined locations. Also in [10] a ride-sharing service is considered. The authors use simulation to estimate the minimal fleet size required for a system that connects a university campus to a train station. This system requires predefined pickup and drop-off locations, while our system does not have this requirement. Moreover, in [11] the authors propose a vehicle-sharing network model to obtain the optimal and near optimal solution fleet size for the urban-scale data. The method obtains a re-organization of the taxi dispatching, without assuming ride-sharing. Instead we provide an explicit mathematical model for the problem. Finally, unlike in [12], where the authors consider elastic vehicle supply, which considers hiring privately-owned freelance autonomous vehicles, we focus on controlling the fleet size without hiring external fleets.

The main contribution of this work can be stated as follows:

- We propose a mixed-integer programming (MIP) problem for online optimization of order dispatching and fleet size, which accounts for several constraints such as desired arrival time and maximum waiting time. The model is flexible enough to accommodate different ride-sharing business models.
- While existing studies focus mainly on metrics such as idle time, waiting time [8] and costs [10], we use the model to assess different configurations of the service. Particularly, we consider a configuration where the service provider owns the fleet and hires drivers as well as configurations where the service provider does not own the fleet but acts as a platform that optimally connects passengers to vehicles. In this case the service provider shares revenues and costs with the drivers and we assess two different sharing schemes.
- We test our model on a number of artificial instances generated to mimic the different configurations of a small-scale service. Our model for online optimization is used in a rolling horizon procedure with periodic re-optimizations based on the arrival of new requests and updated system information (e.g., vehicles position).

The remainder of this article is organized as follows. In Sect. 2 we provide a formal definition of the problem and introduce the corresponding mathematical model. In Sect. 3 we describe our numerical experiments and present results. Finally, we draw conclusions in Sect. 4.

2 Problem Description and Mathematical Model

In this section we provide a description of the problem followed by a mathematical model.

A set of vehicles $\mathcal{K}$, with each vehicle $k \in \mathcal{K}$ initially available at the respective location $o(k)$, is employed to provide first-mile ride-sharing services to a set of customers from their respective location to a designated station d located at $o(d)$. The set of customers is partitioned into a set of mandatory customers $\mathcal{N}_P$, representing the customers whose transportation request has been accepted during a previous optimization phase but not yet fulfilled, and a set of new customers $\mathcal{N}_C$ whose requests have arrived recently and may or not be accepted. We let $o(i)$ be the location of request $i \in \mathcal{N}_P \cup \mathcal{N}_C$. The company is to decide i) which vehicles to dispatch, if not already dispatched, ii) which new requests to accept and iii) how to assign ride-sharing requests to vehicles.

Each vehicle v has V_k passengers on board at the beginning of the operational period. V_k is an input parameter determined by the requests assigned to vehicle k in previous optimization phases. Let Q be the total capacity of a vehicle (we assume a homogeneous fleet). Parameter U_k is equal to 1 if vehicle k has been dispatched in any of the previous re-optimization phases, 0 otherwise. In the latter case V_k is zero. The company bears a fixed cost $\bar{C}$ for each vehicle dispatched and a cost C per unit of travel time. Picking up new customer $i \in \mathcal{N}_C$ yields a revenue P_i. Such customers may however be rejected. The revenue for customers in $\mathcal{N}_P$ has been collected during a previous optimization phase, when the request was accepted, and these customers are now treated as mandatory.

The operating period starts at time T. The travel time between locations $o(i)$ and $o(j)$, with $i \in \mathcal{K} \cup \mathcal{N}_P \cup \mathcal{N}_C$, $j \in \mathcal{N}_P \cup \mathcal{N}_C \cup \{d\}$, is T_{ij}. Each customer has a requested pickup time T_i^P and arrival time T_i^A and we let $T^L := max_{i \in \mathcal{N}_P \cup \mathcal{N}_C}\{T_i^A\}$. The difference between the requested pickup time and the actual pickup time cannot be larger than Δ. Furthermore, each vehicle has a latest arrival time T_k representing the earliest arrival time among the V_k passengers already on board vehicle k at the beginning of the planning phase.

We introduce the following decision variables. Let x_{ij}^k, for $i \in \{k\} \cup \mathcal{N}_P \cup \mathcal{N}_C, j \in \mathcal{N}_P \cup \mathcal{N}_C \cup \{d\}, k \in \mathcal{K}$, be equal to 1 if vehicle k moves directly between $o(i)$ and $o(j)$, 0 otherwise. Let t_k^A be the actual arrival time of vehicle k to the station, for $k \in \mathcal{K}$. Let t_i^P be the actual pickup time of customer i, for $i \in \mathcal{N}_P \cup \mathcal{N}_C$. Finally, let S_k be equal to 1 if vehicle k is dispatched in the current re-optimization phase, 0 otherwise.

The problem is hence

$$\max \quad \sum_{k \in \mathcal{K}} \sum_{i \in \mathcal{N}_C} \sum_{j \in \mathcal{N}_C \cup \mathcal{N}_P \cup \{d\}} P_i x_{ij}^k - \sum_{k \in \mathcal{K}} \bar{C} S_k \tag{1a}$$

$$- \sum_{i \in \{k\} \cup \mathcal{N}_C \cup \mathcal{N}_P} \sum_{j \in \mathcal{N}_C \cup \mathcal{N}_P \cup \{d\}} \sum_{k \in \mathcal{K}} C T_{ij} x_{ij}^k$$

$$\text{s.t.} \quad \sum_{j \in \mathcal{N}_C \cup \mathcal{N}_P \cup \{d\}} \sum_{k \in \mathcal{K}} x_{ij}^k \leq 1 \qquad \forall i \in \mathcal{N}_C \tag{1b}$$

$$\sum_{j \in \mathcal{N}_C \cup \mathcal{N}_P \cup \{d\}} \sum_{k \in \mathcal{K}} x_{ij}^k = 1 \qquad \forall i \in \mathcal{N}_P \tag{1c}$$

$$\sum_{i \in \mathcal{N}_C \cup \mathcal{N}_P \cup \{k\}} x_{ij}^k = \sum_{i \in \mathcal{N}_C \cup \mathcal{N}_P \cup \{d\}} x_{ji}^k \qquad \forall j \in \mathcal{N}_C \cup \mathcal{N}_P, k \in \mathcal{K} \tag{1d}$$

$$\sum_{j \in \mathcal{N}_C \cup \mathcal{N}_P \cup \{d\}} x_{kj}^k = \sum_{j \in \mathcal{N}_C \cup \mathcal{N}_P \cup \{k\}} x_{jd}^k \qquad \forall k \in \mathcal{K} \tag{1e}$$

$$\sum_{i \in \mathcal{N}_C \cup \mathcal{N}_P \cup \mathcal{K}} x_{id}^k \leq 1 \qquad \forall k \in \mathcal{K} \tag{1f}$$

$$t_i^P + T_{ij} \leq t_j^P + T^L(1 - \sum_{k \in \mathcal{K}} x_{ij}^k) \qquad \forall i, j \in \mathcal{N}_C \cup \mathcal{N}_P \tag{1g}$$

$$T + T_{kj} \leq t_j^P + T^L(1 - x_{kj}^k) \qquad \forall j \in \mathcal{N}_C \cup \mathcal{N}_P, k \in \mathcal{K} \tag{1h}$$

$$t_i^P - T_i^P \leq \Delta \qquad \forall i \in \mathcal{N}_C \cup \mathcal{N}_P \tag{1i}$$

$$t_k^A \leq T_i^A + T^L(1 - \sum_{j \in \mathcal{N}_C \cup \mathcal{N}_P \cup \{k\}} x_{ji}^k) \qquad \forall i \in \mathcal{N}_C \cup \mathcal{N}_P, k \in \mathcal{K} \tag{1j}$$

$$t_k^A \leq T_k \qquad \forall k \in \mathcal{K} \tag{1k}$$

$$t_j^P + T_{jd} x_{jd}^k \leq t_k^A + T^L(1 - x_{jd}^k) \qquad \forall j \in \mathcal{N}_C \cup \mathcal{N}_P, k \in \mathcal{K} \tag{1l}$$

$$V_k \leq Q \sum_{j \in \mathcal{N}_C \cup \mathcal{N}_P \cup \{d\}} x_{kj}^k \qquad \forall k \in \mathcal{K} \tag{1m}$$

$$\sum_{i \in \{k\} \cup \mathcal{N}_C \cup \mathcal{N}_P} \sum_{j \in \mathcal{N}_C \cup \mathcal{N}_P} x_{ij}^k + V_k \leq Q \qquad \forall k \in \mathcal{K} \tag{1n}$$

$$S_k \geq \sum_{j \in \mathcal{N}_C \cup \mathcal{N}_P \cup \{d\}} x_{kj}^k \qquad \forall k \in \mathcal{K} \tag{1o}$$

$$S_k \geq U_k \qquad \forall k \in \mathcal{K} \tag{1p}$$

$$x_{ij}^k \in \{0, 1\} \quad \forall i \in \{k\} \cup \mathcal{N}_C \cup \mathcal{N}_P, j \in \mathcal{N}_C \cup \mathcal{N}_P \cup \{d\}, k \in \mathcal{K} \tag{1q}$$

$$t_k^A \in \mathbb{R}^+ \qquad \forall k \in \mathcal{K} \tag{1r}$$

$$t_i^P \in \mathbb{R}^+ \qquad \forall i \in \mathcal{N}_C \cup \mathcal{N}_P \tag{1s}$$

$$S_k \in \{0, 1\} \qquad \forall k \in \mathcal{K} \tag{1t}$$

The objective function (1a) represents the total profit made of the revenue of picking up customers minus dispatching and traveling costs.

Constraints (1b) and (1c) state that new customers may be picked up at most once, while mandatory customers must be picked up exactly once, respectively. Mandatory customers are those already accepted during a previous re-optimization phase. Constraints (1d) are flow conservation constraints, which state that whenever a vehicle visits a customer it must also move to another customer or to the station. Constraints (1e) state that, if a vehicle departs from its original location $o(k)$ it must terminate its journey at the station. Constraints (1f) ensure that each vehicle travels to the station at most once.

Constraints (1g) state that if customers j is picked up by vehicle k immediately after picking up customer i, then the actual picking up time of customer i plus the travel time between customer i and j should be less or equal to customer j's actual pick up time. Constraints (1g) may be improved as described by [13,14]. Similarly, (1h) define the pickup time when the vehicle comes directly from its original location. Constraints (1i) ensure that the difference between actual pick up time and the requested pick up time of each customer do not exceed the maximum waiting time Δ. Constraints (1j) ensure that the arrival time of vehicle k at the station is earlier than the requested arrival time of any of the customers on board. For instance, if customer i is picked up by vehicle k, the right-hand-side will always be equal to T_i^A, which means the actual arrival time of vehicle k needs to be less than or equal to the requested arrival time of customer i. Constraints (1k) ensure that the actual arrival time of vehicle k is earlier than the earliest requested arrival time T_k of the passengers already on board at the beginning of the planning phase. Constraints (1l) define the relationship between pickup and arrival time. For example, if j is the last customer picked up by the vehicle k before arrive at the station, then x_{jd}^k takes value 1, the left-hand-side becomes $t_j^P + T_{jd}$ and the right-hand-side becomes t_k^A, which means that the actual pick up time of j plus the travel time between customer j and station should be equal to the actual arrival time of vehicle k. If j is not the last customer picked up by the vehicle k before arrive at the station, then the left-hand-side becomes t_j^P and the-right-hand side becomes $t_k^A + T^L$, which always holds. Altogether, constraints (1j) and (1k) define an upper bound on t_k^A while (1l) define a lower bound.

Constraints (1m) state that the vehicles that already have customers on board at the beginning of the planning period must be dispatched, while (1n) ensure that the total capacity is not violated. Constraints (1o) set S_k to 1 as soon as vehicle k is dispatched. Constraints (1p) ensure that the vehicles already dispatched in previous re-optimization phases are still available in the current re-optimization phase.

3 Numerical Experiment

In this section we report on the results of our numerical experiments. The scope of the experiments is to assess, in terms of profits and service rates, two different configurations of the service which we refer to as *with fleet control* (wFC) and *without fleet control* (woFC). The former refers to a situation where the service provider owns the fleet and bears all costs and profits. All vehicles are initially idle and the provider decides which of them to dispatch, paying a fixed cost for each dispatched vehicle which covers e.g., the salary of the driver, wear and maintenance. In the configuration woFC the service provider does not own the fleet and acts as platform that connects passengers to vehicles. In this case vehicles are considered to be always available so that the provider does not pay a fixed cost upon dispatching a vehicle. However, in this case, revenues are shared between the driver and the service provider. Particularly, we test two different revenue-sharing schemes inspired by the business configuration adopted by Uber [19]. In the first scheme, which we refer to as woFC-40, the company keeps 40% of the trip fare (thus the driver keeps the remaining 60%) but bears variable costs (e.g., fuel/charge). In the second scheme, which we refer to as woFC-25, the company keeps only 25% [19] of the trip fare but does not cover variable cost.

The different configurations are tested by using an appropriate setting of the parameters in model (1). All problems are solved using the Python libraries of GUROBI 9.5.0 a server equipped with Intel Core i5 CPUs and 16 GB of RAM.

3.1 Instance Generation

We test our model on a number of artificial randomly generated instances that mimic the different configurations of the service. The instances are generated as follows.

The business area is represented by a 4×3 rectangular area with the station located at the center of the area $(2, 1.5)$. We randomly generate travel requests with their respective pickup location, pickup time, drop-off time, and fare. Requests pickup locations are randomly generated in the 4×3 area. For each request, the requested pickup time T_i^P is randomly generated uniformly between 0 and 5 minutes, the requested arrival time T_i^A is the sum of the requested pickup time, the travel time between the pickup location i and the station d, and a random generated buffer time between 5 and 10 minutes. Since the focal rectangular area is continuous, travel times T_{ij} are calculated using Euclidean distances and assuming an average speed of 36 km/h following [15]. The unit cost C of the transportation is set to 11.25\$/h [16] and trip revenues P_i are computed using an hourly rate set to 56.16\$/h with a base fare of \$2.5 following [17].

In the configuration wFC the fixed cost $\bar{C}$ is set to \$2.8 and represents mainly the salary of the driver. This cost is obtained using Lyft salary – \$33.75/h, see [18] – as our reference and considering that our method re-optimizes every 5 minutes. Thus, the fixed cost $\bar{C}$ for each re-optimization is $\$33.75/60*5 = \$2.8$. In Sect. 3.2 we assess the impact of this parameter. In the configurations woFC-40 and woFC-25, the trip fare is reduced to $0.4P_i$ and $0.25P_i$, respectively to mimic the corresponding revenue-sharing scheme. In the configuration woFC-40 the company covers variable costs using the unit transportation cost C cost described above, while in the configuration woFC-25 the company does not cover transportation cost, so $C = 0$. In both cases the dispatching cost is $\bar{C} = 0$.

We generate instances with different number of customers and vehicles. Particularly, we create instance classes named $V|\mathcal{K}|C|\mathcal{N}_C|$ with vehicles in $|\mathcal{K}| \in \{8, 10, 12, 20\}$, and customers, $|\mathcal{N}_C| \in \{6, 8, 12\}$. As an example, $V8C6$ indicates a class of instance with 8 vehicles available for dispatch and 6 new customers in each re-optimization phase. Such instances are perhaps representative of a potential service in a small peripheral station or in a small urban context. Finally, for each instance class we randomly generate 3 instances.

Finally, we consider a one-hour planning horizon with online re-optimization every 5 minutes, leading to a total of 12 re-optimizations for each instance.

It should be noted that at each re-optimization we update the status of the system (i.e., vehicles positions and customers on board) and randomly select the corresponding number of new customers, while considering previously accepted customers as mandatory.

Figure 1 illustrates how information is updated between re-optimizations on an instance with three vehicles and four new customers for each re-optimization phase. Figure 1(a) illustrates the initial position of vehicles (yellow squares), customers (blue circles) and customers that have been assigned to vehicles in the previous re-optimization phases but have not yet been picked up (red circles) – the station is identified by the black triangle. Figure 1(b) shows the routes computed for the vehicles in the corresponding re-optimization phase. It can be noticed that four customers (three new and one mandatory) have been assigned to three vehicles in Route1, Route2, Route3 (their request has been accepted) while one customer has not (the request has not been accepted). Figure 1(c) shows the location and remaining portion of the route of the vehicles before the next re-optimization phase, as well as the location of four new customers (green circles) arrived in the system in the mean time and whose request will be handled in the next re-optimization phase. The four customers assigned to vehicles in the previous optimization phase are now on board the vehicles, while the customer whose request was rejected has left the system. Thus the three vehicles currently have customers on board and are on their way to the station. Nevertheless, their routes may change in the next re-optimization phase in order to pickup new customers.

3.2 Results

We report now on the performance of the different configurations of the service.

Figure 2 reports the dispatch rate, that is the percentage of vehicles dispatched. It can be noticed that in the case wFC, as intuition suggests, the dispatch rate generally increases with the number of customers and decreases with the size of the fleet. When the fleet counts 20 vehicles, there is no case in which the entire fleet is dispatched, indicating that the fleet is larger than needed. On the contrary, in the configurations woFC all vehicles are dispatched, meaning that they are not only available, but actually move from their original location to perform some transportation task. It appears, therefore, that configurations woFC may lead to using more vehicles than are actually necessary.

Figure 3 reports the service rate obtained with the different configurations, that is the number of requests satisfied over the total number of requests received in the one-hour planning horizon. It can be noticed that configuration woFC-25 competes and outperforms the configuration wFC. In the configuration woFC-25 the company is insensitive to transportation costs and does not bear fixed costs, therefore also solutions require a long travel time or would perhaps require an additional vehicle – thus potentially inefficient in a model wFC – become profitable. Such solutions become even more unappealing in the configuration woFC-40 where transportation costs are still born by the company in exchange for a higher revenue share.

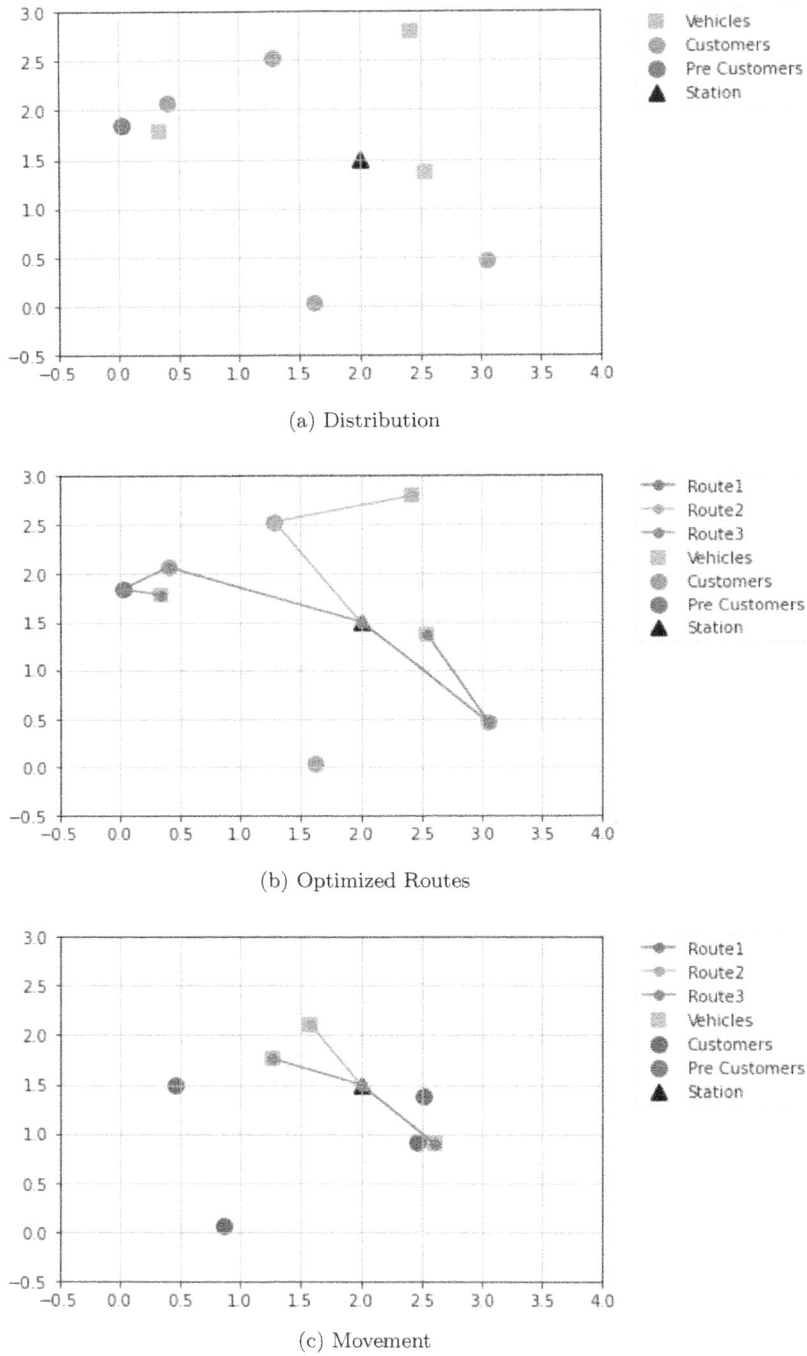

Fig. 1. Illustration of the solving process (Color figure online)

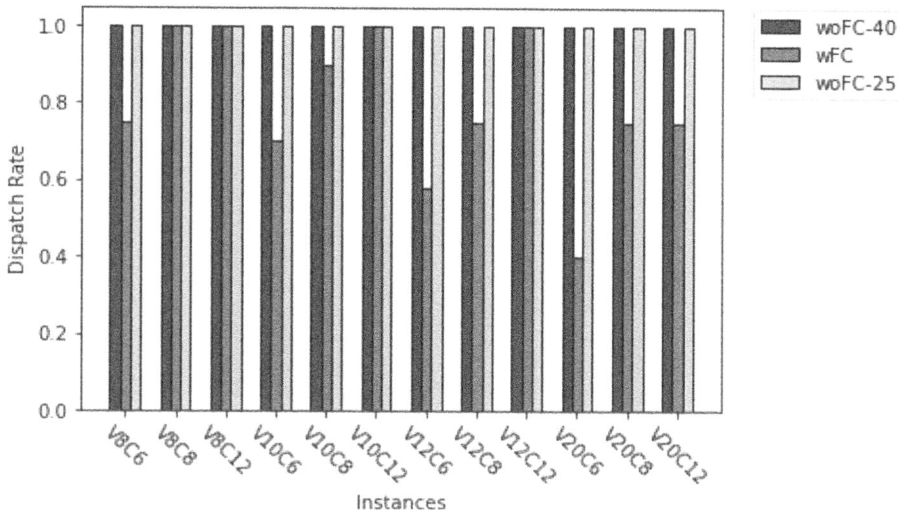

Fig. 2. Dispatch rate for the configuration wFC and woFC. For each instance type the results are the average over three different instances.

Finally, Fig. 4 illustrates that the configuration wFC leads to the highest profits for the company, despite a slightly lower service rate compared to the configuration woFC-25 (see Fig. 3). Both configurations woFC lead to worse profits regardless of the revenue-sharing mechanism.

We report now on the impact of the fixed dispatch cost $\bar{C}$ in the configuration wFC. This in turn sheds light on the effect of using different types of vehicles, maintenance contracts, or salaries. Particularly, we assess dispatch rate, service rate and profit with different values of the fixed dispatch cost $\bar{C} \in \{1.4, 2.1, 2.8, 3.5\}$. Results are reported in Figs. 5, 6 and 7.

Figure 5 shows the intuitive pattern that, as the dispatch cost increases, the dispatch rate decreases. We also observe that the dispatch rate increases with the number of customers. Similarly, in Fig. 6 it can be observed that the service rate increases as the fixed dispatch cost decreases. Nevertheless, the service rate remains rather high for all values of the fixed cost, illustrating that the model is able to find cost-efficient solutions also with fewer vehicles dispatched. Finally, in Fig. 7 we also observe a similar trend, where profits are negatively affected by fixed costs. The effect appears more severe as the number of customers grows.

3.3 Solution Time

Finally, we investigate the solution time. In our numerical experiments we solve each instance in a rolling horizon process. The average solution time and optimality gaps for different instances are reported in Table 1. Average values are computed over three randomly generated instances obtained with same combination of $|\mathcal{N}_C|$ and $|\mathcal{K}|$, 12 re-optimization phases for each instances, and three

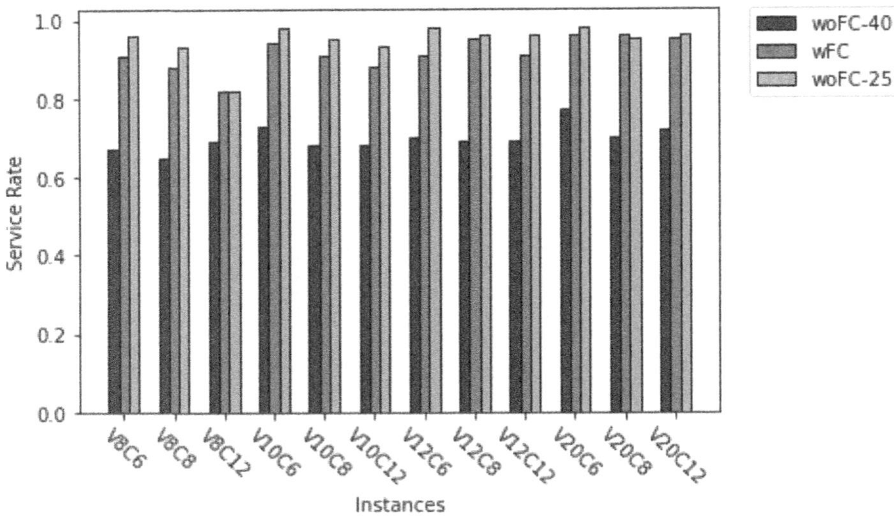

Fig. 3. Service Rate for the configuration wFC and woFC. For each instance type the results are the average over three different instances.

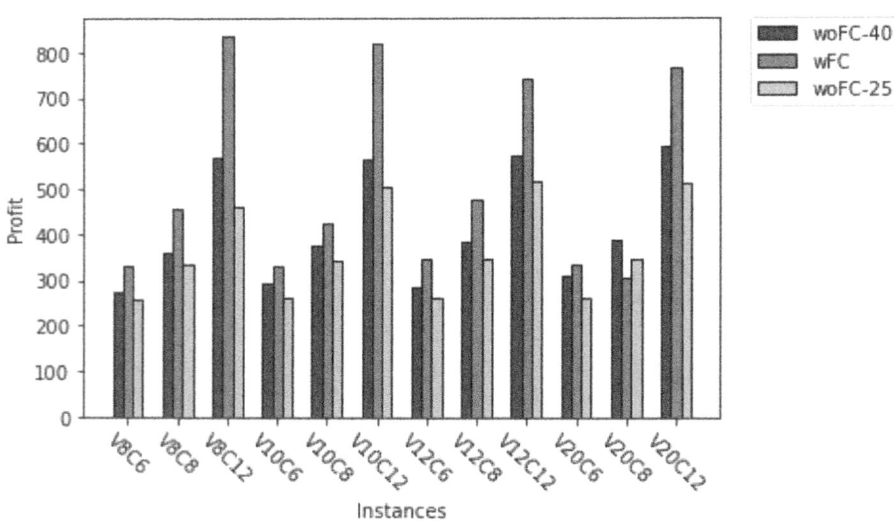

Fig. 4. Profit for the configuration wFC and woFC. For each instance type the results are the average over three different instances.

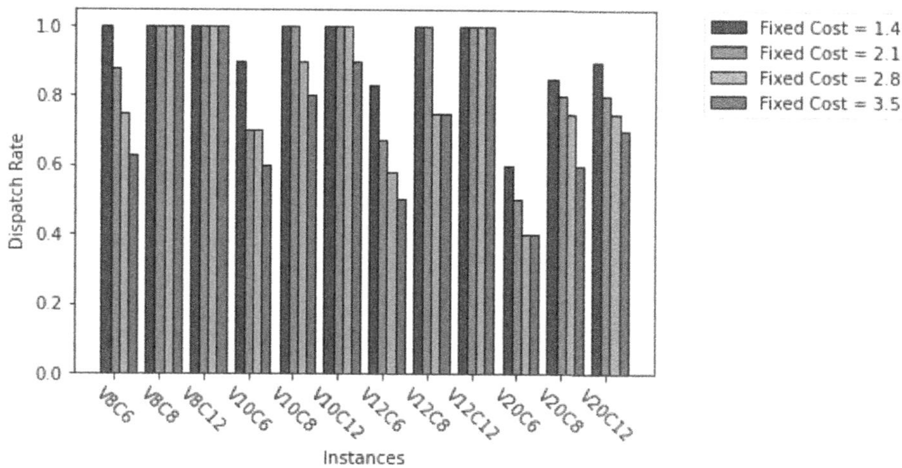

Fig. 5. Dispatch rate with different fixed dispatch costs $\bar{C}$. For each instance type the results are the average over three different instances.

configurations, namely wFC, woFC-40 and woFC-25. Table 1 illustrates that all instances can be solved to provable optimality within 0.5 seconds. There is thus room for scaling up the problems to larger instances which represent more closely a real-life scenario. To this end, Table 2 provides some insights on how the model handles bigger instances. It can be noted that, with a fleet of 20 vehicles, the quality of the solutions decreases with the number of customers.

Table 1. Optimality gap and solution time

Instance	Solution time [s]	Optimality gap
V8C6	0.03	0%
V8C8	0.04	0%
V8C12	0.11	0%
V10C6	0.03	0%
V10C8	0.05	0%
V10C12	0.14	0%
V12C6	0.04	0%
V12C8	0.06	0%
V12C12	0.18	0%
V20C6	0.06	0%
V20C8	0.08	0%
V20C12	0.41	0%

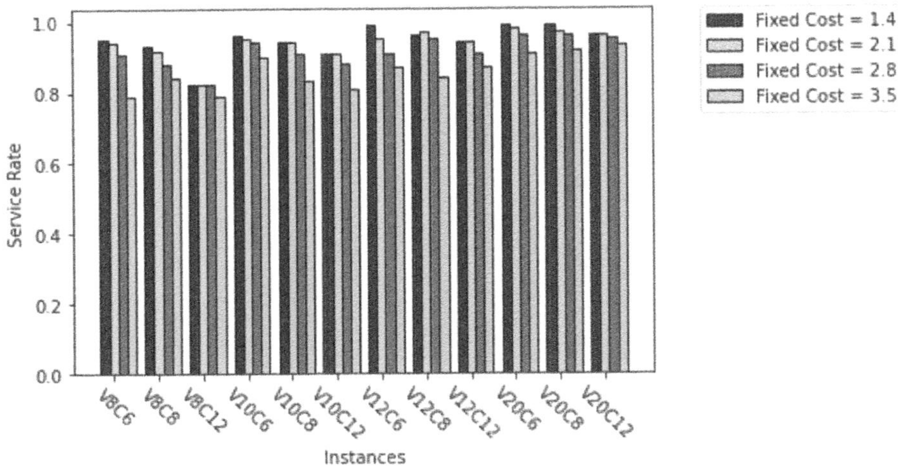

Fig. 6. Service rate with different fixed dispatch costs $\bar{C}$. For each instance type the results are the average over three different instances.

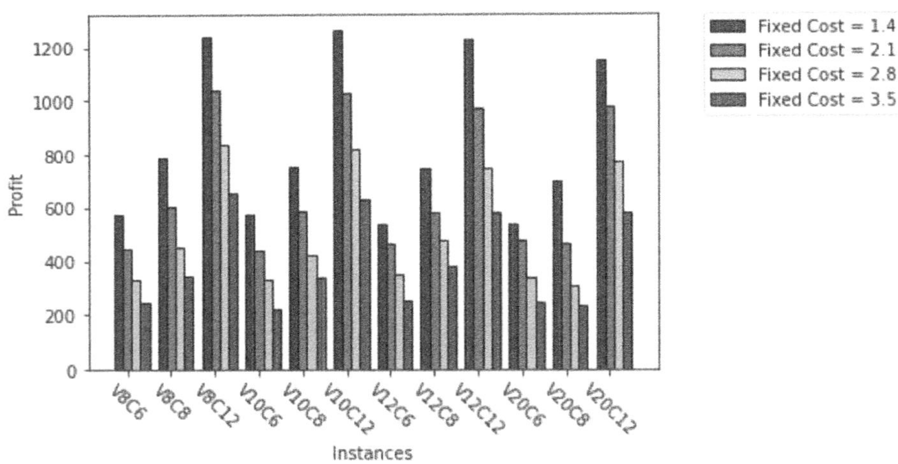

Fig. 7. Profit with different fixed dispatch costs $\bar{C}$. For each instance type the results are the average over three different instances.

Table 2. Optimality gap and solution time on larger instances. For each instance size, maximum and average are taken over three randomly generated instances.

Instance	Avg. sol. time	Avg. gap	Max sol. time	Max gap
V20C20	15.59	0%	300	14%
V20C25	39.54	2%	300	26%
V20C30	96.44	4%	300	41%

4 Conclusion

In this paper we proposed a MIP model for optimal order dispatching and fleet size control in a first-mile ride-sharing service. The model was used in a set of numerical experiments, where we compared different configurations of the service (i.e., business models), with and without fleet control and with different revenue-sharing schemes. Results shows that the configuration with fleet control (i.e., where the company owns the fleet) has a relatively high service rate and outperforms the configurations without fleet control in terms of profits. Results also show that fixed dispatch costs have a critical impact on both service rate and profits. We can observe that, as the fixed cost increases, the number of vehicles dispatched decreases and profits shrink. Nevertheless, service rates remain rather high, showing that the model is able to find cost efficient solutions with fewer vehicles. Finally, the tests illustrate that the model is flexible enough to adapt to different configurations of the service and thus may serve real-life analysis of ride-sharing services. As an example, the model could help assess revenue-sharing mechanisms other than the ones studied in this article.

References

1. Eiichi, T., Russell, T., Tadashi, G.Y.: Recent trends and innovations in modelling city logistics. Procedia - Soc. Behav. Sci. **125**, 4–14 (2014). https://doi.org/10.1016/j.sbspro.2014.01.1451
2. Abubakr, A., Arnob, O.G., Vaneet, A.: DeepPool: distributed model-free algorithm for ride-sharing using deep reinforcement learning. IEEE Trans. Intell. Transp. Syst. 1–14 (2019). https://doi.org/10.1109/tits.2019.2931830
3. New York City Taxi and Limousine Commission (2021). https://www1.nyc.gov/site/tlc/about/tlc-trip-record-data.page
4. Bian, Z., Liu, X., Bai, Y.: Mechanism design for on-demand first-mile ridesharing. Trans. Res. Part B: Methodol. 77–117 (2020). https://doi.org/10.1016/j.trb.2020.03.011
5. Boesch, P.M., Ciari, F., Axhausen, K.W.: Autonomous vehicle fleet sizes required to serve different levels of demand. Trans. Res. Rec.: J. Transp. Res. Board **2542**(1), 111–119 (2016)
6. Pinto, H.K.R.F., Hyland, M.F., Mahmassani, H.S., Verbas, I.O.: Joint design of multimodal transit networks and shared autonomous mobility fleets. Transp. Res. Part C: Emerg. Technol. 2–20 (2019)
7. Treleaven, K., Pavone, M., Frazzoli, E.: Asymptotically optimal algorithms for one-to-one pickup and delivery problems with applications to transportation systems. IEEE Trans. Autom. Control **58**(9), 2261–2276 (2013)
8. Wallar, A., Alonso-Mora, J., Rus, D.: Optimizing vehicle distributions and fleet sizes for shared mobility-on-demand. In: International Conference on Robotics and Automation, ICRA, pp. 3853–3859. IEEE (2019). https://doi.org/10.1109/ICRA.2019.8793685
9. Spieser, K., Treleaven, K., Zhang, R., Frazzoli, E., Morton, D., Pavone, M.: Toward a systematic approach to the design and evaluation of automated mobility-on-demand systems: a case study in Singapore. In: Meyer, G., Beiker, S. (eds.) Road Vehicle Automation. LNM, pp. 229–245. Springer, Cham (2014). https://doi.org/10.1007/978-3-319-05990-7_20

10. Winter, K., Cats, O., de Almeida Correia, G.H., Van Arem, B.: Designing an automated demand-responsive transport system: fleet size and performance analysis for a campus-train station service. Trans. Res. Rec.: J. Trans. Res. Board **2542**, 75–83 (2016)
11. Vazifeh, M.M., Santi, P., Resta, G., Strogatz, S.H., Ratti, C.: Addressing the minimum fleet problem in on-demand urban mobility. Nature **557**(7706), 534 (2018)
12. Beirigo, B.A., Negenborn, R.R., Alonso-Mora, J., Schulte, F.: A business class for autonomous mobility-on-demand: modeling service quality contracts in dynamic ridesharing systems. Transp. Res. Part C: Emerg. Technol. **136** (2022). https://doi.org/10.1016/j.trc.2021.103520
13. Desrochers, M., Laporte, G.: Improvements and extensions to the Miller-Tucker-Zemlin subtour elimination constraints. Oper. Res. Lett. **10**(1), 27–36 (1991)
14. Yuan, Y., Cattaruzza, D., Ogier, M., Semet, F.: A note on the lifted Miller-Tucker-Zemlin subtour elimination constraints for routing problems with time windows. Oper. Res. Lett. **48**(2), 167–169 (2020)
15. Han, J.: Looking Through the Taxi Meter - Analysis of the NYC Green Taxi Data (2019)
16. High fuel prices impoverish New York City taxi drivers. https://www.wsws.org/en/articles/2008/09/taxi-s04.html
17. Taxi Rate New York City. https://www.taxi-calculator.com/taxi-rate-new-york-city/259
18. Taxi Driver salary in New York, NY. https://www.indeed.com/career/taxi-driver/salaries/New-York--NY
19. Uber charges partners 25% fee on all fares. https://www.uber.com/gh/en/drive/basics/tracking-your-earnings/

ILS-RVND Algorithm for Multi-trip Pickup and Delivery Problem, with Split Loads, Profits and Multiple Time Windows

Wahiba Ramdane Cherif-Khettaf[1(✉)], Atef Jaballah[1], and Fernando Ferri[2,3]

[1] LORIA, UMR 7503, Lorraine University, Nancy, France
{wahiba.ramdane,atef.jaballah}@loria.fr
[2] USP University, São Paulo, Brazil
fernando.ferri@usp.br
[3] Mines Nancy-Lorraine University, Nancy, France

Abstract. This paper deals with a real application encountered in the construction sector, which consists in a new variant of the pickup and delivery problem, including several constraints that have never been combined in the same variant, denoted MTPDSPTW. This problem is defined by a set of construction sites that have a delivery demand for construction materials and also a waste removal request. Each construction site has a certain profit which is computed according to the urgency of the pickup and delivery demand. Each site can be visited several times during the day, but the delivery must be done within a set of time windows specified by each site. Heterogeneous vehicles with different availability located at a massification and waste treatment platform must do multiple tours to serve the requests. The objective is to minimize the total travel distance and to maximise the profit. The developed method is based on the Iterated Local Search metaheuristic which uses a Random Variable Neighborhood Descent (RVND) in the Local Search Procedure. Different implementation schemes of the proposed method are tested on set of data instances provided by our industrial partner. The results show the effectiveness of ILS-RVND compared to ILS with a single local search operator. ILS-RVND improves the results of the SBH heuristic by 13.15%.

Keywords: Vehicle routing · Pickup and delivery problem · Split delivery · Vehicle routing problem with profile · Meta-heuristic · Iterated local search · Variable neighborhood descent

1 Introduction

In this paper, we address a real-word problem encountered in the constructions sector and studied in the framework of the ADEME R&D project, denoted DILC.

J. de Armas et al. (Eds.): ICCL 2022, LNCS 13557, pp. 105–119, 2022.
https://doi.org/10.1007/978-3-031-16579-5_8

The project DILC aims to design an innovative platform for optimizing construction site logistics, that is adapted to multi-site ecocity construction projects. The goal is to improve the rate of recycling wastes from the construction site, reduce CHG impacts, and reduce the financial impact for the building companies. The optimization lever studied in this project is the consolidation of the transportation flows and human resources through a physical platform that is modular, removable and mobile, and the development of decision support tools to help the platform managers to optimize their logistics.

The pooling platform aims grouping many delivery building materials from different suppliers, receiving them in pallets according to a schedule corresponding to the progress of construction activities on the construction sites. From the received building materials, ready-to-use kits are prepared on the platform, stored and delivered in pallets to the construction sites. The kit represents the site supply unit, that is, a kit must be delivered in full. It is not possible to split the kit into several deliveries. Each kit is characterized by its ID, the number of pallets it contains, and its weight. The delivery request from the construction sites may involve different kits, and the quantities of material delivery demands are known to sometimes exceed the truck's capacity, which requires to supply the construction sites several times, so splitting the delivery demand is allowed in our case. The quantity of waste is relatively inferior to the quantity of material to be delivered, but can also be split. The platform must also manage the removal of waste from construction sites to the platform. It should be noted that in this study we are interested in Big-bag wastes that can be packed on pallets and concern wastes that are produced with small and medium quantities such as soft plastic, hard plastic, and cardboard. The removal of big-bag wastes can be pooled with the delivery of building materials using a limited and heterogeneous tail-lift truck fleet, whose capacity is given in pallets. The vehicles perform multiple trips between the platform and the construction sites to load the kits at the platform, deliver them to the construction sites, collect waste from the construction sites and unload these wastes in the recycling center located just next to the platform.

The problem studied here is the routing optimization between the pooling platform and the construction sites to mutualize the materiel delivery and the waste removal, and more specifically we present a new variant of the well-known pickup and delivery problem, named MTPDSPTW for the Multi-Trip Pickup and Delivery Problem, with Split loads, Profits and Multiple Time Windows.

The MTPDSPTW belongs to the class of Vehicle Routing Problem with Pickup and Delivery (VRPPD), which has been studied for more than 30 years [9,10], and consists of transporting objects or people between origins and destinations. More precisely, the problem studied in this paper is included in the class VRP with Backhauls (VRPB) where objects or individuals are transported from a depot to linehaul customers and from backhaul customers to a depot [9], and the most adequate VRPB subclass with our problem is the VRP with Divisible Deliveries and Pickups (VRPDDP), which is a special case of the VRPPD, where each customer may have delivery and/or pickup requests that must be served with capacitated vehicles, and the pickup and the delivery quantities can be served, if helpful, in two separate visits [8].

Many variants of VRPPD with several constraints have been proposed in the literature to model real transportation problems (see for example [2, 12]), but very few papers have considered the combination of "pickups and deliveries" and "split deliveries".

We can notice the studies of [6, 7], that considered the combination of the two above constraints. The authors proposed a mixed integer programming (MIP) formulation for this problem and a route construction heuristic based on a cheapest insertion criterion and parallel clustering. Other research focused on the one-to-one pickup and delivery routing problem with split load, where every request originates at one location and is destined for one other location [1]. The vehicle routing problem with simultaneous deliveries and pickups with split loads and time windows have been studied in [13, 14]. The authors proposed a mixed-integer programming model and a hybrid heuristic algorithm enhanced by a local search, where the objective is to minimize both the number of vehicles required and the total travel cost.

In short, we differ from the pickup delivery vehicle routing problems with split load mentioned studies in that we consider, within the same problem, a limited heterogeneous fleet of vehicles, profit, multi-trip and multiple time windows. Combining these constraints into one vehicle routing variant poses significant methodological challenges, and requires more sophisticated classes of neighborhoods to be adequately solved via metaheuristics. Furthermore, this study follows on from the work presented in [3], where a heuristic method named SBH were presented to solve the MTPDSPTW. As such, the key contributions of this work are:

- Modeling a real application in the construction sector as a new variant of pickup and delivery problem named MTPDSPTW that allows simultaneously considering constraints that have never been previously combined in the pickup and delivery variants studied in the literature. More specifically, these are the constraints on heterogeneous fleet of vehicles, multi- trips, splitting demands, profit and time windows. Note that in our problem, profit is associated with a pickup request and/or a delivery request, while in most studies in the literature profit is associated with a customer and includes both pickup and delivery re- quests.
- Efficient ILS-RVND approach that integrates an adaptation of classical neighborhood search as relocate, 2-opt exchange, and swap. A new large neighborhood operator that combines reinsertion and optimization of splitting used as a local search operator and as a perturbation is also proposed. The ILS-RVND enhances the SBH heuristic proposed in our previous research.
- Experimental analyses on real benchmark instances.

The remainder of the paper is organized as follows. In Sect. 2, we describe the problem statement. Solving approaches are presented in Sect. 3. Section 4 summarizes the computational results. Conclusions are given in Sect. 5.

2 Problem Description

The MTPDSPTW can be defined on a complete, undirected graph $G = (V, E)$, where $V = \{0, \ldots, n\}$ is the set of vertices and $E = \{(i, j) : i, j \in V, i \neq j\}$ is the set of edges. Vertex 0 is the pooling platform while the other vertices are the construction sites. A travel time t_{ij} and cost c_{ij} are assigned to each edge (i, j). A fleet of heterogeneous tail lift vehicles is located on the platform. The vehicle fleet is composed by m vehicles with different capacities and time availability. We denote by Q_k the capacity in pallets of the kth vehicle $k \in \{1, \ldots, m\}$, W_k its volume capacity in tons, and by D_k its maximum working time. Each site $i \in V$ has a pickup demand of the zth Big-bag waste denoted by p_z^i, and a delivery demand $d_{z'}^i$ of the z'^{th} kits. Note that, all demands are integer vectors. $\overrightarrow{p_i}$ is in this form $(p_1^i, \ldots, p_z^i)$ which indicates the pickup demand of each type of Big-bag waste. $\overrightarrow{d_i}$ is represented as $(d_1^i, \ldots, d_{z'}^i)$ that describes the delivery demand of each type of kits. A kit can contain one or more pallets and the Big-bag waste unit is the pallet. Thus, all demands of site delivery and pickup are expressed in pallets. In the rest of the paper we denote by $qt(\overrightarrow{vect})$ the size of demand in pallets ($\overrightarrow{vect}$ can be $\overrightarrow{p_i}$ or $\overrightarrow{d_i}$). Sometimes, the demands of sites (delivery and/ or pickup) are greater than the vehicle capacity (for example $qt(\overrightarrow{d_i}) > Q_k$), then the site can be served by the same vehicle with several trips or by several vehicles. Each site can have a priority on its delivery demands or its pickup demands or both. To satisfy these requirements, two real values pp_i and pd_i are associated with each site i and correspond to the pickup profit and delivery profit, respectively. Unlike the literature approaches where the profit is associated with customers, in our model, the profit is associated with each demand.

Each vertex $i \in V \setminus \{0\}$ has a service time s_i which corresponds to the loading/unloading time on site, and a set of time windows $TW_i = \{[e_i^1, l_i^1], [e_i^2, l_i^2], \ldots, [e_i^t, l_i^t]\}$ where e_i^p $p \in \{1, \ldots, t\}$ is the earliest time to begin service at the vertex i and l_i^p is the latest time to finish service at the vertex i. Furthermore, we defined $[e_0, l_0]$ as the single time window of the platform that designates the earliest possible departure from the platform and the latest possible arrival at the platform. The service time s_0 at the platform is given by the sum of the loading time of kits and unloading time of Big-bag waste. This service time is not considered for the first trip of each vehicle since the first vehicle loading can be done independently of its tour. If a vehicle travels directly from site i to site j. The service of site j starts at $b_j = max\{e_j^c, b_i + s_i + t_{ij}\}$ where $e_j^c = min_{1 \leq k \leq |TW_j|}\{e_j^k \mid l_j^k - (b_i + s_i + t_{ij} + s_j) \geq 0\}$ designated the lower bound of the most adequate time window. Note that waiting is not allowed because construction site activities do not allow access to the sites beyond the imposed time constraints.

A feasible solution to our problem is composed of a set of feasible trips assigned to adequate vehicles. A feasible trip is a sequence of nodes that satisfies the following set of constraints:

- Each trip must start and end at the pooling platform.

- Each kit must be delivered in full, no possibility to split the kit into several trips.
- The overall amount of materials delivered and wastes picked along the route must not exceed the vehicle capacity (Q_k, W_k).
- The total duration of each trip calculated as the sum of all travel duration required to visit all the construction sites of the trip sequence, and service time needed for each visit to a construction site during the tour could not exceed D_k.
- Each site can be visited at most once during the trip while respecting one of its time windows.

We seek to construct a feasible solution of a minimum number of trips, and affecting one or several trips to the available vehicles such that:

- The total duration of each vehicle's route, calculated as the sum of all its trips duration, and the sum of the platform's service times don't exceed D_k
- Each vehicle must start at the pooling platform no earlier than e_0 and finish at the pooling platform no later than l_0.
- No more than m vehicles are used;
- Each construction site may be visited several times with the same or different vehicles, so splitting is allowed for delivery requests and pickup requests, and some sites may not be visited at all.
- The sum of the quantities delivered to a given construction site must be less than or equal to its delivery request and the sum of the quantities collected from a given construction site must be less than or equal to its pickup request. This means that the customer can be delivered and/or collected partially.

The objective is to minimize the total distance and maximize the profit, knowing that the profit of a given customer is the sum of the profit of his satisfied pickup demand and his satisfied delivery demand.

3 Solution Approaches

3.1 Iterated Local Search Algorithm

Since the considered problem is NP-hard and in order to solve large instances, we develop an Iterated Local Search (ILS) metaheuristic. This type of method was first used by Martin et al. [5], and has been clearly defined by Lourenço et al. [4] and Stützle [11]. The iterated local search algorithm starts with an initial solution and then finds a local optimum in a pre-defined neighborhood through a local search procedure. The ILS applies perturbation operators to this solution in order to move from this local optimum. An acceptance criterion is used to determine which local optimum will be chosen for the next iteration. This process is repeated until a stopping criterion is satisfied. The developed ILS uses five procedures: (i) generation of an initial solution; (ii) a Local Search which improves the solution initially obtained; (iii) a Perturbation Mechanism that generates a new starting point through a perturbation of the solution returned by the Local Search; (iv) an Acceptance Criterion that specifies if the solution should be accepted or not and (v) a Stopping Criterion that specifies when the ILS procedure should stops. The proposed metaheuristic differs from traditional ILS due to the nature of the neighborhoods used for solution improvement and for perturbation. Three classical Local search operators are adapted to our problem, and a new larger neighborhood operator named Remove-split is proposed. Remove-split operator removes all occurrences of a given client and seeks for a good combination of insertions in different routes in order to cover the maximum of demand. Randomised version of the Remove-split operator is used in the perturbation procedure. The general pseudo-code of the method is displayed in Algorithm 1.

Algorithm 1. Iterated local search ILS

```
1: S_0 ← GenerateInitialSolution
2: S* ← LocalSearch(S_0)
3: repeat
4:     S' ← Perturbation(S*, history)
5:     S*' ← LocalSearch(S')
6:     S* ← AcceptanceCriterian(S*, S*', history)
7: until termination condition met
```

Initial Solution. The initial solution is generated using sequential heuristic called Score Based Heuristic (SBH). This heuristic inserts sites step by step using a score calculated as the weight of 6 criteria. Suppose that i is the last site inserted in the current trip, SBH looks for the next feasible site j minimizing the score. The criteria used are the distance between j and i, the earliest date of arrival in j, the maximum upper limit of the customer's time windows j, the total time available to serve the site j, and a delivery profit (respectively collection) weighted by the cumulative quantity already delivered (respectively cumulative quantity already collected) of the customer j. For more details on this heuristic, please refer to [3].

Local Search Operators. The local search iteratively explores the solution space to improve the quality of the solution. In this study we adapt relocate operator, 2-opt operator, and swap move operator to deal with the constraints of our problem. Furthermore, we propose a new operator named Remove-split operator which consists in removing a given client from all routes and seeks for a good combination of insertions in different routes in order to cover a maximum of demand. The main difficulty in the exploration of the neighborhood consists in the fact that the quantity to be satisfied in delivery and in pick-up of a given client varies with the modification of its position. The variation of the quantities to be collected and to be delivered of a given client implies the modification of the service time of this client and thus the temporal constraints need to be verified for the vehicle and for other clients served by the same vehicle. Note also that the presence of the multi-trip constraint implies the need to maintain synchronization between all the trips of the same vehicle.

The proposed operators are further described below. Note that through the paper we denoted by D_i^l and P_i^l the demand request and the pickup request of the customer i on route R_l, respectively.

- **Relocate operator:** This operator moves a customer to another position in the same route or from the initial route to another. We are talking here about intra- and inter-routes scenarios and rename it as All-relocate (see Fig. 1). For intra-route relocate, we suppose that i and j are two customers in R_l. The customer i is removed from its original position and inserted following j then the new route $R_l = (0, \ldots, j, i, j+1, \ldots, 0)$. For inter-routes relocate, let a customer i in R_l and j a customer in R_k. The customer i is removed from R_l and inserted after j in R_k. The resulting routes are $R_l = (0, \ldots, i-1, i+1, \ldots, 0)$ and $R_k = (0, \ldots, j, i, j+1, \ldots, 0)$

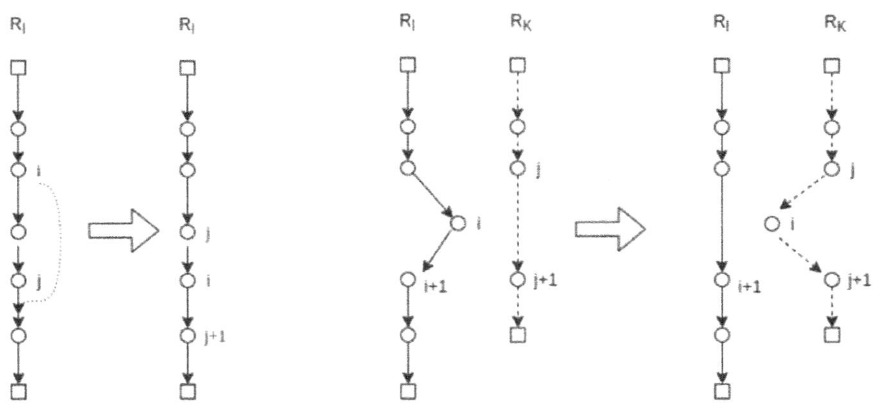

(a) Intra-route relocation (b) Inter-routes relocation

Fig. 1. All-relocate operator.

- **Relocate-split operator:** Suppose that a customer $i \in R_l \bigcap R_k$ and a customer $j \in R_l$. This operator removes the customer i from R_k, then $R_k = (0, \ldots, i-1, i+1, \ldots, 0)$ and it keeps R_l unchanged. It increases D_i^l by D_i^k, seeks a customer j in R_l that can be inserted into R_k, with the quantity D_i^k, and inserts j in R_k (see Fig. 2).
- **2-opt*exchange operator:** Two customers $i \in R_l$ and $j \in R_k$ are chosen. Then, the edges connecting i to $i+1$ and j to $j+1$ are removed and two new edges are created adjoining i to $j+1$ and j to $i+1$ see Fig. 3. We have implemented the intra- and inter-routes 2-opt*exchange operator.

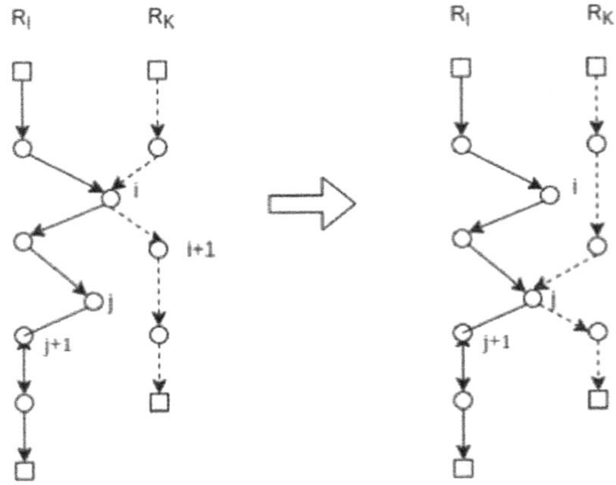

Fig. 2. A relocate split operation.

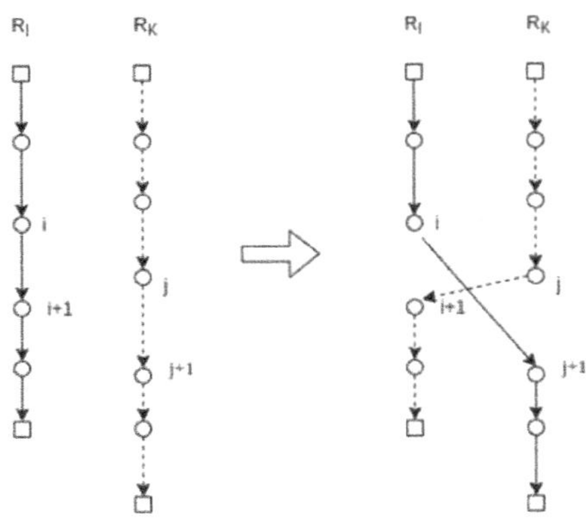

Fig. 3. 2-opt*exchange operator.

- **Swap move operator:** This operator consists in swapping two customers from different routes. More formally, let $i \in R_k$, and $j \in R_l$. This operator interchange the position of i and j. To balance the delivery and pickup quantity, we choose a customer $h \in R_k$ and we split the demand of h between R_k and R_l see Fig. 4. We have implemented the intra- and inter-routes swap move operator.

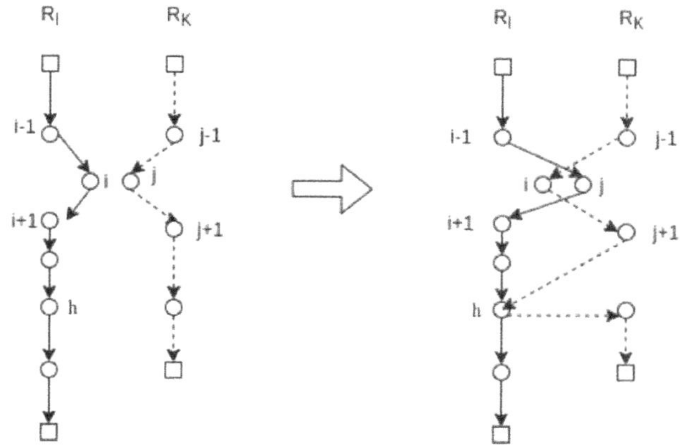

Fig. 4. Swap move operator

- **Remove-split operator**
  This operator consists of removing a customer i from all its current routes and searches for a good combination of insertion of i in all routes in order to cover the maximum demand of the client i. This problem can be viewed as a knapsack problem with an additional constraint that limits the selection to one position at most in each route. We thus use a greedy heuristic with iteratively select the maximum ratio S_k. For each feasible position k of a route R_l, we compute the ratio $S_k(R_l)$ with $S_k(R_l) = Q_{loadk}/D_{insertk}$, where Q_{loadk} represents the maximum quantity in delivery and pickup demand that could be inserted at position k of the route R_l, and $D_{insertk}$ represents the additional distance related to the insertion of i at the position k of the route R_l.
  For example, in Fig. 5, customer $i \in R_l \bigcap R_k \bigcap R_m$ is removed from all routes and reinserted into R_k and R_M. This subset of routes can contain the initial routes of i or other routes.

Perturbation Mechanism. The perturbation mechanism is designed to escape the current local optimum. It can affect the effectiveness of an ILS algorithm, since a strong perturbation of the solution might deliver a similar result as pure randomization, which can decrease opportunities to move toward the global optimal solution. However, a small perturbation may be insufficient to get out of the local optimum. Our perturbation mechanism is based on a randomised version of our Remove-split operator. The description of the perturbation procedure can be found in Algorithm 2. Firstly, a number of perturbation $MaxIter$ is fixed to 20% of the number of visited sites in input solution S (line 2). Next, in each iteration, the algorithm removes randomly a site i from the current solution and reinsert it randomly in one or more new feasible positions (line 6–15). Finally, the input solution S will be sequentially perturbed $MaxIter$ times.

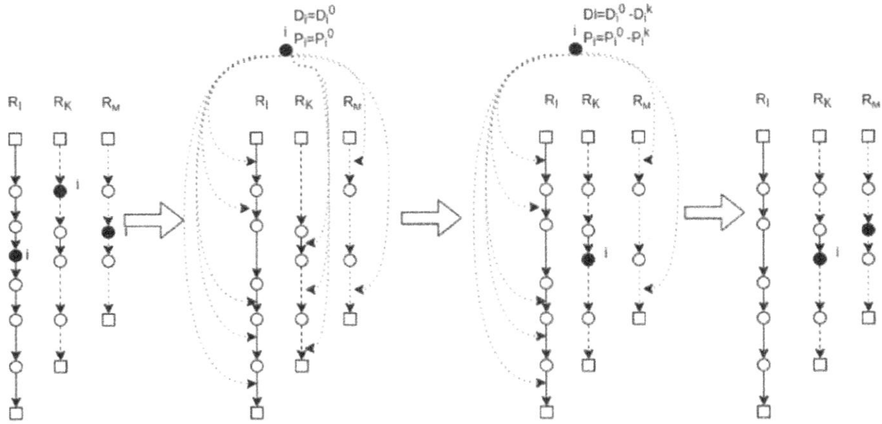

Fig. 5. Remove-split operator

Acceptance Criterion. Some research has proposed to accept solutions which are worse than the best solution according to a definite acceptance criterion. In this paper, simulated annealing acceptance criterion is used. In simulated annealing, the probability p of accepting a solution $S^{'}$ worse than the current solution S is:

$$p = e^{(-\frac{f(S^{'})-f(S)}{T})} \tag{1}$$

where T is the current temperature parameter. The temperature updates are governed by the cooling scheme, which computes the temperature value T_{i+1} at the instant $i+1$ as a function of the previous value T_i at instant i. In this paper, the cooling scheme is defined by $T_{i+1} = \alpha.T_i$.

To determine the initial temperature T_0 of each instance, we introduce a parameter $w \in]0,1[$ to control T_0 indicating that a solution $w\%$ worse than the initial solution S_0 will be accepted with a probability of 0.5.

3.2 ILS-RVND

The ILS-RVND metaheuristic is based on the same principle of classical ILS described in the Sect. 3.1. The difference between the proposed metaheuristic and traditional ILS lies in the nature of the neighborhoods utilised to improve the solution. Instead of relying on local search, it exploits a randomized variable neighborhood descent (RVND). The main steps of ILS-RVND are described by the Algorithm 3. This metaheuristic executes MaxIt iterations (lines 4–22), where a SBH heuristic generates an initial solution (line 5), which is subsequently improved by the ILS (lines 8–17), which implements a local search by means of an RVND (line 9) heuristic to ensure intensification as well as a set of perturbation mechanisms (line 15) in the diversification phase. The parameter S^* represents

Algorithm 2. Perturbation procedure

Input: S
Output $S^{'}$
$MaxIter$ = 20% of number of visited sites
$Iter \leftarrow 0$
while $Iter \neq MaxIter$ **do**
  Choose uniformly at random a site i from list of visited sites LVS.
  Remove i from all trips.
  $d_i \leftarrow qt(\overrightarrow{d_i})$.
  $p_i \leftarrow qt(\overrightarrow{p_i})$.
  Determine the list of possible positions LP of i
  while $d_i! = 0$ and $p_i! = 0$ **do**
    Choose randomly a position x from LP.
    Insert i into x, let a (respectively b) the possible quantity of delivery to be inserted in x (respectively quantity of pickup)
    Update d_i and p_i: $d_i \leftarrow d_i - a$ and $p_i \leftarrow p_i - b$
  end while
  Remove i from the LVS
  $Iter \leftarrow Iter + 1$
end while

the best solution and $MaxIt$ corresponds to the maximum number of perturbations allowed without improvements. Algorithm 4 shows the pseudo code of the RVND procedure. Firstly, an operator list (OL) containing the five operators described in Sect. 3.1 is initialized (line 3). While the operator list is not empty, an operator from OL is chosen randomly and then the best feasible solution is determined (line 6). If the selected operator succeeded in improving the best solution (line 7–10), the solution found by this operator will be considered as the best solution and OL will be up to date. Otherwise, OP is removed from the OL (line 11).

4 Computational Experiments and Discussion

The proposed algorithms are coded in Python programming language and executed in a PC Intel Xeon(R) CPU E5-1603 V3 2.80 GHz with 32 GB of RAM memory and operating system Windows 8. We conducted numerical experiments on real data instances that were provided by our industrial partner. Experiments were conducted on 5 data instances. The number of construction sites for the considered instances is 100 and the number of vehicles is 10, each of these vehicles is characterized by a maximum capacity $Q = 16$.

The characteristics of the instances are:

- The distance between two sites or between a site and the platform is between 1 and 150 km.
- Each site can be served in one, two, or three predefined time windows.

Algorithm 3. ILS-RVND

Input: MaxIt, MaxIterILS
Output S^*
$f^* \leftarrow \infty$
for $i \leftarrow 1$ **to** MaxIt **do**
  $S_0 \leftarrow GenerateInitialSolution$
  $S' \leftarrow S_0$
  $IterILS \leftarrow 0$
  while $iterILS \leq MaxIterILS$ **do**
    $S_0 \leftarrow RVND(N(.), f(.), S')$
    if $AcceptanceCriterion(S_0, S')$ **then**
      $S' \leftarrow S_0$
      $f(S') \leftarrow f(S_0)$
      $IterILS \leftarrow 0$
    end if
    if $f(S') \leq f^*$ **then**
      $S^* \leftarrow S'$
      $f^* \leftarrow f(S')$
    end if
    $S' \leftarrow Perturbation(S')$
    if $f(S') \leq f^*$ **then**
      $S^* \leftarrow S'$
      $f^* \leftarrow f(S')$
    end if
    $IterILS \leftarrow IterILS + 1$
  end while
end for

Algorithm 4. RVND

Input: f(.), S
Output S^*
Initialize the operator List (OL)
while $OL \neq \emptyset$ **do**
  choose randomly a operator OP from OL
  $S' \leftarrow OP(S)$
  if $f(S') \leq f(S)$ **then**
    $S \leftarrow S'$
    Update OL
  else
    Remove OP from the OL
  end if
end while

- For each instance,20% of sites have a load of a delivery request lower than $\frac{1}{3}Q$ and 80% in $[\frac{1}{3}Q, Q]$. The load of a pickup request is lower than $\frac{2}{3}Q$ for all sites, where Q is the pallet capacity of the vehicles.

To evaluate our method, we compared several ILS implementation schemes, by varying the local search operators. Preliminary experiments allowed us to set the parameters of our algorithm as follows: The parameter control of the cooling scheme α was set to 0.9, and the percentage of destruction of the initial solution ϖ is fixed at 20%. Each instance is executed five times for each implementation schema, and each run is limited to 1 h. The experimental results are presented in Table 1, where **Instance** indicates the name of the instance, **Sites** is the number of sites, **#v** is the number of vehicles, **Sol.** is the solution found by the SBH heuristic, **Time.** is the time execution of the heuristic in seconds, **Best S.** is the best solution found by the operator identified in the column header, **Best t.** is the time in seconds to find the best solution in the best run. % **gap.** is the gap between the heuristic solution and ILS solution, were computed using Eq. (2).

$$gap = \frac{Heuristic\_solution - ILS\_solution}{Heuristic\_solution} \times 100 \quad (2)$$

The results obtained show that ILS-RVND is more efficient than ILS based on each local search operator independently. Indeed, the best improvements have been found by ILS-RVND in the majority of cases, except the instance DILC100-1 where the best solutions are obtained by the ILS-Relocate algorithm. The best average gap between the solution found by the SBH heuristic and the ones found by other algorithms is that found by ILS-RVND 13, 15%. However, the computing time of ILS-RVND is more important than the other algorithms. We also notice that when ILS uses a single operator as a local search, the best results are obtained by the "relocate" operator. The average gap obtained is 8, 83% against 5, 51% for ILS-2opt, 5, 38% for ILS-Swap, and 4, 3% for ILS-RemoveSplit. This can be explained by the fact that the Relocate operator represents a complete neighbourhood that allows both moving customers and changing the quantities served to other customers. The Remove-split operator also generates a complete neighbourhood, but the change in quantity only concerns the client that has been removed. We think that it would be interesting in the future to improve this operator by integrating the change in quantity of other customers within the best routes chosen for the reinsertion of the deleted customer. Note also that this operator is more time consuming, and therefore it is expected that it will need more time to achieve competitive performance.

Table 1. Performance comparisons between ILS-annealed with all local search operators and ILS-RVND.

Instance	Sites	#v	SBH		ILS-Relocate			ILS-2 opt			ILS-Swap			ILS-RemoveSplit			ILS-RVND		
			Sol	Time	Best S	Best t	%gap	Best S	Best t	%gap	Best S	Best t	% gap	Best S	Best t	% gap	Best S	Best t	% gap
DILC100-1	100	10	2133,253	2,791	**1961,753**	38,109	**8,039**	2053,356	43,821	3,745	2026,385	54,814	5,010	2104,962	774,597	1,326	1982,106	102,345	7,085
DILC100-2	100	10	578,448	2,926	523,031	55,635	9,580	534,823	46,362	7,542	534,902	37,454	7,528	510,285	3,167	11,784	**451,616**	206,281	**21,926**
DILC100-3	100	10	1224,264	2,637	1102,767	125,105	9,924	1150,493	41,049	6,026	1174,241	22,143	4,086	1204,424	145,448	1,621	**1044,679**	157,347	**14,669**
DILC100-4	100	10	1110,190	3,731	1031,348	75,082	7,102	1060,317	67,264	4,492	1055,999	30,932	4,881	1072,508	4,017	3,394	**988,478**	181,771	**10,963**
DILC100-5	100	10	1094,635	2,788	990,128	73,143	9,547	1031,329	58,158	5,783	1035,185	29,264	5,431	1057,642	612,511	3,379	**972,840**	161,108	**11,126**
Average			1228,158	2,975	1121,805	73,415	8,839	1166,064	51,331	5,518	1165,342	34,921	5,387	1189,964	307,948	4,301	**1087,944**	161,770	**13,154**

5 Conclusion

In this paper, we propose a metaheuristic approach for the Multi-Trip Pickup and Delivery Problem, with Split loads, Profits and Multiple Time Windows. The proposed algorithm, called ILS-RVND is based on Iterated Local Search (ILS) and Randomized Variable Neighbor- hood Descent (RVND). Computational experiments were carried out on 5 real data instances provided by our industrial partner. The experimental results obtained on these instances have confirmed the effectiveness of ILS-RVND compared to other algorithms. As further work, we will test our methods on newly designed data instances and on other benchmark instances of some related problems. Next, we will relax our problem and compare our results with those of the literature. Moreover, we will consider other Local Search procedures and different perturbation mechanisms to improve our method.

References

1. Haddad, M., et al.: Large neighborhood-based metaheuristic and branch-and-price for the pickup and delivery problem with split loads. Eur. J. Oper. Res. (2018). https://doi.org/10.1016/j.ejor.2018.04.017
2. Chentli, H., Ouafi, R., Cherif-Khettaf, W.R.: A selective adaptive large neighborhood search heuristic for the profitable tour problem with simultaneous pickup and delivery services. RAIRO - Oper. Res. **52**(4), 1295–1328 (2018). https://doi.org/10.1051/ro/2018024
3. Jaballah, A., Ramdane-Cherif-Khettaf, W.: Multi-trip pickup and delivery problem, with split loads, profits and multiple time windows to model a real case problem in the construction industry. In: Proceedings of the 10th International Conference on Operations Research and Enterprise Systems, ICORES 2021, Online Streaming, 4–6 February 2021, pp. 200–207. SCITEPRESS (2021). https://doi.org/10.5220/0010253002000207
4. Lourenço, H.R., Martin, O.C., Stützle, T.: Iterated local search: framework and applications. In: Gendreau, M., Potvin, J.-Y. (eds.) Handbook of Metaheuristics. ISORMS, vol. 272, pp. 129–168. Springer, Cham (2019). https://doi.org/10.1007/978-3-319-91086-4_5
5. Martin, O., Otto, S.W., Felten, E.W.: Large-step Markov chains for the traveling salesman problem. Complex Syst. **5**, 299–326 (1991)
6. Mitra, S.: A parallel clustering technique for the vehicle routing problem with split deliveries and pickups. J. Oper. Res. Soc. **59**, 1532–1546 (2008)

7. Mitra, S.: An algorithm for the generalized vehicle routing problem with backhauling. Asia-Pacific J. Oper. Res. **22**(02), 153–169 (2005)
8. Nagy, G., Wassan, N.A., Speranza, M.G., Archetti, C.: The vehicle routing problem with divisible deliveries and pickups. Transp. Sci. **49**(2), 271–294 (2015). https://doi.org/10.1287/trsc.2013.0501
9. Parragh, S., Doerner, K., Hartl, R.: A survey on pickup and delivery problems: Part II: Transportation between pickup and delivery locations. J. für Betriebswirtschaft **58**, 81–117 (2008). https://doi.org/10.1007/s11301-008-0036-4
10. Parragh, S.N., Doerner, K.F., Hartl, R.F.: A survey on pickup and delivery models Part II: Transportation between pickup and delivery locations (2007)
11. Stützle, T.: Local search algorithms for combinatorial problems - analysis, improvements, and new applications. In: DISKI (1999)
12. Sun, P., Veelenturf, L., Hewitt, M., Van Woensel, T.: Adaptive large neighborhood search for the time-dependent profitable pickup and delivery problem with time windows. Transp. Res. Part E: Logist. Transp. Rev. **138**, 101942 (2020). https://doi.org/10.1016/j.tre.2020.101942
13. Wang, Y., Ma, X., Lao, Y., Yu, H., Liu, Y.: A two-stage heuristic method for vehicle routing problem with split deliveries and pickups. J. Zhejiang Univ. Sci. C **15**(3), 200–210 (2014). https://doi.org/10.1631/jzus.C1300177
14. Wang, Y., Ma, X., Lao, Y., Wang, Y., Mao, H.: Vehicle routing problem: simultaneous deliveries and pickups with split loads and time windows. Transp. Res. Rec. **2378**(1), 120–128 (2013). https://doi.org/10.3141/2378-13

The Biobjective Consistent Traveling Salesman Problem

Daniel Díaz-Ríos and Juan-José Salazar-González(✉)

IMAULL, University of La Laguna, 38200 La Laguna, Tenerife, Spain
ddiazrio@ull.edu.es, jjsalaza@ull.es

Abstract. This article deals with the problem of designing a route for each day of a time period to minimize the total travel cost and the discrepancy in the service time to customers visited on different days. In this paper we allow waiting times for the vehicle at customer locations. The literature already includes exact and heuristic approaches for the variant where the first objective is minimized and the second objective is constrained by a given threshold. The variant do not allow waiting times at customer locations, and it is known as Consistent Travelling Salesman Problem. We are not aware of any previous algorithm in the literature to tackle the biobjective problem, and this article describes three compact formulations for it. Each formulation is suitable for approaching the problem through the well-known weighted-sum method for multiobjective optimization, where some Pareto optimal solutions are sequentially determined by systematically changing the weights among the objective functions. We perform a computational study applying the formulations to tackle instances adapted from the TSPLIB library.

Keywords: Travelling Salesman · Time consistency · Branch and cut

1 Introduction

The Traveling Salesman Problem (TSP) is an NP-Hard problem that has been extensively studied in the literature. Given a depot and a set of customers, it consists of finding a minimum-cost circuit so that a vehicle visits each customer exactly once. The Consistent Travelling Salesman Problem (CTSP) is a variant of the TSP introduced by [2] where a time period is given (say, a week), each customer requires service on some (known in advance) days, and one TSP must be solved for each day. The novel requirement in the CTSP is that customers desire to be served consistently in time when visited in different days, meaning that the service times should be similar for each customer. For example, giving service to a customer in the early morning on Monday and in the late evening on Thursday is undesirable. In the literature this requirement has been modelled as a hard constraint (see e.g. [7,8]). Indeed, an input threshold T is given in advance to limit the maximum allowed time inconsistency for each customer visited in several days, and then the routes should be determined to ensure it. While

J. de Armas et al. (Eds.): ICCL 2022, LNCS 13557, pp. 120–131, 2022.
https://doi.org/10.1007/978-3-031-16579-5_9

there are articles where waiting times of the vehicle at the customer locations are forbidden before the services start, better solutions are found when waiting times are allowed. For that reason, in this paper, we assume that the vehicle is allowed to wait along the route. Under this assumption the mathematical problem is more complex since a solution is not only a route for each day, but also the waiting time at each customer location served each day.

Given a route for each day and the waiting times at each customer location, we consider two characteristics. One characteristic is the total travel cost of the routes, not including waiting times. The other feature is the maximum of the time difference between the visits in different days to a customer, over all the customers. The CTSP looks for a solution, minimizing the first feature, while it limits the second feature to T with a hard constraint. However the real-world problem has a multicriteria nature and a CTSP solution also admits other characteristics, like the travel cost of the route in each day (perhaps even including the waiting times), or the maximum waiting time between when a vehicle arrives to a customer and when the service starts at the customer. To reduce the complexity of the exposition in this article, we restrict our analysis to two characteristic, thus leading to a bicriteria optimization problem. The models and implementations can be easily adapted to also include the other characteristics.

Since the two characteristics (the total travel cost and the time inconsistency at customers) evolve in different directions, there does not exist a feasible solution that minimizes the two objective functions simultaneously. In this context, solving the bicriteria problem is finding a Pareto optimal solution, which is a set of routes that cannot be improved in any of the objectives without degrading the other objective. Since there may be a huge number of Pareto optimal solutions, we only aim at generating supporting non-dominated Pareto-optimal solutions, i.e., solutions with objective values on the convex hull of the Pareto frontier. As typically followed when approaching a bicriteria optimization problem, our article models and solves a single-objective problem where the two selected characteristics are linearly combined with a generic weight α, the standard weighted-sum method in multicriteria optimization to generate some Pareto-optimal solutions (see e.g. [5]). We propose three mathematical programming formulations for the single-objective problem and analyse computational experiments using a modern solver to find optimal solutions. The formulations can also be adapted to work on more sophisticated approaches to generate all the Pareto-optimal solutions (see e.g. [3,4]).

2 Problem Definition

Let $G = (V, A)$ be a complete directed graph where $V = \{0, 1, ..., n\}$ is the set of nodes, with 0 representing the depot and $1, ..., n$ representing the customers. Each arc $(i, j) \in A$ is associated with two variables: c_{ij} and t_{ij} representing the travel cost and travel time, respectively, to go from node i to node j. We use $K = \{1, ..., m\}$ to represent the time period (for example, the days of a

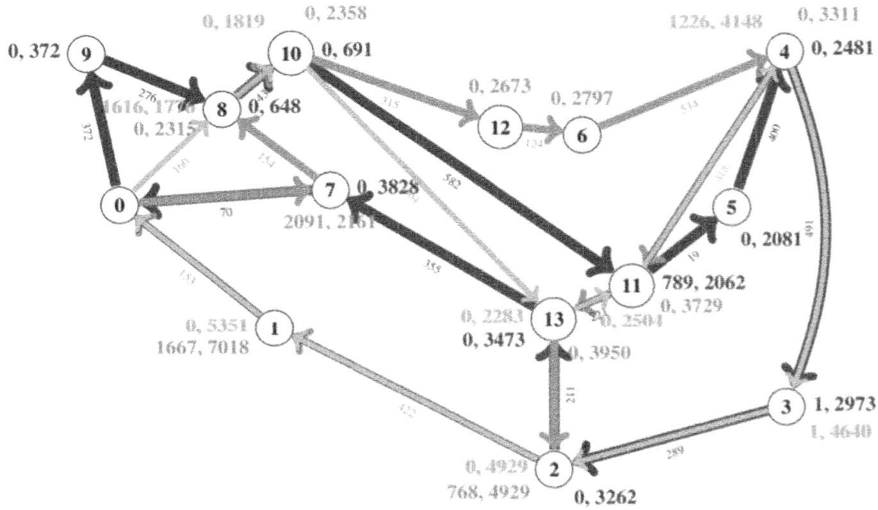

Fig. 1. Optimal solution with $\alpha = 0$. Travel cost: 8414. Time inconsistency: 1667

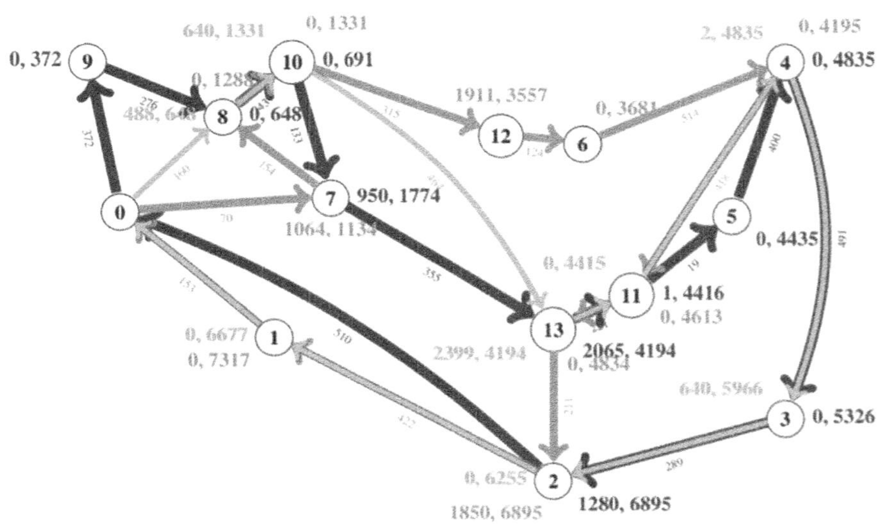

Fig. 2. Optimal solution with $\alpha = 0.1$. Travel cost: 8415. Time inconsistency: 640

week). Each day $k \in K$ is associated with a subset of nodes V_k, representing the customers to be visited in that day, with $0 \in V_k$. The day k is also associated with a set of arcs $A_k = \{(i,j) : i,j \in V_k, i \neq j\} \subseteq A$. Let $G^k = (V^k, A^k)$ be the graph on which a Hamiltonian circuit must be computed to define the route on day k. We assume that waiting times are allowed between the vehicle arrives at

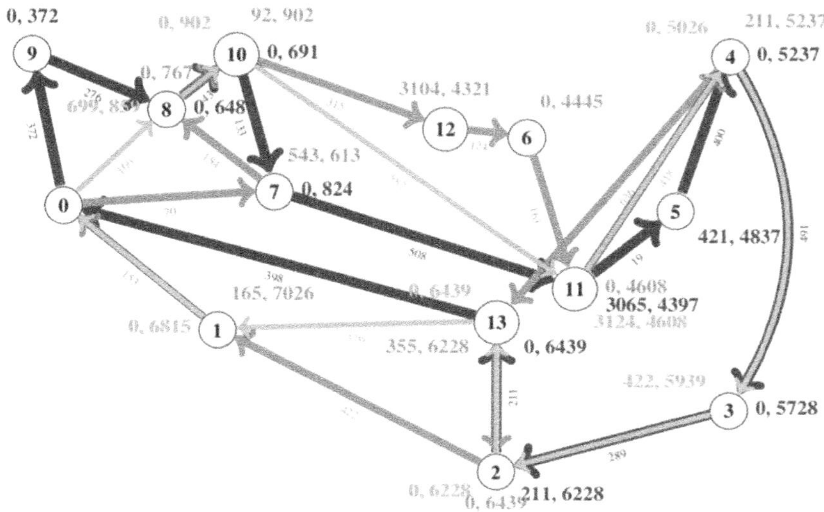

Fig. 3. Optimal solution with $\alpha = 0.27$. Travel Cost: 8572. Time inconsistency: 211

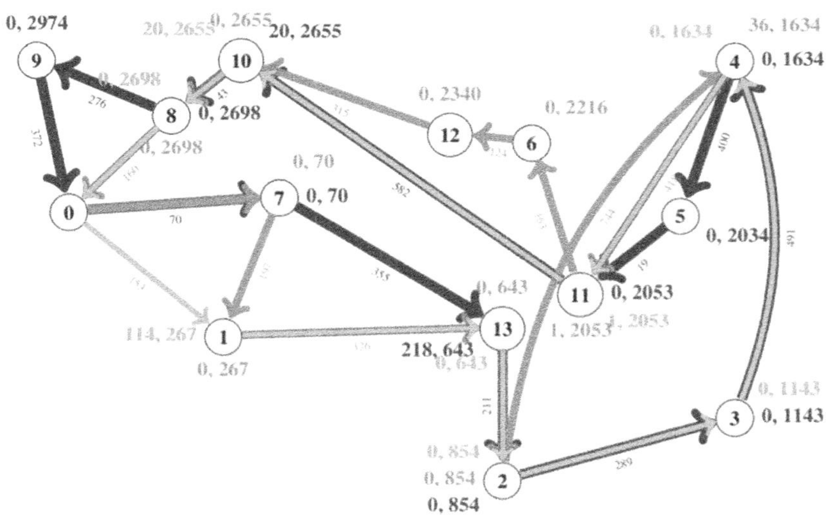

Fig. 4. Optimal solution with $\alpha = 0.3$. Travel Cost: 8652. Time inconsistency: 0

a customer location and before the service starts. To evaluate the two selected characteristics of a problem solution into a single objective function, let α be a given weight in the interval $[0, 1]$ so the cost of the solution is $1 - \alpha$ times the travel cost plus α times the maximum time discrepancy over all the customers.

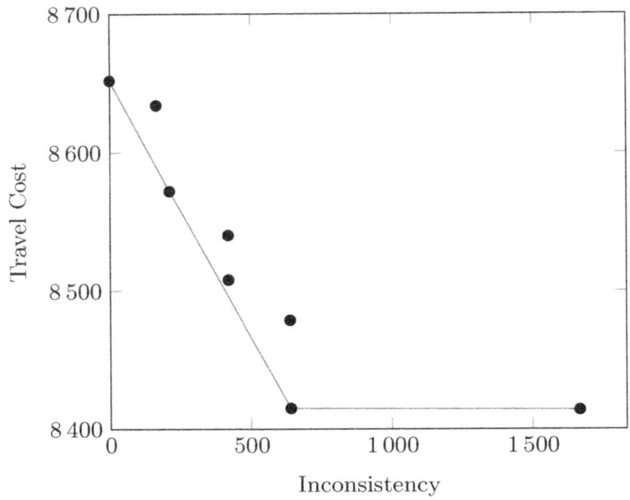

Fig. 5. Pareto frontier

Figures 1, 2, 3 and 4 show the optimal solutions for different values of α using an instance introduced in [7]. It is the `burma14` instance with 13 customers, with travel costs computed from geographic coordinates. Three days are considered (i.e., $|K| = 3$) and every customer requires a visit on each day with probability 0.7. In each figure, we use a different colour for each day, and show a pair of numbers near each customer. The left number is the waiting time of the vehicle at the customer before service starts, which is the right number. The tiny number on an arc shows the travel cost of that arc. Figure 1 corresponds to the solution when $\alpha = 0$, hence the time inconsistencies are not penalized and the result is equivalent to solving three independent TSPs. Figure 2 shows the optimal solution of the problem when $\alpha = 0.1$; the maximum time difference is reduced from 1667 to 640 increasing the travel cost of the routes by only one unit. It is worth mentioning that a solution with the same travel cost could be obtained with the approach in [8] and with any threshold T in the interval $[640, 1666]$. As expected, the more importance we place on time consistency in the objective function, the smaller the maximum time difference and the higher the total path cost. Figure 3 shows the solution when $\alpha = 0.27$, with travel cost equals to 8572 and the maximum time difference reduced to 211. Figure 4 shows the solution for a decision maker accepting a cost of 8652 to reduce the maximum time difference to zero, i.e. there is no inconsistency for any customer. Although α could still be increased to the value 1, no better solution is generated. Figure 5 shows the eight Pareto-optimal points for this bicriteria problem `burma14`. The four points along the blue line (frontier) correspond to the optimal solutions depicted in the previous figures, which are non-dominated Pareto solutions.

3 Mathematical Formulations

In this section we describe three formulations. The three formulations are based on a binary variable x_a^k which takes the value 1 if the vehicle in day $k \in K$ traverses the arc $a \in A^k$ and 0 otherwise. As standard in the literature, with $S \subseteq V^k$ we define $\delta_k^+(S) := \{(i,j) \in A^k : i \in S, j \notin S\}$ and $\delta_k^-(S) := \{(i,j) \in A^k : j \in S, i \notin S\}$. We denote the successors of a node i in day k as $\delta_k^+(i)$ instead of $\delta_k^+(\{i\})$ and the predecessors of node i in day k as $\delta_k^-(i)$ instead of $\delta_k^-(\{i\})$, in addition to $x^k(B)$ instead of $\sum_{a \in B} x_a^k$ where $B \subseteq A^k$. We also define a continuous variable T to represent the maximum time inconsistency of any customer. Therefore the objective function is:

$$\text{minimize} \qquad (1-\alpha) \cdot \sum_{k \in K} \sum_{a \in A^k} c_a x_a^k + \alpha \cdot T \tag{1}$$

Constraints shared by the three formulations are:

$$x^k(\delta_k^+(i)) = x^k(\delta_k^-(i)) = 1 \qquad i \in V^k \tag{2}$$

$$x_a^k \in \{0,1\} \qquad a \in A^k. \tag{3}$$

Formulation 1 uses an additional continuous variable z_i^k to represent the visit time on day k to customer i, and a big value M^k to upper bound the duration of the route in day k. Consequently the problem is formulated as (1)–(3) and

$$z_j^k \geq z_i^k + t_{(i,j)} \cdot x_{(i,j)}^k - M^k \cdot (1 - x_{(i,j)}^k) \qquad k \in K,\ i,j \in V^k \setminus \{0\},\ i \neq j \tag{4}$$

$$z_j^k \geq t_{(0,j)} \cdot x_{(0,j)}^k \qquad k \in K,\ j \in V^k \setminus \{0\} \tag{5}$$

$$z_i^p - z_i^q \leq T \qquad p,q \in K,\ i \in V^p \cap V^q \setminus \{0\}. \tag{6}$$

The constraints (4) are commonly used in vehicle routing problems when dealing with time constraints, they are known as *Miller-Tucker-Zemlin inequalities* (see, e.g. [1]), and they imply that $z_j^k \geq z_i^k + t_{(i,j)}$ when $x_{(i,j)}^k = 1$ with $i,j \in V^k \setminus \{0\}$. Constraints (5) force the same to the depot. Finally time consistency is established with the inequality (6).

Formulation 2 uses a different variable $g_{(i,j)}^k$ with $k \in K$, $(i,j) \in A^k$ to represent the arrival time at customer i on day k only if j is the next location to visit. The expression $\sum_{a \in B} g_a^k$ is abbreviated as $g^k(B)$ for all $B \subseteq A^k$.

$$g^k(\delta_k^+(j)) - g^k(\delta_k^-(j)) \geq \sum_{i \in V^k \setminus \{j\}} t_{(i,j)} x_{(i,j)}^k \qquad k \in K,\ j \in V^k \setminus \{0\} \tag{7}$$

$$0 \leq g_a^k \leq M^k \cdot x_a^k \qquad k \in K,\ a \in A^k \setminus \delta_k^+(0) \tag{8}$$

$$g^p(\delta_p^+(i)) - g^q(\delta_q^+(i)) \leq T \qquad p,q \in K,\ i \in V^p \cap V^q \setminus \{0\} \tag{9}$$

Constraints (7) imply the duration of the route to customer j to be greater than or equal to the duration of the route to its predecessor i plus the time that the vehicle needs to make the journey from i to j. Equations (8) set the value of g_a^k to zero whenever $x_a^k = 0$. The remaining constraints (9) establish just like constraints (6) in the previous formulation, the time consistency. As in the previous formulation, there are big values M^k for all $k \in K$.

Formulation 3 is based on three families of mathematical variables. A first family consider a multi-commodity flow on each day with f_a^{ik} representing the path from the depot 0 to each customer $i \in V_k$ on each day $k \in K$. A second set includes y_i^k representing the idle time of the vehicle at customer i on day k. A third family includes w_j^{ik} representing the idle time on the variable w_j^{ik} if j precedes i. Each feasible solution must verify:

$$f^{ik}(\delta_k^+(0)) - f^{ik}(\delta_k^-(0)) = 1 \tag{10}$$

$$f^{ik}(\delta_k^+(i)) - f^{ik}(\delta_k^-(i)) = -1 \tag{11}$$

$$f^{ik}(\delta_k^+(j)) - f^{ik}(\delta_k^-(j)) = 0 \qquad j \in V^k \setminus \{0, i\} \tag{12}$$

$$0 \leq f_a^{ik} \leq x_a^k \qquad a \in A^k \tag{13}$$

$$y_j^k - N_j^k \cdot f^{jk}(\delta_k^-(i)) \leq w_j^{ik} \leq N_j^k \cdot f^{ik}(\delta_k^-(j)) \qquad i, j \in V^k \setminus \{0\} \tag{14}$$

$$0 \leq w_j^{ik} \leq y_j^k \qquad i, j \in V^k \setminus \{0\} \tag{15}$$

$$\left(\sum_{a \in A^p} t_a f_a^{ip} + \sum_{j \in V^p \setminus \{0\}} w_j^{ip} \right) - \left(\sum_{a \in A^q} t_a f_a^{iq} + \sum_{j \in V^q \setminus \{0\}} w_j^{iq} \right) \leq T \qquad \begin{array}{l} p, q \in K \\ i \in V^p \cap V^q \setminus \{0\}. \end{array} \tag{16}$$

We take N_j^k as an upper bound on the maximum idle time at customer i in day k. The Eqs. (10)–(13) guarantee the existence of a path from the depot to each customer requiring a visit in each day. Inequalities (14)–(15) force w_j^{ik} to take the value y_j^k if j precedes i on day k, and it is zero otherwise. Constraints (16) establish the time consistency.

Formulations 1 and 2 have a weak linear programming relaxation, not only due to the big values involved in the constraint definitions, but also because the well-known subtour elimination constraints are poorly imposed, as [6] demonstrate. Indeed, the two compact formulations can be strengthened by including the following exponential set of inequalities:

$$x^k(\delta_k^+(S)) \geq 1 \qquad S \subset V^k \setminus \{0\}. \tag{17}$$

These inequalities are already implicit in Formulation 3, which has a better linear-programming relaxation when compared to the ones of Formulations 1 and 2, as computationally confirmed in the next section.

4 Preliminary Computational Results

We have implemented computer codes to solve the formulations using Gurobi 9.1.2 through its Python API on a personal computer with Intel(R) Core(TM) i7-10700 CPU @ 2.90 GHz, 24 GB RAM, and Windows 10 Pro. We tested the computer codes on benchmark instances from [7]. These instances were generated with $|K| = 3$ and 5 days, and with a probability for each client to require service on each day of $freq = 0.5$, 0.7 or 0.9. For example, an instance generated with $freq = 0.5$ means that a customer requires service in about half of the days in the time period K. The instances also include three options for the threshold T to limit the time inconsistency in the CTSP, but it is no longer meaningful in our bicriteria problem. Recall that T is unknown in our problem. Instead, we created three instances by using $\alpha = 0$, 0.1 and 0.3. The magnitude of the inconsistency makes useless to solve the problem with larger values for α on these benchmark instances.

We created five computer codes. Codes F1, F2 and F3 are associated with Formulations 1, 2 and 3, respectively. Formulations 1 and 2 were extended with the use of the Subtour Elimination Constraints (17), leading to codes F1+SEC and F2+SEC. Recall that Formulation 3 has these inequalities implicitly. We report computational results on tables with results from the five codes on each instance. The tables report three columns with characteristics of the instances. Column *Incons* shows the value of the maximum time difference obtained in the solution (i.e., the value of T in the best solution found). Column *Travel* shows the total travel cost of the routes. Column *Obj* shows the value of the obtained objective function 1 where the penalty α affects. In addition, for each code, each table reports two columns. Column *Time* shows the number of seconds taken by the MILP solver to solve the formulation with a time limit of one hour. Column *%-gap* is the difference between *Obj* and linear programming bound at the root node, divided by *Obj* and multiplied by 100.

Tables 1, 2 and 3 show how Formulations 1 and 2 benefit significantly from the use of the Subtour Elimination Constraints (17), it can be observed that Formulation 1 reaches the time limit in 21 of the 54 instances, however, applying the subtour elimination in the linear relaxation, the amount of reached time limits is reduced to only 1 case, in addition to reducing the execution time in the remaining cases. Similarly occurs with Formulation 2, where by applying the linear relaxation the number decreases from 31 to 3 time limits reached. In both cases the *%-gap* is significantly reduced. On the other hand Formulation 3 performs better than Formulations 1 and 2 since it reaches the time limit in 18 instances. However, it does not behave better than Formulations 1 and 2 when the subtour elimination constraints are added (i.e., codes F1+SEC and F2+SEC). Quite interestingly, the codes F1+SEC, F2+SEC and F3 produced the same linear programming bounds, never larger than 2%. In terms of computational times F1+SEC is the clear winner followed by F2+SEC. In overall terms, the problem becomes more difficult to solve regardless of the formulation as $|K|$, $freq$ or α increases. When the value of days or the number of nodes to visit each day increases, it is simply a bigger problem. On the other hand, increasing the weight α of the inconsistency T in the objective function makes the instance harder to be solved.

Table 1. Results on ulysses22

$\|K\|$	$freq$	α	Incons	Travel	Obj	F1		F1+SEC		F2		F2+SEC		F3	
						Time	%-gap	Time	%-gap	Time	%-gap	Time	%-gap	Time	%-gap
3	50	0	113	18453	18453.0	0.3	21.6	0.1	0.0	0.3	18.8	0.1	0.0	0.1	0.0
3	50	0.1	0	18463	16616.7	156.7	21.7	0.2	0.1	1793.3	18.8	0.2	0.1	2.5	0.1
3	50	0.3	0	18463	12924.1	28.5	21.7	0.1	0.1	2893.7	18.8	0.2	0.1	2.6	0.1
3	70	0	113	19213	19213.0	1.0	19.4	0.2	0.1	0.9	17.0	0.4	0.1	0.4	0.1
3	70	0.1	113	19213	17303.0	2148.7	19.5	0.2	0.1	351.6	17.0	0.5	0.1	13.8	0.1
3	70	0.3	113	19213	13483.0	221.7	19.6	0.4	0.3	294.4	17.2	0.6	0.3	18.5	0.3
3	90	0	1995	20657	20657.0	56.3	24.9	0.4	0.0	20.5	23.1	0.4	0.0	1.1	0.0
3	90	0.1	52	20718	18651.4	1 h	-	1.8	0.3	1 h	-	1.5	0.3	834.6	0.3
3	90	0.3	0	20724	14506.8	1 h	-	3.2	0.3	1 h	-	1.7	0.3	2395.8	0.3
5	50	0	3191	30412	30412.0	0.3	18.8	0.2	0.0	0.4	16.1	0.2	0.0	0.2	0.0
5	50	0.1	113	20433	27401.0	1 h	-	1.2	0.1	1 h	-	0.7	0.1	8.5	0.1
5	50	0.3	0	30449	21314.3	2323.4	18.9	1.1	0.1	1 h	-	0.5	0.1	13.0	0.1
5	70	0	113	32405	32405.0	2.1	22.1	0.6	0.0	3.5	19.7	0.7	0.0	0.8	0.0
5	70	0.1	113	32405	29175.8	1 h	-	0.5	0.1	1 h	-	1.0	0.1	75.0	0.1
5	70	0.3	113	32405	22717.4	1 h	-	1.4	0.2	1 h	-	2.1	0.2	73.2	0.2
5	90	0	3627	33826	33826.0	53.3	23.1	0.5	0.0	23.0	21.2	0.9	0.0	1.9	0.0
5	90	0.1	148	33904	30528.4	1 h	-	6.6	0.3	1 h	-	10.4	0.3	1 h	-
5	90	0.3	148	33904	23777.2	1 h	-	9.1	0.4	1 h	-	21.8	0.4	1 h	-

Table 2. Results on bays29

$\|K\|$	$freq$	α	Incons	Travel	Obj	F1		F1+SEC		F2		F2 + SEC		F3	
						Time	%-gap	Time	%-gap	Time	%-gap	Time	%-gap	Time	%-gap
3	50	0	319	4270	4270.0	0.3	17.1	0.2	0.0	0.5	16.6	0.2	0.0	0.4	0.0
3	50	0.1	184	4274	3865.0	4.2	17.6	0.6	0.6	208.3	17.1	0.8	0.6	21.0	0.6
3	50	0.3	0	4300	3010.0	4.6	17.7	1.4	0.7	488.8	17.2	1.0	0.7	84.1	0.7
3	70	0	57	5075	5075.0	0.4	14.8	0.3	0.0	1.3	14.4	0.5	0.0	2.0	0.0
3	70	0.1	57	5075	4573.2	11.5	15.0	1.2	0.1	2960.2	14.5	0.9	0.1	53.9	0.1
3	70	0.3	0	5083	3558.1	13.4	15.0	0.4	0.2	1 h	-	1.1	0.2	35.0	0.2
3	90	0	744	5644	5644.0	1.3	10.5	0.7	0.1	7.1	10.0	1.4	0.1	5.4	0.1
3	90	0.1	0	5690	5121.0	3350.5	11.2	8.8	0.9	1 h	-	16.6	0.9	1 h	-
3	90	0.3	0	5690	3983.0	2758.6	11.2	11.9	0.9	1 h	-	39.7	0.9	1 h	-
5	50	0	319	7126	7126.0	0.4	14.6	0.3	0.0	0.7	14.1	0.5	0.0	0.7	0.0
5	50	0.1	184	7130	6435.4	43.8	14.9	2.3	0.3	1 h	-	1.9	0.3	56.7	0.3
5	50	0.3	0	7197	5037.9	84.8	15.4	7.5	1.0	1 h	-	9.1	1.0	659.0	1.0
5	70	0	283	8527	8527.0	0.7	14.0	0.9	0.1	2.6	13.6	1.7	0.1	3.0	0.1
5	70	0.1	57	8542	7693.5	1504.1	14.2	8.6	0.3	1 h	-	12.3	0.3	1047.2	0.3
5	70	0.3	57	8542	5996.5	558.7	14.4	10.9	0.5	1 h	-	20.3	0.5	3447.7	0.5
5	90	0	775	9477	9477.0	1.9	11.3	6.1	0.2	23.2	10.9	14.1	0.2	31.1	0.2
5	90	0.1	240	9512	8584.8	1 h	-	39.6	0.9	1 h	-	112.4	0.9	1 h	-
5	90	0.3	0	9551	6685.7	1 h	-	115.1	1.0	1 h	-	878.4	1.0	1 h	-

Table 3. Results on `dantzig42`

$\|K\|$	$freq$	α	Incons	Travel	Obj	F1		F1+SEC		F2		F2 + SEC		F3	
						Time	%-gap	Time	%-gap	Time	%-gap	Time	%-gap	Time	%-gap
3	50	0	247	1599	1599.0	2.2	22.8	0.4	0.0	1.9	21.4	0.6	0.0	2.2	0.0
3	50	0.1	42	1619	1461.3	1 h	-	9.2	1.5	1 h	-	12.5	1.5	1 h	-
3	50	0.3	0	1631	1141.7	1 h	-	18.4	2.0	1 h	-	23.3	2.0	1 h	-
3	70	0	409	1758	1758.0	134.2	24.5	1.0	0.4	15.6	22.7	1.9	0.4	17.0	0.4
3	70	0.1	0	1787	1608.3	1 h	-	35.4	2.0	1 h	-	135.1	2.0	1 h	-
3	70	0.3	0	1787	1250.9	1 h	-	82.4	2.0	1 h	-	226.7	2.0	1 h	-
3	90	0	487	2041	2041.0	2001.7	23.2	4.4	0.4	1 h	-	13.0	0.4	324.7	0.4
3	90	0.1	30	2046	1844.4	1 h	-	41.9	0.8	1 h	-	130.1	0.8	1 h	-
3	90	0.3	12	2049	1437.9	1 h	-	88.5	1.1	1 h	-	418.0	1.1	1 h	-
5	50	0	452	2678	2678.0	3.5	22.8	0.8	0.0	13.0	21.6	1.1	0.0	3.2	0.0
5	50	0.1	288	2678	2439.0	1 h	-	111.7	1.2	1 h	-	144.2	1.2	1 h	-
5	50	0.3	23	2719	1910.2	1 h	-	1028.9	1.9	1 h	-	1 h	-	1 h	-
5	70	0	494	2936	2936.0	288.7	26.1	5.0	0.2	268.5	24.3	6.6	0.2	45.9	0.2
5	70	0.1	187	2952	2675.5	1 h	-	1699.0	1.5	1 h	-	3238.1	1.5	1 h	-
5	70	0.3	48	2968	2092.0	1 h	-	2664.6	2.0	1 h	-	1 h	-	1 h	-
5	90	0	521	3337	3337.0	2351.9	23.0	28.1	0.3	1 h	-	58.2	0.3	258.0	0.3
5	90	0.1	118	3344	3021.4	1 h	-	454.0	0.9	1 h	-	2083.1	0.9	1 h	-
5	90	0.3	-	-	-	1 h	-	1 h	-	1 h	-	1 h	-	1 h	-

5 Conclusions

This article introduces and addresses a bicriteria optimization variant of the Consistent Travelling Salesman Problem. While waiting times are forbidden in the Consistent Travelling Salesman Problem, our variant allows waiting times for the vehicle at customer locations. This paper describes three Integer Linear Programming models that are suitable to enumerate some Pareto solutions using the weighted-sum method known in Multiobjective Optimization. The first and second formulations outperform the third formulation when they are strengthened with the subtour elimination constraints. As a future direction of research, we plan to implement a Benders' Decomposition Approach for the third formulation. Although in principle generating inequalities also consume time, the advantage of working with a multicriteria problem is that the valid inequalities generated when using a weight α are also valid for a different weight α'. This advantage can be used both for the subtour elimination constraints and for the Benders' cuts, thus potentially saving computational time when solving a sequence of problems.

Acknowledgements. This research has been supported by the Spanish research project PID2019-104928RB-I00.

References

1. Bektas, T., Gouveia, L.: Requiem for the Miller-Tucker-Zemlin subtour elimination constraints. Eur. J. Oper. Res. **236**(3), 820–832 (2014). https://doi.org/10.1016/j.ejor.2013.07.038
2. Groër, C., Golden, B., Wasil, E.: The consistent vehicle routing problem. Manuf. Serv. Oper. Manag. **11**(4), 630–643 (2009). https://doi.org/10.1287/msom.1080.0243
3. Gunantara, N.: A review of multi-objective optimization: methods and its applications. Cogent Eng. **5**(1), 1502242 (2018). https://doi.org/10.1080/23311916.2018.1502242
4. Kirlik, G., Sayın, S.: A new algorithm for generating all nondominated solutions of multiobjective discrete optimization problems. Eur. J. Oper. Res. **232**(3), 479–488 (2014). https://doi.org/10.1016/j.ejor.2013.08.001
5. Marler, R.T., Arora, J.S.: The weighted sum method for multi-objective optimization: new insights. Struct. Multidiscip. Optim. **41**, 853–862 (2010). https://doi.org/10.1007/s00158-009-0460-7
6. Orman, A.J., Williams, H.P.: A survey of different integer programming formulations of the travelling salesman problem (2007)
7. Subramanyam, A., Gounaris, C.E.: A branch-and-cut framework for the consistent traveling salesman problem. Eur. J. Oper. Res. **248**(2), 384–395 (2016). https://doi.org/10.1016/j.ejor.2015.07.030
8. Subramanyam, A., Gounaris, C.E.: A decomposition algorithm for the consistent traveling salesman problem with vehicle idling. Transp. Sci. **52**(2), 386–401 (2018). https://doi.org/10.1287/trsc.2017.0741

Optimized Dispatch of Fire and Rescue Resources

Tobias Andersson Granberg(✉)

Linköping University, ITN, 60174 Norrköping, Sweden
Tobias.andersson.granberg@liu.se

Abstract. A dispatching problem for fire and rescue services is considered, where firefighters have to be allocated to vehicles, and vehicles dispatched to an emergency. A mathematical model for the problem is formulated, capable of managing multiple alarm plans for each emergency considered. The model is solved both exactly and heuristically, using input data from a fire and rescue service area in Skåne, Sweden. The results show that the exact solution method might be too time consuming in some cases, but that the heuristic in most cases finds the optimal solution.

Keywords: Emergency logistics · Optimization · Heuristics · Fire and rescue services

1 Introduction

When modeling fire and rescue services it is often assumed that the first unit to reach an event site (e.g. a traffic accident) will take care of the event all by itself. This follows from the common simplification that all vehicles will turnout from a station, and that all stations have the capacity to handle all possible events. Thus, it is possible to optimize the location of the stations, without regarding the specific manpower or equipment available at a particular station (e.g. [1] and [2]).

In reality, it is common that the types and number of vehicles and personnel varies between different fire stations. For some events, it is therefore necessary to receive a response from multiple stations. For example, a fire in a high-rise building will require a ladder unit, which might not be available at all stations. This has been regarded in some cases, e.g. in [3] where more than one unit is needed, but they are all of the same type. In [4] both engines and ladder units are modeled, but the specific abilities of the units are disregarded, and the objective is to maximize the coverage. A more general model is presented in [5], where each emergency, requires a specific set of vehicles, e.g. one emergency might require two pumpers and one ladder, while another emergency needs one pumper, one ladder, and one HAZMAT vehicle.

An additional complexity that is rarely considered in mathematical models is that the existing station personnel (i.e. the firefighters) seldom can staff all the existing vehicles. Thus, one fire station might not be able to supply all the necessary vehicles to an emergency, even if they physically exist at the station, due to staff shortage. A decision

J. de Armas et al. (Eds.): ICCL 2022, LNCS 13557, pp. 132–146, 2022.
https://doi.org/10.1007/978-3-031-16579-5_10

then must be made regarding which vehicle should be dispatched from which station, taking into account the number of firefighters at each station.

In this paper, fire and rescue resource requirements, i.e. vehicles and personnel, are specifically modeled through the use of alarm plans. An alarm plan states the resource requirements for handling a certain event, i.e. the number of firefighters and vehicles, and which types of vehicles. The problem under consideration is to select which vehicles to send to a specific event, and how to man these with firefighters.

The fire and rescue resource dispatching problem is not very well studied in literature, and often solved by rules of thumb in reality. There have been studies on which unit to send [6] and how may units to dispatch [7]. In [8] two different unit types (engines and ladders) are considered for two different events (serious and not serious), and there is a possibility that units may be busy. This is in contrast to most models dealing with fire and rescue resources, since the risk that a resource will be busy at a given point in time, in most cases is very low. Thus, it is reasonable to assume that they will be available when needed. As this is not true for emergency medical services (ambulances), there has been additional work on the dispatching problem taking into account the potential unavailability of resources, e.g. [9].

In the problem studied here, the unit types, the events and the alarm plans are generalized, so it is possible to model any number and types of resources and accidents. Furthermore, the explicit modeling of allocating firefighters to vehicles in a dispatching context has not been described previously (to the author's knowledge).

The problem is further described, and a mathematical model is presented in Sect. 2. Section 3 describes the solution strategies for solving the model exactly and heuristically. The two solution strategies are compared to each other in terms of solution quality and speed, and the results are presented in Sect. 4. Section 5 discusses how the model can be used practically, and Sect. 6 contains the conclusions and some thoughts on further studies.

2 Problem Statement and Mathematical Model

When there is an incident requiring fire and rescue resources, it is necessary to determine who should go to the incident site, and which vehicles they should use. For each incident there is at least one alarm plan, specifying the resource requirements. Here, a mathematical model is used to select which vehicles that should go, and which firefighter that should travel in which vehicle.

2.1 Alarm Plans

Different events, e.g. building fires or traffic accidents, require different sets of resources. The resources considered here are staff (firefighters) and vehicles of different types. A predefined set of resources needed to handle (the initial phase of) an event is denominated an alarm plan. There is at least one alarm plan for each event, but there may be more than one. As an example, in the test data used, a fire in a single-family building requires two engines, one water supply vehicle and ten firefighters (personnel). An alternative alarm plan for the event is one engine, one water supply vehicle, and one smaller first response vehicle, as well as ten firefighters.

2.2 A Staffing and Dispatch Problem

The problem considered is to select which vehicles and which staff to send to a specific event. This also includes selecting which alarm plan to use, if there are more than one plan defined for the event. The event is characterized by its type and its location. The type will determine which alarm plans that are applicable. The location will determine how long the expected travel times are for the different resources. Each vehicle thus has an expected travel time to the event. Every firefighter has a preparation time, which is the time required to get dressed, collect the necessary equipment, and man a vehicle. The preparation time corresponds to the time span from when a firefighter receives the alarm, until he or she is travelling towards the event. In Sweden, the preparation time is often 90 s for full time firefighters and five minutes for part time firefighters. The latter need time to travel from their workplaces or their homes to the fire station.

The time when a vehicle can leave a station will be determined by the person with the longest preparation time that is allocated to the vehicle. For example, if a vehicle is manned by four firefighters with a preparation time of 90 s, and one firefighter with a preparation time of five minutes, the vehicle will leave the station after five minutes.

Consider the example in Table 1. There are four stations that can send resources to a building fire. Each engine must be manned by five to seven firefighters. The ladders (aerial appliance) must be manned by one to three firefighters, and the tank units (water supply) by one to four firefighters. Full time fire personnel have a preparation time of 90 s and part time personnel have a preparation time of five minutes. The alarm plan requires two engines, one ladder unit, one tank unit, and ten firefighters.

Table 1. Example of resources than can respond to a certain building fire

Station	Vehicles	Personnel	Expected travel time
1	1 engine, 1 ladder, 1 tank	6 full time	5 min
2	1 engine, 1 ladder	5 part time	10 min
3	1 engine	5 part time	8 min
4	1 engine, 1 ladder, 1 tank	6 full time	50 min

One possible solution to the problem, which can be obtained in a greedy fashion, is to man the engine from Station 1 with five firefighters. Then allocate one firefighter from Station 1 to the ladder, and man the engine from Station 3 with five firefighters. Finally, we have to select the tank from Station 4 and man it with one firefighter, since we have already used all personnel at Station 1. The solution is not very good, since the tank unit has a response time of over 50 min. A better solution can easily be found by utilizing the ladder at Station 2 and the tank unit at Station 1 instead. However, to ensure that a better solution is obtained, a more sophisticated method than greedy search is required.

It would also be possible to obtain better solutions by relaxing the constraint that an engine has to be manned by at least five firefighters. The motivation for this constraint is that it is common practice (in Sweden) to travel in a group of five people in the fire engine. Some reasons for this are that the firefighters like to talk tactics and prepare mentally on the way to the event site, and also that they want to arrive at the same time. As a result, when turning out from a smaller station, the firefighters sometimes have to choose whether to bring the ladder or the tank unit, just like in the example. It should be noted that not all fire and rescue services in Sweden operates like this. In fact, a new way of planning and controlling the fire and rescue resources is spreading, where smaller units manned by less firefighters are key factors to shorter response times [10].

2.3 A Mathematical Model

The model, from now on referred to as STAFDIS, solves the problem of selecting which vehicles should respond to a certain event, and which firefighters (personnel) that should man these vehicles.

Sets

E is the set of available vehicles, $e \in E$.
P is the set of available personnel, $p \in P$.
E^p is the set of available vehicles located together with person $p \in P$, $e \in E^p \subseteq E$.
P^e is the set of personnel located together with vehicle $e \in E$, $p \in P^e \subseteq P$
K is the set of defined alarm plans for the event, $k \in K$
N is the set of vehicle types, $n \in N$

Parameters

t_e = the expected travel time for vehicle e to the event
τ_p = the preparation time for person p.
c_{en} = 1 if vehicle e is of type n
d_{kn} = the number of required vehicles of type n in alarm plan k
P_k = the required number of firefighters in alarm plan k
A_e = min number of people required for manning vehicle e
B_e = max number of people that can travel with vehicle e

Variables

y_e = 1 if vehicle e is used in the response
x_{pe} = 1 if person p travels with vehicle e and is used in the response
z_{pe} = 1 if person p travels as a passenger with vehicle e
w_k = 1 if alarm plan k is used
T_p = response time for person p

$$\text{Min} \sum_{p \in P} T_p \tag{1}$$

$$T_p \geq (t_e + \tau_q)(x_{pe} + x_{qe} + z_{qe} - 1) \forall p, q \in P^e; e \in E \tag{2}$$

$$\mathrm{A}_e y_e \leq \sum_{p \in P^e} (x_{pe} + z_{pe}) \leq \mathrm{B}_e y_e \forall e \in E \tag{3}$$

$$\sum_{e \in E^p} \left(x_{pe} + z_{pe}\right) \leq 1 \quad \forall p \in P \tag{4}$$

$$\sum_{k \in K} w_k = 1 \tag{5}$$

$$\sum_{k \in K} d_{kn} w_k \leq \sum_{e \in E} a_{en} y_e \quad \forall n \in N \tag{6}$$

$$\sum_{p \in P} \sum_{e \in E} x_{pe} \geq P_k w_k \quad \forall k \in K \tag{7}$$

$$x_{pe} = z_{pe} = 0 \quad \forall p \notin P^e; e \in E \tag{8}$$

$$x_{pe}, z_{pe} \in \{0, 1\} \quad \forall p \in P; e \in E \tag{9}$$

$$y_e, w_k \in \{0, 1\} \quad \forall e \in E; k \in K \tag{10}$$

$$T_p \geq 0 \quad \forall p \in P \tag{11}$$

The goal of the model is to select personnel and vehicles to satisfy one of the existing alarm plans (in the set K) for the event under consideration, and to minimize the total response time for the personnel active at the event (1). For this, decision variables y_e and x_{pe} are used to determine if vehicle e should be used and if person p should travel with vehicle e.

In the model, a person can also travel with a vehicle as a passenger, which is determined by variable z_{pe}. This is utilized when the alarm plan does not require all the personnel that are sent to the event, but personnel are still required to fulfill the minimum manning conditions (left hand side of (3)). Personnel travelling as passengers will not contribute to the objective function (1). However, the preparation time of the passengers may still affect the response time for active firefighters. This is modeled in (2), which states that the response time for person p is as long as the travel time for the vehicle in which person p is travelling, plus the preparation time for any of the other personnel traveling in the same vehicle.

Constraint (4) states that a firefighter can only travel with one vehicle, and only as either passenger or active personnel. (5) ensures that one single alarm plan is used, and (6) controls that the correct amount of vehicles according to the selected alarm plan are sent to the event. (7) makes sure that enough firefighters are sent to the event, and (8), (9), (10) and (11) are variable declaration constraints.

A final note about the objective function; in (1), the sum of all active personnel's response times is minimized. Other possible options might be to minimize the maximum response time for any resource, or a weighted combination of the first and the last person's response time. One reason for including all personnel is that it is very difficult to predict the effect of the first and the last response in any new incident. For one building fire, the first responder might be able to extinguish the fire easily, and for another, the only thing to do is wait until more resources have arrived before work can start. The same goes for the last arriving unit, which may have a crucial impact on the response in some cases, and a minor impact in other cases. What is true in most cases, is that every person has some impact in managing the incident, and that an early arrival might reduce the damages. Thus, here, the response time for all personnel is included in the objective function to ensure that as many resources as needed arrive as quickly as possible.

3 Solution Strategy

3.1 Exact Solutions

The mathematical model, STAFDIS, can easily be implemented and solved with commercial software, e.g. CPLEX 10 with Concert technology, which is done here. CPLEX can solve realistic problem instances to optimality reasonably quick, from half a second and rarely more than two minutes.

However, in some cases, the problem must be solved numerous times in a short time interval. One example is if you want to use the same modelling principle in a strategic model that can find optimal locations for the resources (or the corresponding fire stations). In such a model, the geography would be divided into a set of zones, each with forecasts of expected number of events of different types. In a solution strategy for this type of location model, e.g. a metaheuristic or a decomposition scheme, it is possible to isolate STAFDIS as a subproblem. In this, the locations of the resources are fixed, but it still needs to be determined which resources should be assigned to which event. To do this, STAFDIS must be solved as many times as there are zones multiplied by the number of event types. For realistic problem instances, this number may become very large, and the solution times required for exact solutions too long to be of practical use.

Another example is when trying to quantitatively evaluate the preparedness (the ability to handle emergencies now and in the future) in different parts of the area (see e.g. [10]). This also includes determining the response times of the responding resources to each emergency that is considered. To do that, it is necessary to know which resources that will respond, information that can be provided by STAFDIS. However, just like in the case for location models, it is necessary to solve the model repeatedly and for many zones and event types, which requires extremely short computational times.

3.2 A Backup Greedy Heuristic

In order to quickly find good solutions to the model, a backup greedy heuristic is constructed. The main objectives with the heuristic, apart from minimizing the objective function, are to avoid clearly unintelligent solutions like the one described in Sect. 2.2, and to be very quick.

The heuristic is based on a greedy philosophy, but looks one step further than greedy. Instead of picking the vehicle with the shortest response time, the backup response time is calculated and used as the greedy selection component. This time is the response time for the next closest vehicle of the same type (should the closest one become unavailable, e.g. due to personnel shortage).

The heuristic starts without any selected vehicles, and then determines the vehicle type that has the longest backup response time. The closest vehicle of this type is manned with the minimum amount of firefighters. Then, the next vehicle type with the now longest backup response time is manned, until all required vehicles have been manned. If additional firefighters are required after this, they are added to already selected vehicles if possible, or a new vehicle is manned.

The pseudocode for the heuristic can be found in Table 2. The notation used is the same as in Sect. 2.3:

Sets

E is the set of available vehicles, $e \in E$.
P is the set of available personnel, $p \in P$.
E^p is the set of available vehicles located together with person $p \in P$, $e \in E^p \subseteq E$.
P^e is the set of personnel located together with vehicle $e \in E$, $p \in P^e \subseteq P$
K is the set of defined alarm plans for the event, $k \in K$
N is the set of vehicle types, $n \in N$

Parameters

t_e = the expected travel time for vehicle e to the event
τ_p = the preparation time for person p.
a_{en} = 1 if vehicle e is of type n
d_{kn} = the number of required vehicles of type n in alarm plan k
P_k = the required number of firefighters in alarm plan k
A_e = min number of people required for manning vehicle e
B_e = max number of people that can travel with vehicle e

Variables

y_e = 1 if vehicle e is used in the response
x_{pe} = 1 if person p travels with vehicle e and is used in the response
z_{pe} = 1 if person p travels as a passenger with vehicle e
w_k = 1 if alarm plan k is used
T_p = response time for person p

The backup greedy heuristic evaluates all alarm plans that exists for the event (Line 1), and selects the one that will provide the lowest objective functions value (Line 25). First, a minimum set of vehicles is found, and the minimum required amount of crew is allocated (the loop starting at Line 3). For each required vehicle type, the response time and the backup response time are calculated (Lines 7 and 8).

The backup response time is a measure of how much the response time will increase if one of the closest required vehicles cannot respond (e.g. due to staff shortage). E.g. assume that there are four engines available, with expected response times 5, 10, 20, and 40 min. If two engines are required for the event, the backup response time would

Table 2. Pseudocode for a backup greedy heuristic for solving STAFDIS

1	FORALL $k \in K$
2	Let $w_k = 1; x_{pe}, z_{pe} = 0 \quad \forall e \in E, p \in P; y_e = 0 \quad \forall e \in E$ and let $P_{alloc} = 0$ be the number of personnel allocated to the event
3	WHILE $\left(\sum_{k \in K} d_{kn} w_k > \sum_{e \in E} a_{en} y_e \quad \exists n \in N\right)$
4	Let E' be the set of not utilized vehicles and N' the set of vehicles types that are still required, where $r_n =$ the number of required vehicles of type n: $E' \subseteq E$ such that $y_e = 0 \quad \forall e \in E'$, and $N' \subseteq N$ such that $r_n = \sum_{k \in K} d_{kn} w_k - \sum_{e \in E} a_{en} y_e > 0$
5	Let P^{eA} be the set of A_e available personnel with the shortest preparation times located together with vehicle $e \in E'$: $P^{eA} \subseteq P^e; \left\lvert P^{eA} \right\rvert = A_e; \tau_p \leq \tau_q \forall p \in P^{eA}, q \in P^e; x_{pe}, z_{pe} = 0 \quad \forall p \in P^{eA}$
6	Let $T^e = t_e + \max_{p \in P^{eA}} \{\tau_p\}$ be the response time for vehicle $e \in E'$
7	Let T^{ni} be the response times for vehicle type n, such that $i = 1$ is the closest vehicle of type n, $i = 2$ the second closest etc.
8	Let $S^n = T^{nr_n+1} - T^{nr_n}$ be the backup response time for vehicle type n and let μ be the vehicle type that satisfy $\max_{n \in N'} \{S^n\}$
9	Let ε be the vehicle that satisfy $\min_{e \in \{E' \mid a_{e\mu} = 1\}} \{T^e\}$ and set $y_\varepsilon = 1$
10	Let $P_{count} = A_\varepsilon$. WHILE $P_{count} \geq 0$
11	Of available personnel that can be allocated to ε, *let* φ be the person with the shortest preparation time, i.e. that satisfy $\min_{p \in \{P^{\varepsilon A} \mid x_{p\varepsilon} = z_{p\varepsilon} = 0\}} \{\tau_p\}$
12	IF $P_{alloc} < P_k$ set $x_{\varphi\varepsilon} = 1; P_{alloc} = P_{alloc} + 1; P_{count} = P_{count} - 1$
13	ELSE set $z_{\varphi\varepsilon} = 1; P_{count} = P_{count} - 1$
14	WHILE $P_{alloc} < P_k$
15	Let T^e be the current response time for vehicle e, and E^{kap} be the set of vehicles that have capacity left to transport more people: $T^e = t_e + \max_{p \in P} \{\tau_p (x_{pe} + z_{pe})\}; E^{kap} \subseteq E$ such that $\sum_{p \in P^e} (x_{pe} + z_{pe}) \leq B_e$

(continued)

Table 2. (*continued*)

16	Of the vehicles that still have capacity left and co-located available personnel, let δ be the vehicle with the shortest response time, i.e. the one that satisfy $\min_{e \in E^{kap}} \{T^e\}$ where $\sum_{p \in P^e} \sum_{l \in E^p} (x_{pl} + z_{pl}) \leq \lvert P^e \rvert$ Furthermore, let ρ be the person that satisfy $\min_{p \in P^\delta} \{\tau_p\}$ where $\sum_{e \in E^p} (x_{pe} + z_{pe}) = 0.$, i.e. of available personnel located with δ, the one with the shortest preparation time
17	IF ($y_\delta = 1$ AND $\tau_\rho - (T^\delta - t_e) \leq 1.5(T^\delta - t_e)$) set $x_{\rho\delta} = 1$; $P_{alloc} = P_{alloc} + 1$
18	IF ($y_\delta = 0$ AND $\lvert P^\delta \rvert - \sum_{p \in P^\delta} \sum_{e \in E} (x_{pe} + z_{pe}) \geq A_\delta$)
19	WHILE $\left(\lvert P^\delta \rvert - \sum_{p \in P^\delta} \sum_{e \in E} (x_{pe} + z_{pe}) < A_\delta \right)$
20	Let ρ be the person that satisfy $\min_{p \in P^\delta} \{\tau_p\}$ where $\sum_{e \in E^p} (x_{pe} + z_{pe}) = 0$
21	IF $P_{alloc} < P_k$ set $x_{\rho\delta} = 1$; $P_{alloc} = P_{alloc} + 1$
22	ELSE set $z_\rho = 1$
23	For all $p \in P$, let $T_p = \max_{q \in P^e; e \in E} \{(t_e + \tau_q)(x_{pe} + x_{qe} + z_{qe} - 1)\}$
24	Let $Z^k = \sum_{p \in P} T_p$ be the evaluation function value for alarm plan k and store all necessary variable values
25	Let κ be the alarm plan that satisfy $\min_{k \in K} \left\{ Z^k \right\}$; export all related variable values; end the algorithm

be 20–10 = 10 min, i.e. the difference between the response times for the third and the second closest resource.

The vehicle type with the longest backup response time is selected, and the vehicle of this type with the shortest response time is manned with the minimum set of personnel available that have the shortest preparation times (Lines 9–13). There might still be personnel required when the necessary vehicles have been manned (Line 14). If so, the heuristic tries to either fill already selected vehicles with more personnel without increasing the response time too much (Line 17; here a factor of 1.5 is used, meaning that the preparation time for the vehicle should not increase by more than 50%) or man a new vehicle with a minimum set of personnel (Line 18–22). The response times for all personnel used in the event (not the passengers) are calculated, and the evaluation function value for the alarm plan is stored (Line 23–24). Finally, the alarm plan with the lowest evaluation function value is selected (Line 25).

Revisiting the example in Table 1, the alarm plan required two engines, one ladder and one tank unit. The backup greedy heuristic would start by manning the tank unit, since this vehicle type has a backup response time of 45 min, i.e. if we cannot select the tank unit at Station 1 we have to pick the one at Station 4. The engine type has a backup response time of two minutes – the difference between Station 2 and 3 – since two engines are required, and it is at the moment possible to man both the engine from Station 1 and the engine from Station 3, which makes the engine at Station 2 the backup unit. The ladder unit type has a backup response time of five minutes. When the tank unit at Station 1 has been manned by one firefighter, the heuristic will man the ladder unit at the same station with one firefighter, thus making it impossible to utilize the engine at Station 1 since it requires at least five firefighters to man. Therefore, the engines at Station 2 and 3 are manned.

In the example above, the backup greedy heuristic manages to avoid a solution where a unit from Station 4 has to be used, which is an improvement from a simpler greedy type of solution strategy. However, in an exact solution, all the personnel at Station 1 would be allocated to the tank and the ladder units, since they together have the capacity to transport seven firefighters. This would result in a total of six passengers (since the engines require a minimum of five firefighters) who would not however contribute to the objective function. The backup greedy heuristic stops trying to allocate personnel to the event as soon as the required number has been reached, and thus would not find the optimal solution in this case.

4 Computational Results

To evaluate the quality of the heuristic solutions, a large set of problem instances are generated and solved both exactly and heuristically. An area consisting of five municipalities in the county of Skåne in Sweden, with a joint fire and rescue service, was used for input data. The five municipalities have in all 11 fire stations comprising 23 units, both full time and part time firefighters. The area was divided into squares with the side 250 m, in all 19732 squares. Each square has a forecast for eight types of expected number of incidents; four types of fire incidents and four types of traffic accidents. For each incident there exists two or three alarm plans.

STAFDIS is here solved as a subproblem to a location problem that aims to find the best locations for the fire and rescue resources. A meta-heuristic is used to find location solutions, moving vehicles and personnel (while ensuring that all personnel have vehicles to travel with, and that there are at least the minimum required staff with each vehicle). STAFDIS is used to determine dispatching strategies for each location solution, for each forecasted incident in the area. This gives different problem instances for STAFDIS. In total, 280 000 instances are solved.

To get a heuristic solution to the problem, the backup greedy heuristic, implemented as a C++ program, is used. For exact solutions, CPLEX 10 is called from a C++ program using ILOG Concert technology. The time it takes for CPLEX to produce a solution is from 0.5 s with a cut-off at 120 s (the cut-off is reached in less than 0.6% of the runs). The heuristic never finds a better solution than CPLEX and takes between 0.01–0.03 ms to find a solution.

280 000 solutions are compared, for four different settings; ptr-locr, ptr-locs, ptp-locr and ptp-locs. In the sets ptr-locr and ptr-locs, the firemen have preparation times 90 s, 5 min or 6 min, just like in reality (ptr = preparation time real). In ptp-locr and ptp-locs (ptp = preparation time perturbed), the preparation times are slightly perturbed, by adding a randomly drawn positive or negative number to each unit's preparation

time. The perturbed times range between 65 and 366 s, which makes the problem a bit more challenging. In the locr-sets, the instance generation (which corresponds to solving the location problem) starts with the current real location for the fire resources (locr = location real), while in the locs-sets, the start solution for the location problem is randomized, i.e. all units and personnel are randomly scattered over the area (although personnel is always located together with a vehicle).

Table 3. Overall statistics from the experiments, reporting the objective function values. Response times in seconds.

	ptr-locr		ptr-locs		ptp-locs		ptp-locr	
	CPLEX	Heuristic	CPLEX	Heuristic	CPLEX	Heuristic	CPLEX	Heuristic
Mean	651.17	655.13	640.11	644.91	705.34	707.89	716.74	720.44
Median	631	636	614	619	666	668	687	691
Min	89	90	89	90	67	70	70	70
Max	1676	1676	1668	1668	1978	1994	1779	1782

Table 3 shows descriptive statistics from the computational experiments. It can be seen that perturbated preparation times give longer response times, as can be expected. Not as intuitive is the fact that randomized start locations for the units (e.g. compare ptr-locr and ptr-locs) give shorter response times. This is because the meta-heuristic solving the location problem works better with randomized start locations, compared to the current stations. It is also evident that while the heuristic does not manage to get as low average response times as CPLEX, the difference is not large.

The difference between CPLEX and the heuristic is further explored in Table 4 and 5. Table 4 shows that while the heuristic solutions on average are a few seconds worse than CPLEX, the median values indicate that most often equally good solutions are found. This is confirmed by Table 5, Row 1, where it is clear that for three of the four settings, in more than 50% of the instances, the heuristic finds as good solutions as CPLEX. The setting ptp-locr seems to be most challenging for the heuristic, and it finds as good solutions as CPLEX in 43.93% of the cases. However, in 86.75% (43.93 + 42.82) of the instances, it finds a solution that is less than one percent worse. For the setting ptr-locr, the heuristic finds a solution that is as good as the one produced by CPLEX in 62.06% of the cases. The solution found by the heuristic is between 0.01% and 1.00% worse than the CPLEX solution in 21.93% of the cases for the same setting.

Looking at the solution times (Row 14) in Table 5, CPLEX seems to find the solution quicker in average in the cases where a randomized start solution is used for the location problem; the locs-settings have shorter mean solutions times than the other two settings. This might be due to the fact that in a start solution based on the current situation, vehicles and firefighters are clustered to stations. Thus, there are more options available when allocating firefighters to vehicles, then when the resources are scattered over the area.

Table 4. Overall differences in objective function values (Heuristic – CPLEX). Times in seconds.

	ptr-locr	ptr-locs	ptp-locs	ptp-locr
Mean	3.95	4.80	2.55	3.70
Median	0	0	0	1
Min	0	0	0	0
Max	202	155	141	155

Table 5. Comparison between CPLEX and the backup greedy heuristic. The numbers show the amount of heuristic solutions that are a certain percentage worse than the solution generated by CPLEX. E.g. Row 3 shows that 4.13–6.50% of the heuristic solutions are between 1 and 2% worse than the equivalent CPLEX solution.

Row	% from CPLEX sol	ptr-locr	ptr-locs	ptp-locs	ptp-locr
1	0	62.06	54.24	56.09	43.93
2	1	21.93	25.43	33.84	42.82
3	2	5.19	6.50	4.13	5.73
4	3	3.29	3.84	2.11	2.54
5	4	2.10	3.33	1.41	1.53
6	5	1.39	2.23	0.91	0.92
7	6	1.01	1.35	0.50	0.51
8	7	0.65	0.88	0.26	0.40
9	8	0.60	0.48	0.20	0.29
10	9	0.40	0.49	0.12	0.23
11	10	0.29	0.29	0.10	0.19
12	50	1.08	0.94	0.33	0.89
13	100	0.01	0.01	0.00	0.01
14	Mean solution time for CPLEX	2.47 s	1.72	1.65 s	2.24 s

Figure 1 shows the same results as Table 5. No clear difference in performance between the settings can be discerned. For ptr-locr and ptr-locs, the heuristic might be considered to perform worse than for the ptp-settings, but ptr-locr also has most solutions of the four settings, as good as CPLEX. For all four settings, 90% of the solutions found by the heuristic are less than 3% worse than the solution found by CPLEX.

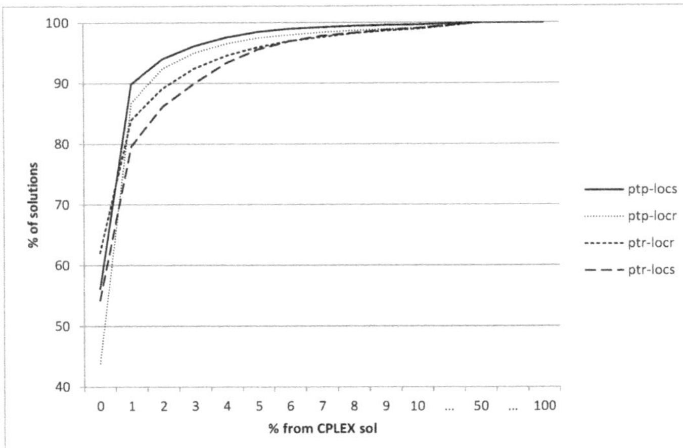

Fig. 1. Comparing the heuristic with the exact solution method

5 Using the Model

For a given event with one or more specified alarm plans, the model will provide a suggestion of which vehicles to dispatch and how to staff these vehicles, in order to minimize the mean response time. In an operational setting, it would be acceptable for an incident manager to wait for a few seconds before getting this suggestion, making it possible to use an exact solution methodology. In the experiments here, the mean solution time for CPLEX was less than three seconds, which might be considered acceptable. However, in some instances it took more than minute, which is too long. Thus, some measures are needed to ensure that the solution time does not exceed a few seconds, since waiting longer is not an option when managing accidents and other emergencies.

In an operational context, it would also be possible to update the expected travel times for the resources. In the model now, a travel time matrix is used, providing quick estimates of travel times from each zone to each other zone in the dataset. Given that each zone is a square with 250 m sides, not too much would be gained by using more exact locations of the resources and the event. However, it would be possible to update the travel time estimation with real time information regarding traffic jams, closed roads, whether conditions, etc., if such information exists.

If the model is to be used as a subroutine for a strategic location model or in preparedness calculations, the computational times for the exact solution method is too long. Spending on average two seconds to solve the problem, and solving it for 19732 zones and 8 event types would take approximately 88 h. Since this has to be done continuously in the preparedness calculation case, or repeatedly as in the station location case, the time to obtain solutions has to be decreased. Using the heuristic, solving the problem takes on average 0.02 ms, which mean that solving for all zones and event types takes about three seconds. Thus, it is more useful in a subroutine than the exact method.

6 Conclusions

From the computational results, it can be concluded that the greedy backup heuristic in most cases finds the optimal or a near optimal solution to the staffing and dispatch problem. The heuristic is also quick enough to be useful as a subroutine for a more extensive location problem solution algorithm, or in a quantitative preparedness measure.

However, since the heuristic does not always find the optimal solution to the sub-problem, it may underestimate the value of a potential good solution being evaluated as a strategic location option. Thus, a solution process for a location model using the backup greedy heuristic, might produce inferior solutions compared to if the exact solutions to the STAFDIS model were used. One interesting study might therefore be to compare the effectiveness of the location problem solution algorithm when solving STAFDIS exactly, compared to when it is solved heuristically.

Another possible study would be to construct a tailored exact algorithm to solve the problem, which is quicker than general purpose solvers like CPLEX, or to expand the backup greedy algorithm to a greedy based meta heuristic, like e.g. Greedy Randomized Adaptive Search Procedure [11] or Fixed Set Search [12]. Another option might be to combine the heuristic with e.g. CPLEX, and use the heuristic to get a good start solution, and use that to warm-start the CPLEX solver.

When exploring new solution strategies, it would also be interesting to study the problem complexity, which was not done here. While it may be a NP-hard problem, this has not been proven. Related to this, it would also be interesting to study how the heuristic performs when the problem size increases.

References

1. Toregas, C., Swain, R., Re Velle, C., Bergman, L.: The location of emergency service facilities. Oper. Res. **6**, 1363–1373 (1971)
2. Yang, L., Jones, B.F., Yang, S.-H.: A fuzzy multi-objective programming for optimization of fire station locations through genetic algorithms. Eur. J. Oper. Res. **181**, 903–915 (2007)
3. Batta, R., Mannur, N.R.: Covering-location models for emergency situations that require multiple response units. Manage. Sci. **1**, 16–23 (1990)
4. Schilling, D.A., Revelle, C., Cohon, J., Elzinga, D.J.: Some models for fire protection locational decisions. Eur. J. Oper. Res. **5**, 1–7 (1980)
5. Pérez, J., Maldonado, S., López-Ospina, H.: A fleet managemnt model for the Santiago Fire department. Fire Saf. J. **82**, 1–11 (2016)
6. Carter, G.M., Chaiken, J.M., Ignall, E.: Response areas for two emergency units. Oper. Res. **20**, 571–594 (1972)
7. Swersey, A.J.: A Markonian decision model for deciding how many fire companies to dispatch. Manage. Sci. **28**(4), 352–365 (1982)
8. Ignall, E., Carter, G., Rider, K.: An algorithm for the initial dispatch of fire companies. Manage. Sci. **28**(4), 366–378 (1982)
9. Bandara, D., Mayorga, M.E., McLay, L.A.: Priority dispatchning strategies for EMS systems. J. Oper. Res. Soc. **65**, 572–587 (2014)
10. Granberg, T.A., Lundberg, J., Ulander, A., Granlund, R.: Supporting dispatch decisions for the fire and rescue services. In: Proceedings of the 2015 IEEE 18th International Conference on Intelligent Transportation Systems, pp. 2562–2567 (2015)

11. Feo, T.A., Resende, M.G.C.: Greedy randomized adaptive search procedures. J. Global Optim. **6**, 109–133 (1995)
12. Jovanovic, R., Tuba, M., Voß, S.: Fixed set search applied to the traveling salesman problem. In: Blesa Aguilera, M.J., Blum, C., Gambini Santos, H., Pinacho-Davidson, P., Godoy del Campo, J. (eds.) HM 2019. LNCS, vol. 11299, pp. 63–77. Springer, Cham (2019). https://doi.org/10.1007/978-3-030-05983-5_5

Industrial Waste Collection Optimization: A Real-World Case Study in Northern Italy

Andrea Chiussi[1,2](✉), Gabriel de Paula Felix[3], Manuel Iori[4], and André Gustavo dos Santos[3]

[1] FMB, Marco Biagi Foundation, University of Modena and Reggio Emilia, Largo Marco Biagi 10, 41121 Modena, Italy
andrea.chiussi@unimore.it

[2] Iren Ambiente Spa, Via Nubi di Magellano 30, 42123 Reggio Emilia, Italy

[3] Department of Informatics, Universidade Federal de Viçosa, Viçosa, MG, Brazil

[4] DISMI, Department of Sciences and Methods for Engineering, University of Modena and Reggio Emilia, 42122 Reggio Emilia, Italy

Abstract. In this work, we present a real case application of a Rollon-Rolloff Vehicle Routing Problem (RRVRP) that arises at a waste collection company in Northern Italy. Compared to other RRVRP applications, where large containers are emptied and moved, our problem presents two additional types of services regarding the collection of bulk waste materials. Moreover, the problem deals with customer selection based on an objective function with two components: outsourcing costs incurred when customers are given to a third-party logistic operator, and internal routing costs. We model the RRVRP as a Mixed Integer Program and we solve it through a commercial solver and a simple but effective Iterated Greedy algorithm. Computational results are provided on 30 real case instances. Solutions provided by the Iterated Greedy are constantly better than the ones implemented by the company, showing that relevant cost reduction can be obtained with a limited computational effort.

Keywords: Rollon-Rolloff Vehicle Routing Problem · Industrial waste collection · Iterated greedy

1 Introduction

The amount of waste generated in cities has been constantly increasing in the last decades, due to population growth and urbanization. As a consequence, an effective waste management is one of the key factors for having sustainable and livable cities. Waste management should also be efficient, because it represents around 20%-50% of the municipal costs [16]. Accordingly to Beliën, De Boeck and Van Ackere [4], who provided an extensive literature review of the field, waste collection is one of the phases with the highest cost in the waste management process, requiring labour intensive activities and massive usage of trucks. Therefore, an efficient routing is essential for the sustainability of the process.

J. de Armas et al. (Eds.): ICCL 2022, LNCS 13557, pp. 147–161, 2022.
https://doi.org/10.1007/978-3-031-16579-5_11

Golden, Assad and Wasil [7] divided waste collection problems into three main categories:

- Residential collection, usually implemented in residential areas as a door-to-door collection with small bins to be served ($<$660 L);
- Commercial collection, usually implemented for serving larger bins (between 660 L and 5000 L) located in predefined public areas, or in medium-small commercial costumers sites;
- Industrial collection, where large volumes of waste have to be collected ($\geq$5000 L) and the servicing of a customer immediately fills the vehicle capacity.

The first category of waste collection can be modeled as a capacitated arc routing problem, while the second one as a capacitated node routing problem. In both cases, the problem differs from the classical Capacitated Vehicle Routing Problems (CVRP) because each vehicle may need more than one visit to waste disposal facilities, given their limited loading capacity. Industrial collection differs from the first two categories because the vehicles have a unit capacity and customers entirely fill this capacity with a single request. In this last category, customers also require different types of services for moving and emptying waste containers. Those services can be categorized in the delivery of empty containers, the substitution of full containers with empty ones, the retrieval of full containers and the emptying of containers at disposal plants and their return to the customer. Industrial waste collection is usually modeled with variants of the Rollon-Rolloff Vehicle Routing Problem (RRVRP), which was firstly presented by Bodin et al. [6], and then extended by Baldacci, Bodin and Mingozzi [3]. It was also adapted to deal with problem specific constraints in Archetti and Speranza [1], Wy et al. [17] and Aringhieri et al. [2], among others. Studies have been published also on a generalization of the RRVRP [9] and on RRVRP with heterogeneous vehicle fleets [5,8,12], all confirming the importance of routing efficiency in this area.

In this article, we present a real case application of the RRVRP with customer selection and problem specific constraints to an industrial waste collection problem faced by Iren Ambiente Spa, a company operating in a large part of Northern Italy. The problem, as other RRVRP, is very complex since, in addition to classical time constraints, it involves the pickup and delivery of different types of containers, operational times at the customer sites depending on the requested services, as well as other specific constraints such as container/customer and container/vehicle incompatibilities. Moreover, in our problem we need to select a subset of customers to be served given the available fleet capacity, and assign the remaining ones to a third-party logistic operator, hence incurring an outsourcing cost. To the best of our knowledge, this feature has been presented, in similar problems, only in [1]. Finally, we propose two additional types of services regarding the collection of bulk waste materials (Fig. 1b), whose operation is performed by the same fleet of vehicles that perform the typical RRVRP service requests proposed by [3,6] (Fig. 1a).

The remainder of the article is structured as follows. In Sect. 2, we describe the problem. In Sect. 3, we present a Mixed-Integer Linear Programming for-

(a) Real case of container loading or unloading in industrial waste collection.

(b) Bulk waste material loading by a vehicle equipped with an orange peel grapple[5].

Fig. 1. Example of real waste collection service requests operated by the company. (Source: https://www.irenambiente.it/raccolta-selezione-e-trattamento-rifiuti.)

mulation (MILP). Section 4 contains the description of the proposed heuristic solution method. Both the MILP and the heuristic algorithm solutions are evaluated in detail and compared with the real solutions implemented by the company in Sect. 5. Finally, concluding remarks are provided in Sect. 6.

2 Problem Description

We are given a set N of customers with different types of requested services, a set M of disposal plants and a depot d. Each requested service has an associated outsourcing cost. The objective of the RRVRP that we face is to determine a set of routes that perform either all the requested services or just a subset of them, by minimizing the sum of (i) total cost due to service outsourcing and (ii) internal operating costs of all routes. The routes should comply with a number of operational constraints.

First of all, the service requests analyzed, usually defined in literature as trip types (see, e.g., [3,6,17]), in our problem can be of seven types, grouped in different sets (S, P, W, R, Y, G, B) whose details are provided below. The set N of customers can be viewed as the union of all the service request sets, and hence $N = (S \cup P \cup W \cup R \cup Y \cup G \cup B)$. Containers are divided into a set $\mathcal{B}$ of different container types. Each service request $i \in N$ is associated with a specific container type $\beta_i \in \mathcal{B}$, which represents the container requested by or collected from the customer site, and an outsourcing cost C_i to be sustained in case the request is not served by the routes but given to a third-party logistic operator. Only for service requests $i \in S, W, R, G, B$ a set of disposal facilities $M_i \in M$ to empty the container is defined, given the waste type filling the container and the contracts with disposal companies. The service request types are:

- W: *empty and return.* A service request $i \in W$ requires, at the customer site, an empty vehicle to load a full container and to carry it to a disposal facility $m \in M_i$ to empty it. After that, the vehicle must return the same container to the customer site. At the end of the service the vehicle is located at i and has no container on it. These are default requests to empty a customer-owned container and are called T1 trips in [3,6].

- S: *swap of a full container with an empty one of the same type.* A service request $i \in S$ requires, at the customer site, a vehicle with an empty container of the same type (β_i) of the full container to be emptied. There, the vehicle must unload the empty container, load the full one and reach a disposal facility $m \in M_i$ to empty it. At the end of the service the vehicle is located at m with an empty container of type β_i on it. These are the default service requests to empty a container when this is not owned by the customer, and are called T2 trips in [3,6].
- P: *delivery of an empty container.* A service request $i \in P$ requires, at the customer site, a vehicle to unload an empty container of the required type (β_i). At the end of the service the vehicle is located at i and has no container on it. These requests are typical for new customers and represent the T3 trips defined in [3,6].
- R: *retrieve of a full container.* A service request $i \in R$ requires, at the customer site, an empty vehicle to load a full container and reach a disposal facility $m \in M_i$ to empty it. At the end of the service the vehicle is located at m and has an empty container of type β_i on it. These represent the T4 trips in [3,6] and model the customer end of service.
- Y: *retrieve of an empty container to bring it to the depot.* A service request $i \in Y$ requires the vehicle to reach the customer without any container. At the customer site the vehicle must load the empty container and reach the depot d. At the end of the service the vehicle is located at d and has no container on it since the empty container retrieved will not be available until a formal control is performed. These are the BTY trips discussed in [17] and, in our case, arise when a customer has a problem with a given container or the customer is a container repairer, so a control at the depot is needed.
- G: *collect bulk material from a container or from the ground*, performed through an orange peel grapple mounted on a hydraulic crane (See Fig. 1b). A service request $i \in G$ requires, at the customer site, a vehicle with the equipment necessary to collect the bulk material from β_i (the ground is considered as a type of container in $\mathcal{B}$ used for these requests) and to reach a disposal facility $m \in M_i$ to empty it. At the end of the service the vehicle is located at m and can either reach the next service request $j \in G$ or return to the depot and change equipment if needed. Only a subset of vehicles can serve these requests, because of the required equipment.
- B: *load bulk waste material from a customer site on an empty container.* These requests are similar to those encountered in S, but the time to unload the empty container and load the full one at the customer site is replaced by a bulk waste loading time. A service request $i \in B$ requires a vehicle at the customer site with an empty container of the required type (β_i). There, the vehicle waits for the bulk material loading and then moves to a disposal facility $m \in M_i$ to empty it. At the end of the service the vehicle is located at m and has an empty container of type β_i on it.

Problem specific constraints that must be fulfilled are the following:

- The fleet of available vehicles is heterogeneous and is composed of different types of tractors that can carry different non-exclusive sets of containers;
- Each tractor can carry only one container at a time;
- Not all tractors can work with all containers types: only a subset H_β of vehicle types can serve a β container type, for $\beta \in \mathcal{B}$;
- A vehicle visits a disposal plant only if required by the service request;
- Each route has a start time (e.g., 6:00) and an end time (e.g., 12:20) that can not be exceeded (overtime duties are not allowed);
- Each customer has a time window in which it can be served;
- There is only one depot (d) that represents the spare containers repository location. The number of containers available at the depot is considered unlimited for all the container types.

Other problem parameters are:

- t_{ij}: travel time between nodes $i, j \in V = (N \cup M \cup \{d\})$;
- τ^L: time required to load an empty/full container;
- τ^U: time required to unload an empty/full container;
- $\tau^G_{\beta_i}$: time to load vehicle in G service requests with β_i type of container;
- τ^B: time to load vehicle in B service requests;
- σ_m: time to empty a container at the disposal facility m;
- σ^G: additional time required in each disposal plant to empty a vehicle for service requests of type G;
- σ^B: additional time required in each disposal plant to empty a vehicle for service requests of type B.

Besides the outsourcing cost C_i of each customer i not directly served by the company vehicles, there is a unit cost c_k for each vehicle k. The cost of the route performed by k is thus obtained by multiplying c_k by the route duration.

In our real case study, the main objective is to reduce the number of customers to be outsourced in order to serve as much customers as possible with the higher service quality provided by the company, making a more efficient usage of internal resources available. For this reason, in our instances outsourcing costs are much larger than internal operating costs, also quantifying a penalty cost to force outsourcing being disadvantageous.

3 Mathematical Model

To better fit the related RRVRP literature, from now on we will refer to customer as a synonym for service requests. Indeed, in case a customer has multiple requests, we can simply split it into multiple customers having the same location.

In the context of RRVPR, it is convenient to apply a reduction of the initial problem by merging all operations into a service and a travel time (see, e.g., [2, 3, 6]). In our case, this implies calculating the service time s_i required to serve request i as shown in (1), and computing a new travel time T_{ij} between two nodes i and j ($i, j \in N \cup \{d\}$) as shown in Table 1. The service time s_i considers all operations that have to be performed within the time window of the request. The travel time T_{ij} considers, instead, all the operations required to move from one node to another (e.g., emptying, loading, unloading, containers' change at depot, etc.). This differentiates T_{ij} from the simple travel time t_{ij} among nodes.

$$s_i = \begin{cases} \tau^U + \tau^L & \forall i \in S \\ \tau^L & \forall i \in R \cup Y \\ \tau^U & \forall i \in P \\ \min_{m \in M_i} \{\tau^L + t_{im} + \sigma_m + t_{mi} + \tau^U\} & \forall i \in W \\ \tau^G_{\beta_i} & \forall i \in G \\ \tau^B & \forall i \in B \end{cases} \tag{1}$$

Table 1. Time matrix T_{ij} definition.

(i, j)	Condition	Equation
(d, j)	$j \in S \cup P \cup B$	$\tau^L + t_{dj}$
(d, j)	$j \in W \cup R \cup Y \cup G$	t_{dj}
(i, j)	$i \in W \cup P, j \in W \cup R \cup Y$	t_{ij}
(i, j)	$i \in W \cup P, j \in S \cup P \cup G \cup B$	$t_{id} + \tau^L + t_{dj}$
(i, j)	$i \in S \cup R, j \in S \cup P, \beta_i = \beta_j$	$\min_{m \in M_i} \{t_{im} + \sigma_m + t_{mj}\}$
(i, j)	$i \in S \cup R, j \in S \cup P, \beta_i \neq \beta_j$	$\min_{m \in M_i} \{t_{im} + \sigma_m + t_{md} + \tau^U + \tau^L + t_{dj}\}$
(i, j)	$i \in S \cup R, j \in G \cup B$	$\min_{m \in M_i} \{t_{im} + \sigma_m + t_{md} + \tau^U + \tau^L + t_{dj}\}$
(i, j)	$i \in S \cup R, j \in W \cup R \cup Y$	$\min_{m \in M_i} \{t_{im} + \sigma_m + t_{md} + \tau^U + t_{dj}\}$
(i, j)	$i \in Y, j \in S \cup P \cup G \cup B$	$t_{id} + \tau^U + \tau^L + t_{dj}$
(i, j)	$i \in Y, j \in W \cup R \cup Y$	$t_{id} + \tau^U + t_{dj}$
(i, j)	$i \in G, j \in G$	$\min_{m \in M_i} \{t_{im} + \sigma_m + \sigma^G + t_{mj}\}$
(i, j)	$i \in G, j \in S \cup P \cup B$	$\min_{m \in M_i} \{t_{im} + \sigma_m + \sigma^G + t_{md} + \tau^U + \tau^L + t_{dj}\}$
(i, j)	$i \in G, j \in W \cup R \cup Y$	$\min_{m \in M_i} \{t_{im} + \sigma_m + \sigma^G + t_{md} + \tau^U + t_{dj}\}$
(i, j)	$i \in B, j \in W \cup R \cup Y$	$\min_{m \in M_i} \{t_{im} + \sigma_m + \sigma^B + t_{md} + \tau^U + t_{dj}\}$
(i, j)	$i \in B, j \in (S \cup P, \beta_i = \beta_j) \cup B$	$\min_{m \in M_i} \{t_{im} + \sigma_m + \sigma^B + t_{mj}\}$
(i, j)	$i \in B, j \in (S \cup P, \beta_i \neq \beta_j) \cup G$	$\min_{m \in M_i} \{t_{im} + \sigma_m + \sigma^B + t_{md} + \tau^U + \tau^L + t_{dj}\}$
(i, d)	$i \in S \cup R$	$\min_{m \in M_i} \{t_{im} + \sigma_m + t_{md} + \tau^U\}$
(i, d)	$i \in Y$	$t_{id} + \tau^U$
(i, d)	$i \in B$	$\min_{m \in M_i} \{t_{im} + \sigma_m + \sigma^B + t_{md} + \tau^U\}$
(i, d)	$i \in W \cup P$	t_{id}
(i, d)	$i \in G$	$\min_{m \in M_i} \{t_{im} + \sigma_m + \sigma^G + t_{md}\}$

To model the case when a set M_i of disposal plants is available for a service request $i \in S, W, R, G, B$, s_i and T_{ij} are calculated using the disposal plant $m \in M_i$ that minimizes respectively the service time s_i (1), in case of service requests $i \in W$, or the time between nodes T_{ij} (Table 1), in case of service requests $i \in S, R, G, B$.

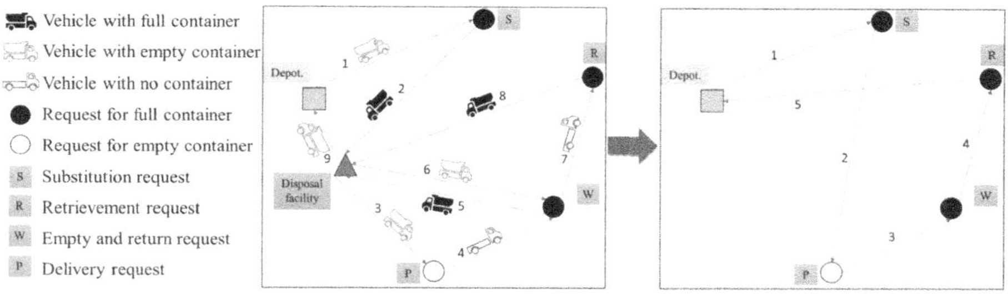

Fig. 2. Problem complexity reduction: on the left an example of a real world feasible route to serve customers with different service requests. Numbers on arcs represents the order of the visits. On the right the same solution on the graph of the reduced problem. All the vehicle operations are modeled in terms of service and travel times.

With this transformation, it is possible reduce the complex problem faced by the company to a CVRP with profits and time windows, as shown next. In Fig. 2 we illustrate an example of the problem reduction from a graph with the depot, fours customers and one disposal facility to a graph considering only the set of requests N and the depot, hiding in the definition of s_i and T_{ij} most of the real problem complexity.

The problem can therefore be defined on a complete graph $G = (V', A')$, where the nodes $V' = (N \cup \{d\})$ are the union of the service requests $N = (S \cup R \cup W \cup P \cup Y \cup B \cup G)$ and the depot $\{d\}$, and A' is the set of arcs connecting the nodes. Given the following parameters:

- K: set of vehicles (each performing a route);
- P_k: vehicle type associated to k;
- β_i: type of container for service request i;
- H_β: set of vehicles that can carry the container type β;
- $[e_i, l_i]$: start and end of the time window of customer i;
- s_i: service time of customer i, calculated as shown in (1);
- T_{ij}: travel time associated with arc $(i, j) \in A'$, calculated as shown in Table 1;
- $[E_k, L_k]$: min start time and max end time of the route performed by k;
- C_i: outsourcing cost for request i;
- c^k: unit-time cost of vehicle k;

and the following variables:

- $x_{ijk} = \begin{cases} 1 & \text{if arc } (i,j) \text{ is used by vehicle } k \\ 0 & \text{otherwise} \end{cases} \qquad \forall i, j \in V', k \in K;$
- $\theta_{ik} \in \mathbb{R}$ vehicle k start time of service at customer i;
- $\theta_{dk} \in \mathbb{R}$ vehicle k end time;

it is possible to formulate the RRVRP by the following `MILP`:

$$\min \sum_{j \in N} C_j \Big(1 - \sum_{i \in V'} \sum_{k \in K} x_{ijk}\Big) + \sum_{k \in K} (\theta_{dk} - E_k) c^k \qquad (2)$$

$$\text{s.t.} \sum_{i \in V'} \sum_{k \in K} x_{ijk} \leq 1 \qquad \forall j \in N \qquad (3)$$

$$\sum_{j \in N} x_{djk} \leq 1 \qquad \forall k \in K \qquad (4)$$

$$\sum_{j \in V'} x_{jik} - \sum_{j \in V'} x_{ijk} = 0 \qquad \forall k \in K, i \in V' \qquad (5)$$

$$\theta_{ik} \geq e_i \qquad \forall i \in N, k \in K \qquad (6)$$

$$\theta_{ik} + s_i \leq l_i \qquad \forall i \in N, k \in K \qquad (7)$$

$$(\theta_{ik} + s_i + T_{ij} - \theta_{jk}) \leq (1 - x_{ijk}) M_{ij} \qquad \forall i \in N, j \in V', k \in K \qquad (8)$$

$$(E_k + T_{dj} - \theta_{jk}) \leq (1 - x_{djk}) M_{dj} \qquad \forall j \in N, k \in K \qquad (9)$$

$$\theta_{dk} \leq L_k \qquad \forall k \in K \qquad (10)$$

$$x_{ijk} = 0 \qquad \forall i, j \in N, k \in K, P_k \notin H_{\beta_j} \qquad (11)$$

$$\theta_{dk} \geq E_k \qquad \forall k \in K \qquad (12)$$

$$x_{ijk} \in \{0, 1\} \qquad \forall i, j \in V', k \in K \qquad (13)$$

where

$$M_{ij} = \max\{l_i + T_{ij} - e_j; 0\} \qquad i, j \in N \qquad (14)$$

$$M_{id} = \max\{l_i + T_{ij} - \min_{k \in K} \{E_k\}; 0\} \qquad i \in N \qquad (15)$$

$$M_{dj} = \max\{\max_{k \in K} \{E_k\} + T_{ij} - e_j; 0\} \qquad j \in N \qquad (16)$$

are large constants used to linearize constraints (8) and (9), as shown in [15]. The objective function (2) is to minimize the sum of total outsourcing costs and total internal operating costs. Constraints (3) ensure that each customer can be visited at most by one route. Constraints (4) ensure that each vehicle departs from the depot only once. Constraints (5) are the classical in-degree and out-degree constraints. Constraints (6) and (7) model the time window requirements. Constraints (8) guarantee valid times between two consecutive services i and j in a route by imposing that the start-time of the service at customer j must be greater than or equal to the start-time of the service at the previous customer plus the service time of the previous customer and the travel time. Constraints (9) are the same as constraints (8), but used when the previous node is the depot. Constraints (10) impose the route time limit. Constraints (11) impose the compatibility of vehicle and container by removing incompatible assignments. Constraints (12) define a lower bound on arrival time at the depot, to avoid a negative component in the objective function in case of empty routes, and (13) define the domain of the variables.

4 Iterated Greedy Algorithm

In this section, we present an Iterated Greedy (`IG`) metaheuristic for the problem. The `IG` metaheuristic was originally proposed by Ruiz and Stützle [13] to

Algorithm 1. Overview of the proposed Iterated Greedy (IG) metaheuristic.

Input: input data
Parameters: $\overline{\eta}_0$, δ
Output: a set of routes $\mathcal{X}^* = (R_1, ..., R_{|K|})$.

$\mathcal{X}^* \leftarrow$ ConstructiveHeuristic()
for $\eta_0 = 1, ..., \overline{\eta}_0$ **do**
    $\mathcal{X}' \leftarrow$ Destruction($\mathcal{X}^*, \delta$)
    $\mathcal{X}'' \leftarrow$ Construction($\mathcal{X}'$)
    if $z(\mathcal{X}'') < z(\mathcal{X}^*)$ **then**
        $\mathcal{X}^* \leftarrow \mathcal{X}''$
    end if
end for
return $\mathcal{X}^*$

Algorithm 2. Constructive heuristic used by IG metaheuristic.

Input: input data
Output: a set of routes $\mathcal{X}^* = (R_1, ..., R_k)$.

$\mathcal{X}^* \leftarrow \{\}$
candidateList $\leftarrow N$
for each *criteria* in $[C1, C2, C3, C4, C5]$ **do**
    $\mathcal{X}' \leftarrow \{\}$
    sortedCL $\leftarrow$ SortService(*candidateList*, *criteria*)
    for each *service* in *sortedCL* **do**
        $\mathcal{X}' \leftarrow$ BestInsertion($\mathcal{X}'$, *service*)
    end for
    if $(z(\mathcal{X}') < z(\mathcal{X}^*))$ **then**
        $\mathcal{X}^* \leftarrow \mathcal{X}'$
    end if
end for
return $\mathcal{X}^*$

solve a scheduling problem and since then has been successfully applied to several optimization problems, either as a pure iterated destruction/reconstruction algorithm or with an additional local search at each iteration (see, e.g., [14]). The choice of an IG algorithm came after some preliminary experiments with single-solution based metaheuristics, which often rely on local search to improve candidate solutions. After trying classical neighborhoods and proposing new ones designed for the problem, we noticed that the several constraints make it difficult to find a feasible move and an improving neighbor. Preliminary tests were performed also with an IG with Variable Neighborhood Descent, providing solutions comparable with the pure IG but in much higher computational times. For this reason, in this article we present only the pure IG algorithm.

Algorithm 1 provides a pseudocode description of the proposed IG metaheuristic. The input of the algorithm is the input data defined in Sect. 3. The best solution found by the heuristic is indicated by $\mathcal{X}^*$, where $\mathcal{X}^* = (R_1, ..., R_{|K|})$ denotes the set of routes forming a feasible solution.

Algorithm 3. Destruction phase function used by `IG` metaheuristic.

Input: $\mathcal{X}, \delta$, input data

1: $r_0 = \min\{\delta \cdot |N|, \sum_{r \in \mathcal{X}} |R_r|\}$
2: **for** $i = 1, ..., r_0$ **do**
3: $\quad \mathcal{X} = \mathcal{X} \setminus$ GETRANDOMSERVICE($\mathcal{X}$)
4: **end for**
5: **return** $\mathcal{X}$

The metaheuristic starts with an initial solution built through a greedy construction algorithm (Algorithm 2) and then goes through several iterations of Destruction (Algorithm 3) and Reconstruction (Algorithm 4) phases where the current best solution is partially destroyed and a new complete candidate solution is reconstructed by a greedy algorithm.

The greedy construction algorithm (Algorithm 2) selects all the requests ordered according to five different criteria $[C1, C2, C3, C4, C5]$ and tries to insert them, one at a time, in the best feasible position. The SORTSERVICE function sorts requests in descending order, based on the values taken in the different criteria: C1 prioritizes outsourcing cost (C_i); C2 prioritizes the closing time $(-l_i)$; C3 the opening time $(-(l_i - e_i))$; C4 prioritizes the ratio between outsourcing cost and opening time $(\frac{C_i}{(l_i - e_i)})$; and finally C5 prioritizes the ratio between outsourcing cost and closing time $(\frac{C_i}{l_i})$. The BESTINSERTION procedure inserts a service in the best feasible position, if any, i.e., it tries all positions in all routes and inserts the service in the feasible position that less increases the cost, or does not insert the service if no feasible position is available. The solution returned by the constructive heuristic, $\mathcal{X}^*$, is the one that provides the minimal cost $z(\mathcal{X}^*)$ among the ones constructed using the five different criteria.

Then, for $\overline{\eta}_0$ iterations, a DESTRUCTION procedure (Algorithm 3) removes at random $\delta\%$ of the total number of requests from the current solution routes, while a RECONSTRUCTION procedure (Algorithm 4) sorts all the outsourced requests at random and tries to insert them in the best position among those that keep the solution feasible. The possibility of the algorithm to remove all the requests in the solution if they are less than $\delta\%$ of the total number of requests was chosen because we found it to be better than a simple restart with a completely new solution. Indeed, this produces a complete random solution (Algorithm 3, line 2) that thus increases the diversification of the algorithm, while a restart would have a more limited effect because of the sorting criterion in Algorithm 2.

The incumbent solution is updated every time the candidate solution has a better objective function value (Algorithm 1, lines 5–6). As shown in the computational experiments, even if the algorithm is simple it provides high quality solutions for the problem in small computational times.

Algorithm 4. Reconstruction phase function used by IG metaheuristic.

Input: $\mathcal{X}$, input data

1: $candidateList \leftarrow N \setminus \mathcal{X}$
2: $sortedCL \leftarrow$ RANDOMSORTING($candidateList$)
3: **for** each *service* in *sortedCL* **do**
4: $\quad \mathcal{X} \leftarrow$ BESTINSERTION($\mathcal{X}, service$)
5: **end for**
6: **return** $\mathcal{X}$

5 Computational Results

In this section, preliminary computational results on real instances are presented. The instances were collected at Iren Ambiente Spa during two different months on two different provinces. Times between nodes (requests sites, disposal plants and depot) have been calculated by an implementation of the Open Source Routing Machine [10], and increased by a 10%, a value empirically determined to model the fact that tractors, and not cars, are used.

Both the MILP and the metaheuristic have been implemented in Python 3.9, and tested on a single-core of an Intel(R) Xeon(R) Gold 6252N CPU running at 2.30GHz, equipped with 16 GB of memory under Windows 10 Pro N operating system. The MILP has been modeled with PuLP version 2.6 [11] and solved with Gurobi version 9.5.1 with a computational time limit (TL) of 3600 s. The time limit for the metaheuristic has not been set, since the number of iterations parameter $\overline{\eta}_0$ already controls the computational time. Moreover, as IG is a non-deterministic algorithm, it was run 10 times for each instance. For the IG the following parameter settings are used: $\overline{\eta}_0 = 4000$ and $\delta = 0.15$. This value of δ was the one, among different values, performing the best on average in preliminary computational results.

An overview of the sizes and the number of service types of the instances is given in Table 2, as well as the percentage of customers visited by the company solution $\mathcal{X}^{\mathcal{R}}$. Table 2 contains two sets of real instances, namely "RE" (Reggio Emilia province) and "PC" (Piacenza province). The "RE" real life instance set has mainly request types that are either swaps (S) or empty and return (W). The second set of instances, "PC", comes from a smaller depot with less routes available and a smaller number of requests that are mainly collection of bulk waste through an orange peel grapple (G) and swaps (S).

The results obtained on these instances are shown in Tables 3 and 4. The corresponding gap between the best dual bound and the best solution value found within the TL for the MILP is reported as $\mathsf{GAP_M} = \frac{|\mathsf{UB_M} - \mathsf{LB_M}|}{|\mathsf{UB_M}|} \cdot 100$, where $\mathsf{UB_M}$ is the cost of the incumbent solution found by the MILP and $\mathsf{LB_M}$ is the best dual bound achieved by the MILP within the TL. The improvement of the MILP or IG solution with respect to the real cost sustained by the firm is defined as $\frac{\mathsf{Z_R} - \mathsf{Z}}{\mathsf{Z_R}} \cdot 100$ where $\mathsf{Z_R}$ is the cost sustained by the company and Z is replaced by $\mathsf{UB_M}$ if we are computing the improvement of the MILP ($\mathsf{IMP_{MR}}$) or $\mathsf{Z_B}$ and $\mathsf{Z_A}$ if we are computing the improvement of the best ($\mathsf{IMP_{BR}}$) or average ($\mathsf{IMP_{AR}}$) solution of

Table 2. Real instances composition. Instances, collected in different areas and periods, are divided in two sets: "RE" with usually more than 30 requests and a majority of W and S types, and "PC" with less than 25 requests and a majority of G and S types.

Instance Name	$\|K\|$	$\|N\|$	Service Types (W, S, P, R, Y, G, B)	$\frac{\|\mathcal{X}^{\mathcal{R}}\|}{\|N\|}\%$
RE001	6	41	(4, 37, 0, 0, 0, 0, 0)	63.41%
RE002	5	38	(9, 28, 0, 0, 1, 0, 0)	63.16%
RE003	5	41	(6, 34, 0, 0, 0, 0, 0)	63.41%
RE004	5	41	(8, 32, 1, 0, 0, 0, 0)	63.41%
RE005	5	36	(8, 28, 0, 0, 0, 0, 0)	63.89%
RE006	5	38	(10, 28, 0, 0, 0, 0, 0)	60.53%
RE007	5	37	(6, 31, 0, 0, 0, 0, 0)	64.86%
RE008	5	35	(7, 28, 0, 0, 0, 0, 0)	62.86%
RE009	5	38	(10, 28, 0, 0, 0, 0, 0)	68.42%
RE010	3	24	(7, 17, 0, 0, 0, 0, 0)	75.00%
RE011	5	36	(9, 27, 0, 0, 0, 0, 0)	66.67%
RE012	6	39	(6, 32, 0, 1, 0, 0, 0)	64.10%
RE013	5	41	(10, 30, 0, 1, 0, 0, 0)	60.98%
RE014	4	27	(13, 12, 2, 0, 0, 0, 0)	70.37%
			AVG	65,08%

Instance Name	$\|K\|$	$\|N\|$	Service Types (W, S, P, R, Y, G, B)	$\frac{\|\mathcal{X}^{\mathcal{R}}\|}{\|N\|}\%$
PC001	3	21	(3, 4, 0, 0, 0, 13, 1)	61.90%
PC002	3	18	(5, 4, 0, 0, 0, 9, 0)	66.67%
PC003	2	15	(2, 4, 1, 0, 0, 8, 0)	60.00%
PC004	2	19	(1, 3, 5, 0, 0, 10, 0)	57.89%
PC005	2	19	(4, 4, 0, 0, 0, 11, 0)	47.37%
PC006	2	16	(2, 1, 0, 0, 0, 13, 0)	50.00%
PC007	3	22	(4, 4, 1, 0, 0, 13, 0)	72.73%
PC008	3	18	(2, 6, 1, 1, 0, 8, 0)	77.78%
PC009	3	22	(3, 5, 0, 0, 0, 14, 0)	59.09%
PC010	4	18	(4, 7, 0, 0, 0, 7, 0)	66.67%
PC011	3	20	(2, 4, 0, 0, 0, 14, 0)	50.00%
PC012	3	14	(4, 2, 0, 0, 0, 8, 0)	42.86%
PC013	2	19	(2, 4, 0, 0, 0, 13, 0)	47.37%
PC014	3	21	(1, 9, 0, 0, 0, 11, 0)	66.67%
PC015	3	23	(6, 4, 1, 0, 0, 12, 0)	65.22%
PC016	3	15	(2, 3, 1, 0, 0, 9, 0)	60.00%
			AVG	59,51%

the IG. Finally, the improvement of IG over the MILP solution is calculated as $\mathsf{IMP_{BM}} = \frac{\mathsf{UB_M} - \mathsf{Z_B}}{\mathsf{UB_M}} \cdot 100$ and $\mathsf{IMP_{AM}} = \frac{\mathsf{UB_M} - \mathsf{Z_A}}{\mathsf{UB_M}} \cdot 100$ if we are comparing the best and the average result of the IG respectively. Computational times, $\mathsf{CPU_M}$ and $\mathsf{CPU_{IG}}$, are reported in seconds throughout the section.

Each row in Tables 3 and 4 reports the cost sustained by the firm, IG and MILP computational results for each one of the 30 test instances. The following information is provided: the average percentage increase of customers visited by the IG ($\Delta|\mathcal{X}^{\mathcal{A}}|$), the average ($\mathsf{Z_A}$) and best ($\mathsf{Z_B}$) objective function computed by the IG along with the corresponding percentage improvements ($\mathsf{IMP_{AR}}$, $\mathsf{IMP_{BR}}$) computed with respect to the real solution and ($\mathsf{IMP_{AM}}$, $\mathsf{IMP_{BM}}$) to the best computed upper bound ($\mathsf{UB_M}$) produced by the MILP. Note that a negative improvement means the compared method performed worse in that case. Finally, the computation time of the IG ($\mathsf{CPU_{IG}}$) is reported as the average over 10 runs.

For most of the instances the solver provides solutions that are better than the real ones, but, accordingly with VRP literature [15], the MILP seems not to have good lower bounds, because, even after a hour of computation, the gap between the upper and lower bound of the model ($\mathsf{GAP_M}$) is still large. This gap has been calculated as a ratio between the difference of upper and lower bound provided by the solver and the upper bound (and not the lower bound), because often the lower bound found after the TL was still equal to 0. Given the poor performance of the proposed MILP, we were not able to prove optimality for any solution, but, for all "RE" instances and for 15 out of 16 "PC" instances the solver was able to find better solutions than the ones provided by the company, with an average improvement among the instances ($\mathsf{IMP_{MR}}$) of 12.09% and 30.13% respectively. Also the IG obtained very good results with respect to both the real cost sustained by the company and the MILP results. Indeed, for all "RE" instances, the best results among 10 runs of IG had an average $\mathsf{IMP_{BR}}$ among the instances of 20.40% compared to the real cost sustained by the company and of 9.46% compared to the MILP solution ($\mathsf{IMP_{BM}}$). For "PC" instances, on

Table 3. "RE" instances with real cost sustained by the company, MILP's and IG's results.

Instance Name	Z_R	UB_M	CPU_M[s]	IMP_{MR}	GAP_M	Z_B	Z_A	$\Delta\lvert\mathcal{X}^{\mathcal{A}}\rvert$	CPU_{IG}[s]	IMP_{BR}	IMP_{AR}	IMP_{BM}	IMP_{AM}
RE001	1557.20	1234.93	3600.00	20.70%	100.00%	1037.84	1064.96	15.00%	42.98	33.35%	31.61%	15.96%	13.76%
RE002	1498.00	1237.21	3600.00	17.41%	100.00%	1109.71	1144.59	6.67%	32.88	25.92%	23.59%	10.31%	7.49%
RE003	1571.00	1540.81	3600.00	1.92%	96.50%	1397.65	1436.28	−5.38%	39.43	11.03%	8.58%	9.29%	6.78%
RE004	1522.00	1457.45	3600.00	4.24%	100.00%	1316.97	1346.39	−4.62%	40.71	13.47%	11.54%	9.64%	7.62%
RE005	1490.00	1287.15	3600.00	13.61%	100.00%	1152.50	1168.66	1.74%	29.73	22.65%	21.57%	10.46%	9.21%
RE006	1585.00	1187.67	3600.00	25.07%	95.46%	1121.30	1160.97	11.74%	32.85	29.26%	26.75%	5.59%	2.25%
RE007	1456.00	1219.83	3600.00	16.22%	100.00%	1083.11	1106.69	−1.25%	31.25	25.61%	23.99%	11.21%	9.28%
RE008	1098.00	999.49	3600.00	8.97%	96.00%	902.87	930.96	2.27%	28.47	17.77%	15.21%	9.67%	6.86%
RE009	1308.00	1213.64	3600.00	7.21%	100.00%	1149.94	1167.07	−4.62%	33.85	12.08%	10.77%	5.25%	3.84%
RE010	579.60	548.57	3600.00	5.35%	100.00%	513.57	524.45	0.00%	10.58	11.39%	9.51%	6.38%	4.40%
RE011	1346.00	1217.45	3600.00	9.55%	100.00%	1065.68	1082.53	1.25%	30.03	20.83%	19.57%	12.47%	11.08%
RE012	1508.20	1381.14	3600.00	8.42%	100.00%	1230.92	1250.76	−1.60%	37.19	18.38%	17.07%	10.88%	9.44%
RE013	1603.00	1470.63	3600.00	8.26%	96.34%	1324.30	1361.09	6.00%	39.20	17.39%	15.09%	9.95%	7.45%
RE014	801.80	623.40	3600.00	22.25%	100.00%	589.46	597.58	5.26%	15.48	26.48%	25.47%	5.44%	4.14%
			AVG	12.09%	98.88%			2.32%		20.40%	18.60%	9.46%	7.40%

Table 4. "PC" real instances composition, real cost sustained by the company with MILP's and IG's results.

Instance Name	Z_R	UB_M	CPU_M[s]	IMP_{MR}	GAP_M	Z_B	Z_A	$\Delta\lvert\mathcal{X}^{\mathcal{A}}\rvert$	CPU_{IG}[s]	IMP_{BR}	IMP_{AR}	IMP_{BM}	IMP_{AM}
PC001	8148.50	5143.91	3600.00	36.87%	100.00%	5143.91	5144.00	23.08%	8.10	36.87%	36.87%	0.00%	0.00%
PC002	6148.50	4141.11	3600.00	32.65%	100.00%	4141.11	4141.11	16.67%	5.48	32.65%	32.65%	0.00%	0.00%
PC003	6113.70	3102.57	3600.00	49.25%	100.00%	3102.57	3102.57	33.33%	4.14	49.25%	49.25%	0.00%	0.00%
PC004	8105.00	6102.47	3600.00	24.71%	100.00%	6102.47	6102.47	18.18%	5.81	24.71%	24.71%	0.00%	0.00%
PC005	10105.60	7101.99	3600.00	29.72%	100.00%	7101.99	7399.27	30.00%	5.89	29.72%	26.78%	0.00%	−4.19%
PC006	8081.50	9062.31	3600.00	−12.14%	100.00%	9062.31	9062.31	−12.50%	4.37	−12.14%	−12.14%	0.00%	0.00%
PC007	6148.50	5138.72	3600.00	16.42%	100.00%	5137.54	5138.62	6.25%	8.92	16.44%	16.42%	0.02%	0.00%
PC008	4148.50	1144.75	3600.00	72.41%	100.00%	1144.64	1144.72	21.43%	4.37	72.41%	72.41%	0.01%	0.00%
PC009	9154.60	4147.41	3600.00	54.70%	100.00%	4147.41	4147.41	38.46%	8.85	54.70%	54.70%	0.00%	0.00%
PC010	6137.40	5118.69	3600.00	16.60%	100.00%	5118.69	5118.69	8.33%	5.93	16.60%	16.60%	0.00%	0.00%
PC011	10114.10	7109.56	3600.00	29.71%	100.00%	7109.56	7109.56	30.00%	7.59	29.71%	29.71%	0.00%	0.00%
PC012	8075.00	7060.46	3600.00	12.56%	100.00%	7060.46	7060.46	16.67%	3.72	12.56%	12.56%	0.00%	0.00%
PC013	10099.00	7087.72	3600.00	29.82%	100.00%	7087.72	7087.72	33.33%	6.07	29.82%	29.82%	0.00%	0.00%
PC014	7148.50	4145.56	3600.00	42.01%	100.00%	4144.91	4244.13	20.71%	8.04	42.02%	40.63%	0.02%	−2.38%
PC015	8148.50	5142.42	3600.00	36.89%	100.00%	5141.32	5141.32	20.00%	9.67	36.90%	36.90%	0.02%	0.02%
PC016	6090.00	5077.10	3600.00	16.63%	100.00%	5077.10	5077.17	11.11%	4.37	16.63%	16.63%	0.00%	0.00%
			AVG	30.13%	100.00%			19.69%		30.13%	29.84%	0.00%	−0.44%

the other hand, IG best solutions among 10 runs provided a IMP_{BR} of 30.13%, although no improvement on average (IMP_{BM} = 0.00%) among the instances. This can be interpreted by supposing that both the MILP and IG probably found optimal or near optimal solution on these smaller instances, but this cannot be confirmed because of the weak lower bounds. If we look also at the average results, it is possible to see the high quality results of the IG. Indeed, on the small-size "PC" instances it provides almost always the same solution value of the MILP, having IMP_{AM} close to 0, while on larger instances, as the "RE" ones, it performs way better having a IMP_{AM} of 7.40%. Average IG results show also an average increase of internally served customers compared to company solutions, even if in some "RE" instances a decrease seems to be beneficial for the objective function, depending on the combination of outsourcing and internal operating costs.

In addition to the high quality level of the solutions that the proposed IG is able to found, we want to stress out also other two main advantages it presents: the simplicity of both the algorithm construction and the parameters tuning, having just one parameter δ driving the diversification in building the solutions and one $\overline{\eta_0}$ driving the computational time, and its velocity, providing very good solutions in less than 10s on "PC" instances and less than 40s on "RE" ones.

Finally, it is possible to notice that for instance PC006 we were not able to improve the result empirically found by the company ($\mathsf{IMP}_{\mathsf{MR}}$, $\mathsf{IMP}_{\mathsf{BR}}$, $\mathsf{IMP}_{\mathsf{AR}}$ are negatives in Table 4). A detailed study of the solutions provided by the company revealed that this happens because the company sometimes applies some movements not modelled in this study: in W customers that are far from depot, if they have the possibility to do so, they make a temporary drop-off of an empty container at the customer site, serve the W request and then pick-up again the empty container to reach the next customer, without going back to the depot to get another one if necessary. This sometimes allows large time savings, as it happened on this particular instance.

6 Conclusions

In this article, we analysed an industrial waste collection case study that lies in the field of Rollon-Rolloff Vehicle Routing Problems. Through data preprocessing we have been able to reduce the size of the underlying graph and hence model the problem as a Capacitated Vehicle Routing Problem with profits and time windows. We first modeled the problem with a Mixed Integer Programming formulation, and then we solved it through an Iterated Greedy algorithm. We executed multiple experiments on real instances collected by the company. Computational results show how the modelling of the problem and the use of a simple Iterated Greedy metaheuristic can lead to significant improvements in the operational costs. Moreover, the speed of the algorithm in providing high quality solutions could make it possible, for the company, to use it as a Decision Support System (DSS), to quickly simulate different scenarios and obtain near-optimal solutions by changing input data and parameters instead of building empirical lower-quality solutions. Indeed, given the complexity of the problem, customers to be outsourced are now often predetermined by the company, which is now evaluating to switch to a model-based planning. To achieve this, an integration of the DSS with the company informative system is needed, as well as the implementation of features such as lunch break, the use of tractors with two trailers, and the possibility of temporary drop-off of containers at customer locations. We are planning to implement these features as future research work.

Acknowledgements. We would like to thank Iren Ambiente Spa for providing case study instances. We also thank two anonymous Reviewers for valuable comments that helped us improve the quality of the paper.

References

1. Archetti, C., Speranza, M.G.: Vehicle routing in the 1-skip collection problem. J. Oper. Res. Soc. **55**(7), 717–727 (2004)
2. Aringhieri, R., Bruglieri, M., Malucelli, F., Nonato, M.: A special vehicle routing problem arising in the optimization of waste disposal: a real case. Transp. Sci. **52**(2), 277–299 (2018)
3. Baldacci, R., Bodin, L., Mingozzi, A.: The multiple disposal facilities and multiple inventory locations rollon-rolloff vehicle routing problem. Comput. Oper. Res. **33**(9), 2667–2702 (2006)
4. Beliën, J., De Boeck, L., Van Ackere, J.: Municipal solid waste collection and management problems: a literature review. Transp. Sci. **48**(1), 78–102 (2014)
5. le Blanc, I., van Krieken, M., Krikke, H., Fleuren, H.: Vehicle routing concepts in the closed-loop container network of ARN-a case study. OR Spectr. **28**(1), 53–71 (2006)
6. Bodin, L., Mingozzi, A., Baldacci, R., Ball, M.: The rollon-rolloff vehicle routing problem. Transp. Sci. **34**(3), 271–288 (2000)
7. Golden, B.L., Assad, A.A., Wasil, E.A.: Routing vehicles in the real world: applications in the solid waste, beverage, food, dairy, and newspaper industries. In: The Vehicle Routing Problem, pp. 245–286. SIAM (2002)
8. Hauge, K., Larsen, J., Lusby, R.M., Krapper, E.: A hybrid column generation approach for an industrial waste collection routing problem. Comput. Industr. Eng. **71**, 10–20 (2014)
9. Li, H., Jian, X., Chang, X., Lu, Y.: The generalized rollon-rolloff vehicle routing problem and savings-based algorithm. Transp. Res. Part B: Methodol. **113**, 1–23 (2018)
10. Luxen, D., Vetter, C.: Real-time routing with OpenStreetMap data. In: Proceedings of the 19th ACM SIGSPATIAL International Conference on Advances in Geographic Information Systems, GIS 2011, pp. 513–516. ACM, New York (2011)
11. Mitchell, S., OSullivan, M., Dunning, I.: PuLP: a linear programming toolkit for python. The University of Auckland, Auckland, New Zealand 65 (2011)
12. Raucq, J., Sörensen, K., Cattrysse, D.: Solving a real-life roll-on-roll-off waste collection problem with column generation. J. Veh. Routing Algorithms **2**(1), 41–54 (2019)
13. Ruiz, R., Stützle, T.: A simple and effective iterated greedy algorithm for the permutation flowshop scheduling problem. Eur. J. Oper. Res. **177**(3), 2033–2049 (2007)
14. Stützle, T., Ruiz, R.: Iterated greedy. In: Martí R., Pardalos P., Resende M. (eds.) Handbook of Heuristics, pp. 547–577 (2018)
15. Toth, P., Vigo, D.: Chapter 5: The vehicle routing problem with time windows. Chapter 5. Society for Industrial and Applied Mathematics (2014)
16. World Bank Group: Solid waste management. http://www.worldbank.org/en/topic/urbandevelopment/brief/solid-waste-management
17. Wy, J., Kim, B.I., Kim, S.: The rollon-rolloff waste collection vehicle routing problem with time windows. Eur. J. Oper. Res. **224**(3), 466–476 (2013)

Solving a School Bus Routing Problem in Rural Areas: An Application in Brazil

Letícia Caldas[1], Rafael Martinelli[1](✉), and Bruno Rosa[1,2]

[1] Departamento de Engenharia Industrial, Pontifícia Universidade Católica do Rio de Janeiro, Rio de Janeiro, Brazil
leticia.caldas@aluno.puc-rio.br, martinelli@puc-rio.br
[2] Secretaria de Estado de Educação do Rio de Janeiro, Rio de Janeiro, Brazil
brunoalexandre@educacao.rj.gov.br

Abstract. School transport is essential to guarantee the access and permanence of students in public schools, especially in rural regions, where students are located in large areas with low density and roads are in precarious situations. The present work aims to apply an Iterated Local Search metaheuristic to route 13,664 students in the rural areas of Rio de Janeiro state, Brazil. To reach this goal, the School Bus Routing Problem is considered with a heterogeneous fleet to minimize the total cost, considering the vehicle capacity constraints and maximum travel distance. The method is applied to the Rio de Janeiro State data to fill the gap between school practices and academic models and quantify potential economic gains. Computational experiments show that when comparing the method's results against the routes used in practice, a reduction of 40.5% in the average cost of the routes and 46.0% in the average mileage per student is obtained.

Keywords: School Bus Routing Problem · Iterated Local Search · Rural school transport · Metaheuristic

1 Introduction

The right to school transport is guaranteed to public school students by the Brazilian Federal Constitution of 1988. Considering the continental dimension of Brazil and its geographic, cultural, and social diversity, the elaboration of public policies at the national level becomes challenging. In addition to these challenges, the economic crisis which began in Brazil in 2014 and the austerity policies adopted resulted in budget cuts, including in the area of education and investments in transport [11].

In this sense, the quality of education spending must be a priority, and the application of optimization techniques can result in significant savings, improving

This research was partially supported by CAPES with Finance Code 001, by CNPq under grant 315361/2020-4, and by FAPERJ under grant E-26/201.417/2022 in Brazil. This financial support is gratefully acknowledged.

J. de Armas et al. (Eds.): ICCL 2022, LNCS 13557, pp. 162–176, 2022.
https://doi.org/10.1007/978-3-031-16579-5_12

efficiency with a high level of service. In most rural regions of Brazil, transport network management activities – establishing routes, selecting students, and selecting vehicles according to cost, safety, capacity, and travel time – are carried out based on the experience and intuition of the responsible person, increasing expenses, travel time and the number of vehicles used [24]. Furthermore, in the rural context, the definition of routes is even more challenging since the students are located in large areas with low density, and most roads are in precarious situations [4]. In many cases, the maximum travel time restriction is reached before vehicle capacity, due to the large distances between the students.

In this sense, the application of optimization techniques, in addition to enabling significant savings, can increase the level of service offered to students. The route optimization performed on vehicle fleets is known in the literature as the Vehicle Routing Problem (VRP). The VRP is a combinatorial optimization problem that consists of determining delivery or collection routes from one or more warehouses, having as destinations points that represent customers or cities, respecting established restrictions [13].

One of the VRP variants is the School Bus Routing Problem (SBRP). The SBRP consists of routing a fleet of school vehicles, where students must be picked up from their residences or pre-determined bus stops and taken to the school [2]. In the SBRP, the depot is usually different from the school, vehicles have a maximum capacity, and there is a restriction on the time the student will stay in the vehicle [20]. In addition, in our application distances from the depot to the first student and from the school to the depot are not considered due to contractual reasons.

The SBRP is similar to the Open Vehicle Routing Problem (OVRP), with vehicles' capacity and distance restriction, classified as an NP-hard problem [20], that is, there are no known algorithms capable of finding an optimal solution in polynomial time [14]. For applications in real large-scale cases, where it is required to consider specific characteristics and constraints, heuristics and metaheuristics are more suitable since they present high-quality solutions in a reasonable time interval [26].

The first publication about the SBRP was done by Newton and Thomas [18]. Fifty years after this first publication on the subject, new approaches and algorithms continue to emerge in the literature, given the potential improvement they can bring to a real environment. The large gap that exists between school practices and academic models is also highlighted by Ellegood et al. [7]. The authors highlight the need for further studies to quantify the benefits of optimization in practice, considering potential economic and social gains.

To fill the gap between school practices and academic models [7] and quantify potential economic gains, we considered real datasets. We apply an Iterated Local Search (ILS) metaheuristic to route 13,664 students in the rural areas of Rio de Janeiro state in Brazil. To reach this goal, the School Bus Routing Problem is considered with a heterogeneous fleet to minimize the total cost, considering the vehicle capacity constraints and maximum travel distance.

The remainder of this paper is organized as follows. Section 2 describes the SBRP. Section 3 reviews some works related to the SBRP and ILS. Section 4 presents our solution approach. Section 5 discusses data collection steps and presents the obtained results with a comparison with the routes currently used. Finally, Sect. 6 presents the concluding remarks of this work.

2 Problem Description

We can define the SBRP according to Hou et al. [9] over a graph with a set of nodes and arcs $G = (V, E)$, where $V = \{0, 1, 2, 3, \ldots, n, n+1\}$ is the set of nodes and $A = \{(i, j), i, j \in V \mid i \neq j\}$ is the set of arcs. When taking students to the school, node 0 corresponds to the depot and node $n+1$ corresponds to the school. The inverse happens when bringing the students home. The node set $C = \{1, 2, 3, \ldots, n\}$ represents the bus stops. Each stop i has a number of students q_i to be served. The nodes representing the school and the depot have no associated demand. Each arc (i, j) has an associated distance $d_{i,j}$. A heterogeneous fleet of vehicles is located at the depot and the set of vehicle types is represented by $M = \{1, 2, 3, ..., K\}$. Each type of vehicle k has a capacity Q_k, a fixed cost f_k and a variable cost per unit of distance traveled v_k. The number of vehicles of type k is represented by h_k.

The objective of the problem is to determine a set of routes with the minimum total cost satisfying the following constraints:

- Each vehicle leaves the depot (or the school), visits a series of stopping points and ends the route at the school (or depot).
- Each stopping point must be visited only once.
- The number of students served by a vehicle cannot exceed its capacity.
- The total travel time for students cannot exceed the maximum travel time or distance allowed D.
- The number of vehicles of type k used cannot exceed h_k.

3 Literature Review

3.1 School Bus Routing Problem

Two literature reviews, recently published about SBRP, reviewed 93 papers [7, 20]. In the following, we will highlight more recent works that are not present in these surveys.

Rosa [23] proposed a methodology to geocode the address of schools and students, calculate the distance and travel time and apply a tool to obtain the routes. The tool uses the Adaptive Large Neighborhood Search (ALNS) metaheuristic. The author considered the same environment as this work, students from the rural area of the state of Rio de Janeiro. The first stage of the proposed methodology, geocoding of schools and students, allowed the development of the computational tests presented in this paper.

Oudouar et al. [19] proposed an approach that consists of generating routes for each school using a basic heuristic, such as Clarke and Wright or Path Scanning, and a clustering algorithm for selecting bus stops. The authors applied the method in real instances of up to 108 students.

In the paper of Avilés-Gonazélez et al. [1], the authors presented the implementation of Simulated Annealing (SA) for SBRP resolution. They used an experiment design technique to obtain statistical support in the selection of parameters. The authors applied the algorithm in a real instance with 41 students and 21 possible stopping points.

Lysgaard et al. [16] used a multistart heuristic and then a framework for mixed integer linear programming. The algorithm was applied in real instances from the literature of up to 101 students. Hou et al. [8] developed a metaheuristic that uses three neighborhood exploration structures to iteratively improve the solution.

Calvete et al. [3] proposed a metaheuristic that makes a partial allocation of students and defines the routes that minimize the total cost. Then, a refinement is made to allocate the remaining students and obtain a feasible solution. The algorithm was applied in instances from the literature with up to 800 students. In 15.18% of the instances, the method obtained a better result than the one from the literature and, in 66.07% of the instances, the same result was found from the literature.

3.2 Iterated Local Search

Some authors have used Iterated Local Search (ILS) in SBRP. The ILS uses a local search to obtain the local minima of a function and, at each iteration, uses a perturbation in the previously obtained locally optimal solution [15]. The strength of the perturbation must be calibrated so that it is not so strong that the solution space is randomly explored and not so weak that the algorithm returns to the solution already visited. The algorithm comprises four components: initial solution, local search, perturbation method, and acceptance criterion.

Dang et al. [6] used ILS in a hybrid metaheuristic to generate a set of solutions and then applies a Set Partitioning (SP) formulation to try to find the optimal route. The SP model is solved by CPLEX and used in instances from the literature. Hou et al. [9] also used a hybrid metaheuristic of ILS with SP and applied in a real instances of the Wuxi City in China, with up to 790 students.

With application in a Brazilian state, the work of Porto et al. [22] proposed a routing method to create better routes that serve students from rural schools in the city of Governador Valadares, in the state of Minas Gerais. The authors considered routing each school, in which the best result was obtained with a heuristic that combined ILS and Random Variable Neighborhood Descend (RVND). Routing for multiple schools was also considered, where the method with the best result was the Record-to-Record. The authors do not consider maximum travel time or distance in the tests performed.

4 Solution Approach

Considering the potential of the application of the ILS in the SBRP and the results obtained in the literature, we choose this metaheuristic as the solution method for the scenario studied.

A solution is represented by a set of vectors, where each vector represents a route to a vehicle. Plus, part of the solution is a vector with distance, total load, cost, and vehicle capacity for each route. Figure 1 shows a solution composed of three routes: R1, R2, and R3. Route information R_i is stored in position i for the distance, load, vehicle, and cost vectors. All routes start and end with element 1 which represents the school or depot. For the trip to the school, the distance to the first student is not considered when calculating the route distance and cost. For the return trip, the distance from the last student to the depot is also disregarded. Those are real aspects of the problem. In the government and drivers contract, the payment is done by km, but only when at least one student is transported. In the example, Route $R1$ has a total distance of 25km and has four students allocated (6, 3, 8, and 2). For this route, a vehicle with a capacity of eight was allocated, which is equivalent to a Kombi according to the available fleet. Finally, the route has a total cost of 32.50. The total distance, load, capacity, and cost of the instance are the sum of the information from R1, R2, and R3 routes.

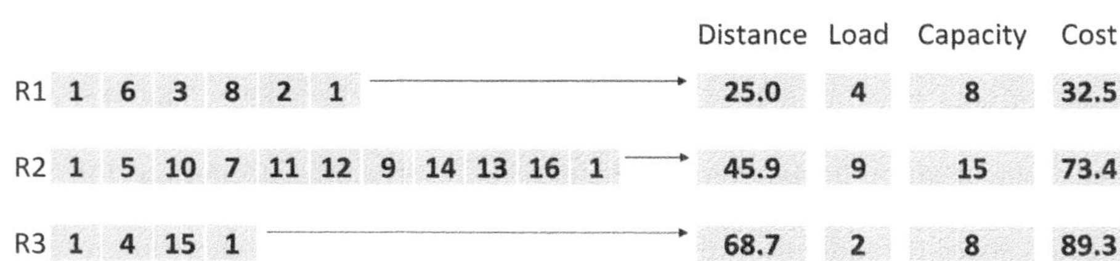

Fig. 1. Solution representation

The constructive algorithm builds the solution from a random choice of the first student to be included in the route. The algorithm uses the nearest neighbor technique from this first student, inserting in the route the student that was not yet visited and that presents the shortest distance to the last element inserted in the route. In addition to the vehicle's maximum capacity, the route must respect the maximum distance or travel time.

To explore the search space, we use classic neighborhood structures of the VRP with intra-route, and inter-route movements [25]. Intra-route moves refer to the Shift, Swap, and Relocate structures. Inter-route moves implemented were Swap and Relocate. The Shift move corresponds to position inversion of consecutive elements of a route. Swap is position inversion of non-consecutive elements in the same or different routes. Finally, Relocate deletes an element from the route with reinsertion in another position on the same or different routes.

In addition to the above movements, we include in the local search the exchange of the route vehicle. As the vehicle type is chosen randomly in the construction, the inclusion of this neighborhood allows the adjustment of the vehicle used in each route according to the number of students allocated.

Seeking to explore the neighborhoods in a systematic way, we use a Variable Neighborhood Descent (VND). Proposed by Mladenovic and Hansen [17] and using First Improvement strategy, when the cost of a neighbor is less than the current solution, the current solution is replaced, and the search returns to the first neighborhood. Otherwise, the search moves to the next neighborhood.

During the Local Search, we decided to allow the violation of the vehicle's capacity. This option was made because the search space could be limited when obtaining only feasible solutions. For cases where the vehicle load exceeds its capacity, the excess load is penalized, and this value is added to the solution's total cost. However, infeasible solutions are never considered as the best solution found during the ILS execution.

An essential element of the ILS is perturbation. In this work, the perturbation applies a limited number of random moves, from the same neighborhoods of the local search.

As acceptance criteria, we use the simulated annealing rule, where the current solution s^* is replaced by the candidate solution $s^{*'}$ given the probability $e^{-(f(s^{*'})-f(s^*))/T}$, where $T > 0$ is the current temperature [12]. The temperature starts with an initial value T_i and decreases on each iteration following the expression $T = T \times r$, where $0 < r < 1$ is the cooling rate. In this work, to define the initial and final temperatures, we use the method proposed by Pisinger and Ropke [21], where the initial and final temperatures are adjusted so that the main algorithm accepts $p_i\%$ of solutions that show up to $p_i\%$ of deterioration and end up accepting $p_f\%$ of solutions with up to $p_f\%$ deterioration. The cooling rate r is defined considering the number of iterations to be performed.

5 Application

5.1 Scenario

The state of Rio de Janeiro is composed of 92 municipalities and it has an estimated population of 17,366,189 people in a territorial area of 43,750,426 km^2 [10]. According to the latest historical series released by the State Center for Statistics, Research and Training of Public Servants of Rio de Janeiro (CEPERJ), the rural population corresponded to 3.4% of the state population in the 2010 demographic census [5].

In 2019, the Rio de Janeiro state had 17,200 students registered to use rural school transport distributed in 357 schools and 83 municipalities. All students are picked up and dropped off daily at their homes or nearby places when access is impossible. The location of boarding points and schools was made available through their latitudes and longitudes. The shift in which the student is enrolled was also made available, which can be morning, afternoon, night, or full time (morning + afternoon). Students were identified in the databases through codes, preserving their identities and not providing personal data.

5.2 Data Collection and Treatment

The directors of each school define students' latitudes and longitudes manually, according to the methodology proposed by Rosa [23]. Before applying the algorithm, the data went through a treatment step to identify inconsistencies.

- We exclude all student records in which latitude and/or longitude were equal to zero or outside the standard format. This step resulted in the deletion of 2072 records.
- We exclude records of students whose latitude and longitude provided a location outside the state of Rio de Janeiro. A total of 586 records were discarded.
- All students from shifts in which more than 70% of students had the same location were excluded. It was assumed that the registration was not performed correctly for these cases. This step resulted in the deletion of 878 records.

Instances. After processing the data, 13,664 students remained in the base. We divided these students into school and shift, generating one instance each. We divided the dataset into two blocks, the first considering the full shift independently, i.e., students from a shift could not be taken to school or to their homes with students from other shifts. The second block includes full-time students so that they would be taken to school together with the students from the morning shift, and at the end of the day, they would return to their homes with the students from the afternoon shift. Considering all scenarios, there is a total of 1,012 instances. Figure 2 shows the distribution of instances in size categories (number of students). On the horizontal axis, it is possible to observe the intervals of the number of students considered for each category. The number of instances of each category is indicated on the vertical axis.

Considering the first block, the largest instance is from the morning shift of school E199. In this instance, 389 students should be routed. In the second block, school E199 also represents the largest instance. However, when including the morning shift with full-time students, 534 students should be routed.

Distance Matrix. To determine the distances between each boarding point to the respective schools, we use the Open Street Maps API with a script in Python. The use of the API was necessary to obtain the real distances. In addition, we consider an asymmetric distance matrix, taking into account the difference between the distances of the round-trip path. Considering the asymmetric matrix is relevant in the rural context since the path between the students' residences and the school often involves roads and highways. Although no law defines

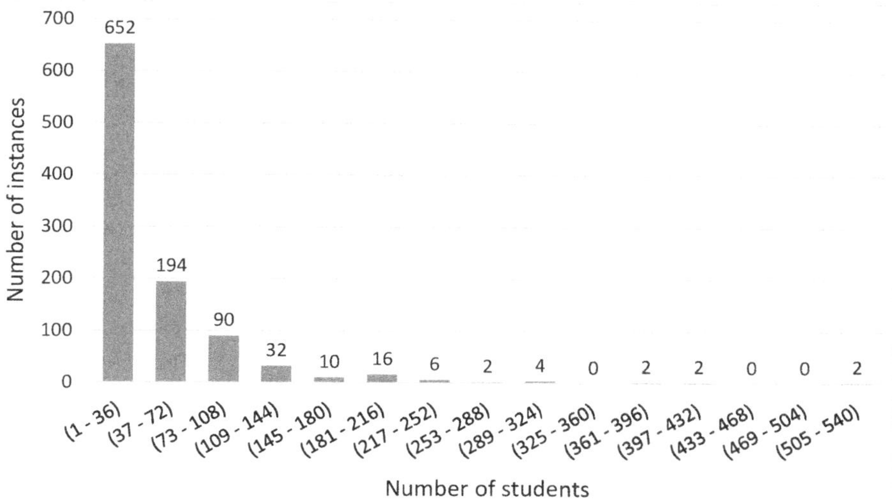

Fig. 2. Instances distribution by number of students

the maximum time or distance of the route taken by students, the government establishes a maximum time of 2 h or 120 km, considering an average speed of 60 km/h.

Fleet. The data provided showed that schools used up to four types of vehicles: kombi, van, minibus, and bus. Table 1 presents the capacity and cost per kilometer of each vehicle. In the government contracting rule, fixed costs are not considered, only variable costs. For this reason, the route cost calculation is done by multiplying only the vehicle's cost per km by the total distance of the route. To determine the fleet available for each instance, we consider that each type of vehicle would have a sufficient number to serve all students.

Table 1. Vehicle characteristics

Vehicle	Capacity	Cost by Km
Kombi	8	1.3
Van	15	1.6
Microbus	22	1.8
Bus	45	2.5

5.3 Computational Experiments

The main code was written in Julia 1.6.1, executed on a machine with Intel® Core™ i7-8700K CPU @ 3.70 GHz, 64 GB of RAM, using only one thread, and Ubuntu 20.04 LTS operating system. The development environment used was Visual Studio Code 1.59.

The first ILS round was carried out with all instances available to calibrate the parameters. We use ten seeds for each instance. We created 27 scenarios with different parameters configurations. For the SA parameters we used the following configurations: (50%–1%), (50%–5%), (50%–10%), (35%–1%), (35%–5%), (35%–10%), (20%–1%), (20%–5%), and (20%–10%). Configuration (50%–1%) means that the algorithm starts with a 50% chance of accepting a solution with up to 50% deterioration, and the probability decreases with each round until the probability is 1%. The number of iterations of the ILS, which is also used to calculate the cooling rate of SA, was set to {50, 75, 100}. Finally, the number of moves considered in the perturbation was set to five.

Considering the lowest total cost obtained among all the instances, the highest total cost, and the average of costs, the best results were obtained with 100 iterations and the following acceptance probabilities: (50%–1%), (20%–1%), and (20%–5%). Since the results obtained were the same for three configurations, we choose to use configuration (50%–1%). This choice was made to obtain larger diversification in the first rounds of the algorithm. A new round was carried out to verify the variation on the results given the number of perturbation moves, considering 1, 3, 5, 7, and 9 moves. We obtained the best solutions considering with five moves. Thus, the final configuration used in the experiments was (50%–1%) for the SA, 100 iterations in the ILS and 5 moves in the perturbation.

To compare the results with the real planning, we selected 79 routes in the dataset. For these cases, we have the information about the students allocated in each route, school, shift, vehicle, total kilometers, and route cost. We group the routes into combinations of school and shift to compare the number of routes used in real-life and the number proposed by the ILS.

For the ILS results, we considered the average total cost of the solutions. Figure 3 shows the comparison between the number of routes, average mileage, average cost, average mileage per student, and percentage of vehicle occupancy. The ILS obtained lower costs in 84% of cases and, considering all scenarios, the average cost of the routes drops from 136.91 to 81.33, a reduction of 40.5%. The number of routes, and therefore the number of vehicles needed, decreased by 8.8%, from 79 to 72. The average distance of the routes decreased by 44%, and the average distance per student decreased by 46%. Finally, the percentage of vehicle occupancy increased from 68% to 73%, indicating a better use of the fleet.

For cases where the ILS did not return a cost less than the original value, we observe the most significant difference in the E164_M instance with a 10% increase in total distance, approximately 16 km. Concerning the total cost, the increase was 5%. The comparison between the results presented by the ILS and the real routes shows the potential of the method used, fulfilling the objective of providing cost reduction considering significant restrictions to ensure the comfort and safety of students, such as reduction of the average mileage per student and the non-use of vehicles above 100% of occupancy.

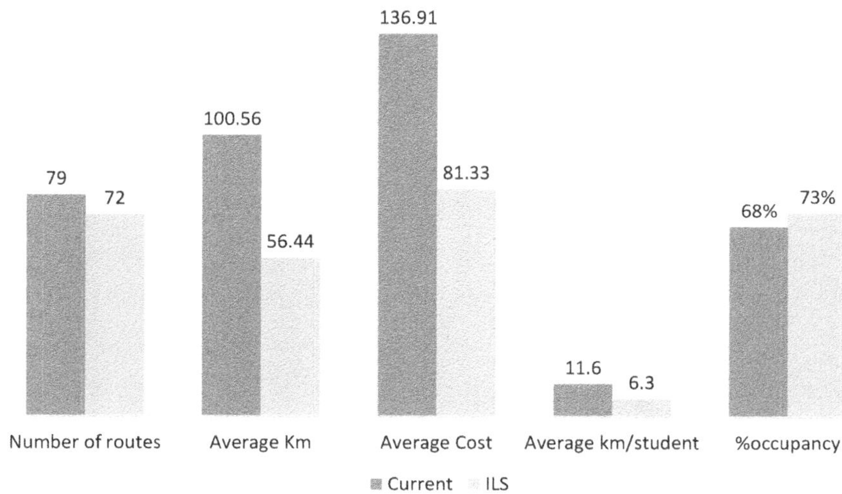

Fig. 3. Performance and occupancy comparison

After validating the results, we applied the method to all 1,012 instances. Figure 4 shows a summary of the results obtained in terms of cost and deviation between the average of the solutions and the best solutions. We divide the instances into groups according to the number of students (horizontal axis of the graph) and, for each group, the following are presented:

- Average Cost*: average of the best costs obtained for the instances in the group
- Average Cost**: average of the average costs obtained for the instances of the group
- Cost Deviation: percentage difference between Average Cost* and Average Cost**

Considering the use of different types of vehicles on the routes, we see in Fig. 5 that the most used vehicles were the Kombi and Van, for 56% and 22% of the routes, respectively. This data is justified when we evaluate together with Fig. 2, which shows a greater number of instances with up to 36 students. Also in this sense, these two smaller vehicles are responsible for transporting 50% of students. Finally, we found that only the vehicle Kombi had an average occupancy lower than 80%. This result is expected because, for all routes with less than 8 students, this type of vehicle is allocated, since it is the minimum capacity.

Presenting the results closer to an application, Fig. 6 shows an illustration of the average cost per municipality through a heat map. The municipality with the lowest average cost obtained 3.92, and the municipality with the highest cost 1,272.63. The map shows a concentration of municipalities with the highest average cost in the northwest Rio de Janeiro.

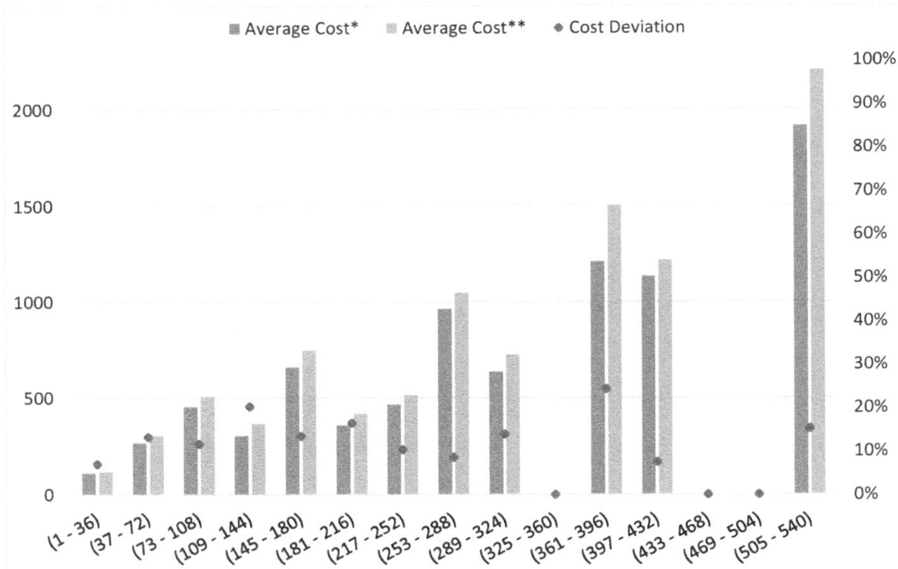

Fig. 4. Average costs and deviations

Figure 7 shows the illustration of the average distance per student in each municipality. The municipality with the lowest indicator had 0.78 km/student, and the municipality with the highest indicator had 133.8 km/student. The average vehicle occupancy is shown in Fig. 8. The municipalities with the lowest occupancy are concentrated in the metropolitan region, with 12.5% occupancy. There is a larger concentration of municipalities with an occupancy percentage above 72% in the Northwest Fluminense and Serrana regions.

Analyzing the computational times, we obtained the results for instances with up to 292 students in up to 52 s, on average. From the instance with 292 students, we observed an exponential increase in computational time.

Still, for the largest instance, with 534 students, we obtained the results in 207 s (3.45 min). It can be noticed then that, for the context of planning and defining the routes, we obtained the results in low computational time, being the application of the method possible in practice.

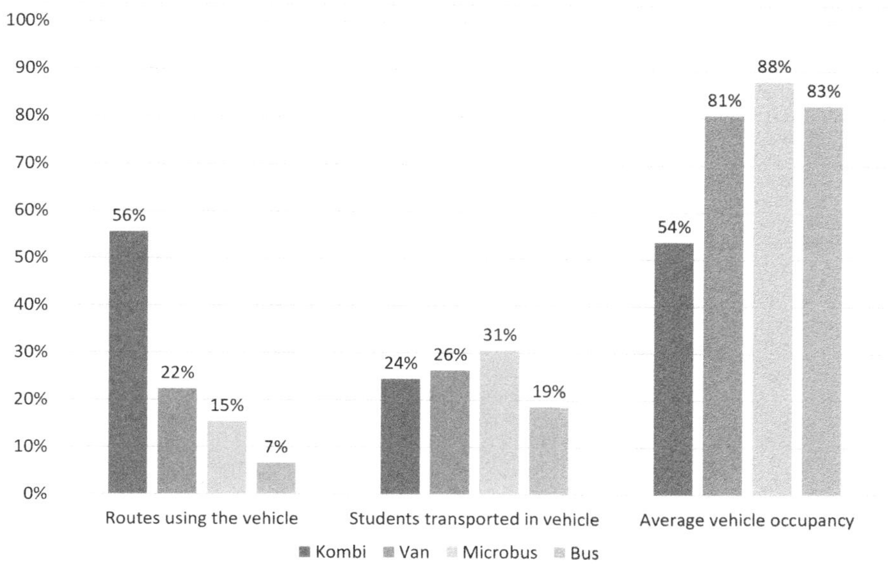

Fig. 5. Vehicle analyses

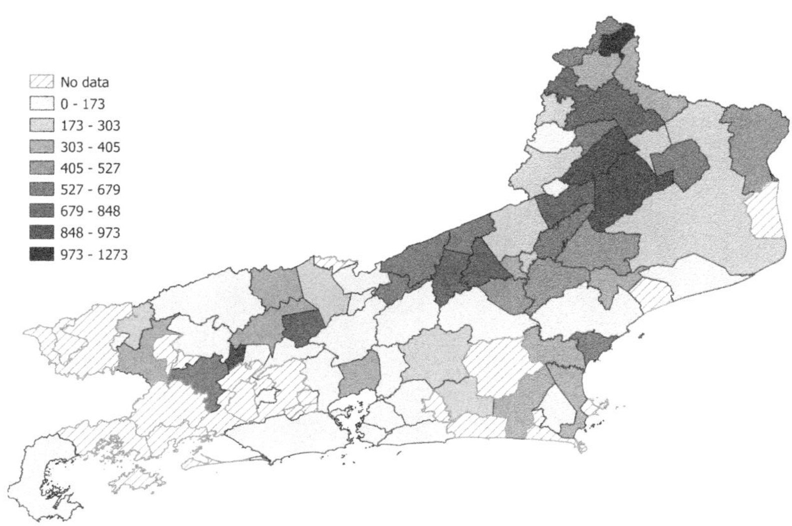

Fig. 6. Average cost per municipality

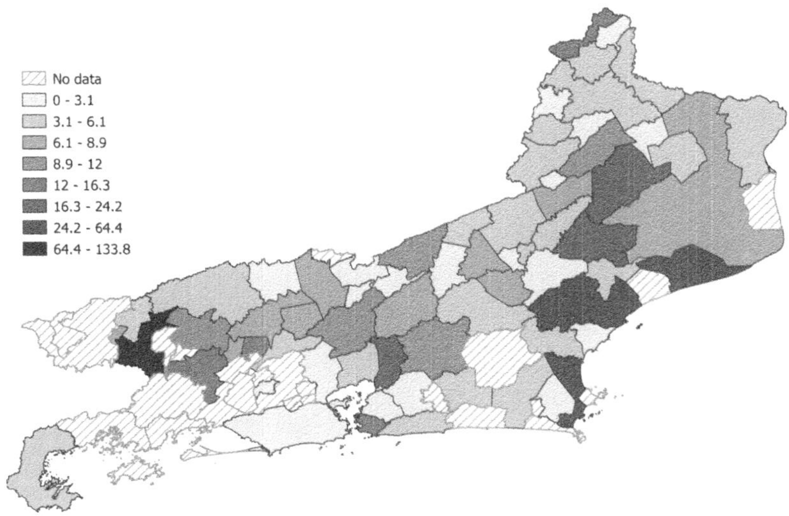

Fig. 7. Average distance per student

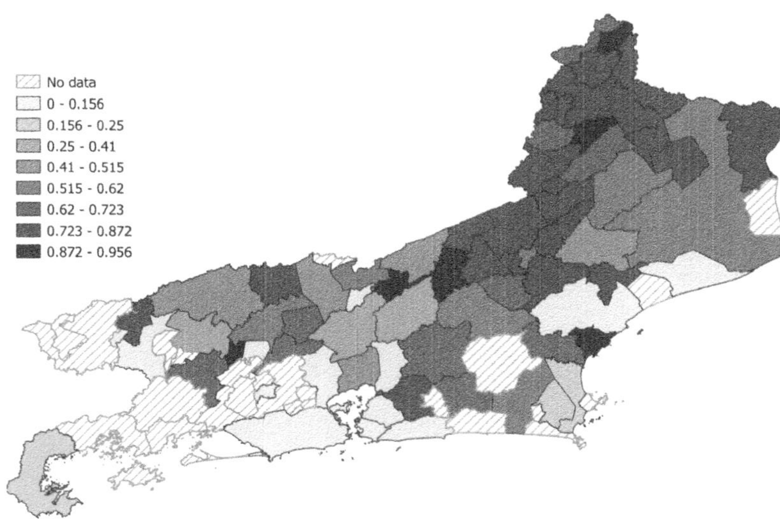

Fig. 8. Average occupancy

6 Conclusions and Future Works

The main objective of this paper was to apply the Iterated Local Search to define rural school transport routes in the state of Rio de Janeiro. For this, we analyze the real location data of students and schools, and after processing the data, we applied the method to the routing of 13,664 students.

Considering the SBRP classification criteria, the application case has as a sub-problem the generation of routes with a single school since the routing is done by each school, not allowing mixed loading. In addition, the data used are from rural areas, characterized by low population density, resulting in greater distances between homes and school units. Thus, in addition to the vehicle capacity, the maximum distance to be covered was also used to restrict the problem.

We analyzed the available data of 79 real routes, allowing comparison with the results of the application of the ILS. The results showed an 8.8% reduction in the number of vehicles needed. The reduction in the average cost of the routes was 40.5%, and the average mileage per student was reduced by 46%. With the validation of the method, we applied the algorithm to the totality of the data, considering 1,012 instances. There was a concentration of municipalities with the highest cost in the state's northwest region. Regarding the average mileage per student, the municipality with the highest indicator had 133.8 km/student. We conclude, therefore, that the algorithm used provides, in low computational time, results that can be assessed by the government as alternatives for reformulating rural school transport routes, bringing financial gains, and increasing the level of service for students.

We suggest, as future work, the consideration of different scenarios of problem characteristics, such as multiple schools and mixed loading. If the variations are performed using the same data set as this study, there is the possibility of presenting comparative analyses. In addition, the variation of the parameters used in the ILS is indicated, including local search and perturbation strategies.

References

1. Avilés-González, J.F., Mora-Vargas, J., Smith, N.R., Cedillo-Campos, M.G.: Artificial intelligence and DOE: an application to school bus routing problems. Wirel. Netw. **26**(7), 4975–4983 (2020)
2. Bektaş, T., Elmastaş, S.: Solving school bus routing problems through integer programming. J. Oper. Res. Soc. **58**(12), 1599–1604 (2007)
3. Calvete, H.I., Galé, C., Iranzo, J.A., Toth, P.: A partial allocation local search matheuristic for solving the school bus routing problem with bus stop selection. Mathematics **8**(8), 1214 (2020)
4. Carvalho, W.L., da Cruz, R.O.M., Câmara, M.T., de Aragão, J.J.G.: Rural school transportation in emerging countries: The Brazilian case. Res. Transp. Econ. **29**(1), 401–409 (2010)
5. Ceperj, F.: População residente por situação do domicílio. estado do rio de janeiro e seus municípios - 1970 a 2010 (2019). http://encurtador.com.br/mFGLV
6. Dang, L.X., Hou, Y.E., Liu, Q.S., Kong, Y.F.: A hybrid metaheuristic algorithm for the bi-objective school bus routing problem. IAENG Int. J. Comput. Sci. **46**(3), 409–416 (2019)
7. Ellegood, W.A., Solomon, S., North, J., Campbell, J.F.: School bus routing problem: contemporary trends and research directions. Omega **95**, 102056 (2019)
8. Hou, Y.E., Dang, L., Dong, W., Kong, Y.: A metaheuristic algorithm for routing school buses with mixed load. IEEE Access **8**, 158293–158305 (2020)

9. Hou, Y.E., Dang, L., Kong, Y., Wang, Z., Zhao, Q.: A hybrid metaheuristic algorithm for the heterogeneous school bus routing problem and a real case study. IAENG Int. J. Comput. Sci. **47**(4), 775–785 (2020)
10. IBGE: Rio de Janeiro (2020). https://www.ibge.gov.br/cidades-e-estados/rj/.html
11. Idoeta, P.A., Magenta, M.: Transporte escolar, livros didáticos e outros programas: o impacto do corte de gastos na educação básica. BBC News Brasil (2019). https://www.bbc.com/portuguese/brasil-48273329
12. Kirkpatrick, S., Gelatt, C.D., Jr., Vecchi, M.P.: Optimization by simulated annealing. In: Readings in Computer Vision, pp. 606–615. Elsevier (1987)
13. Laporte, G.: The vehicle routing problem: an overview of exact and approximate algorithms. Eur. J. Oper. Res. **59**(3), 345–358 (1992)
14. Lenstra, J.K., Kan, A.R.: Complexity of vehicle routing and scheduling problems. Networks **11**(2), 221–227 (1981)
15. Lourenço, H.R., Martin, O.C., Stützle, T.: Iterated local search. In: Glover, F., Kochenberger, G.A. (eds.) Handbook of Metaheuristics. ISOR, vol. 57, pp. 320–353. Springer, Boston (2003). https://doi.org/10.1007/0-306-48056-5_11
16. Lysgaard, J., López-Sánchez, A.D., Hernández-Díaz, A.G.: A matheuristic for the minmax capacitated open vehicle routing problem. Int. Trans. Oper. Res. **27**(1), 394–417 (2020)
17. Mladenović, N., Hansen, P.: Variable neighborhood search. Comput. Oper. Res. **24**(11), 1097–1100 (1997)
18. Newton, R.M., Thomas, W.H.: Design of school bus routes by computer. Socioecon. Plann. Sci. **3**(1), 75–85 (1969)
19. Oudouar, F., El Miloud, Z.: A hybrid heuristic for vehicle routing problem. In: Proceedings of the 4th International Conference on Big Data and Internet of Things, pp. 1–5 (2019)
20. Park, J., Kim, B.I.: The school bus routing problem: a review. Eur. J. Oper. Res. **202**(2), 311–319 (2010)
21. Pisinger, D., Ropke, S.: A general heuristic for vehicle routing problems. Comput. Oper. Res. **34**(8), 2403–2435 (2007)
22. Porto, M.F., Sarubbi, J.F.M., Thiéry, S., da Silva, C.M., Nunes, N.T.R., de Carvalho, I.R.V.: Developing a GIS for rural school transportation in Minas Gerais, Brazil. In: 6th International Multi-Conference on Complexity, Informatics and Cybernetics, IMCIC 2015 and 6th International Conference on Society and Information Technologies, ICSIT 2015-Proceedings, vol. 1, pp. 62–67. Citeseer (2015)
23. Rosa, B.A.B.: Uma Metodologia para Roteamento de Veículos Escolares Utilizando Sistemas de Informação Geográfica. Master's thesis, PUC-Rio (2018)
24. de Souza Lima, F.M.: A mixed load rural school bus routing problem with heterogeneous fleet: a study for the Brazilian problem (2015)
25. Vidal, T., Battarra, M., Subramanian, A., Erdoğan, G.: Hybrid metaheuristics for the clustered vehicle routing problem. Comput. Oper. Res. **58**, 87–99 (2015)
26. Žerovnik, J.: Heuristics for NP-hard optimization problems: simpler is better!? Logist. Sustain. Transp. **6**(1), 1–10 (2015)

Hinterland Intermodal Transport Routing as an Added Value Tool for Port Community Systems: A Colombian Case Study

Adriana Moros-Daza[1(✉)], René Amaya-Mier[1], Guisselle García[1], and Stefan Voß[2]

[1] Departamento de Ingeniería Industrial, Universidad del Norte, Barranquilla, Colombia
{amoros,ramaya,gagarcia}@uninorte.edu.co

[2] Institute of Information Systems (IWI), University of Hamburg, Hamburg, Germany
stefan.voss@uni-hamburg.de

Abstract. In the context of port communities, one of the most commonly used technological developments are Port Community Systems (PCS). The typical service offer of a PCS includes information exchange, electronic exchange of customs declarations and responses, control, tracking and tracing of the goods, and statistics. However, it has been argued that it is necessary to evolve the existing PCS into a renewed version, more suitable to the novel requirements posed by both developed and emerging economies, also incorporating the surge of new technologies. Such renovation should care for integrating new value-added services to the aforementioned typical PCS service offer. Therefore, we propose a new hinterland intermodal routing service to be included to the regular PCS functionality. Such new service is based on the development of a built-in optimization model, delivering a sustainable and cost-effective intermodal transport network. The proposed hinterland intermodal routing service could help mitigating the environmental impact of the Colombian hinterland transport and the national transportation costs, increasing the nation's competitiveness and sustainability through a value-added service of a PCS.

Keywords: Freight transport · Intermodality · Port community systems · Intermodal routing service · Optimization model

1 Introduction

Electronic collaboration is a key business process differentiator. Particularly in logistics, it facilitates transactions and enhances performance and visibility, hence improving the competitiveness of firms in the global markets [7]. The port industry is not an exception, and the electronic collaboration trend increases day

J. de Armas et al. (Eds.): ICCL 2022, LNCS 13557, pp. 177–197, 2022.
https://doi.org/10.1007/978-3-031-16579-5_13

by day [8,38]. In the context of port communities, one of the most commonly used technological developments are Port Community Systems (PCS) [20,45]. A PCS can be defined as an inter-organizational system for promoting commercial services and information exchange between the port to their customers and a variety of stakeholders, such as forwarders, carriers, importers, exporters, customs, among others [20,24,45]. This solution has been used for more than 30 years in different countries to achieve competitiveness in their foreign trade activities [20,31]. The typical services of a PCS are [20]:

- Information exchange between transport operators in the port and for hinterland connections, the port users, customs, port and other authorities, commonly known as Electronic Data Interchange (EDI). Easy, fast and efficient EDI information exchange, re-use and centralisation, is assumed to be available 24/7/365.
- Electronic exchange of customs declarations and customs responses, and cargo releases between private parties and customs.
- Electronic handling of all information regarding import and export of containerized, general and bulk cargo for the port community.
- Status information and control, tracking and tracing goods through the whole logistics chain.
- Processing declarations of dangerous goods with the responsible authorities.
- Processing of maritime and other statistics.

Previous studies [33,35] call for the need to evolve the existing PCS and adapt them to new markets, due to the increase of new technologies and the growth of emerging economies around the world. Moreover, [35,36] report special features, mostly related to the freight hinterland transport processes, to consider in order to increasingly fit the PCS value offer to specifications posed by emerging economies, as is the case of Colombia. One way to meet the specifications of emerging economies and evolve PCS is to include new services as added value. Thus, we propose a hinterland intermodal service as an added value service for the current PCS, taking into account that intermodal freight transport is essential for economical development, assuming given aims to efficiently combine the use of different types of transport, to generate cost efficiencies and environmental savings [10].

In this study, we propose a prototype for a hinterland transportation routing module developed for emerging economies, although of good service for any other contexts. Such prototype measures the impact of use of an intermodal transport network by executing an optimization model. We use the case of Colombia as a testbed and the results of the optimization model are to be used as inputs for the PCS intermodal service.

The paper is composed of the following sections: Sect. 2 includes a description of the current situation of the freight transport in Colombia. Section 3 exposes a brief description of the related works around freight transport optimization. Section 4 discusses the model description for the optimization of the freight transport system in Colombia with the use of intermodality. Section 5 provides the generic system design of the hinterland transport module design for a PCS, with a proposed PCS architecture and a PCS prototype scheme. Finally, Sect. 6 presents the main conclusions and further research directions.

2 Colombian Hinterland Freight Transport

In 1991, Colombia experienced structural changes regarding its logistic activities and its port communities, because of the issue of different laws and policies. One of the most significant laws was Law 001, which modified the Colombian Port Regime and privatized the ports of the country. The main objective was to modernize the system, reduce tariffs and improve port efficiency. The current port system consists of 122 facilities, of which 5 correspond to regional port companies, 7 are private service companies, 9 are public service companies, 10 are coastal docks for smaller ships, 44 are approved docks, and 47 are other kinds of port facilities. The main maritime ports are: the regional port companies of Barranquilla, Cartagena, Buenaventura and Santa Marta [1]. Also, note that although there is rail transport in Colombia, this is only used for a single type of cargo (coal) and is privatized. The hinterland movement of freight is done mostly by road transport or, in some specific cases, by river transport [1,34].

2.1 Road Transport

As mentioned above, the road transport in Colombia is predominant with respect to other types of transport such as rail and river. Investments in Colombia are mostly allocated in infrastructure for the road transport, after a misguided policy which historically put aside other transport modes, most probably due to economic bets towards endogenous industrialization that set competitiveness as a low priority issue [16]. During the 20th century, the Colombian government, as the central country policy maker, historically failed to promote the transportation industry; on the contrary, country politicians, on one hand, were tied to particular business interests, which determined that the deployment of transportation in Colombia, the structure of communication and infrastructure projects, depended on patronage and relationships with specific sectors [9]. On the other hand, we saw the desire of the political class to implement changes, but without a proper budget management nor the skills to solve extant conflicts, i.e., the lack of articulation of the railway lines or the deterioration of these due to technical malpractice. At the times, road transport made up for the insufficiencies of the railway and waterways by facilitating the unification of distribution and consumption centers in the internal market [43]. Currently, the biggest issue of the country regarding freight transport is oriented to network transport. Instead of having a primary network oriented to connect large cities, and large cities with ports and border crossings, it is avoiding cities that are not in the region. Colombia has a primary network traced after 1925 following the vagaries of topography, with higher fuel costs and precarious security. The problem of the Colombian primary road network is not only quantitative (delay in investment), but also qualitative (dysfunctional for trade) [5]. However, the main objective of the Ministry of Transport is the formulation and adoption of policies, plans, programs, projects and economic regulation regarding transportation, transit and infrastructure of the road, maritime, river, rail and air transport modes and technical regulation [29].

2.2 River Transport

In Colombia most of the investments in infrastructure and river transport are made to the Magdalena River. As for the costs of river transport, fuel costs are about 50% to 60% of the total costs of river transport services, in both cases: passenger and freight transport. Taxes on river freight transportation are based on the usage rates of river infrastructure, port taxes, fuel taxes and income taxes. The taxes on fuels are similar to those applied to road transport. There is a significant difference in the fuel used for maritime ships, which is exempt from the aforementioned taxes [30].

2.3 Environmental Impact

Freight transport is one of the biggest generators of CO_2 emissions around the world, and in the same way generates other types of impacts such as the decrease in soil quality, or river erosion. In Colombia, it is expected that the transport sector will increase its energy consumption from 330,000 TJ in 2010 to close to 1,000,000 TJ in 2040, including the effects of the scraping plan. In this scenario, CO_2 emissions could increase from 24 to 64 million tons of CO_2 in the same period [40].

2.4 Intermodal Freight Transport

Nowadays, Colombia has a low productivity in the transport sector. Much of this is reflected by the high informality of road freight transport, only 25% of the companies are formal. Added to this, the average age of the vehicle fleet is among the highest in Latin America [2]. The average age of the vehicle fleet turns out to be approximately 23 years, while in countries such as Germany it is approximately 4 years, United Kingdom 5 years and in Latin American countries such as Peru and Brazil it is approximately 13 years [2]. This implies problems of road and cargo safety and congestion on the highways. In addition, the environmental damage is higher, because the CO_2 emissions generated by this aged vehicle fleet are 1.4 times higher than newer vehicles; proportionally, the transport costs are higher and the quality of the service provided decreases [12]. In addition, port community stakeholders report barriers associated to the hinterland transport in Colombia, such as the lack of loading and unloading areas. This impacts the transport costs, tending to be quite high in the country. While in countries like the United States for every 100 dollars sold, 8 dollars are paid, in Colombia, it turns out to be for every 100 dollars sold, 15 dollars are paid [15]. Another problem regarding the hinterland freight transport is that, on average, the hours expected to transport from an origin to a destination in the same region is 7.4 h, affecting the competitiveness and quality of service provided to the client. The South Central-Amazon region represents a major logistical challenge for the arrival of merchandise, which takes around 18 h [15], as well as for the hiring of a vehicle. Currently, the hinterland freight transport in Colombia is as follows: The cargo arrives at the port, which we call the port of origin, in which the documentation, inspection, unloading, transport of merchandise, and dispatch are carried out. The carrier arrives at the port providing a document that authorizes the entrance to the port to unload a certain amount of cargo. Once everything is verified and approved, the quantity is deducted from the inventory and the truck is removed from the port and starts the journey to its point of destination of the cargo. Once this is reached, the cargo is unloaded.

3 Related Work

This section presents a summary review of influential researches about approaches and procedures used for the design and adaptation of mathematical models that fit the needs of intermodal transport service or network.

Intermodal transport services are well known around the port industry (practitioners) and among scholars [10]. However, not necessary practitioners and scholars consider the same variables in order to optimize the hinterland transport system available in a country [10,18]. Our study is based on the collaboration between scholars and practitioners to create a holistic mathematical model that can support a service platform (PCS) while considering specific needs of port communities.

Our study is based on the linear programming model provided by Sun and Lang [44], which consider the allocation of routes to transport different products through an intermodal transport network. Its formulation allows for characteristics such as an intermodal transport network based on the use of rail networks with flexible service time. In addition, this work takes into account carbon dioxide emissions, as a factor for the analysis of the objective function in terms of the cost implied by these emissions. Another important study is proposed by Bierwirth et al. [6] in which they deal with intermodal transport using road and rail networks for the shipment of large volumes of goods. This case study is applied to the distribution system of a company in Europe, where the impact of costs and the impact of optimal modal split are studied.

Macharis and Bontekoning [25] present a classification of Operations Research (OR) models and techniques implemented in intermodal transport. In this study, the objectives and specific decisions of different operators are categorized, according to the type of decision makers, like, transport operator, network operator, terminal operator and intermodal operator. Verma and Verter [46] propose a bi-objective analytical framework to establish the most appropriate cargo shipment plan for regular and hazardous materials in an intermodal rail/truck transport network. Also [11] provide a mixed-integer linear programming model to examine the impact of planning transport modes and the management of empty containers in intermodal transport, with the aim of minimizing the total cost of transporting empty containers. In 2015, Li et al. [23], proposed an intermodal freight transport network model and a multilevel freight transport planning approach for a container flow control problem. In this research, mode changes are applied in the intermodal terminals, as limitations in the physical logistics infrastructure, time-dependent transport times, and train and barge programming. In order to meet dynamic transport demands and traffic conditions, a backward horizon control approach is proposed and various scenarios are analyzed through the execution of several simulation experiments. The research of [4] proposes a model of sustainable cargo planning with multiple objectives, taking into account several decisions such as the mode of transport (intermodal transport selection), additional services and subcontracting, cargo allocation, transshipment operations, minimization of the total transport cost and CO_2 emissions, and simultaneously maximize customer satisfaction. This is a research applied in real life, to a large-scale international logistics company in Turkey. We should note in passing that a whole bunch of research links this topic to information systems as, e.g., the port-IO system of [17].

Nevertheless, most of the studies about intermodal freight transport systems focus on single cost targets and present hypothetical case studies instead of real-life applications [10,41]. Most of the available studies coincide in using a single directional load flow from the origin to the destinations. It is necessary to consider that both, the export and import of merchandise, must be taken into account in intermodal linear programming models, while satisfying bidirectional demands between cities. Another important aspect are the transshipment operations in ports and terminals, exchange of cargo in ports, usually not taken into account in most models.

4 Model Description

As mentioned above, several studies have been carried out demonstrating the efficiency of intermodal transport based on reduction of costs and environmental impact. One of these works is [22], showing how costs are impacted, specifically by the truck - train combination commonly used in European intermodal transport. The trends in the literature show mostly the difference between costs using an intermodal network and using only a road transport network. It is found that intermodal transport tends to decrease total costs much faster if the distance and amount of cargo increase, indicating economies of scale, while in the road mode it tends to remain constant.

In the study by Murphy and Hall [37] they evaluate not only the costs of the modes of transport used, but also the cost and duration of the transfers between modes, since the particular benefits related to the modal segments in each trip may not compensate the costs and duration of the transfers in terminals or points with high congestion or limited technological and fixed capacity.

Similarly, greenhouse gas (GHG) emissions, like the total transportation costs, are lower due to the use of an intermodal transport network. In a study conducted by Impala [19], in which they compare the scenario in which only trucks are used (basic scenario) and a scenario were trucks and barges are used (intermodal scenario) a considerable reduction is evidenced. Furthermore, it was found that the intermodal scenario represents lower GHG emissions compared with the basic scenario (calculated "per kg" base units). However, this study only considered a limited corridor (just one route) and specific products handled by the company [19].

4.1 Transport Network Description

As mentioned above, the freight transport in Colombia has a strong dependence on road transport, since the infrastructure available in other alternate modes, such as river and railways, underperforms or is insufficient. Because of the former, the current logistic performance of the country has been deteriorated. In order to improve the logistic performance of the country we propose an intermodal transport network, since total costs (e.g. per ton-kilometer) tend to decrease much faster if the distance and the amount of the freight transported increases, while in road transport it tends to remain constant [22]. Another factor on which this configuration is significant is regarding the environmental impact. The GHG emissions come mostly from transport activities. The creation of this network is expected to produce lower emissions due to the use of an intermodal transport compared to the current Colombian scenario with exclusive use of land transport. In order to analyze this problem, a linear programming model was developed.

The linear programming model of transport route selection for the intermodal scenario aims to minimize costs [28]. For this reason it is very important to aim to implement strategies that reduce these costs, increase profits and are able to be nationally and internationally competitive, and that implies being attentive to changes and challenges in adopting intermodal transport schemes to distribute the goods and meet the expectations of customers under criteria of costs, time and environmental impact.

It is important to highlight that the environmental impact is becoming an issue of interest for the transport companies in Colombia, mainly, because of the increase of awareness culture towards environmental sustainability. According to the latest results, green logistics projects have been incorporated into logistics processes. 34.1% of the transport companies in Colombia have been working on environmental efficiency projects; 50.5% of these efforts have focused on the renewal and maintenance of the vehicle fleet and on the adequate schedule of docks, achieving a substantial reduction in emissions of CO_2, approximately 30.1% [15].

In this study, the cities of Barranquilla (BAQ), Cartagena (CTG), Santa Marta (ST), and Buenaventura (BUV) as origin cities were selected (main ports). As destinations were selected departments and big cities with great participation in transport flows such as Bogota (BOG), Cundinamarca (CUN), Valle del Cauca and Cali (VCU), Santander and Barrancabermeja (SAN), Antioquia, Medellin and Caldas (ANT), and Nariño (NAR). All along the river, the terminals located in Gamarra (GAM), Puerto Berrio (PTB), Barrancabermeja

(BARR), and Puerto Salgar (PTS) were taken into consideration. Figure 1 shows the current hinterland routes (connection of each node by road) vs. the intermodal alternative.

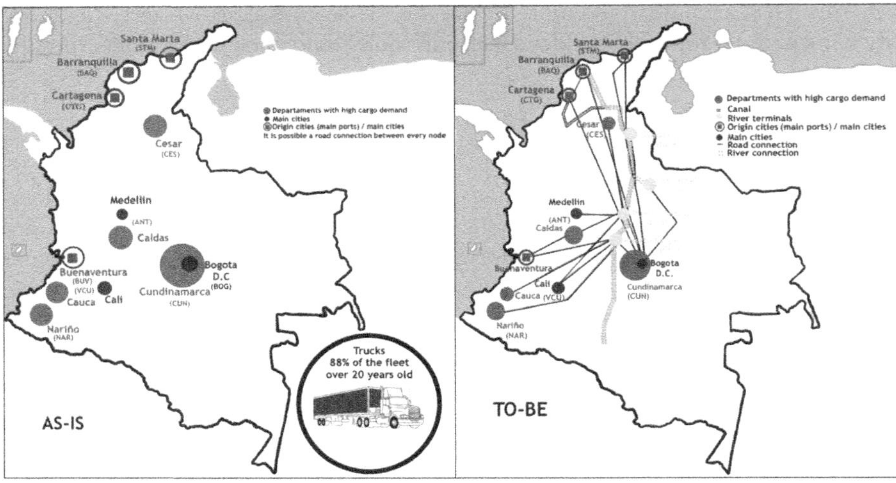

Fig. 1. Nodes and ports considered for the study (AS-IS) - (TO-BE)

4.2 Model Assumptions

For the linear programming model, the following assumptions are taken into account:

- The transport modes to be considered for the model are the river mode (tugboats with barges) and road transport (3-axle truck, 2-axle tractor, 5-axle semi-tractor trailer (3S2) and 6-axle semi-tractor trailer (3S3)). The difference between each type of mode is also related to their capacity; because of this, it will be established how many vehicles or barges are required to transport the cargo from its origin to its destination.
- The capacities corresponding to the trucks are as follows: The 3-axle truck has a fixed capacity of 28 tons, the 2-axle tractor has a capacity of 32 tons, the 5-axle semi-tractor trailer (3S2) has a capacity of 48 tons and the 6-axle semi-tractor trailer (3S3) has a capacity of 52 tons. Regarding the capacity for the barges, each barge has a fixed capacity of 1200 tons and a configuration of six barges per tugboat is allowed to transit in the Magdalena river.
- The cargo transport route must satisfy the demand of a node at a minimum cost. Each node represents an origin or a destination. The route allows a node of interchange or intermodal transshipment. The case can be presented, in which the set of origin cities is not able to satisfy the demand, due to omissions of influential nodes or adverse cases not contemplated in the model.
- The cargo transport route must satisfy the demand of a node with minimum environmental impact. The CO_2 emitted in the routes during transport

activities represent the majority of the total carbon dioxide emissions. In contrast, the amounts of CO_2 emission of the terminal and port operations turn out to be negligible [21].

- The rail network of the country is not taken into account for the modeling, since the infrastructure and the privatization of the networks limits the use of the rail system for any type of cargo other than coal. According to the World Bank, although this type of transport has advantages such as lower operating costs, lower energy consumption and infrastructure capacity, it is not the most efficient for all types of products [39].

4.3 Notations

Table 1 shows the notation used in the optimization model and Table 2 exposes the decision variables of the model.

Table 1. Model parameters

Notation	Description
M_j	Set of cities, $j \in M$
$Mode_k$	Set of transport modes, $k \in Mode$
N_i	Set of city combinations (origin/destination), $i \in N$
P_p	Set of products, $p \in P$
$Arci, k$	Set of arcs (origin/destination i) with its transport mode k
t	Time period, monthly
$A_{i,k,j}$	Matrix of arcs (i, k) with its transport mode, given the city (j) of origin $(+)$ or destination $(-)$
$Cost_i$	Transportation cost between arcs (origin/destination i)
$B_{j,t}$	Offer/demand of each city j in the time period t
$Cco2$	Cost of CO_2 emissions
$U_{j,k}$	Fleet available from city j through the transport mode k
D_i	Distance in km in the arc i
S_k	Tons capacity per transport mode k
FE_k	Emission factor per transport mode k
TC_i	Fuel consumption rate of the transport mode k
$MaxAmb$	Maximum quantity of CO_2 emissions k
Cap_j	Fixed capacity of the node j

Table 2. Model decision variables

Variable	Description
$X_{i,k,p,t}$	Number of tons to be transported of product p through arc i by transport mode k at period time t
$Y_{i,k,p,t}$	Binary variable, 1 if the arc i is open to transport product p by transport mode k at time t, 0 otherwise

A matrix of routes was created in which it is guaranteed that the set of nodes representing the cities or stops are associated with the arcs connecting them; an example is shown in Table 3. This is denoted within the model as $A_{i,k,j}$. It is an MxN matrix, where M represents the cities and N the arcs between the different cities as nodes of origin and destination. The outgoing arcs are expressed by +1 and the incoming arcs by −1, being, respectively, indicators of offer and demand.

Table 3. Matrix of arcs

	i, j	i, l_n	l_n, l_{n+1}	l_{n+1}, j
i	1	1	0	0
l_n	0	−1	1	0
l_{n+1}	0	0	−1	1
j	−1	0	0	−1

4.4 Objective Function

The formulation of the model is based on the minimization of total costs, which are based on the minimization of the sum of the generalized costs corresponding to the transportation of the cargo through the intermodal network (1) and the environmental impact cost generated by carbon dioxide emissions (2).

The transport costs of the route from the origin node to the destination/exchange node are the sum of the linear corresponding components associated to them. These costs represent the variable costs that constitute tolls, fuel, tires and lubricants.

Minimize transport costs

$$\sum_{(i,k)\in arc} \sum_{p\in P} \frac{X_{i,k,p,t}}{S_k} * Cost_i \tag{1}$$

The environmental component of the objective function (2) is based on the distance (unit: KM) of the specified sections from node to node, the volume of cargo that must be moved (unit: Ton) and the emission factor (unit: $kgCO_2$/Ton.KM). According to the emission factors for cargo transport taken from the GHG Protocol tool, the emission factor for articulated vehicles is 0.167 $kgCO_2$/Ton.KM and for barges corresponds to 0.027 $kgCO_2$/Ton.KM.

Minimize emissions costs

$$\sum_{(i,k)\in arc} \sum_{p\in P} D_i * FE_k * TC_k * \frac{X_{i,k,p,t}}{S_k} * Cco2 \tag{2}$$

4.5 Constraints

The restriction (3) corresponds to the flow balance of the cargo sent of product p through arc i, by transport mode k which must be equal to the offer or demand of the node j. In this restriction the matrix $A_{i,k,j}$ represents the routes and links between arcs and cities used.

This restriction is important in the operation of the model, because it is the one that allows controlling the flow balances presented in the interaction of the nodes. For the formulation the study of Barnhart and Wilson [3] was considered, who proposed that the parameter $B_{j,t}$ represents the offer or demand, and it is subject to:

- If $B_{j,t} > 0$, j is an offer node
- If $B_{j,t} < 0$, j is a demand node
- If $B_{j,t} = 0$, j is a transfer node

$$\sum_{(i,k)\in arc} X_{i,k,p,t} * A_{i,k,j} = B_{j,t}, \forall j, \forall p, \forall t \tag{3}$$

Restriction (4) controls that the quantities of product p that must be sent through arc i with transport mode k do not exceed the capacities offered by each city j of the transport resources k.

$$\sum_{(i,k)\in arc} \sum_{p\in P} X_{i,k,p,t} \leq U_{j,k} * S_k * Y_{i,k,p,t} \forall j, \forall k, \forall t \tag{4}$$

Restriction (5) regulates the amount of cargo that can be stored in each node; for the case of the offer nodes this is already regulated with the restriction mentioned above; in the nodes of demand as much as it can store is what is requested for each product, which is regulated by the demand equation. Finally, in the case of the transfer nodes, information on their capacities is acquired. Below is the capacity of these terminals according to CORPOCESAR [14], where it should be noted that on average the cargo stays in a transfer node for about three days, so according to the quantities of the cargo transported it is assumed that they meet this capacity.

- Gamarra: 1'500.000 tons
- Barrancabermeja: 443.000 tons
- Puerto Salgar: 215.967 tons
- Puerto Berrio: 215.967 tons

$$\sum_{(i,k)\in arc} \sum_{p\in P} X_{i,k,p,t} * A_{i,k,j} \leq Cap_j \forall j, \forall t \tag{5}$$

Restriction (6) implies that the carbon dioxide emissions generated through an arc do not exceed the maximum GHG emission parameter $MaxAmb$ reported in ANDEMOS in 2016. This restriction is based on the ages of the vehicles:

- According to the information registered by the Colombian Transport Ministry, 88% of the vehicles of heavy cargo correspond to ages superiors to 20 years. If the vehicle age exceeds more than 20 years, it generates a greater environmental impact. It is estimated that its emissions are 1.4 times ages than those issued by vehicles of lower ages [15].
- The second part of the restriction represents the remaining 12% of the vehicles dating from 1998 until 2018 [15]. The environmental impact generated by the river is very low in comparison with the road one. Because of that there is no differentiating factor for this mode in the restriction.

$$1.4 * \sum_{(i,k)\in arc} \sum_{p\in P} (D_i * FE_k * TC_k * \frac{X_{i,k,p,t}}{S_k}) * 0.88 + 0.12 * \sum_{(i,k)\in arc} \sum_{p\in P} (D_i * FE_k * TC_k * \frac{X_{i,k,p,t}}{S_k}) \\ \leq MaxAmb) \tag{6}$$

4.6 Data

For the development of the model the data was taken from various sources such as:

- Study of the demand of the Colombian river network and cost benefit evaluation, prepared by Steer Davies and Gleave for Cormagdalena [13].
- A tool for consulting the cost of road travel in Colombia, named Infotrip[1].
- An information system of efficient costs for the automotive transport of cargo SICE-TAC[2].
- Colombian Customs' foreign trade statistical system named Comex[3].

The information collected to estimate the demand and offer of the cities that are taken into account in the study, was obtained from the DIAN website, and its tool the Sistema Estadíistico de Comercio Exterior (SIEX)[4] the statistical system of foreign trade. The demand was obtained from the import module, in the chapter of the Customs tariff, Department of Destination tab. The offer was obtained from the same route described above, except for the tab corresponding to the Administration by Customs. For this study we identified 38 types of product families, base on the classification presented by SIEX.

The costs of river freight transport were taken from the study of the Consortium HIDROESTUDIOS - Steer Davies and Gleave [13]. Since the freight matrices of the study are only from the origin cities of Barranquilla and Cartagena, it was assumed that the estimated freight rates for the other connections between river ports were the same as those presented in the study. This was necessary due to the lack of information for the river freight transport in Colombia.

[1] For consulting Infotrip see https://infotrip.net.
[2] For consulting SICE-TAC see http://sicetac.mintransporte.gov.co:8080/sicetacWeb/ejecutar/costos-eficientes.
[3] For consulting the Comex system see http://www.webcomex.com/.
[4] For consulting SIEX see http://websiex.dian.gov.co/.

The road transport costs were extracted from Infotrip and SICE-TAC, the first database only shows the variable costs and the second database the totals, so it will be assumed that the routes that do not appear on the SICE-TAC, will be taken from Infotrip.

4.7 Results

A general analysis is made for the results obtained in the model, which includes monthly results for one year. Figure 2 shows that for the freight transport in Colombia, regardless of the type of product and if only the total costs are taken into account, it will always be better to use the alternate intermodal routes along the river terminals to connect with the destination cities. Also, Fig. 2 shows that the biggest reductions can be obtained in the routes: STM-CUN, STM-ANT, BAQ-ANT, CTG-SAN, BAQ-SAN, BAQ-BOG, and CTG-NAR. It is important to note that those are the routes with an intermodal alternative. While for the routes in which it is necessary to use road transportation only, their costs tend to be quite high compared to those of the intermodal route. In conclusion, it is possible to obtain savings in transport costs using an intermodal route.

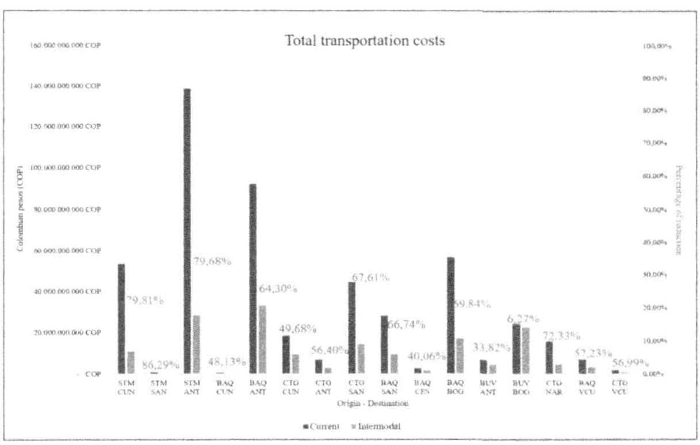

Fig. 2. Transportation cost results per route (origin/destination) (period of time one year)

Figure 3 shows that there is also a reduction regarding CO_2 emissions using an alternative intermodal route. The most significant CO_2 emission reductions are made in the routes: BAQ-ANT, CTG-CUN, CTG-ANT, CTG-SAN, BAQ-SAN, BAQ-BOG, and BAQ-VCU.

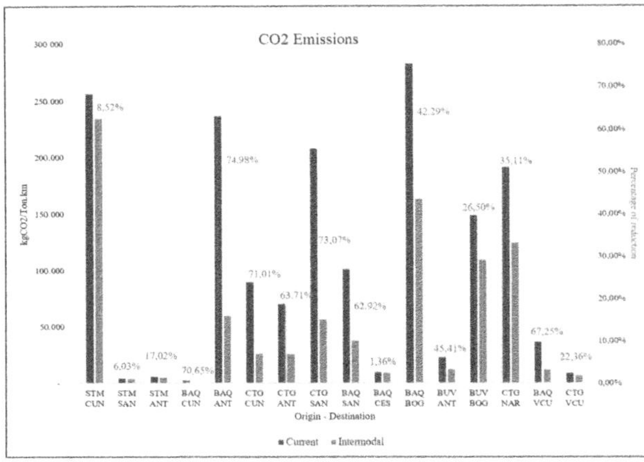

Fig. 3. CO_2 emission results per route (origin/destination) (period of time one year)

Furthermore, the model shows a total reduction of 67% in transportation costs per year and 47% of CO_2 emission on average per year. Finally, as a summary, we can conclude from the results of the mathematical model that:

- It is always more economical to use cargo transshipment in the river for delivering the products in Colombia to their final destination, since the river transport has a greater capacity that enables greater economies of scale. Also, regarding the CO_2 emissions barges are Eco friendlier than trucks. Thus, the intermodal route alternative is more appealing for the system.
- In the case of products with an origin from Buenaventura, road transport is more efficient since this node mainly supplies to its nearby surrounding cities, thus selecting roads as the best transport choice.
- The model chooses as the best intermodal routes to meet the demands: the connections between, origin-Gamarra-destination and origin-Puerto Berrio-destination.
- One of the main results was the average transport cost and CO_2 emission reduction when using the intermodal alternative. The results show that on average the total transport costs could be reduced by 67% and the CO_2 emission by 47%.

However, as a main result we could obtain the most cost-efficient routes for hinterland transport in Colombia for each of the most common 16 origin/destination combinations. Table 4 shows the 16 routes based on the origin and destination of the freight and highlighted in red the route nodes with an intermodal alternative. Also, Table 4 presents a X in the last column if the route has an alternative route using an intermodal transport network.

Table 4. Origin - Destination (routes identification)

Origin	Destination	Route	Alternative intermodal route
SM	CUN	STM - GAM - PTB - CUN	x
SM	SAN	STM - SAN	
SM	ANT	STM - GAM - PTB - ANT	x
BAQ	CUN	BAQ - GAM - PTB - CUN	x
BAQ	ANT	BAQ - GAM - PTB - ANT	x
CTG	CUN	CTG - GAM - PTB - CUN	x
CTG	ANT	CTG - GAM - PTB - ANT	x
CTG	SAN	CTG - SAN	
BAQ	SAN	BAQ - SAN	
BAQ	CES	BAQ - CES	
BAQ	BOG	BAQ - GAM - PTB - BOG	x
BUV	ANT	BUV - ANT	
BUV	BOG	BUV - BOG	
CTG	NAR	CTG - GAM - PTB - NAR	x
BAQ	VCU	BAQ - VCU	
CTG	VCU	CTG - VCU	

5 Generic System Design (Hinterland Transport Module Design)

The generic system design proposes to integrate mobile and web applications, while managing the storage and management of databases on a scalable cloud environment. Thereby, it could connect the importer/exporter with the hinterland transport companies for the schedule, coordination and movement of the cargo.

- Accessibility: A central and inter-operable access to information services for all stakeholders of the port community involved in the hinterland transport of the freight. Internet access is essential to use the transport module.
- Extensibility: The optimization model allows the module to provide environmental statistics regarding the type of route selected to transport the freight.
- Scalability: It refers to the ability of the module to be modified depending on the new requirements of the system in terms of storage power and memory.

– Intuitiveness/Usability: Taking into account the platform on which the prototype of the module (Java Netbeans) was developed, it can be easily restructured and modified by any type of user. An advanced knowledge on computer science is not necessary to make future modifications.

5.1 Service Oriented Architecture

Computer applications have been widely recognized as a help to making business processes more efficient and much faster [27]. However, those applications are based on several/different languages, data structures, protocols and platforms which can lead to high complexity in the information technology infrastructure of a business enterprise [26]. PCS are not the exception [20,32,45], but usually a way to solve the complexity problem is through enterprise application integration as a strategy to merge data from disparate sources. For the PCS architecture we propose a service oriented architecture (SOA), which includes several different computer applications and the integration of a plurality of data sources. SOA has been defined by the World Wide Web Consortium as a set of components which can be invoked, and whose interface descriptions can be published and discovered [42]. It should be noted that the addition from the current PCS architectural scheme is the integration of a freight transport service module. For this module is expected that the data source include systems from providers such as Microsoft and Java, among others. The data sources should include files created or used by applications such as Microsoft Outlook, Word, Excel, Access, as well as files in standard formats such as PNG and PDF, and so forth. Furthermore, it is important to highlight that in order to manage data integration it is necessary to use a graphical user interface (GUI) as a service in a SOA.

5.2 Proposed Prototype

Figure 4 shows a scheme for the hinterland transport routing module interface for a PCS. The added value inputs of the interface are the best cost-efficient intermodal routes of the country. However, for the sake of completeness, the current hinterland alternate routes of the country are also taken into account. As a result, the importer/exporter can arrange in the PCS for the hinterland transport of his/her cargo, devising intermodal options that can reduce the costs and the CO_2 emissions and in spite of his/her lack of familiarity with the local conditions.

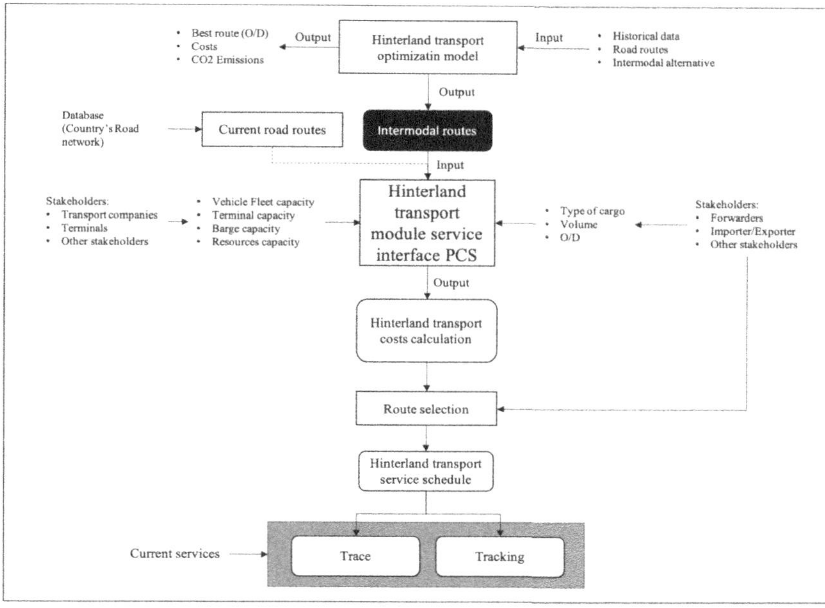

Fig. 4. PCS prototype algorithm scheme – hinterland transport module

As an example of the transport freight module, Fig. 5 presents the proposed prototype user interface. The left side of Fig. 5 shows the minimum requirements that a user needs for programming and scheduling the transport service and the right side shows the different routes that are available based on the users' requirements. Also, the proposed prototype takes into account the process of incorporating new types of users and based on it constantly updates the system.

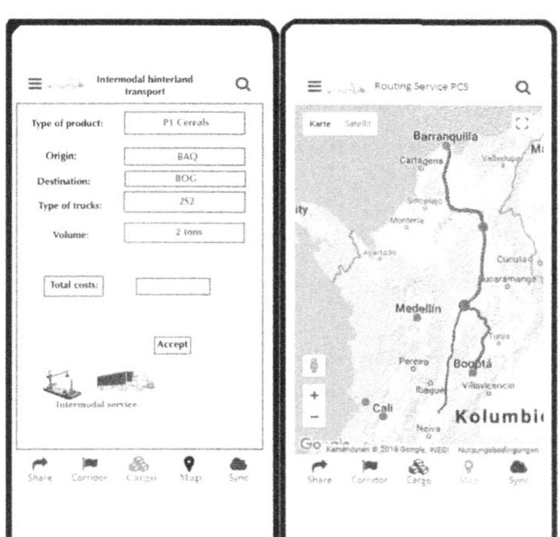

Fig. 5. PCS prototype - hinterland transport module

6 Conclusion

One of the most commonly used technological developments, in the context of port communities, are the Port Community Systems. Basically, those systems focus on: (i) EDI information exchange between all the port community stakeholders, available 24/7/365. (ii) electronic exchange of customs declarations and customs responses, and cargo releases between private parties and customs (iii) electronic handling of all information regarding import and export of containerized, break bulk and bulk cargo for the port community, (iv) status information and control, tracking and tracing of the goods through the whole logistics chain, (v) processing declarations of dangerous goods with the responsible authorities, and (vi) processing of maritime and other statistics.

However, the need to evolve the existing PCS into a renewed version has been argued, more suitable to the novel requirements posed by both developed and emerging economies, and incorporating the surge of new technologies. It was found that such renovation should care for integrating new value-added services to the aforementioned typical PCS services offer. Therefore, we propose a new hinterland intermodal routing service to be included to the regular PCS functionality. The intermodal freight transport has proven to be strategic for the development of national and regional economies, since it enables the efficient interaction of different types of transport to generate positive economic and environmental impacts and facilitation of commercial transactions.

In this work, we introduced an optimization model to mitigate both the environmental impact and transportation costs of the Colombian hinterland. In addition, we proposed to use the results of this model for the creation of an added value transport routing interface for port community systems, in order to fulfill the needs of the Colombian port community as well as to increase the port value-added offer to global users. The optimization model showed that the use of an intermodal hinterland transport network can reduce the total transportation costs about 67% and the CO_2 emission to 47%. This solution could help mitigate the environmental impact of the Colombian hinterland transport and the national transportation costs, increasing the nation's competitiveness and sustainability through a value-added service, which enables programming and coordinating the hinterland transportation system of the import and export cargo of the country.

References

1. Amaya, R., et al.: Intervención sobre Prácticas Integrativas en el Clúster de Logística del Atlántico: Cadenas Logísticas De Comercio Exterior. Ediciones Uninorte (2017)
2. Asociación Colombiana de Vehículos Automotores: Informe Vehiculos Marzo, Colombia 2018 (2018). http://www.andemos.org/wp-content/uploads/2018/04/Informe-Vehiculos-2018-03.pdf

3. Barnhart, C., Wilson, N.: Network problems - transportation operations, planning and control: carrier systems. Lecture Notes (2003). https://ocw.mit.edu/courses/civil-and-environmental-engineering/1-224j-carrier-systems-fall-2003/lecture-notes/lecture4.pdf
4. Baykasoğlu, A., Subulan, K.: A multi-objective sustainable load planning model for intermodal transportation networks with a real-life application. Transp. Res. Part E Logist. Transp. Rev. **95**, 207–247 (2016)
5. Benavides, J.: Plan Maestro de Transporte Intermodal (PMTI) 2015–2035. Report, Financiera de Desarrollo Nacional (FDN) (2015). https://www.repository.fedesarrollo.org.co/handle/11445/2462
6. Bierwirth, C., Kirschstein, T., Meisel, F.: On transport service selection in intermodal rail/road distribution networks. Bus. Res. **5**(2), 198–219 (2012)
7. Bouchard, P., Moros-Daza, A., Voß, S.: Simulation of an AIS system for the port of Hamburg. In: Mes, M., Lalla-Ruiz, E., Voß, S. (eds.) ICCL 2021. LNCS, vol. 13004, pp. 21–35. Springer, Cham (2021). https://doi.org/10.1007/978-3-030-87672-2_2
8. Caldeirinha, V., Nabais, J.L., Pinto, C.: Port community systems: accelerating the transition of seaports toward the physical internet-the Portuguese case. J. Marine Sci. Eng. **10**(2), 152 (2022)
9. Camargo Bonilla, Y.: Historicity of transport in Colombia, a process of transition and rupturas. Tzintzun. Revista de Estudios Históricos **69**, 193–217 (2019)
10. Caris, A., Macharis, C., Janssens, G.K.: Decision support in intermodal transport: a new research agenda. Comput. Ind. **64**(2), 105–112 (2013)
11. Choong, S.T., Cole, M.H., Kutanoglu, E.: Empty container management for intermodal transportation networks. Transp. Res. Part E Logist. Transp. Rev. **38**(6), 423–438 (2002). https://doi.org/10.1016/S1366-5545(02)00018-2
12. Consejo Privado de Competitividad: Consejo privado de competitividad, informe nacional de competitividad 2017–2018 (2018). https://compite.com.co/informe/informe-nacional-de-competitividad-2017-2018/
13. Consorcio HIDROESTUDIOS S - Steer Davies Gleave: Estudio de Demanda de Transporte del Sistema Fluvial del Río Magdalena y evaluación beneficio costo de la instrumentación de un esquema de reactivación de la navegación fluvial. Report (2014)
14. Corporacíon Autónoma regional del Cesar (CORPOCESAR: Resolucion no. 0309 (2014). https://www.corpocesar.gov.co/files/Resolucion03092014DG.pdf
15. Departamento Nacional de Planeacion (DNP: Encuesta nacional logística 2018 (2018). https://onl.dnp.gov.co/es/Publicaciones/SiteAssets/Paginas/Forms/AllItems/Informe%20de%20resultados%20Encuesta%20Nacional%20Log%C3%ADstica%202018.pdf
16. Duque-Escobar, G.: El transporte en Colombia (2007). https://godues.wordpress.com/2007/04/16/el-transporte-en-colombia-2/
17. Heilig, L., Lalla-Ruiz, E., Voß, S.: port-IO: an integrative mobile cloud platform for real-time inter-terminal truck routing optimization. Flex. Serv. Manuf. J. 504–534 (2017). https://doi.org/10.1007/s10696-017-9280-z
18. Heilig, L., Voß, S.: Inter-terminal transportation: an annotated bibliography and research agenda. Flex. Serv. Manuf. J. **29**(1), 35–63 (2016). https://doi.org/10.1007/s10696-016-9237-7
19. Impala: Multimodalismo reduciendo las emisiones de carbono en Colombia. Report (2014). https://www.impalaterminals.com/media/1166/20150101-impala-reducing-carbon-emissions-in-colombia-in-spanish-ie01331s.pdf

20. IPCSA (International Port Community Systems Association): How to develop a port community system), p. 12 (2015). http://www.ipcsa.international/armoury/resources/ipcsa-guide-english-2015.pdf
21. Irannezhad, E., Hickman, M., Prato, C.: Modeling the efficiency of a port community system as an agent-based process. Procedia Comput. Sci. **109**, 917–922 (2017)
22. Janic, M.: Modelling the full costs of an intermodal and road freight transport network. Transp. Res. Part D Transp. Environ. **12**(1), 33–44 (2007)
23. Li, L., Negenborn, R.R., De Schutter, B.: Intermodal freight transport planning - a receding horizon control approach. Transp. Res. Part C Emerging Technol. **60**, 77–95 (2015)
24. Long, A.: Port community systems. World Customs J. **3**(1), 63–67 (2009)
25. Macharis, C., Bontekoning, Y.M.: Opportunities for or in intermodal freight transport research: a review. Eur. J. Oper. Res. **153**(2), 400–416 (2004)
26. Mamou, J.C., Scheffler, L.: Services oriented architecture for handling metadata in a data integration platform. US Patent App. 11/066,321 (2005)
27. Mamou, J.C., Toum, C.: User interface service for a services oriented architecture in a data integration platform. US Patent 7,814,142 (2010)
28. Min, H.: International intermodal choices via chance-constrained goal programming. Transp. Res. Part A General **25**(6), 351–362 (1991)
29. Ministerio de Transporte: Decreto 87 de 2011 (2011). https://www.funcionpublica.gov.co/eva/gestornormativo/norma_pdf.php?i=64906
30. Ministerio de Transporte: Plan Maestro Fluvial de Colombia 2015 (2015). https://www.mintransporte.gov.co
31. Moros-Daza, A., Amaya-Mier, R., Garcia-Llinas, G., Voß, S.: Port community system adoption: game theoretic framework for an emerging economy case study. In: Paternina-Arboleda, C., Voß, S. (eds.) ICCL 2019. LNCS, vol. 11756, pp. 136–153. Springer, Cham (2019). https://doi.org/10.1007/978-3-030-31140-7_9
32. Moros-Daza, A., Amaya-Mier, R., García-Llinas, G., Voß, S.: Port community system design for emerging economies: case study Barranquilla, Colombia. In: International Conference on Industrial Engineering and Operations Management, pp. 308–318. IEEE (2021)
33. Moros-Daza, A., Amaya-Mier, R., Paternina-Arboleda, C.: Port community systems: a structured literature review. Transp. Res. Part A Policy Practice **133**, 27–46 (2020)
34. Moros-Daza, A., Cassandro-De La Hoz, D., Jaller-Martelo, M., Paternina-Arboleda, C.D.: Using advanced information systems to improve freight efficiency: results from a pilot program in Colombia. In: Paternina-Arboleda, C., Voß, S. (eds.) ICCL 2019. LNCS, vol. 11756, pp. 22–38. Springer, Cham (2019). https://doi.org/10.1007/978-3-030-31140-7_2
35. Moros-Daza, A., Lalla-Ruiz, E., Heilig, L., Amaya-Mier, R., Voß, S.: Feasibility study for the adoption of a port community system: the case of Barranquilla, Colombia (2019, submitted)
36. Moros-Daza, A., Solano, N.C., Amaya-Mier, R., Paternina-Arboleda, C.: A multivariate analysis for the creation of port community system approaches. Transp. Res. Procedia **30**, 127–136 (2018)
37. Murphy, P.R., Hall, P.K.: The relative importance of cost and service in freight transportation choice before and after deregulation: an update. Transp. J. **35**(1), 30–38 (1995)

38. Posti, A., Häkkinen, J., Tapaninen, U.: Promoting information exchange with a port community system-case Finland. Int. Supply Chain Manage. Collab. Practices **4**, 455–471 (2011)
39. Revista Dinero: La evolución del transporte ferroviario y vial en Colombia. Semana (2018). https://www.dinero.com/economia/articulo/la-evolucion-del-transporte-ferroviario-y-vial-en-colombia/223410
40. Ruiz-Paz, C.M.: A successful evolution from classical public administration to new public administration. The Colombian Ministry of Environment and Sustainable Development (2014)
41. Schulte, F., Lalla-Ruiz, E., González-Ramírez, R.G., Voß, S.: Reducing port-related empty truck emissions: a mathematical approach for truck appointments with collaboration. Transp. Res. Part E Logist. Transp. Rev. **105**, 195–212 (2017)
42. Sprott, D., Wilkes, L.: Understanding service-oriented architecture. Archit. J. **1**(1), 10–17 (2004)
43. Su, C.S.P., Sanín, J.A.: Historia del transporte y la infraestructura en Colombia (1492–2007), vol. 1. Ministerio de Transporte (2008). https://web.mintransporte.gov.co/
44. Sun, Y., Lang, M.: Modeling the multicommodity multimodal routing problem with schedule-based services and carbon dioxide emission costs. Math. Probl. Eng. **2015**, 406218 (2015)
45. Tsamboulas, D., Ballis, A.: Port community systems: requirements, functionalities and implementation complications. In: Selected Proceedings of the 13th World Conference of Transport Research, Rio de Janeiro (2013)
46. Verma, M., Verter, V., Zufferey, N.: A bi-objective model for planning and managing rail-truck intermodal transportation of hazardous materials. Transp. Res. Part E Logist. Transp. Rev. **48**(1), 132–149 (2012)

Integrated Path Planning and Task Assignment Model for On-Demand Last-Mile UAV-Based Delivery

Jose Escribano(✉), Huan Chang, and Panagiotis Angeloudis

Imperial College London, London SW7 2AZ, UK
jose.escribano-macias11@imperial.ac.uk

Abstract. Recent technological advancements and investments have transformed Unmanned Aerial Vehicles (UAVs) into a credible and reliable tool for the provision of on-demand last-mile logistics services. Nevertheless, few studies have developed integrated task assignment and path planning models that consider dynamic environments and stochastic demand generation. This paper addresses this research gap by developing a reinforcement learning path planning approach, coupled with a task assignment model formulated as a mixed-integer programming problem. The performance of task assignment model is evaluated against a dynamic programming method, and a First-In-First-Out heuristic which serves as the baseline. A case study based on the City of London is proposed to demonstrate the applicability of the integrated model. Results demonstrate the effectiveness of the mixed-integer approach in coordinating the UAV fleet compared to the other methods, with the dynamic programming providing higher returns for large fleet sizes.

Keywords: Path planning · Task assignment · Pickup-and-delivery · Unmanned Aerial Vehicle

1 Introduction

Commercial use of Unmanned Aerial Vehicles (UAVs) has increased in recent years due to their low weight and cost. This is illustrated in several reports that estimate the valuation of the Advanced Aerial Mobility (AAM) market, which envisions the use of UAVs for mobility and freight transportation, to reach $1 trillion by 2040 [9,15].

Last-mile delivery represents a key implementation of AAM as it overcomes the increasing congestion of road networks in urban settlements and provides direct connectivity to low accessibility regions. These multi-agent pickup-and-delivery services leverage swarm control to improve UAV collaboration and optimise aerial operations.

While delivery by UAV swarm is composed of two fundamental problems, task assignment (TA) and path planning (PP), a majority of the research in this

J. de Armas et al. (Eds.): ICCL 2022, LNCS 13557, pp. 198–213, 2022.
https://doi.org/10.1007/978-3-031-16579-5_14

topic has focused on TA alone, commonly modelled as a vehicle routing problem [8,16,17]. This practice ignores the complex urban environments UAVs must navigate through, as well as the accurate representation of battery consumption rates as a result of variable payloads [6].

Within the remit of integrated TA-PP, the literature has proposed several solution methods including linear programming approaches [2,14], metaheuristics [1,4,11,13], heuristics [2,5,12], and learning algorithms [10]. Huang et al. [10] and Zhu et al. [19] proposed a self-organising map neural network combined with a velocity synthesis approach and applied their models to underwater robots. Cai et al. [2] developed a 3D-Dubins Multiple Travelling Salesman process for underwater task assignment and path planning. David et al. [5] presented a Hungarian algorithm coupled with a Hamiltonian motion planning process to plan the trajectories of ground vehicles. Biswas et al. [1] designed a Particle-Swarm Optimisation (PSO)[1] coupled with a Nearest-Neighbour Search task allocation approach. Another Neighbourhood Search algorithm is developed by Chen et al. [4] to solve the multi-agent pickup and delivery problem.

To date, several applications of UAV-based integrated task assignment and path planning has been proposed. Moon et al. [14] developed an Mixed-Integer Linear Programming (MILP) based solution with a potential field-based collision avoidance algorithm. Escribano Macias et al. [7] proposed an integrated routing and trajectory optimisation framework using a Large Neighbourhood Search algorithm. Kuru et al. [12] presented a Hungarian algorithm and Monte Carlo technique to dynamically assign and plan 3D UAV routes. Finally, Huo et al. [11] proposed a simulated-annealing based solution using a swap-and-judge strategy.

As seen above, many studies developed metaheuristics which, while resolving scalability issues, result in suboptimal solutions. In addition, few explored the UAV-based pickup-and-delivery problem in dynamic environments under stochastic demand patterns and payload and battery constraints. This is the subject of this paper.

The optimisation framework proposed in this paper comprises an integrated TA-PP algorithm that optimises profit considering energy cost, customer loss as well as obstacle avoidance. A reinforcement learning approach designs UAV flight paths, and a MILP model performs TA. Furthermore, this paper compares the performance of the MILP against a dynamic programming approach (DP), and a first-in-first-out method (FIFO) that serves as the benchmark.

In summary, the contributions of this paper are two-fold:

1. It proposes an integrated TA-PP comprising of a reinforcement learning PP with a TA methodology in a collaborative and dynamic environment.
2. It evaluates the effectiveness of the TA methods in terms of profitability. A sensitivity analysis is carried out to determine the optimal selection of parameters for the objective function.

[1] PSO is a metaheuristic that utilises agents to search the solution-space through the manipulation of their position and their velocity.

The remainder of the paper is structured as follows. An overview of the modelling framework is presented in Sect. 2, along with a detailed description of the TA and PP algorithms in Sect. 3. The experiment and case study is presented in Sect. 4, followed by conclusions and future works in Sect. 5.

2 Model Framework

This paper presents an on-demand UAV-based pick-up and delivery framework for dynamic environments. The model aims to maximise the profitability of the delivery service by determining the optimal UAV path to the delivery target and the assignment of each task to each member of the UAV swarm while considering battery level, location, and payload. We define the UAV swarm as a group of UAVs which have shared knowledge of the tasks being submitted to the swarm for assignment. These decisions are captured by two interrelated components: a task assignment (TA) algorithm, and a path planning (PP) model. The complete framework is presented in Fig. 1.

The TA algorithm allocates customers to UAVs based on customer waiting times, current battery state of charge, and payloads. Thus, a UAV may be assigned multiple deliveries, in which case the pick-up and drop-off sequence must also be determined provided the UAV has sufficient capacity to pick-up multiple delivery items. The problem is formulated as an MILP and is described in Sect. 3.1.

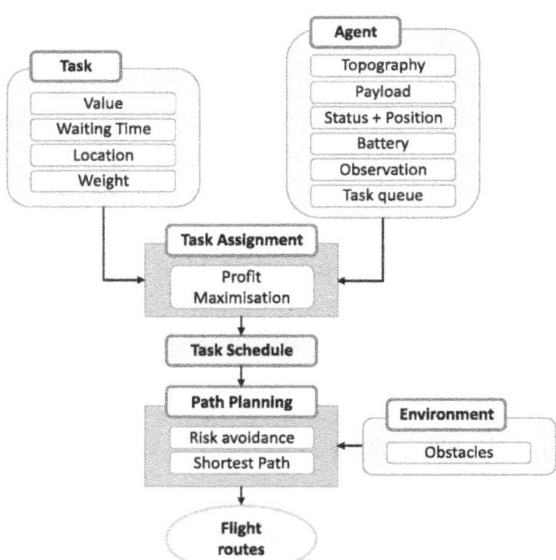

Fig. 1. UAV delivery implementation framework. Agents are indicated in green, with processes in orange, outputs in blue, and final output in yellow. (Color figure online)

The PP process serves to define the UAV path from its current position to the pick-up and drop-off point for each task. Using the UAV weight, location of other members of the swarm, and the surrounding environment, a multi-agent reinforcement learning approach is adopted to minimise collision risk and travel time, where each agent, independently, improve their understanding of the environment and progressively improve their path planning capability as a result of the improved knowledge. Further details on the model are given in Sect. 3.4.

2.1 Modelling Environment

The proposed modelling framework contains two main components: agents and tasks. Agents represent a single UAV in the swarm, while tasks denote the specific job for each agent to complete. An agent contains the following information: a battery capacity B_i, a maximum payload Ψ_i, an observation radius $\mathcal{R}_i$, a database of the explored topography $\mathcal{D}_i$, its current position, a task queue, a path or route to arrive at the destination of the current task that is calculated based on the path planning algorithm, and a state.

At any point, an agent may be in one of the following states:

1. Idle: the agent hovers in place and does not contain a route or task.
2. Pick-up: this task comprises the travelling of the agent to the pick-up location and the actual process of picking up the parcel.
3. Drop-off: as with "Pick-up" but instead of acquiring the parcel, the agent places the payload at the defined destination.
4. Travel to Charger: the agent is moving towards its charging location. Once arriving, the agent task is changed to "Charging".
5. Charging: the agent is charging its battery. Once fully charged, the UAV returns to "Idle" state.

Agent movement through the environment is controlled by the task queue assigned to each agent. A delivery is comprised of two tasks: pick-up and drop-off. Logically, pick-up must always occur before drop-off, but an agent may complete several pick-up tasks in sequence if it has sufficient payload capacity. Every task also contains a specified customer waiting time associated w, a revenue value v, an energy expenditure c, and a status that may be any of the following:

- Unassigned: task not assigned to any agent and is waiting for assignment.
- Ordered: task is assigned to agent but the parcel is yet to be picked-up.
- Picked-up: the agent has collected the parcel, but is yet to be dropped-off at the desired location.
- Completed: the agent has fulfilled the task, and the task is now deleted from the task queue.
- Cancelled: the task has not been fulfilled within w and is deleted from and the task list of any agent. The loss of the customer is added to the total cost.

It is important to note that the agents contain perfect information of all tasks assigned to the swarm.

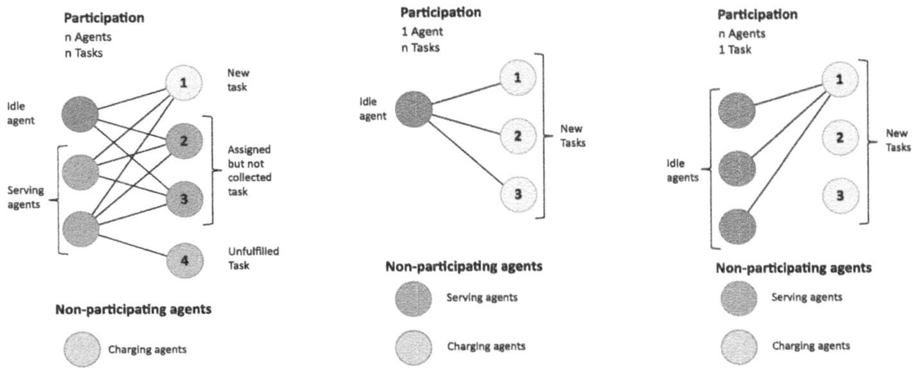

(a) MILP. (b) DP. (c) FIFO.

Fig. 2. Task assignment schematics, where each agent-task connection represents eligibility for task assignment. MILP assigns multiple tasks to a pool of multiple agents. DP assigns multiple tasks to a single idle agent. And FIFO assigns a single task to any of available idle agents.

3 Formulation

This section presents the implementation of the TA and PP algorithms. Three TA models are defined: an MILP, a DP, and a FIFO that serves as a benchmark. A visualisation of their logic is provided in Fig. 2.

3.1 Mixed-Integer Linear Programming Approach

The MILP approach provides a unique property in comparison to the DP and FIFO methods proposed, as it can assign multiple agents to multiple tasks simultaneously. The MILP process is initiated when the following conditions are satisfied: i) an agent changes state, ii) there exists unassigned tasks, and iii) there is at least one agent in state 1–3. Agents in states 4–5 are considered for assignment.

In carrying out task assignment, this method structures the set of tasks as a cost matrix using the following notation:

- An agent location at the start of the assignment A_i for any agent $i \in N$.
- The task set T, comprising of a pick-up and drop-off location (p, d).
- The pick-up and drop-off location set P and D.
- The remaining tasks M_j^i for each agent $i \in N$.
- $y_{j,k}^i$ is a Boolean parameter indicating if transitioning from one location or another is allowed.

Take the example where there are two agents and three tasks. Each agent initiate their assignment at locations A_1 and A_2. Agent 2 has two unfulfilled tasks M_1^2 and M_2^2, while agent 1 has one, M_1^1. Three new tasks T are to be assigned in this process, denoted as a set of pick-up P and a drop-off D locations. There are several logical constraints that can be derived from this example:

1. From their initial position A_i, an agent can travel to any location except any drop-off location D_j, or any remaining task M^i of another agent. Note that an agent can remain in its location A_i if no task is assigned.
   Thus, $y^i_{j,k} = 0\ \forall j \in A_i, \forall k \in D \cup M^i, \forall i, i' \in N : i \neq i'$.
2. From any pick-up location $p\ \forall (p, d) \in T$, an agent can travel to any other location except any agent origin location A_i and $p'\ \forall (p', d') \in T$ when $p = p'$.
   Hence, $y^i_{p,k} = 0\ \forall (p, d) \in T, \forall k \in A_i \cup P : k = p, \forall i \in N$.
3. From any drop-off location $j \in D$, an agent can travel to any other location except any agent origin location A_i, or the pick-up p and drop-off d location of the same task: $(p, d) \in T$ if $d = j$
   Therefore, $y^i_{d,k} = 0\ \forall (p, d) \in T, \forall k \in A_i \cup P : k = p \cup D : k = d, \forall i \in N$.
4. From any remaining task location $j \in M^i$, an agent can travel to any other location except any agent origin location A_i, and other remaining task $k \in M^m$ if $k = j$ and $i = m$, or $i \neq m$.
   So $y^i_{j,k} = 0\ \forall j \in M^i, \forall k \in A_i \cup M^i : k = j, \forall i \in N$.
5. $y^i_{j,k} = 1$ otherwise.

Parameter $y_{j,k}$ captures the constraints in equation set (1). A list of the used nomenclature is provided in Table 1.

Table 1. Variable, parameter and index definitions

Indices		Sets	
i	= Agent	N	= Agents
j, k	= Task	P	= Pick-up tasks $P \subset I$, $P \subset \mathcal{J}$
p, d	= Pick-up and drop-off task $\in T$	D	= Drop-off tasks $D \subset I$, $D \subset \mathcal{J}$
a	= Agent home $a \in A_i$	T	= Drop-off and Pickup task pair $T \subset I$, $T \subset \mathcal{J}$
		I	= Unassigned tasks $I \subset \mathcal{J}$
		M^i	= Assigned and unfulfilled tasks of agent i $M \subset \mathcal{J}$
		A	= Agent "home" location
		$\mathcal{J}$	= All tasks
Parameters			
$v^i_{j,k}$	= Revenue from agent i for completing journey from j, k. [£]		
$c^i_{j,k}$	= Energy expenditure from agent i for completing journey from j, k. [kWh]		
$\omega^i_{j,k}$	= Customer wait time for journey j, k carried out by agent i. [seconds]		
$y^i_{j,k}$	= Equates to 1 if journey j to k by i is possible, and 0 otherwise.		
$\psi^i_{j,k}$	= Payload required by agent i for journey j, k. [grams]		
$\beta^i_{j,k}$	= Energy requirement by agent i for journey j, k. [kWh]		
m^i	= Number of unfulfilled tasks of agent i.		
γ	= Unit energy cost [£/kWh].		
δ	= Relative cost of losing a customer [£]		
Variables			
$x^i_{j,k}$	= Boolean: agent i transitions from task j to k.		

$$\text{Maximise} \quad \pi = \sum_{i \in N} \sum_{j,k \in \mathcal{J}} (v^i_{j,k} - \gamma c^i_{j,k} - \delta \omega^i_{j,k}) x^i_{j,k} y^i_{j,k} \tag{1}$$

$$\sum_{i \in N, k \in \mathcal{J}} y^i_{k,j} x^i_{k,j} \leq 1 \qquad \forall j \in P \tag{1.1}$$

$$\sum_{k \in \mathcal{J}} y^i_{k,p} x^i_{k,p} - \sum_{k \in \mathcal{J}} y^i_{k,d} x^i_{k,d} = 0 \qquad \forall (p,d) \in T, \ \forall i \in N \tag{1.2}$$

$$\sum_{k \in \mathcal{J}} y^i_{j,k} x^i_{j,k} - \sum_{k \in \mathcal{J}} y^i_{k,j} x^i_{k,j} = 0 \qquad \forall j \in P, \ \forall i \in N \tag{1.3}$$

$$\sum_{k \in \mathcal{J}} y^i_{j,k} x^i_{j,k} - \sum_{k \in \mathcal{J}} y^i_{k,j} x^i_{k,j} \leq 0 \qquad \forall j \in D, \ \forall i \in N \tag{1.4}$$

$$\sum_{k \in \mathcal{J}} y^i_{j,k} x^i_{j,k} = m^i \qquad \forall j \in M^i, \ \forall i \in N \tag{1.5}$$

$$\sum_{k \in \mathcal{J}} y^i_{j,k} x^i_{j,k} - \sum_{k \in \mathcal{J}} y^i_{k,j} x^i_{k,j} \leq 0 \qquad \forall j \in M^i, \ \forall i \in N \tag{1.6}$$

$$\sum_{k \in \mathcal{J}} y^i_{a,k} x^i_{a,k} = 1 \qquad \forall a \in A_i, \ \forall i \in N \tag{1.7}$$

$$\begin{aligned} &\sum_{j \in P, k \in \mathcal{J}} y^i_{j,k} x^i_{j,k} - \sum_{j \in P, k \in \mathcal{J}} y^i_{k,j} x^i_{k,j} + \sum_{j \in D, k \in \mathcal{J}} y^i_j x^i_{j,k} - \\ &\sum_{j \in D, k \in \mathcal{J}} y^i_{k,j} x^i_{k,j} + \sum_{j \in M^i, k \in \mathcal{J}} y^i_{j,k} x^i_{j,k} - \sum_{j \in M^i, k \in \mathcal{J}} y^i_{k,j} x^i_{k,j} + \\ &\sum_{a \in A_i, k \in \mathcal{J}} y^i_{a,k} x^i_{a,k} - \sum_{a \in A_i} x^i_{a,a} = 0 \qquad \forall i \in N \end{aligned} \tag{1.8}$$

$$\sum_{j,k \in \mathcal{J}} \psi^i_{j,k} x^i_{j,k} y^i_{j,k} \leq \Psi_i \qquad \forall i \in N \tag{1.9}$$

$$\sum_{j,k \in \mathcal{J}} \beta^i_{j,k} x^i_{j,k} y^i_{j,k} \leq B_i \qquad \forall i \in N \tag{1.10}$$

$$x^i_{j,k} \in \{0,1\} \qquad \forall j,k \in \mathcal{J}, \ \forall i \in N \tag{1.11}$$

$$MTZ \quad constraints \tag{1.12}$$

The objective function (1) calculates the total profit of the operation by considering the total revenue per task, the operational cost to carry out the task, and any lost customers through excessive waiting time.

Constraint (1.1) limits any task is to be assigned to only one agent i. (1.2) ensures that agents are assigned a pick-up and drop-off location for any task j. (1.3) guarantees agents arriving at a pick-up location will also leave said location. Similarly, (1.4) ensures agents arriving at a drop-off location will leave the node, but also allows agents to remain in the drop-off location only if it is the last visit of their schedule.

Constraints (1.5) and (1.6) describe the behaviour of unfulfilled agent tasks M^i. (1.5) ensures all unfulfilled tasks are visited by agent i, while (1.6) is analogous to (1.4).

Constraint (1.7) forces agents to commence the assignment from their starting location A_i. Flow conservation between all tasks is guaranteed through (1.8), and allows agents to not be assigned any task if $x_{A_i,A_i} = 1$.

Constraints, (1.9) and (1.10) ensure payload and battery limitations are satisfied during assignment. The decision variable x is constrained to a Boolean by (1.11), and Miller-Tucker-Zemlin (MTZ) constraints are implemented to eliminate sub-tours.

3.2 Dynamic Programming Approach

The DP approach defined in this paper implements a Dijkstra algorithm that utilises a profit matrix to assign tasks once an agent changes its status to "Idle". Fundamentally, this mirrors the decision variable $x^i_{j,k}$ from equation set (1), where the DP determines the sequence of tasks to be followed by a specific agent. However, there are two main differences with respect to the MILP method: 1) the agent must complete all tasks in order to undergo task assignment, and 2) task assignment to multiple idle agents is carried out sequentially rather than simultaneously.

As a result, the logical constraints 1, 2, and 3 are carried forward from Sect. 3.1. Additionally, constraints (1.8) and (1.9) also apply. The implementation of the DP approach is described in Algorithm 1.

3.3 First-In-First-Out Approach

The FIFO method assigns tasks sequentially to any agent that enters the "Idle" status, provided the agent has sufficient battery and payload capacity to undertake said task. If multiple agents are idle, the FIFO approach maximises profit of that task as defined by Eq. (1). The implementation of the FIFO method is described in Algorithm 2.

3.4 Path Planning Formulation

Once the task sequence is given to the agent, the path planning process derives the shortest trajectory to the target location. In determining the path, we propose a multi-agent reinforcement learning approach, where each agent within the UAV swarm develops a cost matrix G based on its observation range $\mathcal{R}_i$, its current position, and the target destination. The observation radius $\mathcal{R}_i$ denotes the maximum distance an agent is able to detect obstacles and calculate their risk and records their observations in the database $\mathcal{D}_i$. Thus, each agent must navigate through the environment in order to obtain a complete knowledge of the topography.

Algorithm 1. Dynamic Programming

function DP(N, I) ▷ N - agent set, I - tasks
  Initialise $\Gamma_n \leftarrow \epsilon_j^1$ ▷ Γ_n - set of initialised routes. ϵ_j^1 - route to task j
  for i in N **do**
    $\Gamma_n - 1 = \{\}$, $t = 1$
    while $\Gamma_n \neq \Gamma_{n-1}$ **do** ▷ Exit loop if results converged
      $\Gamma_n = \Gamma_{n-1}$
      for j in I **do** ▷ π_j^t - profit of task j at iteration t
        $\pi_j^{t+1} = \pi_j^t$ ▷ If route not explored and satisfies battery B_i and
        for $\epsilon_k^t \in \Gamma_n$ **do** ▷ payload Ψ_i constraints:
          if j **not in** ϵ_k^t **and** $y_{j,\epsilon_k^t} = 1$ **and** $\psi_{\epsilon_k^t} \leq \Psi_i$ **and** $\beta_{\epsilon_k^t} \leq B_i$ **then**
            $\rho = \pi_j^t + v_{j,k}$ ▷ Calculate route profit from k to j
            if $\rho > p_j^{t+1}$ **then**
              $p_j^{t+1} = \rho$ ▷ Update route profit
              $\epsilon_j^{t+1} = \epsilon_k^t + r_{k,j}$ ▷ Update route
            end if
            $\Gamma_{n-1} \leftarrow \epsilon_j^{t+1}$ ▷ Update route list for agent i
          end if
        end for
      end for
      $t = t + 1$
    end while
    $R = \text{Max}(p_j^t \forall \epsilon_j^t \in \Gamma_n)$ ▷ Select task with highest profit
    $i \leftarrow R$ ▷ Assign tasks to agent
  end for
end function

Algorithm 2. First-In-First-Out.

function FIFO(N,I) ▷ N - agent set, I - tasks
  for i in N **do** ▷ π - expected profit
    $\pi_i = -\infty$ ▷ If agent idle and satisfies battery B_i and:
    for j in I **do** ▷ payload Ψ_i constraints:
      if Status_i **is** "Idle" **and** $\Psi_i \geq \psi_j$ **and** $B_i \geq \beta_j$ **then**
        if $\pi_i < \pi_j$ **then**
          Assign Task j to Agent
          $\pi_i = \pi_j$ ▷ update expected profit for agent i
        end if
      end if
    end for
  end for
  return N
end function

The cost matrix G is calculated using a reward matrix S that depicts the objective of minimising path distance and avoiding any risk observed by the agent. For any two points p_1 and p_2 in the map $\mathcal{N}$, the reward S_{p_1,p_2} is described in Eq. (2), where d_{p_1,p_2} is the geometric distance between the two points, and

$\int_{(x,y)\in P_{p_1,p_2}} L(x,y)$ denotes the accumulated risk from p_1 to p_2. K is a risk adjustment coefficient, the effect of which can be observed in Fig. 3.

$$S_{p_1,p_2} = d_{p_1,p_2} + K \int_{(x,y)\in P_{p_1,p_2}} L(x,y) \tag{2}$$

The risk $L(x,y)$ is an accumulated metric of proximity to an obstacle modelled as a normal distribution to the centre of the obstacle. Thus, given a set of obstacles O where each individual obstacle o is located at (X_o, Y_o), the risk exposure at (x,y) is formulated as follows:

$$L(x,y) = 1 - \prod_{o\in O} [1 - l(x,y,x_o,y_o)] \tag{3}$$

where

$$l(X,Y,x,y) = \frac{1}{\sqrt{2\pi\sigma}} e^{-\frac{(X-x)^2+(Y-y)^2}{2\sigma}} \tag{4}$$

In calculating the cost matrix G, an iterative process based on Eq. (5) is used. G is first initialised with all values at ∞ and the destination node at 0. Then, a position p_1 is selected using uniform random distribution until convergence as defined by [18].

Note that the vehicle can only detect risk within its own observation radius $\mathcal{R}$, and any historical data obtained during the mission, defined as the explored topography $\mathcal{D}$. For further details in the implementation of the reinforcement learning model, see [3].

$$G^{k+1} = min(G^k, \sum_{p_2\in\mathcal{N}} S_{p_2,p_1} + G^k_{p_2}) \tag{5}$$

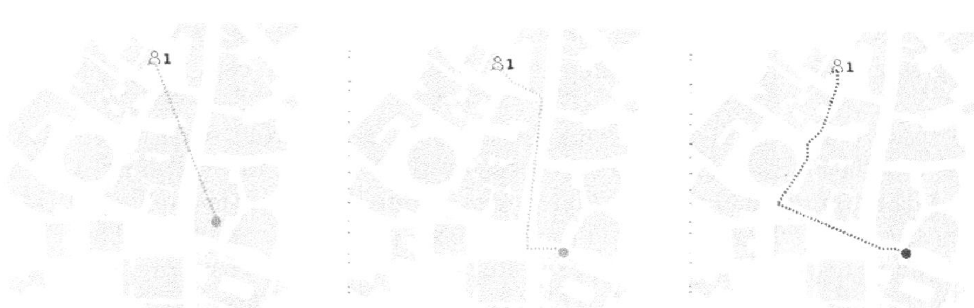

(a) $K = 0$. (b) $K = 10$. (c) $K = 30$.

Fig. 3. Path planning variation with K. Obstacles are shown in light red, and the destination is labelled as 1. As K increases, the agent avoids obstacles more effectively. (Color figure online)

4 Case Study and Simulation

The model described in Sects. 2 and 3 is implemented in Matlab on an Intel Core i9-10980XE CPU, with 256 GB RAM. The case study developed is based on the postal code EC3A in the City of London, comprising an area of 0.5 km^2 (see Fig. 4). The region is discretised into a 80×80 node grid based on the data obtained through ArcGIS.

Demand is assumed to be generated only at side streets and next to buildings as shown in Fig. 4c following a Poisson distribution, with the value of each task calculated based on Eq. (6), where parcel weight is uniform stochastic $\psi \sim U(200, 700)$. The customer waiting time is set to 100 time steps. In total, 30 demand units are generated over a time period of 500 time steps.

$$v = 10 \times U(1, 10) + 0.02\psi \tag{6}$$

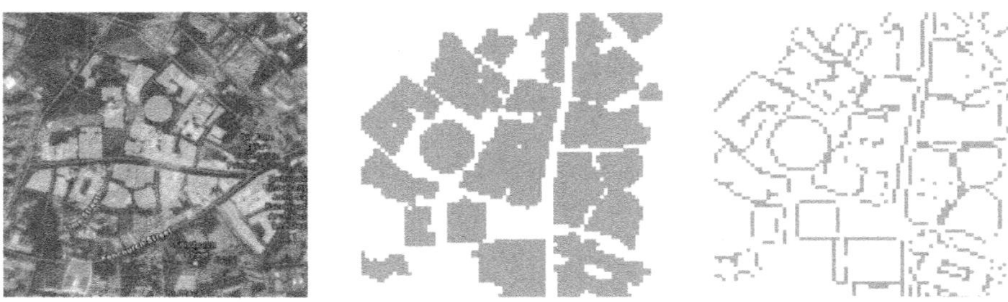

(a) Case study area. (b) Obstacle grid. (c) Demand regions.

Fig. 4. Case study.

We evaluate the performance of the three task assignment approaches by analysing their sensitivity to changes in the unit battery cost γ and the fleet size N.

Figure 5 and the accompanying Table 2 present the profit sensitivity to fleet size and the battery unit cost. We observe that, except for $\gamma < 5$ or $N > 5$, the MILP approach obtains greater profits. Interestingly, as the number of UAV increases, the DP process produces the best performing solution. The FIFO method generally obtains higher profits when operating costs are negligible, $\gamma = 0$. A fleet size of 2 to 3 UAVs ensures highest profits regardless of the TA optimisation model, except when $\gamma = 0$.

These results suggest that if the cost of operation is negligible with respect to the value of the service, a FIFO approach provides fast and reliable task assignment. Instead, in scenarios where the number of orders is significantly higher than the available fleet ($N \leq 3$), the MILP model provides better solutions due to its ability to plan tasks in advance. Finally, the DP model improves profits for smaller order to fleet ratio as agents enter the idle state more frequently.

We further investigate this claim by evaluating the task completion rate in Fig. 6. One can observe that the DP method has a lower order completion rate than both the MILP and FIFO but comparable profits under the same γ and fleet size, suggesting a higher average order value. In addition, while FIFO and MILP obtain similar order completion rates, the MILP provides higher profits particularly for $2 \leq N \leq 3$. Note that, for $N > 3$ the number of tasks completed does not increase further. Meaning that the FIFO approach only provides high quality solutions when fleet size is large enough to ensure all tasks are served without optimal planning, otherwise, the MILP provides a more effective task assignment framework compared to the other two models.

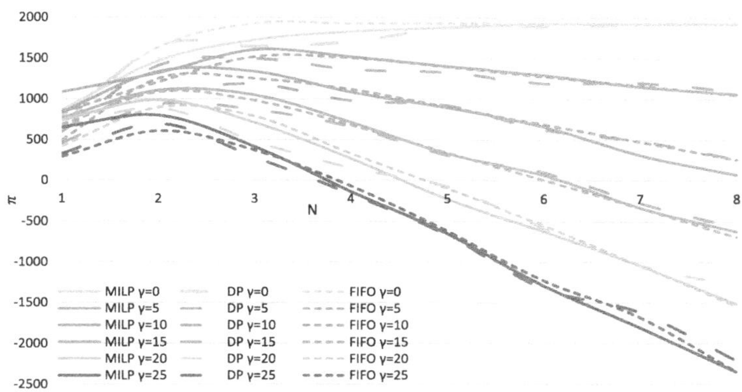

Fig. 5. Profit variation with number of agents and γ.

Table 2. Method with highest profit per agent number and γ. Bold text indicates highest profit for each value of γ, and cell colour intensity denotes profit value.

Agents	$\gamma = 0$	$\gamma = 5$	$\gamma = 10$	$\gamma = 15$	$\gamma = 20$	$\gamma = 25$
1	MILP	MILP	DP	MILP	MILP	MILP
2	DP	DP	**MILP**	**MILP**	**MILP**	**MILP**
3	**FIFO**	**MILP**	MILP	MILP	FIFO	MILP
4	FIFO	MILP	FIFO	MILP	FIFO	FIFO
5	FIFO	MILP	DP	FIFO	DP	FIFO
6	FIFO	MILP	FIFO	DP	FIFO	FIFO
7	DP	DP	DP	DP	DP	DP
8	FIFO	DP	DP	DP	DP	DP

We also evaluate the performance of DP and MILP in term of varying δ value as shown in Fig. 7. Similar to Fig. 5, the MILP provides higher profits for $N \leq 3$. Once the number of agents poses no impediment to the completion of all tasks, the DP records greater profits.

The results suggest that, while the MILP improves profitability in the region of $2 \leq N \leq 3$ where fleet size is insufficient to address all tasks, it underperforms when compared to the DP and FIFO implementations for larger fleet sizes. This may be as a result of the trigger conditions for the MILP execution process, which may result in small time horizons, reducing the impact of its main advantages compared to the other methods.

An exploration of different trigger conditions for the MILP should be explored, for example, potentially through the definition of a fixed activation rate, or by activation through a maximum queue size, which may result in longer planning horizons and improved task assignment. Further work should also on the additional computational requirements these improvements would create, and their feasibility for implementation in real-time for larger case studies.

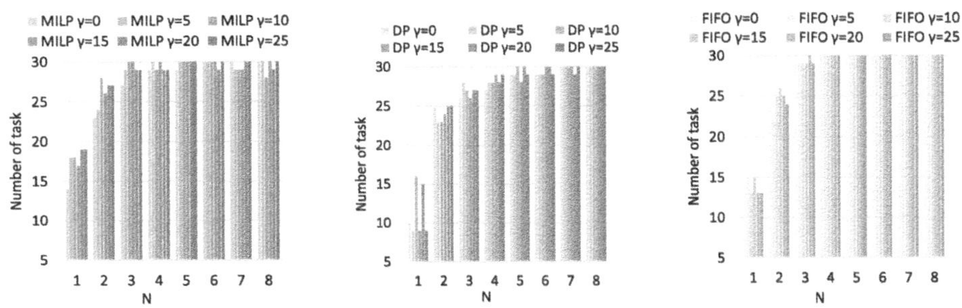

(a) MILP. (b) DP. (c) FIFO.

Fig. 6. Task completion rate variation with γ.

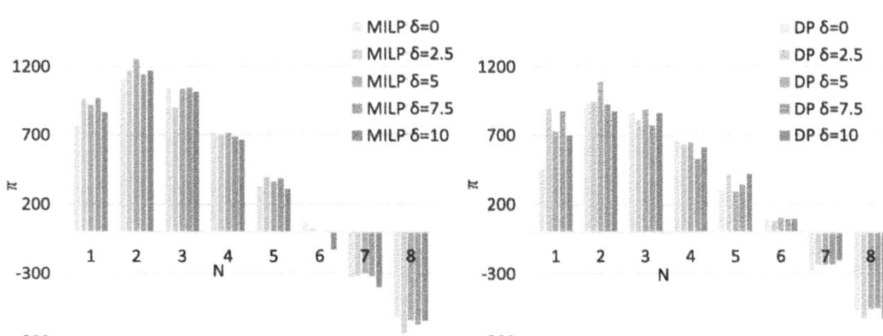

(a) MILP. (b) DP.

Fig. 7. Profit variation with δ.

5 Conclusions and Further Work

This paper has proposed a UAV swarm delivery comprising of a task assignment approach, and a path planning algorithm, which consists of a risk-based learning approach that facilitates optimal path finding with built-in obstacle avoidance. Three implementations of task assignment are evaluated in this paper: a First-In-First-Out method, a Dynamic Programming approach, and a Mixed-Integer Linear Program.

Our results have shown that the MILP assignment provides improved performance in the majority of scenarios, as allows assignment of tasks to agents that have unfulfilled tasks. The FIFO approach yields better results when operational expenditure is negligible, and DP results in higher profit if the number of agents is large compared to the number of orders. Overall, the MILP approach offers higher lever of collaboration within the swarm, and requires fewer agents to the DP and FIFO to obtain maximum income levels.

While this paper shows the effectiveness of aggregating the task assignment and path planning into a single platform, there are simplifications that preclude its implementation. While the risk-aware path planning approach proposed provides shortest routes from origin to destination, it assumes no conflict with other flying platforms outside of the swarm. Under current regulations from the UK Civil Aviation Authority, delivery drones must comply with specific category rules, requiring operational authorisation and available communications with the Air Traffic Service provider. This means that the risk map should update dynamically with updated information of other traffic, and allow evaluation of the operational risk for carrying out the delivery.

Another limitation of the approach is the use of a single swarm of UAVs to test the algorithms. Implementing a multi-swarm environment, with a higher degree of risk for path planning as a result of a higher level of traffic, and order assignment to the multiple swarms would provide a scalable implementation for UAV-based delivery.

In discussing scalability, the problem instance proposed in this paper considers 8 UAVs and 30 orders. Application to a wider region and larger fleet sizes would provide a more realistic implementation of UAV-based pickup and delivery services. This expansion will also allow the investigation of interacting swarms, where UAVs can be interchanged between swarms based on the demand intensity at any point in time. This comprises our future work.

References

1. Biswas, S., Anavatti, S., Garratt, M.: A time-efficient co-operative path planning model combined with task assignment for multi-agent systems. Robotics **8**(35), 1–16 (2019)
2. Cai, W., Zhang, M., Zheng, Y.R.: Task assignment and path planning for multiple autonomous underwater vehicles using 3D Dubins curves. Sensors (Switz.) **17**(7) (2017). https://doi.org/10.3390/s17071607

3. Chang, H., Chen, Y., Zhang, B., Doermann, D.: Multi-UAV mobile edge computing and path planning platform based on reinforcement learning. IEEE Trans. Emerging Topics Comput. Intell. **6**(3), 489–498 (2022). https://doi.org/10.1109/TETCI.2021.3083410
4. Chen, Z., Alonso-Mora, J., Bai, X., Harabor, D.D., Stuckey, P.J.: Integrated task assignment and path planning for capacitated multi-agent pickup and delivery. IEEE Robot. Autom. Lett. **6**(3), 5816–5823 (2021). https://doi.org/10.1109/LRA.2021.3074883
5. David, J., Philippsen, R.: Task assignment and trajectory planning in dynamic environments for multiple vehicles. Frontiers Artif. Intell. Appl. **278**, 179–181 (2015). https://doi.org/10.3233/978-1-61499-589-0-179
6. Dorling, K., Heinrichs, J., Messier, G.G., Magierowski, S.: Vehicle routing problems for drone delivery. IEEE Trans. Syst. Man Cybern. Syst. **47**(1), 70–85 (2017). https://doi.org/10.1109/TSMC.2016.2582745
7. Escribano Macias, J., Angeloudis, P., Ochieng, W.: Optimal hub selection for rapid medical deliveries using unmanned aerial vehicles. Transp. Res. Part C Emerging Technol. **110**(November 2019), 56–80 (2020). https://doi.org/10.1016/j.trc.2019.11.002
8. Grippa, P.: Decision making in a UAV-based delivery system with impatient customers. In: IEEE International Conference on Intelligent Robots and Systems, November 2016, pp. 5034–5039 (2016). https://doi.org/10.1109/IROS.2016.7759739
9. Hader, M.: Advanced air mobility: market study for APAC. Technical report, Roland Berger, Munich, Germany (2022)
10. Huang, H., Zhu, D., Ding, F.: Dynamic task assignment and path planning for multi-AUV system in variable ocean current environment. J. Intell. Robot. Syst. 999–1012 (2013). https://doi.org/10.1007/s10846-013-9870-2
11. Huo, L., Zhu, J., Wu, G., Li, Z.: A novel simulated annealing based strategy for balanced UAV task assignment and path planning. Sensors (Switz.) **20**(17), 1–21 (2020). https://doi.org/10.3390/s20174769
12. Kuru, K., Ansell, D., Khan, W., Yetgin, H.: Analysis and optimization of unmanned aerial vehicle swarms in logistics: an intelligent delivery platform. IEEE Access **7**, 15804–15831 (2019). https://doi.org/10.1109/ACCESS.2019.2892716
13. Macias, J.J.E., Angeloudis, P., Ochieng, W.: Integrated trajectory-location-routing for rapid humanitarian deliveries using unmanned aerial vehicles. In: 2018 Aviation Technology, Integration, and Operations Conference, pp. 1–20 (2018). https://doi.org/10.2514/6.2018-3045
14. Moon, S., Oh, E., Shim, D.H.: An integral framework of task assignment and path planning for multiple unmanned aerial vehicles in dynamic environments. J. Intell. Robot. Syst. Theory Appl. **70**(1–4), 303–313 (2013). https://doi.org/10.1007/s10846-012-9740-3
15. Morgan Stanley Research: eVTOL/Urban air mobility TAM update: a slow take-off. But sky's the limit. Technical report, Morgan Stanley (2021)
16. Rojas Viloria, D., Solano-Charris, E.L., Muñoz-Villamizar, A., Montoya-Torres, J.R.: Unmanned aerial vehicles/drones in vehicle routing problems: a literature review. Int. Trans. Oper. Res. **28**(4), 1626–1657 (2021). https://doi.org/10.1111/itor.12783
17. Thibbotuwawa, A., Bocewicz, G., Nielsen, P., Banaszak, Z.: Unmanned aerial vehicle routing problems: a literature review. Appl. Sci. (Switz.) **10**(13) (2020). https://doi.org/10.3390/app10134504

18. Zhang, B., Liu, W., Mao, Z., Liu, J., Shen, L.: Cooperative and Geometric Learning Algorithm (CGLA) for path planning of UAVs with limited information. Automatica **50**(3), 809–820 (2014)
19. Zhu, D., Huang, H., Yang, S.X.: Dynamic task assignment and path planning of multi-AUV system based on an improved self-organizing map and velocity synthesis method in three-dimensional underwater workspace. IEEE Trans. Cybern. **43**(2), 504–514 (2013). https://doi.org/10.1109/TSMCB.2012.2210212

Dynamic Time Slot Pricing Using Delivery Costs Approximations

Fabian Akkerman(✉), Martijn Mes, and Eduardo Lalla-Ruiz

Department of High-tech Business and Entrepreneurship, University of Twente, Enschede, The Netherlands
{f.r.akkerman,m.r.k.mes,e.a.lalla}@utwente.nl

Abstract. Attended home delivery (AHD) is a popular type of home delivery for which companies typically offer delivery time slots. The costs for offering time slots are often double compared to standard home delivery services (Yrjölä, 2001). To influence customers to choose a time slot that results in fewer travel costs, companies often give incentives (discounts) or penalties (delivery charges) depending on the costs of a time slot. The main focus of this paper is on determining the costs of a time slot and adjusting time slot pricing accordingly, i.e., dynamic pricing. We compare two time slot cost approximation methods, a cheapest insertion formula and a method employing random forests with a limited set of features. Our results show that time slot incentives have added value for practice. In a hypothetical situation where customers are infinitely sensitive to incentives, we can plan 6% more customers and decrease the per-customer travel costs by 11%. Furthermore, we show that our method works especially well when customer locations are heavily clustered or when the area of operation is sparsely populated. For a realistic case of a European e-grocery retailer, we show that we can save approximately 6% in per-customer travel costs, and plan approximately 1% more customers when using our time slot incentive policy.

Keywords: Time slot management · Dynamic pricing · Vehicle routing · Machine learning · Cost approximation

1 Introduction

During the last two decades, many e-commerce initiatives have driven the demand for package delivery services, resulting in several variations of business-to-consumer business models. One of the ultimate value-adding services is last-mile delivery, the delivery of packages to the customer's front door [10]. Home delivery services present great challenges for retailers, service providers, and logistics companies. Logistics must be organized in a way that is efficient, profitable, and satisfies the customers' wishes, while sometimes dealing with stochastic customer arrivals.

In this research, we focus on attended home delivery (AHD), for which it is necessary that the customer is at home at the delivery moment. AHD might

J. de Armas et al. (Eds.): ICCL 2022, LNCS 13557, pp. 214–230, 2022.
https://doi.org/10.1007/978-3-031-16579-5_15

be needed for security reasons (e.g., high-value goods), perishable goods (e.g., groceries), physically large goods (e.g., home appliances), or because services are performed (e.g., product installation) [2]. Many companies that offer AHD services provide their customers with time slots for choosing the delivery moment. Delivery time slots are offered to provide a high customer service and prevent costly delivery failure. When delivery has failed, the goods have to be offered for delivery at a different moment, which will result in additional storage, transportation and planning costs. In the case of perishable goods, the costs of a delivery failure are even higher, since the goods may be spoilt before the next delivery opportunity. An early study shows that AHD costs are often twice the cost of unattended delivery [26]. The AHD customer ordering process is mostly comprised of five steps: (i) the customer fills the online basket, (ii) the customer indicates the required delivery location, (iii) the customer is presented delivery time slots, (iv) the customer chooses a time slot and completes the order, and (v) the order is delivered within the required time window.

Time slots have different delivery charges as part of the company's pricing policy. Often, time slot pricing policies are intended to steer customer behavior towards time slots ("nudge") that are cheaper for the company, i.e., these time slots represent lower transportation costs. By using incentives or penalties, a company can influence customer behavior in choosing a time slot, hence, it is possible to reduce operational costs. The reduction of costs can be done by, e.g., smoothing the demand patterns or the geographical spread of customers over time to reduce demand peaks [2], reducing vehicle routing distance or time, and reducing the required fleet size.

There is limited time to perform many calculations before offering a time slot; recent research suggests that each 100-ms delay in the load time of websites can decrease sales conversion by 7% [3]. Nevertheless, we need to calculate the impact of the time slot offering in terms of, e.g., fuel, salary, vehicle rent, and emissions. In addition, the opportunity costs can be considered, which are the cost of offering a time slot now compared to saving it for potentially more profitable customers that arrive later [25]. The problem is further complicated by uncertain customer arrivals and customer behaviour. Although much research has been conducted on time slot allocation, i.e., the offering of only a subset of the feasible time slots, this study considers the situation in which always all feasible time slots are offered and we can reduce costs by nudging customers to time slots. The contributions of this paper are the application of regression models for approximating transportation costs, a novel parametric rank-based method for modelling customer behavior, and the application of our approach to a realistic time slotting case.

The remainder of this paper is structured as follows. In Sect. 2, we introduce the relevant scientific literature on attended home delivery and time slot management. In Sect. 3, we describe the problem and introduce our approximation and dynamic pricing method. Section 4 introduces the synthetic and European e-grocery retailer cases and in Sect. 5, we validate and illustrate our method using the two cases. Finally, we close with conclusions and future research directions in Sect. 6.

2 Literature

In this section, we give an overview of the state-of-the-art literature considering operational attended home delivery and time slot management. We discuss problem characteristics, solution methods, and cost approximation methods. We close with an overview of the contribution of this paper to the scientific literature.

Since attended home delivery with time slots requires delivery to take place in a specified time interval, it relates to the well-known Vehicle Routing Problem with Time Windows (VRPTW). As part of the VRPTW, the field of AHD is typically divided into the following categories: (i) static time slot allocation, (ii) dynamic time slot allocation, (iii) differentiated pricing, and (iv) dynamic pricing [1,14,25]. Time slot allocation can be summarized by the question: "what time slots should we offer to a customer?" and time slot pricing can be stated as: "what time slots should we incentivize and what time slots should be penalized?". Static methods use forecast data or static rules and can be used to make strategic and tactical decisions, e.g., to decide on the number of time slots and the width of the time slots. For differentiated allocation, the goal is to find what time slots to offer to what delivery area, e.g., certain low-populated areas might be offered fewer time slots, which is a tactical decision. Differentiated pricing tries to find the best static price policy to influence customer behavior. When time slot allocation and pricing happen online, during the decision making, it is called dynamic. Dynamic decisions can consider real-time information about the customer and the current schedule to make better decisions [1,14,25].

We review the state-of-the-art scientific literature on operational decision making techniques for attended home delivery and time slotting, see Table 1 for an overview. We consider the following problem and solution elements: (i) the delivery horizon length, which indicates how many delivery days a customer can choose for delivery, (ii) the customer arrival process, which can be modelled using different probability distributions, (iii) the order generation, which is the way the orders (e.g., quantity, location or time slot) are generated, (iv) the time slot design, which indicates what width and possible overlap of time slots is considered, (v) the time slot allocation method, and (vi) if applicable, the time slot incentive method.

In [6], a model is presented that allows for a flexible horizon, but does not consider days of the week, nor seasonality. The customer arrival process is modelled using a non-homogeneous Poisson process, as inspired by scientific work in revenue management in the airline industry (see [15]). A Markov decision process model is proposed that dynamically adjusts the delivery charges per customer. Optimal prices are calculated based on an "equal profit" policy, which means that the retailer makes the same profit in the remaining booking horizon, regardless the customer choice. Delivery prices can change based on order size, depending on the time left in the booking horizon [6]. In [9], the models are tested on fictitious cases for which customers are uniformly scattered on a 60×60 grid. Their method dynamically determines the feasibility of a time slot insertion, using a combination of insertion heuristics and randomization to determine a feasible schedule. Next, the allocation and size of incentives are determined using a linear

Table 1. Problem and solution elements in AHD and time slotting literature.

Authors	Delivery horizon	Customer arrival process	Order generation	Time slot design	Slot allocation method	Slot incentive method
[6]	Flexible	N/A	Uniform	N/A	Feasibility check	Dynamic, Markov decision process model
[9]	Single-day	Uniform	-	Non-overlapping, 1 or 2-h width	Heuristic feasibility check	Dynamic LP-based model
[11]	-	N/A	Area-based, normal dist.	8 time slots	Dynamic, ESMR	N/A
[12]	Single-day	N/A	Uniform, Demand peaks	8 Non-overlapping, 1-h width time slots	Static/Dynamic, I1 insertion heuristic	N/A
[13]	Single-day	Random	General dist. of nr. of totes $i \in \{1,\ldots,10\}$	4 Non-overlapping, 2-h width time slots	Feasibility check	Dynamic, MILP-model for opportunity costs
[24]	Single-day	Homogeneous Poisson arrivals	General dist. of nr. of totes $i \in \{1,\ldots,10\}$	17 Non-overlapping, 1-hour width time slots	Feasibility check	Dynamic
[25]	Single-day	Time-dependent Poisson arrivals	Normal dist.	27 Partly-overlapping, 1-h width time slots	Heuristic feasibility check	Dynamic, opportunity costs, SDP

programming model, which maximizes the profits related to time slot offerings. The authors conclude the following from their research: (i) incentive schemes can substantially reduce costs, (ii) performance of incentive schemes can be improved using intelligent methods, (iii) incentives can reduce walkaways (lost sales), (iv) it is sufficient to provide incentives to only a few slots (≤ 3), (v) an increase in time slots triggers the need for more sophisticated incentive schemes, (vi) it is easier to persuade customers to choose a wider time window than to let them choose a specific time slot, and (vii) the use of incentives can be critical already in the early stages of making a routing schedule [9].

In [11], a computational study is conducted based on the metropolitan area of Stuttgart, which is divided into nine areas with varying population sizes. Customers can choose between eight time slots. Demand is drawn from the normal distribution and is dependent on the area and the average income in those areas. There is a fixed fleet of four vehicles and capacity is estimated with vehicle routing experiments. The offering of time slots to customers is dynamically determined using the order value. The used method is called "Estimated Marginal Seat Revenue heuristic" (EMSR), as described in [8]. EMSR determines buckets for order values and allocates time slots accordingly, i.e., customers with a high order value, falling in a high-value bucket, will receive more time slot offers than customers with low order value [11]. In a study that also considers metropolitan areas, different travel time patterns are considered to model congestion in the morning peak-hours [12]. Demand for the eight non-overlapping time slots is uniform, and for some experiments demand peaks for time slots are considered. The authors define both static and dynamic approaches to determine the time slot allocation to maximize the number of accepted time slot requests. The static method uses capacity restrictions and a static rule that considers the time windows in which a delivery must be feasible. The dynamic method uses expected, dynamically determined, travel times. The authors expand this method to also have a buffer for lateness and consider stochastic travel times. Their insertion heuristic is a time-dependent adaptation to the well-known I1 insertion heuristic by [21]. In [13], 12 areas are served by a single central depot. A set of 1000 customers can arrive randomly, one at a time, and the size of demand is defined using the number of order totes. The authors develop a mixed-integer linear programming model (MILP) which is integrated into a dynamic programming model for AHD by [25]. The MILP-model maximizes expected profits and is used as an approximation of opportunity costs. The availability of time slots is checked, but time slots are always offered when capacity allows it [13]. The dynamic programming model as described in [25], is the "de facto" framework for dynamic pricing. After doing a heuristic feasibility check, based on [9], the insertion costs are calculated. The pricing solution is dynamic, but for practical reasons it does not differentiate between customers that choose the same time slot and have the same location and order value. In [25], two policies are developed, one only considering the current insertion costs, the other also including the opportunity costs. Their method is tested on a realistic case, for which bookings on a single day arrive as early as 22 days in advance, with most bookings coming in the last three days before the cutoff time. Cancellation and re-scheduling is neglected. They show that dynamic pricing methods that do not consider future expected demands (i.e., opportunity costs) can produce worse results compared to static pricing methods [25]. In a follow-up study, [24] expand their method to use an area-specific cost estimation as input for an approximate dynamic programming approach. They show that the decomposition into smaller areas can successfully reduce computational efforts and estimate the costs [24].

As [20] indicated, attended home delivery literature can also be categorised on the method for including routing costs. Most literature uses the costs resulting from explicit routing decisions, often obtained from a heuristic, since the VRPTW is NP-hard [9,11,12,25]. Alternatively, an approximation of the routing costs, without making explicit routing decisions, can be used, e.g., with Daganzo-approximation [19] or a seed-based approximation method [13,14]. Another option for routing costs approximation, not used before in time slot management research, is the use of regression models, as shown in [16] or [4].

In summary, we observe that the literature considers exclusively time slot allocation or time slot incentives. Those focusing on incentives often state that the closing of time slots for certain customers (i.e., time slot allocation) is a method that results in lost sales and customer dissatisfaction [6]. Hence, dynamic pricing is perceived as the best method, since it can balance the trade-off between lost sales and profits. Also, we see that the topic of cost approximation, being opportunity costs or transportation costs, is much studied. We recognise two different options for dynamic pricing: (i) approximate the costs of a time slot and use this as basis for setting time slot prices [9], or (ii) optimize the time slot prices, such that the behavior of customers is nudged optimally, like is done in the approximate dynamic programming model of [25]. Aside from the previous problem and solution elements, the time slotting literature also differentiates the modelling of customer choice. Most literature either use a probabilistic model, a rank-based model, or the multinomial logit (MNL) model. The latter seems to be the dominant method for the most recent literature. For more information about the MNL model we refer to [22].

The contribution of this paper to the existing scientific literature is threefold. First, we show the application of regression models for approximating transportation costs instead of the currently in use heuristic methods. Second, we present a novel parametric rank-based method for modelling customer behavior that, compared to the currently in use multinomial logit choice model, does not require behavioral data and requires fewer computations. Finally, we apply our solution approach and customer choice model to realistic time slotting case studies together with commercial vehicle routing and time slot allocation software.

3 Problem Formulation

In this section, we give the problem formulation in Sect. 3.1, describe the customer choice model in Sect. 3.2, and show how we attribute transportation costs to customers in Sect. 3.3.

3.1 Problem Characteristics

In this section, the notation of all variables, parameters, and sets is introduced, based on the formulation in [23]. We adhere to the order process as perceived by a customer. This process consists of three steps: (i) customer arrival, (ii) time slot offering, and (iii) time slot selection and confirmation. During a certain period, customers place orders at a retailer, after which the customers are offered a time slot for delivery. As common in these types of problems, we specify this period as $[0, T]$, for which 0 is the first time a customer can place an order and T is the "cutoff time", which is the last moment a customer can place an order. After T, the final delivery schedule is made for a single day, by solving a VRPTW. The customer arrival times are unknown upfront. A customer $i \in \mathcal{C}$ can arrive at any time t_i within the horizon $[0, T]$. Customer orders have a certain size, for example, indicated by weight or volume, q_i. The order quantity q_i is also unknown upfront. Each customer has a delivery service duration, i.e., the time it takes for the deliverer, after arrival at the address, to hand over the package. The service duration is indicated with l_i. The expected delivery duration can be estimated with a fixed time component and a variable time component that is dependent on the order quantity q_i.

After the customer arrival, the customer must be offered a set of time slots for delivery. We consider a single day of delivery time slots, these are all part of the set $\mathcal{T}$, with the earliest time slot beginning after T. The set of offered time slots is denoted $\mathcal{S}_i$, so that $\mathcal{S}_i \subseteq \mathcal{T}$. Time slot offering depends on feasibility and the offering policy. Each time slot $s \in \mathcal{T}$ can be of different length and can be overlapping or non-overlapping. The individual time slot duration is denoted with $[a_s, b_s]$. s is a single element in this set, i.e., $s \in \mathcal{S}_i$. Each time slot that is offered gets a certain incentive to steer customer behaviour. We consider incentives on a continuous scale, part of the incentive set $\mathcal{G}$. The incentives can be dynamically determined and differ per time slot. The incentive given to a certain time slot is $\mathcal{G}_s$. The incentives $\mathcal{G}$ are decimal numbers on the domain $[-1, 1]$, with a negative number indicating a penalty, and a positive number indicating an incentive. During the calculation time z_i, we need to determine (i) what time slots are feasible to offer to customer i, concerning both vehicle capacities and time window constraints, and (ii) the costs of offering a certain time slot. We denote the set of customers that accepted a time slot and need to be planned by $\mathcal{C}'$. The directed graph $\mathcal{G} = (\mathcal{V}, \mathcal{E})$ models the system where nodes $\mathcal{V} = \mathcal{C}' \cup \mathcal{D}$ consist of the set of customers $\mathcal{C}'$ and the set of depots $\mathcal{D}$. Each customer $i \in \mathcal{C}'$ can be served from every depot in the set $\mathcal{D}$. The travel time on edge $(i, j) \in \mathcal{E}$ can be expressed with $\tau_{i,j}$. A single depot $d \in \mathcal{D}$ has a fixed number of vehicles L_d available for delivery. The fleet is homogeneous, where every vehicle has a capacity of H. To make a delivery, a vehicle has to visit the nodes along its route. A vehicle route always starts and ends at the same depot. For the planning of vehicle routes, we consider three constraining factors: (i) the vehicle capacity H cannot be exceeded, (ii) the vehicle routes must start and finish in the interval $[a_d, b_d]$, dependent on depot d, and (iii) the delivery of customers must be done within their selected time slot. A vehicle can leave from a customer i only after the full service duration l_i.

3.2 Customer Choice Model

To model the way customers react to time slot incentives, we develop a new rank-based choice model with a utility theory scoring component. Our approach combines two common methods found in literature, namely, a rank-based model and a parametric utility theory model, see [14] and [22] for recent examples of both modelling types. We model customer preference as follows. A customer has a ranking for all time slots, i.e., the first preferred time slot is ranked highest and the least preferred time slot is ranked lowest, as is normal for rank-based models. The ranking of time slots is based on scores and, therefore, the ranking can be influenced by incentives, similar to models based on utility theory, e.g., the multinomial logit model.

Each customer gives "base scores" to all time slots, expressed with $K_i \subseteq \mathcal{T}$. For our experiments, we use a preference list that includes all time slots, i.e., $|K_i| = |\mathcal{T}|$. We model different types of customers. Some customers can be seen as "rigid", and others are perceived as more "sensitive" to incentives. The level of sensitivity is expressed with f_i, which is a continuous parameter on the scale $[0, 1]$, with 0 being rigid and 1 sensitive. The incentive effectiveness is directly related to the sensitivity parameter f_i of a customer. We do not know the customer sensitivity upfront.

We define the number $\beta_{i,s}$ as the base score of a time slot s, with $\beta_{i,s}$ on the domain $[\frac{1}{|K_i|}, 1]$, with $|K_i|$ being the number of time slots in the base preference list of customer i. The assignment of scores to time slots is done in a decreasing fashion, i.e., the first preference gets the highest score (1), and the last preference gets the lowest score ($\frac{1}{|K_i|}$). The lowest possible score is $\frac{1}{|K_i|}$ instead of 0 because this prevents problems when there are only few time slots and the difference in base score is too large for incentives to have any effect. The equation to determine base scores $\beta_{i,s}$ is given by:

$$\beta_{i,s} = \frac{|K_i| - k_{i,s} + 1}{|K_i|}, \tag{1}$$

where $\beta_{i,s}$ is the base score for time slot s of customer i, $|K_i|$ is the number of time slots in the preference list of customer i, and $k_{i,s}$ is the randomly drawn ranking of time slot s for customer i, where the ranking is an integer number $k_s \in \{1, 2, \ldots, |K_i|\}$. We can influence the ranking of the base preferences using incentives. The incentive decision must be made for all feasible time slots. The incentives we can give are continuous numbers with $\mathcal{G}_s$ on the domain $[-1, 1]$. A negative incentive can be interpreted as a penalty. The incentives are multiplied by the customer sensitivity f_i, and then added to the base preference scores. Next, the list is re-ordered from high to low and the customer chooses the highest ranking time slot that is offered, as common for utility theory models. The total score of a time slot for a customer is expressed with $u_{i,s}$ and is calculated using Eq. 2, as is common for utility theory models [22].

$$u_{i,s} = \beta_{i,s} + f_i \cdot \mathcal{G}_s. \tag{2}$$

3.3 Determining Transportation Costs

To obtain the routing costs per customer, we need to do some transformations with routing data. These transformations are necessary since we need to find the costs of adding a customer, but we only have the total routing costs of the VRPTW, i.e., the total costs need to be divided over the customers. We use a method we call "half-edge partitioning" (HEP), which can be applied to most VRP and VRPTW solutions. HEP is a straightforward, but slightly simplistic method that allocates half of the costs (time or distance) needed to travel an edge to the customer from which the edge departs, and the other half to the customer at which the edge arrives. The edges that depart from and arrive at the depot are partially allocated to their arriving and departing customers, respectively. The other half of these depot edges are equally divided over all customers. The routing costs, expressed in travel time or distance, of a single customer c served by a vehicle that serves a set of customers $\mathcal{C}'$, can be expressed as:

$$\text{Travel costs of customer } c = \frac{1}{|\mathcal{C}'|}(0.5t_{d,f} + 0.5t_{l,d}) + 0.5t_{i,c} + 0.5t_{c,j}, \tag{3}$$

with $t_{i,j}$ being the travel time or distance in the final routing schedule on edge (i, j), where i and j are the locations visited before and after customer location c, respectively. The depot is indicated with d, and customer f and customer l are the first and last customer of a vehicle route, respectively. For our experiments, we use travel time as the cost factor.

4 Solution Approach

In this section, we first describe the cheapest insertion method as cost approximation in Sect. 4.1. Next, we describe the engineered features used in our cost approximation regression model in Sect. 4.2. We show how we obtain training data in Sect. 4.3 and finally, we describe our time slot incentive policy in Sect. 4.4.

4.1 Cheapest Insertion Transportation Cost Approximation

The idea of the cheapest insertion cost approximation is relatively simple: during the booking horizon, we keep track of a preliminary routing schedule that contains all booked customer orders up to the respective moment. This preliminary routing schedule is sequentially constructed using cheapest insertion, and periodically re-optimized after every 20th customer arrival. This re-optimization interval strikes a balance between computational effort and performance for our experiments. We use a commercial vehicle routing solver [17] for re-optimization. When a new customer arrives, the cheapest insertion algorithm calculates how much it would cost, in terms of travel time, to add the new customer to a vehicle route. The cheapest insertion algorithm returns the costs of insertion for every feasible time slot. These costs differ per time slot, since vehicles that serve customers in the same time window may be close by, or alternatively have to make a detour. Cheapest insertion is simple, fast and dynamic, since it uses all current customer information for estimating costs. Nevertheless, it has the disadvantage of being myopic, i.e., it makes the best decision at a point in time, but cannot make a forecast about future customers.

4.2 Regression-Based Transportation Costs Approximation

As discussed in [4], we use a regression model to approximate transportation costs. For this paper, we show the results of random forests regression, since this method is able to fit complex functions without too much computational time. To make transportation costs predictions, we need to supply features to the model. Therefore, we aggregate customer and routing information using area-time slot clusters (ATC), as common in the literature [13,25]. The following information of an ATC is stored: customer locations expressed in latitude and longitude, customer order volume expressed in kilograms, and the routing costs per customer. Aggregation-based features give a synopsis of the characteristics of an *area* and *time slot* cluster (ATC) a customer is in. For every feasible time slot option, we calculate the feature values *before* and *after* the potential insertion of the new customer, to obtain the expected increase in routing costs. The engineered features are based on the features proposed in [4]. Examples of these features are: the number of customers in an ATC, the number of days between customer arrival and the end of the horizon, the distance between the depot and the ATC-centroid, the variance of the angles between customers in an ATC and the depot and the average distance between customers in an ATC. A complete overview of features, including a short description of each feature, and the data partition over which each feature is calculated, can be found in Table 2.

Table 2. Summary of features used for the regression model.

Feature	Feature description	Data partition
Days until the cutoff time (F1)	The number of days left at the arrival of the customer until the cutoff time	N/A
Number of customers in ATC (F2)	The number of customers accepted in the ATC	ATC
Haversine distance from ATC centroid to depot (F3)	The distance from the centroid of all accepted customers in ATC to the depot	ATC
Average distance between customers in an ATC (F4)	The average distance between all accepted customers in ATC	ATC
Variance customer-depot bearing (F5)	The variance of the bearings between the customers in ATC and the depot	ATC
Average customer-depot bearing (F6)	The mean of the bearings between the customers in ATC and the depot	ATC
Area ID (F7)	Binary vector indicating the area	$\mathcal{A}$
Time slot ID (F8)	Binary vector indicating the time slot	$\mathcal{S}$
Variance of time slot population (F9)	The variance of the number of accepted customers per time slot in area $a \in \mathcal{A}$	$a \in \mathcal{A}$
Time slot distance (F10)	The distance measured in time slots between the first and last populated time slot in area $a \in \mathcal{A}$	$a \in \mathcal{A}$
Number of time slots (F11)	The number of booked time slots in $a \in \mathcal{A}$	$a \in \mathcal{A}$

4.3 Obtaining Training Data

We use a simulation model to test different methods and policies. To train our methods, we need to obtain data. We do this by generating a separate set of instances and running full simulations on these. For these training instances, we do not use any nudging policy, i.e., customers choose the offered time slot that has the highest base score $\beta_{i,s}$. We obtain the following data after a simulation run: (i) a final VRPTW-schedule, (ii) all customer locations, and (iii) the time slots chosen by customers.

4.4 Simple Incentive Policy

To test the quality of the cost approximations and the effect they can have on a dynamic pricing policy, we present a simple dynamic pricing policy that uses the approximated costs per time slot, and subsequently, returns time slot prices. The time slot prices are always on the domain $[-1, 1]$ and can be tuned using a parameter. After obtaining a cost approximation for all feasible time slots, given by the set $\mathcal{S} \subseteq \mathcal{T}$, we first calculate the mean $\overline{C}_{\mathcal{S}}$ and standard deviation $\sigma_{C_{\mathcal{S}}}$ of the predicted costs over all feasible time slots. Next, we calculate the difference between the predicted costs for time slot s and the mean estimated costs over all time slots $\mathcal{S}$:

$$\widehat{c}_s = -1 \cdot \left(c_s - \overline{C}_{\mathcal{S}}\right). \tag{4}$$

We multiply with -1 to give higher incentives to the time slots with low costs and vice versa. Next, we use a tunable parameter W multiplied by the standard deviation $\sigma_{C_{\mathcal{S}}}$ to control how much standard deviations distance from the mean $\widehat{c}_s$ is considered large, and adjust the magnitude of incentives accordingly. In our experiments, we tuned W and found that $W = 1.0$ gives best results. In case that $W\sigma_{C_{\mathcal{S}}} \ll \widehat{c}_s$, we cap the incentives to remain in the domain $[-1, 1]$. When the costs for all the time slots are the same, i.e., $\sigma_{C_{\mathcal{S}}} = 0$, no incentives are given:

$$\text{Incentive for time slot s} = \begin{cases} 0, & \text{if } \sigma_{C_{\mathcal{S}}} = 0, \\ -1, & \text{if } \frac{\widehat{c}_s}{W\sigma_{C_{\mathcal{S}}}} \leq -1, \\ \frac{\widehat{c}_s}{W\sigma_{C_{\mathcal{S}}}}, & \text{if} -1 < \frac{\widehat{c}_s}{W\sigma_{C_{\mathcal{S}}}} < 1, \\ 1, & \text{if } \frac{\widehat{c}_s}{W\sigma_{C_{\mathcal{S}}}} \geq 1. \end{cases} \tag{5}$$

5 Case Studies

In this section, we explain the two cases on which we test our transportation cost approximation approach. First, we describe the synthetic case in Sect. 5.1 and then a realistic European e-grocery retailer case in Sect. 5.2.

5.1 Synthetic Case

We generate instances with a single depot from which a fleet of 20 vehicles serves an area of 50 kilometer radius from the depot. The customers are generated in a randomly clustered (RC) pattern, i.e., 80% of the customer belongs to one of the eight customer clusters, while 20% of the generated customers have a random location. During a booking horizon of 21 days, 750 customers can request a time slot. We offer six non-overlapping time slots of 2-hour width. Customers have a base preference list that entails all six time slots, i.e., customers can be nudged to every time slot that is feasible. In practice, VRPTWs have both a vehicle capacity restriction and a time window restriction. For these experiments, we first study the effect of only having a time window (RC-T) restriction, and next, the effect of adding a capacity restriction of 25 customers per vehicle (RC-TC). We use two different customer price sensitivity settings: one for which customers are infinitely flexible (Flex), i.e., customers will always choose the time slot that we nudge; and a second one that uses a sensitivity of $f_i = 1$ (see Sect. 3.2), i.e., customers are sensitive but the time slot with the highest incentive is not necessarily always chosen, since the base scores, before incentives, have influence on the eventual time slot choice.

5.2 European E-grocery Retailer

One of the main contemporary application areas of time slotting is e-grocery retailing, i.e., offering the possibility to order groceries online and delivering them at home. The reason that grocery retailers use time slots for delivery is that the goods are often perishable, so a failed delivery can be costly. Compared to the synthetic case, customers are dispersed over a larger region containing cities and rural areas. The grocery retailer has a heterogeneous fleet, with smaller vehicles used for cities and larger vehicles for rural areas. The retailer offers seven overlapping time slots, and serves from multiple depots (4) with different fleet sizes. For the individual instances, we use order data obtained from the same day of the week, to prevent seasonality differences. The fleet is heterogeneous in terms of vehicle capacity and driving speed. The retailer offers five overlapping time slots of 2-h width, and two time slots of 4 and 5 h width. Customers arrive on a booking horizon of 9 days, and on average instances have ~2000 customer arrivals. Since some of our features are calculated based on the depot location, but we do not know upfront which depot serves a customer area, we always use the main depot for feature value calculations.

6 Computational Experiments

We use a simulation model that mimics customer behavior and integrates commercial time slot allocation and vehicle routing services. The simulation model is built in C# and maintained by the Math Innovation Team from the software development company ORTEC. All cost approximation methods have been trained using the Python Scikit-learn library [18] and are loaded in C# using the ONNX standard artificial intelligence format [7]. The general event structure of the simulator follows the following events: (i) a customer arrives and requests a time slot offering, (ii) a feasibility check for every time slot is done using cheapest insertion and the feasible time slots are offered to the customer, (iii) the customer chooses a time slot, (iv) the customer choice is recorded in the system. A commercial VRP solver is called after every 20th customer arrival to update the intermediate routing schedule, and after the final customer arrival to obtain the final routing schedule. For a full description of the simulation model, we refer to [5,23].

We report six different statistics: (i) the percentage of all customers that could be planned and served, (ii) the average number of time slots that were feasible to offer to a customer, (iii), the percentage of customers that were nudged to a different time slot than their first preference, (iv) the average travel time per customer in minutes, (v) the average waiting time per customer in minutes, and (vi) the average travel distance per customer in kilometers. For both cases, the travel time and the travel distance are calculated with the actual road network costs, using the commercial VRP solver. Traffic congestion has not been accounted when calculating travel times. Waiting time is reported because it is an essential element of VRPTWs: potentially, driving times can be low, however, early arrivals at customer locations result in drivers having to wait.

In the remainder of this section, we first show the results for a synthetic case study in Sect. 6.1, using generated instances based on real data. For these instances, we alter problem attributes to test our approach in different settings. Next, in Sect. 6.2, we use a real case from an European e-grocery retailer to validate our approach in a realistic setting.

6.1 Results for the Synthetic Case

Table 3 summarizes the experimental results. First, we show results for the RC type without time window restriction, that is, RC and RC-C, respectively. Next, we add the time window restriction and show results for the case without a time slot incentive policy. The results show that the addition of time slots, disregarding incentives, causes a significant decrease (19.9%) in the number of served customers for the uncapacitated instance. For the capacitated instances, the difference in served customers is insignificant. However, for both the uncapacitated and the capacitated instances, the addition of time slots causes a large increase in travel time, waiting time, and travel distance, e.g., the travel distance increases by 110.7% and 68.5% for the RC and RC-C instances, respectively.

Table 3. Simulation run statistics on the randomly clustered instances with a time restriction (RC-T) or capacity restriction (RC-TC), using 5 replications.

Offer strategy	Instance	Planned customers (%)	Avg. no. of feasible TS	Nudged customers (%)	Travel time/ customer (min.)	Waiting time/ customer (min.)	Distance/ customer (km)
No time slots	RC	100%	N/A	N/A	9.02	0.38	6.94
No time slots	RC-C	66.7%	N/A	N/A	12.0	0.56	9.66
No incentive	RC-T	80.1%	4.3	N/A	17.46	0.72	14.62
No incentive	RC-TC	66.6%	3.8	N/A	21.74	3.31	16.28
IC	RC-T Flex	84.9%	4.8	80.1%	15.70	0.65	13.15
RFR	RC-T Flex	84.2%	4.8	78.4%	15.68	0.64	14.25
IC	RC-TC Flex	65.9%	3.9	81.3%	21.81	1.81	15.36
RFR	RC-TC Flex	66.6%	3.2	79.4%	24.78	1.01	15.37
IC	RC-T	85.5%	4.7	58.2%	15.54	0.91	12.49
RFR	RC-T	81.9%	4.0	66.5%	16.89	0.86	14.03
IC	RC-TC	66.6%	3.9	58.6%	21.93	4.77	14.98
RFR	RC-TC	66.7%	3.7	66.3%	22.78	4.81	15.96

When we add our incentive policy, either based on the insertion costs (IC) or the random forests regression (RFR) model, we see that we can significantly reduce operational costs and increase the number of served customers for the case with infinitely flexible customers (Flex). For the uncapacitated case, we can plan on average 4.5% more customers and decrease travel distance by 5.5%. For the capacitated case, the incentive policy can reduce travel distance by 5.6%. The IC method most often outperforms the RFR method. Possibly this is caused by the frequent updates of the vehicle routing plan (after every 20th customer arrival), which makes IC more reliable. Finally, we show results for the case with more realistic customer sensitivity, i.e., when time slot incentives do not always have an effect. For most cases, this causes a drop in performance, although we are still able to significantly reduce costs compared to the situation without incentives.

6.2 Results for the European E-grocery Retailer

Table 4 shows the results for the real case study of an European e-grocery retailer. We observe from the "No time slots" experiment that we cannot plan more than 81.1% of the customers due to vehicle capacity restrictions. The addition of time slots causes an increase in travel time and travel distance of 34.5% and 33.9%, respectively. We observe that IC and RFR both can plan more customers when nudging to infinitely flexible customers, compared to the situation without incentives. IC saves 15.7% in travel time and 15.0% in distance per customer, compared with the situation without incentives. RFR improves slightly less compared with the situation without incentives; it saves 7.3% in travel time and 11.2% in distance per customer. Comparing the situation without incentives with the best performing incentive policy setting, we see 0.7% more planned customers, 6.2% less travel time, and 5.3% less traveled distance per customer. Waiting times are low, and the differences between waiting times are insignificant. Again, IC shows somewhat better performance in most statistics, but RFR seems to be the more "active" policy with more nudging.

Table 4. Simulation run statistics for the European e-grocery retailer case, using 2 replications.

Offer strategy	Planned customers (%)	Avg. no. of feasible TS	Nudged customers (%)	Travel time/ customer (min.)	Waiting time/ customer (min.)	Distance/ customer (km)
No time slots	81.1%	N/A	N/A	4.18	0	2.53
No incentive	80.4%	5.6	N/A	5.62	0.03	3.39
IC (Flex)	81.1%	5.7	85.6%	4.74	0	2.88
RFR (Flex)	81.0%	5.6	86.8%	5.21	0.02	3.01
IC	80.5%	5.6	45.4%	5.25	0.02	3.15
RFR	81.0%	5.5	75.1%	5.84	0.08	3.96

7 Conclusions

We explored the possibilities for improving time slot solutions by approximating the costs of adding a customer to a time slot, and subsequently, we studied the effects of dynamic pricing based on these cost approximations. To model customer behavior without the need for a behavioral study, we developed a parametric rank-based customer choice model for which we can influence the ranking of time slots by giving incentives or penalties. We developed a simple incentive policy to test our customer choice model and time slot cost approximation. Our solution approach for approximating the costs of time slots is centered around the prediction of transportation costs using regression models. To improve prediction and reduce noise, we aggregated customers in area-time slot combination (ATC) clusters, after which we trained regression models to predict the travel times to serve an ATC-cluster. We tested our proposed solution on two different cases. First, we ran several experiments with a synthetic case, i.e., a case with generated data using both a time-constrained variant and a capacity-constrained variant. For the second case, we used data from an European e-grocery retailer.

When we compared the situation without time slots, i.e., customers can be planned the whole day, with the situation with time slots, we saw a decrease of the percentage of customers that can be served (∼20%), and a significant increase in travel time, waiting time, and distance per customer. When giving incentives, we can plan 6% more customers and decrease travel time, waiting time and distance per customer by 11% compared to the situation without incentives. Our random forests method often performed similar or slightly worse compared to the insertion costs (IC) method. For the Europen e-grocery retailer case, IC could save in travel times (−15.7%) and distance (−15.0%) per customer, while planning slightly more customers compared to the case without incentives. Our random forests method planned a similar number of customers, and saved 7.3% in travel time and 11.2% in distance per customer, respectively.

Further research can be done on the aggregation structure used for aggregating customers in spatial areas, e.g., using adaptive grids that automatically identify customer clusters. Our rudimentary incentive policy could be improved by improving the cost approximation, e.g., by considering more features or using other supervised learning approaches, e.g., neural networks. The definition of transportation costs is another interesting aspect that requires more research since the half-edge partitioning method we used could be improved to consider more than only travel time or distance. Although we studied the correlation between customer time slots and costs, there is a lacking *causality* between giving incentives and total transportation costs. Hence, the dynamic nature and complexity of the time slotting cause a disconnect between our time slot cost approximation, time slot incentive policy and the final costs. Potentially, a (deep) reinforcement learning model could be valuable for learning this implicit relationship.

Acknowledgements. This paper is based on the master thesis of Fabian Akkerman supervised by Martijn Mes and Eduardo Lalla-Ruiz. We would like to thank Thomas Visser of ORTEC for his advice and assistance during the graduation process.

References

1. Agatz, N., Campbell, A., Fleischmann, M., Nunen, J., Savelsbergh, M.: Revenue management opportunities for internet retailers. J. Revenue Pricing Manage. **12**, 128–138 (2013). https://doi.org/10.1057/rpm.2012.51
2. Agatz, N., Campbell, A.M., Fleischmann, M., Savelsbergh, M.: Challenges and opportunities in attended home delivery. In: Golden, B., Raghavan, S., Wasil, E. (eds.) The Vehicle Routing Problem: Latest Advances and New Challenges. Operations Research/Computer Science Interfaces, vol. 43, pp. 379–396. Springer, Boston (2008). https://doi.org/10.1007/978-0-387-77778-8_17
3. Akamai: Akamai online retail performance report: milliseconds are critical (2017). https://www.akamai.com/uk/en/about/news/press/2017-press/akamai-releases-spring-2017-state-of-online-retail-performance-report.jsp
4. Akkerman, F., Mes, M.: Distance approximation to support customer selection in vehicle routing problems. Ann. Oper. Res., April 2022. https://doi.org/10.1007/s10479-022-04674-8
5. Akkerman, F.: Delivery cost approximations for dynamic time slot pricing, April 2021. http://essay.utwente.nl/86079/
6. Asdemir, K., Jacob, V.S., Krishnan, R.: Dynamic pricing of multiple home delivery options. Eur. J. Oper. Res. **196**(1), 246–257 (2009). https://doi.org/10.1016/j.ejor.2008.03.005
7. Bai, J., Lu, F., Zhang, K., et al.: ONNX: Open neural network exchange (2019). https://github.com/onnx/onnx
8. Belobaba, P.: Air travel demand and airline seat inventory management. Ph.D. thesis, Massachusetts Institute of Technology, Cambridge (1987)
9. Campbell, A., Savelsbergh, M.: Incentive schemes for attended home delivery services. Transp. Sci. **40**, 327–341 (2006). https://doi.org/10.1287/trsc.1050.0136
10. Campbell, A.M., Savelsbergh, M.W.P.: Decision support for consumer direct grocery initiatives. Transp. Sci. **39**(3), 313–327 (2005). https://doi.org/10.1287/trsc.1040.0105
11. Cleophas, C., Ehmke, J.: When are deliveries profitable? Bus. Inf. Syst. Eng. **6**, 153–163 (2014)
12. Ehmke, J.F., Campbell, A.M.: Customer acceptance mechanisms for home deliveries in metropolitan areas. Eur. J. Oper. Res. **233**(1), 193–207 (2014). https://doi.org/10.1016/j.ejor.2013.08.028
13. Klein, R., Mackert, J., Neugebauer, M., Steinhardt, C.: A model-based approximation of opportunity cost for dynamic pricing in attended home delivery. OR Spectr. **40**(4), 969–996 (2017). https://doi.org/10.1007/s00291-017-0501-3
14. Klein, R., Neugebauer, M., Ratkovitch, D., Steinhardt, C.: Differentiated time slot pricing under routing considerations in attended home delivery. Transp. Sci. **53**(1), 236–255 (2019). https://doi.org/10.1287/trsc.2017.0738
15. Lee, T.C., Hersh, M.: A model for dynamic airline seat inventory control with multiple seat bookings. Transp. Sci. **27**(3), 252–265 (1993)
16. Nicola, D., Vetschera, R., Dragomir, A.: Total distance approximations for routing solutions. Comput. Oper. Res. **102**, 67–74 (2019)
17. ORTEC: Vehicle routing solutions. https://ortec.com/en/solutions/vehicle-routing. Accessed 14 July 2022
18. Pedregosa, F., et al.: Scikit-learn: machine learning in Python. J. Mach. Learn. Res. **12**, 2825–2830 (2011)

19. Robuste, F., Daganzo, C.F., Souleyrette, R.R.: Implementing vehicle routing models. Transp. Res. Part B Methodol. **24**(4), 263–286 (1990)
20. Snoeck, A., Merchán, D., Winkenbach, M.: Revenue management in last-mile delivery: state-of-the-art and future research directions. Transp. Res. Procedia **46**, 109–116 (2020). https://doi.org/10.1016/j.trpro.2020.03.170. The 11th International Conference on City Logistics, Dubrovnik, Croatia, 12–14 June 2019
21. Solomon, M.M.: Algorithms for the vehicle routing and scheduling problems with time window constraints. Oper. Res. **35**(2), 254–265 (1987). https://doi.org/10.1287/opre.35.2.254
22. Strauss, A.K., Klein, R., Steinhardt, C.: A review of choice-based revenue management: theory and methods. Eur. J. Oper. Res. **271**(2), 375–387 (2018). https://doi.org/10.1016/j.ejor.2018.01.011
23. Visser, T., Agatz, N., Spliet, R.: Simultaneous customer interaction in online booking systems for attended home delivery. Technical report, ERS-2019-011-LIS, ERIM Report Series Research in Management, Erasmus Research Institute of Management, October 2019. http://hdl.handle.net/1765/120585
24. Yang, X., Strauss, A.: An approximate dynamic programming approach to attended home delivery management. Eur. J. Oper. Res. **263**, 935–945 (2017). https://doi.org/10.1016/j.ejor.2017.06.034
25. Yang, X., Strauss, A.K., Currie, C.S.M., Eglese, R.: Choice-based demand management and vehicle routing in e-fulfillment. Transp. Sci. **50**(2), 473–488 (2016). https://doi.org/10.1287/trsc.2014.0549
26. Yrjölä, H.: Physical distribution considerations for electronic grocery shopping. Int. J. Phys. Distrib. Logist. Manag. **31**(10), 746–761 (2001)

The Green Sequencing and Routing Problem

Giacomo Lanza(✉), Mauro Passacantando, and Maria Grazia Scutellà

Department of Computer Science, University of Pisa, Pisa, Italy
giacomo.lanza@di.unipi.it,
{mauro.passacantando,maria.grazia.scutella}@unipi.it

Abstract. The paper deals with a sequencing and routing problem originated by a real-world application context. The problem consists in defining the best sequence of locations to visit within a warehouse for the storage and/or retrieval of a given set of items during a specified time horizon, by considering some specific requirements and operating policies which are typical of the kind of warehouse under study. A fleet composed of both electric (i.e., equipped with a lithium-ion battery) and conventional (i.e., with internal combustion engine) forklifts is considered. We model the problem in terms of constrained multicommodity flows on a space-time network, and we extend a matheuristic approach proposed for the case of only conventional vehicles. Preliminary computational results are also presented.

Keywords: Green logistics · Warehouse management · Matheuristic

1 Introduction

Warehouses are an essential component of any supply chain. Warehousing concerns receiving, storing, order picking, and shipping of goods. The large majority of the warehouses (especially in Western Europe, according to [8]) are operated pursuing the picker-to-parts principle, i.e., workers walk or drive through the warehouse to perform either picking or put-away operations. The former concern the movement of items from the storage locations towards the output point of the warehouse to respond to a customer order, the latter instead concern the movement of items from the input points of the warehouse towards the storage area to store the items in the assigned storage locations. Picking and put-away are recognized as the most labor and time consuming internal logistics processes, and their careful and efficient planning plays a major role in improving productivity and decreasing the operational costs of a warehouse.

The problem addressing this issue is known in the literature as Sequencing and Routing Problem (SRP). Precisely, the SRP has the scope of defining the

The research has been supported by Polo Universitario Sistemi Logistici di Livorno and funded by project PRA 2020 "Analisi di reti complesse: dalla teoria alle applicazioni" of the University of Pisa.

J. de Armas et al. (Eds.): ICCL 2022, LNCS 13557, pp. 231–244, 2022.
https://doi.org/10.1007/978-3-031-16579-5_16

most efficient sequence of operations to move items within the warehouse to perform order picking and put-away operations, by typically minimizing the total material handling cost or travel efforts (measured either in time or distance traveled by the workers), and respecting some additional and peculiar requirements related to the application context [8].

Warehouses are also major contributors of greenhouse gas emissions in supply chains, especially raised by the use of diesel forklifts [3]. Consequently, besides traditional operational and economic objectives, increasing attention is now given by companies to usually overlooked aspects, such as sustainability and environmental-friendly issues in warehouse management. The *Green* SRP is thus emerging as a new topic of research. It is a variant of the classic SRP where some electric vehicles perform operations within the warehouse. Although the use of electric forklifts has been recognized as a way to both reduce long term management costs [5] and improve healthiness for workers (e.g., reduced noise, better local air quality), it contributes to increasing the problem complexity since peculiar activities, such as the scheduling of recharging periods, as well as the limited autonomy of the vehicles, need to be considered when planning ordinary picking and put-away operations.

A very few contributions discussing SRPs with electric forklifts are available in the literature, highlighting the novelty of the topic. In [7], picking and put-away operations need to be planned by using a fleet of electric forklifts, whose battery may be replaced once the state of charge is too low. A similar problem is discussed in [2], where besides battery replacement also the recharging process of the batteries is considered. Both problems are formulated as job-shop problems.

Recently, [6] addressed a SRP related to a large production site of an Italian company. The SRP is characterized by some specific requirements, originated by the layout design of the warehouse, and also by the particular kind of products stocked, i.e., tissue products for sanitary and domestic use. Conventional vehicles, i.e., with an internal combustion engine, are considered to perform picking and put-away operations. In this paper, we investigate the green extension of the above mentioned problem, where some of the vehicles are electric and equipped with a lithium-ion battery. This technology is considered as the most promising for the near future by the majority of literary sources, for its high efficiency and long lifespan [1]. Indeed, it is also the technology adopted in the studied warehouse.

The paper is organized as follows. The Green SRP is presented in Sect. 2. The main features of the mathematical model proposed for its formulation and an overview of the matheuristic approach used to solve it are described in Sects. 3 and 4, respectively. Section 5 presents some preliminary numerical results on the Green SRP. Finally, Sect. 6 concludes the paper and identifies some future research directions.

2 The Green SRP

The addressed problem is defined in a warehouse characterized by two disjoint areas. The first area is a transit zone connecting the input points of the warehouse, where items wait to be stored, to the storage area. The second area instead is the storage area, where storage locations are situated together with a collection area where, according to the pick-and-sort policy followed, retrieved items are gathered to establish order integrity before loading trucks. Items are homogeneously stocked with respect to their type of product within the storage locations, which have different capacities, depending on their location within the warehouse. The input points and the collection area are capacitated as well.

During a specified time horizon, i.e., an eight hours work-shift, a number of items of different product types require the transportation from the input points to their preassigned storage locations and, at the same time, a certain number of items need to be picked from their storage locations and transported to the collection area. We define these flows of items as *incoming* and *outgoing*, respectively. Incoming items are available at a known *availability date*, while outgoing items are required to reach the collection area before a known *due date*. The amount of items to move and their product types are also known in advance.

The movements of items are performed by capacitated vehicles belonging to two different types of fleets, defined in the following as F1 and F2. The routing of the two fleets of vehicles is restricted to only one of the above described disjoint areas of the warehouse. In particular, F1 can only travel in the transit zone, thus moving incoming items from the input points towards *collectors*, i.e., capacitated zones located at the entrance of the storage area, whereas F2 can only circulate within the storage area, thus moving both incoming items from the collectors towards the assigned storage locations, and outgoing items from the storage locations towards the collection area. Incoming items thus need to follow a two-echelon movement towards their storage locations, using vehicles of fleet F1 and F2 sequentially. In addition, the routing of the vehicles has to be planned by considering:

i) anticipation of outgoing movements with respect to the planned due dates; this is particularly relevant when a shift with a low demand is followed by a shift with a high demand, thus items planned to leave the site in the second shift may be moved towards the collection area already during the first one;
ii) a strict management policy for both picking and put-away operations prescribing that, separately per product type, storage locations have to be emptied/filled up one at a time following a given order of precedence, implying that a new storage location may be utilized for picking/storing only if the previous one in the considered order is already completely empty/full;
iii) safety requirements for workers.

We refer to [6] for a more detailed and comprehensive description of the features above. Here we consider the case where a subset of the vehicles of type F2 are electric and equipped with a lithium-ion battery. The battery is discharged when vehicles move or lift items from the ground, and its state of charge needs to be maintained within a given range to ensure a long lifetime to the battery. As opposed to traditional lead-acid batteries needing full recharging operations, a lithium-ion battery may benefit from partial recharging, which may occur during even short break times between operations at the available charging station. Thus, besides planning the routing of the vehicles in order to move inbound items (from the input points towards the preassigned storage locations) and outbound items (from storage locations towards the collection area), battery charging operations need to be scheduled as well. As in [6], the primary aim is to minimize the travel time of all the vehicles within the warehouse.

3 Mathematical Formulation

The problem is formulated in terms of constrained multicommodity flows on a space-time network, and a Mixed Integer Linear Programming (MILP) model based on this formulation is proposed.

Let $\mathcal{K}$ be the set of the product types, or commodities, requiring movement in a given time horizon. It is composed of the subset of the incoming commodities $\mathcal{K}_{in}$ and the subset of the outgoing commodities $\mathcal{K}_{out}$. Let $\mathcal{V}^1$ and $\mathcal{V}^2$ be the sets of vehicles of type F1 and F2, respectively, in charge of moving commodities inside the warehouse. Moreover, let $\mathcal{V}^E \subseteq \mathcal{V}^2$ denote the subset of the electric vehicles of type F2.

Let $\mathcal{G}^P = (\mathcal{N}^P, \mathcal{A}^P)$ be the directed graph representing the physical network on which vehicles operate. The set of nodes $\mathcal{N}^P$ includes:

- the set $\mathcal{S}^k_{in}$ of the storage locations preassigned to the product types in $\mathcal{K}_{in}$, and the set $\mathcal{S}^k_{out}$ of the storage locations occupied by items of product types in $\mathcal{K}_{out}$ at the beginning of the time horizon;
- the parking areas for vehicles of type F1 and F2, denoted by ω^1 and ω^2, respectively;
- the set $\mathcal{R}$ of the input points (within the transit zone);
- the set $\mathcal{B}$ of the collectors;
- the output point (or collection area) π;
- the available charging station c.

The set of arcs $\mathcal{A}^P$ represents direct connections between pairs of distinct locations of the warehouse. The dynamics of the problem are modelled through a *space-time network* $\mathcal{G} = (\mathcal{N}, \mathcal{A})$. The time horizon is discretized into T time periods of equal length through $T+1$ time instants. The set $\mathcal{N}^P$ is then replicated $T+1$ times, resulting in set $\mathcal{N}$. A node in $\mathcal{N}$ is defined by a couple (i,t), with $i \in \mathcal{N}^P$ and $t \in \{0,\ldots,T\}$, and represents one of the locations of the warehouse at one of the considered $T+1$ time instants. The set of arcs $\mathcal{A}$ is composed of two subsets: the subset of *holding* arcs $\mathcal{A}^H$, including arcs of type $((i,t),(i,t+1))$, for any $i \in \mathcal{N}^P$ and $t \in \{0,\ldots,T-1\}$, used to model *idle time* of items or vehicles in a given node for one time period, and the subset of *moving* arcs $\mathcal{A}^M$, including arcs of type $((i,t),(j,t'))$ with $(i,j) \in \mathcal{A}^P$, $t \in \{0,\ldots,T-\tau_{i,j}\}$ and

$t' = t + \tau_{i,j}$, where $\tau_{i,j}$ denotes the travel time from i to j in the directed graph $\mathcal{G}^P$. The travel time $\tau_{i,j}$ is determined by considering the allowed speed of the vehicles and by assuming that vehicles always follow a shortest path from i to j along the network. The subset of arcs $\mathcal{A}^M$ is thus used to model *movements* of items or vehicles between two different locations in different time periods.

Several parameters are introduced to describe the features of vehicles and incoming and outgoing commodities. We refer to [6] for a complete description. We introduce here only those related to the energy consumption model for the battery.

Let e^{ij} be the battery energy consumed by an electric vehicle in $\mathcal{V}^E$ to move empty along $(i,j) \in \mathcal{A}^P$, while e^{ijk} be the additional battery energy consumed by the vehicle, per unit of load, to move along $(i,j) \in \mathcal{A}^P$ if it is loaded with items of product type $k \in \mathcal{K}$. Moreover, let e^k be the energy consumed by a vehicle to lift one unit of product type $k \in \mathcal{K}$. This operation is necessary only at certain nodes of $\mathcal{N}^P$, i.e., nodes in $S^k_{in} \cup \mathcal{S}^k_{out} \cup \mathcal{B}$. Furthermore, let e^r denote the increase of the battery energy, for one period of time, if the vehicle recharges at the charging station. These parameters have been calculated according to the comprehensive energy consumption model described in [4], which takes into account speed, acceleration, deceleration, load cargo and gradients. Finally, let $[B^-, B^+]$ define the range in which the charge of the battery should always be maintained, while $\psi^v_0 \in [B^-, B^+]$ be the charge that vehicle $v \in \mathcal{V}^E$ has at the beginning of the time horizon. Regarding the battery, $\Theta \in [B^-, B^+]$ will denote the minimum charge required for each electric vehicle at the end of the time horizon. Parameter Θ has been introduced to ensure enough charge at the beginning of the next time horizon, to perform basic operations such as traveling to the charging station.

Now, let us introduce the main families of variables used to formulate the addressed Green SRP. The following four families of variables model the routing of vehicles and commodities along the network. In the variable definition, $\mathcal{A}_{F1}$, $\mathcal{A}_{F2}$, $\mathcal{A}_{in}$ and $\mathcal{A}_{out}$ denote the subsets of arcs of the network where vehicles of type F1, vehicles of type F2, incoming commodities and outcoming commodities are permitted to move, respectively:

- $x^v_{(i,t)(j,t')} \in \{0,1\}$, for any $v \in \mathcal{V}^1$ and $((i,t),(j,t')) \in \mathcal{A}_{F1}$, indicates whether vehicle v passes on the arc $((i,t),(j,t'))$ or not;
- $x^v_{(i,t)(j,t')} \in \{0,1\}$, for any $v \in \mathcal{V}^2$ and $((i,t),(j,t')) \in \mathcal{A}_{F2}$, indicates whether vehicle v passes on the arc $((i,t),(j,t'))$ or not;
- $y^k_{(i,t)(j,t')} \in \mathbb{Z}_+$, for any $k \in \mathcal{K}_{in}$ and $((i,t),(j,t')) \in \mathcal{A}_{in}$, indicates the number of items of product type k passing on the arc $((i,t),(j,t'))$;
- $y^k_{(i,t)(j,t')} \in \mathbb{Z}_+$, for any $k \in \mathcal{K}_{out}$ and $((i,t),(j,t')) \in \mathcal{A}_{out}$, indicates the number of items of product type k passing on the arc $((i,t),(j,t'))$.

Moreover, we define:

- $\psi^v_t \in \mathbb{R}_+$, for any $v \in \mathcal{V}^E$ and $t \in \{1,\ldots,T\}$, which indicates the state of charge of the battery of the electric vehicle v at time t.

The objective function of the MILP model is defined as follows:

$$\min \sum_{v\in\mathcal{V}^1} \sum_{\substack{((i,t),(j,t'))\in\mathcal{A}_{F1}:\\ i\neq\omega^1,\, j\neq\omega^1}} \tau_{i,j}\, x^v_{(i,t)(j,t')} + \sum_{v\in\mathcal{V}^2} \sum_{\substack{((i,t),(j,t'))\in\mathcal{A}_{F2}:\\ i\neq\omega^2,\, j\neq\omega^2}} \tau_{i,j}\, x^v_{(i,t)(j,t')}$$
$$+\psi \sum_{k\in\mathcal{K}_{in}} \sum_{\substack{((i,t),(j,t'))\in\mathcal{A}_{in}:\\ i,\, j\in\mathcal{R}}} y^k_{(i,t)(j,t')} + \xi \sum_{k\in\mathcal{K}_{out}} P^k. \tag{1}$$

It is composed of four parts. The first two summations define the primary optimization goal, i.e., minimizing the travel time of all the vehicles within the warehouse. Notice that arcs entering or leaving the parking areas are not considered for both vehicle types to encourage vehicles to come back to their parking areas when idle, so limiting congestion situations along the network. The third and fourth summations define soft objectives. In particular, the third summation relates to the time of permanence of the items on the input points, so as to favor the movements of items towards other spots of the warehouse. The fourth relates to the anticipation movements to perform. The latter summations are weighted through parameters ψ and ξ, respectively, to state their mutual priorities. Being $\mathcal{N}^-(\pi, t')$ the set of nodes linked to $\pi \in \mathcal{N}^P$ via an entering arc, the terms P^k are defined as follows:

$$P^k = \max\left\{0,\ \sum_{t=0}^{\tilde{T}} d^k_{out}(\pi, t) - \left[u^k_\pi + \sum_{t=0}^{T} \sum_{(j,t)\in\mathcal{N}^-(\pi,t')} y^k_{(j,t)(\pi,t')}\right]\right\} \tag{2}$$

for any $k \in \mathcal{K}_{out}$. The rationale of this penalty is to compare the amount of items of type k at the beginning of the time horizon, i.e., u^k_π, plus the items of type k transported to the collection area π during the considered time horizon, given by the last two addendum of (2), with the overall demand of k from the time instant $t = 0$ to an extended time instant $\tilde{T} > T$, given by the first addendum of (2). Input parameter $\tilde{T}$ relates to the future time periods addressed for the anticipation moves, while $d^k_{out}(\pi, t)$ denotes the number of items of type k which are requested in the collection area at the latest time t. The penalty is equal to 0 if, during the considered time horizon, an amount of items of type k enough to satisfy both the demand of k in the time horizon and also in the extended one, is moved to the collection area. Otherwise, the penalty to be paid is set proportionally to the amount of future demand that cannot be moved in advance.

Several constraints need to be defined to formulate the MILP model, such as flow conservation constraints for incoming and outgoing product types as well as for vehicles, to ensure their correct moving and routing within the warehouse, linking capacity constraints for vehicles and incoming and outgoing flows, demand constraints to ensure the respect of due dates for outgoing product types, location capacity constraints, constraints ensuring the correct application of the management policy in the warehouse, and finally constraints ensuring the security requirements for workers. The latter, in particular, impose that at most one vehicle can be present in any arc of the space-time network, except for the holding arcs representing dwell time at the parking areas.

For the sake of brevity, we do not report the above mentioned constraints, which can be found in [6]. On the other hand, we present below those constraints which regulate the energy behavior of the electric vehicles, since they are peculiar to the Green SRP. In such constraints, M is an input parameter defined as $M = B^+ - B^-$. Moreover, L_j is a parameter which assumes value 1 if $j \in S^k_{in} \cup \mathcal{S}^k_{out} \cup \mathcal{B}$, and 0 otherwise. The constraints are defined as follows:

$$\psi^v_{t'} \leq \psi^v_t - e^{ij} x^v_{(i,t)(j,t')} - \sum_{k \in \mathcal{K}} e^{ijk} y^k_{(i,t)(j,t')} - L_j \sum_{k \in \mathcal{K}} e^k y^k_{(i,t)(j,t')} + M\left[1 - x^v_{(i,t)(j,t')}\right] \quad \forall\, v \in \mathcal{V}^E,\ \forall\, ((i,t)(j,t')) \in \mathcal{A}_{F2}:\ i \neq j, \tag{3}$$

$$\psi^v_{t'} \geq \psi^v_t - e^{ij} x^v_{(i,t)(j,t')} - \sum_{k \in \mathcal{K}} e^{ijk} y^k_{(i,t)(j,t')} - L_j \sum_{k \in \mathcal{K}} e^k y^k_{(i,t)(j,t')} - M\left[1 - x^v_{(i,t)(j,t')}\right] \quad \forall\, v \in \mathcal{V}^E,\ \forall\, ((i,t)(j,t')) \in \mathcal{A}_{F2}:\ i \neq j, \tag{4}$$

$$\psi^v_{t+1} \leq \psi^v_t + e^r x^v_{(c,t)(c,t+1)} + M\left[1 - x^v_{(c,t)(c,t+1)}\right] \quad \forall\, v \in \mathcal{V}^E,\ \forall\, ((c,t)(c,t+1)) \in \mathcal{A}_{F2}, \tag{5}$$

$$\psi^v_{t+1} \geq \psi^v_t + e^r x^v_{(c,t)(c,t+1)} - M\left[1 - x^v_{(c,t)(c,t+1)}\right] \quad \forall\, v \in \mathcal{V}^E,\ \forall\, ((c,t)(c,t+1)) \in \mathcal{A}_{F2}, \tag{6}$$

$$\psi^v_{t+1} \leq \psi^v_t + M\left[1 - x^v_{(i,t)(i,t+1)}\right] \quad \forall\, v \in \mathcal{V}^E,\ \forall\, ((i,t)(i,t+1)) \in \mathcal{A}_{F2}:\ i \neq c, \tag{7}$$

$$\psi^v_{t+1} \geq \psi^v_t - M\left[1 - x^v_{(i,t)(i,t+1)}\right] \quad \forall\, v \in \mathcal{V}^E,\ \forall\, ((i,t)(i,t+1)) \in \mathcal{A}_{F2}:\ i \neq c, \tag{8}$$

$$B^- \leq \psi^v_t \leq B^+ \qquad \forall\, v \in \mathcal{V}^E,\ \forall\, t \geq 0, \tag{9}$$

$$\psi^v_T \geq \Theta \qquad \forall\, v \in \mathcal{V}^E. \tag{10}$$

Constraints (3)–(8) model the state of charge of the battery, which decreases if the vehicle travels along a moving arc, increases if the vehicle idles on a holding arc corresponding to the charging station, or remains constant if the vehicle idles on any other location of the warehouse. Specifically, the discharge of the battery is modelled by constraints (3)–(4). By recalling that a moving arc can be used by at most one vehicle, when a vehicle v travels along a moving arc $((i,t)(j,t'))$ then constraints (3)–(4) imply

$$\psi_{t'}^{v} = \psi_{t}^{v} - e^{ij} - \sum_{k \in \mathcal{K}} e^{ijk} y_{(i,t)(j,t')}^{k} - L_j \sum_{k \in \mathcal{K}} e^{k} y_{(i,t)(j,t')}^{k},$$

thus defining the state of charge of the battery of the vehicle at the time instant t' as the state of charge of the battery of the vehicle at the time instant t minus the energy necessary for the vehicle to move empty on the arc (the second term in the equation), the additional energy used if the vehicle is loaded (the third term in the equation) and the energy used to lift items at location j, if necessary (the last term in the equation). If the arc is not travelled by the vehicle, then constraints (3)–(4) are satisfied since weaker than constraints (9). The latter define the lower and upper thresholds for the ideal operating conditions of the battery. When the vehicle is at the charging station c, i.e., it is on a holding arc of form $((c,t)(c,t+1))$, constraints (5)–(6) define the state of charge of the battery at time instant $t+1$ as the state of charge of the battery at the time instant t plus the energy recharged during one time period at the charging station. Constraints (7)–(8), instead, indicate that the state of charge of the battery remains unchanged if the vehicle is idling on a location of the warehouse other than c. Finally, constraints (10) impose that the state of charge of the electric vehicles at the end of the time horizon is greater than or equal to the minimum threshold Θ. This is to ensure that, at the beginning of the next shift, their state of charge is enough to perform some basic operations rather than being completely discharged.

4 Matheuristic Resolution Approach

In [6], a matheuristic approach based on a decomposition strategy has been proposed for the conventional SRP since real size instances, such as those provided to us by our industrial partner, could not be directly addressed through the state-of-the-art commercial solver CPLEX. The approach has shown a very good performance, as detailed in [6].

Specifically, the original planning horizon is divided into Λ subperiods of equal length. Each subperiod gives rise to a subproblem, whose features are those of the original problem restricted to the considered subperiod. The Λ subproblems are then sequentially solved by using CPLEX in such a way that the final state of the system obtained solving subproblem $\lambda - 1$ becomes the initial state of the system when solving subproblem λ, for any $\lambda = 2, \ldots, \Lambda$. In particular, the state of the system in each subproblem takes into account the position of vehicles and items within the warehouse. Once the Λ subproblems have been solved, in order to construct a solution for the original problem, and thus the complete schedule for the entire time horizon, it is sufficient to concatenate the Λ solutions in an increasing order with respect to the subperiod addressed, i.e., from subperiod 1 to subperiod Λ. The matheuristic approach is summarized in Algorithm 1. We refer to [6] for a more detailed description.

Algorithm 1. The matheuristic approach

1: Divide the time horizon into Λ subperiods
2: **for** $\lambda = 1, \ldots, \Lambda$ **do**
3: Solve the λ-th subproblem
4: **end for**
5: Concatenate the subproblem solutions from 1 to Λ

The matheuristic approach has been extended to deal with the green aspects previously introduced. In particular, the initial state of the system in each subproblem takes into account, in addition to the position of vehicles and items within the warehouse at the end of the previous subperiod, also the state of charge of each battery. Specifically, for any $\lambda = 2, \ldots, \Lambda$, the state of charge of a vehicle, say v, at the initial time instant of subproblem λ, say 0_λ, is defined as $\psi^v_{0_\lambda} = \psi^v_{T_{\lambda-1}}$, where $\psi^v_{T_{\lambda-1}}$ is the state of charge of the battery of vehicle v at the final time instant of subproblem $\lambda - 1$, here denoted by $T_{\lambda-1}$.

5 Numerical Experiments

We present some preliminary results on the Green SRP by solving the set of five artificial instances in the dataset used in [6], suitably generalized to the green context. Generally, such instances turned out to be too difficult to address directly with CPLEX, thus the matheuristic previously introduced has been used to solve the Green SRP. Experiments have been performed by varying the number of the electric vehicles, by analysing both the efficiency of the matheuristic approach in terms of percentage gap and solution time, and also investigating the quality of the returned solutions in terms of some crucial performance indicators suggested by our industrial partner.

The matheuristic has been implemented using the language OPL and solved via CPLEX 12.6 (IBM ILOG, 2016) with a time limit of 3 h. The experiments have been run on an Intel Xeon 5120 with 2.20 GHz and 32 GB of RAM.

5.1 The Reference Case Study

The instances refer to the production site of a company, leader in the tissue sector, which works daily on three shifts of 8 h and produces more than 300 different types of products. Items are arranged in unit-loads and wrapped in so-called columns of pallets. There are 3 input points with capacity 10, 14 and 8 columns, respectively, while the storage area has 858 storage locations, with different capacities ranging from 8 to 17 columns. The number of collectors is 6, with capacities ranging from 2 to 8 columns. Finally, the collection area has a capacity of 700 columns. The fleet of the company is composed of 5 LGV shuttles, corresponding to vehicles of type F1, and 7 forklifts, corresponding to vehicles of type F2, some of which are electric. Both types of vehicles, hereafter LGV and FKL for short, may transport 2 columns at most at the same time.

On average, during each 8 h shift, 320 columns of 9 product types need to be moved from the input points towards their storage locations, while 1110 columns of 28 product types need to be moved from their storage locations towards the collection area. Regarding parameters B^-, B^+ and Θ, related to the state of charge of the battery, they have been set to the 30%, the 80% and the 35% of the total capacity of the battery, respectively. Parameters B^- and B^+ have been set up in accordance with the features described in the user manual of the specific electric FKL used by the industrial partner.

The Green SRP instances have been generated starting from the five artificial SRP instances in the dataset used in [6]. In turn, such five SRP instances have been generated starting from a real dataset provided by the company, which comprises a pool of selected 8 h shifts, by shortening the duration of a shift from 8 to 4 h, and reducing the number of product types and columns to move accordingly. The main features of the Green SRP instances are reported in Table 1. Specifically, the number of available storage locations is reported (column SL) together with the number of the product types in K_{in} and in K_{out} (columns K_{in} and K_{out}, respectively), and the corresponding number of items to move (columns C_{in} and C_{out}, respectively).

Table 1. The Green SRP instances.

Instance	Main features				
	SL	K_{in}	K_{out}	C_{in}	C_{out}
1	10	3	6	142	288
2	4	2	4	108	234
3	9	3	5	78	188
4	4	2	3	132	226
5	8	3	5	134	364
Average	6.6	2.2	4.2	90.8	117.2

5.2 Computational Results

In order to solve the Green SRP by means of the matheuristic approach, we split the time horizon into four subshifts, thus obtaining subshifts of about 60 min. As reported in [6], longer subshifts may lead to hardly solvable subproblems, while shorter subshifts seem to negatively affect the quality of the solutions obtained. The resolution of each subproblem has been performed via CPLEX by stopping the execution as soon as an optimality gap less than 1% or, alternatively, a time limit of 15 min were reached. Most subproblems, however, were solved to optimality. Finally, parameters ψ and ξ in (1) have been set equal to 10, since this combination proved to be very effective in [6].

Each of the five Green SRP instances has been solved three times, by varying the number of the electric vehicles. Specifically, 1, 2 and 3 electric FKL have been considered (recall that the total number of FKL is 7). In the following, we refer to the composition of the fleet of FKL as a pair of numbers in brackets of type ($|\mathcal{V}^D|$ - $|\mathcal{V}^E|$), where the first position indicates the number of traditional FKL used, while the second position gives the number of the electric FLK. After some preliminary tests, we considered three different settings for the initial state of the charge of the electric vehicles, depending on their number. Specifically, if one electric FKL is used, its initial state of charge is set to the half of the range $[B^-, B^+]$; if two electric FKL are used, the range $[B^-, B^+]$ is split into two parts of equal length, and the initial state of charge of one vehicle is set to the half of the first range, while the initial state of charge of the second vehicle is set to the half of the second range; finally, if three electric FKL are used, then the range $[B^-, B^+]$ is split into three parts of equal length, and the initial state of charge of the vehicles is set to the half of the first, of the second and of the third range, respectively.

For each instance, Table 2 reports the time, in seconds, required by the matheuristic to find a solution to the Green SRP for each of the three fleet compositions mentioned before (calculated as the sum of the times needed to solve the subproblems). It also reports the percentage optimality gap, calculated with respect to the optimal value found by CPLEX by solving the Green SRP with only one electric FKL. This is the only variant of Green SRP that CPLEX was able to solve to optimality, and the corresponding optimal values thus represent lower bounds for all the addressed variants. The times required to compute such lower bounds are reported in column LB. Moreover, to perform a comparison with the traditional SRP, the times required by the matheuristic to solve SRP are reported in column (7-0), to emphasize that SRP is the special case of Green SRP with 0 electric vehicles.

Table 2 shows that the Green SRP is more difficult to address than the traditional SRP. In the case of no electric vehicles, the average time required by the matheuristic is in fact about 9 seconds, whereas when electric vehicles are present the time increases a lot, especially in the case of 3 electric FKL. Notice that,

Table 2. Performance of the matheuristic for Green SRP.

Instance	($\|\mathcal{V}^D\|$ - $\|\mathcal{V}^E\|$)							
	(7-0)	(6-1)		(5-2)		(4-3)		LB
	Time	Time	Gap	Time	Gap	Time	Gap	Time
1	10.91	757.73	10.65%	87.10	9.70%	1014.75	8.69%	4496.23
2	5.37	66.99	6.71%	365.52	6.38%	1063.37	7.69%	316.13
3	10.45	14.51	0.32%	106.54	3.09%	124.41	4.87%	1792.26
4	7.54	463.36	2.21%	111.95	20.64%	717.77	21.32%	699.05
5	13.35	1816.47	13.52%	2097.74	6.60%	2530.83	15.00%	4642.82
Avg.	9.53	623.81	6.68%	553.77	9.28%	1090.22	11.51%	2389.30

Table 3. Features of solutions in terms of crucial performance indicators.

	$\|(\mathcal{V}^D\|$ - $\|\mathcal{V}^E\|)$			
	(7-0)	(6-1)	(5-2)	(4-3)
LGV avg. travel time (min.)	75.84	76.56	76.16	76.16
FKL avg. travel time (min.)	122	122.51	122.80	123.03
Conventional FKL avg. travel time (min.)	122	122.20	125.84	117.10
Electric FKL avg. travel time (min.)	-	124.4	115.2	130.93
Electric FKL avg. charging time (min.)	-	10.4	4.6	6.5
Input point avg. idle time per item (min.)	0.127	0.129	0.123	0.131
% of saturation of collection area after 3 h	99.43%	99.43%	98.29%	99.43%
% of saturation of collection area after 4 h	99.43%	99.08%	98.23%	98.12%

as reported in [6], CPLEX was able to optimally solve the five SRP instances in 217 seconds on average, whereas the optimal solution of the Green SRP with just one electric vehicle required about 2389 s seconds on average (see column LB). Nevertheless, the matheuristic is still efficient, being able to find good solutions for the Green SRP with an average optimality gap of about 7% in the case of 1 electric FKL, 9% in case of 2, and 11% in case of 3.

To better analyse the results in Table 2 as well as the quality of the computed solutions, Table 3 reports some aggregated features of the solutions in terms of crucial performance indicators suggested by our industrial partner.

Specifically, the primary goal is analysed in terms of the average time, in minutes, travelled by a LGV and by a FKL over the 5 instances. Disaggregated results are also reported separately for conventional and electric vehicles (averages are calculated over the corresponding number of conventional and electric vehicles used). Moreover, we report the average charging time of the electric vehicles, always in minutes. The secondary goals, i.e., emptying the input points and anticipation moves, are evaluated by considering the average time, in minutes, an incoming item idles on an input point before been moved to an available collector, and the percentage of saturation of the collection area both 60 min before the end of the planning horizon (% of saturation of collection area after 3 h) and also at the end of the planning horizon (% of saturation of collection area after 4 h).

The average time travelled by a FKL (conventional and electric) is almost the same for both the traditional and the Green SRP. However, the number of electric vehicles used strongly influences the usage of the fleet of FKL. This is especially remarkable in the case of 2 electric FKL, where just a few operations are committed to the electric vehicles, whereas more operations are instead performed by conventional vehicles. On the other hand, in the case of 3 electric vehicles, i.e., when almost half of the fleet of FKL is electric, then electric vehicles travel more on average. Interestingly, the average charging time of the battery is greater in the case of a single electric vehicle, probably because, in the absence of conflicts with other electric vehicles towards the unique charging station, it tends to recharge more frequently. The LGV travel time, instead, slightly increases with respect to SRP. This may be explained as an additional way to prevent the discharge of the batteries of the electric FKL, as the majority of the routes from the input points towards the assigned storage locations is built in such a way to favor short trips on-board of electric FKL and longer trips on-board of LGV.

Regarding the secondary goals, being electric FKL not always available, this slightly slows down the rate of the anticipation moves to be performed with respect to SRP. Except for the case in which 2 electric FKL are used, after 3 h of operations the collection area seems not to be affected by the composition of the fleet of FKL (see the row % of saturation of collection area after 3 h and compare with SRP). However, the % of saturation of the collection area after 4 h highlights a lower readiness of the fleets including electric vehicles to promptly respond with replenishment operations when some new space is made available in the collection area. Similarly, the average idle time of incoming items on the input points generally increases with respect to the traditional SRP. Notice that the different impact of the number of electric vehicles on the primary and secondary goals may explain the reduction of time and/or gap sometimes observed in Table 2 when the number of the electric vehicles increases (like instance 1 in the case of one and two electric vehicles).

6 Conclusions

The Green SRP has been proposed and studied, where some of the vehicles of the fleet performing operations within the warehouse are electric. A pool of instances has been solved with a time decomposition matheuristic, which extends the one originally built for the traditional SRP. The experimental results, although preliminary, highlight the greater computational complexity of the Green SRP compared to SRP, and the good performance of the resolution approach in terms of efficiency and quality of the returned solutions. Future research will investigate additional scenarios in terms of number of electric vehicles used, also proposing alternative Green SRP resolution approaches.

References

1. Andwari, A.M., Pesiridis, A., Rajoo, S., Martinez-Botas, R., Esfahanian, V.: A review of Battery Electric Vehicle technology and readiness levels. Renew. Sustain. Energy Rev. **78**, 414–430 (2017)
2. Carli, R., Dotoli, M., Digiesi, S., Facchini, F., Mossa, G.: Sustainable scheduling of material handling activities in labor-intensive warehouses: a decision and control model. Sustainability **12**(8), 3111 (2020)
3. Bartolini, M., Bottani, E., Grosse, E.H.: Green warehousing: systematic literature review and bibliometric analysis. J. Clean. Prod. **226**, 242–258 (2019)
4. Fiori, C., Ahn, K., Rakha, H.A.: Power-based electric vehicle energy consumption model: model development and validation. Appl. Energy **168**, 257–268 (2016)

5. Jiao, M., Pan, F., Huang, X., Yuan, X.: Application potential of second-life lithium-ion battery on forklift. In: 4th International Electrical and Energy Conference (CIEEC), pp. 1–5. IEEE (2021)
6. Lanza, G., Passacantando, M., Scutellà, M.G.: Sequencing and routing in a large warehouse with high degree of product rotation. Flex. Serv. Manuf. J., (2022). Springer. https://doi.org/10.1007/s10696-022-09463-w
7. Lee, S., Jeon, H.W., Issabakhsh, M., Ebrahimi, A.: An electric forklift routing problem with battery charging and energy penalty constraints. J. Intell. Manuf. **33**(6), 1761–1777 (2022)
8. Van Gils, T., Ramaekers, K., Caris, A., de Koster, R.B.: Designing efficient order picking systems by combining planning problems: state-of-the-art classification and review. Eur. J. Oper. Res. **267**(1), 1–15 (2018)

The Long-Haul Transportation Problem with Refueling Deviations and Time-Dependent Travel Time

Silvia Anna Cordieri[1(✉)], Francesca Fumero[2], Ola Jabali[2], and Federico Malucelli[2]

[1] Università di Bologna, Bologna, Italy
silviaanna.cordieri2@unibo.it
[2] Politecnico di Milano, Milan, Italy
{francesca.fumero,Ola.Jabali,federico.malucelli}@polimi.it

Abstract. Basing on the operations of an Italian company, we model and solve a long-haul day-ahead transportation planning problem combining a number of features. Namely, we account for driver hours of service regulations, time-dependent travel times, time-dependent fuel consumption and refueling deviations. The latter stems from the fact that we consider non homogeneous fuel prices at refueling stations. Considering a given origin and destination along with the mentioned features, we propose a mixed integer linear programming (MILP) model that determines the minimum refueling cost route. These costs are established by modeling the time-dependent fuel consumption of the truck, accounting for different travel speeds due to recurrent traffic congestion. Given the challenge in solving the problem, we propose a heuristic algorithm to handle it efficiently. We test our model and algorithm on 42 realistic instances accounting for road network distances. Our result show that our heuristic produces high quality results within competitive run times.

Keywords: Long-haul trucks · Truck scheduling problem · Time-dependency · Refueling deviations · Hours of service regulations

1 Introduction

Long-haul truck transportation is a fundamental activity for goods transportation. In this context, the efficient planning of long-haul trips is complex due to several factors. First, the driver hours of service (HoS) regulations need to be respected. These govern the break times of drivers to guarantee road safety and adequate working conditions (e.g., Goel [14]). Second, traffic conditions, may greatly influence the speed of vehicles and thus lead to time-dependent travel times. Third, such variable speeds have a direct impact on the vehicle fuel consumption. Lastly, an even equally important aspect relates to refueling cost. In particular, the fuel cost may greatly differ from one refueling station to another. In particular, fuel prices are typically higher at stations along highways, when

J. de Armas et al. (Eds.): ICCL 2022, LNCS 13557, pp. 245–259, 2022.
https://doi.org/10.1007/978-3-031-16579-5_17

compared to stations located in rural or urban areas. Such differences, may imply that by deviating from the shortest path one may capitalize on competitive fuel prices.

We thus consider the optimization problem related to long-haul trip planning, accounting for the four previously mentioned factors. Moreover, inspired by a real-world case study in Italy, we consider the setting where a transportation company has contractual arrangements with a number of fuel companies. These entail significant discounts, and effectively restrict the choice of fuel stations to a limited subset of stations. In Italy, fuel prices are established at the beginning of the day by the Italian Ministry of Transport [17], and do not change during the day. Therefore, we study the day-ahead planing problem, where fuel prices do not change during the day and the daily fuel prices are discounted based on contractual agreements. Moreover, we consider the drivers to be employees paid by a fixed salary, thus we do not take into account for drivers cost.

The scientific aim of the paper is to model and solve the long-haul day-ahead truck transportation planning problem with refueling deviations and time-dependent travel time (LHFT). We consider a vehicle that must travel from an origin O to a destination D. The objective is to determine the minimum refueling cost route from O to D, while respecting the HoS regulations and necessary refueling stops. The set of considered fueling stations is limited to the set of contracted ones. These include stations along highways, in rural areas as well as in urban areas. Figure 1 shows an example on how the fuel stations are distributed on the route Milano-Catanzaro. There are 34 contracted stations, as shown in panel (a). Panel (b) shows the shortest path in time with a duration of 11 h and 13 min and a total cost of 94 euros. Panel (c) shows minimum refueling cost path with a duration of 11 h and 50 min and a total cost of 83 euros.

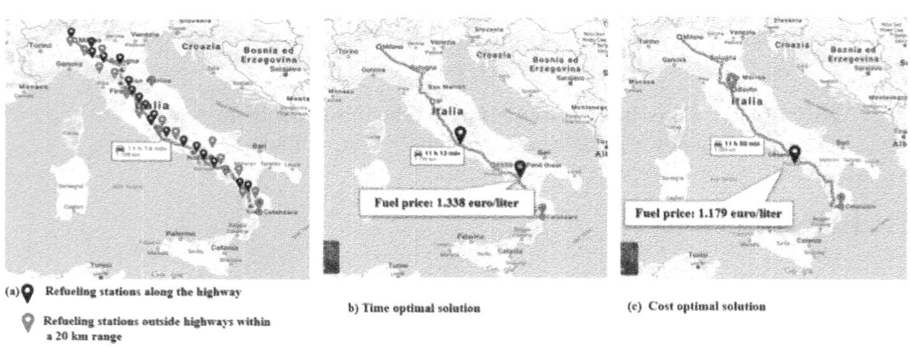

Fig. 1. Milano-Catanzaro: shortest path and minimum refueling cost path example

With respect to the existing literature, one of the main distinctive features of LHFT lies in accounting for time-dependent speeds throughout the day. Specifically, to account for realistic reoccurring traffic conditions, we identify specific hour intervals when congestion may intensify. These are estimated a priori and given as input to the problem. Consequently, the velocity of the vehicle changes according to the time of the day and the intervals defined and the time-dependent speeds lead to time-dependent travel times. The left panels of Fig. 2 show, for a given distance, how a time-dependent speed profile translates into a time-dependent travel time profile (modeling details of this feature are provided in Sect. 3). Furthermore, we consider the influence of time-dependent speeds on the vehicle fuel consumption. Therefore, contrary to what is typically assumed in the literature, fuel consumption is not fixed during the day, but it is dependent upon the predicted traffic conditions at each moment of the day. As such, the LHFT provides a more realistic modeling of fuel consumption, which is then used to find the minimum refueling cost path. The right panel of Fig. 2 provides an example of the resulting optimal solutions of LHFT, depending on different departure times.

We first propose a mixed integer linear programming (MILP) model for the LHFT. We note that the complexity of our problem stems from the fact of having two resources, i.e., fuel and time. This complexity is augmented by having time-dependent travel times and time-dependent fuel consumption. These imply that the resource consumption between two nodes depends on the departure time from the first node. Given the considered case study, our overarching goal was to provide a usable decision support tool for the LHFT. Therefore, the run time required for such a tool included all the data preprocessing necessary for its input. This encompasses retrieving shortest paths between all relevant nodes, as well as computing the time-dependent travel times and fuel consumption profiles for each considered arc. The overall runtime of the MILP with the preprocessing time of its input proved to be impractical. Therefore, we propose a heuristic algorithm for the LHFT, which considerably reduces the optimization runtimes.

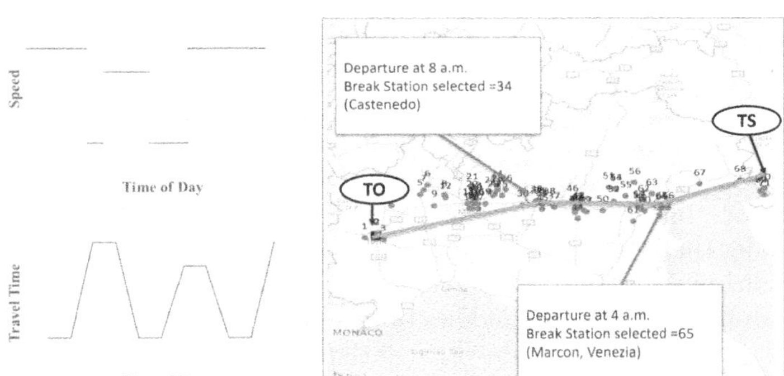

Fig. 2. Time-dependent travel times and optimal LHFT path examples

The main contributions of this paper are as follows. (I) We propose a MILP model for the LHFT that determines the minimum refueling cost path, considering HOS regulations and refueling stops, while accounting for time-dependent travel times and fuel consumption. (II) we propose a computationally efficient heuristic algorithm for the LHFT, and (III) we demonstrate the effectiveness of the proposed model and heuristic on a set of realistic instances.

The remainder of this paper is organized as follows. Section 2 provides a brief overview of the relevant literature. In Sect. 3 we describe the proposed model and the heuristic algorithm. In Sect. 4 we discuss the computational results. Finally, in Sect. 5 we present concluding remarks.

2 Literature Review

In this section we discuss the main contributions related to the long-haul day-ahead truck transportation planning problem with refueling deviations and time-dependent travel time. We classify the literature based on the main modelling features of the treated problems.

Incorporating road network distances has been receiving attention in recent vehicle routing literature (e.g., Ben Ticha et al. [5,6]). Such approaches rely on the so-called customer-based graph, where a node represents a depot, customer, rest station etc. In such cases the shorted path between each pair of nodes is derived from a geographic information system (GIS), and used as input for the optimization problem. We adopt this feature in our study.

Optimizing long-haul trips for an origin and a destination considering the Hours of Service (HoS), but without refueling considerations, has received much attention in the literature. The issue was first addressed by Xu et al. [24] under the title of the truck driver scheduling problem (TDSP). Archetti and Salvelsbergh [1] concentrated finding feasible schedules. Their polynomial algorithm was efficiently modified by Goel and Kok [12] considering the USA HoS regulations. Other countries' HoS regulations were also studied, e.g., Goel and Rousseau [13]. The TDSP was expanded to Vehicle Routing Truck Driver Scheduling Problem (VRTDSP) (e.g., Rancourt et al. [20] and Goel and Irnich [11]). In this problem a given set of customer nodes are to be visited while accounting for HoS regulation. We note that these studies do not take into account for distances on a road network and consider a routing problem rather than a single trip problem.

The role of fuel prices, excluding HoS regulations, has been investigated by several authors, but mostly, again, in the case of routing problems. Bousonville et al. [8] consider the vehicle routing problem with time windows including refueling decisions. Suzuki [22] proposes a heuristic algorithm that extends the traveling salesman problem with time windows to include refueling considerations. Suzuki and Dai [23] consider the bi-objective variable route vehicle refueling problem, accounting for minimizing fuel costs and vehicle mileage. Neves-Moreira et al. [19] study a multi-period vehicle routing problem with the possibility to perform detours to reach refueling stations with lower prices.

Bernhardt et al. [7] study the truck driver scheduling problem with HoS rest periods, breaks and vehicle refueling. In particular, given a route and a set of refueling stations with different fuel prices, the decisions relate to determining when to visit customers, which refueling stations to visit, refueling amounts and driver activities at stop locations. The resulting problem is modeled as a MILP. Mor et al. [18] study a similar problem considering a non restricted set of fuel stations. In particular, relevant fuel stations are considered incrementally using a construction algorithm.

The studies cited this far address the problems using time-invariant data. In several practical applications, this is a simplifying assumption, given the presence of time varying travel times. These lead to time-dependent routing problems, which amount to designing routes in a graph where the travel times vary over the planning horizon (see Gendreau et al. [10] for a comprehensive review). Time-dependent travel times stem from time-dependent speeds which greatly influence fuel consumption. Bektas and Laporte [4] inspect the impact of the vehicle speed on its fuel consumption, while Koç et al. [16] extend this aspect to a heterogeneous vehicle fleet, with three classes of vehicles.

Our work is closely related to that of Bernhardt et al. [7], where the truck driver scheduling problem with rest periods, breaks and vehicle refueling stops is considered. In addition, we consider realistic road networks, and incorporate time-dependent travel times and time-dependent fuel consumption. Furthermore, we propose an effective heuristic algorithm to tackle the resulting problem.

3 Methodology

In Sect. 3.1 we describe a MILP formulation for the LHFT. In Sect. 3.2 we present a heuristic algorithm for the LHFT.

3.1 Model

Given an origin O and a destination D, let F be the set of refueling stations where also resting is allowed. We topologically ordered the elements in F with respect to the distance from the origin. Let $N = \{F \cup O \cup D\}$ be the set of all the nodes considered, while A is the set of arcs connecting each pair of nodes in N.

We consider the European HoS regulations [9]. According to these regulations, truck drivers have to take a break of $p_1 = 0.75$ hours every 4.5 h. This break can be divided into two short breaks of 15 and 30 min, but both of them must be taken within the 4.5 driving hours. Moreover, a driver may drive for at most $p_2 = 9$ hours in a day, after which it is necessary to rest for at least 11 h. Therefore, we define set $K = \{1, 2, 3, 4\}$ to represent the four possible break types. The European Union provides further regulations for truck drivers' driving hours, that go beyond the daily planning. The amount of weekly driving time needs to be limited to 56 h, while the maximum total accumulated driving time during any two consecutive weeks is 90 h. Furthermore, every driver must respect a regular weekly rest period of minimum 45 h and a reduced weekly rest period of a minimum of 24 h [9]. Since our problem deals with single day planning, we decided not to include these further regulations in our model. The maximum fuel capacity of the vehicle is E, while we do not allow the fuel to be lower than

e. The starting fuel at the origin is given and denoted by SF. For each refueling station $i \in F$ the fuel price c_i is given, and refueling time is PT. This is excluded from the required break time, thus if a break and refueling were to take place at the same station, they are done in separation. Every break of type $k \in K$ has a duration of b^k expressed in hours (with $b^1 = 0.25$, $b^2 = 0.5$, $b^3 = 0.75$ and $b^4 = 11$). ST is the starting time from the origin. To avoid frequent refueling stops we limit the total route duration to T_{max}.

We use Eq. (1) based from Barth et al. [2], Scora and Barth [21], and Barth and Boriboonsomsin [3] to estimate fuel consumption of each arc at a given time instant. The parameters of the equation, were taken from the Light Duty vehicle model of Koç et al. [16]. We note that the only parameter we adapted to our study is the vehicle speed v, which varies during the day.

$$F^h = \lambda(k^h N^h V^h d/v + M^h \gamma^h \alpha d + \beta^h \gamma^h d v^2) \tag{1}$$

Similar to Fig. 2 we consider a set of $h \in \{0,..,9\}$ time intervals to model the time-dependent travel times and the time-dependent fuel consumption. For each arc $(i,j) \in A$, we consider T_{ij}^h intervals with $h \in \{1,..,9\}$: each interval is characterized by inclination m_{1ij}^h and an intercept q_{1ij}^h between $h-1$ and h. Similarly, the time-dependent fuel consumption is mapped with inclination m_{2ij}^h and an intercept q_{2ij}^h between $h-1$ and h for $h \in \{1,...,9\}$ and for each arc $(i,j) \in A$. We note that all needed calculations are done a priori considering a time-dependent speed function, which is then imposed on the shortest path distances between each pair of nodes on a road network.

Variable w_i indicates the amount of fuel purchased at fuel station i. Binary variable x_{ij} takes value one if arc $(i,j) \in A$ is selected, and zero otherwise. Variables t_{ij} and f_{ij} take the value of the travel time along the arc and the fuel consumption if arc $(i,j) \in A$ is selected, respectively. Variable τ_{ij} is the arrival time at $j \in N$ from O, if $(i,j) \in A$ is traversed, while variable s_{ij} represents the available amount of fuel upon arrival at $j \in N$ when arc $(i,j) \in A$ is traversed. For $i \in F$, binary variable y_i^k takes the value of one if a break of type $k \in K$ is made at i, and zero otherwise. For $i \in F$, binary variable z_i takes the value of one if a refueling is made at i, and zero otherwise. For $i \in N$ variables $\underline{r}_i$ represents the arrival time at i, while $\overline{r}_i$ represents the departure time from i. Finally, variables $\underline{r}_{ij}^h$ and u_{ij}^h regulate the time-dependent travel time function and the time-dependent fuel consumption function for arc $(i,j) \in A$. Model LHFT-M is a MILP formulation for our problem.

$$[LHFT-M]\quad \min \sum_{i\in F} c_i w_i \tag{2}$$

$$\sum_{j\in N} x_{Oj} = 1,\ \sum_{i\in N} x_{iD} = 1 \tag{3}$$

$$\sum_{j\in N} x_{ji} \le 1,\ \sum_{j\in N} x_{ji} - \sum_{l\in N} x_{il} = 0 \qquad \forall i \in F \tag{4}$$

$$\sum_{k\in K} y_i^k \le \sum_{j\in N} x_{ij} \qquad \forall i \in F \tag{5}$$

$$z_i \le \sum_{j\in N} x_{ij} \qquad \forall i \in F \tag{6}$$

$$\sum_{i\in N} \tau_{ij} + PTz_j + \sum_{l\in N} t_{jl} = \sum_{l\in N} \tau_{jl} \qquad \forall j \in N \tag{7}$$

$$\underline{r}_j = \sum_{i\in N} \tau_{ij} \qquad \forall j \in N \tag{8}$$

$$\overline{r}_i = \underline{r}_i + PTz_i \qquad \forall i \in F \tag{9}$$

$$\overline{r}_i = \underline{r}_i + \sum_{k\in K} b^k y_i^k \qquad \forall i \in F \tag{10}$$

$$\overline{r}_i = \underline{r}_i + PTz_i + \sum_{k\in K} b^k y_i^k \qquad \forall i \in F \tag{11}$$

$$\sum_{l=i|l\in F}^{j} y_l^1 = \sum_{l=i|l\in F}^{j} y_l^2 \qquad \forall i < j \in N \tag{12}$$

$$\underline{r}_j - \overline{r}_i \le p_1 + p_2 \sum_{l=i|l\in F}^{j} \sum_{k\in K} y_l^k \qquad \forall i < j \in N \tag{13}$$

$$\underline{r}_j - \overline{r}_i \le p_2 + p_2 \sum_{l=i|l\in F}^{j} y_l^4 \qquad \forall i < j \in N \tag{14}$$

$$\underline{r}_D - ST + \sum_{k\in K} b^k \sum_{i\in F} y_i^k \le T_{max} \tag{15}$$

$$\sum_{i\in N} s_{ij} + w_j - \sum_{l\in N} f_{jl} = \sum_{l\in N} s_{jl} \qquad \forall j \in N \tag{16}$$

$$\sum_{j\in N} s_{Oj} = SF - \sum_{j\in N} f_{Oj},\ \sum_{j\in N} \tau_{Oj} = ST + \sum_{j\in N} t_{Oj} \tag{17}$$

$$s_{ij} \ge e x_{ij} \qquad \forall (i,j) \in A \tag{18}$$

$$w_i \le E z_i, \qquad \forall i \in F \tag{19}$$

$$\tau_{ij} \le T_{max} x_{ij},\ f_{ij} \le M x_{ij},\ s_{ij} + w_j \le E x_{ij} \qquad \forall (i,j) \in A \tag{20}$$

$$t_{ij} = \sum_{h\in H} m_{1ij}^h \underline{r}_{ij}^h + q_{1ij}^h u_{ij}^h \qquad \forall (i,j) \in A \tag{21}$$

$$T_{ij}^{h-1} u_{ij}^{h-1} \le \underline{r}_{ij}^h \le T_{ij}^h u_{ij}^h \qquad \forall h \in H, \forall (i,j) \in A \tag{22}$$

$$\sum_{h\in H} u_{ij}^h = \sum_{j>i\in N} x_{ij} \qquad \forall i \in N \tag{23}$$

$$\underline{r}_i = \sum_{h\in H} \sum_{j\in N} \underline{r}_{ij}^h \qquad \forall i \in N \tag{24}$$

$$f_{ij} = \sum_{h\in H} m_{2ij}^h \underline{r}_{ij}^h + q_{2ij}^h u_{ij}^h \qquad \forall (i,j) \in A \tag{25}$$

$$y_i^k \in \{0,1\} \qquad \forall k \in K, i \in F \tag{26}$$

$$x_{ij} \in \{0,1\}, s_{ij} \ge 0, t_{ij} \ge 0, \tau_{ij} \ge 0, f_{ij} \ge 0 \qquad \forall (i,j) \in A \tag{27}$$

$$w_i \ge 0, z_i \in \{0,1\} \qquad \forall i \in F \tag{28}$$

$$\underline{r_i} \ge 0, \overline{r_i} \ge 0 \qquad \forall i \in N \tag{29}$$

$$\underline{r_{ij}}^h \ge 0, u_{ij}^h \in \{0,1\} \qquad \forall (i,j) \in A, \forall h \in H \tag{30}$$

The objective function (2) minimizes the total refueling costs. Constraints (3)–(4) ensure path connectivity, while constraints (5)–(6) link the node variables with the arc variables. Constraints (7) update the travel time of each traversed arc. Constraints (8)–(11) keep track of the travel time. Specifically, constraints (8) determine the arrival time at each node, while constraints (9)–(11) determine the departure time after having refuelled, taken a break, or refuelled and taken a break, respectively. Constraints (12)–(14) regulate the breaks according to the EU directives. Specifically, constraints (13) regulate the short breaks, taken at most every 4.5 h, while constraints (14) regulate the long breaks taken at most every 9 h. Constraint (15) regulates the maximum travel time of the whole route. Constraint (16) calculate the available fuel at j when arc (i, j) is traversed. Constraints (17) establish the starting time and the starting fuel conditions of the path. Constraints (18) guarantee that the minimum level of fuel is always respected. Constraints (19)–(20) link the relevant variables. Finally, constraints (21)–(25) regulate the functioning of the time-dependent travel time function, and the fuel time-dependent consumption function.

3.2 Heuristic Algorithm

We aim at providing a usable decision support tool for the LHFT. Therefore, the run time required for such a tool include all the data preprocessing necessary for its input. This comprises extracting the shortest paths between all relevant nodes via a GIS based application, e.g., GraphHopper, as well as computing the time-dependent travel time and fuel consumption profiles for each considered arc. With these considerations, solving the previously described model is time consuming (see Sect. 4.2 for computational details). We therefore chose to develop an efficient heuristic algorithm, which would require computational run times that are more aligned with the considered requirements. In designing the heuristic, we opted for a simple structure which is easily replicable and demands little preprocessing effort.

Due to confidentiality reasons, we cannot disclose the details of all tested parameters. However, we note that the OD pairs in our case study necessitate one or two refueling stops per day. Therefore, our heuristic algorithm is designed to yield one or two refueling stops per day.

Our heuristic algorithm constructs the solution by a forward algorithm and a backward algorithm. The pseudo-codes of these algorithms are shown in Algorithms 1 and 2. Each algorithm produces a solution and we choose the best out of the two as our heuristic solution. We now describe the forward algorithm. We note that the backward algorithm uses the same mechanisms, as the forward algorithm, but in the reverse direction.

The algorithm starts by considering the stations within 4.5 h from a starting node, which is set to the origin, since a short break needs to be taken within such a time span. All these nodes are placed in N_{fuel}. For each station in N_{fuel} we compute an approximate cost. Specifically, the distance between the station and O and the distance between the station and D are summed and we then calculate the total fuel costs entailed by the vehicle traversing that distance, while accounting for the time-dependent speeds. We populate N_{stops} by the subset of stations that are reachable from the starting node within a 4–4.5 h range, since we observed that the LHFT-M usually sets breaks within this range (this is illustrated in panel (a) of Fig. 3). We then select node k with the lowest approximate costs out of N_{stops}, and store k in $N_{stopsfinal}$. We then iterate this process by setting the starting node to node k.

Since $N_{stopsfinal}$ may exclude some stations that are economically convenient, we add the station with minimum approximate cost out of N_{fuel} to $N_{stopsfinal}$, i.e., node q. This is illustrated in panel (b) of Fig. 3. We compute the approximate total fuel consumption TC based on traversing the arcs that connect the ordered set of nodes in $N_{stopsfinal}$, while accounting for the time-dependent fuel consumption. We then examine if q is reachable from O, given the starting fuel level. If it is reachable, we consider that refueling is done at station q, otherwise we consider refueling first at the farthest possible to reach station from the origin out of $N_{stopsfinal}$, and then refueling at q. Once the forward procedure is finished, the backward procedure starts. It performs all the steps done by the forward algorithm but starting from the destination, till the origin. In the end, the solution with minimum costs between the two is chosen.

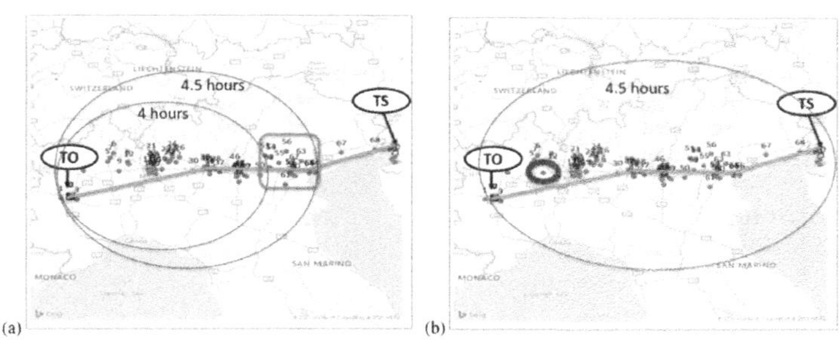

Fig. 3. Cheapest station recovery and insertion

4 Computational Experiments

In this section we present our computational experiments. In Sect. 4.1 we discuss our experimental setting and we present in Sect. 4.2 the results obtained by the computational experiments.

4.1 Experimental Setting

We retrieved distances and travel times between the considered nodes from GraphHopper [15], since it allows choosing between different types of vehicles,

```
Input: Fuel stations N
int ℓ ← ⌊travel time between origin and destination/4.5⌋;
SF ← ⌊fuel in the tank⌋;
Starting node ← O;
N_fuel, N_stopsfinal ← [∅];
for i ≤ ℓ do
    N_stops ← [∅];
    for j in N do
        t_oj:= travel time between Starting node and j;
        if t_oj ≤ 4.5 then
            N_fuel ← j;
            Compute approximate cost of j;
            if t_oj ≥ 4 then
                N_stops ← j;
                k ←node of minimum approximate cost out of N_stops;
                N_stopsfinal←k;
            end
        end
    end
    Starting node ← k;
    i++;
end
q ←node of minimum approximate cost out of N_fuel;
N_stopsfinal←q ;
Compute the total consumption ⇒ TC based on N_stopsfinal;
for each i in N_stopsfinal do
    Compute fuel consumption between O and i ⇒ f_oi;
    if f_oi > SF then
        break
    end
    else
        j ← i
    end
end
if q ≤ j then
    TotCosts= c_q(TC-SF)
end
else
    TotCosts= c_j(f_oq- SF)+c_q(TC- f_oq)
end
```

Algorithm 1: Pseudo-code of the forward algorithm

among which long-haul trucks were present. We was also used Graphhopper to derive the time-dependent speed profile. To do so, we sampled speed data along the main routes during different hours. From these data we constructed the vehicle speed profile, that is used in the algorithm to determine the travel time between two nodes, for each departure hour. The resulting speed profile is described as follows: between 0:00 and 8:00 the speed is 90 km/h, between 8:00 and 10:00 the speed is 60 km/hr, between 10:00 and 16:00 the speed is 85 km/h, between 16:00 and 20:00 the speed is 70 km/h, between 20:00 and 24:00 the speed is 90 km/h. The fuel prices for the various stations were derived from the Italian Ministry of Transport [17] in conjuncture with the contractual agreements of the studied case.

```
Input: Fuel stations N
int ℓ ← ⌊travel time between origin and destination/4.5⌋;
SF ← ⌊fuel in the tank⌋;
Starting node ← D;
N_fuel, N_stopsfinal ← [∅];
for i ≤ ℓ do
    N_stops ← [∅];
    for j in N do
        t_Dj := travel time between Starting node and j;
        if t_Dj ≤ 4.5 then
            N_fuel ← j;
            Compute approximate cost of j;
            if t_Dj ≥ 4 then
                N_stops ← j;
                k ←node of minimum approximate cost out of N_stops;
                N_stopsfinal ←k;
            end
        end
    end
    Starting node ← k;
    i++;
end
q ←node of minimum approximate cost out of N_fuel;
Compute the total consumption ⇒ TC based on N_stopsfinal;
for i in N_stopsfinal do
    Compute fuel consumption between D and i ⇒ f_Di;
    if f_Di > SF then
        break
    end
    else
        j ← i
    end
end
if q ≥ j then
    TotCosts= c_q(TC-SF)
end
else
    TotCosts= c_j(f_Dq- SF)+c_q(TC- f_Dq)
end
```

Algorithm 2: Pseudo-code of the backward algorithm

The computational experiments have been carried out on a single thread of a computer having 4 cores and a processor Intel(R) Core(TM) i5-7200U @2.50 GHz 2.71 GHz with 8 GB. The model was solved with *CPLEX* 12.9.0, whereas the heuristic algorithm was implemented in *Python 3.7*.

We considered 14 OD pairs, which included short, medium and long haul routes. The main parameters related to these OD pairs are presented in Table 1. Some of the routes were fully contained in Italy, whereas others included other European countries. For each OD pair, we considered three possible starting fuel levels: 100%, 75% and 50%. Thus a total of 42 instances are considered. We set the minimum fuel level e to 20% of the full tank, while the parameter E is set to the full tank, which is 1000 liters.

Table 1 describes the instances characteristics.

Table 1. Description of the instances

ID	Name	km	Stations
1	Torino-Reggio Calabria	1340	45
2	Torino-Taranto	1080	46
3	Trieste-Reggio Calabria	1346	32
4	Trieste-Taranto	1045	34
5	Graz-Roma	937	36
6	Wien-Roma	1121	41
7	Torino-Graz	808	80
8	Torino-Trieste	549	69
9	Torino-Roma	689	39
10	Trieste-Roma	673	26
11	Torino-Ancona	558	40
12	Wien-Padova	637	25
13	Tarvisio-Roma	737	32
14	Milano-Graz	682	71

4.2 Numerical Results

Table 2 summarizes the results obtained by CPLEX and by our heuristic on all instances. The run times of CPLEX and of the heuristic include the *Graphhopper* retrieval time of the distances and travel times for each arc, as well as the time-dependency calculation for each arc.

The average CPLEX run time on all instances was more than seven time longer than that of the heuristic. The heuristic produced high quality results, with an average deviation of 2.8% from optimality. The worst case deviation is 8.8%. In more than 60% of the instances (26 out of 42) the heuristic obtained results within a 3% of the optimal solutions. In instances 9–14, the computational time is relatively low. This is due to the density of stations being lower in the vicinity of where refueling and breaks actually occur. Finally, we note that due to the daily time horizon, one refueling stop is made in most instances.

Table 2. Results

ID	Starting fuel [%]	CPLEX			Heuristic			Run Time	Costs [%]
		Run time [s]	Cost [euro]	Fuel [liters]	Run time [s]	Cost [euro]	Fuel [liters]	$\frac{CPLEX}{Heur}$	$\frac{Heur-CPLEX}{Heur}$
1	100	644	145	105	180	149	105	3.6	2.7
1	75	670	180	130	177	185	130	3.8	2.7
1	50	639	214	155	180	220	155	3.6	2.8
2	100	1584	119	86	186	119	86	8.5	0.0
2	75	1674	154	111	134	154	111	12.5	0.0
2	50	1431	188	136	188	188	136	7.6	0.0
3	100	106	133	93	128	133	94	0.8	0.0
3	75	117	169	118	140	180	124	0.8	6.5
3	50	170	205	143	170	216	149	1.0	5.6
4	100	223	113	80	224	119	83	1.0	5.0
4	75	482	140	106	130	147	108	3.7	4.7
4	50	519	175	130	133	181	133	3.9	3.0
5	100	2022	142	101	310	146	105	7.0	2.8
5	75	766	177	126	313	181	130	2.4	2.0
5	50	1083	212	151	312	215	155	3.5	1.5
6	100	3896	156	105	206	158	102	18.9	1
6	75	3941	194	149	212	197	127	18.6	1.6
6	50	3167	231	174	213	235	152	20.0	2
7	100	4000	127	89	310	127	89	13.0	0.0
7	75	4567	166	116	308	166	116	14.8	0.0
7	50	4769	213	149	305	213	149	15.6	0.0
8	100	1153	57	41	204	59	43	5.6	4.1
8	75	1583	92	66	207	94	68	7.6	2.3
8	50	1429	126	91	290	138	97	5.0	8.8
9	100	32	59	53	10	63	55	3.2	6.0
9	75	28	101	91	11	107	91	2.5	5.0
9	50	27	128	115	11	134	117	2.4	5.6
10	100	15	47	32	12	48	35	1.2	2.0
10	75	18	84	57	18	84	60	1.0	0.3
10	50	13	120	84	13	121	85	1.0	0.5
11	100	50	32	23	28	32	25	1.8	3.9
11	75	56	65	48	27	69	53	2.0	5.5
11	50	43	99	73	26	101	78	1.7	2.0
12	100	83	90	65	10	96	67	8.3	7.0
12	75	82	125	90	14	132	92	5.8	5.8
12	50	93	169	107	15	177	124	6.2	5.0
13	100	38	79	55	16	80	54	2.4	1.3
13	75	45	115	80	19	117	79	2.4	1.8
13	50	59	169	117	18	170	116	3.3	0.9
14	100	388	49	33	14	49	33	28.0	0.0
14	75	412	90	63	10	93	63	42.0	3.8
14	50	415	126	88	20	129	90	20.0	2.7
Avg		1043			130			7.6	2.8

5 Conclusions

We proposed a MILP model and a heuristic algorithm for the long-haul day-ahead truck transportation planning problem with refueling deviations and time-dependent travel time. The objective of this problem is to obtain a minimum refueling cost path, while considering refueling stations with different prices, HOS regulations, time-dependent travel times and time-dependent fuel.

Our study was inspired by the operations of an Italian company, and we aimed at providing a usable decision support tool for the LHFT. Therefore, we designed a heuristic that is easily replicable and requires little preprocessing effort.

We have tested our model and heuristic on 42 instances. These include short, medium and long haul travels both on Italian and European routes, at different starting fuel levels. We have shown that the heuristic is considerably faster, when compared to solving the LHFT-M model via CPLEX. Nevertheless, the heuristic produced high quality solutions.

We believe that the heuristic algorithm may be instrumental in handling other relevant routing problems. For example, one could impose the fuel limit at the destination node to be equal to the starting fuel level (or any other user specified value). By doing so, one would add a look-ahead feature that facilitates multi-day planing. Furthermore, the proposed heuristic could be used to periodically estimate the path costs in the context of dynamically changing fuel prices throughout the day.

References

1. Archetti, C., Savelsbergh, M.: The trip scheduling problem. Transp. Sci. **43**, 417–431 (2009)
2. Barth, M., Younglove, T., Scora, G.: Development of a heavy-duty diesel modal emissions and fuel consumption model. Technical report, UCB-ITS-PRR-2005-1, University of California at Berkeley, Institute of transportation Studies (2005)
3. Barth, M., Boriboonsomsin, K.: Real-world CO2 impacts of traffic congestion (2007)
4. Bektaş, T., Laporte, G.: The pollution-routing problem. Transp. Res. Part B Methodol. **45**, 1232–1250 (2011)
5. Ben Ticha, H., Absi, N., Feillet, D., Quilliot, A.: Vehicle routing problems with road-network information: state of the art. Networks **72**, 393–406 (2018)
6. Ben Ticha, H., Absi, N., Feillet, D., Quilliot, A., Van Woensel, T.: A branch-and-price algorithm for the vehicle routing problem with time windows on a road network. Networks **73**, 401–417 (2019)
7. Bernhardt, A., Melo, T., Bousonville, T., Kopfer, H.: Truck driver scheduling with combined planning of rest periods, breaks and vehicle refueling. Technical report, Schriftenreihe Logistik der Fakultät für Wirtschaftswissenschaften der htw saar (2017). http://hdl.handle.net/10419/175088
8. Bousonville, T., Hartmann, A., Melo, T., Kopfer, H.: Vehicle routing and refueling: the impact of price variations on tour length. Herausforderungen, Chancen und Lösungen **II**, 83 (2011)

9. European Union: Your Europe - road transportation workers (2021). https://europa.eu/youreurope/business/human-resources/transport-sector-workers/road-transportation-workers7. Accessed 19 Oct 2021
10. Gendreau, M., Ghiani, G., Guerriero, E.: Time-dependent routing problems: a review. Comput. Oper. Res. **64**, 189–197 (2015)
11. Goel, A., Irnich, S.: An exact method for vehicle routing and truck driver scheduling problems. Transp. Sci. **51**, 737–754 (2017)
12. Goel, A., Kok, L.: Truck driver scheduling in the united states. Transp. Sci. **46**, 317–326 (2012)
13. Goel, A., Rousseau, L.M.: Truck driver scheduling in Canada. J. Sched. **15**, 783–799 (2012)
14. Goel, A.: Truck driver scheduling in the European union. Transp. Sci. **44**, 429–441 (2010)
15. GraphHopper. https://www.graphhopper.com/. Accessed 19 May 2022
16. Koç, C., Bektaş, T., Jabali, O., Laporte, G.: The fleet size and mix pollution-routing problem. Transp. Res. Part B Methodol. **70**, 239–254 (2014)
17. Ministero Dello Sviluppo Economico - Osservatorio Carburanti: Osservatorio carburanti - ricerca per area geografica (2021). https://carburanti.mise.gov.it/ospzSearch/nome. Accessed 17 May 2022
18. Mor, A., Archetti, C., Jabali, O., Simonetto, A., Speranza, M.G.: The bi-objective long-haul transportation problem on a road network. Omega **106**, 102522 (2022)
19. Neves-Moreira, F., Amorim-Lopes, M., Amorim, P.: The multi-period vehicle routing problem with refueling decisions: traveling further to decrease fuel cost? Transp. Res. Part E Logist. Transp. Rev. **133**, 101817 (2020)
20. Rancourt, M.E., Cordeau, J.F., Laporte, G.: Long-haul vehicle routing and scheduling with working hour rules. Transp. Sci. **47**, 81–107 (2013)
21. Scora, M., Barth, G.: Comprehensive modal emission model (CMEM), version 3.01, user guide. Technical report (2006)
22. Suzuki, Y.: A decision support system of vehicle routing and refueling for motor carriers with time-sensitive demands. Decis. Support Syst. **54**, 758–767 (2012)
23. Suzuki, Y., Dai, J.: Decision support system of truck routing and refueling: a dual-objective approach. Decis. Sci. **44**, 817–842 (2013)
24. Xu, H., Chen, Z.L., Rajagopal, S., Arunapuram, S.: Solving a practical pickup and delivery problem. Transp. Sci. **37**, 347–364 (2003)

The Dynamic Drone Scheduling Delivery Problem

Giovanni Campuzano(✉), Eduardo Lalla-Ruiz, and Martijn Mes

University of Twente, 7500 Enschede, AE, The Netherlands
{g.f.campuzanoarroyo,e.a.lalla,m.r.k.mes}@utwente.nl

Abstract. Logistics plays an important role in today's last-mile economy. Therefore, companies constantly seek for improving their delivery system towards more efficient and sustainable management of parcel distribution. In this paper, we study the Dynamic Drone Scheduling Delivery Problem. The objective is to minimize the delayed deliveries by a fleet of drones located in a central drone station, taking into account the uncertain arrival of parcels, soft time windows, and energy requirements. We develop a Markov Decision Processes (MDP) formulation and solve it approximately by implementing a value-based Reinforcement Learning (RL) approach. We compare our approach with several heuristic dispatching policies and provide insights into the efficiency of our RL algorithm when facing different delivery scenarios.

Keywords: Drone scheduling · Battery charging · UAV · Last mile · Reinforcement learning

1 Introduction

The last leg of the transportation chain (end-haul), also known as the last mile [20], concerns delivery activities in highly urbanized city centers and controls the reverse and forward flow of goods from producers to consumers. In this context, the logistics sector is currently facing scenarios of unprecedented change with developments in digitization, autonomous vehicles, urbanization, and increasing customer demands. In particular, the rise of e-commerce has resulted in a significant increase in delivery activities, which encompasses up to 30% of the e-logistics costs [23]. To cope with these demanding tasks, companies have been forced to develop more efficient and sustainable parcel distribution systems, to improve their service's quality, diminish greenhouse gas emissions, and reduce operational costs [4].

The industrial sector and scholars have paid close attention to the advancements in artificial intelligence and automation, placing a collaborative effort to develop and include autonomous vehicles in last-mile operations. Consequently, we see innovative delivery systems using non-traditional delivery vehicles, e.g., drones, cargo bikes, and autonomous robots, which provide several advantages to deal with features such as traffic congestion, speed regulations, time windows,

J. de Armas et al. (Eds.): ICCL 2022, LNCS 13557, pp. 260–274, 2022.
https://doi.org/10.1007/978-3-031-16579-5_18

and so forth. In particular, recent advances in technology have increased the popularity of autonomous drones in last-mile delivery. Nowadays, companies are investigating the parallelization the delivery operations by deploying remotely operated drones that help reduce transportation times and logistics costs (e.g., DHL[1], Wings by Google[2], and Air Prime by Amazon[3]). Autonomous drones have also drawn the interest of the transportation research community, where scholars have devoted their efforts to developing combinations of multiple modes of transport that exploit drones' advantages, i.e., avoidance of traffic congestion and infrastructural issues, fast-flying speeds, mobility, and reduced costs [18]. As a result, new research gaps have been identified, where drones can be employed in a wide range of civil applications, for instance, transportation services, emergency and disaster management, agriculture, and industrial warehouses [5]. Nevertheless, in these applications, the main challenge is to cope with the drone's limitations or requirements that might produce unfeasible solutions, e.g., concerning battery life, maximum payload, no-flying zone restrictions, unsafe landing territory, vulnerability to difficult weather conditions, and mandatory signature for receiving packages. For this reason, drones are mainly involved in applications that require ground vehicles or trucks to support drones' delivery operations, for example, the Flying Sidekick Traveling Salesman Problem [10] and the Traveling salesman Problem with Drone [17].

In this work, we study the Dynamic Drone Scheduling Delivery Problem (D-DSDP), where the objective is to optimize the efficient dispatching of a drone fleet from a station for parcel delivery, considering battery levels, time windows, energy consumption, and uncertain parcel arrivals at a central drone station. The main contributions of this work are as follows:

1. We introduce the Dynamic Drone Scheduling Delivery Problem (D-DSDP) and model the stochastic and time-dependent nature of the problem by means of a Markov Decision Processes formulation.
2. We develop a reinforcement learning approach that can solve realistic instances in a reasonable time, using approximate value iteration with a linear value function approximation.
3. We provide insights into the effect of the selection of parcels based on their time windows and drone battery levels and compare the reinforcement learning approach with different assignation heuristics.

The remainder of this paper is structured as follows. Related literature on the D-DSDP is reviewed in Sect. 2. The D-DSDP is formally described and formulated in Sect. 3. A reinforcement learning approach to face the D-DSDP is presented in Sect. 4. The numerical experiments are performed in Sect. 5. Finally, the main conclusions and future works are stated in Sect. 6.

---

[1] https://www.dhlexpress.be/en/shipping-and-receiving/dhl-parcelcopter/.
[2] https://x.company/projects/wing/.
[3] https://www.amazon.com/Amazon-Prime-Air/b?ie=UTF8&node=8037720011.

2 Literature Review

Literature on drone delivery systems has placed paramount emphasis on transportation systems where drones and trucks work in collaboration [10,11,17,19]. This review, however, focuses on delivery systems where drones are deployed from stations. The reader is referred to [9,12] for reviews on drone applications and drone transportation systems, respectively.

The D-DSDP can be seen as a special case of the Drone Delivery Problem (DDP, [3]), where drones are only allowed to perform round trips to serve customers with their corresponding parcels. The D-DSDP also resembles the Parallel Drone Scheduling TSP (PDSTSP, [10]), with the difference that this delivery system considers only drones. The reader is referred to [13] for a systematic review of the PDSTSP. In [3], authors face the DDP to minimize the makespan and the operational costs. They develop a linear energy consumption model that considers battery and payload to restrict the drone flying range. To solve the DDP, they propose a simulated annealing (SA) algorithm and compare its performance against a MILP formulation. Results show that optimizing the battery weight can provide improvements of up to 80% for the minimum-time DDP. In [2], a MILP formulation and a matheuristic are proposed to solve the multi-objective pick-up and delivery DDP. They consider multiple charging stations and a heterogeneous fleet of drones, where the number of packages that drones can carry is restricted by a maximum weight. A mathematical model that minimizes the maximum distance, number of drones, and the number of batteries is proposed in [22]. This way, the authors develop a MILP formulation that considers drone energy constraints, drone capacity, and time windows to solve instances for up to 10 customers. A pick-up and delivery food distribution case for the DDP is studied in [8], where multiple depots are considered and the demand is predicted in advance. The authors develop a MILP formulation and a heuristic algorithm to solve a dynamic problem. Finally, the reader is referred to [6] for an extensive literature review on truck-and-drone routing problems, mathematical models, problem variants, and heuristic algorithms. Also, the survey [1] provides a relevant literature review on drone distribution systems, which focuses on research issues, solution approaches, and limitations.

We are aware of only one work related to the D-DSDP that studies a delivery system that deploys drones from a central station performing round trips [7]. The authors propose a MILP formulation and a genetic algorithm (GA) for minimizing the number of drones to deliver packages with dynamic arrival and personalized deadlines. Our work mainly differs from it in the solution approach, specific problem features, and the objective function. In our case, first, due to the stochastic nature of this problem, we propose a MDP formulation, which incorporates transportation times, drone energy consumption, battery levels, and uncertain parcel arrivals. Second, we incorporate into our decision space drone charging policies at the central station, while in [7] drones are only allowed to swap the battery for a fully charged one. Third, we focus on minimizing the total costs of the delayed parcels, since we study scenarios with a high-parcel flow to compare our approach with different heuristic policies, whereas in [7] the authors focus on minimizing the number of drones at the station.

As we can observe, literature on drone stations where drones perform round trips for parcel deliveries is being developed. In this regard, we have found a research gap regarding drone delivery systems from a drone station that consider uncertain parcel arrival, drone energy consumption, transportation times, and time windows, when minimizing delayed deliveries. Therefore, in this paper, we aim at filling this research gap by developing a reinforcement learning approach to solve the D-DSDP with the above-mentioned features and outperform myopic policies.

3 Mathematical Model

3.1 Problem Description

In the D-DSDP, a fleet of drones is located in a central station to deliver parcels in the form of round trips. The central drone station faces uncertain parcel arrivals, and the drones have to meet time window and energy consumption requirements. Figure 1 illustrates a drone station with a fleet of drones and a set of known delivery locations.

The D-DSDP consists of a finite horizon, representing a day, where time is discretized in consecutive time periods $t \in \mathcal{T} = \{1, 2, ..., T\}$, from now on called stages. A set of drones $v \in V = \{1, 2, ..., V\}$ should perform round trips to deliver parcels $j \in J = \{1, 2, ..., J\}$ from a central station to their corresponding customers. As shown in Fig. 1, the distribution area is split into different distance classes $d \in \mathcal{D} = \{1, ..., D\}$, which determine the distance of customers to the central drone station. Furthermore, parcels arrive from outside the system according to a stochastic process with a rate $\lambda_{d,t}, \forall d \in \mathcal{D}, t \in \mathcal{T}$. Every parcel is known in the system since it is picked-up by the truck. The time between pickup of the parcel and delivery at the central drone station is indicated by a release period $r \in \mathcal{R} = \{0, ..., R\}$. Once the release period is equal to zero, the corresponding time window $k \in \mathcal{K} = \{0, ..., K\}$ starts decreasing one unit per stage. That is, time windows are related to a parcel release period r and release periods are related to the current stage t. For instance, a parcel that has $r = 2$ and $k = 1$ can be delivered in only one stage, i.e., we first wait two stages from $r = 2$ to $r = 0$, and then there is a time window of one stage to transport the parcel from $k = 1$ to $k = 0$.

Drones have one unit-load capacity and different battery levels $b \in \mathcal{B} = \{0, 1, 2, ...B\}$, where $b = 0$ means the drone has ran out of battery and can only be sent to recharge the battery. Moreover, transporting a parcel $j \in J$ to a customer class $d \in \mathcal{D}$ takes d units of time and battery level. For instance, if a parcel is sent at time $t = 1$ with $d = 2$, and $b = 3$, this means the drone that was sent to $d = 2$ becomes available at time $t = 3$, i.e., $t + d$, and with a battery level of $b = 3 - 2 = 1$. Drones can only charge their battery at one of the Q charging stations at the central station. We assume that charging the battery by one level requires one time unit, i.e., from b to $b + 1$ when going from stage t to $t + 1$. We also assume that the external arrival process of parcels to customer class $d \in \mathcal{D}$ at stage $t \in \mathcal{T}$ is independent of the external arrival process of other parcels at other stages.

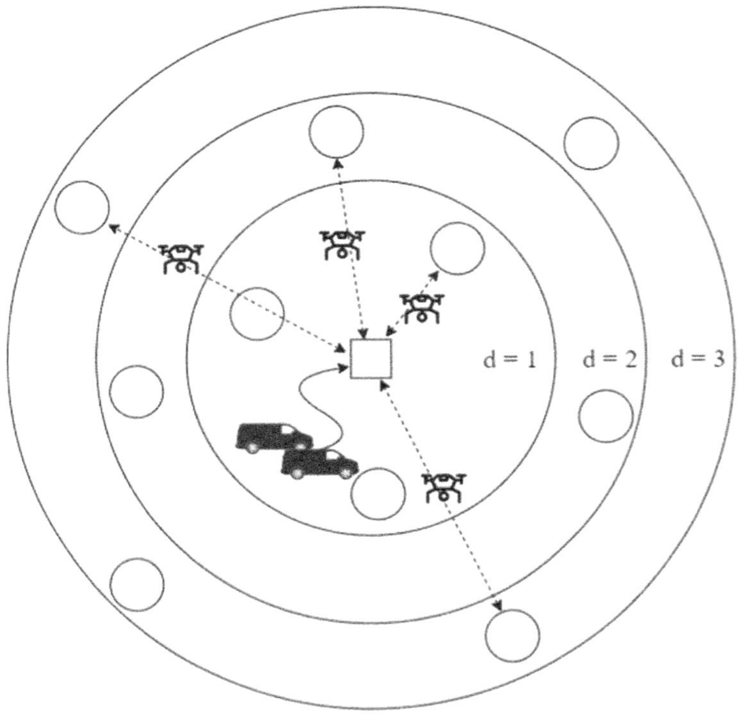

Fig. 1. Illustration of the D-DSDP.

The D-DSDP features two transportation modes. First, we have drones performing round trips from the station to customers. We do not consider transportation costs for drone deliveries, since every parcel has a fixed destination and the system should always bear those costs. Second, if a parcel is not transported by the end of its time window, we consider an alternative transportation mode, i.e., a manned vehicle that performs this transport quickly and at a high cost defined as C^L. Table 1 provides a description of the sets and parameters of the D-DSDP.

3.2 Markov Decision Process Formulation

States: Each period t corresponds to a *stage* in the MDP. Thus, stages are discrete and consecutive. Furthermore, at each stage t, there are $J_{t,d,r,k}$ parcels with distance class d, release stage r, and time window length k at the drone station, and $V_{t,r,b}$ drones with release stage r and battery level b to transport parcels. The state of the system S_t consists of the number of each parcel and

Table 1. Parameters of the D-DSDP.

$\mathcal{T}$:	set of time periods
$\mathcal{D}$:	set of customer classes
$\mathcal{K}$:	set of time periods until expiration of the time window
$\mathcal{R}$:	set of time period until arrival of the parcel
$\mathcal{B}$:	set of battery levels
Q :	number of charging stations at the drone station
$\lambda_{j,t}$:	arrival rate of parcel $j \in J$ at time $t \in \mathcal{T}$
C^L :	Cost of alternative manned transport for late parcels
S_t :	state of the system at period $t \in \mathcal{T}$
V_t :	number of drones available in the system at time $t \in \mathcal{T}$
J_t :	number of parcels in the system at time $t \in \mathcal{T}$

drone type at stage t, as seen in (1). We denote the state space of the system by $\mathcal{S}$, i.e., $S_t \in \mathcal{S}$.

$$S_t = \Big[(J_{t,d,r,k}, V_{t,r,b})\Big]_{\forall d \in \mathcal{D}, r \in \mathcal{R}, k \in \mathcal{K}, b \in \mathcal{B}} \tag{1}$$

Decisions: At each stage $t \in \mathcal{T}$, we have to decide (i) how many drones should transport parcels from the central station and (ii) how many drones should charge the battery. This decision depends on the release time of parcels, the battery level of drones, and the number of drones available to be used. We use variables $\mathcal{X}^V_{t,d,k,b}$ and $\mathcal{X}^C_{t,b}$ to represent the number of drones used to transport parcels for a customer with a distance class d, with time window k, battery level b, and the number of drones sent to charge the battery at a current battery level b, respectively. The decision x_t consists of all decision variables at stage t, as seen in (2), subject to constraints (3)-(6), which define the feasible space of $\mathcal{X}_t$.

$$\mathcal{X}_t = \Big[(\mathcal{X}^V_{t,d,k,b}, \mathcal{X}^C_{t,b})\Big]_{\forall d \in \mathcal{D}, k \in \mathcal{K}, b \in \mathcal{B}} \tag{2}$$

$$s.t.$$

$$\sum_{k \in \mathcal{K}} \sum_{d \in \mathcal{D}} \mathcal{X}^V_{t,d,k,b} + \mathcal{X}^C_{t,b} \leq V_{t,0,b} \qquad \forall b \in \mathcal{B} \setminus \{0\} \tag{3}$$

$$\sum_{\substack{b \in \mathcal{B} \setminus \{0\}, \\ b \geq d}} \mathcal{X}^V_{t,d,k,b} \leq J_{t,d,0,k} \qquad \forall d \in \mathcal{D}, k \in \mathcal{K}, d \leq k \tag{4}$$

$$\sum_{b \in \mathcal{B} \setminus \{B\}} \mathcal{X}^C_{t,b} \leq Q \tag{5}$$

$$\mathcal{X}^V_{t,d,k,b}, \ \mathcal{X}^C_{t,b} \in \mathbb{Z} \cup \{0\} \qquad \forall d \in \mathcal{D}, k \in \mathcal{K}, b \in \mathcal{B} \tag{6}$$

Constraints (3) establish that the maximum number of drones used can not be larger than the drones available. Constraints (4) state that the drones used to transport parcels can not exceed the number of parcels at the drone station and their battery levels should meet the energy requirements, i.e., $b \geq d$. Constraint (5) restrict the maximum number of drones that can be sent to charge the battery at any time period t. Constraints (6) define the nature of the variables.

Stochastic Processes: The transition from S_{t-1} to S_t is influenced by the decision $x_t \in \mathcal{X}_t$ and the exogenous information. Note that the parcel arrival rate and its characteristics, i.e., the time window length, release time, and customer destination, are determined by a probability distribution. To model this stochastic process, we introduce $\hat{J}_{t,d,r,k}$ to represent the number of parcels that arrive at the station with destination d, release time r, and time window k. The exogenous information W_t at stage t consists of all the *new information* represented by $\hat{J}_{t,d,r,k}$, as seen in (7).

$$W_t = \left[\left(\hat{J}_{t,d,r,k}\right)\right]_{\forall d \in \mathcal{D}, r \in \mathcal{R}, k \in \mathcal{K}, b \in \mathcal{B}} \tag{7}$$

A state S_t at stage t occurs as the result of the state of the previous stage S_{t-1}, the decision of the previous stage x_{t-1} plus the exogenous information captured in W_t that became known between the stages. The transition of the tasks is set by the time window k of the parcel, relative to the release time r, the number of parcels transported in the previous stage $t-1$, and the random arrival of new parcels. All of these factors, and index relations, are used to capture the transition of the system. We represent them using the transition function S^M, as shown in (8).

$$S_t = S^M\left(S_{t-1}, x_{t-1}, W_t\left(\hat{J}_t\right)\right) \qquad \forall t \in \mathcal{T} \mid t > 0 \tag{8}$$

Transition of Transportation Tasks' States:

$$J_{t,d,0,k} = J_{t-1,d,0,k+1} - \sum_{b \in \mathcal{B} \setminus \{0\}} \mathcal{X}^V_{t-1,d,k+1,b} + J_{t-1,d,1,k} + \hat{J}_{t,d,0,k} \qquad \forall d \in \mathcal{D}, k \in \mathcal{K} \setminus \{K\} \tag{9}$$

$$J_{t,d,0,K} = J_{t-1,d,1,K} + \hat{J}_{t,d,0,K} \qquad \forall d \in \mathcal{D} \tag{10}$$

$$J_{t,d,r,k} = J_{t-1,d,r+1,k} + \hat{J}_{t,d,r,k} \qquad \forall d \in \mathcal{D}, r \in \mathcal{R} \setminus \{0, R\}, k \in \mathcal{K} \tag{11}$$

$$J_{t,d,R,k} = \hat{J}_{t,d,R,k} \qquad \forall d \in \mathcal{D}, k \in \mathcal{K} \tag{12}$$

Constraints (9) define the number of parcels that become available to be transported at a given period t with a time window k. Constraints (10) define the number of transportation tasks that become available with a maximum time window. Constraints (11) define the transportation tasks that become available with a waiting time r at a stage t. Constraints (12) ensure that the parcels with the maximum waiting time R at a stage t are given by the exogenous information arriving to the system.

Transition of Drones' States:

$$V_{t,0,b} = V_{t-1,0,b} - \sum_{k \in \mathcal{K}} \sum_{d \in \mathcal{D}} \mathcal{X}^{V}_{t-1,d,k,b} - \mathcal{X}^{C}_{t-1,b} + V_{t-1,1,b+1} + \mathcal{X}^{C}_{t-1,b-1} \qquad \forall b \in \mathcal{B} \setminus \{0, B\} \tag{13}$$

$$V_{t,0,B} = V_{t-1,0,B} - \sum_{k \in \mathcal{K}} \sum_{d \in \mathcal{D}} \mathcal{X}^{V}_{t-1,d,k,B} + \mathcal{X}^{C}_{t-1,B-1} \tag{14}$$

$$V_{t,r,b} = V_{t-1,r+1,b+1} + \sum_{k \in \mathcal{K}} \mathcal{X}^{V}_{t-1,r,k,b} \qquad \forall r \in \mathcal{R} \setminus \{0, R\}, b \in \mathcal{B} \setminus \{0, B\} \tag{15}$$

$$V_{t,R,b} = \sum_{k \in \mathcal{K}} \mathcal{X}^{V}_{t,R,k,b} \qquad \forall b \in \mathcal{B} \setminus \{0\} \tag{16}$$

Constraints (13) establish the number of drones available to transport a parcel at a given battery level. Constraints (14) define the number of drones that become available at a maximum battery level. Constraints (15) define the transition of the release time for drones that are transporting a parcel. Constraints (16) set the number of drones that have a maximum release time R at each stage t.

Bellman's Equation: The objective function $C(S_t, x_t)$ at time period t depends on the number of drones used to transport parcels and the use of the alternative transportation mode. We define a variable $z_{t,d}$ as the number of parcels transported to customers with a distance class d by the alternative transportation mode at stage t. This variable is constrained by the transportation tasks' state $J_{t,d,r,k}$ and the number of drones used to transport parcels $\mathcal{X}^{V}_{t,d,k,b}$, as seen in (18). This way, the costs of the decisions can be defined as a function of x_t and S_t, as shown in (17).

$$C(S_t, x_t) = \sum_{d \in \mathcal{D}} C^{L} \cdot z_{t,d} \tag{17}$$

where,

$$z_{t,d} = J_{t,d,0,0} - \sum_{b \in \mathcal{B} \setminus \{0\}} \mathcal{X}^{V}_{t,d,0,b} \qquad \forall d \in \mathcal{D} \tag{18}$$

Bellman's equation enables the sequential minimization of the expected costs over the horizon, i.e., the sum of (17) over all $t \in \mathcal{T}$, since there is uncertainty in the arrival of parcels, and thus the states. We aim to find the policy that minimizes the logistics overhead costs over our planning horizon. Therefore, we define a policy $\pi \in \Pi$ is a function $\pi : S_t \rightarrow x_t$ that maps each state to a corresponding decision. The optimal policy π^* may be found by solving the Bellman optimality equations for each state, as shown in (19). In particular, the transition function S^M allows us to write the expectation in terms of the current state, the corresponding decision, and the given realization. The set of all realizations is denoted by Ω, i.e., $W_t \in \Omega$, $\forall t \in T$, where for each realization $\omega \in \Omega$ there is a probability p^{Ω}_{ω}.

$$V_t^{\pi^*}(S_t) = \min_{x_t \in X(S_t)} \left(C(S_t, x_t) + \sum_{\omega \in \Omega} \left(p^{\Omega}_{\omega} \cdot V_{t+1}^{\pi^*}\left(S^M(S_t, \mathcal{X}_t, \omega) \right) \right) \right), \quad \forall S_t \in \mathcal{S} \tag{19}$$

The probability p^{Ω}_{ω} depends on the realization $\omega \in \Omega$ in three ways. First, it depends on the total number of the arriving parcels, see Equation (22). Second, it depends on the probability that the $\hat{J}_{t,d,r,k}$ parcels will have customer destination class d, release-time r and time-window length k. Third, it depends on a multinomial coefficient β [15] that counts the ways of assigning the total number of arriving parcels j to variable $\hat{J}_{t,d,r,k}$. This coefficient is necessary since the order in which parcels arrive does not matter and their characteristics are allowed to *repeat*. With these three aspects, the probability p^{Ω}_{ω} can be computed using (20).

$$p^{\Omega}_{\omega} = \beta \cdot p^J_j \cdot \prod_{r \in \mathcal{R}, k \in \mathcal{K}, d \in \mathcal{D}, b \in \mathcal{B}} \left((p_d^{D^J} p_r^{R^J} p_k^{K^J})^{\hat{J}^{\omega}_{d,r,k}} \right) \tag{20}$$

where,

$$\omega = \left[(\hat{J}^w_{t,d,r,k}) \right]_{\forall, r \in \mathcal{R}, k \in \mathcal{K}, d \in \mathcal{D}, b \in \mathcal{B}} \tag{21}$$

$$j = \sum_{r \in \mathcal{R}, k \in \mathcal{K}, d \in \mathcal{D}} \hat{J}^w_{d,r,k} \tag{22}$$

$$\beta = \frac{j!}{\prod_{r \in \mathcal{R}, k \in \mathcal{K}, d \in \mathcal{D}} \left(\hat{J}^w_{d,r,k}! \right)} \tag{23}$$

The optimal policy for D-DSDP can be found by solving (19) using dynamic programming. Due to the curses of dimensionality, this is not possible for realistically sized instances. Hence, we develop a reinforcement learning approach to solve this MDP formulation in Sect. 4.

4 Reinforcement Learning Approach

In this section, a detailed description of the RL approach to solve the D-DSDP is presented. This approach is suitable to derive high quality decision policies for

MDP problems that cannot be solved exactly. Such a decision policy is a mapping of states to actions, where the actions account for their long-term effects. More specifically, we use the approximate value iteration algorithm [21]. Algorithm 1 shows the iterative process of the value-based procedure to approximately explore the solution space and converge to a cost approximation of each state of the system. This algorithmic approach works as a combination of Monte Carlo simulation and the Value Iteration algorithm by fitting a linear regression over a set of features F to determine the decision policy π.

Algorithm 1: Approximate Value Iteration Algorithm

Data: $(N, F, \epsilon, \gamma, \overline{V}, \hat{v}, \theta^f)$
1 $\overline{V}, \hat{v}, \theta^f \leftarrow$ *Initialize()*, $\forall f \in F$
2 $n = 1$
3 **while** $n < N$ **do**
4   **for** $t < \mathcal{T}$ **do**
5   **if** $t > 0$ **then**
6             $\hat{v}_t = \min_{x \in \mathcal{X}_t} \left\{ C(S_t, x_t) + \gamma \, \overline{V}_t\left(S^{M,x}(S_t, x_t) \right) \right\}$
7             $\theta^f_t = \theta^f_{t-1} - H_t \phi^f_{t-1} \left(\overline{V}_{t-1}(S^x_{t-1}) - \hat{v}_t \right), \ \forall f \in F$
8         $\tilde{x}_t \leftarrow \epsilon\text{-}greedy(\mathcal{X}_t)$
9         $S^{\tilde{x}}_t = S^{M,\tilde{x}}(S_t, \tilde{x}_t)$
10         $\phi^f_t \leftarrow Compute(S^{\tilde{x}}_t), \ \forall f \in F$
11         $W_{t+1} \leftarrow Random(\Omega)$
12         $S_{t+1} = S^M(S^{\tilde{x}}_t, W^n_{t+1})$
13         $t = t + 1$
14     $n = n + 1$
15 return $\theta^f \ \forall f \in F$

The input data is the number of iterations N, the feature set F, the value ϵ, the learning rate γ, and the initial values for $\overline{V}$, $\hat{v}$, and θ^f. The algorithm starts by setting initial values for $\overline{V}, \hat{v}, \theta^f$, and n (lines 1–2). The iterative process begins in line 3, where a whole horizon $\mathcal{T}$ is run at each iteration n (line 4). We elaborate on the concept of *post-decision* state S^x_t, which refers to the state of the system just after a decision x_t has been made and before the *next-stage* exogenous information W_{t+1} affects the system. The algorithm transitions from state S_t into the *post-decision* state S^x_t by the transition function $S^{M,x}(S_t, x_t)$. If the current stage is larger than 0, the downstream cost $\hat{v}_t$ is computed based on the current policy, that is, make decision x_t (lines 5 - 6). The downstream cost $\hat{v}_t$ represents the direct reward $C(S_t, x_t)$ given x_t, plus the approximated downstream costs of the *post-decision* state (or estimated downstream value) $\overline{V}_t$, i.e., one-step look-ahead with a bootstrap estimate [21]. Then, the linear-regression feature weights $\theta^f \ \forall f \in F$ are updated by computing the error between the previous stage estimated downstream value $\overline{V}_{t-1}$ and the current stage downstream cost $\hat{v}_t$ (line

7). The optimization matrix H_t is implemented to update the feature weights θ^f. For a comprehensive explanation on the optimization matrix we refer to [16]. To properly balance the exploration and exploitation of the decision space, in line 8 the ϵ-greedy decision policy is applied to choose $\tilde{x}_t \in \mathcal{X}_t$ [14]. Then, system transitions into the *post-decision* state $S_t^{\tilde{x}}$ by applying the transition function $S^{M,\tilde{x}}$ (line 9). After this, the features $\phi_t^f \ \forall f \in F$ are computed and stored based on the information provided by $S_t^{\tilde{x}}$ (line 10). Once the exogenous information for the next stage W_{t+1} has arrived (line 11), the algorithm transitions into the next state S_{t+1} by applying S^M (line 12). This process, i.e., from lines 5 - 13, is repeated at every stage $t \in \mathcal{T}$. Then, once n reaches value N, the algorithm returns the learned weights $\theta^f \ \forall f \in F$ to determine the policy π through the value function approximation $\overline{V}_t(S_t^x)$.

5 Numerical Experiments

5.1 Experimental Design

The experiments were executed on a computer equipped with a 1.90 GHz Intel(R) Core(TM) i7-8665U, 16 GB of RAM, and running Windows 10 in 64-bit mode. The instance sets used for the feature selection and the experiments are described in Table 2. In order to select a proper set of features for our RL algorithm, we analyzed the predictive power of a wide set of features. We first ran a long simulation and stored the features' values for all encountered states. Next, for each of the encountered states, we sum the observed costs over the states encountered in the subsequent ten stages, and chose the feature set resulting in the lowest error and the highest predictive power explaining the subsequent 10 stages costs. The final set of selected features for the RL algorithm are the number of drones available per battery level, the number of parcels per release time, the urgent parcels, i.e., that cannot wait one more stage, the non-urgent parcels, the non-urgent parcels per distance class, the total number of parcels in the system, the number of newly arrived parcels, the average distance class over all parcels, and the total travel time to transport all parcels to their corresponding customers. The training times of the RL algorithm were 282 and 644 s for the small and large instance sets, respectively.

5.2 Comparison of the RL Approach with Heuristic Strategies

These experiments study the effectiveness of our RL approach in comparison to four different operational strategies. The procedure of the algorithms is described as follows. The first algorithm chooses an *aleatory decision* at every stage. The second is a *transport-first heuristic* that always prioritizes the transport of parcels and sends drones to charge the battery when they either run out of battery or need to wait. The third is a *charge-first heuristic* that always prioritizes charging the battery of the drones and sends them to transport parcels only when the battery stations are occupied or the batteries of the drones are fully charged.

Table 2. Instance settings.

Set	Meaning	Small instances	Large instances
$\mathcal{T}$:	set of time periods	96	96
$\mathcal{D}$:	set of customer classes	3	3
$\mathcal{K}$:	set of time periods until expiration of the time window	6	6
$\mathcal{R}$:	set of time period until arrival of the parcel	4	4
$\mathcal{B}$:	set of battery levels	10	10
V_t :	number of drones available in the system at time $t \in \mathcal{T}$	10	20
Q :	number of charging stations at the drone station	10	15
$\lambda_{j,t}$:	arrival rate of parcel $j \in J$ at time $t \in \mathcal{T}$	10	20
C^L :	Cost of a delayed parcel	1	1

The last algorithm is a *versatile heuristic* that charges a predefined percentage of drones based on the average battery level of the fleet. Then, the remaining drones are sent to deliver parcels if possible. The results of the different heuristics and the RL algorithm for small and large sets of instances are provided in Table 3, where we consider probabilities $P = \{1/3, 1/3, 1/3\}$ for parcels to be delivered at a customer location $\mathcal{D} = \{1, 2, 3\}$. Furthermore, costs, standard deviations, and horizon running times (time required to run a simulation of 96 stages) are representative of 2000 replications and rounded to the next integer for the final cost, to the second decimal for the deviation, and to the third decimal for the horizon time.

Table 3. Performance comparison of heuristic strategies and the RL algorithm.

Instance size	Small instances			Large instances		
Algorithm	Final cost	Standard deviation	Horizon time (s)	Final cost	Standard deviation	Horizon time (s)
Aleatory heuristic	536	+/−6.80	0.009	1118	+/−14.36	0.015
Transport-first heuristic	516	+/−6.66	0.009	1115	+/−14.28	0.016
Charge-first heuristic	518	+/−6.68	0.007	1118	+/−14.14	0.014
Versatile heuristic	490	+/−6.24	0.007	1097	+/−14.17	0.014
RL algorithm	**447**	**+/−5.59**	**0.111**	**1060**	**+/−13.81**	**0.136**

Results show that the RL algorithm outperforms all the heuristics providing an objective value of 447 and 1060 for the small and large instances, respectively. As expected, the aleatory heuristic is the algorithm that has the worst performance for both sets of instances, which is the same as the charge-first heuristic for the large set of instances. For the whole set of heuristics, we can see standard deviations larger or equal to 6.24 and 14.14, corresponding to the small and large instance sets, whereas the RL algorithm results in smaller standard deviations of 5.59 and 13.81. This shows that the dispersion of the RL algorithm's performance with respect to its objective value is more stable and solid in comparison to the heuristic approaches, but it has larger computational times. In contrast to the heuristics, the RL algorithm needs to evaluate all possible decisions, requiring computing the feature values of all corresponding post-decisions states. However, computation times are still low enough to support online decision making, especially when taking into account that the reported times below 1 s include 96 decision moments and time required for running the simulation. Consequently, we conclude that the RL algorithm is able to explore the solution space and learn from the tested scenarios to make decisions that outperform different operational strategies within reasonable computational times.

5.3 Experiments on Different Instance Scenarios for the RL Approach

The last set of experiments studies how the performance of the best RL algorithm of Sect. 5.2 changes when studying different configuration scenarios. To carry out the experiments, we use the small instance set described in Table 2, which we refer to as *basic instance set*, and vary the time-window length, the number of charging stations, the number of battery levels, and the probabilities $P = \{1/9, 3/9, 5/9\}$ that a given parcel has to be delivered at a customer location $\mathcal{D} = \{1, 2, 3\}$. Regarding the latter, opposed to the original equal probability distribution representing a situation with higher customer density in the city center, the adjusted distribution assumes an equal density, hence more customers at the outskirts of the city. Results are provided in Table 4, where costs, standard deviations and running times are representative of 2000 replications and rounded to the next integer, for the final cost, and to the second decimal, for the deviation.

Table 4. Different instance settings for the RL algorithm.

Instance type	Final cost	Standard deviation	Experiment purpose
Basic instance set	447	+/−5.59	-
Variation 1, $\mathcal{K} = 4$	486	+/−6.17	Smaller time windows
Variation 2, $Q = 5$	472	+/−6.20	Less charging stations
Variation 3, $\mathcal{B} = 5$	464	+/−6.06	Smaller batteries
Variation 4, P	566	+/−7.21	More distant customers

From Table 4, we see that the all the variations increase the final costs and the standard deviations in comparison with the basic instance set. The first variation shows that as the time windows become smaller, parcels can spend less time at the drone station. As such, the instance set becomes more challenging since parcels might not be transported in time. Regarding the second variation, a reduction in charging stations will cause a situation where drones are not able to charge their battery on time for parcels requiring higher energy levels. Results on the third variation show that smaller batteries result in higher final costs. The last variation increases the costs when most of the customers are located on the outskirts. This is more challenging since the RL algorithm should find a policy that allows it to meet time window constraints for distant destinations and, at the same time, to reserve more drones with higher energy levels.

6 Conclusions

We introduced the Dynamic Drone Scheduling Delivery Problem (D-DSDP), which incorporates time windows, release times, charging stations, energy consumption features, and stochastic parcel arrival into the decision-making.

We address the D-DSDP by providing a Markov Decision Processes model and developing an Approximate Value-Iteration Reinforcement Learning algorithm. We carry out two different sets of experiments. In the first set of experiments, we compare the RL algorithm with four dispatching heuristics that resemble decision-making of human planners. Results show that our algorithm is able to outperform the heuristic strategies at the cost of increasing computational times. In the second set of experiments, we test how different instance settings affect the performance of the RL algorithm. We find higher operational costs when the maximum time-window length, the number of charging stations, and the energy levels of the drone batteries are reduced and when most of the customers are located in the outskirts of the city.

With regards to future research, we aim at studying other extensions such as picking up parcels from the customer locations to transport them to the drone station, as single or combined trips. In addition, the D-DSDP can also be extended to an infinite horizon setting.

Acknowledgements. This work was funded by the Chilean National Agency for Research and Development (ANID)/Scholarship Program/DOCTORADO BECAS CHILE/2019 - 72200288.

References

1. Benarbia, T., Kyamakya, K.: A literature review of drone-based package delivery logistics systems and their implementation feasibility. Sustainability **14**(1), 360 (2021)
2. Coelho, B.N., et al.: A multi-objective green UAV routing problem. Comput. Oper. Res. **88**, 306–315 (2017)
3. Dorling, K., Heinrichs, J., Messier, G.G., Magierowski, S.: Vehicle routing problems for drone delivery. IEEE Trans. Syst. Man Cybern. Syst. **47**(1), 70–85 (2016)
4. Jennings, D., Figliozzi, M.: Study of road autonomous delivery robots and their potential effects on freight efficiency and travel. Transp. Res. Rec. **2674**(9), 1019–1029 (2020)
5. Khoufi, I., Laouiti, A., Adjih, C.: A survey of recent extended variants of the traveling salesman and vehicle routing problems for unmanned aerial vehicles. Drones **3**(3), 66 (2019)
6. Liang, Y.J., Luo, Z.X.: A survey of truck-drone routing problem: literature review and research prospects. J. Oper. Res. Soc. China **10**, 343–377 (2022). https://doi.org/10.1007/s40305-021-00383-4
7. Liu, C., Chen, H., Li, X., Liu, Z.: A scheduling decision support model for minimizing the number of drones with dynamic package arrivals and personalized deadlines. Expert Syst. Appl. **167**, 114157 (2021)
8. Liu, Y.: An optimization-driven dynamic vehicle routing algorithm for on-demand meal delivery using drones. Comput. Oper. Res. **111**, 1–20 (2019)

9. Macrina, G., Pugliese, L.D.P., Guerriero, F., Laporte, G.: Drone-aided routing: a literature review. Transp. Res. Part C Emerg. Technol. **120**, 102762 (2020)
10. Murray, C.C., Chu, A.G.: The flying sidekick traveling salesman problem: optimization of drone-assisted parcel delivery. Transp. Res. Part C Emerg. Technol. **54**, 86–109 (2015)
11. Murray, C.C., Raj, R.: The multiple flying sidekicks traveling salesman problem: parcel delivery with multiple drones. Transport. Res. Part C Emerg. Technol. **110**, 368–398 (2020)
12. Otto, A., Agatz, N., Campbell, J., Golden, B., Pesch, E.: Optimization approaches for civil applications of unmanned aerial vehicles (UAVS) or aerial drones: a survey. Networks **72**(4), 411–458 (2018)
13. Pasha, J., et al.: The drone scheduling problem: a systematic state-of-the-art review. IEEE Trans. Intell. Transp. Syst. (2022)
14. Powell, W.B., Ryzhov, I.O.: Optimal Learning, vol. 841. Wiley, Hoboken (2012)
15. Riordan, J.: An Introduction to Combinatorial Analysis. Princeton University Press, Princeton (2014)
16. Rivera, A.E.P.: Anticipatory freight scheduling in synchromodal transport (2018)
17. Roberti, R., Ruthmair, M.: Exact methods for the traveling salesman problem with drone. Transp. Sci. **55**(2), 315–335 (2021)
18. Rojas Viloria, D., Solano-Charris, E.L., Muñoz-Villamizar, A., Montoya-Torres, J.R.: Unmanned aerial vehicles/drones in vehicle routing problems: a literature review. Int. Trans. Oper. Res. **28**(4), 1626–1657 (2021)
19. Schermer, D., Moeini, M., Wendt, O.: A b ranch-and-cut approach and alternative formulations for the traveling salesman problem with drone. Networks **76**(2), 164–186 (2020)
20. SteadieSeifi, M., Dellaert, N.P., Nuijten, W., Van Woensel, T., Raoufi, R.: Multimodal freight transportation planning: a literature review. Eur. J. Oper. Res. **233**(1), 1–15 (2014)
21. Sutton, R.S., Barto, A.G.: Reinforcement Learning: An Introduction. MIT press, Cambridge (2018)
22. Troudi, A., Addouche, S.A., Dellagi, S., Mhamedi, A.E.: Sizing of the drone delivery fleet considering energy autonomy. Sustainability **10**(9), 3344 (2018)
23. Wang, X., Zhan, L., Ruan, J., Zhang, J.: How to choose "last mile" delivery modes for e-fulfillment. Math. Prob. Eng. **2014** (2014)

Integrating Clustering Methodologies and Routing Optimization Algorithms for Last-Mile Parcel Delivery

Angie Ramírez-Villamil[1,2](✉), Jairo R. Montoya-Torres[1](✉), Anicia Jaegler[2], Juan M. Cuevas-Torres[1], David L. Cortés-Murcia[1], and William J. Guerrero[1]

[1] School of Engineering, Universidad de La Sabana, km 7 autopista norte de Bogota D.C., Chia, Cundinamarca 140013, Colombia
{angieravi,jairo.montoya,juancuto, william.guerrero1}@unisabana.edu.co

[2] Kedge Business School, 40 avenue des Terroirs de France, 75012 Paris, France
anicia.jaegler@kedgebs.com

Abstract. This paper aims to design a two-echelon parcel distribution network modeled as the Two-Echelon Vehicle Routing Problem (2E-VRP). In this problem, e-cargo bikes perform the last-mile delivery. In fact, this transportation mode is positioned as a promising alternative to make last-mile delivery. Studies show cost and carbon dioxide equivalent (CO_2e) emissions savings with cargo bikes setup compared to conventional vans. To solve this problem, a three-stage decomposition algorithm is proposed. In the first stage, the non-supervised machine learning clustering method 2D-*k*-means is considered to cluster the clients to the satellites. The second and third stages comprise the second and first echelon routing. The last two stages use a heuristic based on the Nearest Neighbor (NN) procedure. Two local search operators were used as improvement algorithms for the solution given by the NN in the second stage. There are scarce studies that use the 2D-k-means algorithm in this urban distribution network context. Experiments are run using a small instance based on real data from a delivery company in the city of Paris, France. Results show that the fixed costs and the cost of energy consumption of the e-cargo bikes are cheaper than the van used in the first echelon. Also, a reduction of 8.2% in terms of travel time is obtained when the Relocate local search is applied. Additional savings are achieved in performance indicators.

Keywords: Sustainability · Urban logistics · Last-mile delivery · Routing problems · Smart city

1 Introduction

More than 50% of the world's population is located in urban areas [1], and the number is expected to keep growing. As the world population increases, the demand of products will increase. With the strong measures implemented in several countries to deal with the recent outbreak of COVID-19 pandemic, parcel delivery requirements increase because

J. de Armas et al. (Eds.): ICCL 2022, LNCS 13557, pp. 275–287, 2022.
https://doi.org/10.1007/978-3-031-16579-5_19

many businesses are being forced to operate virtually [2], so it contributes to the growth of e-commerce. Parcel delivery service companies are facing the challenge of handling a large number of packages. For this reason, the transportation and mobility sectors are essential to fulfill these demands [3], despite these high costs.

Urban parcel delivery activities have important implications in terms of both traffic and parking. On the one hand, it significantly contributes to congestion and the emission of polluting particles in urban environments. Delivery vehicles account for 15% of urban traffic and more than 20% of CO_2 emissions and congestion [4] while the operations of urban freight transportation represent 25% of CO_2 emissions and between 30 to 50% of other transport-related pollutants in urban areas [5]. On the other hand, pick-up and delivery operations generate an invasion of public space, mostly in city centers. This is because vehicles remain parked while the loading/unloading activity is being performed. This makes it difficult to drive in these areas due to irregular parking practices and congestion [3].

To deal with the externalities related to the emissions caused not only by delivery vehicles but also those associated with other essential activities in cities, the European Commission [6] (p. 9) defined objectives to achieve "essentially CO_2-free city logistics in major urban centers by 2030". Cities are also restricting the access of delivery vehicles in urban centers or in inner-city areas, limiting for example the time of the day with access restriction or the type, emission class, or size of the delivery vehicles that cannot enter. All of these to ensure sustainable living conditions. Even though authorities have the best intentions, these measures worsen the accessibility to customers or places located in restricted areas [7, 8]. To face these challenges, retailers and parcel delivery companies are looking for cost-efficient methods, more environmentally friendly solutions, and different alternatives to deliver parcels in their delivery systems despite the restrictions in city areas.

One possible solution to this problem and the externalities caused by freight transportation networks is the use of innovative transportation modes to improve the efficiency and sustainability of urban parcel distribution systems. Different types of fleets have been studied, such as the use of public transport [9, 10], unmanned aerial vehicles (UAVs) [11], autonomous vehicles [12, 13], delivery robots [14], electric vehicles [15, 16], and cargo bikes [13, 17, 18]. The integration of cargo bikes in the transport infrastructure for urban delivery networks is becoming a modern trend because this transportation mode has the best energy-performance ratio, is efficient in densely inhabited areas, and has zero emissions [19]. In this study, cargo bikes will perform the last-mile delivery (second echelon), so cargo bikes can pick up the parcels at the locations designated as satellites where delivery vans first delivered the packages for further last-mile distribution.

To design the last-mile supply network, the most employed model is the two-echelon distribution network, in which parcels are delivered from a depot to a set of satellites and from there to a set of locations inside the city. This distribution problem is frequently approached by experts as a two-echelon vehicle routing problem (2E-VRP) [20]. Considering the high computational complexity of the problem, different heuristics and metaheuristics have been proposed to optimize these types of distribution networks. For instance, a metaheuristic based on Large Neighborhood Search (LNS) was proposed to handle small-size problems [21]. This metaheuristic was also proposed in [22] where authors introduced a hybrid metaheuristic that combines enumerative local searches and some tailored operators to find the best selections of satellites. An extension of the LNS, the Adaptive Large Neighborhood Search (ALNS) is one of the most applied solution approaches [23–25]. Other solution procedures applied are hybridizations like the GRASP+VND [26], and the graph-based fuzzy evolutionary algorithm hybridized with an iterative evolutionary learning process [27]. If authors deal with multiple objectives, the algorithm can be adapted as a Multi-Objective Evolutionary Algorithm (MOEA) as in [28]. Genetic Algorithms are also generated, for instance in [29] this algorithm was used to reach the best way to deliver parcels with the aim of finding the minimum handling cost. In cases like the presented in [30], authors combine the VND with local search operators to solve medium and large-size instances for the 2E-VRP. In addition, thinking about the eco-friendly 2E-VRP, [31] presented a case study in a logistics enterprise practice in China in which authors used the Clarke & Wright Savings algorithm adding an improvement in the heuristic using a local search phase.

The use of machine learning techniques can speed up algorithms specifically for this problem. A clustering method such as the non-supervised machine learning two-dimensional (2D) k-means is a good approach to cluster the customers to the satellites. Within the scope of this research, few papers applying data science clustering methodologies were found in the literature on two-echelon distribution systems and the 2E-VRP [32–35]. K-means clustering can address the VRP with initial solutions for vehicle routing optimization [36].

The purpose of the paper is to design delivery routes to optimize the total delivery time in the city. We propose a heuristic algorithm with a three-stage decomposition strategy for the 2E-VRP to deal with the high computational complexity of the problem. The heuristic algorithm contains in the first stage a non-supervised machine learning clustering method to allocate the customers to the closest satellite. To generate the routes, an algorithm based on the well-known Nearest Neighbor (NN) routing heuristic is implemented in first and second echelon. Moreover, some local search operators are applied to improve the solution obtained by the NN in the second echelon because this level comprises more complexity. Experiments with the proposed distribution network will be executed and analyzed in a sample of an instance taken from a case study inspired by a delivery company in the city of Paris, France.

The remainder of this article is organized into four sections. The next section discusses the methodology applied in this paper. The third section explains in detail the instance generation, its attributes and reports the results. The fourth section concludes the article and explains some suggestions for future research.

2 Solution Approach: Algorithm and Parameters

2.1 Solution Algorithm

The 2E-VRP is known for its computational complexity (NP-hardness) [23]. Algorithms such as heuristics and metaheuristics are designed to have efficient solution approaches with the ability to find good solutions. When the problem has large-scale instances, these techniques have drawn wide interest in researchers' efforts to solve vehicle routing problems [37].

Decomposition strategies were recently applied to large-scale real-world problems [38], but also were used to overcome the NP-hardiness of the 2E-VRP. These strategies are the most successful approaches [39]. In some studies, the solution is divided into two parts (initial solution phase and optimizing phase) [37]; in cases such as [39–41] authors split the problem into subproblems and solve them separately.

Based on the decomposition strategy, this study splits the problem into three sub-problems with the aim of reduce the complexity but guaranteeing the feasibility and the quality of the solution obtained by aggregating the subproblems. The first subproblem is a two-dimensional (2D) k-means clustering which aims to allocate the delivery points (customers) to predetermined satellites; the second sub-problem determines the routing from satellites to serve the customers (last-mile delivery), and the last sub-problem is to find a set of routes starting from the depots to serve the corresponding satellites (first echelon). A detailed explanation of the subproblems is presented next.

- First subproblem: Customer clustering in the second echelon. The two-dimensional k-means clustering algorithm is performed using customers' geographical coordinates (latitude and longitude). Each customer is assigned to an appropriate cluster which is the satellite.
- Second subproblem: Routing from satellites to customers (second echelon). Based on the decomposition strategy, the problem to be solved at each cluster is modeled as a Capacitated Vehicle Routing Problem (CVRP). Due to the large number of customers that the problem has, the initial solution is obtained by applying the NN heuristic, followed by a local search that contains inter and intra-routes operations to improve the initial solution. A flow diagram of the proposed solution approach is shown in Fig. 1.
- Third subproblem: First echelon routing (from the depots to satellites). The quantity of parcels (expressed in kilograms) required to be delivered to each satellite is obtained from the total demand of the customers of cluster k. The total travel time and the routes in the first echelon are calculated using the NN algorithm.

2.2 Two-dimensional k-Means Clustering Algorithm

Data science methodologies have been extensively applied in different fields. Customer clustering is an effective strategy to reduce the computational complexity of optimization problems [42–44] and to improve the calculation efficiency for large-scale logistics networks [45, 46]. Within the scope of this research, few papers using clustering methodologies were found in the literature about 2E-VRP [32–35]. For example, [34] considered a three-dimensional k-means clustering using customer's geographic coordinates (x, y) and a time parameter (z) that is the value of each service time window interval to solve an initial part of a two-echelon distribution system.

In this paper, a 2D k-means clustering algorithm before route optimization is proposed to reduce the computation complexity. We considered the two dimensions of each customer's geographic location (latitude and longitude), since k-means clustering traditionally groups customers into different clusters on the basis of the two-dimensional Euclidean distance [32, 33]. k is the number of clusters based on the number of satellites in the distribution network. Initially, the algorithm randomly selects the centroid for each cluster k. All the data is processed and the distances from each customer to the centroids are calculated. Each element is assigned to its closest cluster centroid. The new centroids of k clusters are updated. This algorithm continues until all the customers are adjusted in the adequate cluster. Finally, the results of the clustering are saved and are the input to calculate the initial solution for the CVRP optimization. Figure 1 shows the flowchart of this algorithm.

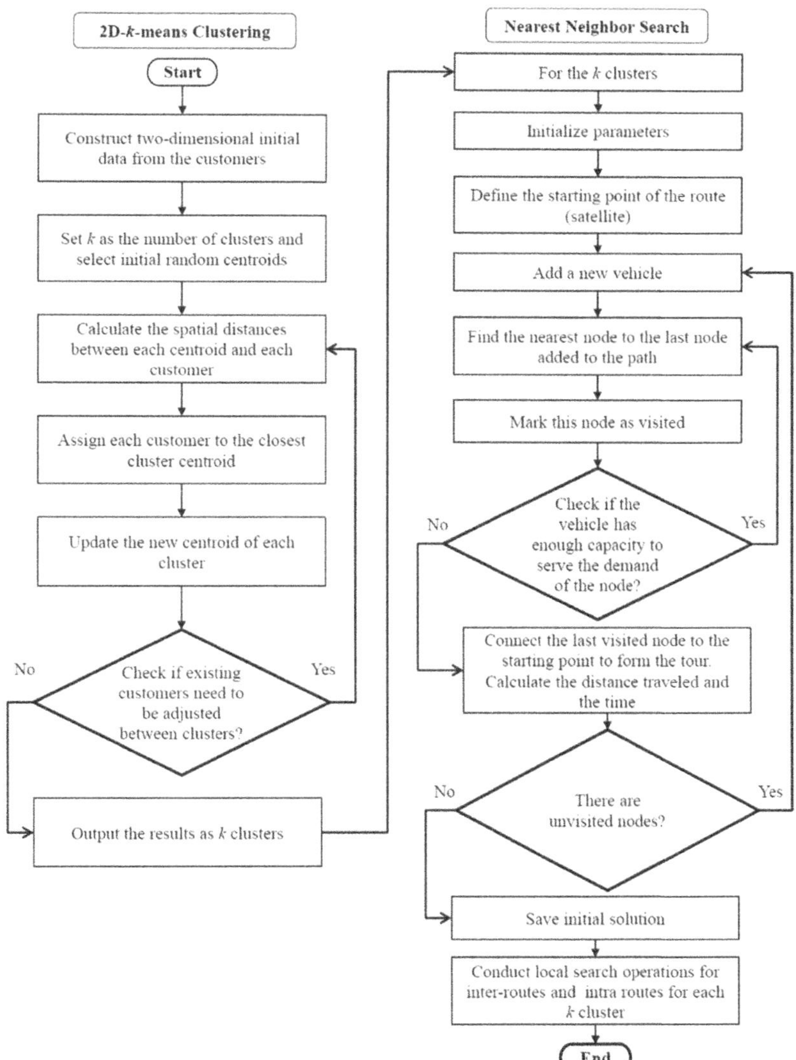

Fig. 1. Flowchart of the solution scheme for the proposed problem.

2.3 Local Search Operators

Two different local search operators are considered to improve the initial solution that was obtained by the NN procedure. The second subproblem is the second echelon routing of the proposed distribution network. For each cluster, the routing problem on the second echelon is a CVRP. In literature, different types of operators have been used to solve routing problems. In this case, relocate and swap operators are proposed as local search for neighborhood solutions.

Relocate local search (RLS)

In this study, the RLS aims to improve a solution by shifting a node in route *n*, before or after another node in a route that is different to *n*, considering that both routes belong to the same cluster. Figure 2 gives an example of this local search. Two routes that are in the same cluster are selected. The first route denoted as "1, 2, 3, 4, 5, 1" is selected as the route that contains the node that will be relocated (node 2). This node will be relocated in the route denoted as "1, 6, 7, 8, 9, 1" in the first position. The new routes "1, 3, 4, 5, 1" and "1, 2, 6, 7, 8, 9, 1" are constructed. The criteria to accept the insertion of the node in a specific route is the following: The insertion is accepted if the demand of the node does not exceed the available capacity of the vehicle in the destination route and if the insertion of that node into the route does give the best improvement in terms of travel time and distance of all possible and feasible combinations.

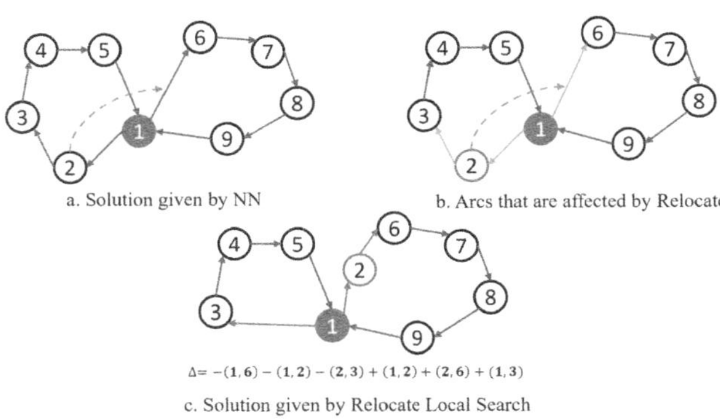

Fig. 2. Representation of Relocate local search (RLS) operator in a distribution network example.

Swap local search (SLS)

The SLS explores not only the exchange of one node of a route with a node located in another route in the same cluster but also intra-route exchanges between two nodes. Figure 3 shows an example of this local search procedure with the same routes of the previous example. First, an initial solution is needed to begin with the local search. Then, an intra route swap is performed to find the best improvement in the objective function. In this step, the solution is updated. In the third step, an inter route swap is conducted in the new solution checking that the new routes do not exceed the vehicle capacity and if there is an improvement in the objective function. If the solution is improved, the solution is updated again. This sequence is carried out until no improvement in the solution is found.

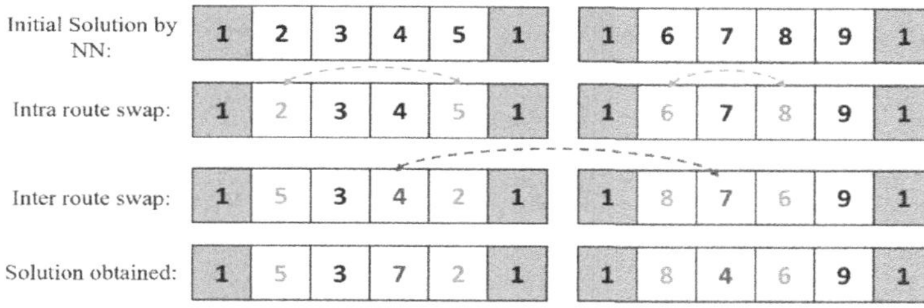

Fig. 3. Explanation of Swap local search (SLS) operator in a distribution network example.

3 Computational Results

The proposed solution procedure is coded in Python, experiments were run on a personal computer with processor Intel® Core™ i7-10510U, CPU at 2.3 GHz and 16 GB RAM. Our experiments evaluate two options of local search operators: RLS and SLS. The distribution network consists of a set of three uncapacitated satellites located inside the city of Paris. A heterogeneous fleet between echelons is considered; in the first echelon, the fleet of vehicles is composed of delivery vans (diesel-fueled) and in the second echelon, e-cargo bikes will perform the last-mile delivery. The transportation modes will have load capacities that are proportional to the type of vehicle but, for the purposes of this study, these are not the actual capacities. In this article, the capacity of the delivery van and e-cargo bike is 45 kg and 8 kg respectively. The instance used for the experiments contains 50 customers.

Regarding the results for the 2D *k*-means clustering. The purpose of the clustering is to minimize the sum of distances between each delivery point and the centroid of its cluster (satellite). Since the case considered in this article contains only 50 customers, the grouping is done in $k = 3$ clusters. Figure 4 shows how the customers that are geographically dispersed in the city are clustered in the three clusters in which the centroid of each group becomes the satellite of their cluster. With this clustering, it can be guaranteed that the e-cargo bikes associated to the satellite or cluster *k* will travel shorter distances and therefore their travel times will be shorter.

Indicators shown in Table 1 are used to analyze the improvements of the solution with the local searches proposed and to see the impact of the distribution network in terms of the number of vehicles, CO_2e emissions, fixed cost, energy consumption and land use. Land use is considered primarily to ensure that the distribution network does not invade public space in large proportions. Fixed costs allow decision-makers to analyze whether the costs associated with operating the scenario are low and to understand if the improvement heuristics generate cost savings. Regarding energy consumption it allows us to quantify the cost of the energy (diesel or electricity) that each transportation mode needs to perform delivery activities.

For the experiments in the second echelon routing (second subproblem), the algorithm based on the NN is used to obtain the initial solution. This solution and the solutions obtained using the local search operators that were explained in section 2: RLS and SLS. In addition, the results with the associated performance indicators are presented in Table 2. These results are presented per cluster and the total values for each solution approach.

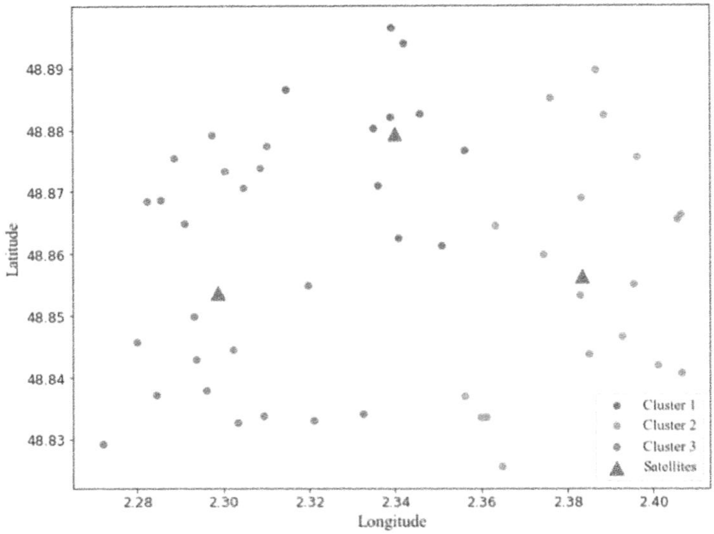

Fig. 4. Results of the 2D *k*-means clustering for last-mile delivery.

Table 1. Factors and parameters to calculate indicators.

Parameter	E-cargo bike	Delivery van
Average speed (*km/h*)	15	30
CO_2e emissions ($kg\ CO_2e/km$)	0.005	0.278
Land use (m^2)	3.48	9.15
Fixed costs (*€/km*)	0.63	1.32
Energy consumption (*€/km*)	0.00126	0.15592

E-cargo bikes performed the last-mile delivery. Due to the duration of the battery, this transportation mode has a limited route duration of 1.5 h per tour. The difference between the solution obtained by the NN and the RLS is 8.2% while between NN and SLS is 5.9% This means that the best results in terms of distance traveled, and travel time are obtained using the RLS improvement heuristic. Moreover, indicators like CO_2e emissions, fixed cost and energy consumption have better values using the RLS, this highlights the importance of having efficient local search operators that allow improvements and savings in last-mile delivery.

The first-echelon results correspond to the third subproblem. It is important to note that as it has only one depot and three satellites it is not necessary to apply a local search procedure to improve the solution obtained by the NN heuristic. The distance traveled by the delivery is 86.9 km taking into account that the depot is located outside the city and must travel on the roads that allow it to arrive at the desired delivery point (satellite). Even so, the average travel speed of the van causes that the complete delivery operation of the first echelon can be done in 2.9 hours with a fixed cost of 114.8 euros and a cost of 13.6 euros in terms of energy consumption using only one vehicle, the CO_2e emitted by the van is 24.2 kg.

Table 2. Second echelon results per indicator for the NN, RLS and SLS solution approaches.

Solution approach n = 50		N° of vehicles	Distance (*km*)	Travel time (*h*)	CO_2e emissions (*kg*)	Fixed cost (€)	Land use (m^2)	Energy consumption (€/*km*)
NN	Cluster 1	3	53.1	3.5	0.27	33.45	10.44	0.067
	Cluster 2	2	35.9	2.4	0.18	22.60	6.96	0.045
	Cluster 3	2	20.0	1.3	0.10	12.60	6.96	0.025
	Total	**7**	**107.7**	**7.2**	**0.54**	**67.83**	**24.36**	**0.135**
RLS	Cluster 1	3	43.1	2.9	0.23	27.15	10.44	0.054
	Cluster 2	2	35.9	2.4	0.17	22.62	6.96	0.045
	Cluster 3	2	19.9	1.3	0.09	12.54	6.96	0.034
	Total	**7**	**98.9**	**6.6**	**0.49**	**62.31**	**24.36**	**0.124**
SLS	Cluster 1	3	46.2	3.1	0.23	29.12	10.44	0.058
	Cluster 2	2	35.1	2.3	0.17	22.11	6.96	0.044
	Cluster 3	2	20.0	1.3	0.10	12.60	6.96	0.025
	Total	**7**	**101.3**	**6.7**	**0.51**	**63.82**	**24.36**	**0.127**

About the global results, Fig. 5 shows a comparison between solution approaches in indicators like distance, travel time and fixed costs. For these three indicators, RLS has a reduction of 5.9%, 3.3% and 2.2% respectively. Regarding CO_2e emissions, the reduction is only 0.12% because the most representative value of CO_2e is emitted by the van while the last mile delivery is executed by e-cargo bikes and the emissions are very low. However, this reduction indicates that RLS makes more sustainable the last-mile delivery. The land use is always 33.5 m^2 because the number of vehicles never changed in the outputs of the three solution approaches considered.

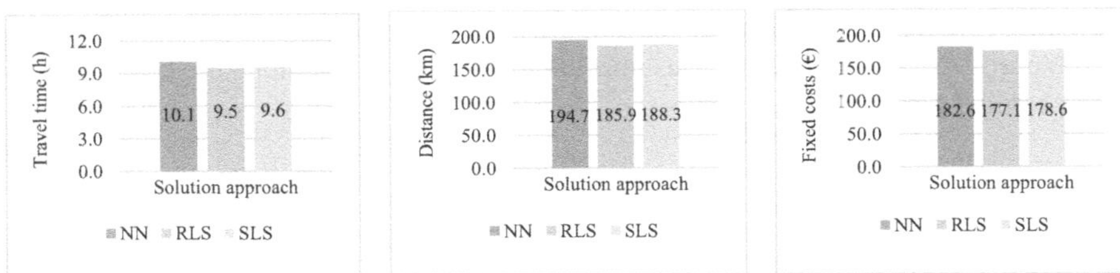

Fig. 5. Global results in terms of travel time, distance, and fixed costs for each solution approach.

4 Conclusions and Perspectives

Two-echelon urban delivery networks are the most common distribution systems applied in city logistics. This paper studied the 2E-VRP in an urban parcel delivery network. To deal with the computational complexity of the problem, we implemented an algorithm with a three-stage decomposition strategy. In the first stage, a 2D-k-means clustering algorithm allocates the customers to the closest satellite. The second and third stages were solved by an algorithm based on the NN routing heuristic. Two different local search operators were applied as improvement phases and their results were compared. The numerical experiments were carried out on a small-size instance. Solutions with this instance using these approaches are obtained approximately in 0.734 seconds for SLS and 0.008 seconds for RLS. However, this study is the first assessment. With the aim of extending this work and obtaining results in larger instances, analyses were made with 100 and 150 delivery points. The RLS improved the solution obtained by the NN in terms of travel time by 9.5% and 13.9% respectively, for the second echelon. When comparing RLS and SLS procedures, RLS seems to explore solutions with unbalanced number of nodes among routes in the second echelon, which explains a better performance.

For future research, several lines are still open. First of all, the application of these solution approaches in the original real-life case study with the real capacity of the vehicles and with more than 90,000 delivery points, to evaluate if RLS remains as the one that gives the best solutions when dealing with a big-size instance. Secondly, the application of metaheuristic algorithms that allow us to escape of the local optima and find better solutions could be very interesting. Other parameters such as service times can be considered. Furthermore, adding new attributes to the problem like mobile satellites or a heterogeneous fleet in the same echelon (using electric vehicles, a mix of cargo bikes with different capacities) could be studied.

References

1. Bac, U., Erdem, M.: Optimization of electric vehicle recharge schedule and routing problem with time windows and partial recharge: a comparative study for an urban logistics fleet. Sustain Cities Soc. **70**, 102883 (2021). https://doi.org/10.1016/j.scs.2021.102883
2. Cortes, J.D., Suzuki, Y.: Last-mile delivery efficiency: en route transloading in the parcel delivery industry. Int. J. Prod. Res. **60**, 2983–3000 (2021). https://doi.org/10.1080/00207543.2021.1907628

3. Calvet, L., Alvarez-Palau, E.J., Viu, M., Castillo, C., Copado, P., Juan, A.A.: Promoting sustainable and intelligent freight transportation systems in the barcelona metropolitan area. Transp. Res. Proc. **58**, 408–415 (2021)
4. Lindholm, M.: Urban freight transport from a local authority perspective-a literature review (2013)
5. Muñoz-Villamizar, A., Santos, J., Montoya-Torres, J.R., Velázquez-Martínez, J.C.: Measuring environmental performance of urban freight transport systems: a case study. Sustain. Cities Soc. **52**, 101844 (2020). https://doi.org/10.1016/j.scs.2019.101844
6. European Commission: White Paper on Transport-Roadmap to a Single European Transport Area - Towards a Competitive and Resource-Efficient Transport System (2011). https://eur-lex.europa.eu/legal-content/EN/TXT/PDF/?uri=CELEX:52011DC0144&from=EN
7. Comi, A.: A modelling framework to forecast urban goods flows. Res. Transp. Econ. **80**, 1–11 (2020). https://doi.org/10.1016/j.retrec.2020.100827
8. Letnik, T., Marksel, M., Luppino, G., Bardi, A., Božičnik, S.: Review of policies and measures for sustainable and energy efficient urban transport. Energy **163**, 245–257 (2018). https://doi.org/10.1016/j.energy.2018.08.096
9. Zheng, C., Gu, Y., Shen, J., Du, M.: Urban logistics delivery route planning based on a single metro line. IEEE Access **9**, 50819–50830 (2021). https://doi.org/10.1109/ACCESS.2021.3069415
10. Azcuy, I., Agatz, N., Giesen, R.: Designing integrated urban delivery systems using public transport. Transp. Res. Part E: Logist. Transp. Rev. **156**, 102525 (2021). https://doi.org/10.1016/j.tre.2021.102525
11. Yuan, Y., Cattaruzza, D., Ogier, M., Semet, F., Vigo, D.: A column generation based heuristic for the generalized vehicle routing problem with time windows. Transp. Res. Part E: Logist. Transp. Rev. **152**, 102391 (2021). https://doi.org/10.1016/j.tre.2021.102391
12. Sonneberg, M.-O., Leyerer, M., Kleinschmidt, A., Knigge, F., Breitner, M.H.: Autonomous unmanned ground vehicles for urban logistics: optimization of last mile delivery operations. Presented at the (2019)
13. Li, J., Ensafian, H., Bell, M.G.H., Geers, D.G.: Deploying autonomous mobile lockers in a two-echelon parcel operation. Transp. Res. Part C: Emerg Technol. **128**, 103155 (2021). https://doi.org/10.1016/j.trc.2021.103155
14. Chen, C., Demir, E., Huang, Y.: An adaptive large neighborhood search heuristic for the vehicle routing problem with time windows and delivery robots. Eur. J. Oper. Res. **294**, 1164–1180 (2021). https://doi.org/10.1016/j.ejor.2021.02.027
15. Juvvala, R., Sarmah, S.P.: Evaluation of policy options supporting electric vehicles in city logistics: a case study. Sustain. Cities Soc. **74**, 103209 (2021). https://doi.org/10.1016/j.scs.2021.103209
16. Settey, T., Gnap, J., Beňová, D., Pavličko, M., Blažeková, O.: The growth of e-commerce due to COVID-19 and the need for urban logistics centers using electric vehicles: Bratislava case study. Sustain. (Switz.) **13**, 5357 (2021). https://doi.org/10.3390/su13105357
17. Janjevic, M., Merchán, D., Winkenbach, M.: Designing multi-tier, multi-service-level, and multi-modal last-mile distribution networks for omni-channel operations. Eur. J. Oper. Res. **294**, 1059–1077 (2021). https://doi.org/10.1016/j.ejor.2020.08.043
18. Caggiani, L., Colovic, A., Prencipe, L.P., Ottomanelli, M.: A green logistics solution for last-mile deliveries considering e-vans and e-cargo bikes. Transp. Res. Proc. **52**, 75–82 (2021)
19. Cempírek, V., Stopka, O., Meško, P., Dočkalíková, I., Tvrdoň, L.: Design of distribution centre location for small e-shop consignments using the Clark-Wright method. Transp. Res. Proc. **53**, 224–233 (2021)
20. Crainic, T.G., Ricciardi, N., Storchi, G.: Advanced freight transportation systems for congested urban areas. Transp. Res. Part C: Emerg. Technol. **12**, 119–137 (2004). https://doi.org/10.1016/j.trc.2004.07.002

21. Kitjacharoenchai, P., Min, B.C., Lee, S.: Two echelon vehicle routing problem with drones in last mile delivery. Int. J. Prod. Econ. **225**, 107598 (2020). https://doi.org/10.1016/j.ijpe.2019.107598
22. Breunig, U., Schmid, V., Hartl, R.F., Vidal, T.: A large neighbourhood based heuristic for two-echelon routing problems. Comput. Oper. Res. **76**, 208–225 (2016). https://doi.org/10.1016/j.cor.2016.06.014
23. Hemmelmayr, V.C., Cordeau, J.F., Crainic, T.G.: An adaptive large neighborhood search heuristic for two-echelon vehicle routing problems arising in city logistics. Comput. Oper. Res. **39**, 3215–3228 (2012). https://doi.org/10.1016/j.cor.2012.04.007
24. Li, H., Wang, H., Chen, J., Bai, M.: Two-echelon vehicle routing problem with time windows and mobile satellites. Transp. Res. Part B: Methodol. **138**, 179–201 (2020). https://doi.org/10.1016/j.trb.2020.05.010
25. Grangier, P., Gendreau, M., Lehuédé, F., Rousseau, L.M.: An adaptive large neighborhood search for the two-echelon multiple-trip vehicle routing problem with satellite synchronization. Eur. J. Oper. Res. **254**, 80–91 (2016). https://doi.org/10.1016/j.ejor.2016.03.040
26. Zeng, Z.Y., Xu, W.S., Xu, Z.Y., Shao, W.H.: A hybrid GRASP+VND heuristic for the two-echelon vehicle routing problem arising in city logistics. Math. Probl. Eng. **2014** (2014). https://doi.org/10.1155/2014/517467
27. Yan, X., Huang, H., Hao, Z., Wang, J.: A graph-based fuzzy evolutionary algorithm for solving two-echelon vehicle routing problems. IEEE Trans. Evol. Comput. 1–14 (2019). https://doi.org/10.1109/TEVC.2019.2911736
28. Eitzen, H., Lopez-Pires, F., Baran, B., Sandoya, F., Chicaiza, J.L.: A multi-objective two-echelon vehicle routing problem. An urban goods movement approach for smart city logistics. In: 2017 43rd Latin American Computer Conference, CLEI 2017, vol. 2017-Janua, pp. 1–10 (2017). https://doi.org/10.1109/CLEI.2017.8226454
29. Wang, Z., Wen, P.: Optimization of a low-carbon two-echelon heterogeneous-fleet vehicle routing for cold chain logistics under mixed time window. Sustain. (Switz.) **12**, 1–22 (2020). https://doi.org/10.3390/su12051967
30. Belgin, O., Karaoglan, I., Altiparmak, F.: Two-echelon vehicle routing problem with simultaneous pickup and delivery: mathematical model and heuristic approach. Comput. Industr. Eng. **115**, 1–16 (2018). https://doi.org/10.1016/j.cie.2017.10.032
31. Li, H., Yuan, J., Lv, T., Chang, X.: The two-echelon time-constrained vehicle routing problem in linehaul-delivery systems considering carbon dioxide emissions. Transp. Res. Part D: Transp. Environ. **49**, 231–245 (2016). https://doi.org/10.1016/j.trd.2016.10.002
32. Wang, Y., Zhang, S., Assogba, K., Fan, J., Xu, M., Wang, Y.: Economic and environmental evaluations in the two-echelon collaborative multiple centers vehicle routing optimization. J. Clean. Prod. **197**, 443–461 (2018). https://doi.org/10.1016/j.jclepro.2018.06.208
33. Wang, Y., et al.: Collaborative two-echelon multicenter vehicle routing optimization based on state–space–time network representation. J. Clean. Prod. **258**, 120590 (2020). https://doi.org/10.1016/j.jclepro.2020.120590
34. Wang, Y., Zhang, S., Guan, X., Fan, J., Wang, H., Liu, Y.: Cooperation and profit allocation for two-echelon logistics pickup and delivery problems with state–space–time networks. Appl. Soft Comput. **109**, 107528 (2021). https://doi.org/10.1016/j.asoc.2021.107528
35. Wang, Y., Li, Q., Guan, X., Xu, M., Liu, Y., Wang, H.: Two-echelon collaborative multi-depot multi-period vehicle routing problem. Expert Syst. Appl. **167**, 114201 (2021). https://doi.org/10.1016/j.eswa.2020.114201
36. Luo, J., Chen, M.-R.: Multi-phase modified shuffled frog leaping algorithm with extremal optimization for the MDVRP and the MDVRPTW. Comput. Industr. Eng. **72**, 84–97 (2014). https://doi.org/10.1016/j.cie.2014.03.004

37. Du, L., He, R.: Combining nearest neighbor search with tabu search for large-scale vehicle routing problem. Phys. Proc. **25**, 1536–1546 (2012). https://doi.org/10.1016/j.phpro.2012.03.273
38. Flaberg, T., Hasle, G., Kloster, O., Riise, A.: Towards solving huge-scale vehicle routing problems for household type applications. In: Network Optimization Workshop. Saint-Remy de Provence (2006)
39. Ostertag, A., Doerner, K.F., Hartl, R.F., Taillard, E.D., Waelti, P.: POPMUSIC for a real-world large-scale vehicle routing problem with time windows. J. Oper. Res. Soc. **60**, 934–943 (2009). https://doi.org/10.1057/palgrave.jors.2602633
40. Ramirez-Villamil, A., Jaegler, A., Montoya-Torres, J.R.: Sustainable local pickup and delivery: the case of Paris. Res. Transp. Bus. Manag. (2021). https://doi.org/10.1016/j.rtbm.2021.100692
41. Muñoz-Villamizar, A., Montoya-Torres, J.R., Vega-Mejía, C.A.: Non-collaborative versus collaborative last-mile delivery in urban systems with stochastic demands. Proc. CIRP **30**, 263–268 (2015)
42. Zhu, E., Zhang, Y., Wen, P., Liu, F.: Fast and stable clustering analysis based on Grid-mapping K-means algorithm and new clustering validity index. Neurocomputing **363**, 149–170 (2019). https://doi.org/10.1016/j.neucom.2019.07.048
43. Cinar, D., Gakis, K., Pardalos, P.M.: A 2-phase constructive algorithm for cumulative vehicle routing problems with limited duration. Expert Syst. Appl. **56**, 48–58 (2016). https://doi.org/10.1016/j.eswa.2016.02.046
44. Ho, G.T.S., Ip, W.H., Lee, C.K.M., Mou, W.L.: Customer grouping for better resources allocation using GA based clustering technique. Expert Syst. Appl. **39**, 1979–1987 (2012). https://doi.org/10.1016/j.eswa.2011.08.045
45. Expósito-Izquierdo, C., Rossi, A., Sevaux, M.: A two-level solution approach to solve the clustered capacitated vehicle routing problem. Comput. Industr. Eng. **91**, 274–289 (2016). https://doi.org/10.1016/j.cie.2015.11.022
46. Defryn, C., Sörensen, K.: A fast two-level variable neighborhood search for the clustered vehicle routing problem. Comput. Oper. Res. **83**, 78–94 (2017). https://doi.org/10.1016/j.cor.2017.02.007

Warehousing and Location

SLAPStack: A Simulation Framework and a Large-Scale Benchmark Use Case for Autonomous Block Stacking Warehouses

Jakob Pfrommer(✉), Alexandru Rinciog, Sohaib Zahid, Michael Morrissey, and Anne Meyer

TU Dortmund University, Faculty for Mechanical Engineering, 44227 Dortmund, Germany
jakob.pfrommer@tu-dortmund.de

Abstract. Block stacking warehouses (BSWs), wherein products are kept in storage on the ground and/or stacked on top of each other, are ubiquitous along the supply chain. With the advent of autonomous forklifts, unmanned BSWs are an impending reality. However, to bridge the gap from isolated vehicles to a fully functioning warehouse, a vehicle control system capable of dealing with the complex interlaced problems associated with BSWs is required. To prove the feasibility of such a control system, we contribute three key elements. Firstly, we introduce SLAPStack, an event discrete simulation framework for BSWs covering all the required decision problems. Secondly, we present WEPAStacks, a large-scale, real-world BSW use case containing data that spans three months of operations. Finally, we use the SLAPStack together with WEPAStacks to test different storage location assignment problem (SLAP) strategies using fixed unit-load selection and dispatching strategies.

Keywords: Autonomous block stacking warehouses · Benchmark dataset · Event discrete simulation · Storage location assignment problem

1 Introduction

Block stacking warehouses (BSWs) have a high practical relevance and are used for varied applications along the supply chain. An example of such is WEPA's large-scale finished goods BSW, presented in this paper, which is used to store output conveyed directly from production. In BSWs, pallets are placed on the floor and stacked on top of each other. Therefore, no expensive infrastructure is required. Pallets can have additional associated information, most importantly a stock keeping unit (SKU). Figure 1 shows the main components of a BSW in a

This work was funded by the German Research Foundation through the Research Training Group 2193; we additionally thank WEPA Hygieneprodukte GmbH for providing the data required to evaluate this work.

J. de Armas et al. (Eds.): ICCL 2022, LNCS 13557, pp. 291–305, 2022.
https://doi.org/10.1007/978-3-031-16579-5_20

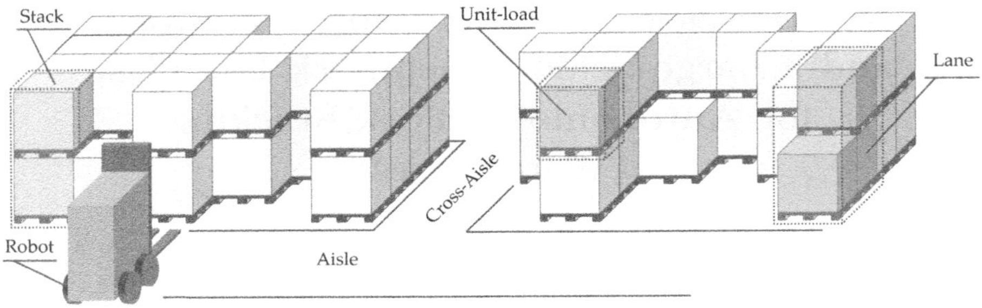

Fig. 1. Example of a block stacking warehouse with a robotic forklift

grid-based layout. Floor space is divided into storage bays and pathways (aisles). Storage bays consist of several lanes consisting of a sequence of stacks.

BSW operation consists of solving a series of interdependent decision problems namely (1) the layout problem, (2) the vehicle dispatching problem (VDP), (3) the storage location assignment problem (SLAP), (4) the unit-load selection problem (ULSP), and (5) the unit-load relocation problem (ULRP). Before operations can start, the layout of the BSW must be set (1). During operation, whenever a pallet arrives at a warehouse source, we need to first dispatch a vehicle to pick it up (2). Then we need to decide where to place the pallet (3). On retrieval orders, a pallet with the correct SKU needs to be selected from the warehouse (4). Having decided which pallet to extract from the warehouse, we once again need to dispatch a vehicle to pick it up and move it to an exit. Additionally, it could make sense to relocate pallets, e.g. when no orders are present, to reduce blockages and improve service times (5). Blockages occur when the pallet to be retrieved is located behind others and relocation is necessary for pallet access. These decisions are taken such that the in- and outbound orders are processed according to an optimization goals, e.g. service or travel time. These problems, coupled with autonomous mobile robots (AMR) form the autonomous block stacking warehouse problem (ABSWP) [15].

Today, BSWs are still mainly operated by human forklift drivers. Human operators structure the storage space based on experience and use a set of rules to stay organized , e.g. dedicated storage locations or class-based storage with zones. Particularly in atypical situations, e.g. warehouse overflows, humans can maintain operations through improvisation. However, the information flow is often lacking, e.g. at shift changes. AMRs on the other hand have well defined communication interfaces, could apply sophisticated algorithms and adapt their strategies depending of the current state. Furthermore, AMRs can work around the clock and could lead to significant operations cost reduction.

To convincingly prove the potential of AMR systems, we need to first demonstrate that they can tackle real world BSW operations. For a minimum viable solution, a control system is needed to accommodate at least three of the five decision problems, namely VDP, ULSP and SLAP. Furthermore, a realistic simulation model fine-grained enough to cover important BSW features is required for investigating whether the orders are serviced successfully without leading to overfull BSW order queues. Third, real world data is needed to test and validate the control system.

The current BSW state of the art reveals a gap with respect to three aspects. Firstly, BSW simulations are either not publicly available, e.g. [3], or overly simplistic, e.g. analytic models with assumptions such as single-command operations and single Input/Output (I/O) point. [4,13]. Secondly, to our knowledge, there are no publicly available BSW datasets. Finally, while individual BSW decision problems have garnered much attention, a holistic ABSWP solution perspective is still missing.

While for VDP and ULSP intuitive heuristic solutions exist, the same cannot be said about SLAP. Without the loss of generality, always dispatching the closest vehicle to a target location (CVL) is a good strategy, if we cannot compute order sequences for the vehicles in advance. Last-in first-out (LIFO) or first-in first-out (FIFO) out are intuitively good strategies, depending on the lane depth, and type of goods stored in the warehouse, e.g. FIFO for perishable goods.

Class-based storage strategies are most popular when it comes to warehouse organization [11]. However, it is often unclear how these strategies are set up and for which use cases they are truly appropriate. The general approach is to first define fixed zones within the warehouse for each class. Then SKUs are assigned to these zones based on some popularity metric like the number of picks for a certain time period (see e.g. [5]). When storing SKUs, the zone associated with the particular SKU class is selected for storage. Under closer inspection, this approach reveals a series of questions with no definitive answer, e.g. How many zones do we use? How do we draw the zones within the warehouse? How often do we redraw the zones?

The goal of this work is to provide a believable, minimally viable solution for ABSWP. To that end we make the following contributions: (1) We offer SLAPStack, a fine-grained simulation framework covering three of the five ABSWP decision problems, (2) provide and discuss WEPAStacks, a large-scale real-world BSW use case dataset provided by WEPA, and (3) evaluate 16 SLAP strategies in terms of their ABSWP fit given LIFO as a fixed solver for ULSP and CVL for VDP. We start our elaboration with the related work in terms of warehouse simulation and SLAP in Section (2). This is followed by the description of SLAPStack and WEPAStacks in Sections (3) and (4) respectively. In Section (5) we present our computational experiments. We draw our conclusions in Section (6).

2 Related Work

Simulation Frameworks: While there are no publicly available simulation frameworks targeting BSWs, some exist for related domains. A type of warehouse that became popular in industrial applications in recent years is the robotic mobile fulfillment system (RMFS). In RMFS items are stored on movable shelves (pods) that are transported by robots to pick stations. The goods-to-man order-picking system shares many properties with autonomously organized BSWs (e.g.

grid-based layout and AMRs). The main difference is that the robots run dual-command cycles to pick stations and drive under the pods. These pods are usually directly accessible (no multi-deep lanes) and are not stacked which results in less blockages in these storage systems. Several open-source simulation frameworks have been introduced starting with Alphabet Soup [9] and the more recent frameworks RAWSim-O [12] as well as RWARE [2,14].

Alphabet Soup is an event- and agent-based simulation framework written in Java that contains realistic models for robot behavior. It allows to study multiple decision problems like SLAP, the assignment of pods to pick stations, the replenishment of pods or the assignment of picking orders to pick stations [9]. In RAWSim-O a similar approach is used to build a simulation framework in C#. For this particular implementation a 2D and 3D visualization is available [12]. RWARE is a multi-agent simulation environment built on the Gym API in Python with the purpose to be used for reinforcement learning. It therefore is a leaner implementation compared to the detailed RAWSim-O [2,14].

Storage Location Assignment Problem: Storage strategies concerning SLAP can be categorized according to the availability of information: no information (SLAP-NI), product information (SLAP-PI), and item information (SLAP-II) [7]. Simple storage storage rules in the category SLAP-NI are often based on time or distance. Well known are closest-open-location (COL) or random [7]. Using COL as a storage strategy is tantamount to simply choosing the closest available open location relative to the order entry point for storage.

For SLAP-PI is available on a product level. This is for example conducted by analyzing the historical data for each SKU, also known as profiling (e.g. amount of picks per SKU over time). Based on this information, SKUs can be assigned to dedicated storage locations or to zones within the warehouse [5,7]. A well-known metric to assign items to dedicated storage locations is the Cube Order per Index. It represents the ratio of the required storage space and the demand rate per SKU [10]. For the class-based (CB) storage strategy, where a storage area is divided into a number of zones, each zone usually corresponds a class. SKUs are assigned to these classes based on Pareto's Law (e.g. in case of three classes the well known ABC storage strategy). For instance the products with the highest number of picks over time are assigned to the most desireable zone [5]. Hausman et al. [8] compare a random-based, a dedicated turnover-based, and CB storage strategies in an automated storage and retrieval system. The CB strategy assigns SKUs into classes based on turnover and assigns the class with higher turnover to the zone with the smaller travel times. The turnover-based strategy achieves the best results. Recent publications by Rimélé et al. [16–18] address adaptive storage strategies in RMFS. They compare several storage strategies in an event discrete simulation with learning approaches [16]. In [18] they use Monte Carlo Tree Search guided by a neural network trained in a supervised fashion inspired by [21] to predict actions. The learning-based approaches outperform the rule-based strategies.

SLAP-II requires detailed information, e.g. the due date for each item, to calculate the duration-of-stay [6]. In our use case the item due dates are not known in advance.

3 SLAPStack Simulation Framework

SLAPStack is an event discrete simulation embedding three of the five decision problems from Sect. 1, namely SLAP, ULSP and VDP. The implementation follows the architecture from [19]. The interaction between the simulation and a decision making algorithm (agent) is defined by the OpenAI Gym interface. The gym interface consists mainly of the functions `init`, `reset`, `step` [1].

The simulation usage begins by calling the `reset` function, which returns the initial simulation `state`. Thereafter, `step` is called on a loop until the simulation terminates (indicated by the `done` flag). `step` takes an action as a parameter and runs the simulation until the next action, e.g. storage allocation, is required. The `step` function exposes the current warehouse state together with an optional reward signal. The `state` serves to inform the agent action.

Analogously to [19], agents can take direct actions, i.e. select a storage location for delivery/retrieval, or chose from a set of user defined `WarehousePolicy` objects, which in turn take the direct action. The agent state and the reward can be jointly configured by means of a custom `OutputConverter` object.

An in depth elaboration of the simulation implementation would burst the frame of this work. Since SLAPStack is open-source (available with supplementary details and figures at [20]), in what follows, we only discuss key aspects of our simulation framework just enough for researchers to get started with our code. To that end we discuss the simulation inputs and initialization. A brief elaboration of the event management during a simulation step follows. Lastly, we sketch the mechanisms reflected by the simulation state. We use the typewriter font to indicate variables present in the implementation.

3.1 Inputs and Initialization

The main simulation parameters are given by the warehouse layout, an order list, a number of AMRs together with their speed, the warehouse unit distance (of each tile), a set of initial SKUs and an optional storage strategy for ordering the initial SKUs. The layout is an integer matrix with specific integer encodings for storage locations, aisles, walls and docks inbound docks (see Sect. 4.2). Each tile in the matrix is assumed to have a symmetric spatial expansion corresponding to the `unit_distance` parameter. The orders are lists of objects containing five fields namely type, arrival time in seconds, SKU, batch, and week number. The order type is either `delivery` or `retrieval`. The batch integer encodes the production lot for type `delivery` and each truckload for type `retrieval`. The week number enables the easy aggregation of order information.

During initialization four three-dimensional matrices, specifically the storage matrix S, the vehicle matrix V, the arrival-time matrix T and the batch matrix B are populated. The first matrix dimensions (width and length) reflect the given layout. The user defined `initial_pallets_storage_strategy` is used to select positions for the placement of the `initial_skus`. V is initialized by randomly sampling AMR positions from the collection of aisle positions.

Having initialized the state matrices, the simulation proceeds to create `Retrieval` and `Delivery` events and to add them to the the main event queue, i.e. the `future_events` heap, wherein the events are sorted by their arrival time. Then, the first event is popped from the heap, its handle function gets executed which leads to a state update and the initial state is returned. Depending on the order type, the `decision_mode` variable is set in the state to either `Delivery` or `Retrieval` to indicate the type of decision the agent is supposed to make. Aside from (S, V, T, B), the `State` contains several objects dedicated to managing specific state information, namely `AMRManager`, `LocationManager`, `Trackers`, `RouteManager` as well as a copy of the simulation input parameters save for the orders and initial SKUs.

3.2 Step and Event Management

The simulation maintains six types of self handling `Events` of either `Order` (`Delivery/Retrieval`) or `Transport` type. The `Transport` types, which model the AMR movement through the warehouse, are `DeliveryFirstLeg` (drive empty to an I-point for pickup), `DeliverySecondLeg` (transport pallet to a free storage location), `RetrievalFirstLeg` (drive empty to the storage location for pickup), and `RetrievalSecondLeg` (transport pallet to an O-point). `Transport` events are directly associated with an `Order` event. `Events` can be either blocking, i.e. they require an agent decision, or non-blocking, meaning that the next heap event can be handled.

The environment's `step` function, works in three stages: During stage (1), the event associated with the current mode is created and added to `future_events`. In stage (2), the event with the smallest occurrence time is popped from the `future_events` heap and its `handle` function is called to update the environment state including the system time. These steps are repeated until a blocking event is encountered. Stage (3) handles the updates of the `legal_actions` state property, marks current AMR positions and returns control to the agent.

`Transport` events are created either as a result of an Agent action (`DeliverySecondLeg`, `RetrievalFirstLeg`), or they are created automatically as part of the handling logic of a different event (`DeliveryFirstLeg`, `RetrievalSecondLeg`). To enable the agent to track the transport routes, `Transport` events are additionally maintained in a `running_transport` queue to which they are added on creation and removed on completion. During stage (3) of `step`, this queue is processed by calling `partial_handle` on all contained events, which leads to the active AMR positions being updated in the state.

Whenever a `Delivery` gets popped from the `future_events` heap, an AMR must be selected and moved to the source to pick up the order. For now, dispatching decisions (i.e. AMR selection) are hard-wired into the simulation. The closest AMR to the respective source will be picked for the job. A `DeliveryFirstLeg` event is then created associating the chosen AMR with the triggering order. During `Transport` event creation, the AMR route and travel time are computed using the Dijkstra shortest path algorithm and the event is added to both `future_events` and the `running_transport` queues.

`DeliveryFirstLeg` events are blocking. When such an event is retrieved from the heap, the agent controlling the simulation needs to select an appropriate open storage location for the order contained in `DeliveryFirstLeg`. As a result of the agent action, a `DeliverySecondLeg` is created and added to the heap. Analogously to its `DeliveryFirstLeg` counterpart, the event completion time and the route taken are saved in the event properties. The order object carried by the `DeliveryFirstLeg` is passed on to the current event prior to adding the `Transport` to `future_events` and `running_transport`.

When `Retrieval` orders arrive, the execution halts for the agent to pick an appropriate occupied position for the requested SKU. The closest free AMR to the picked position is then chosen for retrieving the SKU. The route between the vehicle and target position is calculated along with the required travel time and saved within a new `RetrievalFirstLeg` event along with the `Retrieval` order.

When the `handle` function is called on a `RetrievalFirstLeg`, a `Retrieval-SecondLeg` event is created and the order saved within the former event is passed along to the latter. A route is computed between the reached SKU position and the sink associated with the carried `Retrieval` order. The `RetrievalSecondLeg` is then added to the appropriate event queues. When popping and handling `RetrievalSecondLeg` and `DeliverySecondLeg` events, the AMR is simply released without any new events being created.

The event chain lain down does not consider the situation in which all AMRs are busy transporting other orders. If no AMR is available on `Order` arrivals, the respective `Delivery` or `Retrieval` order will be added to the `queued_delivery_orders` or `queued_retrieval_orders` respectively. During stage (1) of the `step` function the order queues are processed by AMRs in a FIFO fashion whenever they become free again.

3.3 State Management Mechanisms and Routing

The state management serves three distinct purposes, namely caching for simulation speedups (`RouteManager`), enforcing the correct simulation logic (`LocationManager` and `AMRManager`) and providing the simulation control with raw and aggregated state information (S, V, T, B and `Trackers`). The state is updated on event occurrence by the event's handle function.

The `LocationManager` is mainly used to maintain structures for the fast retrieval of occupied position indexed by SKU as well as the open storage locations. The current implementation limits the options available for placing pallets to avoid what we call "Swiss cheese" situations, i.e. creating holes in blocks of storage through improper placement of pallets. To that end, the legal delivery actions are the subset of open locations corresponding to the immediate lane border relative to the aisle.

Three further mechanisms that impact legal actions are maintained by the `LocationManager`, namely lane purity, lane locks and pallet shifting. For the lane purity mechanism, whenever SKUs get placed in an empty lane, the lane gets assigned to that particular SKU. Whenever a new SKU is to be stored in the warehouse, the simulation form the set of legal actions by listing the positions in the lanes assigned to this particular SKU together with the unassigned lanes. If no adequate positions are available, but there are otherwise open positions in the warehouse, then any open positions are considered legal actions. The lane lock mechanism works as follows: Whenever an agent selects a position for either delivery or retrieval, the lane of the respective position gets locked. As a result, the lane positions cannot be used for neither retrieval nor delivery until the locking event finishes.

The pallet shifting mechanism ensures that retrieving SKUs from the back of a lane does not lead to Swiss cheese. When selecting the legal actions for a particular `Retrieval` order, the first candidate set is, analogously to delivery, the outermost positions (border set) in every lane which contain the required SKU. If the border set for a particular SKU is empty but matching SKUs are available in the warehouse at deeper positions in the lanes, we allow retrieval from such positions. The AMR incurs a time penalty for every pallet it shifts away to reach the desired position. The hole that results from such a retrieval is plugged by pushing all pallets inward towards the bottom of the lane.

All routes in SLAPStack are complete grid-cell sequences along the shortest path between an AMR position and its target, e.g. dock or storage locations. To speed up route computation, Dijkstra is performed on a routing graph comprised of a subset of all grid-cells, namely aisle and dock positions. Furthermore, routes are cached by the `RouteManager` for later reuse.

4 WEPAStacks Benchmark

Along with our open-source simulation, SLAPStack, we publish the novel benchmark dataset WEPAStacks based on the in- and outbound flow of a large-scale BSW from WEPA. WEPA is one of the largest hygienic paper manufacturers in Europe with production plants and warehouses in currently six European countries. BSWs play a key-role for the storage of their goods, especially for situations where additional storage capacity has to be added on short notice.

4.1 Warehouse Setup

The BSW in this use case contains only finished goods on pallets (Fig. 2b). The warehouse has a maximum capacity of 19512 storage locations (6504 locations on the ground with stacking up to three levels). Figure 2a shows the footprint of the warehouse. The light-gray area represents aisles, the white areas with separating lines are storage bays and the dark-gray areas outline the warehouse boundaries (surrounding wall and the truck loading zone). All aisles are wide enough to allow two-way traffic. This does not apply to the lanes. The pallets arrive at four input points (I-points) on conveyor belts from the production lines. Forklift drivers pick up the pallets at I-points and deliver them to a storage location in the warehouse. When a retrieval order arrives, pallets are picked up and transported to O-points. O-points represent the truck loading staging areas where pallets are provided at each dock door for shipping. The truck loading process is executed by external truck drivers and thus not part of our use case.

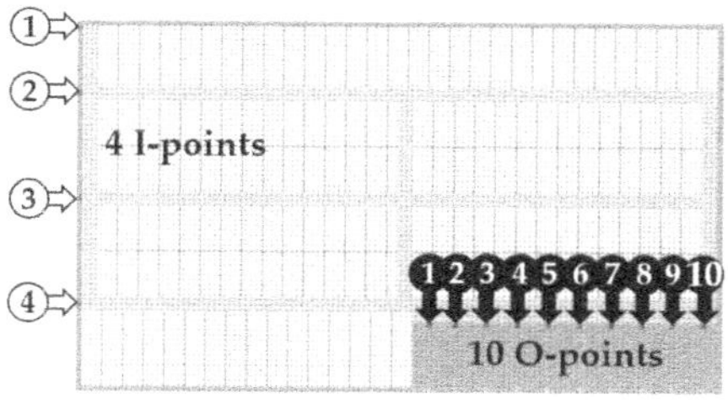

(a) Warehouse Layout

(b) Warehouse Interior

Fig. 2. Top view on the warehouse layout in (a). The aisle and loading zone is shown in (b)

4.2 Dataset and Assumptions

The obtained dataset from WEPA consists of three components: the warehouse layout, the initial fill level per SKU, and the daily in- and outbound flow volume per SKU for a time period of three months (89 d). The vehicle fleet is not provided since the number of manually operated forklifts is not transferable to an automated system and must be determined. All pallets are assumed to be unit-loads that can be stacked up to three levels. In reality pallet height and weight as well as the stacking capability of different SKUs varies. To anonymize the data and generate the detailed in- and out-bound order history with exact arrival times required by SLAPStack, we made the following assumptions.

For the inbound flow, we used the fact that WEPA's production is highly automated and achieves steady outputs within production batches, but often requires long changeover times. As such we set the within production batch times are sampled from 60 to 120 s per pallet. The changeover times between production batches take from 30 to 120 min. Both are calculated via a uniform distribution. SKUs can be produced on all production lines around-the-clock. The arrival times are the cumulative sum of the sample times.

For outbound flow, the products are mainly shipped via full truck loads of 33 pallets per truck. The standard opening hours of the warehouse are from 06:00-22:00. On weekends and public holidays the warehouse is usually closed, but there can be exceptions. The truck arrival times over the 16 opening hours follow a distribution with peaks in the morning hours and after lunch time. The loading time per truck in minutes is drawn uniformly at random from the interval $[45, 90]$. The times vary depending on the provisioning of pallets from storage and the skills of the truck drivers. The orders consist of six parameters namely the type (delivery or retrieval), the SKU (number from 1 to 136), the order arrival time (absolute time in seconds counting from zero), the dock door (number from 1 to 4 from top to bottom for delivery and 1 to 10 from left to right for retrieval), the batch number (number of production batches from 1 to 1498 for delivery and of truckload batches from 1 to 7496 for retrieval), and the week number (from 1 to 14). Each order represents a single pallet.

WEPAStacks presents autonomous BSWs with a feasibility challenge: The ABSWP decisions need to be taken in such a way, that trucks never queue up at O-points and the production never needs to halt. This can be translated into the following (virtual) buffer constraints: For trucks not to queue up, the number of queued retrieval orders cannot exceed 330 (truck capacity $\times$ 10 Ω-points). For deliveries we set a cumulative virtual buffer of 240 matching the maximum production capacity of one hour per line (60 pallets).

5 Experiments

In this section we discuss the experiment setup derived from the WEPA use case and compare the performance of several CB storage policies as well as a variation of COL. We use a fixed ULSP strategy, namely LIFO, and a fixed VDP strategy which is, for now, hardwired in the simulation, namely CVL.

5.1 Experiment Setup

The SLAP strategies chosen for evaluation are based on the popular COL and CB strategies. For the latter, we consider different parameter variations that fit the WEPA use case. We modified COL to use the pure-lane mechanism described in Sect. 3.3 by choosing the closest open pure lane (COPL) for delivery instead of any location. Therefore, the traditional COL is only encountered in situations where no pure lanes are available for a particular SKU.

Our CB SLAP strategies are implemented as follows. (1) We use the current SKU amounts in the warehouse to estimate the relative space to be booked to a zone for a particular SKU. (2) We compute our zones in two steps: First we create a geometric progression for the percentage of space assigned to each zone. For three zones, for instance, this will result in a sequence close to 10%, 30%, and 60% of the available storage space. The more popular SKUs get assigned to the smaller zone. In a second step we order all lanes in the warehouse with respect to the average distance between lane access points and I- and O-points and distribute these (sorted) lanes according to the percentages computed in the first step. (3) On delivery, after choosing the appropriate SKU zone, we decide on the free slot within the zone using COPL. (4) If the target zone is full, we pick the next best zone. (5) We redraw the zones every 1000 orders.

We define the SKU popularity based on which we assign SKUs to classes in one of five ways to empirically investigate their impact on WEPAStacks. (i) SKU Turnover time—T: The SKU turnover time we define as the average time between delivery and retrieval over all pallets of a particular SKU (see [8]). Higher turnover times are less popular. (ii/iii) Picks Past/Future—PP/F: We denominate pick popularity past/future as the cumulative SKU amounts over all retrieval orders of the past/future, the higher the pick number, the higher the popularity (e.g. PP [5]). (iv, v) SKU Throughput Past/Future—TP/F: By SKU throughput we mean the cumulative SKU amounts over all processed delivery and retrieval orders of the past/future. Higher cumulative amounts map to a higher popularity.

The coarse-grained future information for PF and TF is available for WEPA-Stacks on a weekly basis. While knowing the future SKU amounts is plausible, the exact delivery and retrieval times are not available to us. Hence this future information cannot be used for T-strategies. This, however, is not necessarily the case for every BSW use case.

For each of the five popularity definitions we test a storage strategy version with two, three, and five classes. This amounts to a total of 16 storage strategies: COPL, T2 to T5, PP2 to PP5, PF2 to PF5, TP2 to TP5, and TF2 to TF5. Within this nomenclature, the numbers represent the respective number of classes. The following parameters complete our setup: The simulation uses 40 AMRs, a unit distance of 1.4 m, a constant AMR speed of 2 m per second and a pallet shift penalty of 20 s per pallet.

5.2 Results

Table 1 shows the results achieved by the four best and four worst SLAP heuristics in terms of average service time, total distance traveled by AMRs, the maximum length of the delivery and retrieval queues, average end-state entropy, average turnover time (over all SKUs), and system throughput.

Table 1. Metric values for the four best and four worst storage strategies. Rows are sorted by the average service time and the best results achieved are set in bold.

Metric							
Storage Strategy	Average Service Time (s)	Total Distance (km/AMR)	Max. Delivery Queue	Max. Retrieval Queue	Average Lanewise Entropy	Average Turnover Time (days)	Average Hourly Throughput
COPL	**310.02**	**2648.83**	192	**293**	2.05	14.71	193.66
T5	317.69	2753.01	**188**	**293**	1.99	14.91	193.66
T2	335.03	2751.95	220	**293**	1.86	14.14	193.66
TF2	371.49	2732.78	490	**293**	1.91	14.26	**193.67**
	...						
PF2	650.06	2751.62	749	**293**	2.08	**14.07**	193.66
PP5	669.68	2756.39	1465	**293**	2.00	14.73	193.66
TP3	734.92	2745.33	947	**293**	1.94	14.11	193.66
PF5	749.89	2747.61	1581	**293**	**1.78**	14.57	193.66

In terms of service time, we see that the time between order arrival and order completion is, on average, between 310.02 and 749.89 s. If all 10 Ω-points are occupied, this corresponds to an average provisioning time of 43 $(\frac{310.02\ \text{s} \cdot 33\ \text{pallets} \cdot 10\ \Omega\text{-points}}{40\ \text{AMRs} \cdot 60\ \text{s/min}} = 42.62775\ \text{min})$ and 103 min for the best and worst strategy respectively. Both of these times are acceptable given that around

71 trucks need to be loaded daily in the present use case ($\frac{71 \text{ trucks} \cdot 103 \text{ min}}{40 \text{ AMRs} \cdot 60 \text{ min/h}} = 12.19$ h). Judging the SLAP strategies by maximum delivery queue length, however, relativizes these results: Only COPL, T2, and T5 respect the virtual delivery buffer limit of 330 palettes.

We define the average lanewise entropy as $LE := \sum_{SKU \in L} p_{SKU} \cdot \mathbf{log}(p_{SKU})$, where L is a lane and p_{SKU} the relative SKU amount in the lane. LE takes values between 0 and ∞, with lower values signaling order and higher ones increasing disorder. The values in Table 1 show that all our storage strategies generate a significant amount of disorder in the warehouse, with COPL being the messiest feasible storage strategy and T2 the neatest. In terms of turnover and throughput, our results register little variation. This suggests that these metrics are dominated by the order sequence rather than the AMR behavior.

Figures 3 and 4 show the evolution of six different metrics, namely the delivery queue length (3a), average service time (3b), fill level (3c), lanewise average entropy (3d), average utilization (4a) and snapshot utilization (4b) over the span of the simulation for the four best SLAP strategies. Four aspects which we refer to as Feasibility Bottleneck, Lane Homogeneity Impact, Disorder Management and ULRP Potential, become evident from an analysis of our results.

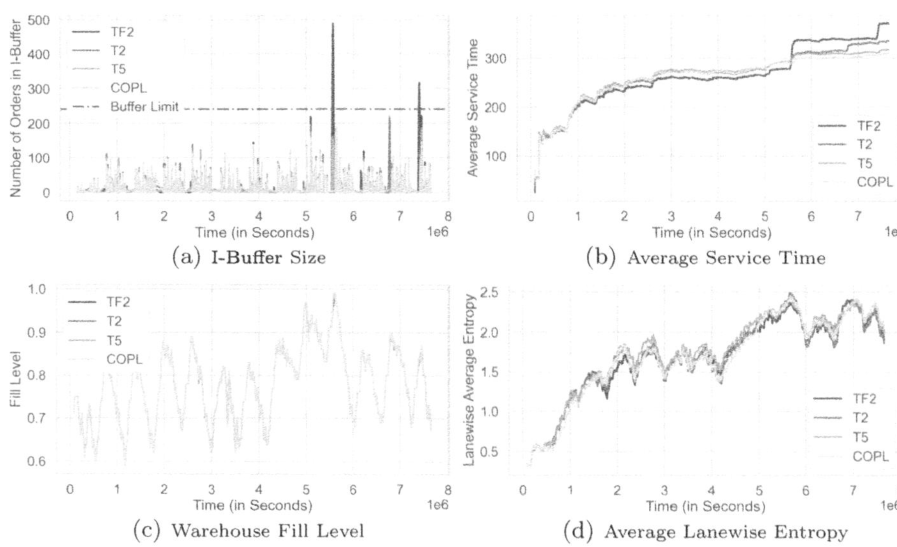

(a) I-Buffer Size (b) Average Service Time

(c) Warehouse Fill Level (d) Average Lanewise Entropy

Fig. 3. Behavioral comparison of the four best storage strategies.

Feasibility Bottleneck: Finding SLAP heuristics that represent feasible ABSWP solutions in conjunction with CVL and LIFO is challenging. Figure 3 shows that TF2 exceeds the buffer limit (Fig. 3a) in situations of high entropy (Fig. 3d) and a high fill level (Fig. 3c). Hence the only viable candidates are COPL, T5 and T2. A possible explanation for COPL being the best solution in spite of the high entropy it generates, may be the more homogeneous distribution of disorder generated by deferring the use of classes. The retrieval buffer limit is kept by all four best strategies (Table 1).

Lane Purity Impact: There seems to be an overall positive correlation between entropy (Fig. 3d) and service time (Fig. 3b). Note that the warehouse is originally fairly well organised, because all 13942 initial pallets are placed using TF3 with no zone re-computation. The warehouse order degenerates with time independently of storage strategy, because of a vicious circle where pure lanes gradually become less available given a higher fill level and more disorder. This could suggest that the AMR system is more efficient when there is less disorder in the warehouse. However, more experiments are required to isolate the impact of fill level and entropy on service time.

Disorder Management: From Table 1 and Fig. 3 we see that our SLAP strategies lead to high LE values. In large BSWs with many SKUs, such as ours, human operators could quickly lose track of the SKU locations. An AMR system on the other hand, could handle the high degree of entropy.

ULRP Potential: From the Fig. 4a we can see that the average AMR utilization is at most 25%. This is natural, since the warehouse is closed for retrieval during the night and for both retrieval and delivery during (most) weekends (Fig. 4b). During such periods, AMRs can be used to rearrange the SKUs within the warehouse to re-establish lane purity, thereby ensuring faster service times during periods with more frequent order arrivals.

(a) Average Utilization (b) Utilization

Fig. 4. AMR average and snapshot utilization over.

6 Conclusion

Our contributions were threefold. Firstly, we introduced SLAPStack, a novel, fine-grained and configurable simulation framework covering three of the five main operational decision problems of BSWs. In its current form, SLAPStack is suitable for investigating layout problem, SLAP, and ULSP strategies. Given SLAPStack's modular architecture, the framework is easily extensible to enable the testing of VDP and ULRP solutions. Secondly, we discussed WEPAStacks, a large-scale real-world benchmark dataset containing the in- and outbound flow as well as the exact layout of a real warehouse managed by WEPA. We open-sourced both SLAPStack and WEPAStacks through [20]. Thirdly, we used both simulation and dataset to explore 16 different SLAP strategies given fixed ULSP and VDP strategies (LIFO and CVL respectively).

Three of the 16 SLAP strategies managed the in- and outbound orders such that no delays were incurred by production and outbound trucks. Therefore, we achieved our goal of providing a minimally viable solution for the WEPAStacks ABSWP. The results reveal COPL to be the best strategy in terms of average service time and AMR travel distance. Furthermore, we drew four general conclusions for the WEPAStacks use case: We identified the delivery queue length as the *feasibility bottleneck*, hypothesized the *lane purity impact* on the operational warehouse performance, noted the advantage of a AMR system in terms of *disorder management* and underlined the *ULRP potential* for ABSWPs.

Our current work opens up a wide avenue of research. On the one hand, SLAPStack needs to be extended to cover more use cases, be closer to direct AMR interaction and embed the missing ABSWP decision problems in a configurable fashion. To these ends, an explicit pallet-shifting and conflict-free routing mechanism must be implemented and two new decision modes dedicated to unit load relocation and vehicle dispatching must be added. Given the low average utilization of the AMRs and the improved service times in case of less disorder, reshuffling strategies for the ULRP are particularly promising areas of future inquiry. A wider-reaching SLAPStack would allow for the better evaluation and validation of ABSWP solutions.

On the other hand, SLAPStack coupled with WEPAStacks, already offers a solid testbed for more sophisticated decision algorithms for the constituent problems individually and as an ensemble. Since our simulation framework implements the OpenAI Gym interface, Reinforcement Learning approaches can be used for control. Furthermore, decision algorithms could consider more, or even all, the available planning information (the currently queued orders, AMR positions etc.) to reach better solutions, e.g. through (stochastic, ML guided etc.) search. Last but not least, the metrics monitored by SLAPStack allow for the construction of datasets and training of Supervised Learning approaches.

References

1. Brockman, G., et al.: Openai gym. CoRR abs/1606.01540 (2016). http://arxiv.org/abs/1606.01540
2. Christianos, F., Schäfer, L., Albrecht, S.: Shared experience actor-critic for multi-agent reinforcement learning. Adv. Neural. Inf. Process. Syst. **33**, 10707–10717 (2020)
3. Clements, K., Sweeney, K., Tremont, A., Muralidhara, V., Kuhl, M.E.: Evaluation of warehouse bulk storage lane depth and ABC space allocation using simulation. In: Winter Simulation Conference (WSC), pp. 2239–2249 (2016)

4. Fontana, M.E., Cavalcante, C.A.V.: Use of promethee method to determine the best alternative for warehouse storage location assignment. Int. J. Adv. Manuf. Technol. **70**(9), 1615–1624 (2014). https://doi.org/10.1007/s00170-013-5405-z
5. Frazelle, E.H.: World-Class Warehousing and Material Handling. McGraw-Hill Education, New York (2016)
6. Goetschalckx, M., Ratliff, H.D.: Shared storage policies based on the duration stay of unit loads. Manag. Sci. **36**(9), 1120–1132 (1990)
7. Gu, J., Goetschalckx, M., McGinnis, L.F.: Research on warehouse operation: a comprehensive review. Eur. J. Oper. Res. **177**(1), 1–21 (2007)
8. Hausman, W.H., Schwarz, L.B., Graves, S.C.: Optimal storage assignment in automatic warehousing systems. Manag. Sci. **22**(6), 629–638 (1976)
9. Hazard, C.J., Wurman, P.R., D'Andrea, R.: Alphabet soup: a testbed for studying resource allocation in multi-vehicle systems. In: Proceedings of AAAI Workshop on Auction Mechanisms for Robot Coordination, pp. 23–30. Citeseer (2006)
10. Heskett, J.L.: Cube-per-order index-a key to warehouse stock location. Transp. Distrib. Manag. **3**(1), 27–31 (1963)
11. Le-Duc*, T., De Koster, R.B.: Travel distance estimation and storage zone optimization in a 2-block class-based storage strategy warehouse. Int. J. Prod. Res. **43**(17), 3561–3581 (2005)
12. Merschformann, M., Xie, L., Li, H.: Rawsim-o: a simulation framework for robotic mobile fulfillment systems. arXiv preprint arXiv:1710.04726 (2017)
13. Öztürkoğlu, Ö.: A bi-objective mathematical model for product allocation in block stacking warehouses. Int. Trans. Oper. Res. **27**(4), 2184–2210 (2020)
14. Papoudakis, G., Christianos, F., Schäfer, L., Albrecht, S.V.: Benchmarking multi-agent deep reinforcement learning algorithms in cooperative tasks. In: Proceedings of the Neural Information Processing Systems Track on Datasets and Benchmarks (NeurIPS) (2021)
15. Pfrommer, J., Meyer, A.: Autonomously organized block stacking warehouses: a review of decision problems and major challenges. Logistics J. Proc. **2020**(12) (2020)
16. Rimélé, A., Gamache, M., Gendreau, M., Grangier, P., Rousseau, L.M.: Robotic mobile fulfillment systems: a mathematical modelling framework for e-commerce applications. Int. J. Prod. Res. **60**(11), 3589–3605 (2021)
17. Rimélé, A., Grangier, P., Gamache, M., Gendreau, M., Rousseau, L.M.: E-commerce warehousing: learning a storage policy. arXiv:2101.08828 (2021)
18. Rimélé, A., Grangier, P., Gamache, M., Gendreau, M., Rousseau, L.M.: Supervised learning and tree search for real-time storage allocation in robotic mobile fulfillment systems. arXiv:2106.02450 (2021)
19. Rinciog, A., Meyer, A.: Fabricatio-rl: a reinforcement learning simulation framework for production scheduling. In: 2021 Winter Simulation Conference (WSC), pp. 1–12. IEEE (2021)
20. Rinciog, A., Meyer, A.: Slapstack. GitHub Repository (2022). https://github.com/malerinc/slapstack.git
21. Silver, D., et al.: Mastering the game of go without human knowledge. Nature **550**(7676), 354 (2017)

Locating Hydrogen Production in Norway Under Uncertainty

Šárka Štádlerová(✉), Trygve Magnus Aglen, Andreas Hofstad, and Peter Schütz

Department of Industrial Economics and Technology Management, Norwegian University of Science and Technology, 7491 Trondheim, Norway
sarka.stadlerova@ntnu.no
https://www.ntnu.edu/

Abstract. In this paper, we study a two-stage stochastic multi-period facility location and capacity expansion problem. The problem is motivated by the real-world problem of locating facilities for green hydrogen in Norway. We formulate a model with modular capacities. Investment in a facility and expansion costs represents long-term costs. For each capacity, we define a convex short-term production cost function which enables to capture economies of scale in investment as well as in production. The objective is to minimize the total expected investment, expansion, production and distribution costs while satisfying demand in each scenario. We solve the problem using sample average approximation. The results from solving the problem show that the stochastic problem leads to lower installed capacity in the opening decisions than the expected value problem.

Keywords: Stochastic facility location · Capacity expansion · Hydrogen supply chain

1 Introduction

In February 2020, Norway adopted more ambitious emission reduction targets than agreed upon in the Paris Agreement. The new target is to reduce greenhouse gas (GHG) emissions by at least 50% towards 2030, compared to the 1990 level [35]. To achieve this goal, the emissions from the transport sector also need to be halved. With a share of more than 30%, the transportation sector is an important contributor to total GHG emissions [37].

One of the key instruments for achieving the emission reduction targets is to use green hydrogen as a zero-emission energy carrier [37]. Only hydrogen coming from a CO_2-free production process can be considered a green zero-emission

This work was performed within MoZEES, a Norwegian Center for Environment-friendly Energy Research (FME), co-sponsored by the Research Council of Norway (project number 257653) and 40 partners from research, industry and the public sector.

J. de Armas et al. (Eds.): ICCL 2022, LNCS 13557, pp. 306–321, 2022.
https://doi.org/10.1007/978-3-031-16579-5_21

fuel. Electrolysis (EL) using energy from renewable sources is the most mature technology for green hydrogen production [16]. EL is a quite flexible production technology and can produce in a range of $20 - 100\%$ of installed capacity [27]. The production costs are subject to economies of scale as higher production quantities result in lower average unit costs [15].

In order to start the transition towards hydrogen in Norway, municipalities can require the usage of hydrogen as fuel when public transport contracts for ferries, high-speed passenger vessels, and coastal routes are renewed. Hydrogen is also a promising energy carrier for long-distance buses and heavy trucks [11]. The Norwegian government is also working on designing possible low- and zero-emission requirements for offshore supply vessels [30]. The conversion potential to zero-emission energy carrier of the offshore fleet with respect to the fleet composition and future demand is presented in [32]. Future hydrogen demand is highly uncertain because the market share of hydrogen vehicles in the road traffic sector and the future energy carrier in the offshore sector are also subject to uncertainty.

In this paper, we study the problem of locating hydrogen production facilities in Norway under uncertain demand. We formulate our problem as a two-stage stochastic multi-period facility location problem with capacity expansion. We consider modular capacities in order to model economies of scale. The goal is to minimize expected investment, expansion, production and distribution costs of satisfying the customer demand. We distinguish between long-term investment costs and short-term operational costs to capture economies of scale in investment and production. This approach also enables the modelling of different utilization of the installed capacity. The problem is solved using sample average approximation (SAA). We compare the first-stage solution of the stochastic problem (SP) and the expected value problem (EVP) and discuss the value of the stochastic solution. We analyse the hydrogen production infrastructure and provide a managerial insight into the investment capacity of new facilities.

The remainder of this paper is structured as follows: we first provide an overview of related work to deterministic and stochastic facility location and capacity expansion problems in Sect. 2. We formulate the mathematical model for the stochastic two-stage multi-period facility location problem in Sect. 3. The solution approach is presented in Sect. 4. Case study and Computational results are discussed in Sects. 5 and 6, respectively. We conclude in Sect. 7.

2 Related Work

We structure the related work into three main parts. First, we focus on literature related to deterministic facility location and capacity expansion problems before we continue with two-stage facility location and supply chain design problems. Finally, we present literature related to SAA.

Deterministic multi-period facility location and capacity expansion problems with modular capacities are studied in [10,41]. In these papers, both capacity expansion and capacity reduction are allowed. Expansion is modelled as new-building of another facility at a given location while capacity reduction means closing some or all of the facilities at a given location. An approach where capacity expansion is modelled as a modification of an existing facility is presented in [18–20,43]. In [43], the number of capacity expansions is limited, and capacity reduction is not allowed. In [18], capacity expansion and reduction are allowed multiple times. An extended version of the model from [18] for multiple commodities is presented in [19,20]. See also the review [26,28] for an overview over multi-period facility location problems.

Uncertainty in demand in two-stage stochastic problems is more commonly found in single-period facility location problems. The first-stage decisions usually refer to the opening of facilities and determining their capacities, while the second-stage decisions are related to distribution and demand satisfaction. A model with random demand and non-linear cost function to model economies of scale is discussed in [4,39]. The problem in [39] is solved using Lagrangian relaxation. A two-stage facility location problem with depots is presented in [24] and also solved by Lagrangian relaxation. The model presented in [24] can be solved by an effective genetic algorithm as shown in [12]. A two-stage multi-period facility location model with a capacity expansion is studied in [7]. The authors compare two model formulations: In the first model, capacity expansion is a part of the first-stage decisions while in the second model, capacity expansion is a second-stage decision. A multi-stage formulation of a multi-period stochastic problem is discussed in [3].

Supply chain network design problems are similar to facility location problems and have received lots of attention. A study on designing the hydrogen supply chain under uncertain demand with a similar decision structure to [4], [39] is presented in [21,31]. The first-stage decisions correspond to investing in production and storage capacity during the planning horizon while the second-stage decisions correspond to the distribution plan. A two-stage stochastic programming model for minimizing the total daily costs of the hydrogen supply chain with uncertain demand is presented in [9]. Compared to previous work in the hydrogen supply chain, the authors provide emission, energy consumption and risk costs. An early literature review on dynamic facility location and supply chain problems with stochastic data can be found in [34]. A review on facility location problems under uncertainty is provided in [42] and a recent summary on facility location problems under uncertainty is presented in [6,14].

The SAA algorithm allows for solving large two-stage stochastic problems with a binary first stage. See [25] and [22] for the details on methodology. The application of SAA to a facility location problem where the availability of opened facilities is uncertain is presented in [13]. A similar problem with facility disruptions is discussed in [23]. The authors combine SAA with a scenario decomposition algorithm to solve the problem. A combined solution approach of SAA and Benders decomposition for a supply chain design problem with uncertain demand is studied in [38]. A supply chain design problem with a model that captures short-term as well as long-term demand uncertainty is discussed in [40]. In order to increase the number of scenarios in the sample, SAA combined with dual decomposition is applied to solve the problem.

3 The Mathematical Programming Model

We study a stochastic two-stage multi-period facility location and capacity expansion problem with uncertain demand. The objective is to minimize the total expected costs.

3.1 Problem Description

We formulate our problem as a two-stage stochastic multi-period facility location and capacity expansion problem. The goal is to minimize the sum of expected discounted investment, expansion, production and distribution costs while satisfying demand in each scenario. The decisions when and where to open and which capacity to invest in are taken before the uncertainty is disclosed. In the second stage, decisions covering capacity expansion, production, and distribution are taken. Capacity expansion is allowed only once in each scenario and only in the sense of increasing the capacity level. Once a facility is opened, it cannot be closed.

We consider a set of candidate locations and a set of customers. For each facility-customer combination, we have specific unit distribution costs. However, not all customers can be served from all facilities. The investment costs are given by the installed capacity while the production costs depend both on installed capacity and production quantity. Note that investment and production costs can depend on location. The production quantities can vary from the installed capacity. However, there is a lower and an upper limit. The lower limit is given by the minimum production quantities for each capacity. The installed capacity represents the upper limit for production. This upper limit can be extended by expansion.

We model the investment and capacity decision as a discrete choice from a set of modular capacities. Expansion is then modelled as a jump between available capacities. We consider opening a small facility and expanding it as a more expensive alternative to opening a large facility right away. These extra costs are modelled as a one-time payment when expanding. However, the short-term production costs are independent of whether the capacity results from expansion or from opening the facility right away.

For each available capacity, we provide a piecewise linear convex short-term production cost function which enables a variation in production quantities. This approach enables to capture the economies of scale in investment as well as in production. Figure 1 shows our long-term (dashed line) and short-term (solid line) production costs. The capacity index of installed modular capacity is denoted k and Q_k is the appropriate quantity. The total costs for production at installed capacity k are denoted C_k. For each capacity k, we define a short-term production costs function $f_k(q)$ that enables production in a range between minimum and maximum limit. However, higher utilization of installed capacity leads to lower unit costs. This approach of modelling investment and production costs is similar to the one in [39].

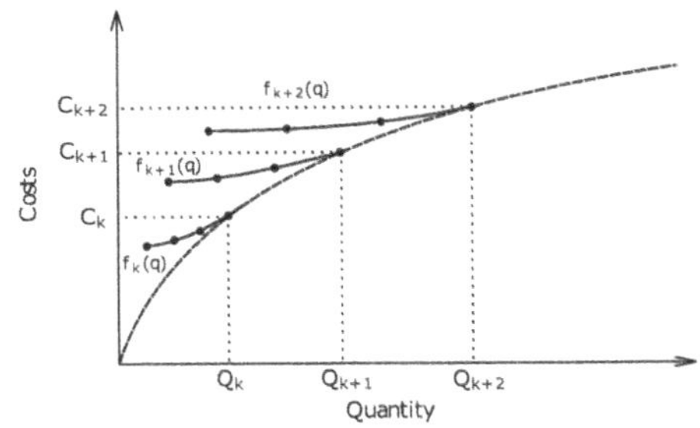

Fig. 1. Long-term and short-term production costs

3.2 Mathematical Formulation

Let us first introduce the following notation:

Sets

$\mathscr{B}$ Set of breakpoints of the short-term cost function
$\mathscr{I}$ Set of possible facility locations
$\mathscr{J}$ Set of customer ports
$\mathscr{K}$ Set of available discrete capacities
$\mathscr{S}$ Set of scenarios
$\mathscr{T}$ Set of time periods
$\mathscr{T}_1$ Set of time periods corresponding to the first-stage, $\mathscr{T}_1 \subset \mathscr{T}$

Parameters and Coefficients

C_{ik} investment costs at location i for capacity point k;
D^s_{jt} demand at customer j in period t, and scenario s;
E_{ikl} costs of expansion at location i from capacity in point k to capacity in point l;
F_{ibk} costs at location i at breakpoint b of the short-term cost function of capacity k;
L_{ij} 1 if demand at location j can be served from facility i, 0 otherwise;
Q_{bk} production volume at breakpoint b of the short-term cost function, for capacity point k;
T_{ij} distribution costs from facility i to customer j;
y_{ikl0} initial facility variable;
δ_t discount factor in period t;
p^s probability of scenario s;

Decision Variables

x^s_{ijt} amount of customer demand at customer location j satisfied from facility i in period t in scenarios s;
y^s_{iklt} 1 if facility is operated in location i in period t, with originally installed capacity k, and operated capacity l in scenario s, 0 otherwise;
μ^s_{bilt} weight of breakpoint b at location i for capacity point k in period t and scenario s.

We present a two-stage stochastic multi-period model. The model is given as:

$$\begin{aligned}\min \sum_{s\in\mathcal{S}} p^s \Bigg[&\sum_{i\in\mathcal{I}}\sum_{k\in\mathcal{K}}\sum_{t\in\mathcal{T}} \delta_t C_{ik}\left(y^s_{ikkt} - y^s_{ikk(t-1)}\right) + \\ &\sum_{i\in\mathcal{I}}\sum_{k\in\mathcal{K}}\sum_{l\in\mathcal{K}:l>k}\sum_{t\in\mathcal{T}} \delta_t E_{ikl}\left(y^s_{iklt} - y^s_{ikl(t-1)}\right) + \\ &\sum_{b\in\mathcal{B}}\sum_{i\in\mathcal{I}}\sum_{l\in\mathcal{K}}\sum_{t\in\mathcal{T}} \delta_t F_{ibl}\mu^s_{bilt} + \sum_{i\in\mathcal{I}}\sum_{j\in\mathcal{J}}\sum_{t\in\mathcal{T}} \delta_t T_{ij} x^s_{ijt}\Bigg],\end{aligned} \tag{1}$$

subject to:

$$\sum_{k\in\mathcal{K}}\sum_{l\in\mathcal{K}:l\geq k} y^s_{iklt} \leq 1, \qquad i\in\mathcal{I}, t\in\mathcal{T}, s\in\mathcal{S}, \tag{2}$$

$$\sum_{k\in\mathcal{K}}\sum_{l\in\mathcal{K}:l>k} y^s_{iklt} = 0, \qquad i\in\mathcal{I}, t\in\mathcal{T}_1, s\in\mathcal{S}, \tag{3}$$

$$\sum_{t'=1}^{t-1} y^s_{ikkt'} \geq \sum_{l\in\mathcal{K}:l>k} y^s_{iklt}, \qquad i\in\mathcal{I}, k\in\mathcal{K}, t\in\mathcal{T}, s\in\mathcal{S}, \tag{4}$$

$$\sum_{l\in\mathcal{K}:l\geq k} y^s_{iklt} \geq \sum_{l\in\mathcal{K}:l\geq k} y^s_{ikl(t-1)}, \qquad i\in\mathcal{I}, k\in\mathcal{K}, t\in\mathcal{T}, s\in\mathcal{S} \tag{5}$$

$$y^s_{iklt} - y^s_{ikl(t-1)} \geq 0, \qquad i\in\mathcal{I}, k\in\mathcal{K}, l\in K : l>k, t\in\mathcal{T}, s\in\mathcal{S}, \tag{6}$$

$$\sum_{b\in\mathcal{B}} \mu^s_{bilt} = \sum_{k\in\mathcal{K}} y^s_{iklt}, \qquad i\in\mathcal{I}, l\in\mathcal{K}, t\in\mathcal{T}, s\in\mathcal{S}, \tag{7}$$

$$\sum_{j\in\mathcal{J}} x^s_{ijt} = \sum_{b\in\mathcal{B}}\sum_{l\in\mathcal{K}} Q_{bl}\mu^s_{bilt}, \qquad i\in\mathcal{I}, t\in\mathcal{T}, s\in\mathcal{S}, \tag{8}$$

$$\sum_{i \in \mathcal{I}} x_{ijt}^s = D_{jt}^s, \qquad j \in \mathcal{J}, t \in \mathcal{T}, s \in \mathcal{S}, \quad (9)$$

$$x_{ijp}^s \leq L_{ij} D_{jt}^s, \qquad i \in \mathcal{I}, j \in \mathcal{J}, t \in \mathcal{T}, s \in \mathcal{S}, \quad (10)$$

$$\frac{1}{|\mathcal{S}|} \sum_{s' \in \mathcal{S}} \sum_{l \in \mathcal{K}: l \geq k} y_{iklt}^{s'} = \sum_{l \in \mathcal{K}: l \geq k} y_{iklt}^s, \qquad i \in \mathcal{I}, k \in \mathcal{K}, t \in \mathcal{T}, s \in \mathcal{S}, \quad (11)$$

$$y_{iklt}^s \in \{0, 1\}, \qquad i \in \mathcal{I}, k \in \mathcal{K}, l \in \mathcal{K} : l \geq k, t \in \mathcal{T}, s \in \mathcal{S}, \quad (12)$$

$$x_{ijt}^s \geq 0, \qquad i \in \mathcal{I}, j \in \mathcal{J}, t \in \mathcal{T}, s \in \mathcal{S} \quad (13)$$

$$\mu_{bilt}^s \geq 0, \qquad b \in \mathcal{B}, i \in \mathcal{I}, k \in \mathcal{K}, t \in \mathcal{T}, s \in \mathcal{S}. \quad (14)$$

The objective function (1) is equal to the expected discounted costs of investment, expansion, production and distribution costs. Restrictions (2) guarantee that only one facility is opened at a given location and that this facility is operated at only one capacity at a time. Constraints (3) ensure that we are allowed to open facilities in the first stage, but not to expand them. Restrictions (4) make sure that only previously opened facilities can be expanded and constraints (5) ensure that a facility can be expanded but cannot be closed. Capacity expansion is allowed only once during the planning horizon in each scenario. The variable y_{iklt}^s contains information about the initially installed capacity k as well as the capacity l at which it is currently operated. After expansion, the operated capacity l is higher than the installed capacity k. Inequalities (6) ensure that capacity index l can change only once. Equations (7) guarantee that production is allocated only to opened facilities and that the short-term production cost function depends on the operated capacity. Equations (8) express the requirement that the whole production has to be distributed to customers. Equations (9) ensure demand satisfaction in each scenario, while constraints (10) specify if customer j can be served from facility i.

Constraints (11) are the non-anticipativity constraints (see e.g. [36]) that ensure that the opening capacity k is the same in all scenarios. Once a facility has been opened with capacity k in a given scenario s, it has to be operated at a capacity $l \geq k$. Hence, the right-hand side, $\sum_{l \in \mathcal{K}: l \geq k} y_{iklt}^s$, is equal to 1. The left-hand side then ensures that the facility is opened with capacity k in all scenarios, even though it might be operated at different capacities l in different scenarios.

Restrictions (12)–(14) are the binary and non-negativity requirements for the decision variables. The variables are defined for each scenario. However, investment decisions must be taken before the uncertainty is disclosed.

4 Solution Approach

We use the SAA algorithm [22,25] to solve our two-stage stochastic multi-period model with binary variables. A description of the algorithm can also be found in [38] and [40], but we summarize it here for the sake of completeness. Using the SAA approach, the problem is repeatedly solved with a smaller set of scenarios.

First, a random sample $\xi^1, ..., \xi^n$ with a size N is generated. Then the expectation $\mathbb{E}[Q(y, \xi)]$ is approximated by the sample average function $\frac{1}{N}\sum_{n=1}^{N} Q(y, \xi^n)$. We approximate our problem with the following SAA problem:

$$\min \left\{ \hat{g}(y) = c^T y + \frac{1}{N} \sum_{n=1}^{N} Q(y, \xi^n) \right\} \tag{15}$$

With increasing sample size, the optimal solution of (15), $\hat{y}_N$ converges to the optimal solution of the original problem with probability one. In practical implementations, the sample size is often chosen with respect to the computational effort. As we have issues solving our model with more than 10 scenarios, we follow the approach from [38]. The authors show that a higher number of samples can be more efficient than increasing the number of scenarios.

Let M be the number of independent samples and v_N^m the optimal objective function of a problem for $m = 1, ..., M$. The average objective function value is then computed as:

$$\overline{v}_{N,M} = \frac{1}{M} \sum_{m=1}^{M} v_N^m \tag{16}$$

Equation (16) represents a statistical lower bound (LB) on the objective function value for the original problem [25,29].

Let $N' >> N$ be the reference sample representing the true uncertainty in the problem and $\overline{y}$ a feasible first-stage solution. Then, the objective function of the original problem for a given solution $\overline{y}$ can be calculated as:

$$\widetilde{g}_{N'}(\overline{y}) = c^T \overline{y} + \frac{1}{N'} \sum_{n=1}^{N'} Q(\overline{y}, \xi^n) \tag{17}$$

Equation (17) provides an upper bound (UB) on the optimal objective function value. Having the lower and upper bound estimates, we can compute the estimated optimality gap as:

$$gap_{N,M,N'}(\overline{y}) = \widetilde{g}_{N'}(\overline{y}) - \overline{v}_N^m. \tag{18}$$

5 Case Study

In this section, we provide the real-world input data used for solving the problem of locating hydrogen production in Norway under uncertainty.

5.1 Facilities and Production

We consider 17 candidate locations for the opening of new facilities on the Norwegian west coast. The candidate locations are taken from [33]. We approximate the facility capacity by 8 discrete points and provide the investment and production costs at full capacity utilization for EL in Table 1.

Table 1. Investment and production costs at full capacity utilization for EL [43]

Discrete capacity	1	2	3	4	5	6	7	8
Capacity [tonnes/day]	0.6	3.1	6.2	12.2	30.3	61.0	151.5	304.9
Investment EL [mill. €]	1.4	6.0	11.2	20.5	46.5	87.2	197.7	371.5
Production EL [€/kg]	1.95	1.61	1.53	1.45	1.43	1.42	1.40	1.38

There are minimum production requirements for electrolysis, as the production rate can decrease towards 20% of the installed capacity. We approximate the short-term production costs by a convex piecewise linear function with three linepieces. We define four breakpoints at 20%, 50%, 80%, and 100% of installed production quantity. The 20% breakpoint represents the minimum production requirement based on the technical specifications for electrolysis, and the 100% breakpoint represents full utilization of installed capacity. Each breakpoint is characterized by a specific production quantity and production costs. We can produce arbitrary quantities from the range between 20 – 100% of the installed capacity by a linear combination of two neighbourhood breakpoints. The short-term costs at a breakpoint are calculated based the a model provided in [17]. We assume that the investment and production costs are independent of facility location.

We calculate the expansion costs E_{ikl} as: $E_{ikl} = (C_{il} - C_{ik}) \cdot (100 + \alpha)\%$. The expansion costs are equal to the difference between investment costs of opening a facility with capacity l and a facility with capacity k, where $k < l$, plus an additional mark-up α. In our case, the mark-up α is 10%

Table 2. Hydrogen distribution costs in [€/km/kg H_2] [8]

Distance [km]	1–50	51–100	101–200	201–400	401–800	801–1000
Costs	0.00498	0.00426	0.00390	0.00372	0.00363	0.00360

We use the distribution costs for compressed hydrogen provided by [8]. We consider demand points that aggregate customer demand from the whole municipality, and if a demand point is located in the same municipality as a facility, we assume zero distribution costs. The reason is that the starting point for our case study is the production of hydrogen for maritime transportation. The demand points for this sector are limited to ports. For locations along the Norwegian coastline, we assume that hydrogen production will take place in port or close to the port with negligible distribution costs. This assumption has then been extended to municipalities producing hydrogen for other sectors than maritime for reasons of consistency. We set the distance limit between a production facility and a customer to 1000 km km. See Table 2 for the distribution costs for compressed hydrogen. The production cost and distribution cost data for our case are identical to the from [43]. For simplification, we assume that the discount factor is equal to one in each period.

5.2 Demand

We consider three main demand components. In the maritime sector, the hydrogen demand estimations are based on current ferry routes and the assumption that the new public contracts will require hydrogen as an energy carrier [1,32]. The demand estimations in the land-based sector from [11] are based on the emission reduction goal within 2030 stated in [37]. In the offshore sector, we use the hydrogen demand estimations from [2]. These estimations are based on the medium penetration scenario from [32] which calculates the energy consumption for ammonia. However, hydrogen fuel alternative is just as likely to occur [45]. These different demand components are shown in Fig. 2 together with the expected demand level and the maximum potential hydrogen demand consisting of all three components. The maritime demand is quite certain. Thus, it represents the minimum demand level and is present in all demand scenarios.

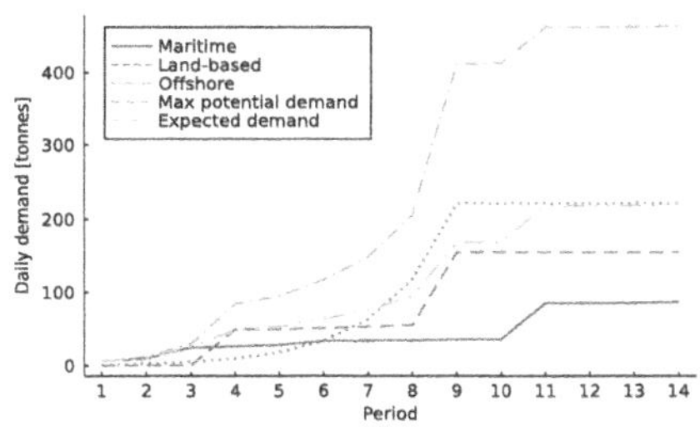

Fig. 2. Demand development

We aggregate individual customer demand into 70 demand points located in Norway. These demand points consist of 51 ports that are relevant for the maritime and the offshore sector and 19 municipalities with the highest road traffic volumes according to the statistic provided in [44]. Based on the traffic volumes statistic [44], we divide the road traffic demand among the different municipalities. We remove municipalities with demand lower than 3.65 tonnes H_2/year. However, not all customers, respectively demand points, have demand in all scenarios.

Our planning horizon is 14 periods. Demand is non-decreasing during the whole planning horizon in all considered sectors. In the maritime sector, demand is slightly increasing until period 10 and there is a jump in period 11 when the coastal route Bergen-Kirkenes is to be operated on hydrogen fuels. The jumps in the land-based sector correspond to the strategic government plan to start with the transition towards hydrogen for buses and trucks. The offshore sector will not start the transition towards hydrogen before period 4.

The market share of hydrogen vehicles and hydrogen-driven offshore supply vessels is highly uncertain. We consider demand in the land-based sector and offshore sector to represent a conversion potential and assume that the probability of reaching the maximal potential demand is low. Therefore, we assume that our demand scenarios are not evenly distributed between the minimum and the maximum potential demand. We assume the expected value to be a weighted average of minimum and maximum demand with coefficients 0.65 and 0.35, respectively.

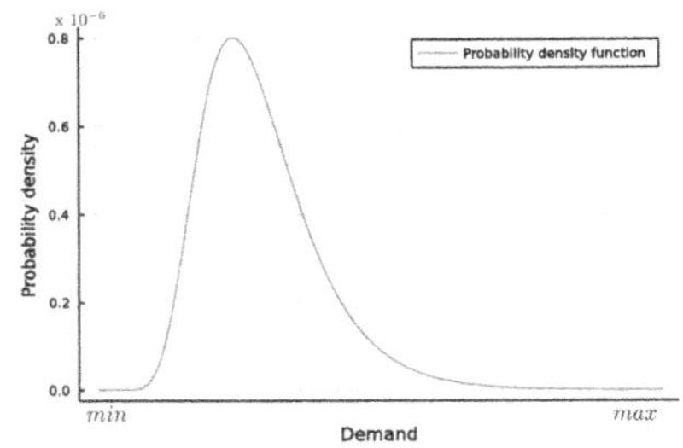

Fig. 3. Probability density function for hydrogen demand

We expect that scenarios with lower demand consisting of maritime demand and a share of the land-based and offshore sector are more likely to occur than very optimistic hydrogen scenarios with very high demand. Thus, we need a left-skewed distribution with a low probability of extreme values to sample the scenarios from. We therefore assume a log-normal distribution, $D \sim Lognormal(\mu, \sigma^2)$. The expected value $E(D)$ is given by the previously computed expected demand level and we assume the standard deviation to be $\sigma = 0.3$ as this value still allows some of the high demand scenarios to occur. The probability density function of our log-normal distribution is shown in Fig. 3.

6 Computational Results

The model is implemented in Julia 1.6.5 and solved using Gurobi Optimizer version 9.5. All calculations have been run on a computer with two 3.6 GHz Intel Xeon Gold 6244 CPU (8 core) processors and 384 GB RAM.

The problem (15) is solved for $M = 50$ SAA problems where each of the problems has a sample size of $N = 10$. The reference sample size is $N' = 1000$ and we evaluate the performance on the reference sample for each of the 50 SAA solutions. We choose to solve the problems (15) with relative optimality gap $\gamma' < 2\%$.

Table 3. Evaluation of the SP and the EEV

Problem	LB [x10^6 €]	UB [x10^6 €]	$gap_{N,M,N'}(\overline{y})[\%]$
SP	1381.2	1455.2	5.36
EEV	-	∞	-

We show the best statistical lower and upper bound of the SP in Table 3 and compare the results with the EVP. We calculate the expected value of the EVP solution (EEV) and compare the results with the SP. The value of the stochastic solution is: $VSS = EEV - SP$ [5]. The results show that the EVP solution is infeasible. Thus, the VSS goes to infinity. This shows that even if the EVP problem is easier to solve and we can find an optimal solution, it is important to consider the uncertainty in our problem.

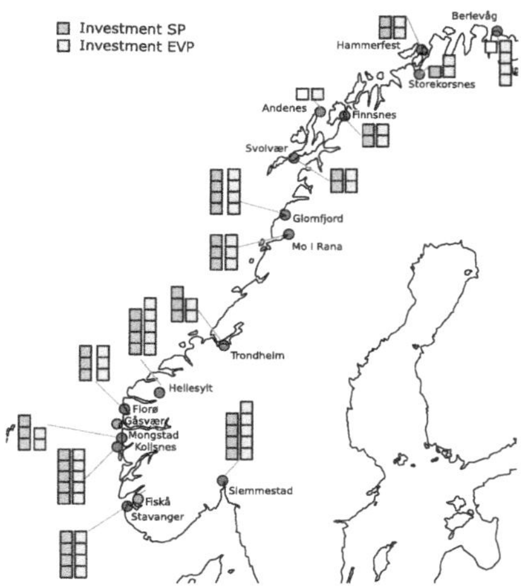

(a) Location and opening capacity of hydrogen facilities in the SP and the EVP

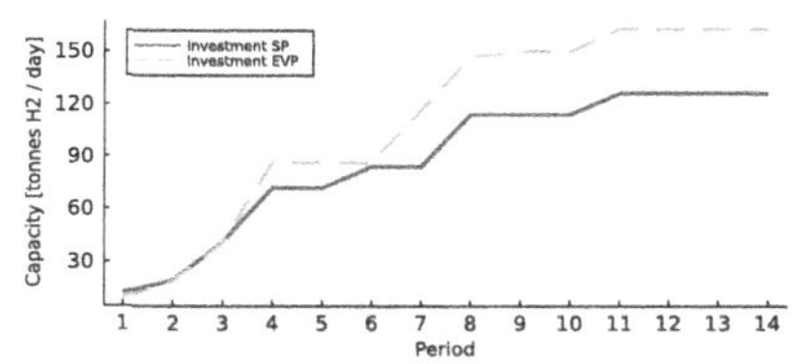

(b) Opening capacity in the SP and the EVP

Fig. 4. First-stage decisions: Investment in the SP and the EVP

To analyze the first stage decisions, we study the opening decisions in the SP and the EVP. Figure 4a illustrates the facility locations and the opening size of facilities before expansion. When comparing the number of opened facilities, we open 13 facilities in the SP and 15 facilities in the EVP. However, in general, the differences between the SP and the EVP are very small. The main differences can be seen in the northern part of Norway where we do not open a facility in Berlevåg and Andenes in the SP. Thus, we install more capacity in the EVP in comparison to SP. However, the infeasibility comes from the south-western part of Norway even if the number of opened facilities is equal. Please note that the difference between capacity 2 and 3 is only 3.1 tonnes daily while the difference between capacity 4 and 5 is 18.1 tonnes daily. Thus, we install more capacity in the EVP as we open two large facilities in Hellesylt and Slemmestad. Most of the land-based demand is located in the south-western part of Norway and this area is also affected a lot by the offshore demand. Thus, here, we observe the highest differences between the scenarios and the large capacities installed for the EVP cause infeasibility for scenarios with low demand. In the EVP, we cannot fulfil the minimum production requirements for scenarios with low demand due to the large facilities in Hellesylt and Slemmestad.

The development of installed capacity in the first stage in the SP and the EVP solution can be seen in Fig. 4b. The installed capacity is almost the same in the first three periods because the differences between scenarios are low until period three. Then, both lines indicate growing capacity. However, the installed capacity in SP is considerably lower. The solution of the SP leads to more conservative investment decisions and additional capacity is installed in the expansion step. The expected demand level is considerably higher than the minimum demand so the EVP problem leads to more extensive investments than the SP which is also the reason for the infeasibility of the EVP.

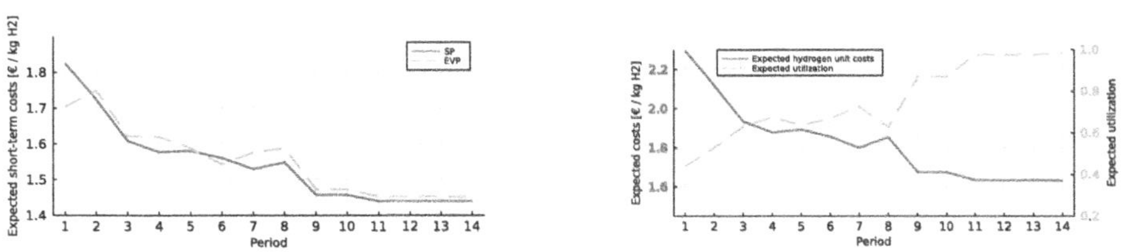

(a) Expected unit short-term costs in the SP and the EVP

(b) Expected unit costs and expected capacity utilization in the SP

Fig. 5. Expected hydrogen costs

For illustration, we show the expected unit short-term costs in the SP and the EVP in Fig. 5a. Please note that we show results for a feasible subset of scenarios in the EVP. The EVP provides lower costs in the first period due to the lower installed capacity (see Fig. 4b) resulting in higher utilization. In the following periods, the costs in the SP are, in general, lower. However, the costs are very similar because expansion in the second stage provides a lot of flexibility to adjust the infrastructure as a reaction to growing demand. Expected unit hydrogen costs and expected utilization for the SP are shown in Fig. 5b. The expected unit hydrogen costs have a decreasing tendency that is in line with the growing capacity (see Fig. 4b) and increasing utilization. The unit production costs have two peaks in period 5 and 8 that are related to a decrease in capacity utilization as lower utilization results in higher unit costs. In expectation, unit production costs are decreasing together with increasing capacity and its utilization which indicates the presence of economies of scale in hydrogen production.

7 Conclusion

We study the optimal hydrogen production infrastructure under uncertain demand in Norway. We present a model for a two-stage stochastic multi-period facility location problem with capacity expansion. The problem is hard to solve and using commercial software, we can solve it with 10 scenarios. Therefore, we use SAA to solve the problem. This approach provides good solutions with an estimated gap between the lower and the upper bound of 5.36%.

The quality of the solution is limited by the number of scenarios we can solve the problem with. Implementing an efficient solution method in order solve the problem with more scenarios and thus improve the solution quality is a natural extension of this work.

Another extension of this work is to study how the investment structure will change when we modify the underlying demand distribution.

Expansion in the second stage provides a lot of flexibility in terms of reaction to growing demand. It is worth considering, how the investment decisions will change for different models. We can consider a multi-stage model, or a more restrictive model where expansion is the first-stage decision and only decisions regarding demand allocation are taken in the second stage. In future work, uncertainty in costs might be considered as well.

References

1. Aarskog, F.G., Danebergs, J.: Estimation of energy demand in the Norwegian high-speed passenger ferry sector towards 2030. IFE/E-2020/003, Halden, Norway (2020)
2. Aglen, T.M., Hofstad, A.: Designing the hydrogen supply chain for maritime transportation. Master's thesis, Department of Industrial Economics and Technology Management, NTNU, Trondheim, Norway (2022)
3. Ahmed, S., King, A.J., Parija, G.: A multi-stage stochastic integer programming approach for capacity expansion under uncertainty. J. Global Optim. **26**(1), 3–24 (2003). https://doi.org/10.1023/A:1023062915106
4. Balachandran, V., Jain, S.: Optimal facility location under random demand with general cost structure. Naval Res. Logistics Quart. **23**(3), 421–436 (1976)
5. Birge, J.R., Louveaux, F.: Introduction to Stochastic Programming, 2nd edn. Springer Science & Business Media, New York (2011). https://doi.org/10.1007/b97617
6. Correia, I., da Gama, F.S.: Facility location under uncertainty. In: Laporte, G., Nickel, S., da Gama, F.S. (eds.) Location Science, pp. 177–203. Springer, Cham (2015). https://doi.org/10.1007/978-3-319-13111-5_8
7. Correia, I., Melo, T.: Integrated facility location and capacity planning under uncertainty. Comput. Appl. Math. **40**(5), 1–36 (2021). https://doi.org/10.1007/s40314-021-01560-0
8. Danebergs, J., Aarskog, F.G.: Future compressed hydrogen infrastructure for the domestic maritime sector. IFE/E-2020/006, Halden, Norway (2020)
9. Dayhim, M., Jafari, M.A., Mazurek, M.: Planning sustainable hydrogen supply chain infrastructure with uncertain demand. Int. J. Hydrogen Energy **39**(13), 6789–6801 (2014)
10. Dias, J., Captivo, M.E., Clímaco, J.: Dynamic location problems with discrete expansion and reduction sizes of available capacities. Investigação Operacional **27**(2), 107–130 (2007)

11. DNV GL: Produksjon og bruk av hydrogen i Norge (2019). Rapport 2019–0039, Oslo, Norway, (in Norwegian)
12. Fernandes, D.R., Rocha, C., Aloise, D., Ribeiro, G.M., Santos, E.M., Silva, A.: A simple and effective genetic algorithm for the two-stage capacitated facility location problem. Comput. Ind. Eng. **75**, 200–208 (2014)
13. Gade, D., Pohl, E.: Sample average approximation applied to the capacitated-facilities location problem with unreliable facilities. Proc. Inst. Mech. Eng. Part O J Risk Reliab. **223**(4), 259–269 (2009)
14. Govindan, K., Fattahi, M., Keyvanshokooh, E.: Supply chain network design under uncertainty: a comprehensive review and future research directions. Eur. J. Oper. Res. **263**(1), 108–141 (2017)
15. Hirth, M., et al.: Norwegian future value chains for liquid hydrogen, : NCE Maritime CleanTech, Report liquid hydrogen 2019. Stord, Norway (2019)
16. IRENA: Green hydrogen: a guide to policy making. International Renewable Energy Agency (2020)
17. Jakobsen, D., Åtland, V.: Concepts for large scale hydrogen production. Master's thesis, Department of Energy and Process Engineering, NTNU, Trondheim, Norway (2016)
18. Jena, S.D., Cordeau, J.F., Gendron, B.: Dynamic facility location with generalized modular capacities. Transp. Sci. **49**(3), 484–499 (2015)
19. Jena, S.D., Cordeau, J.F., Gendron, B.: Solving a dynamic facility location problem with partial closing and reopening. Comput. Oper. Res. **67**, 143–154 (2016)
20. Jena, S.D., Cordeau, J.F., Gendron, B.: Lagrangian heuristics for large-scale dynamic facility location with generalized modular capacities. INFORMS J. Comput. **29**(3), 388–404 (2017)
21. Kim, J., Lee, Y., Moon, I.: Optimization of a hydrogen supply chain under demand uncertainty. Int. J. Hydrogen Energy **33**(18), 4715–4729 (2008)
22. Kleywegt, A.J., Shapiro, A., Homem-de Mello, T.: The sample average approximation method for stochastic discrete optimization. SIAM J. Optim. **12**(2), 479–502 (2001)
23. Li, X., Zhang, K.: A sample average approximation approach for supply chain network design with facility disruptions. Comput. Ind. Eng. **126**, 243–251 (2018)
24. Litvinchev, I., Ozuna Espinosa, E.L.: Solving the two-stage capacitated facility location problem by the Lagrangian heuristic. In: Hu, H., Shi, X., Stahlbock, R., Voß, S. (eds.) ICCL 2012. LNCS, vol. 7555, pp. 92–103. Springer, Heidelberg (2012). https://doi.org/10.1007/978-3-642-33587-7_7
25. Mak, W.K., Morton, D.P., Wood, R.K.: Monte Carlo bounding techniques for determining solution quality in stochastic programs. Oper. Res. Lett. **24**(1–2), 47–56 (1999)
26. Melo, M.T., Nickel, S., Saldanha-Da-Gama, F.: Facility location and supply chain management-a review. Eur. J. Oper. Res. **196**(2), 401–412 (2009)
27. NEL Hydrogen: Efficient electrolysers for hydrogen production (2015). https://wpstatic.idium.no/www.nel-hydrogen.com/2015/03/Efficient_Electrolysers_for_Hydrogen_Production.pdf/. Accessed May 02 2021
28. Nickel, S., Saldanha-da Gama, F.: Multi-period facility location. In: Laporte, G., Nickel, S., Saldanha-da Gama, F. (eds.) Location Science, pp. 303–326. Springer, Cham (2019). https://doi.org/10.1007/978-3-319-13111-5
29. Norkin, V.I., Pflug, G.C., Ruszczyński, A.: A branch and bound method for stochastic global optimization. Math. Program. **83**(1), 425–450 (1998)

30. Nærings- og skeridepartementet: Grønnere og smartere morgendagens maritime næring (2020). https://www.regjeringen.no/no/dokumenter/meld.-st.-10-20202021/id2788786/. Accessed 03 Sep 2022. (in Norwegian)
31. Nunes, P., Oliveira, F., Hamacher, S., Almansoori, A.: Design of a hydrogen supply chain with uncertainty. Int. J. Hydrogen Energy **40**(46), 16408–16418 (2015)
32. Ocean Hyway Cluster: 2030 hydrogen demand in the Norwegian domestic maritime sector (2020). OHC HyInfra project, Workpackage C: Mapping future hydrogen demand
33. Ocean Hyway Cluster: Interactive map - potential maritime hydrogen in Norway (2020). OHC HyInfra project, Workpackage C: Mapping future hydrogen demand
34. Owen, S.H., Daskin, M.S.: Strategic facility location: a review. Eur. J. Oper. Res. **111**(3), 423–447 (1998)
35. Regjeringen: A european green deal: Norwegian perspectives and contributions (2021). https://www.regjeringen.no/contentassets/38453d5f5f5d42779aaa3059b200a25f/a-european-green-deal-norwegian-perspectives-and-contributions-20.04.2021.pdf. Accessed 03 Sep 2022
36. Rockafellar, R.T., Wets, R.J.B.: Scenarios and policy aggregation in optimization under uncertainty. Math. Oper. Res. **16**(1), 119–147 (1991)
37. Samferdselsdepartementet: Nasjonal transportplan 2022–2033 (2021). https://www.regjeringen.no/no/dokumenter/meld.-st.-20-20202021/id2839503/?ch=1. Accessed 03 Sep 2022. (in Norwegian)
38. Santoso, T., Ahmed, S., Goetschalckx, M., Shapiro, A.: A stochastic programming approach for supply chain network design under uncertainty. Eur. J. Oper. Res. **167**(1), 96–115 (2005)
39. Schütz, P., Stougie, L., Tomasgard, A.: Stochastic facility location with general long-run costs and convex short-run costs. Comput. Oper. Res. **35**(9), 2988–3000 (2008)
40. Schütz, P., Tomasgard, A., Ahmed, S.: Supply chain design under uncertainty using sample average approximation and dual decomposition. Eur. J. Oper. Res. **199**(2), 409–419 (2009)
41. Shulman, A.: An algorithm for solving dynamic capacitated plant location problems with discrete expansion sizes. Oper. Res. **39**(3), 423–436 (1991)
42. Snyder, L.V.: Facility location under uncertainty: a review. IIE Trans. **38**(7), 547–564 (2006)
43. Štádlerová, Š, Schütz, P.: Designing the hydrogen supply chain for maritime transportation in Norway. In: Mes, M., Lalla-Ruiz, E., Voß, S. (eds.) Computational Logistics, pp. 36–50. Springer, Cham (2021). https://doi.org/10.1007/978-3-030-87672-2
44. Statistics Norway: Statistics Norway: 12579: Road traffic volumes (2018). https://www.ssb.no/en/statbank/table/12579/. Accessed 11 Feb 2021
45. Ulstein Design: Zero-emission operations in offshore construction market (2021). https://ulstein.com/news/zero-emission-operations-in-offshore-construction-market. Accessed 04 May 2022

Oblivious Stacking and MAX k-CUT for Circle Graphs

Martin Olsen(✉)

Department of Business Development and Technology, Aarhus University, Aarhus, Denmark
martino@btech.au.dk

Abstract. Stacking is an important process within logistics. Some notable examples of items to be stacked are steel bars or steel plates in a steel yard or containers in a container terminal or on a ship. We say that two items are *conflicting* if their storage time intervals overlap in which case one of the items needs to be rehandled if the items are stored at the same LIFO storage location. We consider the problem of stacking items using k LIFO locations with a minimum number of conflicts between items sharing a location. We present an extremely simple online stacking algorithm that is oblivious to the storage time intervals and storage locations of *all other items* when it picks a storage location for an item. The risk of assigning the same storage location to two conflicting items is proved to be of the order $1/k^2$ under mild assumptions on the distribution of the storage time intervals for the items. Intuitively, it seems natural to pick a storage location uniformly at random in the oblivious setting implying a risk of $1/k$ so the risk for our algorithm is surprisingly low. Our results can also be expressed within the context of the MAX k-CUT problem for circle graphs. The results indicate that circle graphs on average have relatively big k-cuts compared to the total number of edges.

Keywords: Oblivious algorithms · MAX k-CUT · Stacking · Circle graphs

1 Introduction

We consider a storage area with a continuous flow of items entering and leaving the area. The storage area consists of k storage locations accessible in a LIFO manner. If we want to retrieve a target item from a storage location, we have to deal with all the items present at the storage location that have arrived later than the targeted item. The items that have arrived later but have not left yet are conflicting with the targeted item so we focus on the problem of assigning storage locations to the items with a minimum number of conflicts among items sharing a location. We refer to this problem as *stacking* since each storage location acts as a stack data structure.

J. de Armas et al. (Eds.): ICCL 2022, LNCS 13557, pp. 322–335, 2022.
https://doi.org/10.1007/978-3-031-16579-5_22

The stacking problem is an important problem within logistics with many applications such as shipment of containers [3,18], track assignment for trains (the storage locations are train tracks) [6,8] and stacking of steel bars or steel plates [11,12,16]. Actually, a storage location can be any place where items potentially block each other as described earlier: a truck, a train wagon, a shelve in a warehouse, etc.

We can rephrase the problem as a graph problem if we construct a graph with a vertex for each item and an edge between two vertices if the corresponding items are conflicting. Now the objective is to color the vertices using k colors with a minimum number of edges connecting two vertices with the same color or, equivalently, to maximize the cardinality of the set of edges connecting vertices with different colors. The latter set of edges is typically called the *cut* and the problem is commonly known as the MAX k-CUT problem. The MAX k-CUT problem is a famous graph problem appearing in many contexts. The MAX k-CUT problem is closely related to the coloring problem where the objective is to use as few colors as possible with no edges connecting vertices with the same color. For the MAX k-CUT problem the number of colors is known a priori as opposed to the coloring problem where the number of colors is output by the algorithm.

1.1 Related Work

An *offline* stacking algorithm has access to all information on all the items before the assignment of storage locations is carried out in contrast to an *online* stacking algorithm where a decision on where to store an item is made without access to any information on future items.

First, we consider related work for the coloring version of stacking where the objective is to use as few storage locations as possible with no conflicts. Upper and lower bounds for the competitive ratio for online coloring are presented by Demange et al. [8] and Demange and Olsen [7]. Olsen and Gross [14] have developed a polynomial time algorithm for online coloring with a competitive ratio that converges to 1 in probability if the endpoints of the storage time intervals are picked independently and uniformly at random. Olsen [13] has also shown how to use Reinforcement Learning to improve online stacking heuristics.

The offline version of coloring is NP-hard for unbounded stack capacity [1] and for fixed stack capacity $h \geq 6$ [6] and the computational complexity for $2 \leq h \leq 5$ is an open problem (to the best of our knowledge).

We now take a look at related work for the MAX k-CUT version of stacking where the number of storage locations is given and where the objective is to minimize the number of conflicts among the items. Handling shipping containers that block each other in a stack is known as *rehandling* or *shifting*. Tierney et al. [18] show how to compute the minimum number of shifts offline in polynomial time using a fixed number of stacks (storage locations) with bounded capacity. The MAX k-CUT version of stacking is at least as hard as the coloring problem as can be easily seen by reduction from the coloring problem. The offline version is even NP-hard for $k = 2$ (unbounded capacity) [15].

For the offline version of MAX k-CUT for graphs in general, we can achieve an approximation ratio $1 - \frac{1}{k}$ with a simple polynomial time algorithm but it is not possible to achieve an approximation ratio better than $1 - \frac{1}{34k}$ if $NP \neq P$ [10]. Finally, it should be mentioned that Coja-Oghlan et al. [5] examine the MAX k-CUT problem in random graphs.

1.2 Contribution

For the remaining part of the paper, we focus on the MAX k-CUT version of stacking so from now on we assume that our goal is to minimize the number of conflicts between items stored at the same location using k storage locations.

Our main aim is to investigate the case where an online algorithm does *not* have access to the storage time intervals for the items already stored and does *not* keep track of the locations of these items but *only* has access to the arrival time and the departure time for an entering item when it has to pick a storage location for that item. In other words, the algorithm is *oblivious* to the time intervals for *all other items* and the storage locations assigned to items in the past. We will refer to such an algorithm as an *oblivious stacking algorithm*. Such an algorithm is extremely simple to implement and it can even be used in a scenario with several disconnected stacking agents. To the best of our knowledge, we are the first to examine this type of stacking algorithms but such oblivious algorithms have been examined for other problems (for example routing [2,4]).

Intuitively, it might look a little strange to consider the oblivious setting since it seems hard to do anything better than to assign a random storage location to an entering item if we do not have any information on the other items. The risk of assigning the same storage location to two conflicting items is $1/k$ if we use the random strategy. We present an extremely simple algorithm for oblivious stacking where this risk is reduced dramatically to the order $1/k^2$ under the assumption that the storage time intervals are produced by a model proposed by Scheinerman [17]. In short, our online stacking algorithm is as simple as an algorithm can be and it has a surprisingly good performance using a minimum amount of information. The algorithm is based on the intuition that the risk of a conflict between two items is low if the *centers* of their storage time intervals are close to each other since such items only will have a conflict if the lengths of their storage time intervals are roughly the same. The basic principle of our algorithm is to place items at the same storage location if the centers of their storage time intervals are close to each other or far apart.

Our algorithm can be used on its own but it can also be used as a part of a hierarchical approach to divide the items into k groups with only a few conflicts in each group. We can for example divide a steel yard or a container terminal into a few areas and then use our algorithm to assign an area to each item in a preprocessing step. For each area, we then apply a local stacking algorithm to assign a specific storage location to each item (the local algorithms do not have to be identical).

The stacking conflict graphs described earlier are so called *circle graphs* – also known as *interval overlap graphs* (more details in Sect. 2). From a graph theory perspective, we offer a contribution for an audience interested in circle graphs and show that our algorithm computes a k-cut with expected cardinality satisfying $E(|cut|) \geq (1 - O(1/k^2))E(m)$ for random circle graphs represented by an extended version of the Scheinerman model (m denotes the number of edges). This indicates that random circle graphs on average have relatively big k-cuts compared to the number of edges m in contrast to random graphs of the Erdős-Rényi type [5].

The problem that we consider is formally defined in Sect. 2 where we also present our algorithm and the first model for generating the instances. The performance of our algorithm is analyzed in Sect. 3 using average case analysis where we compute the exact risk that our oblivious algorithm assigns two conflicting items to the same storage location. In Sect. 4 we extend our model for generating the instances and demonstrate that the risk is low (of the order $1/k^2$) even in a more generic setting. Finally, our results are related to circle graphs/interval overlap graphs.

2 Preliminaries

2.1 The Problem

Two intervals $[a, b]$ and $[c, d]$ are said to *overlap* if and only if the intervals intersect and neither is contained in the other: $a < c < b < d$ or $c < a < d < b$. Two items are conflicting if and only if their storage time intervals overlap since shifting/rehandling is necessary exactly in this case if the items are stored at the same location. A graph with vertices representing intervals and edges representing overlaps is commonly known as an *interval overlap graph*. A *circle graph* is a graph where vertices represent chords of a circle with an edge between two vertices if the corresponding chords intersect. Gavril [9] has shown that a graph is an interval overlap graph if and only if it is a circle graph. In other words, a conflict graph for stacking is an interval overlap graph/circle graph implying relevance of our results, as already mentioned, for a broader audience interested in the MAX k-CUT problem for such graphs. It should be noted that the connection between stacking and interval overlap graphs/circle graphs was established by Avriel et al. [1].

To sum up, the problem considered in this paper can be formally and concisely defined as follows where the items are represented by their storage time intervals:

Definition 1. *The MAX k-CUT STACKING problem:*

- *Instance: A set of n intervals $\mathcal{I}_n = \{I_1, I_2, \ldots, I_n\}$*
- *Solution: A coloring of the intervals using colors $\{1, 2, 3, \ldots, k\}$ with a maximum cardinality cut where the cut is the set of unordered pairs of overlapping intervals with different colors*

An example of a MAX k-CUT STACKING instance and an optimal solution is displayed in Fig. 1 for $n = 4$ and $k = 2$. The corresponding interval overlap

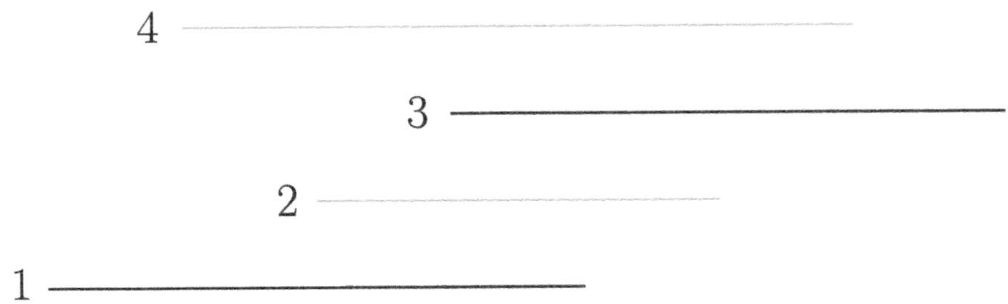

Fig. 1. An example of a MAX k-CUT STACKING instance for $n = 4$ and $k = 2$ and an optimal solution. The coloring uses the colors gray and black. (Color figure online)

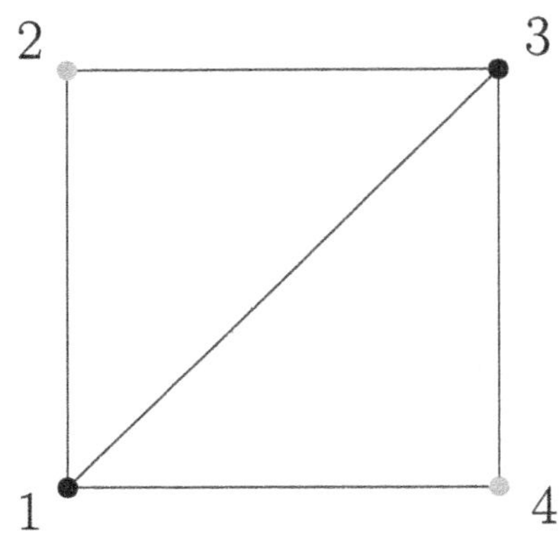

Fig. 2. The conflict graph for the MAX k-CUT STACKING instance in Fig. 1. The cut $\{\{1,2\},\{2,3\},\{1,4\},\{3,4\}\}$ has cardinality 4: $|cut| = 4$.

graph/circle graph is shown in Fig. 2. The intervals/vertices have received a gray or a black color producing a cut with cardinality 4: $|cut| = 4$. The optimal solution has only one conflict between items stored at the same location.

Please note that there is a one-to-one correspondence between the colors and the storage locations. It should also be noted that we consider storage locations with unbounded capacity. According to Kim et al. [11], this assumption is not critical considering stacking of steel plates since many plates can be stacked together because the thicknesses of the plates are very small. If our algorithm is used in a hierarchical approach as described in Sect. 1.2 then it also makes sense to assume that the capacity is unbounded so there are applications where this assumption is justified.

2.2 The Instance Model

We will use a simple stochastic model for generating the instances introduced by Scheinerman [17] in his work on random interval (intersection[1]) graphs:

[1] Two overlapping intervals intersect but the converse is not necessarily true.

Definition 2. *The Scheinerman Model [17]: The centers of the intervals in $\mathcal{I}_n$ are drawn independently using a uniform distribution on $[0,1]$ and the lengths of the intervals are drawn independently using a uniform distribution on $[0,L]$ for some number L.*

In order to be able obtain exact results for the analysis to follow, we assume the following:

$$1/\left(\frac{k}{k-1}L\right) \in \mathbb{Z} \ . \tag{1}$$

This means that $L = \frac{k-1}{kz}$ for some $z \in \mathbb{Z}$.

Our second model for generating instances (defined later in Sect. 4) allows us to use an arbitrary bounded continuous probability density function for the lengths where L denotes an upper bound of the lengths. It is important for us to emphasize that the second model is a lot more flexible than our first model but qualitatively the results obtained for the two models are the same. As already stated, the assumption (1) facilitates exact computations.

2.3 The Algorithm

Our algorithm works as follows. The interval $[0,1]$ is split into $\frac{k-1}{L}$ consecutive intervals $J_1, J_2, \ldots, J_{\frac{k-1}{L}}$ with length $\frac{L}{k-1}$. We now color the J-intervals with the colors $\{1,2,\ldots,k\}$ in a circular manner such that J_i receives color $(i-1) \bmod k+1$. Please note that (1) implies that the final interval receives the color k and has 1 as its right endpoint.

Let an item represented by the storage time interval $I = [x,y]$ with center $c(I) = (x+y)/2$ enter the storage area. The algorithm locates the J-interval containing the center and assign the color of this J-interval to the entering item ($A(I)$ denotes the color assigned to I by the algorithm):

$$A(I) = \left\lfloor \frac{(k-1)c(I)}{L} \right\rfloor \bmod k+1, \quad I \in \mathcal{I}_n \ . \tag{2}$$

The dynamics of the algorithm is illustrated in Fig. 3 showing an example with $k = 3$ and $L = 1/3$. This is a very simple online algorithm that only considers

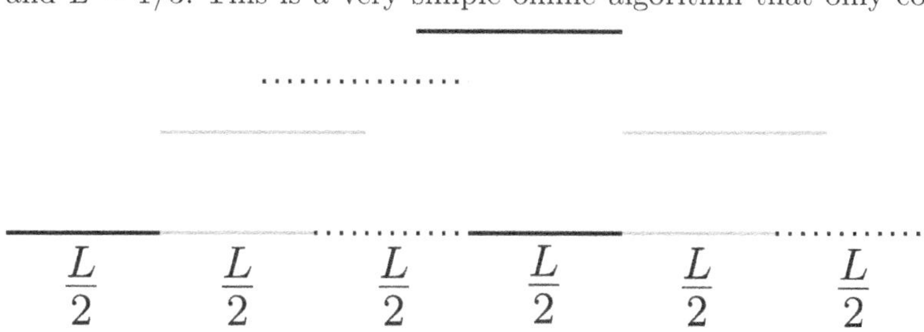

Fig. 3. The figure shows how our algorithm works for $k = 3$ and $L = 1/3$. The items are represented by the four storage time intervals at the top. An item receives the color of the J-interval at the bottom containing the center of the storage time interval for the item.

information on the current interval. As earlier mentioned, we refer to such an algorithm as an *oblivious* algorithm. The running time per interval is $O(1)$.

The intuition behind our algorithm is as follows. If two intervals receive the same color then there are two possibilities: 1) The centers of the intervals belong to different J-intervals in which case the intervals are not overlapping, or 2) The centers of the intervals belong to the same J-interval in which case the centers are close to each other implying a low risk of an overlap since an overlap only occurs if the lengths of the intervals are roughly the same. In other words, we will observe relatively few overlapping intervals with the same color.

3 Analysis of the Scheinerman Model

The intuition will now be verified using exact computations. The key observation is as follows: two intervals are not likely to overlap if their centers are close to each other. We now present a lemma quantifying this observation based on the Scheinerman model (Definition 2). Let $C = d$ denote the event that the distance between the centers of two intervals is d and let OV denote the event that two intervals overlap.

Lemma 1. *For two intervals drawn using the Scheinerman model we have the following:*

$$\Pr(OV \mid C = xL) = \begin{cases} 4x - 6x^2 & , \ 0 \le x \le 0.5 \\ \frac{1}{2}(2-2x)^2 & , \ 0.5 < x \le 1 \\ 0 & , \ 1 < x \end{cases}$$

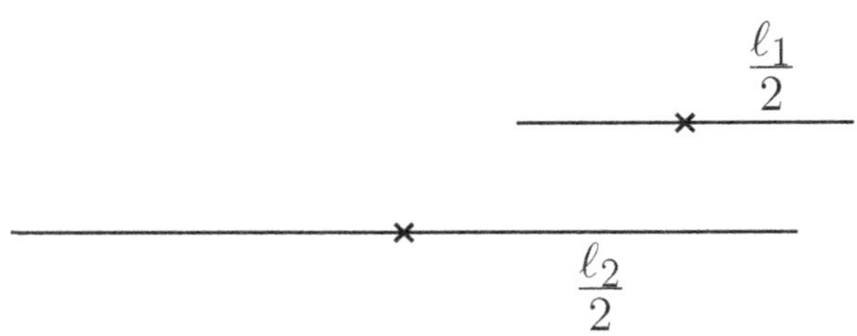

Fig. 4. Two intervals with lengths $\ell 1 < \ell_2$ and distance d between the centers overlap if and only if $d < \frac{\ell_1}{2} + \frac{\ell_2}{2} \wedge d + \frac{\ell_1}{2} > \frac{\ell_2}{2}$.

Proof. Consider two intervals with lengths ℓ_1 and ℓ_2 with $\ell_1 < \ell_2$ (see Fig. 4). Let d denote the distance between the centers of the intervals. The intervals overlap if and only if

$$d < \frac{\ell_1}{2} + \frac{\ell_2}{2} \wedge d + \frac{\ell_1}{2} > \frac{\ell_2}{2} \ . \tag{3}$$

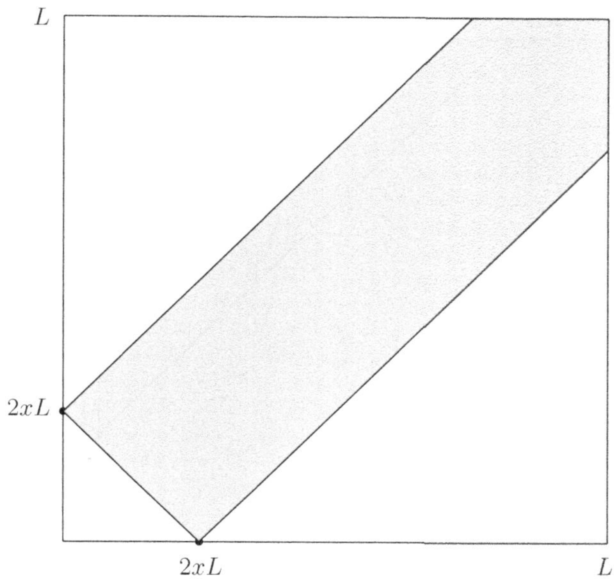

Fig. 5. The square $[0, L] \times [0, L]$ represents the possible pairs of lengths for the two intervals. The gray region illustrates the cases where the two intervals overlap given $C = xL$ for $x \leq 0.5$. (Color figure online)

The gray region in Fig. 5 contains all pairs (ℓ_1, ℓ_2) – including intervals with $\ell_1 > \ell_2$ – that correspond to overlapping intervals with $d = xL$ for $x \leq 0.5$. The conditional probability $\Pr(OV \mid C = xL)$ is computed as the area of the gray region divided by L^2:

$$\Pr(OV \mid C = xL) = 1 - 2x^2 - (1 - 2x)^2 = 4x - 6x^2 \ , \ \ x \leq 0.5 \ .$$

The case $0.5 < x \leq 1$ is handled in a similar way (see Fig. 6):

$$\Pr(OV \mid C = xL) = \frac{1}{2}(2 - 2x)^2, \ \ 0.5 < x \leq 1 \ .$$

□

We can see that the risk of an overlap is close to 0 if the centers are close to each other and that the risk is highest if the distance between the centers is $\frac{1}{3}L$. The risk decreases for higher distances between the centers than $\frac{1}{3}L$ and reaches (not surprisingly) 0 for distances above L.

Even though our algorithm is oblivious to information on other items than the entering item, it has a very low risk of assigning the same storage location to two conflicting items compared to a random stacking strategy. The risk is of the order $1/k^2$ assuming that the instances are generated using the Scheinerman model. Our next lemma expresses the exact risk where SC denotes the event that two

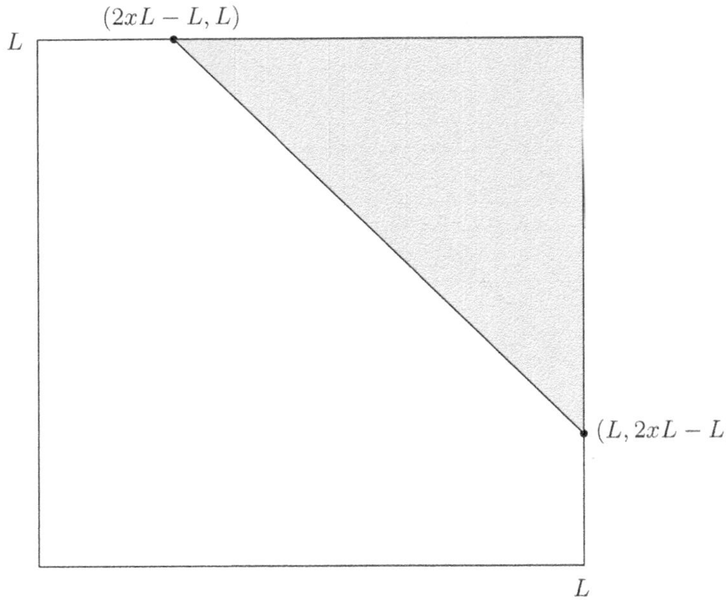

Fig. 6. The square $[0, L] \times [0, L]$ is once again representing the possible pairs of lengths for the two intervals. The gray region now illustrates the cases with an overlap given $C = xL$ for $0.5 < x \leq 1$ (Color figure online)

intervals receive the same color (= storage location) by our algorithm. As stated earlier, we assume that L satisfies (1) in order to enable exact computations.

Lemma 2. *For two intervals drawn using the Scheinerman model with L satisfying (1) the following holds for $k \geq 3$:*

$$\Pr(SC \mid OV) = \frac{12}{8-3L}\left(\frac{4}{3(k-1)^2} - \frac{1}{(k-1)^3}\right) .$$

Proof. It is well known and straightforward to show that the probability density function for the distance between two random numbers chosen uniformly at random in $[0, a]$ is as follows:

$$g_a(x) = \frac{2}{a^2}(a - x) , \ 0 \leq x \leq a . \tag{4}$$

Let SI denote the event that the centers of the intervals belong to the same J-interval. There are $\frac{1}{k} \cdot \frac{k-1}{L}$ intervals for each color implying

$$\Pr(SI \mid SC) = \frac{k}{k-1}L .$$

The maximum length of an interval is L so $\Pr(OV \cap \overline{SI} \mid SC) = 0$ where $\overline{SI}$ is the complementary event of the event SI. This means that

$$\Pr(OV \mid SC) = \Pr(OV \cap SI \mid SC) \ .$$

The event SI implies the event SC ($SI \cap SC = SI$):

$$\Pr(OV \cap SI \mid SC) = \Pr(OV \mid SI) \cdot \Pr(SI \mid SC) \ .$$

We can now apply Lemma 1 and (4) and use the law of total probability (we also use the fact that $\frac{1}{k-1} \leq \frac{1}{2}$ for $k \geq 3$):

$$\begin{aligned}
\Pr(OV \mid SC) &= \Pr(OV \mid SI) \cdot \Pr(SI \mid SC) \\
&= \int_0^{\frac{1}{k-1}} g_{\frac{1}{k-1}}(x) \Pr(OV \mid C = xL) dx \cdot \Pr(SI \mid SC) \\
&= \int_0^{\frac{1}{k-1}} 2(k-1)^2 \left(\frac{1}{k-1} - x\right) (4x - 6x^2) dx \cdot \frac{k}{k-1} L \\
&= kL \left[4x^2 - 4x^3 - \frac{8}{3}(k-1)x^3 + 3(k-1)x^4\right]_0^{\frac{1}{k-1}} \\
&= kL \left(\frac{4}{3(k-1)^2} - \frac{1}{(k-1)^3}\right) \ .
\end{aligned}$$

We once again use the law of total probability and Lemma 1 and compute the probability that two intervals overlap. This time we use $g_1(x)$ from (4):

$$\begin{aligned}
\Pr(OV) &= \int_0^1 g_1(x) \Pr(OV \mid C = x) dx \\
&= \int_0^{1/2L} \left(4 \cdot \frac{x}{L} - 6\left(\frac{x}{L}\right)^2\right) 2(1-x) dx + \int_{1/2L}^{L} \frac{1}{2}\left(2 - 2 \cdot \frac{x}{L}\right)^2 2(1-x) dx \\
&= \int_0^{1/2} L\left(4t - 6t^2\right) 2(1 - Lt) dt + \int_{1/2}^{1} L\frac{1}{2}(2 - 2t)^2 2(1 - Lt) dt \\
&= \frac{2}{3}L - \frac{1}{4}L^2 \ .
\end{aligned}$$

The assumption (1) on L implies

$$\Pr(SC) = \frac{1}{k} \ .$$

To prove the lemma, we now apply Bayes Theorem:

$$\begin{aligned}
\Pr(SC \mid OV) &= \frac{\Pr(OV \mid SC) \Pr(SC)}{\Pr(OV)} \\
&= \frac{L}{\frac{2}{3}L - \frac{1}{4}L^2} \left(\frac{4}{3(k-1)^2} - \frac{1}{(k-1)^3}\right) \\
&= \frac{12}{8 - 3L} \left(\frac{4}{3(k-1)^2} - \frac{1}{(k-1)^3}\right) \ .
\end{aligned}$$

□

We are now ready to present the main theorem of our paper for $k \geq 3$.

Theorem 1. *Let a set of intervals $\mathcal{I}_n$ be drawn using the Scheinerman model with L satisfying (1). The algorithm (2) computes a cut of the corresponding MAX k-CUT STACKING instance for $k \geq 3$ such that*

$$\frac{E(|cut|)}{E(m)} = 1 - \frac{12}{8-3L}\left(\frac{4}{3(k-1)^2} - \frac{1}{(k-1)^3}\right)$$

where m denotes the number of edges in the corresponding interval overlap graph/circle graph.

Proof. By using linearity of expectation we obtain the following:

$$\begin{aligned}\frac{E(|cut|)}{E(m)} &= \frac{\Pr(OV \cap \overline{SC})\binom{n}{2}}{\Pr(OV)\binom{n}{2}} \\ &= \frac{\Pr(OV) - \Pr(OV \cap SC)}{\Pr(OV)} \\ &= 1 - \Pr(SC \mid OV) \ .\end{aligned}$$

The theorem follows from Lemma 2. □

4 Analysis of the Extended Scheinerman Model

Our results are now extended to a more generic model for generating the instances where we allow the lengths of the intervals to be drawn using any (fixed) bounded continuous probability density function with L as an upper bound on the lengths. This model is very flexible even for L satisfying (1) since L is an upper bound on the lengths. In this section we show that the risk of assigning the same color to two overlapping intervals is also of the order $1/k^2$ for the generic instance model.

Definition 3. *The Extended Scheinerman Model: The centers of the intervals in $\mathcal{I}_n$ are drawn independently using a uniform distribution on $[0,1]$. The number L is an upper bound on the lengths of the intervals and the lengths are drawn independently using a bounded continuous probability density function f, $f(\ell) \leq B$.*

Theorem 2. *Under the same assumptions as in Theorem 1 the following holds for algorithm (2) for the extended Scheinerman model:*

$$\frac{E(|cut|)}{E(m)} \geq 1 - O(k^{-2}) \ .$$

Proof. Now assume that the intervals are drawn using the extended Scheinerman model. By a slight modification of the proof of Lemma 1, we get the following for $x \leq 0.5$:

$$Pr(OV \mid C = xL) \leq L^2B^2(4x - 6x^2) \ .$$

We revisit the proof of Lemma 2 and establish an upper bound for $\Pr(OV \mid SC)$ using the factor L^2B^2:

$$\Pr(OV \mid SC) \leq L^2B^2 \cdot kL \left(\frac{4}{3(k-1)^2} - \frac{1}{(k-1)^3}\right) .$$

The probability of receiving the same color has not changed, $\Pr(SC) = \frac{1}{k}$, so Bayes Theorem can once again ensure that the theorem holds. We just have to make sure that the conditional probability is well defined – in other words that $\Pr(OV) > 0$: There exists an ℓ_0 such that $f(\ell_0) > 0$. Let $\epsilon > 0$ be a sufficiently small positive number. Let ℓ_1 and ℓ_2 denote the lengths of two intervals drawn using the extended Scheinerman model. By using (3) and independence we can verify that $\Pr(OV) > 0$:

$$\Pr(OV) \geq \Pr(|l_1 - l_0| < \epsilon \wedge |l_2 - l_0| < \epsilon \wedge \epsilon < d < \ell_0 - \epsilon) > 0 .$$

This concludes the proof. □

The theorem implies a corollary that is targeted at an audience with an interest in circle graphs/interval overlap graphs. The corollary indicates that these graphs on average have k-cuts with a relatively high cardinality compared to the number of edges.

Corollary 1. *Let $\mathcal{I}_n$ be drawn using the extended Scheinerman model. For the circle graph/interval overlap graph represented by $\mathcal{I}_n$ we have the following for $k \geq 3$*

$$\frac{E(|cut|)}{E(m)} \geq 1 - O(k^{-2})$$

where "cut" denotes the maximum size k-cut.

Conclusion

We have presented an extremely simple oblivious stacking algorithm with a surprisingly low risk – of the order $1/k^2$ – of assigning two conflicting items to the same storage location under mild assumptions on the distribution of the storage time intervals. The algorithm can easily be used in a distributed setting with disconnected stacking agents. The principle guiding the algorithm is to assign the same storage location to two items if the centers of their storage time intervals are close to each other implying a low risk of a conflict. This principle can probably be used in other stacking algorithms/heuristics.

Our algorithm can be used on its own but there is also a possibility that it can be used in a preprocessing step since the items are split into k groups with only a few conflicts to handle in each group. As an example, each group could correspond to an area of a container terminal with $k << n$. Our algorithm could be used to assign an area to each container in the preprocessing step and a local stacking algorithm could pick a specific storage location for the container in the particular area.

References

1. Avriel, M., Penn, M., Shpirer, N.: Container ship stowage problem: complexity and connection to the coloring of circle graphs. Discrete Appl. Math. **103**(1–3), 271–279 (2000)
2. Bansal, N., Blum, A., Chawla, S., Meyerson, A.: Online oblivious routing. In: SPAA 2003, Proceedings of the Fifteenth Annual ACM Symposium on Parallel Algorithms, pp. 44–49. Association for Computing Machinery, Inc (2003). https://doi.org/10.1145/777412.777420
3. Borgman, B., van Asperen, E., Dekker, R.: Online rules for container stacking. OR Spectrum **32**(3), 687–716 (2010). https://doi.org/10.1007/s00291-010-0205-4
4. Busch, C., Magdon-Ismail, M., Xi, J.: Optimal oblivious path selection on the mesh. IEEE Trans. Comput. **57**(5), 660–671 (2008). https://doi.org/10.1109/TC.2008.23
5. Coja-Oghlan, A., Moore, C., Sanwalani, V.: MAX k-CUT and approximating the chromatic number of random graphs. Random Struct. Algorithms **28**(3), 289–322 (2006). https://doi.org/10.1002/rsa.20096
6. Cornelsen, S., Stefano, G.D.: Track assignment. J. Discrete Algorithms **5**(2), 250–261 (2007). https://doi.org/10.1016/j.jda.2006.05.001
7. Demange, M., Olsen, M.: A note on online colouring problems in overlap graphs and their complements. In: Rahman, M.S., Sung, W.-K., Uehara, R. (eds.) WALCOM 2018. LNCS, vol. 10755, pp. 144–155. Springer, Cham (2018). https://doi.org/10.1007/978-3-319-75172-6_13
8. Demange, M., Stefano, G.D., Leroy-Beaulieu, B.: On the online track assignment problem. Discrete Appl. Math. **160**(7–8), 1072–1093 (2012)
9. Gavril, F.: Algorithms for a maximum clique and a maximum independent set of a circle graph. Networks **3**(3), 261–273 (1973). https://doi.org/10.1002/net.3230030305
10. Kann, V., Khanna, S., Lagergren, J., Panconesi, A.: On the hardness of approximating Max k-Cut and its dual. Chicago J. Theor. Comput. Sci. **1997**(2) (1997)
11. Kim, B., Koo, J., Sambhajirao, H.P.: A simplified steel plate stacking problem. Int. J. Prod. Res. **49**(17), 5133–5151 (2011). https://doi.org/10.1080/00207543.2010.518998
12. König, F.G., Lübbecke, M., Möhring, R., Schäfer, G., Spenke, I.: Solutions to real-world instances of PSPACE-complete stacking. In: Arge, L., Hoffmann, M., Welzl, E. (eds.) ESA 2007. LNCS, vol. 4698, pp. 729–740. Springer, Heidelberg (2007). https://doi.org/10.1007/978-3-540-75520-3_64
13. Olsen, M.: Online stacking using RL with positional and tactical features. In: Kotsireas, I.S., Pardalos, P.M. (eds.) LION 2020. LNCS, vol. 12096, pp. 184–194. Springer, Cham (2020). https://doi.org/10.1007/978-3-030-53552-0_19
14. Olsen, M., Gross, A.: Probabilistic analysis of online stacking algorithms. In: Corman, F., Voß, S., Negenborn, R.R. (eds.) ICCL 2015. LNCS, vol. 9335, pp. 358–369. Springer, Cham (2015). https://doi.org/10.1007/978-3-319-24264-4_25
15. Pocai, R.V.: The complexity of SIMPLE MAX-CUT on comparability graphs. Electron. Notes Discrete Math. **55**, 161–164 (2016). https://doi.org/10.1016/j.endm.2016.10.040

16. Rei, R.J., Pedroso, J.P.: Tree search for the stacking problem. Ann. Oper. Res. **203**(1), 371–388 (2013). https://doi.org/10.1007/s10479-012-1186-2
17. Scheinerman, E.R.: An evolution of interval graphs. Discrete Math. **82**(3), 287–302 (1990)
18. Tierney, K., Pacino, D., Jensen, R.M.: On the complexity of container stowage planning problems. Discrete Appl. Math. **169**, 225–230 (2014). https://doi.org/10.1016/j.dam.2014.01.005

How Can a Refrigerated Warehouse Be Used to Store Energy?

Marco Repke[1(✉)], Ann-Kathrin Lange[1], and Carsten Eckert[2]

[1] Hamburg University of Technology, Am Schwarzenberg-Campus 1, 21073 Hamburg, Germany
Marco.Repke@gmx.de, Ann-Kathrin.Lange@tuhh.de
[2] HPC Hamburg Port Consulting GmbH, Am Ballinkai 1, 21129 Hamburg, Germany
C.Eckert@hpc-hamburg.de

Abstract. Refrigerated warehouses are essential for a well-functioning cooling supply chain. Here, the ambient temperature is regulated around the clock, while the refrigeration system is turned on in recuring time intervals. The idea of this paper is to use the refrigerated warehouse as a virtual battery. The temperature inside the warehouse is cooled down when the market price is low. Thus, the energy is stored and the use of the refrigeration system during times of high electrical prices is avoided. This concept can be seen as a part of the demand side management, where monetary incentives are provided to electricity consumers to adapt their load profile in a grid supporting manner. The use case is based on the electricity price of the day-ahead-market. The characteristics of this electricity market require an electricity price prediction. This is based on the availability of renewable energy sources and the predicted electricity demand. The implementation is done via a time-driven discrete simulation model of a real refrigerated warehouse operating in the normal cooling range (above 0 °C). The simulation models first control option is the use of deterministic strategies which result in a decrease of the electricity cost of up to 7%. The second more complex control option via the so-called solution finding exploits electricity cost savings of 37%. To receive satisfactory results, a highly detailed implementation in the warehouse and well predicted electricity price have proven to be necessary. Therefore, this study can be seen as a first step on the way to use refrigerated warehouses as virtual batteries.

Keywords: Demand side management · Load management · Discrete simulation · Refrigerated warehouse · Energy efficiency · Virtual battery · Energy storage

1 Introduction

In order to act against the climate crisis, the transition from fossil- to regenerative energy sources is required. In Germany, the dominant sustainable energy sources for electricity generation are photovoltaics and wind energy. In 2020, they generated more than 70% of the electricity from renewable sources (Fraunhofer Institute for Solar Energy Systems

J. de Armas et al. (Eds.): ICCL 2022, LNCS 13557, pp. 336–350, 2022.
https://doi.org/10.1007/978-3-031-16579-5_23

2021). Besides their positive climatic impact, a central disadvantage is their availability. Fossil energy sources can be used continuously, while photovoltaics and wind energy depend on the weather. As a solution, the electricity supply can be adjusted by using storage technologies, such as battery or pumped storages. However, this requires high investment costs and, in the case of pumped storage power plants, special geological conditions. At the same time, both technologies lead to an energy loss during storage due to their energy efficiency of maximum 85% (Federal Ministry for Economic Affairs and Climate Action, Lund et al. 2015, p. 794).

To avoid these losses, this paper evaluates an alternative approach of adjusting the electricity demand. Especially electricity-intensive companies are focused to act in a grid-supporting way, where they decrease their energy demand during times with low energy production and lift the demand during a surplus of electricity. This form of consumption adjustment is called demand side management.

Refrigerated warehouses are predestined for this concept. They are mainly used in food logistics and are essential for a well-functioning supply chain. To maintain cold chains, 11% of the worldwide generated electricity is used (Gao 2019, p. 1). Accordingly, refrigerated warehouses are characterized by a high electricity demand. In addition, electricity consumption takes place around the clock at mostly irregular intervals due to the thermal inertia of the refrigeration system.

The novelty in this paper lies in minimization of electricity costs by prediction of electricity prices and adjustment of the cooling cycles constrained by a detailed simulation. An overview about the research status quo of demand side management of refrigerated warehouse is given in Sect. 2. An existing refrigerated warehouse, which is mainly used for fruits and vegetables, is taken as use case. By using time-driven discrete simulation, a thermodynamical model focusing on the temperature curve of this warehouse is developed, validated and evaluated (Sect. 3). The model considers logistical aspects like warehouse movements as well as the thermal energy storage of the stored goods. To evaluate the opportunities of a demand side management, different temperature control options are applied based on electricity price predictions. Here deterministic strategies and a complex solution finding are implemented and tested in the simulation model. Finally, the evaluation of the simulation model is done (Sect. 4) ending in a critical assessment of the findings (Sect. 5).

2 Literature Review

The approach of implementing demand side management has been of scientific interest over the past years. Logenthiran et al. (2012) use an optimization model in which a network of consumers with different loads are synchronized as energy-efficiently as possible. In the industrial sector, this cooperation can save up to 10% of electricity costs. Li et al. (2017) use a dynamic simulation model to investigate the implementation of an electrical storage unit as well as of a thermal energy storage unit on the electricity cost of a refrigerated warehouse. This set up supports the shift of loads from the high-cost hours during the day to the nighttime hours with lower electricity prices. As a result, electricity cost reductions of over 50% can be realized. Murrant and Radcliffe (2018) elaborate on the possibility of thermal energy storage using Liquid Air Energy Storage systems. This involves cooling down the air to the point of liquefaction, storing it, and using it for cooling later. Countries with a high percentage of renewable energy sources and, at the same time, many refrigerated warehouses are the preferred users of this technology. Zong et al. (2009) use a genetic search algorithm, which can mainly evaluate stochastic and non-linear behavior. It is used to design a decision model that adjusts the cooling cycles of a refrigerated warehouse according to the predicted availability of wind energy. The authors conclude that the implementation of this control in a refrigerated warehouse is feasible and could lower the electricity cost. Fikiin (2015) has developed a decision support system to help integrate wind energy into the power grid. Using wind availability data, an electricity price forecast and a model of the refrigerated warehouse to make decisions about the operation of the refrigeration system. Goli et al. (2011) use several refrigerated warehouses in California to examine the potential of demand side management and the obstacles of the implementation. In particular, the implementation of automated load management on a web-based communication protocol has been highlighted as efficient. Furthermore, it is emphasized that the clear communication of financial and sustainability factors raises the awareness of decision makers towards demand side management. Ma et al. (2015) use constrained optimization to model a cooperative demand side management of several refrigerated warehouses. These are combined in a smart grid so that the electricity consumption is coordinated among them. In this process, the adjustment of one's power consumption is rewarded, but at the same time uncooperative behavior of individual actors is actively penalized. It is shown that cooperative demand side management produces about 2% higher savings in electricity costs compared to individual demand side management.

Hence, it can be said that already some research studies investigate the demand side management of refrigerated warehouses in relation to renewable energy. However, these are mostly not based on such a comprehensive simulation model of the cooling process as it is part of this paper. Furthermore, the models do not compare the quality of the prediction with the actual occurring electricity price. In addition, the consideration of different control options of the refrigeration system does not take place in the found papers. Hence, the following research question is investigated in this paper:

What is the impact of implementing different temperature control options on the electricity consumption and electricity cost of a refrigerated warehouse?

3 Model Description

In this paper, the examination of demand side management of refrigerated warehouses is done by a discrete simulation model with the simulation software Tecnomatix Plant Simulation version 16. In detail, a time-driven simulation model is applied where the simulation time progresses in constant time steps (Wenzel 2018, p. 10). A scheme of the simulation with the different steps is visualized in Fig. 1.

To maintain a practical simulation while keeping the required accuracy, the step size in which the simulation time moves is set to one minute. Here, individual points in time are used to generate discrete values which are connected to get an approximation of the actual temperature curve. This temperature curve, resulting from the thermodynamic model, is the first part of the simulation model. As second part, an electricity price

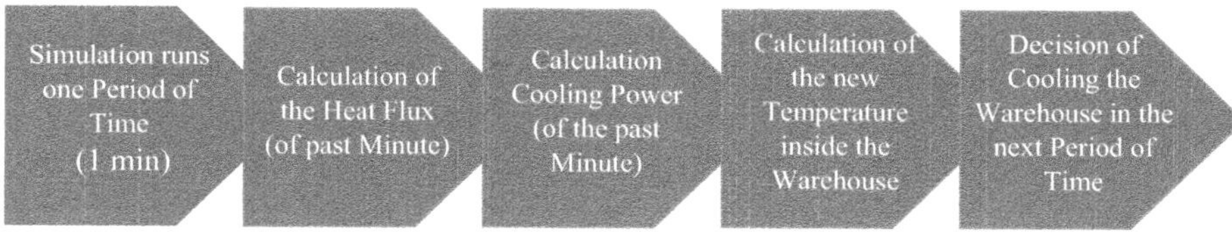

Fig. 1. Repetitive scheme of the simulation model

forecast is developed. Both parts are merged by implementing the control options of the refrigerated warehouse. The relation of the different parts is visualized in Fig. 2.

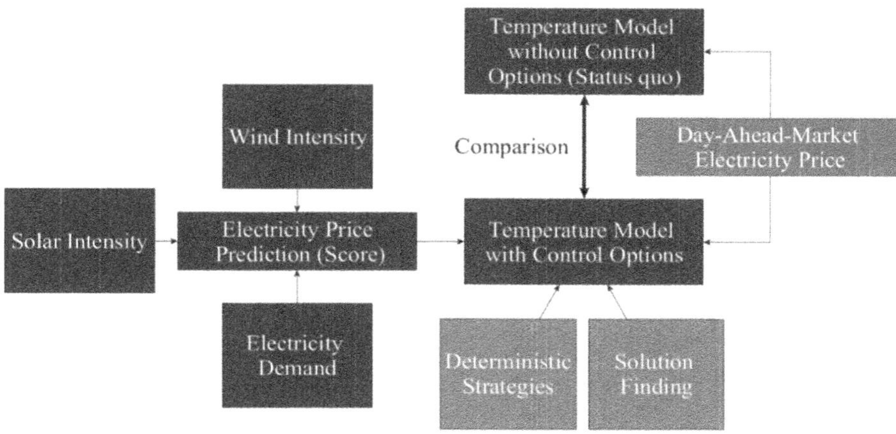

Fig. 2. Structure of the developed simulation model

3.1 Temperature Model

A precise calculation of the temperature curve of the refrigerated warehouse is the foundation of the simulation model. For this purpose, a thermodynamic model based on Breidert (2013), Maurer (2016) and Breidert et al. (2016) is set up. This approach is originally used for statical dimensioning of refrigeration systems and has been modified for the realization in the simulation model. It was chosen, because it contains all factors influencing the temperature inside the warehouse while allowing the implementation of the required logistical processes. In the thermodynamic model, some factors were simplified for the implementation e.g. the missing consideration of air streams inside the warehouse. Therefore, the parameter heat flux was calibrated after the validation to improve the quality of the simulation results. The modelling happened based on the use case and the actual data of a refrigerated warehouse in Germany. The warehouse mostly stores fruits and vegetables and operates in the normal cooling area above 0 °C.

In the simulation model, all heat inputs of the refrigerated warehouse are represented (see Fig. 3). It considers the most relevant logistical operations (like warehouse jobs executed with a forklift), all significant building specific parameters of the warehouse (like the isolation) and good specific characteristics like the heat transfer coefficients and the surface area. The heat fluxes (shown in Fig. 3 with a red single arrow) result in heat inputs into the system. In contrast, the red double arrows can lead to heat input or output depending on the temperature difference. The blue arrow represents the heat discharge through the refrigeration system. The total heat flux is determined by cumulating the heat inputs and outputs of the respective time period.

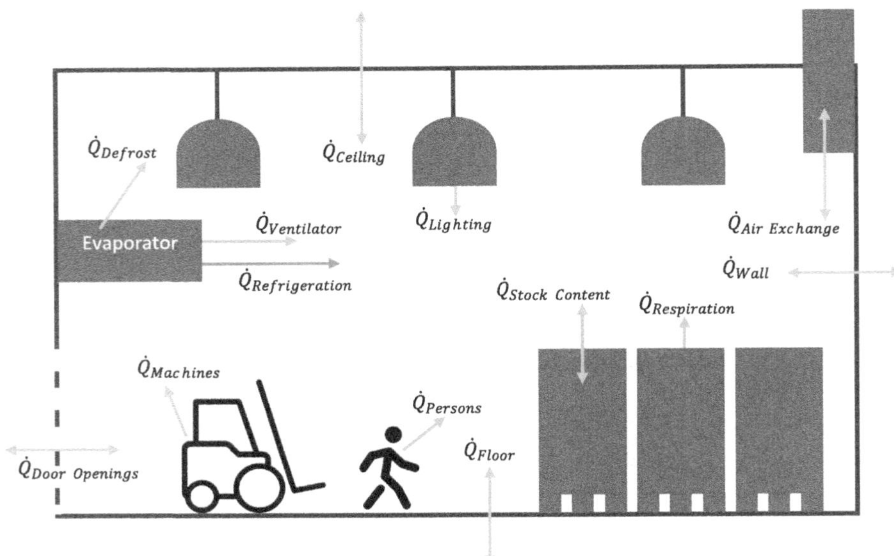

Fig. 3. Temperature model of the refrigerated warehouse

The refrigeration system is the crucial part of the refrigerated warehouse. In the evaluated use case, the stored goods (fruits and vegetables) are very sensitive regarding the temperature. The quality suffers from either a higher or a lower temperature and deviations from the required quality are often punished by fees. Therefore, the setting of the refrigeration system could have a large financial impact.

In the use case, a compression refrigeration system is used. In those systems, the compressors are switched on, when the highest feasible temperature is reached. The compressors enable the cooling process and are turned off once the lowest feasible temperature is reached. In the investigated warehouse, the goods are stored in the range of normal refrigeration (above 0 °C). The specific storage temperature of each good is set with a range of 1 °C. This means that a temperature range of plus / minus 0.5 °C around the target temperature is used. In the investigated use case of the storage, a temperature between 7.6 °C and 8.6 °C is maintained.

The heat transfer from the air inside the warehouse to the cooling system is done by evaporators and the transfer from the cooling system to the outside is enabled by the condensers. To ensure that a large volume of air can be cooled and heat can be discharged to the outside air, fans are installed on both the evaporator and the condenser to ensure air circulation (Reisner and Reisner 2016, p. 40 ff). These fans, along with the compressor as the main consumer, are the electricity-intensive components of the refrigeration system. Hence, the electricity consumption of the warehouse mainly takes place during the discrete times when the cooling is executed. Resulting from the described temperature model, the status quo of the cooling process can be modeled.

For the validation of the simulation model, many different techniques have been applied. Three of them are further described. At first, the simulation was checked by the *face validity* test (Rabe et al. 2009, p. 109). Here, the model behavior and the results were presented to the technical director of the refrigerated warehouse. During the discussions he confirmed the high level of accuracy of the results. Additionally, a *trace analysis* was performed (Rabe et al. 2009, p. 107). Here, the behavior of the model was followed step by step in a test setup. Thereby, it was confirmed that the refrigerating system works in the simulation according to the intensions. For the *statistical validation* (Rabe et al. 2009, p. 103) of the temperature model, the simulated temperature curve is compared to a temperature curve from real data of the evaluated use case. Both curves are plotted for an exemplary period of time (shown in Fig. 4).

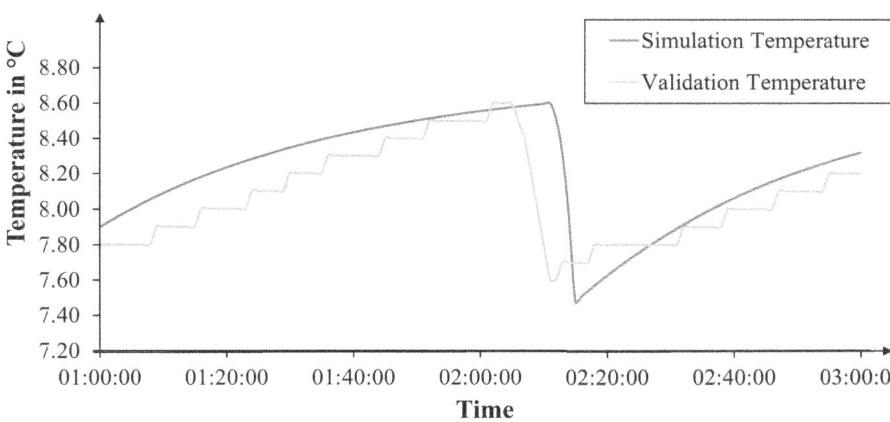

Fig. 4. Validation of the temperature model

In Fig. 4, it can be seen that the validation and simulation data differ only slightly from each other. In detail, an average difference of 0.16 °C between the values of both curves occurs. This outlines a high accuracy of the simulation model. Especially the timespans without warehouse movements are simulated quite well. Here, no cargo is moved and the door remains closed which leads to an even distributed amount of heat input. Despite the fact, that some differences of the temperature could occur in phases with many warehouse movements, the model offer a valid functionality and is well suited for this simulation study.

3.2 Electricity Price Forecast

Since electricity is a non-storable commodity, its market price is highly volatile compared to other goods (Ciarreta et al. 2017, p. 680). Thus, from a business perspective cost potentials should be exploited by using electricity at low-cost times. This potential could be utilized by participating in the electricity stock exchange rather than purchasing electricity from a provider to long term fixed prices. The question arises whether it is better to participate in the intraday or the day-ahead market. In contrast to the forward market, short-term price fluctuations are passed on in both markets, which enables the implementation of a demand side management. The difference between both markets is the timespan. While in intraday markets electricity can be traded up to five minutes before the delivery, the participants of the day-ahead-market have to announce their hourly electricity demand at the day before delivery at 12 a.m. Afterwards, the Merit-Order is formed and the electricity price is determined by the marginal costs of the least expensive electricity supplier to cover all the demands (Bundesnetzagentur 2022 b).

Pricewise, the intraday and day-ahead markets are related. Bader (2017) has shown that the intraday price can be derived from the day-ahead price in a normally distributed manner. Thus, it can be assumed that no relevant advantage can be generated by systematically covering the power demand on the intraday market compared to the day-ahead market. In addition, depending on the time of purchase, there are strong price fluctuations on the intraday market and consequently the electricity procurement is more uncertain. In contrast, electricity price forecasting can reduce the uncertainty of the day-ahead market. So, it can be justified that the day-ahead market is proposed for the electricity procurement in this paper. As this market requires a decision about the hourly electricity demand at the day before consumption, a forecast is necessary. The volatile availability of renewable energy sources in combination with the relatively inflexible conventional energy sources causes fluctuations in the electricity supply. Accordingly, the availability of renewable energy sources can be used as forecast indicator for electricity price (Cerjan et al. 2019, p.19). The corresponding weather data can be taken from freely accessible weather database of the German Weather Service. Wind farms are mainly located in the north of Germany. Some of the largest are on the North Sea coast, which is why the wind strengths of the Spiekeroog weather station are used as reference values for wind power. German solar parks, are more decentralized. Here, one of the largest generation plants is located near Regensburg. The solar radiation from the weather station there is used in the forecast. The global solar irradiation is considered as a characteristic value for the power generation of the solar cells.

In addition to supply factors, the electricity demand flows into the electricity price forecast. This can be mapped based on the description of Bader (2017) as well as the consideration of real electricity consumption data from the database Electricity Market Data (SMARD) (Bundesnetzagentur 2022 a). According to this, the electricity demand is lower at night (9 p.m. to 7 a.m.) than during the day. Demand peaks exist during the week in the morning between 8 a.m. and 10 a.m. and in the evening between 6 p.m. and 7 p.m. On weekends and holidays, a relatively balanced demand can be seen throughout the day, with increased demand in the two evening hours (6 p.m. and 7 p.m.). It should be noted that these times are indicative, and reality sometimes deviates from them.

3.3 Explanation of Control Options

The control options are implemented to take advantage of low electricity prices by using the cooling system to a high extend. At the same time, the feasible temperature range of the good is maintained. The control options are applied to merge the electricity price prediction and the temperature model of the warehouse. The prediction creates a forecast as an evaluation of each hour of the simulated day. Here, a ranking is formed which is realized in the simulated warehouse by the different control options of the refrigeration system. As first control option, the generated deterministic strategies are exemplarily shown in Fig. 5. These strategies compare the forecasted electricity prices of each hour and define different cases, where the cooling process of the warehouse is triggered. The bars in Fig. 5 represent the respective hourly forecasted electricity price. Here, fictional prices are used to explain the deterministic strategies. At the times where the bars are marked in red the active switching on of the refrigeration plant takes place.

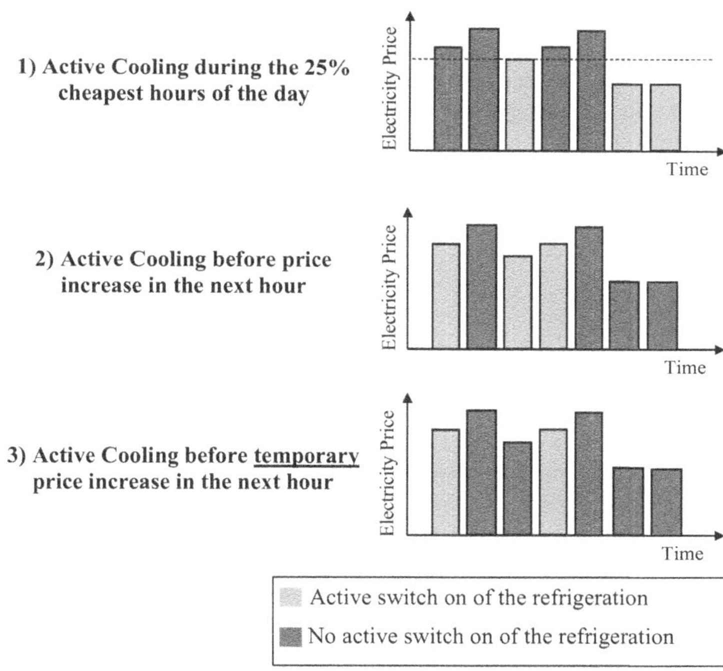

Fig. 5. Visualization of the control strategies

The first strategy states that cooling should take place in the presumably cheapest 25% of the hours of each day. For this purpose, the hours are sorted based on the forecast values. It is continuously checked whether the current simulated hour is one of the 25% cheapest hours. The second strategy specifies that cooling should only take place when an increase in the electricity price is expected in the coming hour. In the third strategy, this approach is extended. It leads to cooling when a temporary increase in electricity price is expected. This is characterized by a rising electricity price in the coming hour and a price decrease in the next hour. Strategy three is intended to bypass the middle hour with the higher price while keeping the number of cycles low. The strategies are only used to supplement the temperature-based cooling. Accordingly, cooling also takes place when the maximum temperature (1 °C temperature range) is reached. The goal of all deterministic strategies is to shift the temperature-based cooling to the least expensive hours. The execution of the cooling based on the strategies is checked in the 50th minute of each hour. If the refrigeration system is activated, the warehouse temperature is reduced to the minimum in the current hour. Like this, the electricity price of the current hour is used in the best possible way with respect to the following hours.

Besides the implementation of the deterministic strategies, the solution finding is developed as second control option to represent a more complex control of the refrigerated warehouse. This approach variates the factors time and intensity of each cooling cycle. Different possible solutions are generated by activating the refrigeration system stepwise earlier. In detail, the cooling takes place at a warming of 0.3 °C, 0.6 °C and at the maximum temperature range of 1 °C. Similar to this, the warehouse is not only cooled down to the minimum but stepwise to other temperatures higher than the minimum if they are feasible. By following this procedure, each cooling cycle leads to many possible options which are simulated and generate many other options again. This results in an exponential growth of possible solutions, which are evaluated by the electricity price forecast. Finally, the solution with the lowest electricity price is chosen and could be used to support the discission of cooling for the warehouse operator.

4 Evaluation

The evaluation contains three different parts analyzing electricity price prediction, deterministic strategies and solution finding. The prediction model based on the weather conditions and the demand is evaluated by comparing the predicted price with the actual electricity price. Here, comprehensive data from 2019 is used. The comparison is done sample wise for some periods of time. One of them is plotted below in Fig. 6.

In Fig. 6, the electricity price (left y-axis) is shown in dark blue and the score (right y-axis) in red. In the prediction, the score behaves in the opposite direction to the electricity price. Thus, a high score predicts a low electricity price and vice versa. To facilitate a better comprehension of the diagram, the right y-axis is inverted.

Figure 6 shows that the prediction model reproduces some price fluctuations accurately, but other fluctuations less precise. In detail, just about 5% of the hourly electricity price is predicted within an accuracy of 1 € per MWh. The reasons for the deviations may be that other factors influencing the electricity price had a greater impact in the period under review. For example, electricity imports and exports, maintenance of the production plants or fluctuations in demand may have been decisive. The last factor is already part of the prediction model but could have a higher impact as conventional fossil energy plants still keep a high share of the overall electricity production. Reviewing the database of regenerative energy, the use of representative weather data from many weather stations could also improve the prediction model.

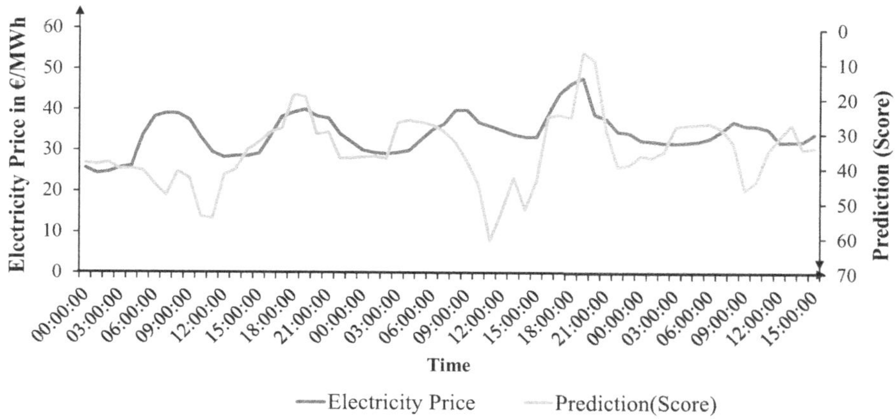

Fig. 6. Comparison of the electricity price prediction and the actual price

In the further evaluation, the model behavior is investigated under the premise of a correct prediction. Therefore, real price data are used instead of the predicted values. During the execution of experiments, the described deterministic strategies were evaluated using different settings. In detail, a combination of the factors size of the warehouse, degree of filling and number of performed warehouse jobs is made. All in all, 72 experiments are defined to evaluate the cooling strategies for different scenarios. For each experiment, 20 simulation runs are used, where one day is selected randomly, simulated and compared to the current status quo of a pure temperature-based cooling of the warehouse. The evaluation took place on the basis of the defined output parameters electricity consumption, electricity costs and number of cooling cycles. The respective values of the status quo were taken as a basis and the relative changes after application of the deterministic strategies were recorded. The evaluation is visualized in Fig. 7.

As can be seen in Fig. 7, strategy one reduces electricity costs by about 3% and strategy three by about 7%. In contrast, strategy two causes an increase in electricity costs of about 9%. As a reason for the described observation, an exemplary electricity cost curve can be considered (see Fig. 8). As it can be seen there, on weekdays there is a typical load curve in which electricity price peaks occur especially in the morning and evening hours. Using the first strategy, active cooling is used in the most favorable 25% of the hours, which are mostly during midday or at night. Hence there is a chance that active cooling will take place before the high price peaks. Here, it must be remembered that based on the temperature range of 1 °C, usually only one hour between two cooling cycles can be bridged.

However, since the electricity price increases over several hours at peak times and with strategy one the first hour is mostly bypassed, temperature-driven cooling can be triggered during the price peak. This scenario can be avoided by using the third strategy. Here, active cooling is not triggered until a price decrease is expected at the second hour after cooling. Thus, the refrigeration system is not switched on during the price increase, but before the price peak. In this way, the hour of the electricity price peak can be bypassed at the morning and evening times. This explains the slightly better

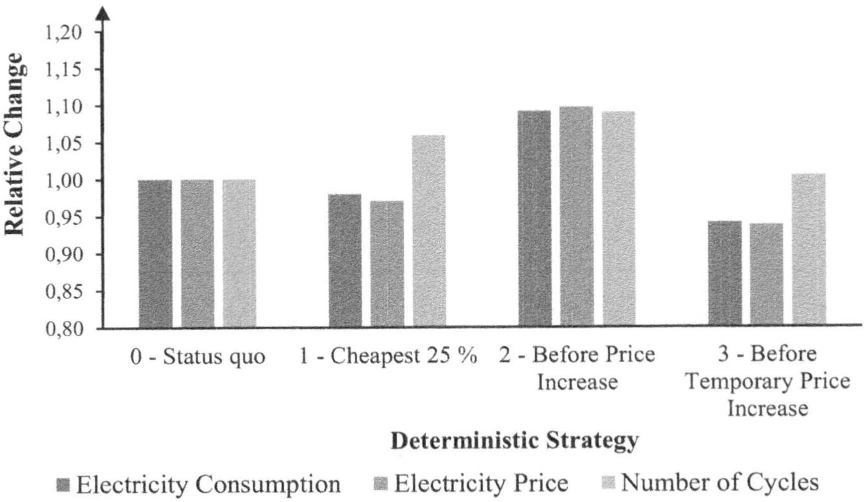

Fig. 7. Performance of the deterministic strategies with real price data

performance compared to strategy one. At the same time, strategy two performs worse than the status quo. One possible explanation is that slight price increases already occur before the morning and evening peaks. Especially during the weekends, the electricity price increases many times in a smaller manner (see Fig. 8). Also, price increases occur over several hours before the morning and evening peak during weekdays. Hence, the warehouse is cooled down many times, which is reflected in the number of cooling cycles. The temperature inside the warehouse stays at the lower area of the feasible range more often which rises the electricity consumption (as explained after Fig. 9).

In addition, with strategy two, there is the risk that cooling down already occurs before the price peaks, so the temperature-related cooling must take place accordingly close to the highest electricity price. Overall, the poor performance of strategy two is due to the large number of possible cases of unfavorable cooling behavior.

The number of cooling cycles can be considered as a further output parameter. The analysis of Fig. 7 shows that all strategies lead to an increase of the cooling cycles compared to the status quo. It is also visible that the number of cooling cycles increases only slightly with strategy three, since the requirements to activate the cooling are strict. In contrast, active cooling can be applied up to six times per day with strategy one and up to 24 times per day with strategy two, given a high number of price fluctuations.

As last part of the evaluation, the implemented solution finding is analyzed. By varying the timing and intensity of the cooling processes, a plan is developed to cool the warehouse as cost-effective as possible. In detail, a variety of different solutions for the problem is evaluated in the simulation and the most favorable one is chosen. The experiments with solution finding have been carried out for one day of simulation and with a correct electricity price prediction for each hour of the day. Figure 9 compares the temperature plot of the solution finding with the status quo of the temperature-based solution.

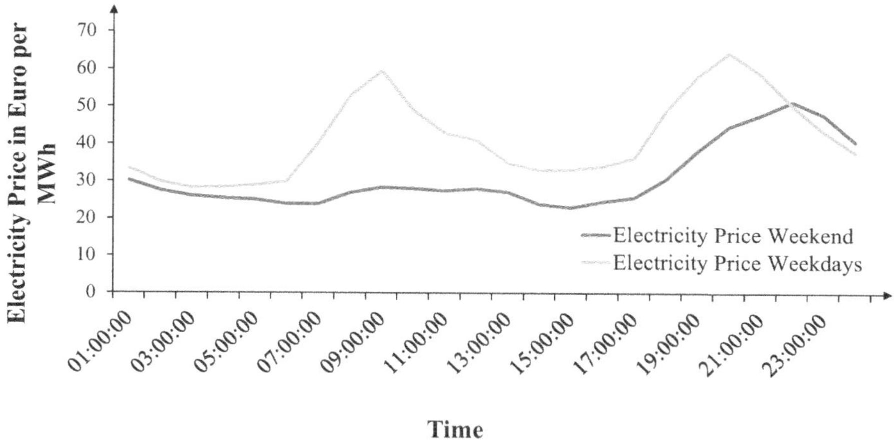

Fig. 8. Exemplary electricity price during weekdays and on weekends

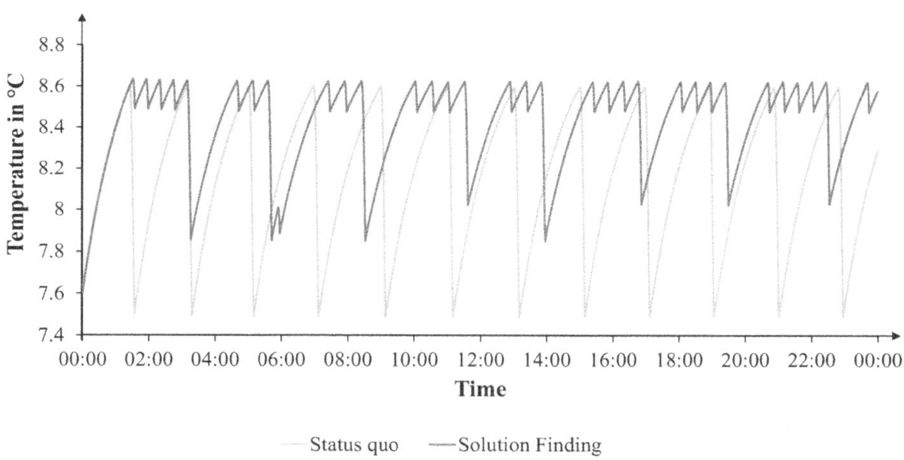

Fig. 9. Cooling cycles of solution finding compared to status quo

The temperature curve in Fig. 9 reveals serious differences between the status quo and the best possible solution determined by the solution finding. In detail, the cooling is done more frequent and takes place in shorter cooling cycles. As a result, the temperature is predominantly kept within the maximum possible temperature range of 8.3 °C to 8.6 °C. This can be justified by the fact that if the temperature is higher, the temperature difference between outside and inside the warehouse is lower (Evaluation was done in summer with an outside temperature over 15 °C). Consequently, the temperature curve grows slower. By keeping the temperature rise as flat as possible, less electricity has to be used for cooling.

At the same time, a stronger cooling down takes place in the developed solution at favorable hours. However, the cooling is not done to the minimum, but down to

7.9 °C and 8 °C, respectively. This behavior could be explained by the fact that the steep temperature rise in the minimum temperature ranges outweighs the advantage of using the favorable electricity price to a great extent.

The qualitative evaluation of the solution finding is supplemented by a quantitative evaluation in the following Fig. 10. Here, the control option is compared with the status quo of purely temperature-based cooling. The comparison is done with the parameters power consumption, power costs and number of cycles as relative to the status quo.

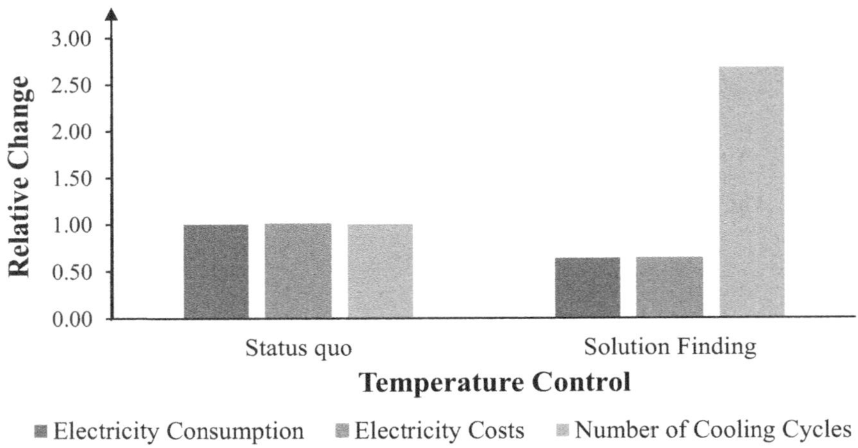

Fig. 10. Performance of the solution finding

Figure 10 illustrates the high potential of adjusting the cooling cycles using the solution finding control option. Thus, approximately 37% of the electricity consumption and electricity costs can be saved. At the same time, the solution finding results in a cycle rate of 2.6 times the status quo. Due to the refrigeration system being more frequently switched on and off, there may be more failures and higher maintenance costs. At the same time, the higher temperature in the warehouse increases the core temperature of the stored goods. Consequently, a lower resistance to temporarily higher ambient temperatures (for example during the handling process) may occur. Accordingly, careful considerations should be made before implementing such a cooling plan. Only in this way the identified cost potentials can be used and the quality of storage can be ensured at the same time.

5 Conclusion

Refrigerated warehouses are significant consumers of electricity and can be used in a grid-supporting manner due to their fluctuating power consumption. This finding was confirmed in the research of this paper. Possible cost savings through the implementation of simple deterministic strategies were partially confirmed. With the most effective strategy, an average saving of the electricity procurement costs of 7% has been achieved.

Due to the implementation effort of the control strategies, the savings are relativized from an operational point of view. The relatively low benefit can be justified by the small temperature range of 1 °C and by the existing weaknesses of the implemented control strategies. Furthermore, the potential of a more sophisticated approach described as solution finding control option is proven. Here, high cost potentials can be exploited by a saving of electricity costs of 37%.

Another conclusion of this paper is that the electricity price prediction of this simulation model using a simple method based on weather and demand data is not sufficiently accurate. This could change while the share of renewable energy rises. Nevertheless, additional work is needed to improve the electricity price prediction and enable the supposed demand side management on an operational basis.

Regarding the solution finding model, the simulation showed that a large computational process capacity is needed to evaluate the exponential growing number of possible solutions. Here, the solution could be further enhanced by a larger simulation timeframe, a more powerful computer or the implementation of operations research heuristics.

A general recommendation proven by this paper is to keep the temperature inside the refrigerated warehouse close to the upper temperature boundary. This approach can already reduce electricity consumption and enable electricity cost savings without changes in electricity procurement. Further investigations regarding the proposed solution should be carried out into the possible consequences of a long-term high cycle rate on the refrigeration system. In particular, increasing maintenance costs can be expected if the refrigeration system is switched on and off frequently. As part of further research, the investigation of storage conditions with a higher temperature range as in deep-freeze warehouses (-18 °C to -30 °C) should follow. As there is a higher timespan between the cooling cycles, such a use case would be promising to be more costs saving and could have a higher contribution to grid stability.

To conclude, it is technically possible to use a refrigerated warehouse as a virtual battery. Nevertheless, for the investigated refrigerated warehouse operating with a 1 °C temperature range, the supposed demand side management does not have enough potential for its implementation. This assessment relies on the current electricity price curve. When there is a higher fluctuation of the electricity price and a higher dependency of the price to the current availability of renewable energy sources, the approach of this paper could gain in relevancy.

References

Bader, A.: Entwicklung eines Verfahrens zur Strompreisvorhersage im kurzfristigen Intraday-Handelszeitraum, RWTH Aachen Universität (2017)

Breidert, H.-J., Schittenhelm, D., Hoffmann, M.: Formeln, Tabellen und Diagramme für die Kälteanlagentechnik, 6th edn. VDE-Verlag, Berlin (2016)

Breidert, H.-J.: Projektierung von Kälteanlagen, 4th edn. VDE-Verlag, Berlin, Offenbach (2013)

Bundesnetzagentur a: market data. https://www.smard.de/home/downloadcenter/download-marktdaten. Accessed 07 May 2022

Bundesnetzagentur b: This is how the electricity market works. https://www.smard.de/page/home/wiki-article/446/384. Accessed 07 May 2022

Cerjan, M., Petričić, A., Delimar, M.: HIRA model for short-term electricity price forecasting. Energies **12**(3), 568 (2019). https://doi.org/10.3390/en12030568

Ciarreta, A., Muniain, P., Zarraga, A.: Modeling and forecasting realized volatility in German-Austrian continuous intraday electricity prices. J. Forecast. **6**(36), 680–690 (2017)

Federal Ministry for Economic Affairs and Climate Action. https://www.bmwk.de/Redaktion/EN/Textsammlungen/Energy/storage-technology.html. Accessed 02 May 2022

Fikiin, K.: Temperature control strategies for smarter energy use in refrigerated warehouses. New Food **18**(4), 76–79 (2015)

Fraunhofer Institute for Solar Energy Systems, Public Net Electricity Generation in Germany 2020: Share from Renewables Exceeds 50 percent. https://www.ise.fraunhofer.de/en/press-media/news/2020/public-net-electricity-generation-in-germany-2020-share-from-renewables-exceeds-50-percent.html. Accessed 02 May 2022

Gao, H.: analysis of new energy-saving technology for cold chain logistics. In: IOP Conference Series: Earth and Environmental Science, vol. 252, pp. 1–5 (2019)

Goli, S., McKane, A., Olsen, D.: Demand response opportunities in industrial refrigerated warehouses in California. In: ACEEE Summer Study on Energy Efficiency in Industry, pp. 78–89 (2011)

Li, X., Campana, P.E., Li, H., Yan, J., Zhu, K.: Energy storage systems for refrigerated warehouses. In: Energy Procedia **143**, pp. 94–99 (2017)

Logenthiran, T., Srinivasan, D., Shun, T.Z.: Demand side management in smart grid using heuristic optimization. IEEE Trans. Smart Grid **3**(3), pp. 1244–1252 (2012)

Lund, P.D., Lindgren, J., Mikkola, J., Salpakari, J.: Review of energy system flexibility measures to enable high levels of variable renewable electricity. Renew. Sustain. Energy Rev. **45**, pp. 785–807 (2015)

Ma, K., Hu, G., Spanos, C.J.: A cooperative demand response scheme using punishment mechanism and application to industrial refrigerated warehouses. IEEE Trans. Ind. Inf. **11**(6), 1520–1531 (2015)

Maurer, T.: Kältetechnik für Ingenieure. VDE-Verlag, Berlin (2016)

Murrant, D., Radcliffe, J.: Analysis of when and where the integration of LAES with refrigerated warehouses could provide the greatest value to Europe. Energy Procedia **151**, pp. 144–149 (2018)

Rabe, M., Spieckermann, S., Wenzel, S.: Verification and Validation for Simulation in Production and Logistics. Springer, Berlin, Heidelberg (2009)

Reisner, K., Reisner, T.: Fachwissen Kältetechnik, 6th edn. VDE-Verlag, Berlin, Offenbach (2016)

Wenzel, S.: Simulation logistischer systeme. In: Tempelmeier, H. (ed.) Modellierung logistischer Systeme. FL, pp. 1–34. Springer, Heidelberg (2018). https://doi.org/10.1007/978-3-662-57771-4_1

Zong, Y., et al.: Application genetic algorithms for load management in refrigerated warehouses with wind power penetration. In: 2009 IEEE Bucharest PowerTech, pp. 1–6 (2009)

CrossLog: Automatic Mixed-Palletizing for Cross-Docking Logistics Centers

Pedro Rocha[1], António G. Ramos[1](✉), and Elsa Silva[2]

[1] INESC TEC and School of Engineering, Polytechnic of Porto, Porto, Portugal
pedro.f.rocha@inesctec.pt, agr@isep.ipp.pt
[2] INESC TEC, Porto, Portugal
emsilva@inesctec.pt

Abstract. The CrossLog project aims to investigate, study, develop and implement an automated and collaborative cross-docking system (aligned with Industry 4.0) capable of moving and managing the flow of products within the warehouse in the fastest and safest way. In CrossLog, the ability to generate intelligent three-dimensional packing patterns is essential to ensure the flexibility and productivity of the cross-docking system while ensuring the stability of the palletised load. In this work, a heuristic solution approach is proposed to generate efficient pallet packing patterns that simultaneously minimise the total number of pallets required and address the balance of weight and volume between pallets. Computational experiments with data from a real company demonstrate the quality of the proposed solution approach.

Keywords: Mixed pallet loading · Heuristics · Volume and weight balance

1 Introduction

In a context of a paradigm shift from a 'forecast-led supply-chain' to a 'responsive demand-driven supply-chain' environment, numerous challenges emerge. The customization of the offer, accessibility, convenience, navigability, and customer experience, in space and time, are truly fundamental. Recently, we have witnessed a proliferation of proximity stores/supermarkets spaces characterised by being larger in number, smaller in size than traditional hypermarkets, and without storage capacity *per se*. This raises the question of how to supply this type of shop efficiently and effectively, reducing the effort associated with logistics operations in a context of high volume and mix.

In the age of digitalisation, to satisfy consumer needs, companies need to develop and adopt efficient, fast and agile logistics processes to provide the best shopping experience, with cross-docking emerging as the natural evolution of conventional logistics. Currently, this process still relies heavily on human labour. Its automation becomes complex when considering the number of variables in these systems and the frequency with which they change. However, with

J. de Armas et al. (Eds.): ICCL 2022, LNCS 13557, pp. 351–365, 2022.
https://doi.org/10.1007/978-3-031-16579-5_24

increasingly adaptable and flexible automation solutions, there is the possibility of automating cross-docking operations, making the process more agile and reducing human effort.

The main objective of the CrossLog project is to develop and implement an automated and collaborative cross-docking system capable of moving and managing the flow of products within the warehouse quickly and safely. The handling of objects is carried out using a set of modules (industrial conveyors, highly advanced robotic units and artificial vision systems) that interact with each other and communicate with an intelligent decision support system responsible for managing flows and the intelligent palletizing system.

Within the scope of the CrossLog project, an intelligent three-dimensional palletizing system was developed to decide the allocation of products of different sizes on the pallet. The main goal of the intelligent palletizing system is to generate efficient and safe three-dimensional packing patterns that contribute to increase the availability and efficiency of the mobile palletizing unit. Features related to cross-docking, such as the arrival of pallets at different points in time, the availability of products, and the temporary storage of products, are handled by the intelligent decision support system developed under the CrossLog project.

The rest of this paper is organised as follows. Section 2 is dedicated to the description of the problem. In Sect. 4 it is detailed the solution approach proposed to solve the problem, with a description of the different variants considered and the corresponding algorithms. The computational experiments analysis is described in Sect. 5. Finally, in Sect. 6 some conclusions are presented.

2 Problem Description

The intelligent palletizing system problem addressed in this paper belongs to the wider combinatorial optimisation class of Cutting and Packing (C&P) problems. According to the typology proposed by Wäscher *et al.* (2007) for C&P problems, the addressed problem is classified as a 3-Dimensional Single Bin Size Bin Packing Problem (3D-SBSBPP).

The 3D-SBSBPP addressed in this work can be stated as follows: A given set of small items of parallelepiped shape $k(k = 1, ..., K)$, known as box types $B = b_1, b_2, ..., b_K$, each box type in quantity n_k, assumed to be a rigid body with the centre of gravity located at its geometric centre and characterised by its depth (d_k), width (w_k), height (h_k) and weight (p_k) is to be loaded orthogonally into a large object of parallelepiped shape, designated as pallet C, characterised by its depth (D), width (W) and height (H).

The problem is a multi-objective one. The main goal is to minimise the number of pallets, and the second has the purpose of defining the way boxes are distributed between the pallets. In this second priority objective, three different options are considered:

- Maximise the volume usage of the pallets (VU). The aim is to maximize the volume usage of each pallet. With this objective one of the pallets typically has a reduced volume usage.

- Balance the weight of the pallets (WB). The objective is to generate packing arrangements where pallets have similar weights.
- Balance the volume of the pallets (VB). The objective is to generate packing arrangements where the sum of the volume of the boxes loaded on each pallet is similar.

The objectives must be met while satisfying the following constraints:

- the boxes must not overlap;
- all boxes must lie entirely within a pallet;
- each box must be placed in accordance with one of its possible orientations;
- the total weight loaded into a pallet cannot exceed its maximum permissible weight (weight limit constraint);
- each box must maintain its packing position undisturbed during cargo loading (static stability constraint);

The solution to the problem should provide the set of boxes to be loaded in each pallet and the location of each box inside the pallets.

3 Related Work

The literature shows several methods for solving 3D-SBSBPP problems, but only a few can cope with the size and requirements that the industry is looking for. Mixed integer linear programming based solution approaches are presented in Chen *et al.* (1995), Junqueira *et al.* (2012) and Paquay *et al.* (2016), however, are not able to solve large problems as the ones found in practice.

In contrast, different heuristics and exact methods, such as those presented in Faroe *et al.* (2003), Martello *et al.* (2007), Fekete *et al.* (2007), and Zhu *et al.* 2012) disregard many practical and logistical constraints.

A review of the literature on practical constraints in 3D-SBSBPPs is presented in Wäscher (2013) and Zhao *et al.* (2016). More recently, a literature review on solution approaches for packing problems on-line and offline has been published in Ali *et al.* (2022).

A literature work dealing with problems similar to that presented in this work is Gzara *et al.* (2020), considering practical constraints such as vertical support, load bearing, pallet weight limits, and planogram sequencing. In vertical support, an item is considered supported by having 70% of its area supported or its four corners sitting on top of items underneath. Load bearing refers to the ability of an item to withstand the weight placed on top. The weight of the pallet is the limit of the total weight of the items in a pallet, and the sequencing of the planogram refers to the ordering of items that enables efficient pallet emptying of the items in the store. A matheuristic approach based on column-generation is proposed, where the pricing sub-problem is a two-dimensional layer generation problem combined with second order cone programming and graphs. The main difference from the problem analysed in this work is the balance of weight and volume of the pallets generated.

4 Solution Approach

The proposed solution approach developed to address the described 3D-SBSBPP is based on an iterative procedure that loads one pallet at a time. Given a set of selected items, the algorithm loads them in a single pallet using the container loading algorithm with static stability (CLA-SS) proposed by Ramos *et al.* (2016). Then it uses a compaction procedure to reduce the height of the pallet. This procedure is repeated until there are no more boxes to load.

The CLA-SS algorithm used to load the pallet tries to maximise the pallet volume usage with an assortment of items while considering the maximum pallet allowed weight, nonoverlap, and stability constraints.

Two variants were developed to address the different secondary objectives. The first is centered on the secondary goal of maximizing the volume usage of the pallets. The second variant is centred on the weight or volume balance of the pallets.

The first variant starts with trying to pack all the items on a single pallet. However, if there is a subset of items that were not loaded on the pallet, a new pallet is added and the subset is loaded. The last pallet will not have a high volume usage in most situations.

The second variant was devised to improve safety during transport. Two main issues often arise in transport, the dynamic stability of the pallet (Ramos *et al.*., 2015; Ramos & Oliveira, 2018) and the axle weight distribution of the cargo on trucks (Silva *et al.*, 2018; Ramos *et al.*, 2018). As such, the second variant aims at balancing the volume or the weight of the pallets. By balancing the volume, the pallets are expected to be similar in height, which contributes to the dynamic stability of cargo. Balancing the weight can obtain a more balanced distribution of the pallets' weight on the container floor and contribute to a better axle weight distribution.

The second variant differs from the first variant in determining the subsets that are to be loaded in each iteration. The variant uses an assignment approach that is based on an item-to-pallet allocation algorithm (I2PAA) that estimates the minimum number of required pallets and assigns items to the pallets during an initialisation phase. The assignment is done by sorting the items in non-ascending order of size (item weight or volume) and assigning them to pallets using a roll-robin heuristic. This enables more evenly balanced pallets regarding either weight or volume, which increases the vehicle's dynamic stability or the axle weight balance compared to the first variant.

The pseudocode of the pallet building algorithm is presented in Algorithm 1. This algorithm is common to both variants. The main difference is that all items are immediately assigned to the first pallet in the first variant. At the end of each iteration, the remaining items are assigned to the next pallet, while in the second variant, items are assigned to pallets based on the weight or volume of the item. If in a given pallet some boxes cannot be loaded, a reassignment procedure for the not yet loaded items is performed. The pseudocodes for the initial assignment and reassignment procedures of the second variant are shown, respectively, in Algorithm 2 and Algorithm 3.

Algorithm 1. Pallet Construction Algorithm

```
procedure BuildingPallet(P)
    Load instance files and prepare output files
    Configures parameters of the algorithm
    Run Initial Item Assignment Algorithm
    Saves current instance as PrevInstance
    Defines current pallet and compaction state
    do
        Initialise stability Matrices
        Prepare Decoder and Container Structures and define Objective Function
        Run Compaction Heuristic using Genetic Algorithm
        Reset Objective Function
        Check current compaction phase and selects next step
        if Phase = Compact $Max_{OCCUP}$ & Status = $Leftover_{ZERO}$ then
            Save Current Solution as LastSolution
            Reduce maximum allowed pallet height
            RELOAD PrevInstance for $Min_{HEIGHT}$ phase
        end if
        if Phase = Compact $Max_{OCCUP}$ & Status = $Leftover_{MANY}$ then
            Save Current Solution as LastSolution
            Prepare next $Max_{OCCUP}$ phase - > Run Item Re-Assignment Algorithm
            Return LastSolution
        end if
        if Phase = Compact $Min_{HEIGHT}$ & Status = $Leftover_{ZERO}$ then
            Save Current Solution as LastSolution
            Reduce maximum allowed pallet height
            RELOAD PrevInstance for $Min_{HEIGHT}$ phase
        end if
        if Phase = Compact $Min_{HEIGHT}$ & Status = $Leftover_{MANY}$ then
            Prepare next $Max_{OCCUP}$ phase - > Run Item Re-Assignment Algorithm
            Return LastSolution
        end if
        Clear stability Matrices
    while (Number of unassigned items > 0)
end procedure
```

4.1 Packing and Compaction Phase

The packing and compaction phase consists of an iterative process that uses the CLA-SS to build a single pallet considering the constraints of volume, weight, non-overlap, and stability. This process uses two secondary objective functions: maximising volume occupation or minimising pallet height.

Independently of the secondary objective, each pallet is loaded using the same two-step procedure. First, given a set of boxes, the CLA-SS tries to load them on a single pallet to maximise the volume usage of the pallet. Secondly, considering the loaded boxes on the pallet compacts the cargo arrangement by minimising the height of the pallet.

The compaction phase iteratively reduces the maximum height allowed for the pallet until it cannot load any item onto the pallet. This compaction phase returns pallets with maximised volume usage and minimised height.

Depending on the item assignment characteristic, different pallet configurations will emerge:

Weight balance produces pallets with similar weights, although their occupied volumes may differ depending on the density of the items. May produce extra pallets if the item assignment heuristic assigns very large items to one pallet exceeding the allowed volume limit.

Volume balance produces pallets with similar volumes, but this generates pallets with significant differences in total weight. May produce extra pallets if the item assignment heuristic assigns very heavy items to one pallet that exceeds the allowed weight limit.

This packing and compaction phase returns pallets with their volume occupation maximised, and their height minimised considering their assortment of items.

4.2 Second Variant Assignment of Boxes

The initialisation and re-assignment phases can be configured to generate different pallet allocations: maximising the occupation of all pallets except the last where height minimisation is preferred, or balancing the weight (or volume) across the minimum number of estimated pallets used, aiming to produce pallets with similar occupied weight (or similar volume).

The initialisation phase of the second variant requires estimating the minimum number of pallets able to pack all items successfully and then adequately assigning the items to those pallets considering the balancing preference of either weight or volume.

It starts by ordering the items into a non-ascending sequence by the selected characteristic (volume or weight) and then assigning them to the pallets using a round-robin heuristic. Considering the assignment by weight, items are ordered from heaviest to lightest (as observed in Fig. 1a). When selecting assignments by volume, items are ordered from largest to smallest (as presented in Fig. 1b). In these examples, the assortment of items is assigned using a round-robin heuristic to four pallets (P1, P2, P3, and P4).

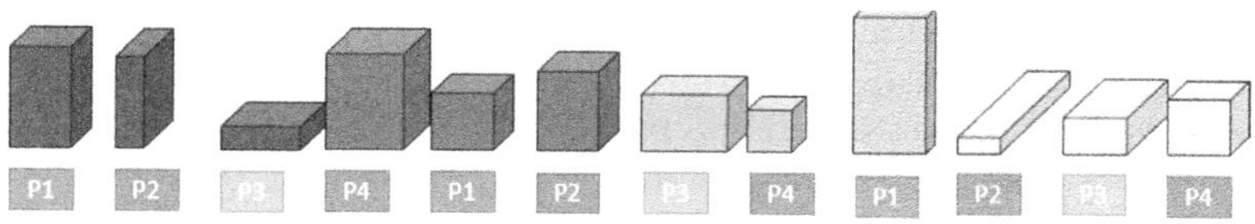

(a) Weight Balance

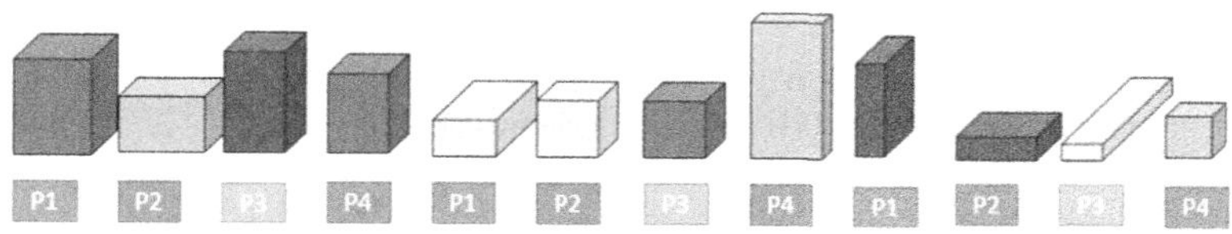

(b) Volume Balance

Fig. 1. Assignment strategies

Algorithm 2. Initial Assignment Algorithm

procedure ASSIGNMENT(I, P)
    Initialises weight and volume data arrays
    Defines pallet item assignment algorithm parameters
    Compute minimum number of pallets used, considering total weight and volume of items
    if OPT selected is 1 **then**
        Select items on WEIGHT array descending
        Round-robin item allocation to pallets
        Validation of weight, volume, and maximum allowed WEIGHT considering balanced flag
    else
        if OPT selected is 2 **then**
            Select items on VOLUME array descending
            Round-robin item allocation to pallets
            Validation of weight, volume, and maximum allowed VOLUME considering balanced flag
        end if
    end if
end procedure

The item reassignment process runs after the packing and compaction of any pallet is verified (when maximum volume occupation and minimum height are achieved) and assigns all items not yet compacted into pallets considering the chosen strategy (weight or volume balancing).

The general steps of the item re-assignment process are shown in the pseudocode in Algorithm 3.

Algorithm 3. Re-Assignment Algorithm

```
procedure ReAssignment(I, P)
    Selects items not yet placed into pallets
    Initialises weight and volume data arrays
    Defines pallet item re-assignment algorithm parameters
    Update estimation of pallet occupation ratio
    Compute minimum number of pallets left, considering total weight and volume of unallocated items
    if OPT selected is 1 then
        Select items on WEIGHT array descending
        Round-robin item allocation to pallets
        Validation of weight, volume, and maximum allowed WEIGHT considering balanced flag
    else
        if OPT selected is 2 then
            Select items on VOLUME array descending
            Round-robin item allocation to pallets
            Validation of weight, volume, and maximum allowed VOLUME considering balanced flag
        end if
    end if
end procedure
```

5 Computational Experiments

Computational experiments were performed using a set of instances to estimate the behaviour of the pallet building algorithm, comparing multiple options (maximisation of occupation, balancing by volume and balancing by weight). The computational experiments were conducted on an AMD Ryzen Threadripper PRO 3995WX with 16 cores, 256 Gb Ram DDR4 3200 Mhz, under Windows 10.

The genetic algorithm parameters used in the algorithm are based on those used by Ramos *et al.* (2016). The parameters are presented in Table 1.

Table 1. Genetic algorithm parameters used in all computational experiments.

Parameters	Values
Top	15%
Bottom	15%
Crossover probability	0.7
Population size	20 × number of boxes
Number of populations	2
Exchange between pop	Every 15 generations
Stopping criteria	After 150 generations

5.1 Instance Characteristics

The instances are a set of real-world instances that contain enough items to fill at least three full pallets but no more than five. This is the average order size in real-world scenarios for our specific case, but the instance size can be significantly larger in some situations.

The size of the pallet is fixed at $1200 \times 800\,\text{mm}^2$, with a maximum height of 1500 mm, representing $1.44\,\text{m}^3$ of the available volume. The maximum allowed weight for each pallet was set at 800 kg. The set of items in each instance has different assortments, ranging from weakly heterogeneous to strongly heterogeneous, considering item weight and dimensions.

The characteristics of the instances are presented in Table 2. Computational experiments were performed using a set of instances to estimate the behaviour of the pallet building algorithm, comparing multiple options (maximisation of occupation, balancing by volume and balancing by weight).

Table 2. Instance characteristics.

Instance name	# Item types	# Items	Total item weight (kg)	Total item volume (m^3)	Estimated Min # pallets
1751	98	135	892.93	2.70	3
2306	152	222	1323.57	3.52	3
2659	123	189	1081.27	3.00	3
2702	119	193	1127.69	2.71	3
2723	172	236	1123.55	4.33	4
2725	142	207	948.04	2.86	3
2727	105	145	879.43	2.85	3
2731	102	155	1053.72	2.54	3
2732	140	174	1261.55	3.54	3
2742	91	120	683.01	2.65	3
3417	94	184	1085.36	2.53	3
3510	104	152	1082.55	2.84	3
4125	96	183	1278.35	3.42	3
Average	118.31	176.54	1063.15	3.04	3.08

The lower bound for the number of pallets is obtained by rounding up the division of the total volume of the items by the volume of the pallet multiplied by a factor of 0.85. The factor was defined based on the average volume usage of 90.58% obtained by Ramos *et al.* (2016) for strongly heterogeneous instances. The estimated number of pallets for each instance is presented in the last column of Table 2.

5.2 Results

Using the first variant that tries to maximise the occupation of the pallets, the algorithm allocates all items to the first pallet and, after finding the best compaction, pushes all remaining items to be packed into the next pallet. This approach tries to iteratively maximise the occupation of each pallet considering the set of items available. The results for the first variant can be shown in Table 3.

The second variant uses the balancing approach of weight or volume, and its results can be seen in Table 4 and Table 5, respectively. Each table contains the values obtained for all built pallets, comparing volume usage percentage, pallet weight, and maximum height (considering the top of the highest item placed on the pallet). Notice that the full pallet contains a maximum volume of 1.44 m^3.

Table 3. Results of the first variant

OCP.	Volume usage(%)				Weight (kg)				Height (mm)			
instance	P1	P2	P3	P4	P1	P2	P3	P4	P1	P2	P3	P4
1751	94.5	86.1	7.1	-	430.2	412.5	50.2	-	1500	1498	428	-
2306	96.0	87.5	60.9	-	411.6	556.0	356.0	-	1498	1499	1338	-
2659	95.0	87.2	26.0	-	434.6	513.4	133.3	-	1500	1500	587	-
2702	94.1	82.1	12.1	-	557.5	497.0	73.2	-	1498	1494	281	-
2723	94.6	93.8	79.7	32.6	324.1	236.3	377.3	185.8	1500	1500	1500	598
2725	93.3	85.8	19.4	-	439.8	394.4	113.9	-	1499	1500	445	-
2727	94.8	87.3	15.5	-	301.8	496.9	80.8	-	1498	1498	434	-
2731	94.3	80.0	2.0	-	630.9	408.8	14.0	-	1500	1500	206	-
2732	95.5	92.7	57.7	-	647.2	281.1	333.2	-	1496	1500	1200	-
2742	92.4	89.2	2.8	-	400.4	264.9	17.7	-	1500	1498	302	-
3417	94.6	79.3	2.0	-	637.3	428.6	19.5	-	1500	1500	280	-
3510	93.9	85.5	17.9	-	640.8	357.0	84.8	-	1500	1498	436	-
4125	93.8	92.0	51.4	-	535.8	464.9	277.7	-	1496	1500	1044	-

Comparing all these results, Table 3 clearly shows that the first pallets in all instances are the ones with the highest total volume of items compacted and show a reduction for every additional pallet. The average pallet volume usage, not including the last pallet of each instance is 90.2%. These results are in line with those obtained by Ramos *et al.* (2016) for highly heterogeneous instances.

Both the results of Table 4 and Table 5 show a similar occupation between all pallets. The most consistent balancing strategy is the balancing by volume, which distributes into similar pallet occupations while still reducing the number of pallets. The weight-balancing strategy also manages to balance the pallets, but not as well as the previous strategy. It is also observed that when the estimated number of pallets is exceeded the balance is not achieved (e.g. Instance 2306 in Table 4).

Table 4. Results of the second variant with weight balance

WGH.	Volume usage (%)				Weight (kg)				Height (mm)			
instance	P1	P2	P3	P4	P1	P2	P3	P4	P1	P2	P3	P4
1751	58.4	64.1	65.2	-	317.4	298.9	276.7	-	1048	1500	1497	-
2306	88.3	70.8	84.4	0.9	511.3	374.0	431.1	7.1	1324	1061	1266	162
2659	76.1	65.5	66.4	-	418.6	343.3	319.3	-	1340	1191	1191	-
2702	64.4	66.8	57.0	-	452.1	348.7	326.9	-	1200	1480	987	-
2723	70.0	68.2	79.4	83.0	291.0	284.7	277.5	270.3	1346	1499	1497	1500
2725	62.6	66.3	69.5	-	336.8	314.8	296.4	-	1195	1483	1486	-
2727	84.2	49.8	63.7	-	362.1	279.2	238.2	-	1500	899	1193	-
2731	65.7	64.2	46.3	-	413.2	395.6	244.9	-	1200	1500	854	-
2732	89.4	70.0	86.5	-	530.8	403.6	327.1	-	1500	1338	1500	-
2742	55.6	63.7	65.0	-	240.3	232.3	210.5	-	1039	1462	1498	-
3417	61.6	57.5	56.7	-	402.3	344.7	338.3	-	1049	1493	1487	-
3510	70.3	63.4	63.6	-	389.6	352.9	340.1	-	1348	1498	1492	-
4125	86.3	68.6	82.3	-	460.5	444.5	373.4	-	1500	1198	1500	-

Table 5. Results of the second variant with volume balance

VOL.	Volume usage (%)				Weight (kg)				Height (mm)			
instance	P1	P2	P3	P4	P1	P2	P3	P4	P1	P2	P3	P4
1751	64.2	62.6	60.8	-	314.2	320.1	258.7	-	1184	1497	1500	-
2306	88.3	81.8	74.2	-	570.3	374.8	378.4	-	1499	1497	1348	-
2659	75.1	69.2	63.8	-	343.5	383.6	354.1	-	1347	1176	1174	-
2702	65.9	62.5	59.8	-	425.8	343.5	358.4	-	1199	1490	1498	-
2723	77.8	76.5	75.5	71.0	289.1	298.6	283.5	252.3	1350	1499	1498	1476
2725	68.7	66.2	63.6	-	357.3	274.3	316.4	-	1199	1496	1490	-
2727	73.5	64.9	59.3	-	301.6	297.0	280.9	-	1350	1146	1144	-
2731	65.2	63.6	47.4	-	386.4	462.2	205.2	-	1199	1500	850	-
2732	88.6	86.4	70.8	-	515.2	438.8	307.5	-	1497	1500	1344	-
2742	68.8	59.9	55.7	-	235.1	214.5	233.4	-	1199	1060	1060	-
3417	62.2	58.9	54.8	-	367.3	349.3	368.8	-	1189	1495	948	-
3510	67.5	65.8	64.1	-	351.3	409.7	321.6	-	1200	1470	1498	-
4125	82.5	81.0	73.8	-	430.8	466.7	380.9	-	1497	1498	1349	-

The average computational times are higher in the first variant and lower in the second variant with volume balance. The values of the computational times for each instance and secondary objective are presented in Table 6.

Table 6. Computation time for each instance, considering each objective function.

	TIME (s)		
instance	OCP.	WGT.	VOL.
1751	206	241	182
2306	1066	529	441
2659	711	673	519
2702	656	503	458
2723	1169	378	339
2725	993	691	641
2727	441	505	293
2731	470	430	384
2732	601	313	255
2742	191	144	138
3417	865	664	548
3510	394	231	238
4125	551	434	306
Average	639	441	365

5.3 Examples of Palletized Instances

Figures 2, 3, and 4 show an example of a full palletization, considering the two variants and the secondary objectives. In Fig. 2, the first variant tries to use the maximum volume using all available items, generating pallets filled to the maximum limit and minimising the height of the last pallet.

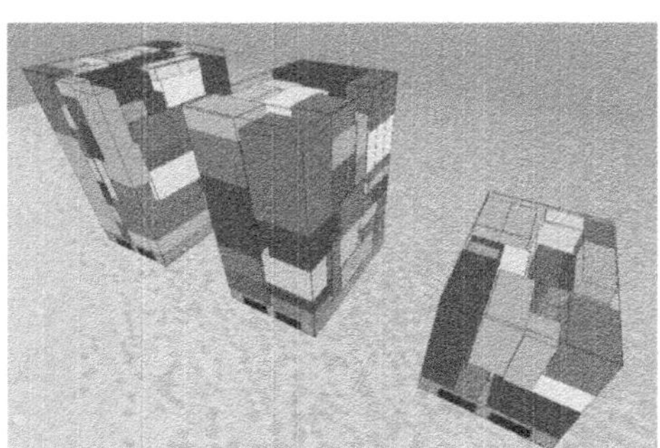

Fig. 2. Pallets generated using the first variant

Figure 3 balances the assignment of items according to weight, which generates pallets of similar size if the density of the items is similar.

Fig. 3. Pallets generated using the second variant with weight balance

Fig. 4. Pallets generated using the second variant with volume balance

Figure 4 shows the assignment of items based on a volume balance that tries to have all pallets filled with the same volume of items.

6 Conclusions

In this work, we have addressed the mixed palletizing problem, the aim was to minimise the number of pallets used and ensure a balanced distribution of the boxes with respect to weight and volume in the pallets. A solution approach considers two different variants, one centred on maximizing the volume usage of the pallets and the other on the pallets' weight or volume balance. In the solution approach the packing and compaction phase are conducted with the CLA-SS algorithm. Computational experiments considering data from a real-world company were performed to evaluate the efficiency of the solution approach considering both variants. Analysing the results, it is clear that the second variant obtained solutions with a better weight and volume balance. The average computational time is smaller for the second variant compared to the first one. It is important to improve the lower bound used to estimate the minimum number of pallets in future work.

Acknowledgements. This work is co-financed by the ERDF - European Regional Development Fund through the Operational Programme for Competitiveness and Internationalisation - COMPETE 2020 under the PORTUGAL 2020 Partnership Agreement and through the Portuguese National Innovation Agency (ANI) as part of project "POCI-01-0247-FEDER-039895 CrossLOG-1". The third author is financed by National Funds through the FCT - Fundação para a Ciência e a Tecnologia, I.P. (Portuguese Foundation for Science and Technology), with reference DL57/2016/CP1452/CT0006.

References

Ali, S., Ramos, A.G., Carravilla, M.A., Oliveira, J.F.: On-line three-dimensional packing problems: a review of off-line and on-line solution approaches. Comput. Ind. Eng. **168**, 108122 (2022)

Bortfeldt, A., Wäscher, G.: Constraints in container loading - a state-of-the-art review. Eur. J. Oper. Res. **229**(1), 1–20 (2013)

Chen, C.S., Lee, S.M., Shen, Q.S.: An analytical model for the container loading problem. Eur. J. Oper. Res. **80**(1), 68–76 (1995)

Faroe, O., Pisinger, D., Zachariasen, M.: Guided local search for the three-dimensional bin-packing problem. INFORMS J. Comput. **15**(3), 267–283 (2003)

Fekete, S.P., Schepers, J., der Veen, V., Jan, C.: An exact algorithm for higher-dimensional orthogonal packing. Oper. Res. **55**(3), 569–587 (2007)

Gzara, F., Elhedhli, S., Yildiz, B.C.: The pallet loading problem: Three-dimensional bin packing with practical constraints. Eur. J. Oper. Res. **287**(3), 1062–1074 (2020)

Junqueira, L., Morabito, R., Yamashita, D.S.: Three-dimensional container loading models with cargo stability and load bearing constraints. Comput. Oper. Res. **39**(1), 74–85 (2012). Special Issue on Knapsack Problems and Applications

Martello, S., Pisinger, D., Vigo, D., Boef, E.D., Korst, J.: Algorithm 864: general and robot-packable variants of the three-dimensional bin packing problem. ACM Trans. Math. Softw. (TOMS) **33**(1), 7-es (2007)

Paquay, C., Schyns, M., Limbourg, S.: A mixed integer programming formulation for the three-dimensional bin packing problem deriving from an air cargo application. Int. Trans. Oper. Res. **23**(1–2), 187–213 (2016)

Ramos, A.G., Oliveira, J.F.: Cargo stability in the container loading problem - state-of-the-art and future research directions. In: Vaz, A.I.F., Almeida, J.P., Oliveira, J.F., Pinto, A.A. (eds.) APDIO 2017. SPMS, vol. 223, pp. 339–350. Springer, Cham (2018). https://doi.org/10.1007/978-3-319-71583-4_23

Ramos, A.G., Oliveira, J.F., Gonçalves, J.F., Lopes, M.P.: Dynamic stability metrics for the container loading problem. Transp. Res. Part C Emerg. Technol. **60**, 480–497 (2015)

Ramos, A.G., Oliveira, J.F., Gonçalves, J.F., Lopes, M.P.: A container loading algorithm with static mechanical equilibrium stability constraints. Transp. Res. Part B Methodol. **91**, 565–581 (2016)

Ramos, A.G., Silva, E., Oliveira, J.F.: A new load balance methodology for container loading problem in road transportation. Eur. J. Oper. Res. **266**(3), 1140–1152 (2018)

Silva, E., Ramos, A.G., Oliveira, J.F.: Load balance recovery for multi-drop distribution problems: a mixed integer linear programming approach. Transp. Res. Part B Methodol. **116**, 62–75 (2018)

Wäscher, G., Haußner, H., Schumann, H.: An improved typology of cutting and packing problems. Eur. J. Oper. Res. **183**(3), 1109–1130 (2007)

Zhao, X., Bennell, J.A., Bektaş, T., Dowsland, K.: A comparative review of 3D container loading algorithms. Int. Trans. Oper. Res. **23**(1–2), 287–320 (2016)
Zhu, W., Zhang, Z., Oon, W.-C., Lim, A.: Space defragmentation for packing problems. Eur. J. Oper. Res. **222**(3), 452–463 (2012)

Supply Chain and Production Management

A Framework on Centralised to Decentralised Logistics Control Structures Applied in Two Case Studies

Meike Hopman, Ruben Fransen(✉), Jaco van Meijeren, and Irene Zubin

TNO Sustainable Transport and Logistics, The Hague, The Netherlands
ruben.fransen@tno.nl

Abstract. Developments on digitalisation and automation in transport and logistics create new possibilities in the organisation of supply chains. New technologies can disrupt existing control structures, establish new forms of control and improve the efficiency and flexibility of operations. This paper provides a framework to analyse the trade-offs and conditions that best apply to each control structure from centralised to decentralised. A centralised control structure is characterised by one party (control tower) that collects and analyses data to come to optimal operational decisions on a system level. In opposition, a decentralised control structure is characterised by each unit in the logistics chain taking independent decisions (self-organisation) based on local intelligence and autonomy. A 2 × 2 control structure matrix is created, with each corner defining a different type of logistics control structure. The framework is then applied in two practical case studies in which simulation models are developed to show the impact of different logistics control structures. Results show the effects of different control structures in one supply chain and under which circumstances and for which type of logistics chain, each logistics control structure is most suitable.

Keywords: Centralised or decentralised organisation · Container logistics · Multi-agent simulation · Self-organising logistics (SOL) · Supply chain management

1 Introduction

The increasing technological development on digitalisation and automation in transport and logistics creates new possibilities in the organisation of supply chains. Real-time connectivity and improved data sharing enables innovative methods of decision making which can change the control structure of logistics operations. More (autonomous) data driven decision making can be applied in different control structures, ranging from central coordination (control tower approach) to decentral coordination (self-organising approach). On one hand, a central control structure is characterised by one party (control tower) that collects and analyses data to come to optimal operational decisions, which are then communicated to various parties in the logistics chain. Consequently, decisions are made globally based on globally-available information. This control tower approach

J. de Armas et al. (Eds.): ICCL 2022, LNCS 13557, pp. 369–381, 2022.
https://doi.org/10.1007/978-3-031-16579-5_25

offers potential for optimisation of efficiency at system level. In this way, the interests of the chain can be placed above individual interests, and standardised communication takes place via one system.

In opposition, a decentral control structure is characterised by each unit in the logistics chain (e.g. a parcel, a container, a vehicle or a hub) taking independent decisions (self-organisation) based on local intelligence and autonomy, aiming for more flexible operations. A mixed approach between centralised and decentralised control, could combine the advantages of both forms, aiming at improving efficiency for the operations that require a central organisation and providing flexibility for the operations that can be performed at a local level.

In a centralised control structure, the advantages of a centralised system are reduced communication errors within the chain, and a large degree of predictability and accountability. However, a lot of responsibility rests within one party, which makes this control mode sensitive due to a single point of failure. Questions whether logistics parties can develop a feasible control tower or whether data can be exchanged, processed, optimised and returned fast enough, are still open.

Self-organising logistics (SOL) comes into scope when operators and carriers make decentral decisions to organise their logistics operations and no longer require control towers or other centralised forms of decision making. Less communication and fast direct local response to unexpected events can be identified as organisational advantages, along with not having the requirement of developing, operating and maintaining a central control infrastructure. There are however questions on how supply chains can become more self-organising, what the impact is on performance and what properties are essential for successful implementation.

Building on a previous publication on the implementation of self-organising logistics from Quak [1], in this contribution we develop a framework to define different logistics control structures ranging from central to decentral. The aim is to analyse the trade-offs and conditions that best apply to each control structure, by applying this framework into two practical case studies. To do so, a two-step methodology was followed. First, a set of interviews and brainstorming sessions were conducted to answer the following research question: "What are the factors that affect the type of logistics control structure and what are their possible development directions?" Subsequently, two use cases were analysed with simulation models in order to answer the following research question: "What is the effect of different control structures and under which circumstances and for which type of logistics chain, is each logistics control structure most suitable?".

This paper is based on the research conducted for the SOLPort project (Self Organising Logistics in the Port), carried out by a consortium of the following partners: TNO, SmartPort, Port of Rotterdam, University of Twente, Pharox, Distribute, NPRC, Intel and Ab Ovo. The project was partly financed by TKI Dinalog (Dutch Top Sector Logistics).

2 Background

The term self-organisation refers to a dynamic process in which an overall order is achieved through local interactions between parts of an initially disordered system [2]. In the logistics sector, self-organisation can be found in hybrid forms in which elements from a centralised control structure and a decentralised control structure are combined using automated processes and real-time system information. Self-organising logistics (SOL) systems can be seen as a network of nodes of different nature: nodes can be locations operated by humans and supported by IT systems (e.g., seaports, container terminals and warehouses) but also intelligent moving objects that are capable of automated decisions (e.g., trucks and barges) [3]. These nodes should have access only to the data that is relevant to accomplish their tasks and should communicate with other nodes in the network to optimise the logistics chain. To achieve that, SOL-systems should ensure secure and efficient communication, extended sensors monitoring and adequate robustness [4].

Most studies on SOL systems focus on fully decentralised approaches. For example, Wycisk [5] describes how self-organisation can improve the performance of a logistics chain, allowing for more autonomy at a decentral and local level. However, as already explored in Pan [6], it is important that, although defined as decentralised systems, self-organising logistics should also be able to work towards a common goal and thus should be able to oversee the whole logistics chain. Moreover, recent studies started to take central coordination into account when exploring the possibilities of self-organising logistics. In Feng [7], a decentral agent decision-making framework with central coordination is developed, showing how including a vertical and horizontal collaboration can improve the system performances.

Linked to the work of Feng [7], this research explores decentral structures with a central escalation channel. This central escalation channel is activated when decentral agents deviate from the system boundaries (e.g., when key performance indicators are exceeded) to intervene and bring the system back to its standard values. While previous studies focused on SOL-systems as a decentralised control structure or on the combination of decentralised and centralised control, this research examines the differences between centralised and decentralised control and tests them on two case studies, to gain practical knowledge on the impacts that different control structures could have on a logistics chain.

3 Methodology and Research Setup

In the previous study from Quak [1], the possibilities of self-organising logistics were discussed through serious gaming sessions and living labs (i.e. real-life experiments). In this contribution, we broadened the scope and created a framework for analysing different logistics control structures, ranging from completely centralised (control tower approach) to fully decentralised (self-organising approach), considering also in-between approaches. Subsequently, we applied this framework to two case studies, to quantitatively assess the different control structures with simulation models.

The research was structured in two phases. First, interviews and brainstorming sessions were conducted to define the framework. Consequently, the framework was tested through the simulation modelling of two case studies.

3.1 Interviews and Brainstorming Sessions

To define the important aspects and development directions of logistics control structures, four interviews and brainstorming sessions were conducted between August and December 2018 with experts in the logistics field. The aim was to enrich the existing definitions of centralised and decentralised control structures. As a result, the first research question is answered: "What are the factors that affect the type of logistics control structure and what are their possible development directions?".

The interviews started with defining the concepts of centralised and decentralised control structures. The discussions then moved towards the aspects of new mixed control structures, which led to the creation of a control structure matrix with two axes, and the definition of four logistics control structures. During the interviews and the follow-up brainstorming sessions, each control structure was analysed, to understand the preconditions and the perspectives that should be taken into account. Current practical examples of control structures were put in perspective with respect to the control structure matrix, so to understand how logistics chains are currently organised and how they could be improved in the future.

3.2 Case Studies and Simulation Models

In the SOLport project, two case studies (i.e. practical experiments) were performed, in which different control structures (from centralised to decentralised) were compared with each other. The first case study concerns dry bulk inland shipping, whereas the second case study deals with container hinterland transport by road. In the elaboration of these experiments, a link was made with the control structures previously formulated in the framework, which makes them extensive examples of an application of different logistics control structures.

To analyse the case studies, simulation models were used. The simulation models were developed and calibrated based on real data. To gain insight into the effects of the different control structures applied to different logistics chains, multiple scenarios were run for each case study. The results of the simulation models provide an answer to the second research question: "What is the effect of different control structures and under which circumstances and for which type of logistics chain, is each logistics control structure most suitable?".

Set Up Case Study 1 – Dry Bulk Inland Shipping. The first case study was performed by the inland shipping cooperative NPRC and the research institute TNO, and pertains the inland waterway transport of bulk goods from one production facility to three different consumption locations, which is fully executed by barges. The consumption locations have limited stock capacities and the barge fleet has to guarantee the receiver a security of supply, i.e. a minimal amount of available stock.

The current logistics control structure consists of a central planner that oversees the process and allocates load to barges, while ensuring sufficient stock at the consumption locations. Each barge in the fleet is an individual enterprise with their own interests and preferences. This gives the skippers the urge to have a role in the decision making process of the operations they have to execute. The details on the physical and organisational flows were provided by barge cooperation NPRC and the receiver in this supply chain. For the details regarding the planning and execution processes, the logistics manager at NPRC and one of the barge skippers had been interviewed. Based on the information collected in the interviews, as well as real-world data, scheduling heuristics have been designed and integrated into a newly developed simulation model.

Description of the Simulation Model. An agent based model was developed to simulate this case study. Agents are the barges, the production facility and the three consumption locations. Agents simulate both the physical processes of sailing, berthing and (un)loading and the organisational processes of shipment and (un)load slot allocation. The model provides an aggregate representation of the essential physical processes as this research focusses on the organisational aspects of logistics control structures. Three different scenarios were analysed: one with a centralised control structure and two with a decentralised control structure. The first scenario is a representation of the current practice with a central planner. The decision heuristic of the central planner was implemented by assigning barges to the unload location with the earliest expected stock depletion. The second and third scenarios represent two forms of self-organising logistics where barges decide for themselves to which location and at which unload slot they will go, based on their own specific preferences. The difference between the second scenario ('standard decentral') and the third ('flexible decentral') scenario is the time at which the unloading decision is made by each individual barge. In the standard decentralised scenario the choice is made at the same time as in the centralised scenario: both the load and the unload slots are immediately scheduled as soon as the barge is empty and leaves the consumption location to sail back to the production facility. In the flexible decentralised scenario, decisions about the unload slot are made by the barge only a few hours before it reaches the unload location. In this way, more accurate information on delays and stock levels can be taken into account.

To prevent undesired outcomes in the two SOL scenarios, an escalation method was implemented. In the case that an unload location foresees critical low stock levels, it can claim priority for a barge visit and therewith overrule the preferred location decision of the barge. Implementing this heuristic prevents unwanted stock depletion, but also reduces decision autonomy of the barge skippers. In the case that multiple locations use this priority claim simultaneously, then the central scheduling rule of the earliest stock depletion is used.

Set Up Case Study 2 – Container Hinterland Transport by Road. The second case study is performed by Distribute and Combi Terminal Twente (CTT) and concerns self-organising logistics for the last-mile container transport from a hinterland container terminal by a fleet of trucks [8]. Each container has its own specifications, such as client location, and pick-up and delivery windows. The challenge is to assign containers to trucks such that all containers are transported in an efficient manner.

The current logistics control structure consists of human planners that manually assign containers to trucks with a centralised decision-making process. The assignment is based on a list of attributes, which can change and can be updated by each party during the process.

Description of the Simulation Model. To simulate different control structures (from central to decentral) a multi-agent simulation system was developed, in which containers and trucks are represented as agents. The simulation model explores seven scenarios with their own control strategy with different levels of self-organising logistics. These decentralised decision-making processes enable the agents to autonomously schedule their activities following a local sealed-bid auction mechanism. The auction mechanism is based on the Vickrey auction from Mes [9], in which agents only have information from their neighbours (decentralised approach) using sensors and local communication protocols. When a container reaches the terminal, it opens an auction and each truck can place a bid expressed by price, expected departure time and expected arrival time. Once the bid is accepted, the container communicates the decision to the winning truck, creating a new schedule. In some of the scenarios, a scanning mechanism is triggered after a fixed amount of time (threshold), in which a human planner or the SOL-system re-evaluates or confirms the decisions.

4 Framework for Logistics Control Structures

During the first phase of the research, as described in Sect. 3.1, interviews and brainstorming sessions were conducted to define the framework for logistics control structures as described in Hopman [10]. Gathering the information provided by the experts during the interviews, it was possible to identify two important criteria for defining the type of control – decision level and information – and their two possible directions – global or local. As a result, a control structure matrix is created, with four logistics control structures (Fig. 1).

Decisions can be made on a local or global level. In the case of global-level decisions, there is a (third) party who oversees (a part of) the logistics chain and makes operational decisions for different agents (e.g. logistics parties or vehicles). In the case of local-level decisions, every logistics party in the chain is responsible for its own operational choices.

Information can be exchanged on a global or local level. In the case of global-level information, all the necessary data is available and exchanged through the entire logistics chain. In the case of local-level information, data is known only within a specific party and it is shared in a very limited way. This limitation concerns the number of parties (e.g., data is only shared with the previous and the next parties in the logistics chain), but also the content of the shared data (e.g., only aggregates or specific data that are required for the logistics process are shared).

4.1 Control Structure Matrix

Based on which level decisions are made and information is exchanged, a 2 × 2 matrix is created (Fig. 1), with each corner defining a different type of control structure. The figure presents four possible controle structures along the two axis, level of information exchange and level of decision making.

The top left corner defines a central logistics organisation with one large control tower. Decisions are made on a global/central level based on information that is available

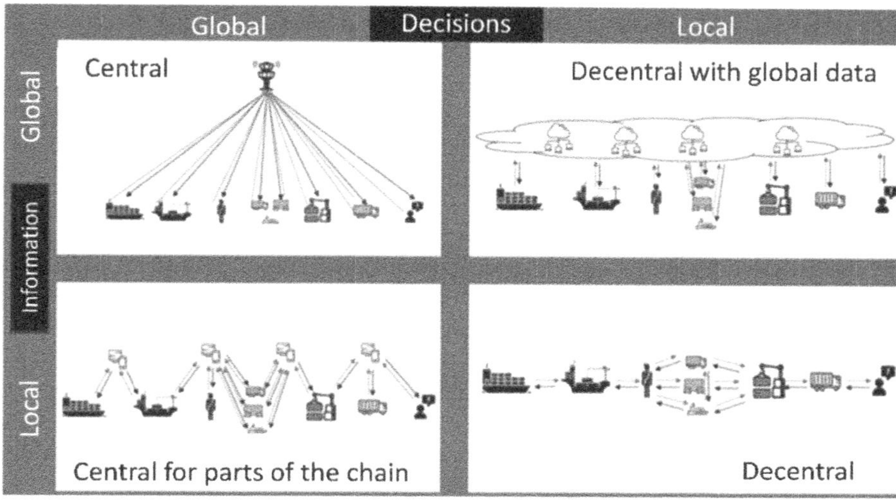

Fig. 1. The 2 × 2 matrix with four different control structures.

on a global/central level. The advantage of this control structure is that the control tower has the overview of all processes and can optimise decisions on a system level. Some of the disadvantages include having a single point of failure, a high chance of mistrust from companies, low willingness to share data with the control tower, the complexity of collecting and processing lots of data (possibly in a standardised way), and optimise processes and communicate actions with all stakeholders in a short period of time. It is possible to invest in and maintain back-up facilities to improve uptime of a central control tower, but this does not take away the reliability of the supply chain on the presence of a control tower. This structure is especially relevant for situations where the system perspective is very important and for situations that are rather predictable.

In complete opposition, the bottom right corner defines a decentral logistics organisation, also called self-organising logistics. In this control structure, agents in the logistics chain can make their own (local) decisions based on the information they have directly available. Advantages are that only a limited amount of data has to be shared and that agents can optimise their own decisions in a responsive and flexible way without dependency on a central organisation, which creates high autonomy. A disadvantage is that there is no optimization at system level which might lead to unwanted results at system level. Escalation levels should be introduced to avoid this. This structure is most relevant in situations that are very dynamic, where fast and flexible decisions are required often and in situations where autonomy of agents is important.

The top right corner combines local-level decisions with globally-shared information in a decentral logistics organisation with global data. Information on logistics processes and possible disturbances is sent to a global data infrastructure with a standardised way of communication and information is available for all the parties involved in the logistics chain to make operational decisions based on individual performance indicators. This control structure can potentially allow for a better utilisation of assets and less delay in the logistics chain, using as much as possible real-time information. On the other hand, since different parties are involved in the logistics chain, it might be a challenge to properly coordinate all operational processes. Moreover, the lack of predictability (due to the local-level decisions) can be harmful for long-term investments. The application of a decentralised logistics organisation with global data is suitable when coordination and data exchange between different parties are crucial for making individual decisions in dynamic circumstances.

Lastly, the bottom left corner combines global-level decisions with locally-shared information in a central logistics organisation with several smaller control towers. Each of the smaller control towers (e.g. an organisation or a digital platform) oversees and manages a specific part of the logistics chain by collecting locally-shared information and by making operational decisions. To realise this control structure it is important that the control towers are jointly accepted by the parties involved and that they are able to efficiently collect and process data. Compared to central operations, the smaller control towers can better cope with dynamic conditions, while the system perspective is taken into account and clarity about the motivations behind decisions is provided.

An overview of the characteristics and trade-offs for each control structure is shown in Fig. 2.

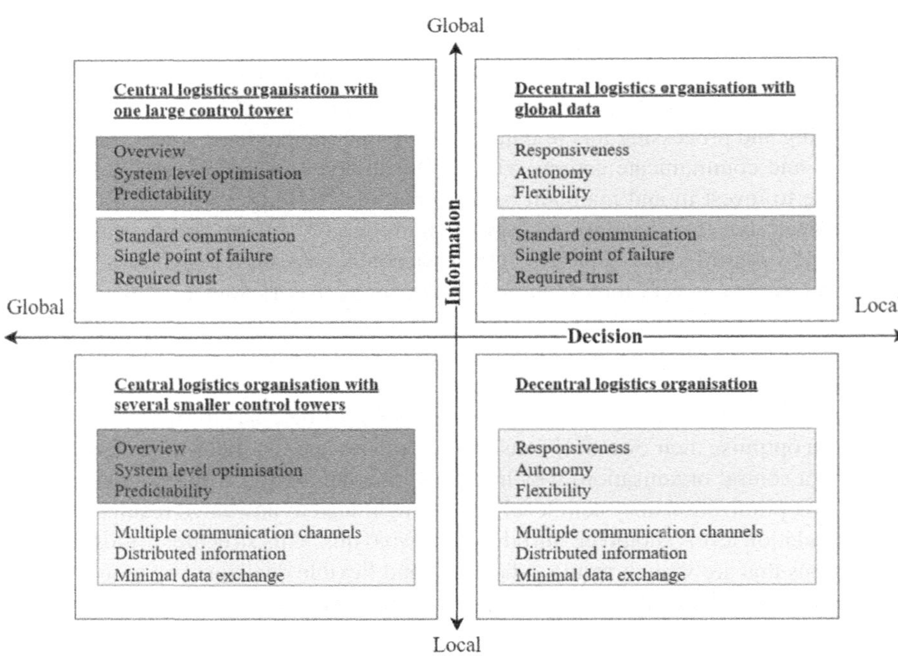

Fig. 2. Control structure matrix with characteristics for global (dark green) and local (light green) decisions and for global (dark orange) and local (light orange) information (Color figure online).

5 Application of the Framework in Two Case Studies

The second phase of the research includes the application of the logistics control structure framework in two case studies: dry bulk inland shipping and container hinterland transport by road. Different logistics control structures were simulated for each case study. All results can be found in Fransen [11] and De Bruin [8] and are summarised below.

5.1 Dry Bulk Inland Shipping

The developed simulation model represents real world operations and performances in the case of a centralised control structure (current practice) and was used to compare three different logistics control structures (*centralised, standard decentralised* and *flexible decentralised*). The main difference between the scenarios is how barges are assigned to the unload slots and locations.

Results show that both a centralised and decentralised approach are able to supply the requested annual volume of dry bulk to the consumption locations. The variation in turnover per ship is much bigger in the decentralised scenarios, since in this control structure, skippers choose their unload location based on individual preferences, which has a clear effect on the distribution of ships across the different locations, hence on the turnover.

For what concerns the stock levels, results show that different control structures lead to different stock levels per unload location. In the centralised control scenario, there is less variation and thus more stability and certainty regarding the stock levels. In contrast, both self-organising logistics structures (decentralised scenarios) have a much greater variation in stock levels, which is caused by the individual unload preferences of the different barges. To ensure the security of supply for the receiver, an escalation method was implemented in the decentralised scenarios, but the simulation model still shows that decentral organisation can lead to sub-optimal performance from a system perspective.

Another aspect that differs between centralised and decentralised control structures is the priority claim by consumption locations. In case of self-organising logistics, a priority claim is often needed to ensure security of supply while dealing with the higher variation in stock level. Location preferences by skippers play an important role in the priority claim that is required for (other) consumption locations and therefore the preferences of skippers have a high influence on the outcome.

For the shipper, security of supply and a stable stock level are extremely important. To guarantee this, a central control structure is more suitable. On the other hand, the interests of a skipper are better represented in the case of a decentralised control structure, in which they have more flexibility and autonomy. As an inland shipping cooperation, NPRC is the connecting factor between skippers and shippers and, when choosing a logistics control structure, a trade-off has to be made between different interests of these parties. It is a balancing act with the freedom of choice for skippers on one hand and the security of supply for shippers on the other hand, which variation can be assessed by setting different system rules. Based on the results of the simulation and the characteristics of the case study (e.g. a predictable flow of goods and a well-organised supply chain), a centralised control structure is most suitable. In case that a decentralised control structure is chosen, it is important to create system rules in such a way that skippers only have freedom of choice within the limits necessary to meet system requirements. When the system rules are more strict, there is less freedom of choice for the skippers and the situation will be more similar to a centralised control structure.

5.2 Container Hinterland Transport by Road

The developed simulation model represents real world operations for the container hinterland transport by road at CTT, and was used for comparing seven different scenarios, with each scenario having an increased level of self-organisation.

Results show that increasing the level of self-organisation does not lead to substantial changes in meeting the established deadlines. The differences in the on-time deliveries are less than 1% and thus considered neglectable. Furthermore, increased levels of self-organisation do not bring many changes in the loading and unloading turnaround times. However, these average turnaround times are significantly lower in the two scenarios in which overruling of the system is not allowed.

The simulation of scenarios with a different level of self-organisation, leads to interesting results on the efficiency of last-mile container transport. For configuring a self-organising fleet of trucks, trade-offs should be made on different performance aspects for the container terminal and its clients. A positive aspect of a more self-organised control structure is the opportunity of continuously scanning for better options, which allows for merged trips (i.e. one trip in which the delivery of a container to one client is combined with the pick-up of a container at another client). Having more merged trips leads to higher efficiency in transporting a container. Therefore, within a SOL-system agents can increase the percentage of loaded driving time and consequently decrease the total driving distance. The simulation model shows that the self-organising scenarios have a better performance on driving time and driven kilometres. However, this also leads to a more dynamic system with spontaneous overruling and merging trips, which requires more communication between trucks and thus more connectivity and flexibility from the truck drivers.

Based on the results of the simulation, a decentralised form of control should be preferred for the container hinterland transport at CTT. Introducing a SOL-system drastically reduced the dependence on manual planning and increased operational performance, which in turn leads to reduced costs. The optimal degree of self-organisation should be evaluated for each specific case study and preferences with respect to the different performance indicators using simulation.

6 Conclusions and Further Research

This research defines a framework to analyse different logistics control structures and tests this framework by applying it in two case studies.

The first part concerns the creation of the framework and aims to answer the following research question: “What are the factors that affect the type of control and what are their possible development directions?”.

Based on a set of interviews and brainstorming sessions, it was possible to identify the trade-offs that should be made between a completely centralised control structure and a completely decentralised one. Consequently, a 2 × 2 matrix was created, with the axes decision-level and information-level and with the two possible directions of global and local (as shown in Fig. 2). The results are four logistics control structures, each corresponding to one quarter of the matrix: central logistics organisation with one large control tower, central logistics organisation with several smaller control towers, decentral logistics organisation with global data and decentral logistics organisation with local data.

The second part concerns the simulation analysis of two case studies, to test the framework and to answer the following research question: "What is the effect of different control structures and under which circumstances and for which type of logistics chain, is each logistics control structure most suitable?".

Simulation models were developed for the case of dry bulk inland shipping for NPRC and the case of container hinterland transport for CTT. For the case study of dry bulk inland shipping, three different scenarios were simulated, one with a centralised control structure and two with a decentralised control structure. For the case study of container hinterland transport, seven scenarios were simulated, each with an increased level of self-organisation. By comparing the performance indicators of each scenario and taking into account the real world characteristics of the case studies it was possible to identify the most suitable control structure for each of the case studies and therefore answer the second research question.

Both case studies show that self-organisation can be successfully implemented for the logistics operations in the simulation models. Applying self-organisation in real world dynamics requires an approach that can handle undesired outcomes at system level (e.g. an escalation mechanism). In current centrally-organised logistics, this is generally resolved by human flexibility.

The case study of dry bulk inland shipping has a stable and predictable flow of goods, it is well organised and there is the need for a high security of supply at the consumption locations. Simulation results show that a decentral organisation leads to a decrease on performance levels, such as the stability of stock levels. Consequently, a central control structure is more suitable. With respect to the matrix in Fig. 2, this case study should be positioned in the top-left section, with global-level decisions and globally shared information. A self-organising logistics control structure is advised only in the case that the benefits outbalance the decrease in system performances, or when a control tower approach with globally-available information is not achievable.

The case study of container hinterland transport by road is defined by a flexible chain, in which minimal data is exchanged and a high responsiveness is required due to the dynamic circumstances. Simulation results show that performances can be improved if a self-organising control structure is introduced. The main benefit lies in the possibility of decision overruling, which represents a very flexible way of planning. For these reasons, a decentralised control structure is more suitable. With respect to the matrices in Fig. 1 and Fig. 2, this case study should be positioned in the bottom-right section, within local-level decisions and locally shared information.

Choosing a feasible logistics control structure is not a choice between two extremes (central and decentral), but rather identifying a point on the scale between central and decentral such that a specific control structure best suits the different interests and needs of the parties involved. In this context, more research is needed to find the balance between a centralised and decentralised control structure. On a general term, more practical use cases are required to study the effects of different control structures on the performances of a logistics chain, and to understand how to implement a new control structure in practice.

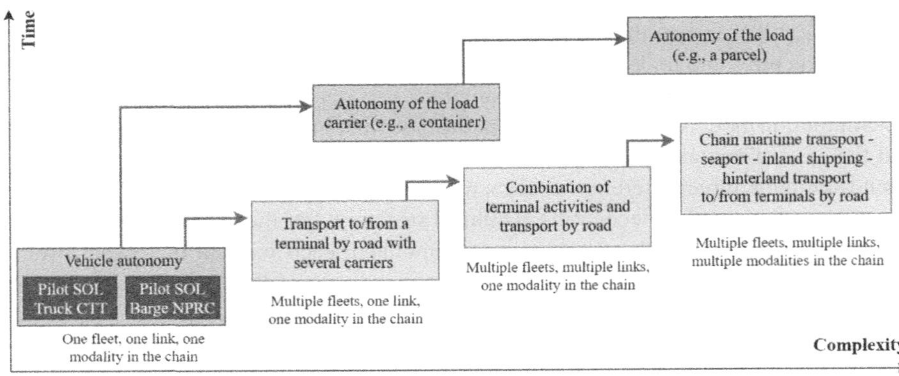

Fig. 3. Vision for further research on self-organisation.

The current research can be enriched in two ways, as displayed in Fig. 3. On one hand, future studies should focus on placing higher intelligence in a lower level of the chain (blue development in Fig. 3), such as assigning autonomy at a load carrier level (e.g., a container) or even at a load level (e.g., a parcel). On the other hand, the focus should be on extending the scope of the logistics chain (red development in Fig. 3), going from a configuration with one fleet, one link in the logistics chain and one modality (like in the NPRC and CTT case studies), to a configuration with multiple fleets, links and modalities in the logistics chain.

References

1. Quak, H., Van Kempen, E., Hopman, M.: Moving towards practical implementation of self-organizing logistics–making small steps in realizing the PI vision by raising awareness. In: Proceedings of the 5th Physical Internet Conference (2018)
2. Bartholdi, J.J., Eisenstein, D.D., Lim, Y.F.: Self-organizing logistics systems. Annu. Rev. Control **34**(1), 111–117 (2010)
3. Solanki, M., Daniele, L., Brewster, C.: Enabling self organising logistics on the web of things. In: Workshop on the Web of Things: Enablers and Services for an Open Web of Devices, Berlin (2014)
4. Jedermann, R., et al.: Transport scenario for the intelligent container. In: Hülsmann, M., Windt, K. (eds.) Understanding Autonomous Cooperation and Control in Logistics, pp. 393–404. Springer, Heidelberg (2007). https://doi.org/10.1007/978-3-540-47450-0_25

5. Wycisk, C., McKelvey, B., Hülsmann, M.: "Smart parts" supply networks as complex adaptive systems: analysis and implications. Int. J. Phys. Distrib. Logist. Manag. **38**(2), 108–125 (2008)
6. Pan, S., Trentesaux, D., Sallez, Y.: Specifying self-organising logistics system: openness, intelligence, and decentralised control. In: Borangiu, T., Trentesaux, D., Thomas, A., Leitão, P., Barata Oliveira, J. (eds.) Service Orientation in Holonic and Multi-Agent Manufacturing. SCI, vol. 694, pp. 93–102. Springer, Cham (2017). https://doi.org/10.1007/978-3-319-51100-9_9
7. Feng, F., Pang, Y., Lodewijks, G., Li, W.: Collaborative framework of an intelligent agent system for efficient logistics transport planning. Comput. Ind. Eng. **112**, 551–567 (2017)
8. De Bruin, D.: Self-organizing logistics in container hinterland planning, Twente: University of Twente (2020)
9. Mes, M., van der Heijden, M., van Harten, A.: Comparison of agent-based scheduling to look-ahead heuristics for real-time transportation problems. Eur. J. Oper. Res. **181**(1), 59–75 (2007)
10. Hopman, M., van Meijeren, J.: Logistieke aansturingsvormen van centraal tot decentraal. TNO, Den Haag (2020)
11. Fransen, R., Hopman, M.: SOLport praktijkcasus - aansturing logistieke keten droge bulk via de binnenvaart. TNO, Den Haag (2020)

Risk-Aware Procurement Optimization in a Global Technology Supply Chain

Jonathan Chase, Jingfeng Yang, and Hoong Chuin Lau(✉)

School of Computing and Information Systems, Singapore Management University, 80 Stamford Rd, Singapore 178902, Singapore
{jdchase,hclau}@smu.edu.sg, jfyang.2018@phdcs.smu.edu.sg

Abstract. Supply chain disruption, from 'Black Swan' events like the COVID-19 pandemic or the Russian invasion of Ukraine, to more ordinary issues such as labour disputes and adverse weather conditions, can result in delays, missed orders, and financial loss for companies that deliver products globally. Developing a risk-tolerant procurement strategy that anticipates the logistical problems incurred by disruption involves both accurate quantification of risk and cost-effective decision-making. We develop a supplier-focused risk evaluation metric that constrains a procurement optimization model for a global technology company. Our solution offers practical risk tolerance and cost-effectiveness, accounting for a range of constraints that realistically reflect the way the company's procurement planners operate.

Keywords: Supply chain · Risk analysis · Procurement optimization

1 Introduction

The COVID-19 pandemic has revealed vulnerabilities in global supply chains, creating supply, demand, and logistics challenges that required immediate action, forcing supply chain executives to re-chart their courses. Other recent headline-grabbing supply chain challenges include the blocking of the Suez Canal by the Ever Given, and the Russian invasion of Ukraine, a significant producer of the world's food supply. However, while these 'Black Swan' scenarios attract global attention, supply chains must also deal with more ordinary, but also more frequent disruptions, such as natural disasters, labour disputes, tax policy changes, and transport disruptions. Supply chain resilience is a company's ability to navigate unexpected supply chain disruptions with its existing capabilities. In other words, supply chain resilience is the ability to react to problems and recover from them without significant impact on operations and customer timelines. Most of the short-term tactics to mitigate disruption involve reallocating production lines to other products, re-balancing workforce, shutting down production, and finding alternative logistics models and suppliers. Large companies can employ dedicated teams to handle this workload, therefore in this paper, we develop a

J. de Armas et al. (Eds.): ICCL 2022, LNCS 13557, pp. 382–396, 2022.
https://doi.org/10.1007/978-3-031-16579-5_26

medium-term procurement optimization method to provide a risk-robust procurement strategy that reduces the burden on short-term emergency response teams. Since supply chain disruption data can be challenging to acquire from third-party vendors, with the impact of a disruption event being difficult to accurately quantify, we develop a risk evaluation metric that assigns a risk score to suppliers based on multiple risk categories that allows direct optimization without the need to generate disruption scenarios from inadequate data.

The contributions of this paper are as follows. First, we develop a supplier risk score metric from multiple sources, performing factor analysis to identify key risk factors that lead to supply chain disruption. Second, based on the risk scores, we formulate a risk-constrained optimization model that generates a parts procurement strategy for a global computer manufacturing firm. We then compare our optimization model against a baseline greedy approach, and evaluate the cost-effectiveness of our plan against historical procurement data obtained from the procurement department.

2 Literature Review

A critical review on supply chain risk has been conducted in [5], which reviewed existing approaches for quantitative supply chain risk management by setting the focus on the definition of supply chain risk and related concepts. An end-to-end supply chain risk management process (SCRMP) was proposed in [10] for managers to assess and manage risks in supply chains. The structured approach can be divided into the phases of risk identification, measurement, and assessment; risk evaluation; and mitigation and contingency plans. For supply chain risk assessment, [1] proposed a fuzzy-based integrated framework. It first identifies risks based on an expert's knowledge, historical data, and supply chain structure. Then the proposed fuzzy inference system is used to calculate the aggregated total risk score, considering the risk management parameters and risk predictability. [4] carried out a case study for supplier risk assessment based on expert rating and supplier clustering. 72 existing suppliers were evaluated and clustered into 3 different clusters, and each cluster had 17 risk criteria with scores to help decision makers select the best suppliers. A graph-based model is proposed in [9] to measure the structural redundancy for supply chain resilience. The approach focuses on the resilience of the supply chain network against disruptions. Critical supply chain components are identified and the percentage of plants disrupted is calculated in their real-world case. Recently, supply chain risk management (SCRM) with artificial intelligence is also emerging. [2] provided a comprehensive review of supply chain literature that addresses problems relevant to SCRM using approaches that fall within the AI spectrum.

Optimization methods have been applied to a range of supply chain and logistics problems, mitigating risk and accounting for uncertainty. The classic Newsvendor Problem [7] makes advance purchasing decisions in the face of demand uncertainty, while supply chain disruption can be addressed using a portfolio approach that uses multiple time periods to estimate the impact of delay on the delivery time of an order [8]. For problems where the impact of disruption can be accurately quantified, it is appropriate to employ stochastic optimization to account for uncertainty, typically solved deterministically for multiple generated scenarios [6]. However, where available data does not permit the accurate realization of scenarios to optimize on, methods that draw directly on risk to constrain the scope of optimization can be employed, either introducing risk minimization as a joint objective with cost minimization, or through risk as a constraint on a cost minimization problem [3]. It is this last case that is the most appropriate for the technology company use case in this work.

3 Problem Description

In this paper we consider a global technology company that supplies a wide range of computer products encompassing both software and hardware for both consumers and businesses. To provide hardware solutions, such as enterprise-level servers, parts are obtained from a range of third-party suppliers, and then assembled according to customer orders. Contracts are arranged with each supplier on a long-term basis, with part procurement decisions taken for the medium term (3–6 months). In the event of supply disruption, a dedicated team is responsible for meeting demand from any sources available, with the goal of this work being to generate a risk-aware medium term procurement plan that reduces the burden on the disruption-response team. Parts supplied to the company may belong to 'Alternative Parts Groups' (APGs), where member parts in the group may be substituted for each other based on similar technical specifications in order to satisfy demand. Suppliers may optinally specify minimum purchase levels and rebate schemes in their contracts, where exceeding a threshold quantity of eligible parts purchased triggers a percentage discount on purchased parts. Since suppliers may not charge identical prices for the parts in an APG, and have varying risk levels, an effective risk-tolerant procurement strategy should balance cost, rebates, and risk.

It can be challenging to quantify risk in the real world, as many methods, particularly those employing machine learning, require a large quantity of consistent and accurate data on past disruptions, which may be difficult or time-consuming to obtain. To overcome this challenge, we develop a risk-score metric for each supplier, identifying a range of risk categories and formulating a representative score. These scores provide input to our risk-constrained optimization model that recommends a procurement strategy which minimizes the net cost of meeting part demand while not exceeding a chosen risk tolerance.

4 Supplier Risk Analysis

In this section, we present our risk analysis model. The technology company has several important products that need to be evaluated for risk. Our goal is to develop an automated resiliency metric, which is represented by a risk score from 0 to 10 (low to high), for the suppliers that deliver parts critical to products where supply chain risk is an essential consideration. Supply risk is a multidimensional concept that encompasses various risk factors such as supplier failure, disruption/loss of a supplier, non-suitable essential parts, late deliveries, and disruption due to catastrophic events. We decompose the risk analysis into the following five steps, as depicted in Fig. 1: (1) examine which risk categories must be addressed for each product, as well as which risk criteria must be evaluated within each broad risk category; (2) based on the selected risk criteria, collect related data from both internal and external (third-party companies) sources for analysis; (3) reduce the dimensionality of selected risk criteria, focusing on the most important factors; (4) calculate the risk score for each supplier; and finally, (5) dynamically update the risk score calculation method with feedback from suppliers.

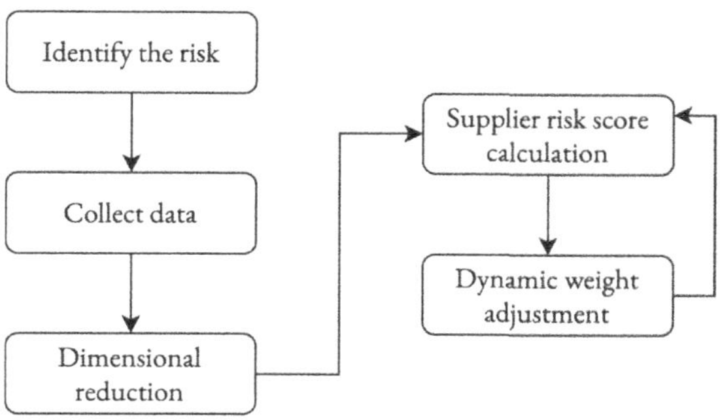

Fig. 1. Framework for risk analysis model

4.1 Risk Criteria Identification

First, we identify which criteria are appropriate for the risk assessment from the supplier perspective. Through literature review and detailed discussion with supply chain experts in our company, we produced a set of risk evaluation categories. The initial round of analysis identifies 12 different risk categories, such as socio-political, manufacturing, or financial, risks, which are then reduced to 6 in the second round of discussion. Finally, 13 risk criteria are chosen for further consideration in our supplier risk assessment.

4.2 Supplier Risk Score Calculation

Following the selection of risk criteria, the next step is to collect relevant data for each criterion from both internal and external third-party sources. The following data types were obtained from internal and external databases:

- Internal data: product information, market condition, supply business leverage data, financial data;

- External data: macroeconomic data (Economist database), socio-political data and rational data (e.g., geopolitical, legal), manufacturing and catastrophic data (Resilinc database);

Each of the criteria has a numerical value from 0 to 10 (after normalization) that represents the criterion's risk score (the higher the value, the greater the risk). Figure 2 shows an example of the data used to calculate the supply risk score. The first three columns contain supplier information, such as name, country, and city. The fourth column indicates whether or not the vendor is a subcontractor. The risk score data for selected criteria is contained in the remaining columns.

SUPPLIER	COUNTRY	CITY	SUBCONTRACTOR	CREDIT	RECOVERY	SOURCING	GEOPOLITICAL	MACROECONOMIC	RESILIENCY	...	POLITICAL
A	CHINA	ZHONGSHAN	0	1.00	1.00	8.00	6.00	3.00	3.00	...	5.00
B	CHINA	DONGGUAN	0	2.00	2.00	7.00	6.00	3.00	4.00	...	5.00
C	THAILAND	CHONBURI	0	5.00	1.00	6.00	6.00	4.00	4.00	...	6.00
D	CHINA	WUXI	1	3.00	10.00	9.00	6.00	3.00	6.00	...	5.00
E	SINGAPORE	SINGAPORE	0	0.00	5.00	9.00	6.00	3.00	5.00	...	2.00

Fig. 2. Sample of data collected for the calculation of supplier risk score

The final step in calculating supplier risk is to aggregate all of the risk score data into a single total. We utilize the weighted sum approach to determine the final risk score here because of the method's interpretability. We first introduce the notations for risk score calculation as follows:

- r_i: risk score for supplier i;
- w_i: weight assigned for criterion c_i;
- c_i: risk criterion i.

We then use a weighted sum to calculate the final risk score:

$$r_i = w_1 \cdot c_1 + w_2 \cdot c_2 + \cdots + w_n \cdot c_n \tag{1}$$

There may be a strong inter-correlation between each risk criterion, and the risk data with 19 criteria is too large and difficult to understand and manage. Hence we use a factor analysis to examine the relationships between these criteria and group them into a small number of factors, which is a common data dimension reduction technique. Factor analysis also allows us to discover intrinsic links and better comprehend the data.

4.3 Factor Analysis

In this part, we take the product anonymized as "A0001" in our company, which is a high-performance computer, as an example, and examine the correlation between different risk criteria using the risk data obtained. Figure 3 depicts the relationship between various risk criteria. The correlation coefficient ranges from

−1 to +1, and the closer the value is to +1, the higher is the positive linear relationship between the variables. It can be seen, for example, that the corruption perception index has high correlations with other risk criteria, such as infrastructure risk, labour market risk, tax policy risk, financial risk, foreign trade, payments risk and so on.

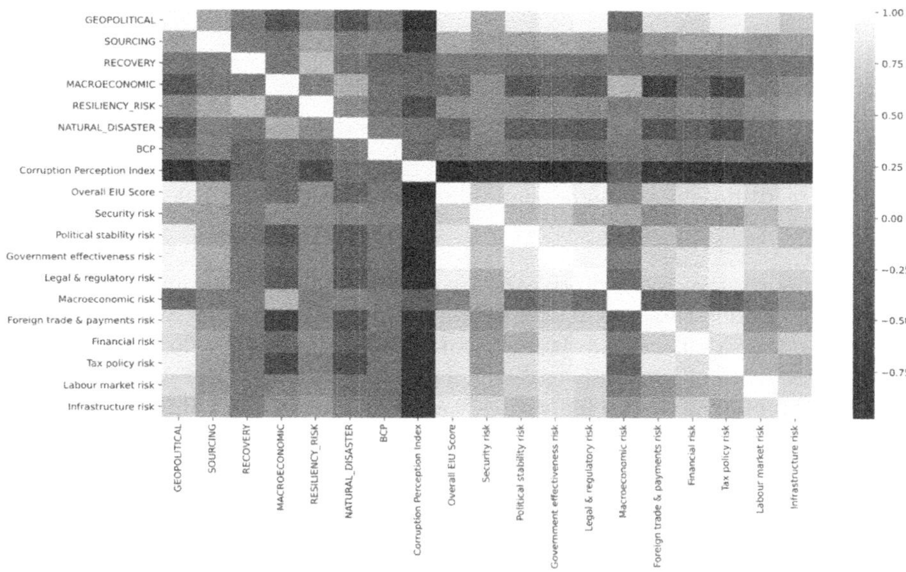

Fig. 3. Correlation matrix of 19 risk criteria for enterprise server product

The results of the factor analysis is shown in Fig. 4a. When conducting a factor analysis, it is frequently necessary to determine how many component variables to keep. Here, we determine the number of factors based on Kaiser Criterion that proposes to extract factors with an eigenvalue greater than 1. The eigenvalue in factor analysis is a measure of how much of the observed variables' common variance is explained by a factor. The larger the eigenvalue is, the more variance the factor can explain than a single variable (risk criterion). Based on this, we select four factors for the supplier risk data. The factor loading of a variable quantifies the extent to which the variable is related to a given factor. It finds most of the risk criteria can be included in factor 1, while the business continuity planning (BCP) risk can be treated as an independent factor.

4.4 Score Calculation

We calculate risk scores for each supplier using the processed risk data from factor analysis. Through extensive brainstorm meetings with experts from different departments in the company (e.g., financial, supply chain, procurement, and so

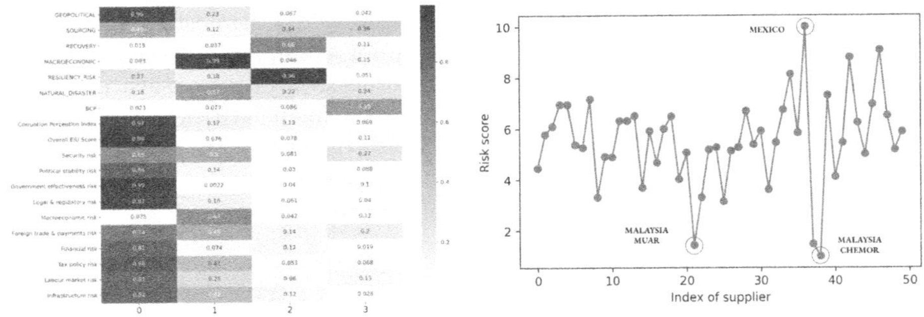

(a) Results of the factor analysis

(b) Supplier risk score

Fig. 4. Results for factor analysis and supplier risk score calculation

on), all quantitative risk criteria are rated as of low, medium and high importance. The higher the importance of the risk criteria, the greater the weight assigned in the calculation of the risk score. Using product "A0001" as an example, the risk score of 50 suppliers is calculated and displayed in Fig. 4b. We highlight the supplier with the highest risk score in Mexico and the two suppliers with the lowest risk in Malaysia.

5 Risk-Aware Supply Chain Optimization

In our problem, the procurement planner needs to make purchasing plans on computer parts that are subsequently assembled into products for end users such as desktop computers and rack mount servers. Some parts are cheap and required in large quantities while others are expensive specialized components that have high cost but low demand quantity. Internally, parts obtained from suppliers are given a part number (PN) with each PN obtainable from a single supplier. To enable choice among a selection of suppliers, parts may be grouped into APGs, defined by equivalent specifications. For example, consider a range of storage components, different brand hard disks with the same capacity and RPM values may be grouped into an APG. The demand for parts is defined by APG, although parts are purchased by PN from suppliers.

Since contracts with suppliers are typically agreed on a long term basis, our goal is not to recommend suppliers, but uses an established list of contracted suppliers to recommend a default risk-aware part procurement strategy. In addition to the per-part cost of suppliers, two additional factors must be considered. Firstly, suppliers may offer rebates on some of the parts they sell in the form of either a percentage discount or as a per-part discount, if a target quantity of eligible parts is purchased. Since either a percentage discount or a per-part discount can each be expressed in terms of each other, we only implement the percentage discount, and express the per-part discount contracts in terms of percentages. Incentives are not typically agreed for a single part but across all parts ordered from a supplier matching a particular technical specification and importance in the supply chain. Since APGs are an internal concept and apply across suppliers, it cannot be assumed that there will be a convenient correspondence between APG membership and rebate eligibility. Secondly, in order to maintain a good relationship with each supplier, a minimum purchase level per supplier should be achieved, such that a percentage of the demand for each APG is allocated to each supplier that offers parts in that APG.

The notation used in the optimization methods introduced in this section is given in Table 1.

Table 1. Key notations used in optimization solutions.

Indices	
i	Supplier index from set $\mathcal{I}$
j	Part index from set $\mathcal{J}$
k	Alternative Parts Group set index from set $\mathcal{K}$ Each k is a set of parts, $j \subset \mathcal{J}$
l	Incentive index from set $\mathcal{L}$. Each l is uniquely linked to 1 supplier i. Each l is a set of parts, $j \subset \mathcal{J}$
Decision variables	
$y_{i,j}$	Number of part j obtained from i,
$z_{i,j}$	Binary variable indicating if the incentive threshold is crossed for supplier i and for part j
$\zeta_{i,l}$	Variable indicating the number of part j qualifying for rebate
Parameters	
r_i	Risk score of supplier i, normalized to $[0, 1]$
ψ, ψ_j	Risk tolerance level for whole system and for part j individually
$c_{i,j}$	Per-part cost of obtaining j from i
$\theta_{i,j}$	Minimum purchase threshold imposed by supplier i for part j which becomes 0 if disrupted under scenario s
$\lambda_{i,l}$	Incentive threshold for supplier i for scheme l
$\mu_{i,j}$	Rebate percentage if incentive threshold is crossed for i on part j
d_k	Demand for part group k
$\gamma_{i,j}$	Capacity for supplier i, part j

5.1 'Bang for Buck' (B4B) Baseline

The first method to consider is a simple ranking-based approach that does not use scenarios, where suppliers are ordered by their risk score, and, once any minimum order requirements have been satisfied, parts are allocated with priority to the lower risk suppliers, meeting incentive thresholds until all demand has been met. If demand remains after incentives have been satisfied, a default allocation increment should be set, to allocate remaining demand incrementally to each supplier in turn. The best value for the default increment would be a subject for experimentation. The resulting solution will generate two values: the cost of the solution, and the risk score of the solution. The method of calculating overall risk score can be left open for further development, but a reasonable metric would be to express the risk as a percentage or probability in the range [0, 1] of all supplier risk scores, normalised to the [0, 1] range, multiplied by the proportion of all required parts obtained from them, as shown in (2). These two output values will provide a basis for comparison with other methods. The usable output of the method is a default allocation strategy in terms of the numbers of parts that should normally be ordered from suppliers.

$$risk = \sum_i \sum_j r_i \cdot \frac{y_{i,j}}{\sum_j d_j} \tag{2}$$

The algorithm is as follows:

1. Sort the list of suppliers in ascending order of risk score.
2. Allocate parts to buy from each supplier with minimum spend agreement, enough to satisfy the minimum. If there is still unsatisfied part demand, continue.
3. Going through the supplier list in order: if any have rebate incentives, satisfy them. If at any point the total demand is satisfied, end the algorithm. If the end of the list is reached with remaining demand, continue. Given that multiple parts can be part of an incentive scheme, move to the next supplier as soon as the incentive scheme is satisfied.
4. If unsatisfied demand for an APG remains, the leftovers can be distributed among the suppliers with parts in that APG in increments, with priority given to the suppliers with lower risk scores.

5.2 Risk-Constrained Optimization (RCO) Model

Risk-Constrained Optimization (RCO) is a methodology developed in engineering design to optimize performance while remaining within key safety limits [3]. A typical formulation maximizes or minimizes a quantity while ensuring that the probability of failure for a given plan remains below a chosen safety threshold. Thus, rather than considering the cost of failure and trading the cost off with the potential benefits of a plan, failure is a hard constraint to be avoided. We can employ an analogous idea in a the context of this supply chain problem, where, instead of considering the probability of a disruption in the supply chain, we set a limit on the total risk permitted in the system using the risk score in (2).

Our risk-constrained approach needs to account for the features required by our company, namely APGs, rebates, and minimum purchase requirements. The formulate the following set of rules for the optimization to enforce:

- The cost of the allocation is the total cost of buying the required parts from the suppliers at their per-part cost, offset by any rebates that are activated.

- Any minimum spend requirements with suppliers must be met (in this case, this is as a percentage of the demand for each APG that the supplier offers parts for).
- If the number of parts that are part of a rebate scheme with a supplier exceeds the incentive threshold quantity, a percentage rebate is applied to offset the total cost of those parts.
- There are no reductions to capacity or increases in cost due to disruption events, so the total demand for parts must be met. Since parts are members of Alternate Part Groups (APGs), demand satisfaction is counted for the total demand for each part group.
- The risk score for the allocation cannot exceed a set threshold.

$$\min \sum_i \sum_j \left(y_{i,j} c_{i,j} - \mu_{i,j} c_{i,j} z_{i,j} \right) \tag{3}$$

$$\sum_{j \in k} y_{i,j} \geq \theta_{i,k} \quad \forall i, k \tag{4}$$

$$\lambda_{i,l} \zeta_{i,l} \leq \sum_{j \in l} y_{i,j} \quad \forall i, l \tag{5}$$

$$z_{i,j} \leq \gamma_{i,j} \zeta_{i,l} \quad \forall i, l, j \in l \tag{6}$$

$$z_{i,j} \leq y_{i,j} \quad \forall i, j \tag{7}$$

$$\sum_i \sum_{j \in k} y_{i,j} \geq d_k \quad \forall k \tag{8}$$

$$\sum_i \sum_j r_i \frac{y_{i,j}}{\sum_j d_j} \leq \psi \tag{9}$$

$$\sum_i r_i \frac{y_{i,j}}{d_j} \leq \psi_j \tag{10}$$

Equation (3) is the objective we want to minimize, combining the per-part cost with any rebate offset. Equation (4) enforces the minimum purchase requirement for the parts in each APG offered by a supplier. (5)–(7) determine if the threshold required to activate a rebate on a particular part has been crossed and therefore the amount of parts that are discounted. (8) ensures that the demand for each APG is satisfied. (9) and (10) ensure that the risk tolerance threshold is not crossed for either the whole problem, or per-part if there are critical individual parts for which the user wishes to specify a particular risk tolerance level.

5.3 Numerical Results

For the purpose of verifying our model, we constructed a number of test cases from anonymized data provided by the company's procurement department. We present results of cases with single APGs, and then for a full dataset over various 3-month periods. Both the B4B and RCO methods were implemented in

Python 3.9, with the optimization solution generated using the CPLEX library, on a desktop computer powered by an Intel Core i7 3.40 GHz with 16 GB RAM.

Comparison Against Baseline. We first evaluate the performance of the B4B baseline method by generating results for a single APG with 3 suppliers, each offering a single compatible part model. The price and risk parameters for each supplier are given in Table 2, with a total demand for the part of 208, and minimum purchase requirement of 10% of demand per supplier. In Fig. 6a we plot the B4B and generate cost values obtained by our risk-aware model with varying risk constraints to serve as a Pareto Front, with the Balance Point indicating the optimal cost obtainable for the risk of the B4B solution. The vertical gap indicates the cost saving achievable at that risk level. As expected, our risk-aware model is able to achieve a considerably better cost performance against the B4B method across all risk levels. Given the superior performance of the RCO, we focus on attempting to outperform the cost totals for historical data in the following results.

Table 2. Parameters used for performance analysis against baseline.

Supplier	Price	Risk
0110	142.558	0.37
0106	155.867	0.15
0107	120.913	0.48

Single APG Results. To verify the correctness of the behaviour of our optimization model, four APGs were considered independently as illustrated in Fig. 5. For each APG, there was a choice of supplier, each offering a different part. The APGs were chosen to highlight two purchasing dynamics - in 'Scenario 1', one supplier offered a lower price, while the other offered a lower risk, while in 'Scenario 2', the supplier with the lower price also offered lower risk. In Scenario 2, there is a clear preference for one supplier over the other, but when the rebate schemes were introduced, for some APGs, the dynamics changed.

For APG 26, the introduction of a rebate transformed the scenario from a trade-off between price and risk into a straightforward preference for one supplier over the other, with only the minimum required allocation of 10% being given to the other supplier. APG 1 gave the reverse behaviour, with a fixed optimal decision without rebate, but when rebates were made available, the allocation changed as illustrated in Fig. 6b, as the risk constraint changed.

For APG 8, the solution was stable and remained stable with rebates, as expected, while the opposite was the case for APG 35. However, for APG 35, the exact minimum point for the scenario with rebate changed because at looser risk tolerances, rather than choosing the minimum value of the costlier part, our optimization model chooses to buy a slightly higher quantity in order to cross the rebate threshold, resulting in a solution with a lower net cost, than choosing the minimum value and buying the remaining demand from the cheaper part, as shown in Fig. 7.

Price vs Risk:
Scenario 1: Lower Price-High Risk vs Higher Price-Lower Risk
Scenario 2: Lower Price-Lower Risk vs Higher Price-Higher Risk

	APG	PNs	Supplier Risk	Price w/o Rebate	Price with Rebate
Scenario 1 → Scenario 2	APG 26	Supplier 11: PN 67	5.52	**120.75**	112.75
		Supplier 8: PN 75	**5.56**	119.57	**113.59**
Scenario 2 → Scenario 1	APG 1	Supplier 8: PN 56	5.56	99.5	**94.53**
		Supplier 10: PN 64	**6.23**	**101.9**	93.75
Scenario 1 → unchanged	APG 35	Supplier 11: PN 44	5.52	**214.06**	**201.06**
		Supplier 8: PN 77	**5.56**	168.16	159.75
Scenario 2 → unchanged	APG 8	Supplier 11: PN 54	5.52	235	215
		Supplier 8: PN 79	**5.56**	**236.42**	**224.60**

Fig. 5. Single APG test cases with purchasing dynamics changing as rebate becomes available.

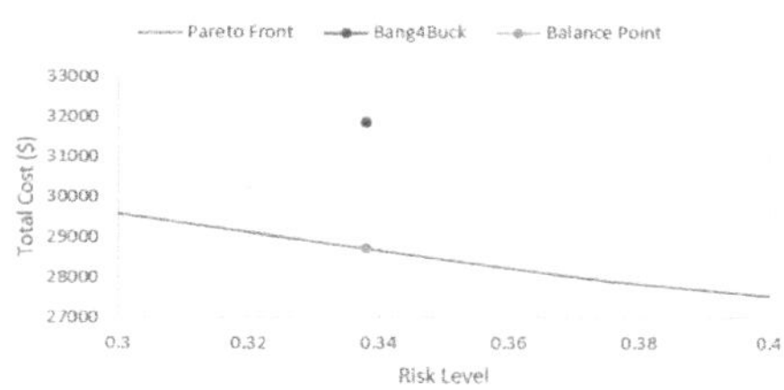

(a) Pareto Front showing the optimal trade-off between risk and cost for a single part, with the B4B result plotted for comparison.

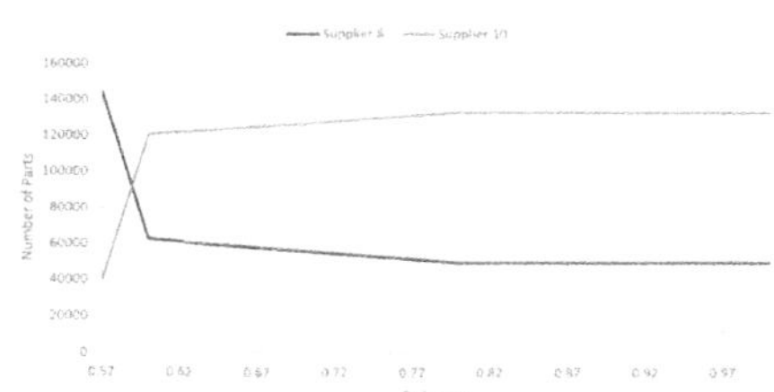

(b) Cost-Risk trade-off for APG 1 when rebates are available.

Fig. 6. Results to verify correctness of RCO, impact of rebates, and performance against the baseline.

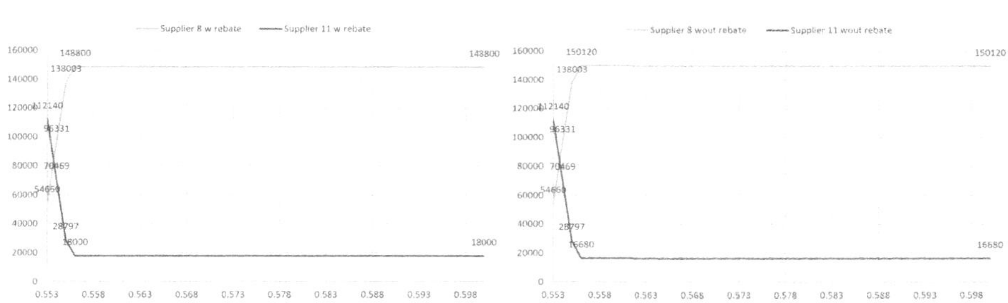

Fig. 7. Cost-risk trade-off for APG 35 with rebate (left) and without rebate (right). For the case with rebate, the lowest value for the costlier part is chosen to be the rebate threshold, as the net cost proves lower than buying the minimum undiscounted part.

These results indicate that when there is a choice of two different parts available to satisfy the demand, the model is able to find solutions that are not immediately obvious to a human observer, but which prove more cost-effective overall. However, since incentive schemes can be satisfied by parts bought from multiple APGs, these examples do not reflect the complexities of actual procurement.

Full Dataset Results. We considered a 3-month period from Jan-Mar 2021, comparing the quantity of parts purchased and the net cost of our optimization model against historical data. We chose a 3-month period, as the threshold number of parts required to trigger a rebate in the provided data was determined by the total quantity purchased in 3 months. Parts with no membership in either an APG nor contributing to a rebate scheme were discarded from both datasets, as they involved no decision-making. The dataset for this 3-month period featured 5 suppliers and 78 PNs after unnecessary parts had been removed. 3 suppliers had incentive schemes, of which 2 were triggered in the historical data. The optimization was able to trigger all 3 while satisfying demand, ultimately purchasing a slightly higher number of parts in order to achieve a lower net cost overall (4.3% cost reduction). Since additional parts could be added to inventory, this should not be a significant concern for the supply chain. Further, as shown in Fig. 8, even a version of the optimization without access to rebates was able to achieve a slightly better cost performance, indicating that more cost-effective part purchases were possible.

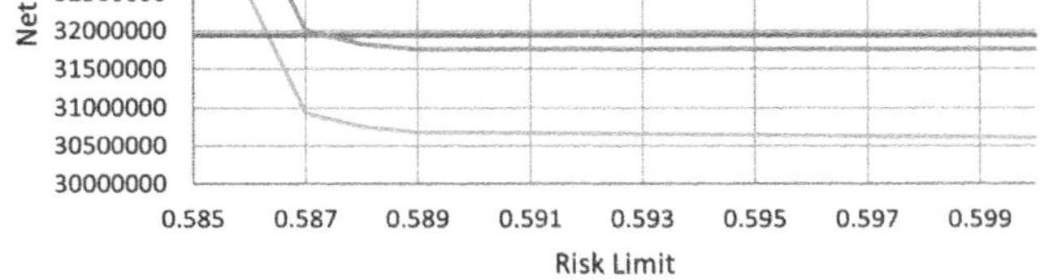

Fig. 8. Net cost values for historical and optimized data as well as optimization without rebates with changing risk tolerance.

By focusing on 3 APGs (APG 7, APG 11, and APG 15) which featured some of the largest savings, some insights are available into why the optimization is able to improve on the historical cost. For APG 7 and 11, the optimizer chooses a smaller selection of parts over the minimum required purchase, with the historical purchases selecting some parts with high cost. For APG 15, the result changes with the availability of rebates. When rebates are available, the optimizer balances the demand between two similarly priced parts, but when rebates are not available, the strictly cheaper part is heavily favoured. This adaptation to the presence of rebates illustrates why the optimization is able to achieve improved cost performance even when rebates are unavailable.

Finally we ran our optimization model on 3 other 3-month periods: April to June, June to August, and August to October. In each case, the goal was to determine whether more rebates could be activated by the optimization. For April to June, the number of parts purchased for Suppliers 8, 10, and 11, the three with rebate schemes, was sufficient to provide a rebate for all, but in the historical purchases, while the allocation to Supplier 8 doubled the rebate threshold, Supplier 10 and Supplier 11 fell short, resulting in only 1 supplier activating their rebates. For June to August, there was a similar case, but Supplier 11 was also activated with only Supplier 10 missing out. For August to October, the total allocated to the three suppliers was inadequate to trigger the rebate for all 3, but an increase from 1 activated supplier to 2 may have been possible. In fact, the optimization was able to achieve rebates on all 3 suppliers in each of the 3 periods, because, due to the consideration of APGs, purchases could be re-allocated from the 2 remaining rebateless suppliers, Supplier 4 and Supplier 7. This resulted in an allocation that was more even between the three suppliers (though still preferring Supplier 8 as in the historical data), but also assigned more parts to the 3 Suppliers and therefore gained discounts for all. The only exception to this was for the case where the risk constraint was set to the tightest limit feasible, in which case Supplier 11 was ignored as far as possible, and therefore could not achieve the rebate threshold while also satisfying the risk constraint.

From these results, we conclude that considering APGs and incentive schemes that encompass multiple parts, it is possible to take a holistic approach to procurement that results in a global cost reduction that may be challenging for planners to identify due to the scale and complexity of the possible solutions.

6 Conclusions and Further Work

Further developments of this project could pursue a number of possible avenues. The first is the research and development of quantifiable risk impact, allowing realistic scenarios to be generated, and thus a stochastic optimization scenario-based approach could be reconsidered. The second approach could be to consider additional 'risk' metrics, such as quality of parts provided. Thus an additional focus on the proportion of defective parts provided by suppliers may enrich the model beyond focusing on supply disruption type risks. Third, some of the assumptions used in the experimental part of the project could be further examined. In particular, it is assumed that for suppliers with multiple risk scores connected to different sites, the scores should be averaged to get the overall supplier risk, but this may be too simplistic to achieve the best cost-risk balance.

Finally, it is also assumed that all parts in an APG are equally viable and there is no inherent preference for one over another that may lead to a decision that is not purely cost-focused. Examining the impact of changing these assumptions will lead to different purchasing decisions. For example, changing the risk calculation to the maximum site risk rather than the average could lead to much greater variation between suppliers and therefore the allocation dynamic and range of possible risk tolerance tuning will change.

The real-world problem of risk-tolerant cost-effective part procurement is a complex one, with many factors being included in decisions that may not all be reflected in the models in this work. However, the results presented for the problems shown indicate that when correctly specified, an optimization model can find a solution that is much more mathematically explainable and scalable than those that can be derived by simple greedy methods or human planners.

References

1. Aqlan, F., Lam, S.S.: A fuzzy-based integrated framework for supply chain risk assessment. Int. J. Prod. Econ. **161**, 54–63 (2015)
2. Baryannis, G., Validi, S., Dani, S., Antoniou, G.: Supply chain risk management and artificial intelligence: state of the art and future research directions. Int. J. Prod. Res. **57**(7), 2179–2202 (2019)
3. Beck, A.T., Gomes, W.J.S., Lopez, R.H., Miguel, L.F.F.: A comparison between robust and risk-based optimization under uncertainty. Struct. Multidiscip. Optim. **52**(3), 479–492 (2015). https://doi.org/10.1007/s00158-015-1253-9
4. Er Kara, M., Oktay Fırat, S.Ü.: Supplier risk assessment based on best-worst method and k-means clustering: a case study. Sustainability **10**(4), 1066 (2018)
5. Heckmann, I., Comes, T., Nickel, S.: A critical review on supply chain risk-definition, measure and modeling. Omega **52**, 119–132 (2015)
6. Kleywegt, A.J., Shapiro, A., Homem-de Mello, T.: The sample average approximation method for stochastic discrete optimization. SIAM J. Optim. **12**(2), 479–502 (2002)
7. Mohammadivojdan, R., Merzifonluoglu, Y., Geunes, J.: Procurement portfolio planning for a newsvendor with supplier delivery uncertainty. Eur. J. Oper. Res. **297**, 917–929 (2021)
8. Sawik, T.: A portfolio approach to supply chain disruption management. Int. J. Prod. Res. **55**(7), 1970–1991 (2017)
9. Tan, W.J., Zhang, A.N., Cai, W.: A graph-based model to measure structural redundancy for supply chain resilience. Int. J. Prod. Res. **57**(20), 6385–6404 (2019)
10. Tummala, R., Schoenherr, T.: Assessing and managing risks using the supply chain risk management process (SCRMP). Supply Chain Manag.: Int. J. **16**, 474–483 (2011)

Freight Costs Versus Service Level: Optimizing the Distribution of a Materials Trader

Thomas Bömer(✉) and Anne Meyer(✉)

TU Dortmund University, 44221 Dortmund, Germany
{thomas.boemer,anne2.meyer}@tu-dortmund.de

Abstract. Constantly rising freight rates can force traders to reduce transportation costs at the expense of their service promise of next-day delivery. In this paper, we examine the potential freight costs savings for the local distribution network considering two temporal and one spatio-temporal consolidation concept: Consolidation Period, Delivery Profiles, and Area Forwarding & Milk Runs. We examine the potential savings arising from these concepts using the 2020 orders from a local distribution center of a German materials trader as a case study. We describe the problems and solution methods of these concepts both on the tactical and the operational planning levels. For the Area Forwarding & Milk Run concept we additionally introduce an effective math-heuristic to solve the instances of the case study. For all three consolidation methods significant savings can be achieved. A consolidation for two days saves 11.6 % of the freight costs. Using delivery profiles lead to cost cuts of up to 8.9 %. The transport concept selection between area forwarding and milk runs achieves a maximum reduction of freight costs of 23.8 %. These findings can be used by departments within the company—such as supply chain management, transport or sales—to assess whether freight costs savings justify the lowering of the service level.

Keywords: Delivery profiles · Milk runs · Freight costs

1 Introduction

Due to constantly rising freight costs, our project partner, a large German materials trader, searches for ways to reduce freight costs in its distribution network at the expense of service level reduction. Today, the company offers customers a next day delivery service. To this end local distribution centers and the area forwarding concept are used. If longer delivery times are accepted, consolidation is a way to counter the freight costs pressure: Temporal consolidation combines several small shipments to one individual customer into one larger shipment. Spatial consolidation combines multiple customers into one tour. The service level is mainly determined by the delivery time. Since consolidation often reduces shipment frequency and thus extends delivery times, the shipper has to trade off freight costs against service level.

J. de Armas et al. (Eds.): ICCL 2022, LNCS 13557, pp. 397–411, 2022.
https://doi.org/10.1007/978-3-031-16579-5_27

Spatial consolidation can be achieved using specific transport concepts. A typical transport concept is area forwarding: All shipments for an area are reported to a logistics service provider who plans and executes the tours. Tariffs are given in the form of a cost matrix with costs decreasing as the weight and/or distance increase. The logistics service provider is responsible for building cost-efficient tours. A less used concept is the milk run: Milk runs are regular, for example weekly, round trips to supply several customers. Milk run planning is carried out by the shipper. The calculation of the costs is based on the actual trip duration and distance. Since the cost calculation is independent of the freight weight, the risk associated with underutilized milk runs is carried by the shipper [13].

In our study, we investigate the saving potential of three consolidation concepts for frequent customers with an average frequency of at least one delivery per week. Other customers are not affected by the concepts. The first two consolidation concepts, *Consolidation Period* and *Delivery Profiles*, are purely based on temporal, while the third, *Area Forwarding & Milk Runs*, also takes spatial consolidation effects into account. We propose models for the optimization problems related to the application of each concept, including a math-heuristic algorithm for milk run planning.

To evaluate the concepts, we apply them to the order data of a one-stage local distribution network of our project partner. The dataset includes the 28,000 non-divisible shipments of around 1,400 customers from the year 2020. Currently, all next-day delivery shipments use area forwarding. Area forwarding costs are determined based on distance and shipment weight according to a degressive tariff matrix. The findings of our study prompted a cross-departmental (e.g. supply chain management, transport, and sales) discussion within the company, to assess whether lowering the freight rate savings at the expense of service-level is justified.

The outline of this paper is as follows: Sect. 2 describes the consolidation concepts and related optimization problems. Section 3 introduces related work. Section 4 presents our solution approaches. Section 5 covers the real-world case study, including the parameter settings and computational results. Section 6 concludes the findings and points out further research subjects.

2 Concepts for Balancing Service Level and Freight Costs

In this section, we introduce the three addressed consolidation concepts and the related tactical and operational decisions that need to be taken. Table 1 gives an overview of the relationship between concepts and decisions.

Consolidation Period. Consolidation Period is a temporal consolidation concept. In its simplest form, it holds back the shipments of the same customer until a defined consolidation period elapsed. The period duration can be determined separately for individual customers or globally, for all customers. The resulting larger shipments reduce freight costs of area forwarding, but lower the service level due to a longer delivery time.

Table 1. Tactical and operational decisions

Concept	Tactical decision	Operational decision
Consolidation period	Consolidation duration determination	Shipment overload
Delivery profiles	Delivery profile assignment	Shipment overload
Area forwarding & Milk runs	Transport concept selection and milk run scheduling	Milk run overload

On the tactical level, the consolidation duration has to be determined. The longer a consolidation period is, the more freight costs can be saved, but the more cuts in the service level have to be made. Additionally, the shipper has to make the operational decision of choosing which shipments should be combined if the weight of consolidated shipments of a customer exceeds the maximum shipment weight once or even multiple times.

Delivery Profiles. Delivery Profiles is also a temporal consolidation concept. It assigns customer shipments to fixed weekdays. For example, a customer with a shipment frequency of two shipments per week is assigned to a profile with shipments on Monday and Wednesday. Demand on days without shipments is shifted to the previous shipment day. This leads to larger and thus cheaper shipments for an area forwarding tariff. In the Delivery Profile concept, profiles can be assigned to customers based on their historic shipment frequency. Therefore, the service level adaptation is more compatible with high-frequency customers. For example, a customer with a historic frequency of four shipments per week still receives a maximum of four shipments per week, but on fixed weekdays. Delivery profiles make the shipment process easier to plan for the customer and shipper. The customer can prepare the necessary equipment or staff for the unloading process. The shipper can assign the profiles in such a way that the distribution center workload is leveled over the weekdays. However, to achieve a balanced distribution, low variability in demand and shipment frequency is beneficial.

Similar to the concept of Consolidation Period, the shipper has to make the operational decision with respect to which shipments should be combined if the weight of consolidated shipments of a customer exceeds the maximum shipment weight once or multiple times.

Area Forwarding & Milk Runs. Area Forwarding & Milk Runs is a spatio-temporal consolidation concept in which some customers are supplied through milk runs. Customers that are not assigned to a milk run are serviced as per the area forwarding concept. Milk runs apply delivery profiles in combination with periodic round trips to supply fixed customers. For example, a milk run is performed every Monday and Wednesday including customers X, Y and Z. Tariffs for milk runs are based on tour distance and duration. Hence, the price for the tour is fixed and unrelated to the weight of the shipments. Due to this tariff, which differs from area forwarding tariffs, the shipper can obtain additional savings compared to Delivery Profiles. However, if the milk runs are underutilized, the shipper has a higher risk of cost than in a pure area forwarding network. The effects on the service level are comparable to those of delivery profiles.

The optimization problem on a tactical level is to make a transport concept selection between area forwarding and milk runs for each customer and to schedule the milk runs over the week while respecting tour duration and capacity restrictions. The problem is introduced as the *Transport Concept Selection and Milk Run Scheduling Problem* (TC-MRS) in [10]. Variations in demand can cause milk run overload situations in which the shipments of customers in a milk run exceed the milk run vehicle weight capacity. Hence, on the operational level, a decision needs to be made regarding which shipments should be transported via milk run and which should be carried out via area forwarding.

3 Related Work

In this section, we introduce the current work addressing the tactical decisions considered in this paper.

Consolidation Duration Determination. Three main temporal consolidation policies can be distinguished (see e.g. [1,6]), namely the quantity, time and hybrid policies. The quantity policy holds back the shipment until a weight threshold Q is reached. The time policy dispatches a shipment every T periods. T either starts immediately after the last shipment or with the costumers first demand. A combination of the prior policies is the hybrid policy: Shipments are released after a weight threshold is accumulated or a defined number of periods are passed.

For the determination of the parameters Q and T, a balance between storage costs and freight costs must be found. T_{max} is often necessary to guarantee a maximum delivery time. According to [6] the parameter selection for Q and T is to a large extent a management decision.

Only very few real-world studies reporting savings can be found in literature. Bookbinder and Higginson [1] investigate the use-case of a fiber glass producer and show that the consolidation of daily to weekly shipments can reduce 23% of freight costs. In [2] the quantity policy saves 0.66% to 25.79% on artificial instances.

Delivery Profile Assignment. In [8] the assignment of delivery profiles in combination with a transport concept selection between direct transport and area forwarding for a multi-level logistics network is investigated. A heuristic is used as an initial solution for an integer optimization model. Transport concept selection and delivery profiles together achieve savings up to 59% for a real-world dataset. The value for delivery profiles only is slightly lower.

The authors of [14] also pursue the goal of minimizing warehousing and freight costs in a two-stage inbound logistics network by using area forwarding in conjunction with delivery profiles. A preprocessing algorithm calculates inventory holding and capital commitment costs for each supplier. Thereafter, an initial heuristic solution is improved using an integer optimization model. On average savings of 17% with a maximum of 36% can be reached for a case study of a German truck manufacturer. In [15] the approach of [14] is enhanced with the aim to achieve better robustness against demand uncertainty. Compared to the deterministic approach in [14], the new approach increases savings by an additional 2.98% points.

Meyer et al. [11] propose a two-stage approach for assigning delivery profiles to customers in a two-stage long-haul truck network. First, all suppliers determine their frequency by solving a dynamic lot size model. In a second model, suppliers are assigned to delivery profiles, such that the total transport quantities over the weekdays are leveled out. In their case study, the number of tours was reduced by 7% compared to a random profile assignment.

In [5] a model for assigning delivery profiles to minimize freight costs in a multi-commodity network considering multiple tariff systems and inventory costs is presented. The approach uses multiple heuristics to determine initial solutions based on shortest arc algorithms and linear programming. The initial solution is improved upon using local search. In their case study, the authors achieve a solution that is 14% better than a supply chain design software solution.

Transport Concept Selection and Milk Run Scheduling. In [7] the authors present a model considering milk runs for transport concept selection in a two-stage inbound logistics network with optional cross-docking. To solve this model, a combination of harmony-search and simulated-annealing heuristics is used. However, no evaluation on real-world instances is provided.

An exact a-priori-column generation approach for TC-MRS is proposed by Meyer and Amberg [10]. In a pre-processing step, all possible milk run tours are determined. Then, the set of tours is used in a mixed integer program that is solved by a mixed integer programming solver. On real-world data, a cost reduction of 15% is achieved for frequent customers.

In [9] an approach for TC-MRS in a two-stage network using a genetic algorithm and Clark and Wright's algorithm is presented. The authors' approach is able to solve instances of 12 customers optimally. Instances of 50 customers are solved in less than eleven seconds.

4 Solution Approaches

In this section, we present our solution approaches for each concept. First, we address the tactical decision problems. Then, we present the solutions for the operational decision problems.

4.1 Consolidation Period Application

We apply a time policy to the material trader's dataset. We use the same duration of the consolidation period for all customers. The first demand of a customer marks the beginning of the consolidation period. We determine the resulting savings for consolidation periods of 2, 3, 4, and 5 days.

4.2 Delivery Profile Assignment

Based on the approach in [11], we assign delivery profiles in such a way that the shipment weight leaving the distribution center is leveled over the weekdays. We determine permissible shipment profiles in advance and then solve a mathematical model for delivery profile assignment using a mixed integer programming solver.

Permissible Delivery Profiles. As was the case in [11], only inventory optimal profiles are permissible. Table 2 shows the inventory optimal delivery profiles for a cycle time of five working days and shipment frequencies of one to five days per working week [3]. Each array represents a feasible pattern for the respective frequency. Days with shipments are represented by 1, days without by 0. For example, the pattern [10100] allows shipments every Monday and Wednesday.

Table 2. Inventory optimal delivery profiles

Frequency	Profiles
1	[10000] [01000] [00100] [00010] [00001]
2	[10100] [01010] [00101] [10010] [01001]
3	[11010] [01101] [10110] [01011] [10101]
4	[11110] [01111] [10111] [11011] [11101]
5	[11111]

Delivery Profile Assignment Model. This model assigns each customer to a delivery profile so that the shipment weight is leveled over working weekdays. Let $\mathcal{S} = \{1, 2, ..., |\mathcal{S}|\}$ be the set of customers and $\mathcal{T} = \{1, 2, ..., |\mathcal{T}|\}$ the set of days. $\mathcal{F} = \{1, 2, ..., |\mathcal{T}|\}$ represents the set of possible frequencies. We use $\mathcal{P}_s$ to denote the set of permissible profiles for a customer $s \in \mathcal{S}$. The parameter α_{spt} has a value of 1 if profile $p \in \mathcal{P}_s$ contains a shipment on day $t \in \mathcal{T}$ for customer $s \in \mathcal{S}$. Otherwise, α_{spt} is equal to 0. Parameter q_s is the average shipment weight of customer $s \in \mathcal{S}$.

We use the variable n to represent the maximum total shipment weight over the periods. The variable x_{sp} is 1, if the profile $p \in \mathcal{P}_s$ for customer $s \in \mathcal{S}$ is selected, otherwise it is 0. See Table 3 for an overview of the variable definitions.

Table 3. Overview of parameters and sets of model (1)

Parameters:	$\mathcal{S}$	Set of customers
	$\mathcal{T}$	Set of days
	$\mathcal{F}$	Set of frequencies
	$\mathcal{P}_s$	Set of feasible profiles for customer $s \in \mathcal{S}$
	f_s	Average frequency of customer $s \in \mathcal{S}$
	α_{spt}	1, if day $t \in \mathcal{T}$ in profile $p \in \mathcal{P}_s$ of customer $s \in S$ is used, else 0
	q_s	Average shipment weight for customer $s \in \mathcal{S}$
Variables:	n	Maximum total shipment weight
	x_{sp}	1, if profile $p \in \mathcal{P}_f$ for the transport to customer $s \in \mathcal{S}$ is chosen with frequency f_s, else 0

$$\min n \tag{1a}$$

subject to

$$\sum_{s \in \mathcal{S}} \sum_{p \in \mathcal{P}_s} x_{sp}\, \alpha_{spt}\, q_s \leq n \qquad \forall\, t \in \mathcal{T} \tag{1b}$$

$$\sum_{p \in P_s} x_{sp} = 1 \qquad \forall\, s \in \mathcal{S} \tag{1c}$$

$$x_{sp} \in \{0, 1\} \qquad \forall\, s \in \mathcal{S}, \forall\, p \in \mathcal{P}_s \tag{1d}$$

$$n \geq 0 \tag{1e}$$

The objective function (1a) minimizes the maximum total shipment weight. The variable n along with Constraints (1b) form the linearization of the maximum operators in the objective function. Constraints (1b) sum up the customer-specific shipment weights per day for each customer who is assigned to a profile that provides a delivery on that day. The Constraints (1c) assign each customer to exactly one profile. The Constraints (1d) and (1e) determine the variable domains.

4.3 Math-Heuristic for the TC-MRS

For the TC-MRS, we propose a math-heuristic algorithm based on the exact approach in [10]. Meyer and Amberg [10] perform a complete a priori tour generation to create a set of all feasible and cost-optimal tours. Afterward, the tour set is used in a set cover model to find the optimal solution. The problem is $\mathcal{NP}$-hard. The number of feasible tours grows exponentially with the number of customers. Therefore, this algorithm is only applicable to a limited number of customers. Our approach addresses this problem by partly substituting the tour generation phase with a heuristic procedure.

TC-MRS Optimization Model. This model assigns each customer to area forwarding or to a milk run tour from a set of milk run tours that was generated a priori. The parameters $\mathcal{T}, \mathcal{S}, \mathcal{P}_s$ and α_{spt} are the same as in the model from Subsect. 4.2. Each vehicle type $k \in \mathcal{K}$ has a set of executable milk run tours $\mathcal{R}_k$. Each tour $r \in \mathcal{R}_k$ respects the maximum vehicle capacity and tour duration. The set of vehicle types is denoted by $\mathcal{K}$ and the set of all vehicles of type k is defined as $\mathcal{L}_k = \{1, 2, ..., |\mathcal{L}_k|\}$. Parameter a_{krs} is 1 if customer s is served in tour r by the vehicle type k, and 0 otherwise. The parameter c^R_{kr} designates the freight costs of the milk run tour $r \in \mathcal{R}_k$ executed by a vehicle of type $k \in \mathcal{K}$. The parameter c^{AF}_s denotes the freight costs for the customer $s \in \mathcal{S}$ assigned to area forwarding.

The variable u_{sp} is equal to 1, if the delivery profile $p \in \mathcal{P}_s$ is assigned to customer $s \in \mathcal{S}$, and 0 otherwise. Variable z_{klrt} encodes whether vehicle $l \in \mathcal{L}_k$ of type $k \in \mathcal{K}$ is used for the milk run $r \in \mathcal{R}_k$ on day $t \in \mathcal{T}$. In this case, the variable is equal to 1, otherwise it takes a value of 0. Variable x_s is 1, if the customer $s \in \mathcal{S}$ is assigned to area forwarding, and 0 otherwise. Table 4 gives an overview of all sets and parameters.

Table 4. Overview of parameters and sets of model (2)

Parameters:	$\mathcal{T}$	Set of days in the planning horizon (system cycle time)
	$\mathcal{S}$	Set of customers
	$\mathcal{P}_s$	Set of feasible profiles for customer $s \in \mathcal{S}$
	$\mathcal{K}$	Set of available vehicle types
	$\mathcal{L}_k$	Set of available vehicles of type $k \in \mathcal{K}$
	$\mathcal{R}_k$	Set of feasible milk run tours with vehicle type $k \in \mathcal{K}$
	α_{spt}	1 if day $t \in \mathcal{T}$ is used in profile $p \in \mathcal{P}_s$ of customer $s \in \mathcal{S}$, else 0
	a_{krs}	1, if customer $s \in \mathcal{S}$ in tour $r \in \mathcal{R}_k$ is visited by vehicle type $k \in \mathcal{K}$, else 0
	c^R_{kr}	Freight costs for the tour $r \in \mathcal{R}_k$ of vehicle type $k \in \mathcal{K}$
	c^{AF}_s	Freight costs, if customer $s \in \mathcal{S}$ is assigned to area forwarding
Variables:	u_{sp}	1, if profile $p \in \mathcal{P}_s$ is assigned to customer $s \in \mathcal{S}$, else 0
	z_{klrt}	1, if vehicle $l \in \mathcal{L}_k$ of type $k \in \mathcal{K}$ is used on tour $r \in \mathcal{R}_k$ in day $t \in \mathcal{T}$, else 0
	x_s	1, if customer $s \in \mathcal{S}$ is assigned to area forwarding, else 0

TC-MRS

$$\min \sum_{k \in \mathcal{K}} \sum_{l \in \mathcal{L}_k} \sum_{r \in \mathcal{R}_k} \sum_{t \in \mathcal{T}} z_{klrt} c^R_{kr} + \sum_{s \in \mathcal{S}} x_s c^{AF}_s \tag{2a}$$

subject to

$$x_s + \sum_{p \in \mathcal{P}_s} u_{sp} = 1 \qquad \forall s \in \mathcal{S} \tag{2b}$$

$$\sum_{r \in \mathcal{R}_k} z_{klrt} \leq 1 \qquad \forall k \in \mathcal{K}, \forall l \in \mathcal{L}_k, \forall t \in \mathcal{T} \tag{2c}$$

$$\sum_{p \in \mathcal{P}_s} u_{sp} \alpha_{spt} - \sum_{k \in \mathcal{K}} \sum_{l \in \mathcal{L}_k} \sum_{r \in \mathcal{R}_k} z_{klrt} a_{krs} = 0 \qquad \forall s \in \mathcal{S}, \forall t \in \mathcal{T} \tag{2d}$$

$$u_{sp} \in \{0, 1\} \qquad \forall s \in \mathcal{S}, \forall p \in \mathcal{P}_s \tag{2e}$$

$$z_{klt} \in \{0, 1\} \qquad \forall k \in \mathcal{K}, \forall l \in \mathcal{L}_k, \forall t \in \mathcal{T} \tag{2f}$$

$$x_s \in \{0, 1\} \qquad \forall s \in \mathcal{S} \tag{2g}$$

The objective function (2a) minimizes the freight costs for the selected milk runs and area forwarding customers. Constraints (2b) ensure that each customer is assigned to exactly one transport concept. Constraints (2c) restrict each vehicle to at most one tour per day. Furthermore, Constraints (2d) links the profile and the assignment decision: If a profile is chosen for a customer, for each day in which a shipment takes place, exactly one tour has to exist in which the customer is assigned to an available vehicle. All further constraints determine the binary variable structure.

Milk Run Tour Set Generation. The set of feasible milk run tours is generated in two steps. In the first step, a complete tour generation up to a small number of customers is performed using the approach of [10]: From every limited size subset of customers the shortest tours meeting the maximum tour length are calculated via dynamic programming. The tours are added to the set of feasible tours if the capacity constraints for the tour hold for the respective vehicle type.

In a second step, we enrich the set of feasible milk run tours. To do so, we solve a standard *Capacitated Vehicle Routing Problem* (CVRP) heuristically for each vehicle type considered. Each time an interim solution for the CVRP is found, the tours in the solution are saved. If they are not part of the set of feasible milk run tours for the respective vehicle type yet, they are added to the set. To solve the CVRP, we use the Vehicle Routing library from Google OR-Tools [12]. To solve the CVRP we use the path-cheapest-arc algorithm to find the first solution and guided local search to improve the solution.

Please note that the milk run tours start at the distribution center of the materials trader and end with the last customer, as we assume that the tours are outsourced to logistics service providers having their own vehicle depots.

4.4 Overload Situations

As described in Sect. 2, we face two overload situations on an operational level. The first one occurs when consolidated shipments of the same customer exceed the maximum shipment weight (multiple) times. In this case, an operational decision has to be made concerning the way in which to combine the shipments to minimize the resulting freight costs. Forming the largest possible shipments leads to the biggest cost reduction. The problem of creating shipment sets that are maximal with respect to weight can be formulated as the *Multiple Subset Sum Problem* (MSSP). To formulate the problem as a MSSP, we provide one consolidation shipment (bin) less than necessary in the model to assign all consolidated shipments of the same customer. For example, if the maximum shipment weight is 25,000 kg and the sum of the consolidated shipment weights of the same customer is 60,000 kg, we provide $\lfloor \frac{60,000}{25,000} \rfloor = 2$ bins. The shipment weight of the bins is maximized. The leftover shipments are combined to an additional one.

In the second overload situation, the shipment weights of the customers assigned to a milk run exceed the weight capacity of the respective milk run vehicle. To solve this problem, we maximize the area forwarding costs covered by the milk run. The optimization problem to select a maximum subset of shipments by area forwarding costs while meeting the maximum shipment weight capacity of the milk run vehicle can be formulated as a *0–1 Knapsack Problem* (01KP). Leftover shipments are transported via area forwarding. We solve both, the MSSP and the 01KP, using a mixed integer solver.

5 Case Study of a German Materials Trader

In this section, we evaluate the freight costs saving potential for one of the material trader's distribution center based on data for the year 2020. We start the section by providing information about the use case. We then discuss the parameter settings of our optimization models and conclude with an analysis of the computational results.

5.1 Use Case Description

The dataset includes around 28,000 non-divisible shipments of around 1,400 customers. The distribution center operates five days a week. Each customer is supplied at most once a day. All shipments are executed via area forwarding by a logistics service provider with the service level promise of next-day delivery. Costs for the area forwarding are calculated according to a degressive transport price matrix taking into account the shipment weight and the euclidean distance to the customer. Above a weight of 10,000 kg, a full truckload tariff is applied such that the shipping costs do not increase any further. The shipments are supplied by vehicles with a maximum weight capacity of either 6,500 kg, 12,000 kg, or 25,000 kg.

Around 75% of the materials trader's customers have an average shipment weight below 1,000 kg. On the one hand, this is disadvantageous for the application of milk runs, due to the number of customers needed to utilize the whole vehicle capacity. On the other hand, this enhances the potential of temporal consolidation, because shipments under 1,000 kg are very expensive in the tariff structure of this use case.

In terms of shipment frequency, 86.9% of the customers receive a shipment less than once per week, which is counterproductive for consolidation. However

13.1% of customers that have a weekly frequency above one receive 59.4% of shipments and are responsible for 63.8% of the freight costs. This implies a substantial saving potential for a relatively small group of frequent customers.

5.2 Parameter Setting

Since Delivery Profiles and Area Forwarding & Milk Runs are most promising in case of frequent customers that are, to a certain extent, stable in terms of the weekly frequency and weight, we filtered the set of customers for our study as follows: We applied the all three concepts to 123 (8.8%) customers with an average weekly shipment frequency of one and a coefficient of variation in weekly shipment frequency and weight ≤ 1.33. The coefficient of variation is calculated by dividing the standard deviation by the mean value. These customers have a shipment share of 46.06%, a freight costs share of 52.03% and a freight weight share of 65.28%. The other 91.2% of customers are not affected by the concepts. The filtered customers are reachable in less than 3.5 h. Area forwarding costs are determined from the materials trader's tariff matrix for all concepts.

We consider the concept of Consolidation Period with durations from two to five days and a cycle time of five days for delivery profiles and milk runs, because the material trader has a five-day working week. The average shipment frequency and weight of customers are calculated based on historical data. The maximum frequency is five shipments per week. For the TC-MRS, we assume three vehicle types with weight capacities of 6,500 kg, 12,000 kg, and 25,000 kg. Since we assume that a milk run is executed by a logistics service provider, the vehicle number per vehicle type is unlimited. The set of feasible milk run tours is determined as described in Subsect. 4.3. Table 5 shows vehicle type dependent costs per km, which we used for milk runs. Costs per hour and the markup rate are equal for all vehicle types. The markup rate includes further costs and the profit of the logistics service provider. Due to the fact that the costs are only estimates, we vary the milk run costs by taking 80% (0.8) and 120% (1.2) of the estimation. We used the *openrouteservice.org* API to calculate driving times and route distances. Additionally, we assume 20 min of service time per stop and a maximum tour duration of nine hours. In case of consolidation shipment overload, i.e. the MSSP, we assume a maximum shipment weight of 25,000 kg. For the milk run overload situation, we use the respective milk run vehicle capacity as the maximum capacity for the 01KP.

Table 5. Milk run vehicle tariffs.

Max. weight capacity [kg]	Costs per km [€]	Costs per h [€]	Markup rate [%]
6,500	0.3	35	15.5
12,000	0.4	35	15.5
25,000	0.6	35	15.5

For the math-heuristic solution algorithm, we set a maximum tour length of three customers for the complete tour generation and a maximum run time of ten minutes per CVRP. The run time for the TC-MRS is limited to 30 min. We implemented all models in Python 3.8. All models, except the TC-MRS, are solved with Google OR-Tools. We solved the TC-MRS using the Gurobi solver [4]. All calculations were made on a machine with Intel-Core i7 processor (2.80 GHz), 16 GB RAM and Windows 10 (64 bit) as the operating system.

5.3 Computational Results

The baseline for all scenarios is given by the company's shipping expenses resulting if all shipments are executed via area forwarding with next day delivery. All freight costs savings relate to the total freight costs over all 1,400 customers. Figure 1 shows the freight costs savings of the Consolidation Period concept with a duration of two to five days (left), Delivery Profiles consolidation (middle) and Area Forwarding & Milk Runs consolidation with variation in milk run cost factors (right).

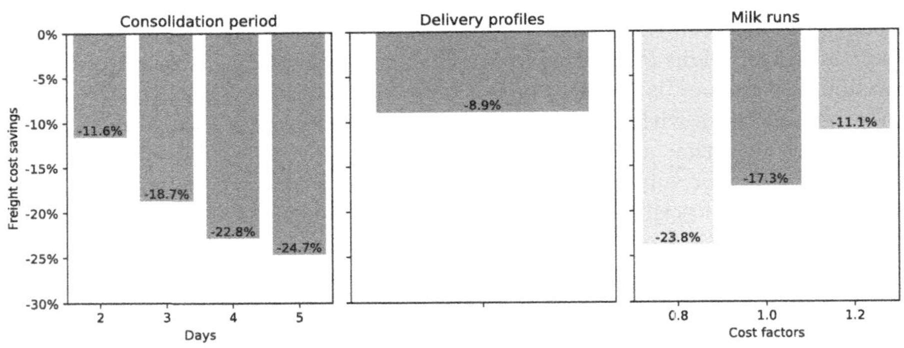

Fig. 1. Freight costs reduction.

As expected, in the case of the Consolidation Period concept, the savings increase with increasing consolidation period duration. The purely temporal consolidation can save 11.6% of freight costs for a duration of two days and up to 24.7% for the five days case. The additional cost savings for each extra day of consolidation thereafter declines.

The application of delivery profiles can save 8.9% on freight costs. This shows that Delivery Profiles achieve fewer freight costs savings than the temporal consolidation concept with a consolidation period of two days. However, the application of Delivery Profiles reduces the service level to a smaller extent, because the profiles are assigned based on the historical average shipment frequency.

With the Area Forwarding & Milk Run concept the company could save 17.3% in the basic milk run costs scenario. In the scenario with a milk run cost factor of 0.8, even higher savings of 23% can be achieved. In the scenario with a milk run cost factor of 1.2 we still obtain a freight costs reduction of 11.1%.

Aside from the freight costs reduction, we tried to achieve a leveling of the shipment weights in the distribution center by applying delivery profiles. Table 6 shows the shipment weight share of all 1400 customers per weekday without and with the application of delivery profiles. In the current situation, where no shipment profiles are employed, the share of shipment weight on Monday is large while the share on Friday is small.

Table 6. Shipment weight share per weekday

Scenario	Monday	Tuesday	Wednesday	Thursday	Friday
Without delivery profiles	26.3%	21.3%	21.3%	22.6%	8.4%
With delivery profiles	25.9%	20.2%	20.0%	21.5%	12.5%

The usage of delivery profiles for the selected customers can increase the share on Friday, but does not significantly reduce the overload situation on Monday. Hence, the success of shipment leveling is limited. The reasons for this limited success could be that the customers considered for delivery profiles do not have a shipment share that is large enough or that the irregular customers have a high shipment weight share on Mondays.

Figure 2 shows the weight capacity usage of the planned milk runs over all scenarios. The overall capacity usage is very high. The median is 85.8%. This high weight capacity usage leads to a lot of milk run overload situations in which shipments have to be taken over by area forwarding. Over all scenarios, an average of 24.5% of the freight weight of customers that are assigned to milk runs has to be transported via area forwarding. It is therefore even more surprising that the concept performs so well despite these additional costs.

The use of Area Forwarding & Milk Runs can double the savings compared to Delivery Profiles in the standard case of milk run costs. Even with a milk run cost factor of 1.2, Area Forwarding & Milk Runs can lead to 2.2% points more savings than Delivery Profiles. Area Forwarding & Milk Runs (cost factor 1.0) can save almost as much freight costs as a Consolidation Period with a duration of three days. At the same time, the usage of milk runs would have much less impact on the service level due the customer-specific delivery profiles. However, planning and maintaining milk runs, instead of simply using area forwarding or delivery profiles, is considerably more complex for the company. As such, extra costs have to be considered.

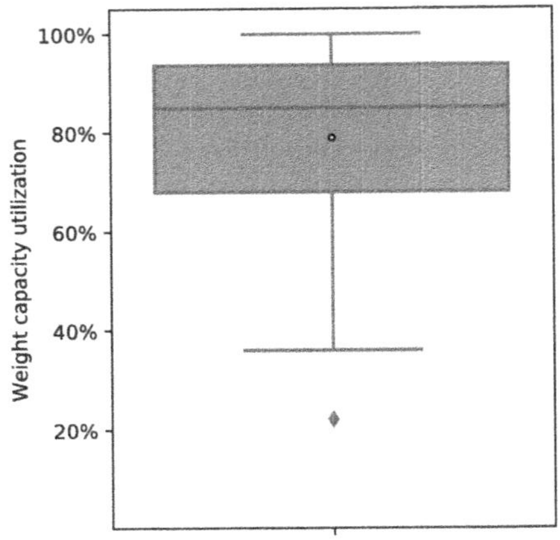

Fig. 2. Milk run weight capacity usage

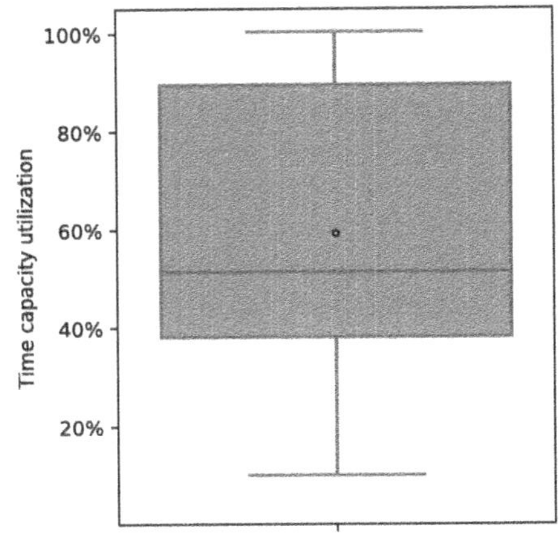

Fig. 3. Milk run duration capacity usage

Furthermore, the risk of violating the maximum tour duration exists. Figure 3 shows the planned milk run duration capacity usage for all cost factor scenarios. The median is 55.3%. This suggests that the maximum tour duration restriction is less likely to be violated than the weight capacity. For long milk runs, situations in which customers do not receive a shipment are more frequent, which leads to shorter travel times.

For a quick assessment of the performance of the math-heuristic, we compared our solutions for instances with 20 customers to the optimal solutions determined by the approach in [10]. The math-heuristic approach is able to find the optimal solution for these small instances.

6 Conclusion

In this paper, we investigated the three following concepts to realize freight costs reductions for a German materials trader based on temporal and spatial consolidation: Consolidation Period, Delivery Profiles, and Area Forwarding & Milk Runs. All three concepts were able to decrease the freight costs significantly when compared with the company's historic cost baseline. A Consolidation Period of two days can already lead to a cost reduction of 11.6%. Delivery profiles can lead to savings of 8.9%. Area Forwarding & Milk Runs yield savings between 11.1% and 23.8% depending on the milk run cost level.

Furthermore, we proposed an effective math-heuristic algorithm for solving the TC-MRS. The approach adapts the work of [10] and partly replaces the complete tour generation phase with a heuristic tour generation. This enables the generation of solutions for instances with more than 100 customers, as was the case in our computational study.

In future work, we plan to incorporate the stochasticity of the demand into the TC-MRS model and develop new heuristics for the stochastic version.

Acknowledgments. This research was funded by the Deutsche Forschungsgemeinschaft (DFG, German Research Foundation) - Projektnummer 276879186.

References

1. Bookbinder, J.H., Higginson, J.K.: Probabilistic modeling of freight consolidation by private carriage. Trans. Res. Part E: Logistics Trans. Rev. **38**(5), 305–318 (2002)
2. Çetinkaya, S., Mutlu, F., Lee, C.Y.: A comparison of outbound dispatch policies for integrated inventory and transportation decisions. Eur. J. Oper. Res. **171**(3), 1094–1112 (2006)
3. Fleischmann, B.: Transport and inventory planning with discrete shipment times. In: Speranza, M.G., Stähly, P. (eds.) New Trends in Distribution Logistics, vol. 480, pp. 159–178. Springer, Heidelberg (1999). https://doi.org/10.1007/978-3-642-58568-5_8
4. Gurobi Optimization, LLC: Gurobi Optimizer Reference Manual (2022). https://www.gurobi.com
5. Harks, T., König, F.G., Matuschke, J., Richter, A.T., Schulz, J.: An integrated approach to tactical transportation planning in logistics networks. Trans. Sci. **50**(2), 439–460 (2014)
6. Higginson, J.K., Bookbinder, J.H.: Policy recommendations for a shipment-consolidation program. J. Bus. Logistics **15**(1), 87–112 (1994)
7. Hosseini, S.D., Akbarpour Shirazi, M., Karimi, B.: Cross-docking and milk run logistics in a consolidation network: a hybrid of harmony search and simulated annealing approach. J. Manuf. Syst. **33**(4), 567–577 (2014)
8. Kempkes, J.P., Koberstein, A., Suhl, L.: A resource based mixed integer modelling approach for integrated operational logistics planning. In: Dangelmaier, W., Blecken, A., Delius, R., Klöpfer, S. (eds.) IHNS 2010. LNBIP, vol. 46, pp. 281–294. Springer, Heidelberg (2010). https://doi.org/10.1007/978-3-642-12494-5_26
9. Kocaoglu, Y., Cakmak, E., Kocaoglu, B., Taskin Gumus, A.: A novel approach for optimizing the supply chain: a heuristic-based hybrid algorithm. Math. Prob. Eng. **2020**, 1–24 (2020)
10. Meyer, A., Amberg, B.: Transport concept selection considering supplier milk runs - an integrated model and a case study from the automotive industry. Trans. Res. Part E: Logistics Trans. Rev. **113**, 147–169 (2018). Making connections: Supply chain innovation research collaboration
11. Meyer, A., Cardeneo, A., Furmans, K.: A two stage approach for balancing a periodic long-haul transportation network. In: Hu, B., Morasch, K., Pickl, S., Siegle, M. (eds.) Operations Research Proceedings 2010. Operations Research Proceedings, pp. 257–262. Springer, Heidelberg (2011). https://doi.org/10.1007/978-3-642-20009-0_41
12. Perron, L., Furnon, V.: Or-tools. https://developers.google.com/optimization/
13. Projektgruppe Standardbelieferungsformen: Standardbelieferungsformen der Logistik in der Automobilindustrie. In: Recommendation 5010 (2008)
14. Schöneberg, T., Koberstein, A., Suhl, L.: An optimization model for automated selection of economic and ecologic delivery profiles in area forwarding based inbound logistics networks. Flex. Serv. Manuf. J. **22**(3), 214–235 (2010)
15. Schöneberg, T., Koberstein, A., Suhl, L.: A stochastic programming approach to determine robust delivery profiles in area forwarding inbound logistics networks. OR Spectrum **35**(4), 807–834 (2013). https://doi.org/10.1007/s00291-013-0349-0

Reference Model for Data-Driven Supply Chain Collaboration

Anna-Maria Nitsche[1,2(✉)], Christian-Andreas Schumann[2], and Bogdan Franczyk[1,3]

[1] Leipzig University, Augustusplatz 10, 04109 Leipzig, Germany
anna-maria.nitsche@uni-leipzig.de
[2] University of Applied Sciences Zwickau, Kornmarkt 1, 08056 Zwickau, Germany
[3] Wrocław University of Economics, Komandorska 118/120, 53-345 Wrocław, Poland

Abstract. This paper presents a strategic reference model for data-driven supply chain collaboration (SCC) designed based on the principles of design science research and the process model for empirically grounded reference modelling. Increasingly competitive and global supply networks require the wider application of collaborative supply chain management. Thus, the different aspects of SCC, including inter-organizational exchange of data and knowledge as well as the integration of novel technologies such as artificial intelligence are essential factors for organizational growth. This paper attempts to fill the gap of a missing overview of this field by providing the results of the development of a comprehensive framework of data-driven SCC. Due to the interdisciplinary focus and approach combining information systems, design science and management research, the paper contributes to the academic debate by providing a macro level perspective on the topic of SCC and a conceptualization and categorization of data-driven SCC. Furthermore, this paper presents a valuable contribution to practice and supply chain processes in organizations across sectors by delivering an adaptable strategic reference framework for application in collaborative processes.

Keywords: Empirically grounded reference modelling · Supply Chain Collaboration · Artificial intelligence · Information systems · Design science research

1 Introduction

The wider application of collaborative supply chain management (SCM) is a requirement of increasingly competitive and global supply networks. Trends such as global integration, population growth and urbanization, digitalization, and automation, as well as social and environmental concerns put supply chain networks under increasing pressure [1–3]. While these challenges drive the development of collaborative supply chain networks [4], cross-industry logistics cooperation for digitalization [5] and supply chain transparency [6–8], organizations and managers also turn towards technological solutions. In the logistics sector, where, according to a German study, approximately half of companies consider themselves to be trendsetters or innovators [5], inter-organizational exchange

J. de Armas et al. (Eds.): ICCL 2022, LNCS 13557, pp. 412–424, 2022.
https://doi.org/10.1007/978-3-031-16579-5_28

of data and knowledge as well as the integration of novel technologies such as artificial intelligence (AI) are essential factors for organizational growth and competitiveness [9–11].

Despite the comprehensive challenges facing supply chain collaboration (SCC), the disruptive influence of technology on physical and information flows, and the relevance of SCC [3, 4, 12–14], a uniform orientation framework for data-driven SCC is currently not available [4] as research often focuses on specific aspects of data-driven SCC such as flexibility [e.g. 15] or computational experiments [e.g. 16]. This paper thus fills the gap of a missing overview of this field by proposing a comprehensive strategic framework of data-driven SCC. Due to the interdisciplinary focus and approach combining information systems (IS), DSR and management research, the paper contributes to the academic debate by suggesting a macro level perspective on the topic of SCC and a conceptualization and categorization of data-driven SCC. Furthermore, this paper presents a contribution to practice and supply chain processes in organizations across sectors by delivering a strategic reference framework for application in collaborative process management and development. The remainder of the paper presents key concepts, the research approach and methods, as well as the modelling results and discussion.

2 Key Concepts

SCC is a relevant research area within the field of SCM research that has become increasingly heterogenous and comprehensive over the last years [4]. SCC is defined as "seven interweaving components of information sharing, goal congruence, decision synchronization, incentive alignment, resources sharing, collaborative communication, and joint knowledge creation" [14, p. 55] while collaboration is characterized as "a mutually shared process where two or more firms display mutual understanding and a shared vision, and the firms in question voluntarily agree to integrate human, financial, or technical resources with the aim of achieving collective goals" [17, p. 35]. Barratt [18] similarly states that trust, mutuality, information exchange, openness, and communication are the basic components of a collaborative culture.

A development from technology-enabled to technology-centric SCM can be observed as information management plays a central role [19]. As digital transformation profoundly impacts organizational strategy and change [20], also regarding collaborative SCM processes, "today and looking at the near future [...] the supply chain is as good as the digital technology behind it" [21, p. 9]. AI is widely considered to be of growing importance and high potential for supply networks as well as the underlying IS [e.g. 22–24]. AI aggregates the "philosophies of machines to think, behave and perform either same or similar to humans" [25, p. 869] and can be defined as "the branch of computer science that is concerned with the automation of intelligent behavior" [26, p. 1]. Data-driven collaboration refers to collaborative processes that are prescribed by relevant data structures [27]. As data-driven collaboration is "happening or done according to information that has been collected" [28], it is determined by, or dependent on, the collection or analysis of data.

3 Research Approach and Methods

DSR has been an established part of research for the last 30 years [29] and is useful for bringing together different disciplines as well as related non-academic organizations. It is suitable to create and evaluate information technology solutions for SCC due to its construction-oriented and problem-solving approach [30, 31]. This paper intends to contribute a DSR artefact in the form of a strategic model, the *Reference Model for Data-Driven Supply Chain Collaboration*. The model characteristics are illustrated in Table 1 [based on 32]. Reference modelling addresses all levels and business fields of enterprises, including strategic and organizational aspects, the design of IS, the description of organizations, business process (re-)engineering, and knowledge management [33, 34].

Table 1. Typology of reference models (appropriate categories underlined) [based on 32, p. 98].

Characteristic		Description			
Model-related	Aspect	Aspect-specific		Multi-aspect	
	Formality	Not formal	Semi-formal		Formal
	Subject	Technical concept	Data processing concept		Implementation
	Objective	Organizational system model		Application System Model	
	Sector	Industry	Trade	SCC	Other sectors
	Task	Support	Purpose		Steering
Method-related	Fulfilment of requirements	Reference model-unspecific		Reference model-specific	
Technology-related	Representation	Print		Computer-aided	
Organization-related	Availability	Unpublished		Published	

A prevalence of analytical and theoretical concepts over empirically developed reference models is acknowledged within DSR [35], which is also described as a worrying "wide gap between theoretical and empirical research in a real science" [35, p. 338]. The approach chosen for this paper bridges the gap between theoretical and empirical construction methods and enables a human-centered perspective on data-driven SCC.

The construction of the *Reference Model for Data-Driven Supply Chain Collaboration* within the DSR artefact development is based on the process model for empirically grounded reference modelling [36] as a deductive approach [37]. The process model has been applied in various contexts [e.g. 38] and consists of five phases, namely planning, model construction, validation, practical testing, and documentation (see Fig. 1).

Phase I of the reference modelling approach covers model-related planning, including the problem identification and definition as well as method-related, organizational, technological and project planning. The steps within this phase are based on the four

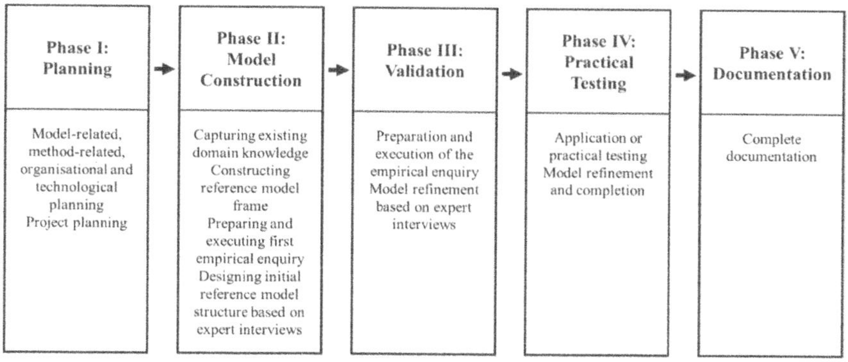

Fig. 1. Reference modelling approach [based on 36].

design areas for reference modelling [39]: organization, model, method, and technology. The model-related planning is concerned with the definition of the reference model domain (i.e. data-driven SCC), which is referred to as the problem definition [40]. Method-related planning is tasked with the selection of appropriate problem-solving and model representation techniques. In addition to the process model for empirically grounded reference modelling [36], natural language is chosen as the representation technique. Organizational planning covers the definition and documentation of a research design, the identification of the experts to be involved in the modelling process as well as coordination of these activities. Technological planning is concerned with the selection of appropriate technologies to support the modelling process, including the model construction, the documentation of the reference model and the recording and analysis of the expert interviews. A top-down approach for complex tasks has long time been established as suitable to achieve different levels of abstraction [40] and is chosen for the project planning.

The second phase is the model construction phase which comprises capturing existing domain knowledge, constructing the reference model frame, preparing and executing the first empirical enquiry, and designing the initial reference model structure. The construction of the reference model frame is useful for structuring the expert interviews and for constructing and documenting the reference model. First, general domain knowledge of logistics process and collaboration modelling is used, including the distinction of different focus levels [e.g. 41] and the Supply Chain Operations Reference Model (SCOR) [42]. The model is intended to include business to customer (B2C) as well as business to business (B2B) collaboration [e.g. 43]. Based on the reference model frame, the first empirical enquiry is prepared and executed to enable the first construction cycle of the reference model based on the experts' domain knowledge. The preparation comprises the identification, examination, and selection of interview participants (IPs), and the creation of an interview guide. To acquire experts for the interviews, we use homogenous purposeful sampling [44]. To incorporate both academic and business-oriented viewpoints and experiences, the qualitative sample comprises four scholarly experts and three experts with a practical SCC background from different industries in Germany and the UK (see Table 2). Thus, the empirical inquiry is based on a total of 14 in-depth semi-structured interviews (seven per round of interviews) in February/March 2021 (first empirical enquiry, 98 pages of transcript) and May/June 2021 (second empirical enquiry, 123 pages of transcript). The interview guide for the first empirical inquiry is structured according to the ARIS concept [45, 46] and the St. Gallen approach to business engineering [47–50]. The transcripts of the interviews are analyzed during iterative sessions of reading and coding using template analysis based on a priori as well as a posteriori coding [44, 51, 52] and the qualitative analysis software Nvivo. Following the first empirical enquiry, the initial reference model structure is designed.

Table 2. Overview of expert interview participants.

IP No	Background	Organization size
IP1	Academic, DE	Public service
IP2	Academic, DE	Public service
IP3	Academic, UK	Public service
IP4	Academic, UK	Public service
IP5	Logistics services, DE	SME
IP6	Retail/e-commerce, UK	Corporate
IP7	Industry conglomerate, DE	Corporate

Phase III is the validation phase which consists of the preparation and execution of the second empirical enquiry and the model refinement. The lists of correction proposals gathered during each expert interview form the basis for the further model refinement. The interview guide for the second empirical inquiry is based on the interview findings from the first round.

Phase IV is tasked with the application or practical testing and the subsequent model refinement and completion. Thus, the *Reference Model for Data-Driven Supply Chain Collaboration* is conceptually applied to a last mile supply chain and logistics network context.

A complete documentation is carried out in the fifth and last phase to ensure increased comprehension and validity.

4 Modelling Results and Discussion

The first empirical enquiry focuses on the following aspects: functions and processes; organization, strategy, and control; data, information systems, and AI/ML. Based on the IPs' suggestions regarding the framework's potential structure and content, the initial model draft is developed. At the beginning, the IPs are asked to define SCC to establish the different perspectives on the topic. The definitions provided by the IPs highlight the focus on togetherness within supply networks as well as the change from competition between organizations to competition between value chains. Overall, there can be different directions, activities as well as degrees of collaborative behavior due to the high complexity of this topic. According to the experts, a re-appearing core aspect of collaboration is the exchange of data and information. Additionally, some experts stressed the harmonizing and superordinate function of SCM and logistics within and across organizations. The objectives of collaboration are described as similar to the general aims of SCM, and include overall success and competitiveness of the value chain, coordinated behavior, customer satisfaction and high service levels, harmonization, smooth flow and efficiency, cost and time savings, high quality and performance, overall optimization, transparency, and risk and disruption avoidance. Following the first empirical enquiry, the IPs' statements are used to design the initial reference model structure.

The second empirical enquiry focuses on the discussion of the initial model draft, the application context of collaborative last mile networks and the influence of AI, as well as the expert evaluation of the strategic *Reference Model for Data-Driven Supply Chain Collaboration*. Based on the IPs' feedback and the subsequent discussion among the research team, the initial model draft is revised and finalized (see Fig. 2). The final *Reference Model for Data-Driven Supply Chain Collaboration* is visualized as a three-dimensional cube. The model distinguishes between the dimensions of collaboration agents, collaboration orientation, and collaboration type. The collaboration agents describe the different actors involved in the collaboration process. These actors can be actual people but also organizations or other entities such as machines and algorithms. The collaboration orientation is the second dimensions and refers to the focus level, i.e. operational, tactical, or strategic collaboration. Some collaborations can take place on an operational level, for example sharing infrastructure or order information. Strategic collaboration could include setting sustainability goals or location strategy planning. The third dimension distinguishes the collaboration types of minor, repeat, and partnership. Depending on the intensity of the collaboration, the type minor could describe a non-standardized exchange of information or one-off interactions, while the type partnership could include the coordination of research and development activities or long-term financial commitments.

The smaller sub-cubes contained within the three-dimensional cube are connected via the communication level (shaded in grey) which can vary in its intensity, depending on the collaboration process characteristics. For instance, a partnership collaboration between several agents might require relatively intense communication. Similarly, the communication is based on both system 1 and system 2 thinking [53]. As the experts consistently highlighted the exchange of data and information as a core aspect of collaboration, the communication level can be regarded as the key enabler of collaborative processes.

Across the communication level, smaller circles depict the actual collaboration process which can connect two or more sub-cubes and thus incorporate an operational, tactical and/or strategic orientation among one or more agents in a minor, repeat, or partnership collaboration type.

The collaboration process circles can be further detailed by zooming in (Fig. 2 on the right). Collaboration is based on general prerequisites such as laws and regulations. The collaboration process comprises three categories (people, process, system) which can be further divided into sub-categories. The people category contains interaction-focused elements (e.g. knowledge sharing, coordination), human-focused elements (e.g.

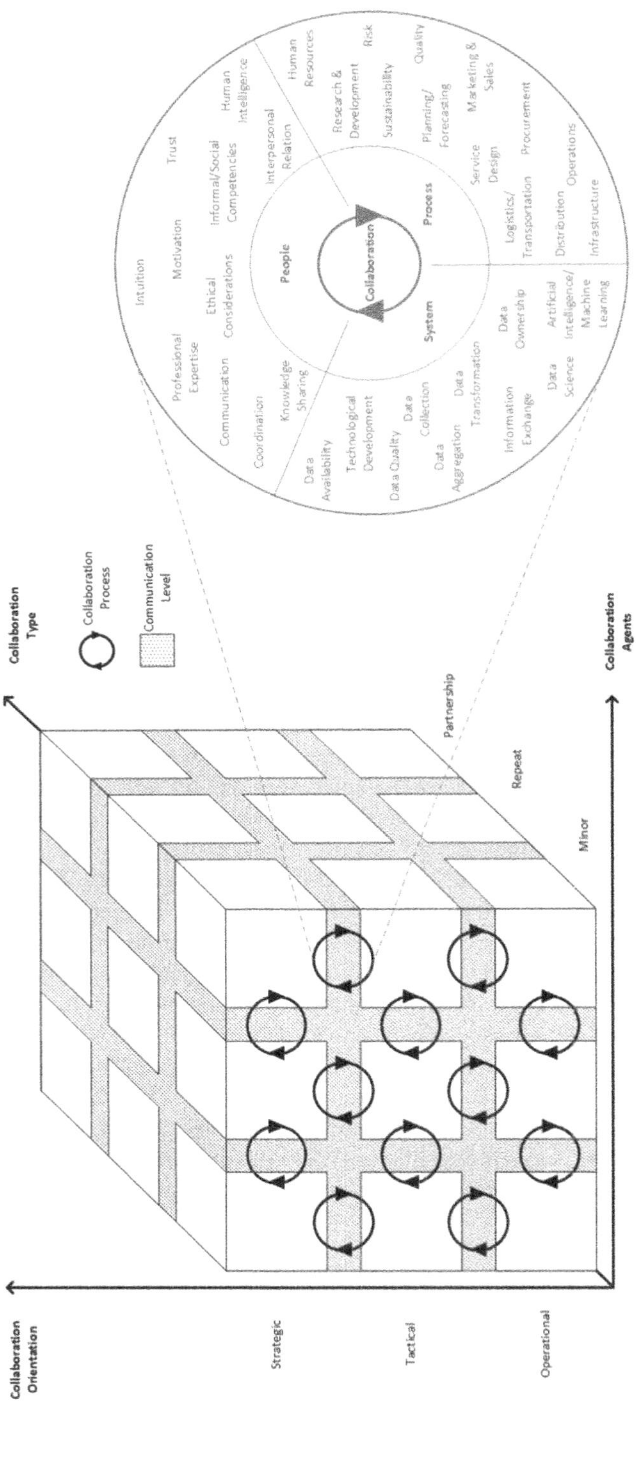

Fig. 2. Reference model for data-driven supply chain collaboration

intuition, professional expertise), and intelligence-focused elements (e.g. interpersonal relation, informal/social competencies). This category can also be applied to organizational entities. The process category contains operational (e.g. distribution) and management processes (e.g. sustainability management). Lastly, the system category comprises relevant elements that enable data-driven collaboration, including data collection and information exchange. The sub-category AI and machine learning can further be broken down according to the different available tools such as supervised learning, agent-based models, and artificial neural networks.

While the model itself proposes a conceptualization and framing of data-driven SCC on a strategic level, instantiations could focus more on a practical process level. Researchers and managers using this model could use the three-dimensional cube to first determine the collaboration characteristics along the three dimensions before further zooming into the collaboration process categories to define relevant areas for management and further development of collaborative processes.

To further highlight the potential model application, an exemplary last mile use case description is provided (see Fig. 3). The example refers to a collaboration between two delivery service providers who share urban depots to provide more environmentally friendly last mile services. The collaboration agents can thus be specified as delivery agent X and delivery agent Y. This collaboration could be classified as a strategic partnership as the aim of both collaborators is to increase last mile sustainability, including social, environmental, and economic aspects. Within the collaboration process, the delivery service providers, i.e. the involved collaboration agents, could use the zoom-in depiction of the collaboration process to discuss their partnership regarding their processes, the people involved in the collaboration, and the underlying systems such as information technology systems. As their shared goal is to enhance the sustainability management and information exchange, they could discuss which categories and components within the collaboration process are relevant for their collaboration. For instance, they could agree to define collaboration sustainability goals according to the UN sustainable development goals 11 (sustainable cities and communities) and 13 (climate action) [54]. In addition, they could decide to implement sharing of additional delivery order information based on data collection enabled through sensors.

The application of this strategic model in specific use cases could thus enable the collaborators to define the type and focus of their collaboration more clearly. In addition, the collaboration process circle to extend and improve the individual components of their collaborative process with a balanced approach to all three collaboration categories (people, process, and system).

This research project applies a formative-summative design-evaluate-construct-evaluate pattern [55]. The expert evaluation of the initial model draft and the estimated revised model (see Table 2) are based on the principles of proper reference modelling, the recommendations for DSR evaluation [56] and the framework for evaluation in design sciences [57]. As the interviewees are both from a business and academic background, practical and scholarly evaluation perspective are included.

The main critical points mentioned by the experts are the ease of use and the level of detail/completeness. According to the IPs, the required detail and thus completeness of the model depends on the user and the use context. Accordingly, the model is not

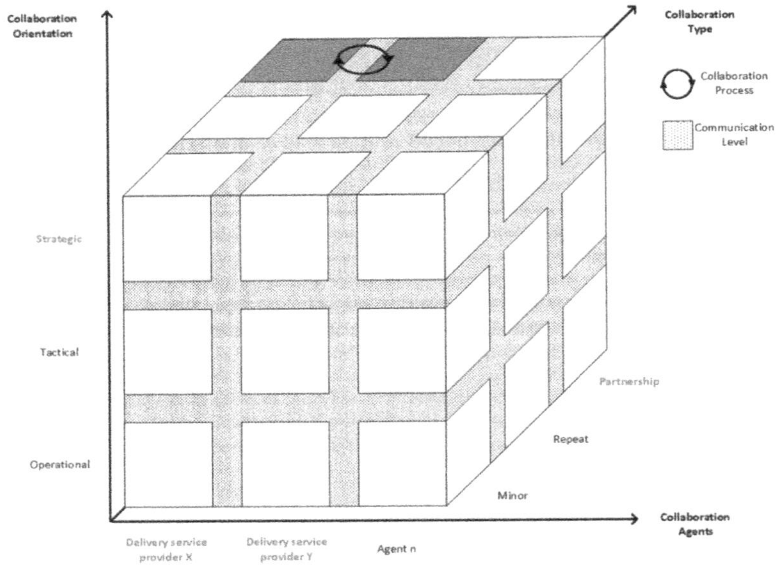

Fig. 3. Last mile collaboration use case example.

Table 3. Expert evaluation feedback averages (evaluation scale 1 = low to 5 = high).

Feedback criteria	Initial model	Revised model
General adequacy	4.17	4,58
Accuracy/correctness	4.14	4.43
Clarity/unambiguity/consistency/systematic structure	4.07	4.75
Level of detail/completeness	3.79	4.00
Internal validity	4.33	4.42
Ease of use	3.71	3.93
Relevance/usefulness/appropriateness	3.93	4.57
Adaptability/generalizability/comparability	4.14	4.50

applicable to every situation and serves as a strategic blueprint for instantiations in different sectors. The ease of use similarly depends on previous knowledge of the user regarding scientific models and can thus be problematic. We intend to further develop the model as an interactive web application including detailed instructions and explanations to enable a more accessible and intuitive model use.

While the research presented in this paper adheres to the seven design-research guidelines [30], the chosen modeling and evaluation approach suffer from several limitations. First, the process model for empirically grounded reference modelling is limited regarding its focus on qualitative methods for data generation. Second, the results of the empirical enquiry and thus the model itself are restricted due to the selection of experts and their respective background. While experts from both a business and academic background are included in the modeling process, opinions and suggestions remain subjective. Third, the artefact evaluation approach is limited as no evaluation method can assess all potential evaluation criteria.

5 Conclusion

This paper presents the results of the systematic empirically based development of a strategic *Reference Model for Data-Driven Supply Chain Collaboration*. The wider application of collaborative SCM is a requirement of increasingly competitive and global supply networks as inter-organizational exchange of data and knowledge as well as the integration of novel technologies such as AI are essential factors for organizational growth and competitiveness. This paper thus fills the gap of a missing overview of the field by proposing a framework of data-driven SCC.

The results contribute to the academic debate on data-driven SCC by providing a comprehensive interdisciplinary conceptualization and categorization combining IS, DSR and management research approaches. Future research avenues include the further analysis of the collaboration dimensions and process categories. Furthermore, this paper presents a valuable contribution to supply chain processes in organizations of different sectors by providing a macro level perspective on the topic of SCC. In addition, the paper suggests an adaptable reference framework for managers focusing on strategic collaboration development and information management. The further development of the model as an interactive web application is intended to enable a more accessible and intuitive model use.

Acknowledgment. This work was supported by the tax revenues on the basis of the budget adopted by the Saxon State Parliament under Grant SAB/100379142.

References

1. Hölderich, P., et al.: City-Logistik neu gedacht - Impulse für das Stuttgarter Rosensteinviertel. IHK (2020)
2. Witten, P., Schmidt, C.: Globale trends und die Konsequenzen für die Logistik der letzten Meile. In: Schröder, M., Wegner, K. (eds.) Logistik im Wandel der Zeit – Von der Produktionssteuerung zu vernetzten Supply Chains, pp. 303-319. Springer, Gabler, Wiesbaden (2019).https://doi.org/10.1007/978-3-658-25412-4_1
3. Schönberg, T., Wunder, T., Huster, S.W.: Urban logistics 2030 in Germany: Stronger together: Keep the Wild West scenario at bay with cooperation. BVL International (2018)
4. Nitsche, A.-M., Schumann, C.-A., Franczyk, B., Reuther, K.: Mapping supply chain collaboration research: a machine learning based literature review. Int. J. Logistics Res. Appl. 1–29 (2021)
5. Kohl, A.-K., Pfretzschner, F.: Logistikmonitor 2018: Der Wirtschaftszweig in Zahlen. Bundesvereinigung Logistik e.V., Statista GmbH (2018)
6. Zanker, C.: Branchenanalyse Logistik: Der Logistiksektor zwischen Globalisierung, Industrie 4.0 und Online-Handel. Hans-Böckler-Stiftung (2018)

7. Kersten, W., von See, B., Lodemann, S., Grotemeier, C.: Trends und Strategien in Logistik und Supply Chain Management – Entwicklungen und Perspektiveneiner nachhaltigen und digitalen Transformation. Bundesvereinigung Logistik e.V. (2020)
8. Kersten, W., Seiter, M., von See, B., Hackius, N., Maurer, T.: Trends and strategies in logistics and supply chain management – digital transformation opportunities. BVL International (2017)
9. Gesing, B.: Sharing Economy Logistics: Rethinking logistics with access over ownership. DHL Customer Solutions Innovation (2017)
10. Backhaus, A., et al.: Logistik 2020: Struktur- und Wertewandel als Herausforderung. Gipfel der Logistikweisen: Initiative zur Prognose der Entwicklung der Logistik in Deutschland (2020)
11. Junge, A.L., Verhoeven, P., Reipert, J., Mansfeld, M.: Pathway of Digital Transformation in Logistics: Best Practice Concepts and Future Developments. Universitätsverlag TU Berlin, Berlin (2019)
12. Glöckner, M.: Foundational research artifacts of cloud logistics: development of selected artifacts for virtualizing, categorizing and encapsulating resources and services of logistics within reusable modules. Wirtschaftswissenschaftlichen Fakultät der Universität Leipzig, Leipzig (2019)
13. Soosay, C.A., Hyland, P.: A decade of supply chain collaboration and directions for future research. Supply Chain Manag. Int. J. **20**, 613–630 (2015)
14. Cao, M., Zhang, Q.: Supply Chain Collaboration: Roles of Interorganizational Systems, Trust, and Collaborative Culture. Springer-Verlag, London (2013)
15. Khanuja, A., Jain, R.K.: The conceptual framework on integrated flexibility: an evolution to data-driven supply chain management. The TQM Journal (2021)
16. Long, Q.: A framework for data-driven computational experiments of inter-organizational collaborations in supply chain networks. Inf. Sci. **399**, 43–63 (2017)
17. Richey, R.G., Adams, F.G., Dalela, V.: Technology and flexibility: enablers of collaboration and time-based logistics quality. J. Bus. Logist. **33**, 34–49 (2012)
18. Barratt, M.: Understanding the meaning of collaboration in the supply chain. Supply Chain Manag. Int. J. **9**, 30–42 (2004)
19. Sharma, A., Rana, N.P., Nunkoo, R.: Fifty years of information management research: a conceptual structure analysis using structural topic modeling. Int. J. Inf. Manag. **58**, 1–27 (2021)
20. Hanelt, A., Bohnsack, R., Marz, D., Antunes Marante, C.: A systematic review of the literature on digital transformation: insights and implications for strategy and organizational change. J. Manag. Stud. **58**, 1159–1197 (2020)
21. Panetto, H., Iung, B., Ivanov, D., Weichhart, G., Wang, X.: Challenges for the cyber-physical manufacturing enterprises of the future. Annu. Rev. Control. **47**, 200–213 (2019)
22. Toorajipour, R., Sohrabpour, V., Nazarpour, A., Oghazi, P., Fischl, M.: Artificial intelligence in supply chain management: a systematic literature review. J. Bus. Res. **122**, 502–517 (2021)
23. Min, H.: Artificial intelligence in supply chain management: theory and applications. Int. J. Log. Res. Appl. **13**, 13–39 (2010)
24. Collins, C., Dennehy, D., Conboy, K., Mikalef, P.: Artificial intelligence in information systems research: a systematic literature review and research agenda. Int. J. Inf. Manag. **60**, 1–17 (2021)
25. Dhamija, P., Bag, S.: Role of artificial intelligence in operations environment: a review and bibliometric analysis. TQM J. **32**, 869–896 (2020)
26. Luger, G.F.: Artificial intelligence: Structures and Strategies for Complex Problem Solving. Pearson Education, Inc. (2009)

27. Müller, D., Reichert, M., Herbst, J.: Data-driven modeling and coordination of large process structures. In: Meersman, R., Tari, Z. (eds.) OTM 2007. LNCS, vol. 4803, pp. 131–149. Springer, Heidelberg (2007). https://doi.org/10.1007/978-3-540-76848-7_10
28. CUP: Data-Driven. Cambridge Dictionary Online. Cambridge University Press, Cambridge (2021)
29. Peffers, K., Tuunanen, T., Niehaves, B.: Design science research genres: introduction to the special issue on exemplars and criteria for applicable design science research. Eur. J. Inf. Syst. **27**, 129–139 (2018)
30. Hevner, A.R., March, S.T., Park, J., Ram, S.: Design science in information systems research. MIS Q. **28**, 75–105 (2004)
31. Gregor, S., Hevner, A.R.: Positioning and presenting design science research for maximum impact. MIS Q. **37**, 337–355 (2013)
32. vom Brocke, J.: Referenzmodellierung: Gestaltung und Verteilung von Konstruktionsprozessen. Logos Verlag Berlin, Berlin (2003)
33. Fettke, P., Loos, P., Zwicker, J.: Using UML for reference modeling. In: Rittgen, P. (ed.) Enterprise Modeling and Computing with UML, pp. 171–202. IGI Global, Hershey, PA (2007)
34. Becker, J., Delfmann, P.: Referenzmodellierung: Grundlagen. Springer-Verlag, Techniken und domänenbezogene Anwendung (2013)
35. Fettke, P., Loos, P.: Referenzmodellierungsforschung. Wirtschaftsinformatik **46**(5), 331–340 (2004). https://doi.org/10.1007/BF03250947
36. Ahlemann, F., Gastl, H.: Process model for an empirically grounded reference model construction. In: Fettke, P., Loos, P. (eds.) Reference Modeling for Business Systems Analysis, pp. 77–97. Idea Group Publishing, London (2007)
37. Rehse, J.-R., Fettke, P., Loos, P.: A graph-theoretic method for the inductive development of reference process models. Softw. Syst. Model. **16**(3), 833–873 (2015). https://doi.org/10.1007/s10270-015-0490-0
38. de Kinderen, S., Kaczmarek-Hess, M.: Multi-level modeling as a language architecture for reference models: on the example of the smart grid domain. In: 2019 IEEE 21st Conference on Business Informatics (CBI), pp. 174–183 (2019)
39. Lehrstuhl für Wirtschaftsinformatik (insb. Prozesse und Systeme), Universität Potsdam. https://enzyklopaedie-der-wirtschaftsinformatik.de/wi-enzyklopaedie/lexikon/daten-wissen/Informationsmanagement/referenzmodellierung/index.html?searchterm=referenzmodell
40. Schütte, R.: Grundsätze ordnungsmäßiger Referenzmodellierung: Konstruktion konfigurations-und anpassungsorientierter Modelle. Springer-Verlag, Wiesbaden (1998)
41. Müller, E., Ackermann, J.: Modellierung von Logistikstrukturen mittels 3-Ebenen-Modell und Strukturtypen. In: Delfmann, W., Wimmer, T. (eds.) Strukturwandel in der Logistik: Wissenschaft und Praxis im Dialog, vol. 5, pp. 274–285. DVV Media Group, Hamburg (2010)
42. APICS: SCOR Supply Chain Operations Reference Model Version 12.0. APICS (2017)
43. Villarreal, P.D., Salomone, E., Chiotti, O.: Modeling and specification of collaborative business processes. In: Rittgen, P. (ed.) Enterprise Modeling and Computing with UML, pp. 13–44. IGI Global, Hershey (2007)
44. Saunders, M., Lewis, P., Thronhill, A.: Research Methods for Business Students. Pearson Education Ltd, Harlow (2016)
45. Scheer, A.-W.: Wirtschaftsinformatik: Referenzmodelle für industrielle Geschäftsprozesse. Springer, Berlin (2013)
46. Scheer, A.-W.: ARIS - House of Business Engineering: Konzept zur Beschreibung und Ausführung von Referenzmodellen. In: Becker, J., Rosemann, M., Schütte, R. (eds.) Entwicklungsstand und Entwicklungsperspektiven der Referenzmodellierung, pp. 3–15. Westfälische Wilhelms-Universität, Münster, Institut für Wirtschaftsinformatik (1997)
47. Österle, H.: Business Engineering: Prozess-und Systementwicklung. Springer, Berlin (1995)

48. Österle, H., Blessing, D.: Ansätze des Business Engineering. HMD **42**, 7–17 (2005)
49. Österle, H., Senger, E.: Prozessgestaltung und IT: Von der Unternehmens-zur Konsumentensicht. Controlling Management **55**, 80–88 (2011)
50. Winter, R.: Business engineering navigator: Gestaltung und Analyse von Geschäftslösungen "Business-to-IT". Springer-Verlag (2010)
51. King, N.: Using templates in the thematic analysis of text. In: Cassell, C., Symon, G. (eds.) Essential Guide to Qualitative Methods in Organizational Research, p. 256. Sage Publications, London (2004)
52. Sang, K.J.C., Sitko, R.: Qualitative data analysis approaches. In: O'Gorman, K.D., MacIntosh, R. (eds.) Research Methods for Business and Management, pp. 140–154 (2015)
53. Kahneman, D.: Thinking, fast and slow. Farrar, Straus and Ciroux, New York (2011)
54. United Nations. https://sdgs.un.org/goals
55. Sonnenberg, C., vom Brocke, J.: Evaluations in the science of the artificial – reconsidering the build-evaluate pattern in design science research. In: Peffers, K., Rothenberger, M., Kuechler, B. (eds.) DESRIST 2012. LNCS, vol. 7286, pp. 381–397. Springer, Heidelberg (2012). https://doi.org/10.1007/978-3-642-29863-9_28
56. Peffers, K., Rothenberger, M., Tuunanen, T., Vaezi, R.: Design science research evaluation. In: Peffers, K., Rothenberger, M., Kuechler, B. (eds.) DESRIST 2012. LNCS, vol. 7286, pp. 398–410. Springer, Heidelberg (2012). https://doi.org/10.1007/978-3-642-29863-9_29
57. Venable, J., Pries-Heje, J., Baskerville, R.: FEDS: a framework for evaluation in design science research. Eur. J. Inf. Syst. **25**, 77–89 (2016)

Heuristics for the Single-Item Dynamic Lot-Sizing Problem with Rework of Internal Returns

Steffen Rudert(✉) and Udo Buscher

Faculty of Business and Economics, TU Dresden, 01069 Dresden, Germany
steffen.rudert@mailbox.tu-dresden.de

Abstract. While external product returns from customers are well-studied in the dynamic lot-sizing literature, the same is not true for internal returns resulting from imperfect production. We approach this problem by considering a basic dynamic single-product lot-sizing model in which some of the items produced do not meet quality requirements and, therefore, must be reworked. The objective is to minimize the sum of setup and inventory costs for new production and rework while fully satisfying demand. To this end, three heuristics are developed, based essentially on two production policies that can efficiently coordinate new production and rework for different parameter constellations. This is confirmed by a computational study in which the developed heuristics yielded highly competitive results compared to those obtained with a commercial solver.

Keywords: Dynamic lot sizing · Defectives · Rework · Heuristics

1 Introduction

Increased environmental awareness among large segments of the population, increasingly restrictive environmental legislation in many countries, and economic incentives have led companies to become increasingly concerned about product-return management and to take this subject into consideration in addition to their regular manufacturing activities. Sources of product returns can be external to the company as well as internal. In the case of external returns, a distinction can be made between distribution returns and customer returns. The former comprises of returns because of damage, end of shelf life, and contamination, while the latter includes returns related to end-of-use, end-of-life, repair, and warranties (Shaharudin et al. (2015)). In contrast, internal return flows occur when products generated within the manufacturing processes fail to meet the specified requirements.

Herein, we focus on how product returns are addressed in the context of the single-item dynamic lot-sizing problem. This has fundamental importance for dynamic lot-sizing, and since the seminal contribution of Wagner and Whitin

J. de Armas et al. (Eds.): ICCL 2022, LNCS 13557, pp. 425–440, 2022.
https://doi.org/10.1007/978-3-031-16579-5_29

(1958), a large number of publications with numerous extensions have been published. In their review paper, Brahimi et al. (2017) listed a variety of different extensions including limited production capacity, backlogging, lost sales, demand and production time windows, perishability, and carbon emission constraints. Product returns have also been included previously in dynamic lot-size planning. While the literature extensively includes external returns in dynamic lot-sizing, the same is not true for internal returns.

Despite significant efforts, it is only rarely that production is completely defect-free. If the proportion of defective units is subject to uncertainties, this is discussed in the literature under the term 'random yield' (Yano and Lee (1995)). However, for the sake of simplification, it is often assumed that based on experience, the proportion of defective units can be specified with sufficient accuracy. Depending on the defect, products can either be reworked or must be discarded. If they can be reworked, a distinction can be made as to whether they are in such a condition that they meet all the requirements for faultless new products (as good as new condition) or whether they are to be sold as second-hand goods.

The problem considered in this paper can be described as follows. There is a deterministic and time-varying demand that has to be satisfied by production in lots. In addition, unreliable production leads to a certain proportion of a production lot that fails to meet the quality requirements (so-called defectives). All defective units are reworked so that they meet all quality requirements. Thus, we assume that both a priori perfect products and reworked products are identical and serve as so-called serviceables to satisfy demand. The task is to determine the production and rework lots under complete demand satisfaction in such a way that the total costs, which consist of setup and inventory-holding costs for new production and rework, are minimized over the planning period.

The remainder of the paper is organized as follows. After reviewing the related literature in Sect. 2, we present two fundamental production and rework strategies and their cost functions in Sect. 3. We then embed them in three constructive heuristics and illustrate them with small numerical examples in Sect. 4. In Sect. 5, we conduct a small computational study to compare the solutions of the heuristics with those of a commercial solver. In Sect. 6, we provide conclusions.

2 Literature

Kilic and van den Heuvel (2019) denoted the problem that involves customer returns in dynamic lot-sizing as the economic lot-sizing problem with remanufacturing (ELSR). If, by contrast, internal returns are generated due to unreliable production, the term economic lot-sizing problems with rework (ELSRW) will be used in the following. The main difference between these two approaches lies in the sources that are responsible for generating products that do not meet the specified requirements (defectives). While an externally specified influx of customer returns is usually assumed for the ELSR, the ELSRW is characterized by the fact that the defectives occur in the course of production. Despite this crucial difference, both approaches involve similar planning tasks.

First, determining the quality of the product returns needs to be done with the help of an inspection process. Devoto et al. (2021) and Piñeyro and Viera (2021) considered explicitly heterogeneous product returns in the ELSR. This extends beyond simply deciding whether or not the returns can be reworked. Previously published papers that have explicitly considered a disposal option for defectives have been provided, for example, by Golany et al. (2001) and Pan et al. (2009).

In both ELSR and ELSRW, there must be clarity as to whether remanufacturing or rework is conducted on a separate line (off-line) or on a common line with new production (in-line). For the ELSR, Teunter et al. (2006) assumed that joint setup costs occur when new production and remanufacturing take place on one line, while separate setup costs occur when separate lines are used. Helmrich et al. (2014) demonstrated that the ELSR with separate setup costs is NP-hard when all costs are time-invariant, while the ELSR with joint setup costs is NP-hard in general. Consequently, the use of heuristic methods for solving this problem is obvious. Teunter et al. (2006) presented three heuristics for solving the ELSR, where the Silver-Meal based approach was adopted and improved by Schulz (2011). Various metaheuristics such as the tabu search (Li et al. (2014)), the differential evolution algorithm (Parsopoulos et al. (2015)), and the variable neighborhood search algorithm (Sifaleras et al. (2015)) have also been used to solve this problem.

As described above, the literature focuses almost exclusively on external returns. The consideration of internal return flows is mostly represented in models whose scope far exceeds beyond the problem described above as ELSRW. Goerler and Voß (2016) introduced an ELSRW for multiple products with limited capacity for joint new production and rework on one line. Additionally, back-ordering and minimum lot-size constraints are considered. For another rich ELSRW considering multiple products, capacity constraints, lifetime constraints, joint setups, and disposal option, Goerler et al. (2020) proposed a late acceptance hill-climbing matheuristic (LAHCM). Recently, van Zyl and Adetunji (2022) presented an extensive model that incorporates both internal and external returns and uses Wagner/Whitin-based approaches to solve the problem.

In this paper, however, we focus on internal returns and thus on the basic version of the ELSRW with separate setup costs and we derive cost functions for two fundamental production and rework policies. This allows us to develop a deeper understanding of the interplay between production and rework based on the respective setup and inventory costs. Subsequently, it enables the development of efficient heuristics that provide competitive results compared to commercial solvers.

3 Fundamental Production and Rework Policies

3.1 Basic Considerations

The planning problem considers a production system whose imperfect production process leads to a certain fraction β of defective products. The defective units can be reworked to be as good as new. There is a finite planning horizon with T periods and the task is to satisfy given positive demands d_t in every period t (cf. for notation Table 1). The demand can be satisfied by either newly manufactured products or reworked products and both can be stored in a so-called serviceable inventory at a cost rate h_s and defective units in a rework inventory at a cost rate h_d. The associated inventories at the end of period t are denoted by $I_{s,t}$ and $I_{d,t}$. Since new production and rework are performed on separate lines, setup costs R_p and R_r for production and rework are incurred whenever a production lot p_t or rework lot r_t is performed in a period t. Moreover, with the chosen formulation, we follow the common practice in the literature that the unit production costs for new production and rework are negligible (see, e.g., Kilic and van den Heuvel (2019) with further references). In addition, we assume that neither disposal of defectives nor back-ordering is allowed. The objective is to determine a production schedule that minimizes total costs while fully satisfying the demand. The problem described here is NP-hard, see Rudert and Buscher (2022).

Table 1. Notation

Indices		R_p	Setup cost for production
t	Actual period	R_r	Setup cost for rework
T	End of the planning horizon	**Variables**	
k	Production period	p_t	Production amount in period t
l	End of production lot	r_t	Rework amount in period t
m	Rework period	$r_{k,l}$	Sum of rework amounts from period k to l
b	Number of reworks at one lot	y_t	Binary variable for production setup
Parameters		z_t	Binary variable for rework setup
d_t	Demand at period t	$I_{s,t}$	Inventory of serviceables at the end of period t
$d_{k,l}$	Demand from period k to l	$I_{d,t}$	Inventory of defectives at the end of period t
β	Defective rate at production	C	Total cost
h_s	Holding cost per serviceable	C^{PO}	Total cost using production only
h_d	Holding cost per defective	C^{MR}	Total cost using multiple rework

In the following, the two fundamental policies, production only (PO) and multiple rework (MR), are first explained; then, the associated cost functions are derived in the following subsections. If PO is applied between periods k and l, then no rework occurs. Hence, inventories of serviceables I_s and of defectives I_d can be separated (see the lower and upper parts of the left side of Fig. 1). The serviceables inventory of the upper part serves to fulfill the demand, while defectives are stored throughout (k, l). In contrast, in the example given, MR performs a rework twice (a first rework in period 2 ($m_1 = 2$) and a second rework in period 4 ($m_2 = 4$)). Since both, new and reworked products, satisfy demand in periods k through l, their inventories are combined in the upper part to clearly illustrate the overall lower inventory compared to PO.

As a consequence, the production volume of PO must be larger than that of MR in order to obtain the same number of serviceables to completely satisfy demand throughout (k, l). In detail, for MR $p_k = d_{k,l}$ is sufficient while PO

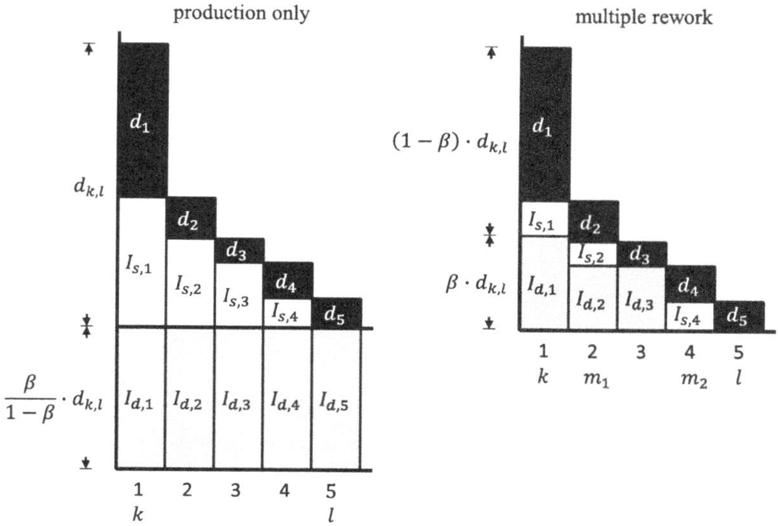

Fig. 1. Inventory for production only and for multiple rework

needs $p_k = \frac{d_{k,l}}{1-\beta}$. For both cases $(1-\beta) \cdot p_k + r_{k,l} = d_{k,l}$ must be valid. As $n = 0$ for PO, $(1-\beta) \cdot p_k = d_{k,l}$ yields to $p_k = \frac{d_{k,l}}{1-\beta}$. For the standard MR case, all produced defective items are reworked ($r_{k,l} = \beta \cdot p_k$) and consequently $(1-\beta) \cdot p_k + \beta \cdot p_k = d_{k,l} = p_k$. Another consequence of PO is that the defectives inventory is transferred from one lot to another. For the example here, $I_{d,5}$ of the PO case will be the starting inventory of the next lot in $k = 6$ which we will refer to as $I_{d,k-1} > 0$ in this paper. It should be noted that the defective rate β is 33% for this example to clearly visualise the defectives inventory and thus the difference between PO and MR. Next, we explain cost expressions for both cases in detail.

3.2 Production Only

There are two inventories in our model, serviceables and defectives, whose respective costs we derive separately. We start with the inventory of serviceables. The **inventory of perfect-quality items** comprises the amount of all demands from periods k to l. After each period in which demand has been satisfied, it is necessary to store the remaining units until the next period. The resulting inventory of serviceables for the production only policy from k to l are

$$I_s^{PO} = \sum_{i=k+1}^{l} d_{i,l}. \tag{1}$$

For the **inventory of defectives**, all items are held until the end of this lot and the duration of the lot is $(l-k+1)$. Defectives generated by production are

$\beta \cdot p_k = \beta \cdot \frac{d_{k,l}}{1-\beta}$. In addition, there may be leftovers if PO has already been used before ($I_{d,k-1} > 0$) and both parts together yield (2).

$$I_d^{PO} = (l - k + 1) \cdot \left(I_{d,k-1} + \frac{\beta}{1-\beta} d_{k,l} \right) \tag{2}$$

As there is no rework, no rework setup costs R_r occur; only production setup costs R_p (3). The total costs of using policy production only from period k to l are

$$C_{k,l}^{PO} = h_s I_s^{PO} + h_d I_d^{PO} + R_p. \tag{3}$$

3.3 Multiple Rework

As shown above, the PO policy produces defectives inventory carried over from lot to lot ($I_{d,k-1} > 0$). This initial stock of defectives influences the production volume of MR. For PO there is no rework and, therefore, no influence on the production volume. For MR, $p_k = d_{k,l}$ is exchanged with $p_k = \max\{0; d_{k,l} - I_{d,k-1}\}$. Hence, the production volume is reduced by the initial stock of defectives and could also be zero for $I_{d,k-1} > d_{k,l}$. In this case, demand would be satisfied completely by rework. The **inventory of perfect-quality items** can be determined with the help of three segments: (I) until the first rework, (II) between rework actions, and (III) after the last rework.

(I): Until the first rework ($m_1 - k$), the full number of produced items ($(1-\beta) \cdot p_k = (1-\beta) \cdot \max\{0; d_{k,l} - I_{d,k-1}\}$) is in stock but is reduced by each period's demand. For each period i, the sum of the demand from k to i is withdrawn from this initial stock. The sum of these withdrawals is $\sum_{i=k}^{m_1-1} d_{k,i}$. In most cases, there may be items left in stock at the period before rework: $(1 - \beta)d_{k,l} - d_{k,m-1} > 0$. The first part of the inventory of serviceables is the initial stock of perfect-quality items multiplied by the duration of the first part ($m_1 - k$) reduced by the withdrawals.
(II): The middle part applies the same logic used for the PO calculation. Each rework covers demand from the rework period up to the last period before the next rework. This inventory is also reduced each period due to demand fulfilment. For the time span between first and second rework, the resulting inventories from $t = m_1$ to $t = m_{1+1} - 1 = m_2 - 1$ are $\sum_{e=m_1+1}^{m_2-1} d_{e,m_2-1}$. This calculation must be conducted for all rework activities; thus, m_1 is replaced by m_j. The calculation runs from the first ($j = 1$) to the last but one ($j = b - 1$) rework and yields the second part of I_s^{MR}, see (4).
(III): After all defectives have been reworked, the same logic is applied again, and the calculation for the inventory of perfect-quality items is the sum of $\sum_{q=m_b+1}^{l} d_{q,l}$.

All three parts together yield the inventory of serviceables from period k to l for the multiple rework policy.

$$I_s^{MR} = (1-\beta) \cdot \max\{0; d_{k,l} - I_{d,k-1}\} \cdot (m_1 - k) - \sum_{i=k}^{m_1-1} d_{k,i} + \sum_{j=1}^{b-1} \sum_{e=m_j+1}^{m_{j+1}-1} d_{e,m_{j+1}-1} + \sum_{q=m_b+1}^{l} d_{q,l} \tag{4}$$

For the **inventory of defectives**, too, it makes sense to distinguish between three segments: (I) before the first rework, (II) between rework actions, and (III) excess inventory of defectives.

(I): All defectives that will be reworked during this lot ($\beta \cdot d_{k,l}$) are held in stock until the first rework ($m_1 - k$).
(II): Between rework actions, the defectives remain at a constant level and can be used for future rework: $\sum_{i=1}^{b-1}(m_{i+1} - m_i) \cdot d_{m_{i+1},l}$.
(III): Some defectives may remain in stock at the end of the production lot (if $I_{d,k-1} > d_{k,l}$). Consequently, this excess inventory ($\max\{0; I_{d,k-1} - d_{k,l}\}$) is stored during the complete duration of the lot ($l - k + 1$). All three parts together yield the inventory of defectives from period k to l for the multiple rework policy.

$$I_d^{MR} = (m_1 - k) \cdot \beta \cdot d_{k,l} + \sum_{i=1}^{b-1} (m_{i+1} - m_i) \cdot d_{m_{i+1},l} + (l - k + 1) \cdot \max\{0; I_{d,k-1} - d_{k,l}\} \tag{5}$$

The total costs for using the multiple rework policy from k to l now show that setup for rework may be incurred several times ($b \cdot R_r$).

$$C_{k,l}^{MR} = h_s I_s^{MR} + h_d I_d^{MR} + R_p + b \cdot R_r \tag{6}$$

The rework periods may be determined using the procedure below:

Step 1: Determine *first* rework $m_1 = m^*$ using

$$d_{k,m^*-1} \leq (1-\beta) \cdot p_k < d_{k,m^*}.$$

Step 2: Search *second* rework m_i backward from l to $m_1 + 1$ using

$$(h_s - h_d) \cdot d_{m_i,l} \cdot (m_i - m_1) > R_r.$$

If true then fix *second* rework $m_b = m_i$ and values for p_k, m, n, $I_{d,l}$ else continue searching.

Step 3: Search for next rework m_i backward from $i = m_b - 1$ to $m_1 + 1$ using

$$(h_s - h_d) \cdot d_{m_i,m_b-1} \cdot (m_i - m_1) > R_r$$
$$(h_s - h_d) \cdot d_{m_b,l} \cdot (m_b - m_i) > R_r.$$

If both are true then fix *third* rework $m_{b-1} = m_i$.

else continue searching.

Step 4: Search for next rework m_i backward from $i = m_b - 2$ to $m_1 + 1$ using ...

The first rework m^* at step 1 is necessary as the initial inventory of serviceables $(1-\beta)p_k$ can no longer fulfil demand d_{k,m^*}. For additional reworks, the savings due to lower storage costs of defectives ($h_d < h_s$) must exceed the additional rework setup costs R_r. At step 2, the equation must hold for the additional rework. For all upcoming reworks from step 3 onward, one equation for the new and one for the former must hold simultaneously.

For $h_s \leq h_d$, a single rework as early as possible is the most economical: $r_k = \beta p_k$. For $h_s > h_d$, it is most cost-effective to rework as late as possible and only a minimum amount of reworked products is needed to satisfy each demand. While the former case is simple, the latter is covered by our procedure.

4 Heuristic Algorithms

4.1 Basic Algorithm

This section starts with the development of a constructive heuristic in subsection (4.1), which is extended in subsection (4.2) in two ways. The basic algorithm explores the solution space by systematically calculating various lot sizes and chooses the best solutions. Our implementation here uses a forward algorithm for calculating all lot sizes (k, l) for each given l. For each $k > 1$, the best cost solution is chosen as the predecessor.

Our algorithm starts at $l = 1$ and sets $k = 1$ (step 1). It calculates PO and MR, using the sub-routine as described above, for each lot and chooses the one with lower costs (step 2). However, due to the assumption that both inventories and, thus, also the defectives inventory, must be cleared at the end of the planning horizon, it becomes necessary to start rework from a certain point in time. Each time a new production lot is started, $p_k + I_{d,k-1} \leq d_{k,T}$ must apply. This prevents overproduction as p_k is allowed only up to the sum of all upcoming demand minus the initial stock of defective items. As the production volume for PO is higher than for MR, the PO option will not be available if this condition is not met and MR must be chosen in this case.

After deciding to choose PO or MR, all parameters for this (k, l) combination are fixed: production volume p_k, rework periods m, rework volumes n, and final inventory of defectives $I_{d,l}$. The total costs comprise the costs of this actual lot plus the best cost predecessor. This predecessor is found by selecting the minimum costs of the existing solutions that cover the demand up to one period before this lot $\left(\min\limits_{1 \leq i \leq e} \{C_{i,e=k-1}\}\right)$.

Afterward, if the end of the planning horizon is reached ($k = l = T$), the algorithm is terminated. Otherwise, if $k = l$, it increases l by one period and goes to step 2 or, if $k < l$, it increases k by one period and also goes to step 2.

Combining all steps together, the basic algorithm reads as follows:

Step 1: $l = 1$, $k = 1$.

Step 2: Determine rework.

$$\text{If } (C^{PO} < C^{MR}) \text{ then } C_{k,l} = C^{PO}_{k,l} + \min_{1 \le i \le e} \{C_{i,e=k-1}\}$$
$$\text{else } C_{k,l} = C^{MR}_{k,l} + \min_{1 \le i \le e} \{C_{i,e=k-1}\}.$$

Fix p_k, m, n, $I_{d,l}$.

Step 3: If $k = l = T$ then go to end

else if $k = l$ set $l = l + 1$ and $k = 1$ and go to Step 2
else set $k = k + 1$ and go to Step 2.

We present a numeric sample to illustrate our algorithm. The cost parameters are $h_s = 1$, $h_d = 1$, $R_p = 50$, $R_r = 50$, and $\beta = 5\%$. The algorithm chooses to produce every period and to rework at the last period $t = 10$ only (see Table 2). This example with its solution may appear to be quite simple, but it works well to illustrate the improvements of the algorithm. As defectives holding costs at each period are less than rework setup costs, PO is chosen every period, and this is done according to the decision rule of the basic algorithm. Hence, rework activities are not balanced throughout the planning horizon, and therefore, we name the basic algorithm NB in the following. In the next section we demonstrate how this can be improved.

Table 2. Numeric sample of the basic algorithm (NB)

t	d	k	l	m	p	$(1-\beta)p$	βp	n	I_s	I_d	R	$h_s I_s$	$h_d I_d$	C	C_{cum}
1	89	1	1	0	93.68	89.00	4.68	0.00	0	4.68	50	0	4.68	54.68	54.68
2	107	2	2	0	112.63	107.00	5.63	0.00	0	10.32	50	0	10.32	60.32	115.00
3	83	3	3	0	87.37	83.00	4.37	0.00	0	14.68	50	0	14.68	64.68	179.68
4	106	4	4	0	111.58	106.00	5.58	0.00	0	20.26	50	0	20.26	70.26	249.95
5	94	5	5	0	98.95	94.00	4.95	0.00	0	25.21	50	0	25.21	75.21	325.16
6	91	6	6	0	95.79	91.00	4.79	0.00	0	30.00	50	0	30.00	80.00	405.16
7	110	7	7	0	115.79	110.00	5.79	0.00	0	35.79	50	0	35.79	85.79	490.95
8	104	8	8	0	109.47	104.00	5.47	0.00	0	41.26	50	0	41.26	91.26	582.21
9	120	9	9	0	126.32	120.00	6.32	0.00	0	47.58	50	0	47.58	97.58	679.79
10	105	10	10	10	57.42	54.55	2.87	50.45	0	0.00	100	0	0.00	100.00	779.79

4.2 Improvements

As stated above, our heuristic algorithm would check for every lot PO vs. MR and selects the one with the lower cost. In some instances, this would create high holding costs of defectives and concentrate rework at the end of the planning horizon. The first improvement to our basic algorithm is the **balancing** of rework activities to avoid this phenomenon. This is incorporated by adding the cumulated holding costs for defectives as an additional decision rule between PO and MR. Consequently, rework would also be conducted if cumulated holding costs of defectives exceed rework setup costs, although PO would result in a lower total cost for this single period than MR would.

To calculate the costs for the new decision criterion from the last known rework onward, the information needs to be transferred from lot to lot. The calculation of the cumulated defective holding cost at the end of lot (k, l) is λ_l and differs for PO and MR. For PO, λ_l includes all defectives' holding costs of the actual lot as there is no rework. In addition, it includes costs from previous lots back to the last known rework, which is λ_{k-1}. Thus, the cumulated defective holding cost for the production only policy is

$$\lambda_l^{PO} = h_d I_d^{PO} + \lambda_{k-1}. \tag{7}$$

Differing from that, there are rework activities at MR, and therefore, cumulated holding costs start from the last rework of the actual lot and do not include costs from previous lots. Thus, the final defectives inventory of the actual lot $(I_{d,l})$ is multiplied by the duration from the last rework until the end of this lot $(l - m_b + 1)$ and by the costs per defective item h_d. The cumulated defective holding cost for the multiple rework policy is

$$\lambda_l^{MR} = I_{d,l} \cdot (l - m_b + 1) \cdot h_d. \tag{8}$$

Consequently, the criterion of the balancing improvement is ϕ.

$$\phi : \lambda_l^{PO} < R_r. \tag{9}$$

More precisely, our improved algorithm to which we refer as BA in the following, checks $\lambda_l^{PO} < R_r$ in the case of $C_{k,l}^{PO} < C_{k,l}^{MR}$ and only chooses PO if both inequalities are fulfilled. We incorporate this into our algorithm by modifiying step 2. For BA it reads as follows:

Step 2: Determine rework.

$$\text{If } \left(\left(C_{k,l}^{PO} < C_{k,l}^{MR} \right) \wedge \phi \right) \text{ is true then } C_{k,l} = C_{k,l}^{PO} + \min_{1 \leq i \leq e} \{C_{i,e=k-1}\}$$
$$\text{else } C_{k,l} = C_{k,l}^{MR} + \min_{1 \leq i \leq e} \{C_{i,e=k-1}\}.$$

Fix p_k, m, n, $I_{d,l}$, λ_l.

The result, applying the improved algorithm BA, is shown in Table 3. Differing from NB, rework is now started already in $t = 5$ as the cumulated defective holding cost would exceed R_r at this period. The next rework is placed at $t = 9$ as the cumulated defective holding cost would, again, exceed R_r. Since the end of the planning horizon is reached at the next period, there will be a third rework at $t = 10$. The BA improvement reduces the total costs from 779.79 of NB to

Table 3. Numeric sample of the balanced algorithm (BA)

t	d	k	l	m	p	$(1-\beta)p$	βp	n	I_s	I_d	R	$h_s I_s$	$h_d I_d$	C	C_{cum}
1	89	1	1	0	93.68	89.00	4.68	0.00	0	4.68	50	0	4.68	54.68	54.68
2	107	2	2	0	112.63	107.00	5.63	0.00	0	10.32	50	0	10.32	60.32	115.00
3	83	3	3	0	87.37	83.00	4.37	0.00	0	14.68	50	0	14.68	64.68	179.68
4	106	4	4	0	111.58	106.00	5.58	0.00	0	20.26	50	0	20.26	70.26	249.95
5	94	5	5	5	73.74	70.05	3.69	23.95	0	0.00	100	0	0.00	100.00	349.95
6	91	6	6	0	95.79	91.00	4.79	0.00	0	4.79	50	0	4.79	54.79	404.74
7	110	7	7	0	115.79	110.00	5.79	0.00	0	10.58	50	0	10.58	60.58	465.32
8	104	8	8	0	109.47	104.00	5.47	0.00	0	16.05	50	0	16.05	66.05	531.37
9	120	9	9	9	103.95	98.75	5.20	21.25	0	0.00	100	0	0.00	100.00	631.37
10	105	10	10	10	105.00	99.75	5.25	5.25	0	0.00	100	0	0.00	100.00	731.37

731.37. However, the accumulation of reworks at the end of the planning horizon may occur using BA and we will present a second improvement to address this.

The **look-ahead** (LA) criterion compares the costs if, now, no rework would be conducted until the end of the planning horizon to the costs of a rework setup at the actual lot. Thereby, it reduces futile reworks, especially at or next to the end of the planning horizon.

When the BA criterion overrules the cost comparison of PO vs. MR and would select MR, the LA criterion can overrule the BA criterion and select PO. This prevents a rework whenever it is near the end of the planning horizon and, additionally, another rework occurs in $t = T$ to clear the defective stock. By reducing this unnecessary rework, the LA criterion also balances rework activities throughout the planning horizon. Please note, however, that it is used only in combination with the BA criterion and is calculated by assuming that, from this point onward, there will be no rework. Following this, the demand from the actual lot up to one period before the end of the planning horizon should be covered solely by PO and generate defective items $\frac{\beta}{1-\beta} \cdot d_{k,T-1}$. Together with the initial stock of defectives $I_{d,k-1}$, they will be stored for $(T-k)$ periods. Multiplying by the cost per defective item h_d yields the additional decision criterion ψ for the BA LA algorithm.

$$\psi : \left(\frac{\beta}{1-\beta} \cdot d_{k,T-1} + I_{d,k-1} \right) \cdot (T-k) \cdot h_d < R_r \tag{10}$$

For the BA algorithm, the BA criterion ϕ must be true to allow for PO in the case of $C_{k,l}^{PO} < C_{k,l}^{MR}$. For the new BA LA algorithm, PO will be selected if $C_{k,l}^{PO} < C_{k,l}^{MR}$ and ϕ or ψ are true. The BA criterion ϕ is true if the cumulated defectives holding costs are less than the rework setup costs. The LA criterion ψ is true if the maximum sum of future defectives holding costs are less than the rework setup costs. The combined BA LA improvement will allow PO for both, thus if ϕ is true or ψ is true or both. Hence, the purpose of the LA criterion ψ is only to overrule the BA criterion ϕ. The modified step 2 for BA LA reads as follows.

Step 2: Determine rework.

$$\text{If } \left((C^{PO}_{k,l} < C^{MR}_{k,l}) \wedge (\phi \vee \psi)\right) \text{ is true then } C_{k,l} = C^{PO}_{k,l} + \min_{1 \leq i \leq e} \{C_{i,e=k-1}\}$$
$$\text{else } C_{k,l} = C^{MR}_{k,l} + \min_{1 \leq i \leq e} \{C_{i,e=k-1}\}.$$

Fix p_k, m, n, $I_{d,l}$, λ_l.

Table 4 shows the effect of the BA LA improvement as the futile rework at $t = 9$ of Table 3 is eliminated. For this example, BA LA thus finds the optimal solution with a total cost of 703.74 compared to 731.37 for BA and 779.79 for NB.

Table 4. Numeric sample of the balanced look-ahead algorithm (BA LA)

t	d	k	l	m	p	$(1-\beta)p$	βp	n	I_s	I_d	R	$h_s I_s$	$h_d I_d$	C	C_{cum}
1	89	1	1	0	93.68	89.00	4.68	0.00	0	4.68	50	0	4.68	54.68	54.68
2	107	2	2	0	112.63	107.00	5.63	0.00	0	10.32	50	0	10.32	60.32	115.00
3	83	3	3	0	87.37	83.00	4.37	0.00	0	14.68	50	0	14.68	64.68	179.68
4	106	4	4	0	111.58	106.00	5.58	0.00	0	20.26	50	0	20.26	70.26	249.95
5	94	5	5	5	73.74	70.05	3.69	23.95	0	0.00	100	0	0.00	100.00	349.95
6	91	6	6	0	95.79	91.00	4.79	0.00	0	4.79	50	0	4.79	54.79	404.74
7	110	7	7	0	115.79	110.00	5.79	0.00	0	10.58	50	0	10.58	60.58	465.32
8	104	8	8	0	109.47	104.00	5.47	0.00	0	16.05	50	0	16.05	66.05	531.37
9	120	9	9	0	126.32	120.00	6.32	0.00	0	22.37	50	0	22.37	72.37	603.74
10	105	10	10	10	82.63	78.50	4.13	26.50	0	0.00	100	0	0.00	100.00	703.74

5 Computational Study

We computed various data sets for our three algorithms (NB, BA, and BA LA) and compared them to solutions obtained by Gurobi using two different settings. First, we used Gurobi at a time limit of 60 s to obtain optimal or near-optimal solutions (denoted by G-60). For a second setting, we set the time limit of Gurobi to the mean runtime of our best algorithm BA LA in terms of cost delta to the optimal solution (denoted by G-TL). All tests were conducted on a Windows Server 2012 R2 with Intel(R) Xeon(R) CPU E5-4627 v2 @ 3.3 GHz processors with 32 cores, of which 4 were used for the computations, 768GB RAM and Gurobi 8.1 as the MILP solver. The results of all computations are summarised in Table 5.

To obtain highly meaningful results, we solved a whole set of different problem instances. For this purpose, we chose the following parameters: $\beta = 1\%$; 5%; 10%; 20%, $h_s = 1$, $h_d = 0.5$; 1.0; 2.0, $R_p = R_r = 50$; 250; 500; 2000. Thus, there are a total of $4 * 3 * 4 * 4 = 192$ test instances. For each of these parameter constellations, 10 demand series were used (two each for the five different demand patterns) according to the demand function given in Teunter et al. (2006). The calculations were computed for different lengths of the planning horizon $T = 10$;

Table 5. Computation times and cost deltas of Gurobi and the heuristic algorithms

	G-60		NB		BA		BA LA		G-TL	
T	rt [s]	gap [%]	rt [s]	ΔC [%]	rt [s]	ΔC [%]	rt [s]	ΔC [%]	rt [s]	ΔC [%]
10	0.072	0.00	0.019	0.52	0.023	0.35	0.018	0.20	0.021	12.80
20	0.799	0.00	0.075	1.65	0.090	0.68	0.073	0.43	0.082	12.07
40	23.027	0.96	0.337	3.63	0.498	0.79	0.431	0.58	0.491	6.73
80	52.855	6.18	2.269	5.96	2.767	0.54	3.086	0.34	3.928	3.01
160	58.467	11.37	17.724	7.91	21.078	-0.07	19.753	-0.14	24.623	0.86

20; 40; 80; 160 to show the performance of our algorithms for smaller and larger problem sizes. Thus, a total of $5 \cdot 1,920 = 9{,}600$ data sets were used.

The results in Table 5 are listed from left to right for Gurobi with a time limit of 60 s (G-60), basic heuristic algorithm not balanced (NB), balanced (BA), balanced and look-ahead (BA LA), and Gurobi with a time limit of the mean runtime of BA LA (G-TL). The mean runtime in seconds (rt) and the cost delta to G-60 (ΔC) for 1,920 samples are shown for each solution procedure and each T respectively. Hereby, ΔC denotes the costs of applying the heuristic algorithms or G-TL minus the costs of G-60. For G-60, the mean computed gap to the optimal solution is provided instead of the cost delta to the optimal solution.

We start by analysing the **computation times** of the solution methods, and we can see that Gurobi needs significantly more time compared to the heuristic solutions. It should be noted that the Gurobi runtimes for $T = 40; 80; 160$ are restricted due to the time limit of 60 s. Our heuristic algorithms show little variance for the computation time between the three options. Only NB may need less runtime compared to BA and BA LA, especially for larger problem sizes.

For the **quality** of the obtained solutions, we can see that G-60 yields optimal solutions for $T = 10; 20$. For $T = 40; 80; 160$ there is an optimality gap, but for $T = 40; 80$, it still shows the best solutions. Only for $T = 160$, BA and BA LA yield a lower mean of the total cost compared to Gurobi, indicated by negative values of ΔC. Also, the mean cost deltas of our three algorithms improve from NB to BA and to BA LA for each T. Both, BA and BA LA, show cost deltas significantly below 1% for all lengths of the planning horizon compared to G-60.

When the time limit for Gurobi is set very restrictively, as for G-TL, the cost deltas to G-60 can be quite high. They are above 10% for $T = 10; 20$ but decrease with increasing problem size. Although the time limits for $T = 40; 80; 160$ are also restrictive, Gurobi shows better basic solutions if the available time is higher than a certain minimum time. For the problem sizes provided here, BA and BA LA always yield solutions at a lower cost compared to G-TL at about the same runtime.

Now we focus only on the results of our algorithm BA LA. We observe that the solution quality differs for various input data. Table 6 shows cost deltas to G-60 for $T = 20$ and is designed as a heatmap, with entries highlighted in red associated with long computation times. We use $T = 20$ as Gurobi solves all samples optimally and, thus, we can compare BA LA to the optimal solution.

Table 6. Cost delta to optimal solution in [%] for BA LA for different input data

	h_d	0.5				1.0				2.0			
	β	1%	5%	10%	20%	1%	5%	10%	20%	1%	5%	10%	20%
R_p	R_r												
50	50	0.45	0.72	0.93	0.74	0.19	0.39	0.54	0.42	0.14	0.57	0.42	0.00
	200	0.06	2.07	2.96	3.56	0.08	0.42	0.77	1.15	0.98	0.93	1.42	1.82
	500	0.05	0.50	3.97	4.89	0.00	0.78	0.73	1.43	0.53	1.05	0.65	1.83
	2000	0.03	0.05	1.03	2.73	0.00	0.00	0.18	1.15	0.00	0.08	0.37	1.02
200	50	0.15	0.44	0.63	0.42	0.09	0.12	0.00	0.00	0.11	0.02	0.00	0.00
	200	0.00	0.76	1.06	1.07	0.03	0.55	0.67	1.08	0.23	0.70	0.87	0.00
	500	0.00	0.56	2.45	1.73	0.00	0.66	0.90	1.18	0.23	0.71	0.91	1.24
	2000	0.00	0.16	0.55	2.15	0.00	0.00	0.13	0.59	0.00	0.07	0.44	1.19
500	50	0.19	0.15	0.44	0.04	0.06	0.04	0.00	0.00	0.01	0.00	0.00	0.00
	200	0.00	0.21	0.42	1.06	0.03	0.22	0.16	0.00	0.16	0.09	0.05	0.00
	500	0.00	0.26	1.08	0.84	0.00	0.43	0.16	0.37	0.34	0.13	0.22	0.00
	2000	0.00	0.06	0.30	0.99	0.00	0.00	0.02	0.60	0.00	0.08	0.36	0.70
2000	50	0.04	0.01	0.00	0.08	0.00	0.00	0.00	0.00	0.00	0.00	0.00	0.00
	200	0.05	0.23	0.17	0.16	0.01	0.00	0.00	0.00	0.09	0.00	0.00	0.00
	500	0.00	0.39	0.34	0.63	0.00	0.13	0.03	0.00	0.01	0.04	0.00	0.00
	2000	0.00	0.01	0.05	0.16	0.00	0.00	0.03	0.19	0.00	0.00	0.30	0.00

As there are 10 demand patterns used for each parameter combination, each entry in the table represents the average of 10 computations. Recalling the data from Table 5 we know that the mean cost delta of BA LA is 0.43% for $T = 20$.

High cost deltas can be observed for (1) higher values of defective rate β, (2) smaller values of holding cost per defective item h_d, (3) smaller values of production setup costs R_p, and (4) medium-high values of rework setup costs R_r. The largest cost delta in the amount of 4.89% results consistently for the parameter combination $R_p = 50$, $R_r = 500$, $h_d = 0.5$, $\beta = 20\%$. If β is reduced from 20% to 10% with otherwise unchanged parameters, the second-highest deviation results in the amount of 3.97%. By setting $h_s = 1$ and varying h_d from 0.5 over 1 to 2, we can conclude whether, and if so how, the ratio of inventory cost rates affects the performance of the heuristics. Table 6 shows that the heuristics presented have particularly small cost deltas when $h_s < h_d$ holds. In the opposite case ($h_s > h_d$), slightly increased cost deltas can be observed for otherwise-unchanged parameter constellations.

6 Conclusions

This paper has addressed the case of imperfect production with rework, which is widely neglected in the dynamic lot-sizing literature. To gain several basic insights, we have considered a simple but nonetheless fundamental problem. For two production policies (PO and MR), associated cost functions were explicitly derived, and three heuristics were developed based on these. The basic algorithm NB uses only the best cost solution of PO vs. MR. The first improvement BA consists of balancing rework activities by involving cumulated holding costs for defectives. The second improvement LA is to look-ahead from the actual lot and modify the rework policy accordingly. All algorithms showed substantially less computational effort and both improvements yielded very competitive results of less than 1% cost delta compared to Gurobi operating at a time limit of 60 s. Also, we illustrated how the performance of our algorithms varies with varying input data cost parameters.

There are some limitations at this paper. We use only two special characteristics of the model to build the problem specific algorithms, PO and MR. It can be shown that for optimal solutions there is sometimes overproduction of serviceables and this could also be integrated in the solution procedure. Besides, our algorithms are constructive heuristics that need their full runtime and cannot be used with time limits. Moreover, the procedure for determining rework is a greedy heuristic and could also be improved.

If $\lambda_l^{PO} < x \cdot R_r$ rather than $\lambda_l^{PO} < R_r$ is chosen as the decision criterion ϕ, it can be shown that better results can be obtained to varying degrees for both $x < 1$ and $x > 1$. This needs further research and could narrow the gap between our algorithms and Gurobi even more.

Appendix

The following MIP formulation has been used to calculate the optimal solutions using Gurobi as the commercial solver.

$$\min \textstyle\sum_{t=1}^{T} h_s \cdot I_{s,t} + h_d \cdot I_{d,t} + y_t \cdot R_p + z_t \cdot R_r \tag{11}$$

subject to

$$I_{s,t} = I_{s,t-1} + (1-\beta) \cdot p_t + r_t - d_t \quad \forall t = 1, \ldots, T \tag{12}$$

$$I_{d,t} = I_{d,t-1} + \beta \cdot p_t - r_t \quad \forall t = 1, \ldots, T \tag{13}$$

$$p_t \leq d_{t,T} \cdot y_t \quad \forall t = 1, \ldots, T \tag{14}$$

$$r_t \leq d_{t,T} \cdot z_t \quad \forall t = 1, \ldots, T \tag{15}$$

$$I_{s,0} = I_{d,0} = I_{d,T} = I_{s,T} = 0 \tag{16}$$

$$p_t, r_t, I_{s,t}, I_{d,t} \geq 0, d_t > 0 \quad \forall t = 1, \ldots, T \tag{17}$$

$$y_t, z_t \in \{0; 1\} \quad \forall t = 1, \ldots, T \tag{18}$$

References

Brahimi, N., Absi, N., Dauzère-Pérès, S., Nordli, A.: Single-item dynamic lot-sizing problems: an updated survey. Eur. J. Oper. Res. **263**(3), 838–863 (2017)

Devoto, C., Fernández, E., Piñeyro, P.: The economic lot-sizing problem with remanufacturing and inspection for grading heterogeneous returns. J. Remanufact. **11**(1), 71–87 (2020). https://doi.org/10.1007/s13243-020-00089-5

Goerler, A., Voß, S.: Dynamic lot-sizing with rework of defective items and minimum lot-size constraints. Int. J. Prod. Res. **54**(8), 1–14 (2016)

Goerler, A., Lalla-Ruiz, E., Voß, S.: Late acceptance hill-climbing matheuristic for the general lot sizing and scheduling problem with rich constraints. Algorithms **13**, 1–26 (2020)

Golany, R., Yang, J., Yu, G.: Economic lot-sizing with remanufacturing options. IIE Trans. **33**, 995–1003 (2001)

Helmrich, M.J.R., Jans, R., van den Heuvel, W., Wagelmans, A.P.: Economic lot-sizing with remanufacturing: complexity and efficient formulations. IIE Trans. **46**, 67–86 (2014)

Kilic, O.A., van den Heuvel, W.: Economic lot sizing with remanufacturing: structural properties and polynomial-time heuristics. IISE Trans. **51**(12), 1318–1331 (2019)

Li, X., Baki, F., Tian, P., Chaouch, B.A.: A robust block-chain based tabu search algorithm for the dynamic lot sizing problem with product returns and remanufacturing. Omega **42**, 75–87 (2014)

Pan, Z., Tang, J., Liu, O.: Capacitated dynamic lot sizing problems in closed-loop supply chain. Eur. J. Oper. Res. **198**, 810–821 (2009)

Parsopoulos, K., Konstantaras, I., Skouri, K.: Metaheuristic optimization for the single-item dynamic lot sizing problem with returns and remanufacturing. Comput. Ind. Eng. **83**, 307–315 (2015)

Piñeyro, P., Viera, O.: The economic lot-sizing problem with remanufacturing and heterogeneous returns: formulations, analysis and algorithms. Int. J. Prod. Res. (2021). https://doi.org/10.1080/00207543.2021.1925771

Rudert, S., Buscher, U.: On the complexity of the economic lot-sizing problem with rework of defectives. Dresdner Beiträge zur Betriebswirtschaftslehre, Nr. 182/22. TU Dresden, Dresden (2022). https://doi.org/10.25368/2022.322

Schulz, T.: A new silver-meal based heuristic for the single-item dynamic lot sizing problem with returns and remanufacturing. Int. J. Prod. Res. **49**(9), 2519–2533 (2011)

Shaharudin, M.R., Govindan, K., Zailani, S., Tan, K.C.: Managing product returns to achieve supply chain sustainability: an exploratory study and research propositions. J. Cleaner Prod. **101**(101), 1–15 (2015)

Sifaleras, A., Konstantaras, I., Mladenović, N.: Variable neighborhood search for the economic lot sizing problem with product returns and recovery. Int. J. Prod. Econ. **160**, 133–143 (2015)

Teunter, R.H., Bayindir, Z.P., van den Heuvel, W.: Dynamic lot sizing with product returns and remanufacturing. Int. J. Prod. Res. **44**(20), 4377–4400 (2006)

van Zyl, A., Adetunji, O.: A lot sizing model for two items with imperfect manufacturing process, time varying demand and return rates, dependent demand and different quality grades. J. Remanufact. 1–26 (2022). https://doi.org/10.1007/s13243-022-00110-z

Wagner, H.M., Whitin, T.M.: Dynamic version of the economic lot size model. Manage. Sci. **5**, 89–96 (1958)

Yano, C.A., Lee, H.L.: Lot sizing with random yields: a review. Oper. Res. **43**(2), 311–334 (1995)

A Carbon-Aware Planning Framework for Production Scheduling in Mining

Nurul Asyikeen Binte Azhar[1,2](✉), Aldy Gunawan[1], Shih-Fen Cheng[1], and Erwin Leonardi[2]

[1] School of Computing and Information Systems, Singapore Management University, 80 Stamford Road, 178902 Singapore, Singapore
{nurula.a.2020,aldygunawan,sfcheng}@smu.edu.sg

[2] Rio Tinto Ltd., Tower 3, 12 Marina Boulevard, Marina Bay Financial Centre, 018982 Singapore, Singapore
{asyikeen.azhar,erwin.leonardi}@riointo.com

Abstract. Managing the flow of excavated materials from a mine pit and the subsequent processing steps is the logistical challenge in mining. Mine planning needs to consider various geometric and resource constraints while maximizing the net present value (NPV) of profits over a long horizon. This mine planning problem has been modelled and solved as a precedence constrained production scheduling problem (PCPSP) using heuristics, due to its NP-hardness. However, the recent push for sustainable and carbon-aware mining practices calls for new planning approaches. In this paper, we propose an efficient temporally decomposed greedy Lagrangian relaxation (TDGLR) approach to maximize profits while observing the stipulated carbon emission limit per year. With a collection of real-world-inspired mining datasets, we demonstrate how we generate approximated Pareto fronts for planners. Using this approach, they can choose mine plans that maximize profits while observing the given carbon emission target. The TDGLR was compared against a Mixed Integer Programming (MIP) model to solve a real mine dataset with the gaps not exceeding 0.3178% and averaging 0.015%. For larger instances, MIP cannot even generate feasible solutions.

Keywords: Operations research and management · Resource capacity planning · Lagrangian relaxation · Sustainability

1 Introduction

Logistics in mining involves extensive planning and management of the flow of excavated raw materials starting from the mine pit, through an extensive series of processing, until the shipment of desired end products. A mining compound comprises of multiple operational facilities. Besides the massive mine pit where valuable raw materials are excavated, there are also processing facilities (e.g.,

Supported by Enterprise Singapore.

J. de Armas et al. (Eds.): ICCL 2022, LNCS 13557, pp. 441–456, 2022.
https://doi.org/10.1007/978-3-031-16579-5_30

crushing), refining facilities (e.g., hydrometallurgy), storage facility (i.e., stockpiles), and waste facilities (e.g., dump and tailings pond). Each of these facilities is supported by various resources with their corresponding capacity limits. A generic logistics system of a mine is outlined in Fig. 1.

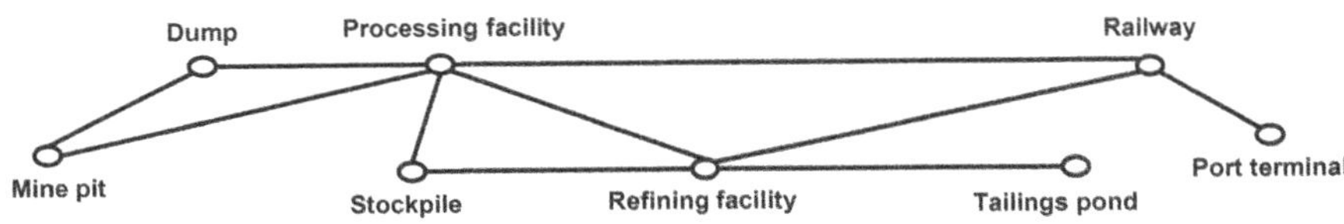

Fig. 1. A schematic diagram of a generic mine logistics system.

The logistics management of a mining compound comprises of forecasting, planning, and scheduling activities across strategic, tactical, and operational levels [15]. Strategic models determine the three dimensional shapes or outlines of the mine, known as the final pit limit. Tactical models determine the production schedule that consists of block extraction, its sequencing, and processing decisions after extraction. Meanwhile, operational models determine the deployment of resources such as machinery to support production scheduling.

In this paper, we focus on the planning at the tactical level, which falls under the planning phase of the five mining phases (Fig. 2); it is generally accepted to be the most critical cost factor [9]. Tactical planning over the entire life span of a mine (in decades) has been solved as a *precedence constrained production scheduling problem* (PCPSP) in the literature, which dictates operational decisions of machine types, quantity, apportionment, and maintenance [15]. As such planning problems are known to be NP-hard [11], the focus of most past research works are thus on the development of effective and efficient heuristics.

INVESTMENT DECISION

Phase	Exploration	Planning	Implementation	Production	Reclamation
Activities	Deem economic viability by inspecting and measuring ore deposits	Detailed estimates on costs, environmental effects, financing, expected revenue, ore tonnage and grade, mining and production schedule	Prepare infrastructure (e.g. road and rail), heavy equipment, processing facilities (e.g. smelters), operational facilities (e.g. employee housing), and environmental management system (e.g. waste removal)	In **operation**	Rehabilitate at end of life
Relative cost	-	**Highest**	**High**	**Low**	-

Fig. 2. Summary of activities for each mine phase and their influences on costs.

To generate an actionable long-term plan given the vast swath of the mining area, planners usually have to discretize the landmass of the mine pit into three-dimensional blocks, and decide the sequence of blocks to be excavated. In order to stay feasible, the mining plan has to minimally satisfy geometric constraints at the mining pit (e.g., surface blocks have to be excavated before reaching underground blocks) and various resource consumption constraints at the downstream facilities. However, to optimize the performance of the mining plan, we have to also consider the estimated block processing cost and profit (based on geological survey), and predicted market demands over the planning horizon. In the literature, these factors are usually incorporated by the net present value (NPV) of estimated profit over a decade-long planning horizon [12].

Besides profit consideration, there are increasing concerns on the environmental impacts of the open-pit metal mining due to its scale and complex refining processes [16]. In particular, the planner now needs to also consider carbon emissions along the whole production process. This push is also observed in other industries such as manufacturing [22]. Carbon costing is increasingly pertinent as more countries participate in, develop, and consider emissions trading systems (ETS) [10] as well as emission taxes. In this paper, we aim to augment past research on mine planning to consider important environmental side constraints, so that the computed mining plans can be carbon-aware by construction.

Our approach is based on the generic PCPSP formulation [5], where the objective is still to maximize the NPV, yet with a new set of constraints on carbon emission per time period. To solve realistic-scale instances, we propose an efficient *temporally decomposed greedy Lagrangian relaxation* (TDGLR) approach, which is tested on a real-world-inspired mine dataset and two benchmark instances from MineLib [5]. We demonstrate how we generate approximated Pareto fronts for planners to choose mining plans that maximize profits while observing the given carbon emission targets. When the TDGLR was compared against a Mixed Integer Programming (MIP) model, the solution gap was an average of 0.015% for a real dataset.

2 Related Work

The logistical challenges in mine planning have been examined from strategic, tactical and operational levels. Over the years, research on how sustainability elements can be incorporated into mine planning has multiplied [23]. This increased in tandem with the pressure by shareholders for mining giants to establish actionable sustainability goals to slash emissions [16]. Most research on mining sustainability are qualitative using methods such as life cycle analysis (LCA) and decision making trial and evaluation laboratory (DEMATEL). Meanwhile, quantitative research using techniques in operations research, artificial intelligence or machine learning pales in comparison [23].

Sustainability within mining is manifested through both life cycle of the mine and mined ore. The former enhances mine operations to reduce its environmental footprint while the latter governs the life span and retirement of mined ores [8]. The sustainability of mining operations have four key characteristics of reducing inputs, outputs, land disruption, and environmental as well as safety hazards at the end of mine life [2]. Sustainability within mine planning relates to the mine life cycle of reducing inputs, outputs and land disruption.

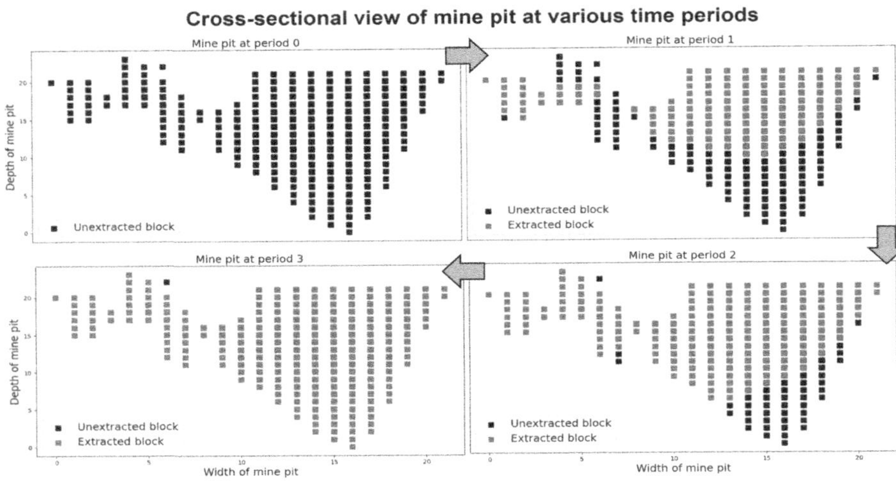

Fig. 3. Block extraction sequence from year to year, following precedence and resource constraints, for MineLib's newman1 instance using MIP

At the operational level, the focus is on reducing carbon-related costs at operational facilities and transportation network. Valderrama et al. [18] considered carbon emissions from operating facilities and inter-facility transport with an MIP model. Meanwhile, Attari and Torkayesh [1] considered carbon emissions from transport between facilities and to the customers using a multi-objective MIP. Correspondingly, Canales-Bustos, Santibañez-González and Candia-Véjar [3] designed a multi-objective hybrid particle swarm optimization algorithm to minimize total costs of investments and transport, deviations between product quality and goals, and carbon emissions from facilities and vehicles. These perspectives disregard block extraction and sequencing decisions.

At a strategic level, Rimélé, Dimitrakopoulos and Gamache [17] primarily addressed reducing land disruption by optimizing the sequence of ore extraction with an in-pit waste disposal which allows dumping of non-profitable extracted ores at available areas within the pit instead of transporting to temporary dumps. Hence, haulage costs are minimized as these waste do not need to be moved back from the dumps to the pit during the mine rehabilitation phase. Indirectly, the reduction of inputs (fuel) and outputs (carbon emissions) are also addressed. Succeeding research [7,14] consider effective use of dumps by simultaneously optimizing extraction sequence, dump capacity and related costs.

However, such perspective prioritizes profits ahead of environmental footprints instead of examining the trade-offs. Xu et al. [21] examined trade-offs that reduce outputs and land disturbance. These environmental costs form part of the Dynamic Programming formulation for optimum ore extraction sequence. Meanwhile, Wang et al. [19] focused on the processing of extracted ores. They solved both resource efficiency and NPV in a multi-objective using a Non-dominated

Sorting Genetic Algorithm, displayed as a Pareto front. Xu et al. [20] then confined the formulation to the pit limit; it determined if ores should be extracted, but disregards the sequence and subsequent processing decisions. Their multi-objective formulation minimized ecological costs and, concurrently maximized NPV as well as social benefits. The metrics used built upon Xu et al. [21]. We build upon these works by tackling the tactical perspective of PCPSP that reflects decisions in a real-world mine of block extraction, sequencing and processing. We also adopt the carbon costing framework [20] and plot our solutions as a Pareto front.

3 Problem Definition

The PCPSP determines mining activities from start to end; it provides investors a valuation of a mine's worth based on extraction and processing decisions of valuable mineral ores [9]. Components of a mine include the pit, dump, stockpiles, processing plants and corresponding heavy machinery. Within the pit, mineral ore deposits are discretized into equally sized blocks for the modelling purpose. Each block has its unique associated value and set of precedence constraints due to the geology. This affects the overall extraction sequence across time periods, as exemplified in Fig. 3, and how the ore is processed. Upon extraction, the block is sent to processing facilities where it is reduced according to requirements such as through crushing, grinding and screening. Next, the material undergoes refining to enhance the quality and derive various types of desired end products. This value chain, lamentably, consumes ample raw materials and produces detrimental by-products, as exemplified in Fig. 4.

3.1 Carbon Costing Framework

As shown in Fig. 4, energy as input and air pollution as output appear constantly throughout. Hence, we focus on incorporating carbon costing in the enhanced PCPSP formulation. The metric for carbon emissions is adopted from Xu et al. [20]. They defined $\mathcal{C}_{i,e}$ to be the carbon emission cost from consuming energy. It is the cost associated with the absorption of carbon dioxide generated during ore excavation, and processing or refining.

The formula mainly comprises the ore extracted from the pit and sent for further processing $\mathcal{Q}_{i,o}$ and the amount of material extracted and treated as waste $\mathcal{Q}_{i,w}$. These quantities are multiplied against the amount of energy consumed using coal to extract per unit tonne of materials, either ore or waste, from the pit e_m and the energy consumed to process per unit tonne of ore e_p. These are further multiplied against the carbon factor of coal f_c, the conversion coefficient of carbon dioxide from carbon f_a and the absorption cost of carbon dioxide $\mathcal{C}_c$.

$$\mathcal{C} = \frac{(\mathcal{Q}_{i,o} + \mathcal{Q}_{i,w})e_m + \mathcal{Q}_{i,o}e_p}{1000} f_c f_a \mathcal{C}_c \qquad (1)$$

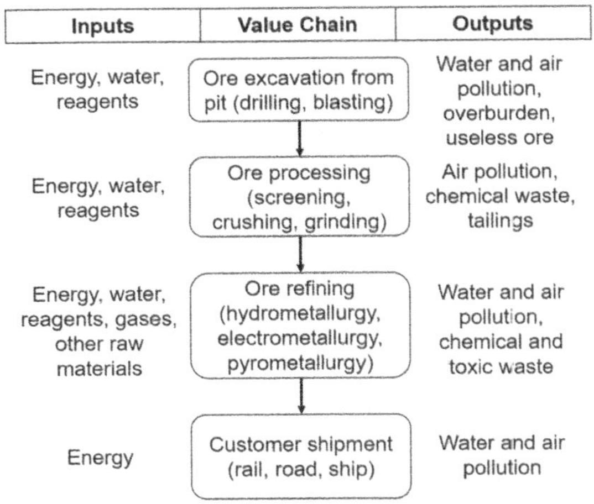

Fig. 4. Inputs and outputs along the mining value chain

3.2 Enhanced PCPSP Mathematical Formulation

The PCPSP is a scheduling problem that aims to maximize the NPV while meeting operational, regulatory as well as economic constraints such as mineral ore grade (i.e. percentage content), equipment availability, and processing plant capacity [5]. In doing so, expertise required stretches across multiple domains such as geology, chemistry, engineering, economics, and customer relations. Geologists assess the estimated ore components and grades based on multiple drill samples as well as structure of materials surrounding the ore; each block has unique and diverse components. These samples are continuously taken throughout the mine life span. Based on these information, mining engineers assess the structure, methods and equipment to access the ore. For accessed ores, geologists and chemists determine the type of processing and refining required for different ores (e.g. iron, copper, gold and silver) and its grade. This results in varying products. The ores and grades are monitored by economists to estimate the economic value of each block based on demand and supply worldwide. Meanwhile, the demand by current and potential customers are evaluated by customer relations. All these complicate mine scheduling.

Mine scheduling research mostly rely on real-world case studies as mining operations are unique and shaped by geo-metallurgical factors [15]. However, this leads to solution techniques that cannot be directly compared with others. The publicly available MineLib library [5] attempts to close this gap with generalized mathematical formulations and instances for three problem variants, whereby PCPSP is the most complex problem. We adopt the PCPSP formulation to enable other researchers to build upon our work.

The generic formulation for the PCPSP [5] denotes $\mathcal{B}$ as the set of blocks, $\mathcal{B}_b$ is the subset of predecessors for block $b \in \mathcal{B}$, and $\mathcal{D}$ is the set of destinations. The profit $\tilde{p}_{bdt}$ is obtained by extracting block b and processing it at destination

d at period t. The amount q_{bdr} of operational resource $r \in \mathcal{R}$ is used to extract block b and process it at destination $d \in \mathcal{D}$. The binary decision variable x_{bt} equals to 1 if block b is extracted by period t and 0 otherwise. The continuous decision variable y_{bdt} represents the portion of block b sent to destination d at period t. The objective function of PCPSP maximizes discounted total profits for periods $\mathcal{T}$. The profit $\tilde{p}_{bdt}$ for a period $t \in \mathcal{T}$ is computed by $\frac{p_{bd}}{(1+\alpha)^t}$ where α is the discount factor. The associated value of a block depends on the ore composition and its grade, estimated by geologists. The discounted value reflects the importance of extracting a more valuable block earlier rather than later.

$$\textbf{(PCPSP)} \quad \mathbf{Z} = \max \sum_{b \in \mathcal{B}} \sum_{d \in \mathcal{D}} \sum_{t \in \mathcal{T}} \tilde{p}_{bdt} y_{bdt} \tag{2}$$

Constraint (3) imposes precedence requirements for all blocks and time periods. It stipulates that block b' must be extracted in the same period as, or prior to, block b since block b' is a predecessor of block b. This constraint is determined by mining engineers based on the type and composition of materials (e.g. sand, silt, clay) surrounding the desired ore and the ore itself. That information is provided by geologists.

$$\sum_{\tau \leq t} x_{b\tau} \leq \sum_{\tau \leq t} x_{b'\tau} \quad \forall b \in \mathcal{B},\, b' \in \mathcal{B}_b,\, t \in \mathcal{T} \tag{3}$$

Constraint (4) requires that if a block is extracted, it must be fully sent to one or more destinations and if a block is not extracted, it is not sent to any destination. The choice of destination depends on the ore composition, if any, and grade of the ore. It is also affected by customer demands.

$$x_{bt} = \sum_{d \in \mathcal{D}} y_{bdt} \quad \forall b \in \mathcal{B},\, t \in \mathcal{T} \tag{4}$$

Constraint (5) restricts block extraction to at most once over the horizon.

$$\sum_{t \in \mathcal{T}} x_{bt} \leq 1 \quad \forall b \in \mathcal{B} \tag{5}$$

Constraint (6) ensures minimum $\underline{\mathcal{R}}_{rt}$ and maximum $\bar{\mathcal{R}}_{rt}$ use of every operational resource r are satisfied for each period t. The operational resource include diggers, haulage trucks, grinders, and various processing plants that are overseen by mining engineers and technicians.

$$\underline{\mathcal{R}}_{rt} \leq \sum_{b \in \mathcal{B}} \sum_{d \in \mathcal{D}} q_{bdr} y_{bdt} \leq \bar{\mathcal{R}}_{rt} \quad \forall r \in \mathcal{R},\, t \in \mathcal{T} \tag{6}$$

Constraint (7) corresponds to general side constraints with lower and upper bounds $\underline{a}$ and $\bar{a}$ respectively. It can model more complex mining scenarios such as grade constraints. The grade of ores desired are based on customer demands worldwide and market outlook. The ore grade cutoff affects the destination of the block, constraint (4), as well.

$$\underline{a} \leq \mathcal{A}y \leq \bar{a} \tag{7}$$

Finally, constraints (8) and (9) reflect the range of values.

$$x_{bt} \in \{0,1\} \quad \forall b \in \mathcal{B}, t \in \mathcal{T}, \tag{8}$$

$$y_{bdt} \in [0,1] \quad \forall b \in \mathcal{B}, d \in \mathcal{D}, t \in \mathcal{T}. \tag{9}$$

To enhance this PCPSP generic formulation with carbon cost constraints, we define c_{bdrt} as the discounted carbon costs emitted by operational resource $r \in \mathcal{R}$ when extracting or processing block b at destination $d \in \mathcal{D}$ for a period $t \in \mathcal{T}$. The carbon constraint (10) ensures the maximum carbon emissions $\bar{\mathcal{C}}_t$ are not exceeded for each period t.

$$\sum_{b \in \mathcal{B}} \sum_{d \in \mathcal{D}} \sum_{r \in \mathcal{R}} c_{bdrt} y_{bdt} \leq \bar{\mathcal{C}}_t \quad \forall t \in \mathcal{T} \tag{10}$$

The carbon costing constraint would be paramount within the system of tradeable carbon emissions, or carbon credit trading. This system falls under market-based instruments advocated to reduce carbon dioxide emissions. Economies that are unable to decrease their carbon dioxide emissions to the allocated permits can purchase from those that have decreased beyond their permits [24]. Hence, constraint (10) enables miners to monitor emissions against allocated permits and the cost of purchasing carbon credits.

4 Methodology

Since the PCPSP is a NP-hard problem, conventional Lagrangian relaxation for larger instances proved unsuccessful; initial solutions were not found. Hence, we propose a temporally decomposed greedy Lagrangian relaxation (TDGLR) algorithm for the PCPSP, summarized in Algorithm 1. It reduces the problem space using time windows and a cone selection for each window.

In Algorithm 1, the sliding time window w is implemented through lines 2, 3, 18 and 19. Meanwhile, the enhanced cone selection is implemented in lines 5 and 6. Next, an initial solution is found by Lagrangian relaxation in lines 7 and 8 that is faster than an exact MIP approach. It is then checked and fixed by the greedy heuristic in line 10 for feasibility.

4.1 Block Pre-selection Heuristic

Blocks are pre-selected during each time window for a Lagrangian relaxation MIP. The heuristic accounts for maximum resource available in each time window $\bar{\mathcal{R}}$, amount of resource required by each block q, upper bound resource multiplier

Algorithm 1. Temporally decomposed greedy Lagrangian relaxation framework (TDGLR)

Input: Block model $\mathcal{B}$, destinations $\mathcal{D}$, predecessor edges $\mathcal{E}$, time periods $\mathcal{T}$, resources $\mathcal{R}$, resources required per block q, resource bounds $\bar{\mathcal{R}}$, profit of block when sent to destination $\mathcal{P}_{bd}$, general side constraints
Parameter: Time window size w, upper bound resource multiplier ρ, iterations for Lagrangian relaxation $\mathcal{I}$
Output: Set of extracted blocks, extraction period, block destination and net present value of profit

$G \leftarrow ConstructDAG(\mathcal{B}, \mathcal{E})$
$t_s \leftarrow 0$
$t_e \leftarrow w$
while $t_s < \mathcal{T}$ **do**
  $cones \leftarrow ConeCalc(\mathcal{B}, \mathcal{D}, \mathcal{E}, \mathcal{R}, q, \bar{\mathcal{R}}, \mathcal{P}_{bd}, DAG)$
  $\mathcal{S} \leftarrow GetSubsetBlocks(cones, \mathcal{R}, \bar{\mathcal{R}}, q, w, \rho)$
  for i in $\mathcal{I}$ **do**
    $(x^*, y^*) \leftarrow LR(t_s, t_e, \mathcal{S}, \mathcal{D}, \mathcal{E}, \mathcal{R}, \bar{\mathcal{R}}, q, \mathcal{P}_{bd})$
  end for
  $(\hat{x}, \hat{y}) \leftarrow LF(x^*, t_s, \mathcal{B}, \mathcal{D}, \mathcal{E}, \mathcal{R}, q, \bar{\mathcal{R}}, \mathcal{P}_{bd})$
  $\hat{\mathcal{B}} \leftarrow BlocksExtractedinPeriod(t_s, \hat{x})$
  if $t_s > 0$ and $\hat{\mathcal{B}} = 0$ **then**
    break
  end if
  $\mathcal{B} \leftarrow \mathcal{B}.drop(\hat{\mathcal{B}})$
  $G \leftarrow UpdateDAG(\hat{\mathcal{B}})$
  $profit \leftarrow CalcDiscProfit(\hat{x}, \hat{y}, t_s, \mathcal{P}_{bd})$
  $t_s \leftarrow t_s + 1$
  $t_e \leftarrow min(t_e + 1, \mathcal{T})$
end while
return period, destination, profit

ρ, profit of block when sent to destination $\mathcal{P}_{bd}$ and the set of predecessor edges $\mathcal{E}$ for the block model set $\mathcal{B}$.

Each block in the block model set $\mathcal{B}$ has a set of preceding blocks that has to be excavated before the block of interest. This set, together with the block of interest, can be regarded as a cone due to the shape formed. Cone sets are determined for each block, and the maximum profit that can be derived using the associated resource are calculated. The cones are sorted by descending ratio of profit to resource, instead of only profit by [13]. In doing so, the heuristic juggles between maximizing both profit and resource.

4.2 Temporally Decomposed Lagrangian Relaxation

At each time window, a Lagrangian relaxation problem is solved for a subset of blocks derived from 4.1. In the Lagrangian relaxation problem, constraint 6 is dualised and incorporated into the objective function using Lagrangian multipliers λ and the time dimension is removed as follows:

$$Z^*(\lambda) = \sum_{b\in\mathcal{B}} \sum_{d\in\mathcal{D}} \tilde{p}_{bd} y_{bd} + \sum_{r\in\mathcal{R}} \lambda_r \cdot (\bar{R}_r - \sum_{b\in\mathcal{B}} \sum_{d\in\mathcal{D}} q_{bdr} y_{bd}) \tag{11}$$

$Z^*(\lambda)$ is the Lagrangian objective function where λ_r defines the vector of Lagrangian multipliers for constraint 6. To initiate, λ is set as 0. To optimize the Lagrangian multiplier λ so that the profit objective is maximized, a subgradient descent is used [6]. The Lagrangian multipliers are updated at each iteration, where θ is the step size, using:

$$\lambda_r \leftarrow \lambda_r + \theta \cdot (\bar{R}_r - \sum_{b\in\mathcal{B}} \sum_{d\in\mathcal{D}} q_{bdr} y_{bd}) \tag{12}$$

The step size θ is calculated with the following formula where μ is the step-size multiplier and $\underline{\mathcal{Z}}$ is the lower bound solution to the original PCPSP objective:

$$\theta = \frac{\mu \cdot (\underline{\mathcal{Z}} - \mathcal{Z}(\lambda))}{\left|(\bar{R}_r - \sum_{b\in\mathcal{B}} \sum_{d\in\mathcal{D}} q_{bdr} y_{bd})\right|^2} \tag{13}$$

The step size multiplier μ are of the values $0 \leq \mu \leq 2$ where μ is initially set as 2. Whenever the objective value of $Z^*(\lambda)$ fails to improve within a set number of iterations, the value of μ is adjusted by $\mu \leftarrow \frac{1}{2} \cdot \mu$ [6].

4.3 Greedy Heuristic

Results from the Lagrangian relaxation may either be infeasible due to violation of some resources and/or carbon credits or feasible, but with under utilized resources and/or carbon credits. Hence, blocks are removed or added to the solution using a greedy method based on the best profit of a certain block when sent to a destination. While doing so, precedence constraints are respected by maintaining the block model set $\mathcal{B}$ and predecessor edges $\mathcal{E}$ within a DAG.

The blocks considered for removal and addition are at the fringes of the solution to potentially minimize the resource required. The overall framework of this heuristic is displayed in Algorithm 2. Line 1 calculates the residual of resources at all destinations based on greedy assignment of blocks to the most profitable destination. Line 3 checks for any resource and carbon costs violation. If none, more profitable blocks are extracted. Otherwise, the least profitable blocks are removed. Subsequently, line 11 handles resources or carbon costs that are possibly under utilized.

5 Experiments

We use a real-world inspired data from an operating copper and gold mine, namely Wilma. It is a small-sized open pit mine. The data was transformed to

Algorithm 2. Fix feasibility of Lagrangian relaxation solution and maximize resource use

Input: $\mathcal{B}$, $\mathcal{D}$, $\mathcal{E}$, $\mathcal{R}$, q, $\bar{\mathcal{R}}$, $\mathcal{P}_{bd}$, Lagrangian relaxation solution of extracting block x^*
Output: Extract block $\hat{x}$, block portion to destination $\hat{y}$

$res_r \leftarrow \bar{R}_r - \sum_{b\in\mathcal{B}} \sum_{d\in\mathcal{D}} q_{bdr} y_{bd}$
$\mathcal{G} \leftarrow ConstructDAG(\mathcal{B}, \mathcal{E})$
if $res_r \geq 0, \forall r$ **then**
  $x^+, y^+ \leftarrow AddBlocks(\mathcal{G}, x^*, \mathcal{B}, \mathcal{D}, \mathcal{R}, q, \bar{\mathcal{R}}, \mathcal{P}_{bd}, res_r)$
  $\hat{x} \leftarrow x^* + x^+$
  $\hat{y} \leftarrow y^* + y^+$
else
  $x^-, y^-, res_r \leftarrow RemoveBlocks(\mathcal{G}, x^*, \mathcal{B}, \mathcal{D}, \mathcal{R}, q, \bar{\mathcal{R}}, \mathcal{P}_{bd}, res_r)$
  $\hat{x} \leftarrow x^* - x^-$
  $\hat{y} \leftarrow y^* - y^+$
  $x^+, \hat{y} \leftarrow AddBlocks(\mathcal{G}, \hat{x}, \mathcal{B}, \mathcal{D}, \mathcal{R}, q, \bar{\mathcal{R}}, \mathcal{P}_{bd}, res_r)$
  $\hat{x} \leftarrow \hat{x} + x^+$
  $\hat{y} \leftarrow y^* + y^+$
end if
return $\hat{x}, \hat{y}$

fit the generic formulation with further mock-ups. We supplement this dataset with two copper MineLib benchmark instances of Kd and Marvin. Kd is a copper mine in North America while Marvin is a famous copper and gold test mine. The number of blocks $|\mathcal{B}|$, precedence $|\mathcal{B}_b|$, time periods $|\mathcal{T}|$, destinations $|\mathcal{D}|$ and operational resource $|\mathcal{R}|$ constraints are in Table 1.

Table 1. Key characteristics of dataset

Name	Block	Precedence	Periods	Destinations	Resources
Wilma	1,960	7,263	4	3	3
Kd	14,153	219,778	12	2	2
Marvin	53,271	650,631	20	2	2

5.1 Experimental Setup

By using the TDGLR and MIP, the generic PCPSP formulation (without carbon constraint) was first run to produce its respective optimal profit and discounted carbon cost. The cost is then used to estimate the range of values for the carbon upper bound $\bar{C}_t$ for experimentation in the enhanced PCPSP formulation (with carbon constraint). For this enhanced PCPSP formulation, the TDGLR algorithm was evaluated against the MIP, solved by CPLEX. We experiment with at least 30 values of $\bar{C}_t$. These experiments generate multiple Pareto-optimal solutions $\mathcal{Z}$ and their corresponding discounted carbon emission cost $\mathcal{C}$.

Finally we compare the results between the TDGLR and MIP with respect to the percentage gap, distance and diversity metrics. The percentage gap evaluates the gap between the profit obtained by MIP, $\mathcal{Z}_1$, and the TDGLR, $\mathcal{Z}_2$:

$$\text{Percentage gap} = \frac{\mathcal{Z}_1 - \mathcal{Z}_2}{\mathcal{Z}_1} * 100\% \tag{14}$$

Next, the distance metric evaluates the convergence of the TDGLR to the non-dominated MIP front [4]. It first measures the minimum Euclidean distance, d_{kl}, between a solution from the TDGLR, k, and all solutions from the MIP, l. It then finds the average across all $\mathcal{N}$ solutions:

$$\text{Distance metric} = \frac{\sum_{k=1}^{\mathcal{N}} \min d_{kl}}{\mathcal{N}} \tag{15}$$

Lastly, the diversity metric evaluates the even spread of solutions over the Pareto front [4]. It uses the Euclidean distance, d_i, between successive solutions and the average, $\bar{d}$ of all d_i. Next, d_f measures the Euclidean distance between the extreme solutions of the true Pareto-optimal front. Meanwhile, d_l is the Euclidean distance between the extreme solutions of the obtained solution set. Overall, a value below one and close to zero indicates better diversity.

$$\text{Diversity metric} = \frac{d_f + d_l + \sum_{i=1}^{N-1} |d_i - \bar{d}|}{d_f + d_l + (\mathcal{N} - 1)\bar{d}} \tag{16}$$

The model was built entirely using Python with the core packages of Cvxpy and NetworkX. Cvxpy is an optimization package that formulates mathematical programming flexibly and accesses the CPLEX solver, whereas NetworkX creates and manipulates DAGs. Algorithm 1 was executed on a Linux operating system with the second generation Intel Xeon Scalable Processors (Cascade Lake), sustained all core Turbo frequency of 3.6 GHz, single core turbo frequency up to 3.9 GHz, 48 CPU and 192 Gb RAM.

The initial solution for the lower bound of the Lagrangian relaxation is produced using CPLEX solver with an MIP gap of 0.1. The value of the step size multiplier μ in the sub-gradient descent optimisation is adjusted whenever the objective value of $Z^*(\lambda)$ fails to improve within ten iterations. The Lagrangian relaxation runs for 100 iterations unless the decrease in the objective values begin to stagnate or the gap between the upper and lower bound has reached a gap threshold of $1e^{-9}$. There are also limits to the depth first search when adding blocks if resource constraints are yet to be violated. Once 10 consecutive attempts to add blocks result in resource violation, the greedy process terminates.

5.2 Results

For the three instances, we visualize the evolution of profit and carbon upper bound pairs in Fig. 5 that produce a convex approximate Pareto optimal front.

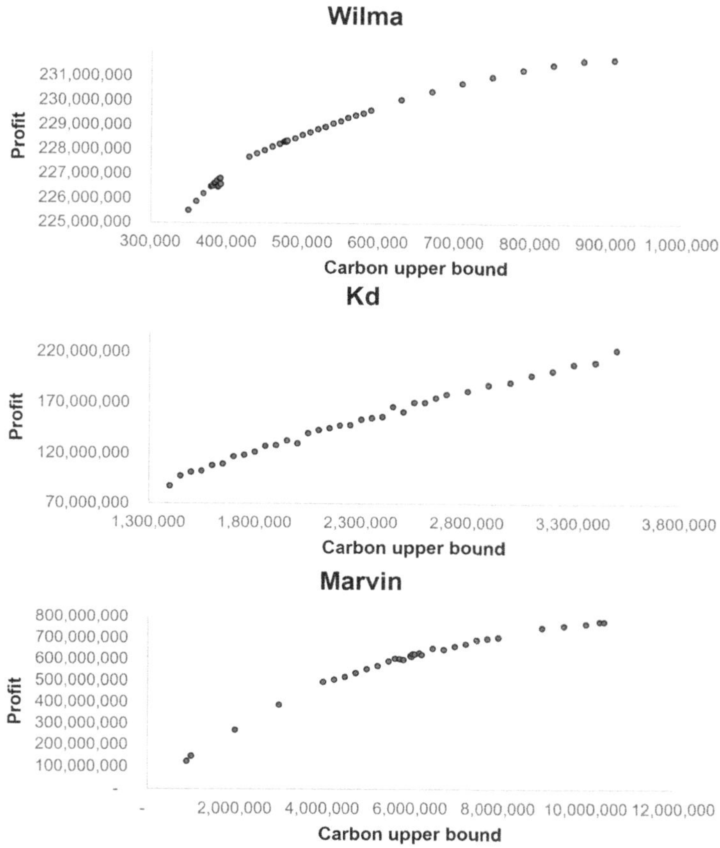

Fig. 5. Approximate Pareto front of profit against carbon upper bound

The solutions along this front may be of interest to miners to determine a palatable trade-off between maximizing profits and minimizing carbon costs.

Table 2 summarizes the statistical comparison of the computation times between the TDGLR and MIP while Fig. 6 displays the various computation times across the carbon upper bounds. The computation times for the MIP are between 36 s to 8.4 min. Meanwhile, the computation times for the TDGLR range from 15 to 65 s. Figure 6 shows that the computation time for the MIP is faster than the TDGLR for lower carbon upper bounds, but the computation time increases drastically for larger carbon upper bounds. Conversely, the computation time for the TDGLR generally decreases as the carbon upper bound increases, indicating the difficulty level of solving the problem decreases as the carbon upper bound increases. On average, the TDGLR is more efficient than the MIP in solving the enhanced PCPSP formulation. This efficiency is most apparent when solving the larger instances, Kd and Marvin. After 12 hours, the

Table 2. Computation time comparison between TDGLR and MIP (seconds)

Method	Minimum	Maximum	Average	Median
TDGLR	14.5	64.6	36.5	30.3
MIP	36.4	504.3	67.1	37.5

MIP is still unable to provide a solution for both instances whereas the TDGLR was able to solve in about 2.92 and 1.91 hours respectively for Kd and Marvin. Hence, the TDGLR is able to efficiently solve the NP-hard PCPSP for larger instances that is more reminiscent of a real-world mine.

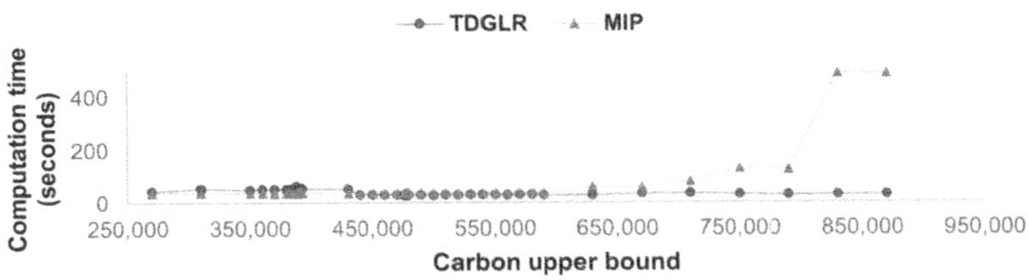

Fig. 6. Comparison of computation time between TDGLR and MIP

Table 3. Performance metrics of TDGLR against Non-dominated MIP solutions

Average percentage gap	Distance metric	Diversity metric
0.015%	0.000135	0.998

The TDGLR is also compared to the MIP with the performance metrics of percentage gap, distance and diversity metrics, displayed in Table 3. As an exact method, the MIP is expected to provide better results than TDGLR and forms the non-dominated front. The percentage gap between the profit derived from the MIP, $\mathcal{Z}_1$, and that of the TDGLR, $\mathcal{Z}_2$, was compared for each value of the carbon upper bound. These gaps are shown in Fig. 7 for the Wilma instance. The gap ranged from 0% to 0.3178% with an average gap of 0.015%. The distance metric of 0.000135 is very close to zero and concurs with the close convergence of the TDGLR to the MIP. Meanwhile, the diversity metric of 0.998 is below one, but far from zero. This indicates the TDGLR can be improved to provide better distribution of solutions. Overall, the TDGLR appears to provide reliable solutions for the enhanced PCPSP formulation. Unfortunately, these metrics cannot be applied for the larger instances of Kd and Marvin due to the shortcoming of the MIP as highlighted earlier.

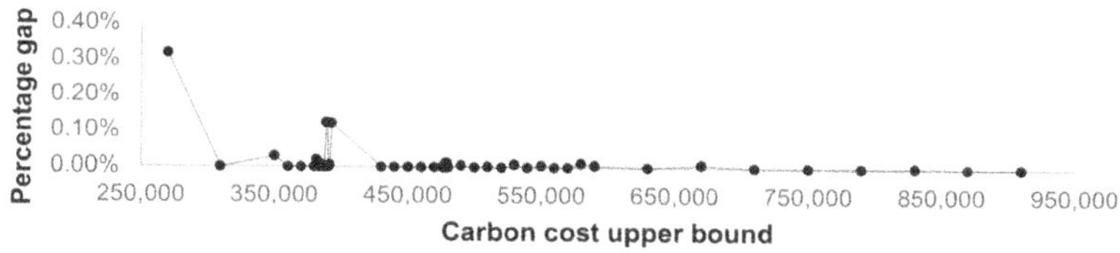

Fig. 7. Percentage gap between MIP and TDGLR solutions for Wilma

6 Conclusion

In this paper, we propose the temporally decomposed greedy Lagrangian relaxation (TDGLR) approach that handles the flow of materials from the mine pit to production facilities for the open pit mine. It handles the logistical considerations throughout this value chain. Our TDGLR approach is sustainability-aware, and can cater to a wide variety of environmental considerations. We augment a collection of real-world instances from an operating mine and the MineLib with sustainability requirements, to demonstrate how our approach could be utilized in realistic planning settings. Our computational approach can effectively generate Pareto fronts over the dimensions of carbon cost and the NPV of profits. This provides an ideal interface for planners to simultaneously consider economic and environmental considerations.

To the best of our knowledge, this is the first such model for the open pit mining planning using the generic PCPSP formulation. Our approach can be extended to other types of environmental considerations, and it can help the mining industry achieve Goal 9 of the United Nations' Sustainable Development Goals (SDG). Further considerations may include the cost of treating water and waste such as tailings. Owing to the limitations of Lagrangian relaxation, we can also formulate the problem as a multi-objective and further explore the use of meta-heuristic evolutionary algorithms instead as future work.

Acknowledgements. This work is supported by Enterprise Singapore under the grant 20-IPPII-T-001-B-1 and Rio Tinto Ltd.

References

1. Attari, M.Y.N., Torkayesh, A.E.: Developing benders decomposition algorithm for a green supply chain network of mine industry: case of Iranian mine industry. Oper. Res. Perspect. **5**, 371–382 (2018)
2. Calas, G.: Mineral resources and sustainable development. Elem. Int. Mag. Mineral. Geochem. Petrol. **13**(5), 301–306 (2017)
3. Canales-Bustos, L., Santibañez-González, E., Candia-Véjar, A.: A multi-objective optimization model for the design of an effective decarbonized supply chain in mining. Int. J. Prod. Econ. **193**, 449–464 (2017)
4. Deb, K., Agrawal, S., Pratap, A., Meyarivan, T.: A fast elitist non-dominated sorting genetic algorithm for multi-objective optimization: NSGA-II. In: Schoenauer, M., et al. (eds.) PPSN 2000. LNCS, vol. 1917, pp. 849–858. Springer, Heidelberg (2000). https://doi.org/10.1007/3-540-45356-3_83

5. Espinoza, D., Goycoolea, M., Moreno, E., Newman, A.: MineLib: a library of open pit mining problems. Ann. Oper. Res. **206**(1), 93–114 (2012). https://doi.org/10.1007/s10479-012-1258-3
6. Fisher, M.L.: The Lagrangian relaxation method for solving integer programming problems. Manage. Sci. **27**(1), 1–18 (1981)
7. Fu, Z., Asad, M.W.A., Topal, E.: A new model for open-pit production and waste-dump scheduling. Eng. Optim. **51**(4), 718–732 (2019)
8. Gorman, M.R., Dzombak, D.A.: A review of sustainable mining and resource management: transitioning from the life cycle of the mine to the life cycle of the mineral. Resour. Conserv. Recycl. **137**, 281–291 (2018)
9. Hustrulid, W.A., Kuchta, M., Martin, R.K.: Open Pit Mine Planning and Design, Two Volume Set and CD-ROM Pack. CRC Press, Boca Raton (2013)
10. ICAP: Emissions trading worldwide: Status report 2022. ICAP Berlin (2022)
11. Johnson, D.S., Niemi, K.: On knapsacks, partitions, and a new dynamic programming technique for trees. Math. Oper. Res. **8**(1), 1–14 (1983)
12. Johnson, T.B.: Optimum open pit mine production scheduling. California Univ Berkeley Operations Research Center, Technical report (1968)
13. Kenny, A., Li, X., Ernst, A.T., Thiruvady, D.: Towards solving large-scale precedence constrained production scheduling problems in mining. In: Proceedings of the Genetic and Evolutionary Computation Conference, pp. 1137–1144 (2017)
14. Levinson, Z., Dimitrakopoulos, R.: Simultaneous stochastic optimisation of an open-pit gold mining complex with waste management. Int. J. Min. Reclam. Environ. **34**(6), 415–429 (2020)
15. Newman, A.M., Rubio, E., Caro, R., Weintraub, A., Eurek, K.: A review of operations research in mine planning. Interfaces **40**(3), 222–245 (2010)
16. Reid, H., Denina, C.: Rio says climate change "at heart of strategy" after investors demand action, April 2022. https://www.reuters.com/business/energy/investors-urge-rio-tinto-cut-indirect-emissions-2022-04-08/
17. Rimélé, M.A., Dimitrakopoulos, R., Gamache, M.: A stochastic optimization method with in-pit waste and tailings disposal for open pit life-of-mine production planning. Resour. Policy **57**, 112–121 (2018)
18. Valderrama, C.V., Santibanez-González, E., Pimentel, B., Candia-Vejar, A., Canales-Bustos, L.: Designing an environmental supply chain network in the mining industry to reduce carbon emissions. J. Clean. Prod. **254**, 119688 (2020)
19. Wang, X., Gu, X., Liu, Z., Wang, Q., Xu, X., Zheng, M.: Production process optimization of metal mines considering economic benefit and resource efficiency using an NSGA-II model. Processes **6**(11), 228 (2018)
20. Xu, X., Gu, X., Qing, W., Zhao, Y., Wang, Z.: Open pit limit optimization considering economic profit, ecological costs and social benefits. Trans. Nonferrous Met. Soc. Chin. **31**(12), 3847–3861 (2021)
21. Xu, X., et al.: Production scheduling optimization considering ecological costs for open pit metal mines. J. Cleaner Prod. **180**, 210–221 (2018)
22. Yağmur, E., Kesen, S.E.: Bi-objective optimization for joint production scheduling and distribution problem with sustainability. In: Mes, M., Lalla-Ruiz, E., Voß, S. (eds.) ICCL 2021. LNCS, vol. 13004, pp. 269–281. Springer, Cham (2021). https://doi.org/10.1007/978-3-030-87672-2_18
23. Zeng, L., Liu, S.Q., Kozan, E., Corry, P., Masoud, M.: A comprehensive interdisciplinary review of mine supply chain management. Resour. Policy **74**, 102274 (2021)
24. Zhang, Z., Folmer, H.: The choice of policy instruments for the control of carbon dioxide emissions. Intereconomics **30**(3), 133–142 (1995). https://doi.org/10.1007/BF02927268

Multi-shift Worker Assignment Problem with a Heterogeneous Workforce in Semi-automated Electronics Production

Nadine Schiebold(✉)

Faculty of Business and Economics, TU Dresden, 01069 Dresden, Germany
nadine.schiebold@tu-dresden.de
https://tu-dresden.de/bu/wirtschaft/bwl/lim

Abstract. To face the challenges of today's competitive industry, this work studies a real-world problem in semi-automated electronics production. It considers a worker assignment problem with a heterogeneous workforce in the multi-shift environment of protective device manufacturing. Simultaneously with multi-skilled workers, requested orders are assigned to workstations and shifts. One of the main particularities is the restriction of possible assignments of workers and orders to workstations according to qualifications. Additionally, this paper considers sequence-independent family setup times, disparate workstations, and a time limit for completing the orders. A mixed-integer linear programming model is introduced that minimizes the makespan calculated by the last shift used for production. The model is tested using real-world data. Additionally, this contribution examines the influence of the workforce with the help of scenario analysis and solves 49 test instances. The solutions serve as input and support for production planners and personnel planning. Furthermore, this work reveals production problems such as a lack of workers and qualifications.

Keywords: Worker assignment · Heterogeneous workforce · Multi-shift · Semi-automated production

1 Introduction

In electronics production and other manufacturing sectors workers carry out most tasks, which is why workers influence the performance more than machines [2]. Workers are highly diverse. They can differ in physiology, age, training, experience, and much more. This diversity influences the productivity and flexibility of production systems, which are both very important in Industrial Revolution 4.0 environments [6]. Therefore, the consideration of a heterogeneous workforce plays a crucial role in production systems.

The real-world problem considered in this work comprises worker assignment in a multi-shift environment. Orders and workers are assigned to workstations

J. de Armas et al. (Eds.): ICCL 2022, LNCS 13557, pp. 457–471, 2022.
https://doi.org/10.1007/978-3-031-16579-5_31

and shifts. The workers in the real-world problem differ in their skills, which is why worker-station incompatibilities exist. The electronics production considered combines manual and automated workstations and is therefore specified as semi-automated. Besides the level of automation, workstations differ in the type of order tasks that they can process and the capacity, calculated with individual limitation factors. The contribution of this work is the discussion of a new problem motivated by practical experience as well as support of production planners and personnel scheduling.

The remainder of this paper is organized as follows. Section 2 provides a brief literature review focusing on multi-skilled worker assignment problems. Section 3 describes the problem and its particularities in detail. The mathematical formulation of the problem is introduced in Sect. 4 and computational results follow in Sect. 5. Finally, Sect. 6 concludes this work and gives a summary and possibilities for future research.

2 Literature Review

This section discusses the literature on problem structures similar to the semi-automated electronics production considered. The three main particularities are emphasized and researched: heterogeneous workforce, heterogeneous workstations and a multi-shift environment.

First, the focus of this review lies on literature with a heterogeneous workforce. This problem aspect is modeled in various ways. Most literature includes worker-dependent processing times, where workers need individually different times to process tasks. Infeasible worker-task combinations could be modeled by setting the operation time of a task to infinity when the task is infeasible for a worker, e.g. [7,8]. Other approaches consider workers with different skill levels, e.g. [6,10]. Workers can only perform tasks that have the same (or a lower) skill level. Incompatibilities between workers and tasks are not representable by simple adjustments. The workers heterogeneity is given via a skill matrix in the considered problem, such as in [3,5,9]. A skill matrix indicates whether a worker can perform a task or not.

Second, workstations are not homogeneous in the considered problem as they are in most literature. The different processing tasks of orders have special requirements for workstations and incompatibilities exist for certain task-workstation combinations. Additionally, workstations differ in their capacity, i.e., in the time they are available within a shift. The reason for this lies in the company's production specifics and is discussed further in Sect. 3. [1] introduced machine types and a binary parameter specifying whether a task can be processed by the machine type or not. In contrast, [3] implemented station-dependent processing times. This approach could be adapted to our problem by setting a processing time to infinity if the workstation is not able to process the task.

Third, the total number of orders can not be processed within one shift and can not be easily divided into smaller fitting groups. Therefore, orders and workers are assigned to multiple shifts. The consideration of multi-shift environments in the literature is mostly motivated by parameters changing over time. Examples are varying part demands and costs of machines and workers, as in [6] and a varying product mix in [4]. [9] considered the extension of the planning horizon to one week divided into several shifts and the assignment of orders and workers to cells and shifts, as in this paper.

The contribution of [9] addresses a similar problem. A set of workers must cover all qualifications in total. It is acceptable for one worker to have all the required qualifications alone, while all the others have only one each. This may result in a surplus or shortage of qualifications. In this contribution, each qualification must be covered by one worker.

None of the mentioned articles combined all analyzed criteria: heterogeneous workforce, heterogeneous workstations and multiple shifts. Furthermore, none included automated workstations with no need of an assigned worker. Ultimately, the literature does not provide an approach to solve the real-world problem considered.

3 Problem Description

The problem considered in this paper is motivated by a real-world multi-shift worker assignment problem in electronics production. The manufacturer has 14 production cells. Two parallel cells produce the most recent products with the highest sales (Cell 1 and Cell 2 in the following). Since those are most important, this contribution focuses on that two cells. Their portfolio comprises overcurrent and feeder protection in medium-voltage and high-voltage systems, for example. The cells have four groups of workstations for assembly (A), testing (T), final assembly (F), and packing (P) production tasks. Those groups are designated as processes in the following. The number of workstations per process is identical for both cells: six assembly stations and two stations each for testing, final assembly, and packing. The workstations differ in their maximum capacity. The differences lie in their efficiency and the progressiveness of the equipment. For implementation, limiting factors are defined for the groups of workstations, which limit the possible processing time within a shift. The higher the possible processing time in a shift, the more profitable the station. The difference between the two cells lies in the level of automation. While the housing assembly workstation (first workstation of process A) is manual at Cell 2, Cell 1 has three robots for these tasks (automated workstation).

The production takes place in a three-shift system. Each day is divided into an early, a late, and a night shift. Each shift is seven hours long (κ^{work}) and there is a one-hour break between the shifts, during which no production takes place. It follows, every eight hours a new shift starts (κ^{dur}). Within a week, the worker is available in the same shift type (for example, the early shift) every day if not absent. The workers are heterogeneous and therefore not arbitrarily interchangeable within the assignment problem. In relation to the practical problem, this is due to the workers' skills. The worker skill profile differs in two aspects. On the one hand, workers differ in their capabilities for different cells.

Table 1. Data extract of the workers' skill profiles

Worker ID	Cells 1 and 2				Assigned to (Fig. 1)
	A	F	T	P	
2	x	x	x	x	Assembly 2
5	x	x	x	x	Assembly 3
6	x	x		x	Packing 1
7	x	x	x	x	Assembly 4
8	x	x		x	Packing 2
10	x	x	x	x	Final assembly 1
16	x				Assembly 5
22	x	x	x	x	Final assembly 2
23	x				Assembly 6
25	x	x	x	x	Testing 1
29	x	x	x	x	Testing 2

In addition to the cells considered in this paper, the electronics manufacturer operates 12 other cells for different and discontinued products. Workers may be capable of operating orders at those excluded cells as well. Workers unable of operating on Cell 1 and Cell 2 are left out of the database beforehand. On the other hand, workers master different numbers of the four processes within a cell. If a worker masters a process on one of the two considered cells then he or she also masters it on the other.

Table 1 shows an extract of the database with eleven workers. Seven workers master all four mentioned processes which are abbreviated in the table with A, F, T and P. Workers 6 and 8 can not process testing tasks and Workers 16 and 23 can process assembly tasks only. Note that the missing workers like Workers 1, 3, and 4 are excluded from the database due to their incapability for Cell 1 and 2. The last column shows the assignment of the workers to the workstations of Cell 1 in the example given in Fig. 1.

Each of the workstations has to be occupied by precisely one worker who has the appropriate qualification for the corresponding process. The robot station on Cell 1 makes an exception and does not need any worker. Note that even if not all of the workstations of a process are needed to process all orders, a minimal number of workstations has to be mated.

Each order consists of a certain number of identical devices, given as order quantity. The time to process one single device is the base processing time of the order. Furthermore, each order belongs to a product family, whereby sequence-independent family setup times must be respected. Additionally, each order has day-based time limits: the earliest start date and due date. The assignment of the order must take place between the limits. An order consists of 35 to 40 tasks of each of the four processes (A, F, T, P). To assign an order to a cell, all tasks of the same process are assigned to the group of workstations of that process. The tasks of an order can not be splitted between the two cells.

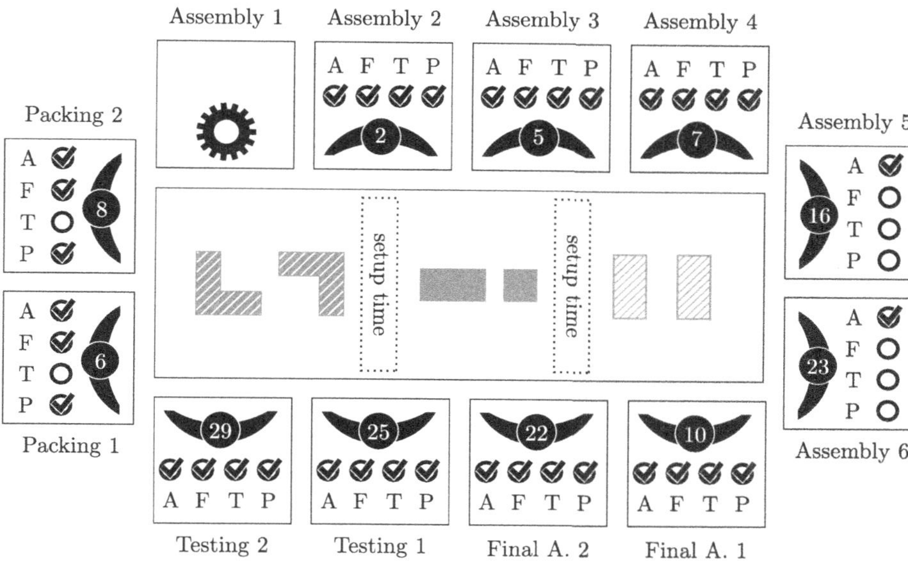

Fig. 1. Illustration of Cell 1 with all workstations mated

In the problem analysis it turns out that the following two assignment problems appear simultaneously: First, the assignment of orders to workstations and shifts taking into account family setup times. Second, the assignment of workers to workstations and shifts considering the worker skill sets.

To give a better understanding of the problem described, Fig. 1 shows an illustration of Cell 1 with all its workstations. Six devices are shown in the middle of the figure as shapes with different patterns. The patterns mark different product types where sequence-independent setup times appear between the production. The workstations are shown as boxes around the devices. Cell 1 contains six Assembly, two Final Assembly (Final A.), two Testing, and two Packing stations, starting clockwise at the top. All workstations are mated, except for the first assembly station, which is the automated station at Cells 1 and has no need for an assignment. The eleven assigned workers are taken from the data extract in Table 1 and marked with their unique identification number (ID). For each worker, the corresponding skill sets are given in Table 1 and additionally represented in the figure as checkboxes. Each of the four checkboxes per worker (A, F, T, P) is marked if the worker is skilled in the process and not otherwise. Note that a worker must meet the skill corresponding to their assigned workstation and it is irrelevant which other skills the worker has. For example, the worker assigned to the Assembly 2 workstation must have the assembly skill (A) checked in their skill set. The remaining skills (F, T, P) correspond to the other workstations Final Assembly, Testing and Packing, respectively.

4 Mathematical Problem Formulation (MILP)

In the following, we introduce a mixed-integer linear program (MILP) for the described problem. We define the set of cells as C, the set of shifts as S, the set of workers as W, the set of orders as O, and the set of product families as F. Furthermore, Table 2 introduces the parameters and the decision variables. Note that the cells' workstations are aggregated for each process p, so no set of workstations is defined. Orders and workers are assigned to shifts and a group of workstations of one cell belonging to the same process p. The average capacity of all group workstations defines a group's maximum capacity.

Table 2. Parameters and decision variables

Parameters	
κ^{dur}	Duration of one shift (including working time κ^{work} and break)
κ^{work}	Maximum working time in a shift
δ_o	Number of devices contained in order $o \in O$
τ_{op}	Base processing time of all tasks of process p of one device of order $o \in O$
ϵ_o^{S}	First shift $s \in S$ that satisfies earliest start date of order $o \in O$
ϵ_o^{D}	Last shift $s \in S$ that satisfies due date of order $o \in O$
σ_f	Setup time of product family f
λ_{cp}^{LB}	Lower bound for the number of operating workstations of process p in cell c
λ_{cp}^{UB}	Upper bound for the number of operating workstations of process p in cell c
l_p^c	Maximum capacity of process p workstations of cell c, $l_p^c \in [0, 1]$
r_p^c	Number of robot stations in cell c for process p
α_w^s	Binary parameter indicating if worker $w \in W$ is available in shift $s \in S$
β_{wp}^c	Binary parameter indicating if worker $w \in W$ can perform process $p \in P$ in cell $c \in C$
Decision Variables	
z^{cs}	1, if cell $c \in C$ is used in shift $s \in S$, 0 otherwise
y_o^{cs}	1, if order $o \in O$ is processed in cell $c \in C$ in shift $s \in S$, 0 otherwise
x_{wp}^{cs}	1, if worker $w \in W$ is assigned to process $p \in P$ in cell $c \in C$ in shift $s \in S$, 0 otherwise
v_p^{cs}	Number of workstations that operate process $p \in P$ in cell $c \in C$ in shift $s \in S$, $v_p^{cs} \in \mathbb{N}$
u_f^{cs}	1, if any order belonging to product family $f \in F$ is produced in cell $c \in C$ in shift $s \in S$, 0 otherwise

$$\min \quad C_{\max} \tag{1}$$

$$\text{s.t.} \quad s \cdot \kappa^{\text{dur}} \cdot z^{cs} + \kappa^{\text{work}} \leq C_{\max} \quad \forall\, c \in C, s \in S \tag{2}$$

$$\sum_{c \in C} \sum_{s \in S} y_o^{cs} = 1 \quad \forall\, o \in O \tag{3}$$

$$y_o^{cs} \leq z^{cs} \quad \forall\, c \in C, s \in S, o \in O \tag{4}$$

$$y_o^{cs} \leq u_{f_o}^{cs} \quad \forall\, c \in C, s \in S, o \in O \tag{5}$$

$$y_o^{cs} = 0 \quad \forall\, c \in C, o \in O, s \in S : s < \epsilon_o^{\text{S}} \vee s > \epsilon_o^{\text{D}} \tag{6}$$

$$v_p^{cs} \geq \frac{\sum_{o \in O} \tau_{op} \cdot \delta_o \cdot y_o^{cs} + \sum_{f \in F} \sigma_f \cdot u_f^{cs}}{\kappa^{\text{work}} \cdot l_p^c} \quad \forall\, c \in C, s \in S, p \in P \tag{7}$$

$$v_p^{cs} \leq \frac{\sum_{o \in O} \tau_{op} \cdot \delta_o \cdot y_o^{cs} + \sum_{f \in F} \sigma_f \cdot u_f^{cs}}{\kappa^{\text{work}} \cdot l_p^c} + 1 \quad \forall\, c \in C, s \in S, p \in P \tag{8}$$

$$\sum_{c \in C} \sum_{p \in P} x_{wp}^{cs} \leq 1 \quad \forall\, w \in W, s \in S \tag{9}$$

$$v_p^{cs} - r_p^c \cdot z^{cs} = \sum_{w \in W} x_{wp}^{cs} \quad \forall\, c \in C, s \in S, p \in P \tag{10}$$

$$x_{wp}^{cs} \leq \alpha_w^s \cdot \beta_{wp}^c \quad \forall\, c \in C, s \in S, p \in P, w \in W \tag{11}$$

$$z^{cs} \cdot \lambda_{cp}^{\text{LB}} \leq v_p^{cs} \quad \forall\, c \in C, s \in S, p \in P \tag{12}$$

$$v_p^{cs} \leq z^{cs} \cdot \lambda_{cp}^{\text{UB}} \quad \forall\, c \in C, s \in S, p \in P \tag{13}$$

The objective is to minimize the makespan. Since the scheduling of the orders is not considered, makespan does not correspond to the end of the processing time of the last job. Indeed, the makespan equals the maximum working time in the final shift ($s \cdot \kappa^{\text{dur}} \cdot z^{cs} + \kappa^{\text{work}}$) in which orders are still being produced and workers are assigned, as realized by Constraints (2). Constraints (3) ensure the satisfaction of the order demand. Each order o (and every contained device) has to be processed exactly once. It is therefore assigned to precisely one cell and shift (cell-shift combination). Constraints (4) guarantee that cell c is used in shift s ($z^{cs} = 1$) if any order o is assigned to that cell-shift combination. Constraints (5) ensure that processing an order o in a cell-shift combination leads to setting up the corresponding product family f_o ($u_{f_o}^{cs} = 1$). Constraints (6) prevents the scheduling of orders before their earliest possible start date and after their due date. Constraints (7) and (8) determine the number of workstations needed to process all assigned orders according to the total processing time and the maximum working time of process p. The total processing time of process p is the product of the base processing times of all assigned orders multiplied by their order quantity ($\sum_{o \in O} \tau_{op} \cdot \delta_o \cdot y_o^{cs}$) plus the setup times ($\sum_{f \in F} \sigma_f \cdot u_f^{cs}$). The maximum working time in a shift (κ^{work}) is limited by l_p^c for process p in cell c. The number of workstations must be at least the division of total processing time and maximum working time, but not higher than this term plus one. Constraints (9) limit the use of worker w to one station s within one shift s. Constraints (10) ensure that each manual workstation needed in one shift is operated by a worker. Since robot stations do not need the assignment of workers, the number of manual stations is the number of all stations minus the number of robot stations ($v_p^{cs} - r_p^c \cdot z^{cs}$). Workers can only be assigned if they are present and qualified for the assignment, which Constraints (11) guarantee. Compliance with the lower and upper bounds for the number of operating workstations of process p in cell c is ensured by Constraints (12) and (13).

5 Computational Results

5.1 Experiment Data and Scenarios

The model is tested with real-world data obtained from a protective device manufacturer. Table 3 shows the cell data of the groups of workstations for each process at Cells 1 and 2. The table includes the maximum capacity as percentage of the work time of 420 min (l_p^c) and the lower bounds for the number of operating workstations (λ_{cp}^{LB}).

Table 3. Maximum capacity and lower bounds of the workstation groups for each process on Cells 1 and 2

Process p	Cell 1		Cell 2	
	l_p^1	λ_{1p}^{LB}	l_p^2	λ_{2p}^{LB}
Assembly (A)	88.50%	2	76.00%	3
Final assembly (F)	88.25%	1	79.00%	1
Testing (T)	100.00%	1	83.00%	1
Packing (P)	86.50%	1	83.00%	1

The data set contains 2955 orders in total and is divided into seven weeks. One week contains orders whose production can start in the workweek from Monday to Friday, i. e., the earliest start date is in that week. Some orders can start on Mondays, whereas others can start on Wednesdays at the earliest for logistical reasons. Table 4 shows the number of total orders ($|O|$) and the number of orders ready from Mondays (#orders(Mon)) and Wednesdays (#orders(Wed)), respectively, for each week. To get a better idea of the problem sizes, the number of devices included in the orders is given in the columns #devices(Mon) and #devices(Wed).

The database includes 57 workers, which differ in the number of available shifts and obtained skills. In average, 14 workers are available per shift with differences between early (⌀18), late (⌀13.6), and night shift (⌀10.7). A total of 34 workers obtain the skills for all four processes (A,F,T,P), whereas 12 workers are skilled for assembly only and the remaining 11 are either skilled for (P), (F,P), or (A,F,P). The testing skill in total is represented the least of all.

Table 4. Total number of orders per week, number of orders and devices starting on Monday and Wednesday

Week	$\|O\|$	#orders(Mon)	#devices(Mon)	#orders(Wed)	#devices(Wed)
1	313	135	360	178	530
2	382	180	447	202	553
3	573	270	738	303	1006
4	449	224	547	225	624
5	470	216	743	254	519
6	418	194	502	224	590
7	350	184	529	166	533

The problem is solved in different scenarios to analyze the workers' influence on the solution. Roughly two cases are distinguished, first the best-case scenario and second the worst-case scenario. In both cases, workers are successively removed from the database. In three steps, five workers are assigned to the excluded cells and are thus no longer available for Cells 1 and 2. In the following, we assume that a worker is less dispensable the more processes he masters. Every worker gets a skill priority, which is the sum over the processes a worker masters. For example, if a worker has all four qualifications the skill priority is four. In addition, workers are more valuable if they are available for many shifts. Any day the worker does neither work the early, late, nor night shift counts as absent.

The database of all 57 workers is sorted according to the skill priority and the number of absent shifts. For the best-case scenario, the workers are sorted according to ascending skill priority first and decreasing number of absent shifts second. In contrast, workers are sorted according to decreasing skill priority first and ascending number of absent shifts second in the worst-case scenario.

Table 5. Scenario analysis: extraction of top worker data after sorting according best-case and worst-case scenario

Best-case scenario							Worst-case scenario						
Worker ID	A	F	T	P	$\sum\uparrow$	Absences $\downarrow$	Worker ID	A	F	T	P	$\sum\downarrow$	Absences $\uparrow$
84	x				1	36	66	x	x	x	x	4	11
77	x				1	35	79	x	x	x	x	4	12
33	x				1	32	64	x	x	x	x	4	13
16	x				1	24	88	x	x	x	x	4	14
68	x				1	21	93	x	x	x	x	4	14
23	x				1	20	96	x	x	x	x	4	15

The workers listed at the top after sorting according to the scenarios will be removed from the database successively. The first six positions of both scenarios are shown in Table 5. Looking at the best-case scenario, all workers have only one qualification, which is the skill priority is 1 ($\sum$). The skill is for assembly tasks in each case (marked with x). Therefore, the sequence is defined by the number of absent shifts (Absence). All workers listed top after sorting according to the worst-case scenario have the same skill priority and are skilled in each process (assembly, testing, final assembly, and packing). As in the best-case scenario, the number of absent shifts defines the sequence. Workers 88 and 93 are indifferent considering both sorting categories.

The basis scenario is defined as Scenario 0 and contains all 57 workers in the database. The reduction of workers result in six additional scenarios: 1a, 1b, 1c, 2a, 2b, and 2c. Thereby, number 1 represents the best-case instances, number 2 represents the worst-case instances, and the letters a, b and c point to the number of remaining workers (52, 47, 42). Figure 2 shows the skill set as combination of processes and the number of workers able to operate them for each scenario. The reduction of workers leads above all to reduced assembly skills in the best-case scenario. In the worst-case scenario all removed workers are skilled for all four processes, which reduces the number of testing-skilled workers to 19 out of 42 workers in Scenario 2c.

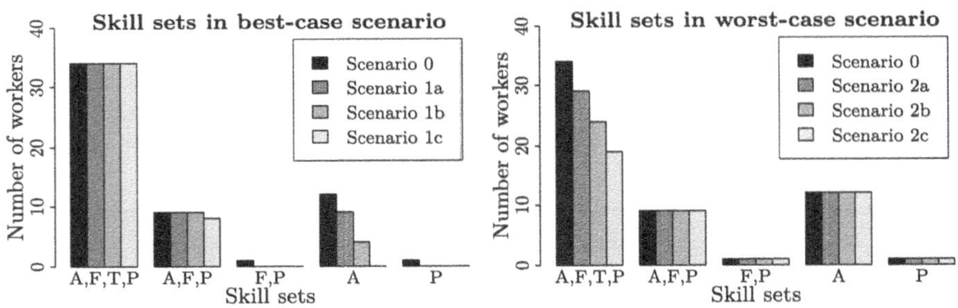

Fig. 2. Skill sets as combinations of processes of all workers in best-case and worst-case scenario

Considering seven different scenarios in seven weeks result in 49 test instances in total. The availabilities of all 49 instances are given in Table 6 as the average number of available workers per shift. The total number of workers is given in column $|W|$. The average number of available workers per shift throughout the week is given in the following columns (⌀W(w1) to ⌀W(w7)). Due to the lower bounds for the processes in Cell 1 and 2, at least five workers are needed to produce on Cells 1 and six for Cell 2, respectively. It follows that in every shift with less than 11 workers available, only one of both cells can produce orders. Weeks 3, 6, and 7 show fewer numbers of available workers than the other weeks.

5.2 Results

The model is implemented in C# with .NET 6.0 using Gurobi 9.5 as solver. All tests are performed on a Windows Server 2016 Standard with Intel(R) Xeon(R)

Table 6. Availability displayed as number of average available workers per shift

Scenario	$\|W\|$	⌀W(w1)	⌀W(w2)	⌀W(w3)	⌀W(w4)	⌀W(w5)	⌀W(w6)	⌀W(w7)
0	57	15.07	15.47	13.47	14.60	14.27	13.40	12.60
1a	52	13.67	14.40	12.40	13.53	13.73	12.47	11.53
2a	52	13.47	13.87	11.87	13.00	12.73	11.87	11.00
1b	47	12.67	13.40	10.87	12.07	12.13	11.33	10.40
2b	47	11.87	12.47	10.60	11.67	11.40	10.60	9.67
1c	42	11.33	11.80	9.87	10.73	10.53	10.00	8.93
2c	42	10.40	10.87	9.93	10.53	9.93	9.07	8.27

Gold 6136 CPU @ 3.0 GHz processors with 16 cores and 128 GB RAM. However, we limit the number of cores to 12, and the memory consumption is only a small fraction of the available memory.

31 of the 49 instances are solved to optimality in under one hour. Solutions with an optimality gap of 7.8 % on average are gained on another 16 instances. The two remaining instances could not be solved since they are infeasible. Table 7 gives an overview of all results in the appendix. The table includes the average number of cells opened per shift ($\varnothing C$) and the total number of shifts used for producing all orders ($|S|$). Considering only productive shifts result in a $\varnothing C$-value between 1 and 2 for each instance. Furthermore, the table shows the assignment rate of workers (Wor[%]), the objective value in minutes (Obj), the computational time in seconds (Time[s]), and the optimality gap (Gap[%]) grouped by best- and worst-case scenario.

The smaller instances of weeks 1 and 2 can be handled efficiently within one workweek regardless of how many and which workers are assigned to other cells and therefore not available. There are one to four shifts unused, which provide a buffer for further orders. Additionally, further workers are available within the used shifts. Figure 3 shows the assignment rates of the workers in all 15 shifts of Week 2 in scenarios 0 and 2a. The bars can be interpreted as follows. The heights of the bars give the total number of available workers, all assigned workers are marked in gray, and the white parts are not assigned and still available workers. The workers' assignment rates 80.48 % for Scenario 0 and 91 % in Scenario 2a given in the titles are calculated excluding unused shifts.

The orders of the third week could not be processed within one workweek in any of the scenarios. Even if all workers are available in Cells 1 and 2 (scenario 0), all orders that could not be completed in one workweek must be processed in two shifts on Monday of the following week. This is inadmissible since the next week is planned without those remaining orders of Week 3. To solve this issue, planners should consider bringing forward orders to previous weeks to avoid a delay.

The scenarios of Weeks 4, 5, 6, and 7 give mostly permissible solutions with all orders completed on Thursday or Friday of the corresponding week. The workers'

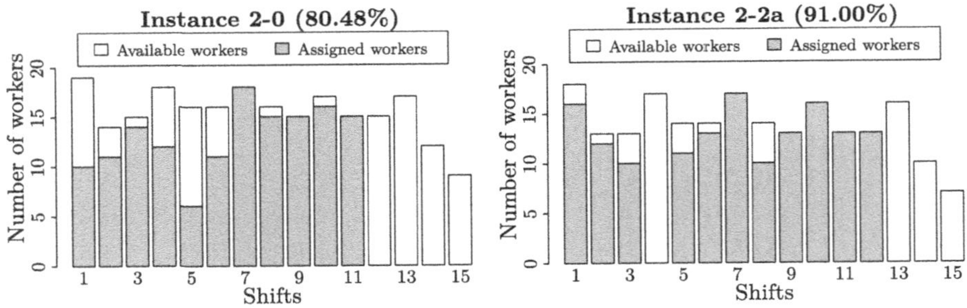

Fig. 3. Workers rate of assignment in Scenario 0 and 2a of Week 2

assignment rates are higher compared to Weeks 1 and 2. As an example, Fig. 4 shows scenarios 0 and 2a of Week 5 and can be interpreted analogously to Fig. 3.

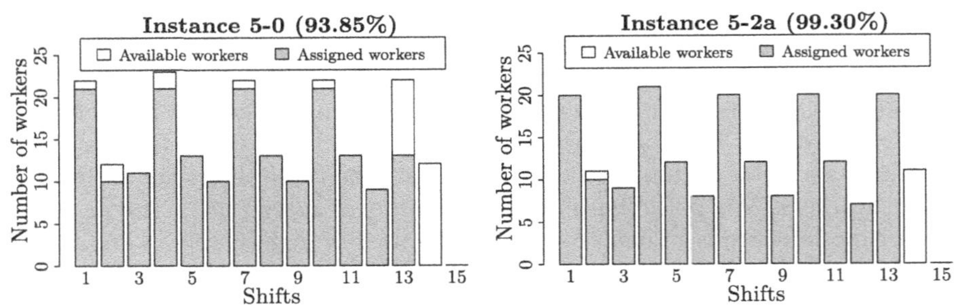

Fig. 4. Workers rate of assignment in Scenario 0 and 2a of Week 5

The following instances make an exception: 5–2b, 5–2c, 6–2c, 7–1c, and 7–2c. The three instances 5–2b, 5–2c, and 6–2c need one or several additional shifts in the following week and are therefore inadmissible. The instances of the seventh week with only 42 workers are infeasible. That is because it is the last week and orders can not be postponed. Since permissible solutions exist for all three weeks, planners should schedule the necessary workers for Cells 1 and 2.

The workstations are the second resource besides the workforce. The utilization of workstations differs between the processes. The average over all instances is 89.62 % for assembly, 82.76 % for final assembly, 66.25 % for testing, and 44.80 % for packing. The assembly workstations are utilized the most but they do not represent a bottleneck in any instance. The utilization of packing workstations is the smallest and indicates a low workload of the workers assigned to them. Note that even if a workstation is underutilized, a worker will be committed to the station for the entire 420-minute work period.

6 Conclusion and Future Research

This work studies a multi-shift worker assignment problem with a heterogeneous workforce in semi-automated electronics production. The problem includes two parallel cells, which differ in the level of automation. Additionally, it considers family setup times, stations with no need for a worker, and time limits for processing orders. This work introduces a mixed-integer linear program with the objective to minimize the makespan represented as the last used shift in the planning horizon. Seven weeks are solved in seven different scenarios, which leads to 49 real-world instances. With a time limit of one hour, all feasible instances are solved with an average optimality gap of 2.66 % using Gurobi. The solutions are practical input for production planners, which can be used as a planning basis. They reveal problems like insufficient workforce or conspicuously high numbers of orders to process within one week.

Various directions exist for further research. Firstly, future works can extend the problem by including all external cells to determine the optimal number and allocation of workers for Cells 1 and 2 simultaneously. Furthermore, softening the immutability of the worker assignment can improve the solution. The possibility of switching workstations or cells enables filling up workers' shifts. For example, workstation utilizations less than 50 % are predestined for assigning workers to two workstations within one shift. This means that one worker processes tasks on one workstation and switches stations halfway through. Furthermore, scheduling of the orders and tasks could be added to determine the best order sequence within a shift. Another option to improve the solution is to introduce work on Saturdays or the possibility of buying another robot. Those measures can be evaluated by including costs for assignments on weekends and additional automated stations. Multi-criteria approaches are suitable due to the trade-off between reducing makespan and increasing costs or vice versa. A further extension of the problem could be incorporating setup carry-over between shifts. Thereby, future works should strike a balance between solution improvement and the increase in complexity. Lastly, to realize longer planning horizons or to find a good solution early on, heuristic approaches such as metaheuristics or matheuristics can be developed.

Acknowledgements. The author would like to thank Tony Alexander of Siemens AG for his support in elaborating on the problem and obtaining the data.

Appendix

Table 7. Overview of the results of all test instances

W	Sce	Best-case scenario (1)						Worst-case scenario (2)					
		⌀C	|S|	Wor[%]	Obj	Time[s]	Gap[%]	⌀C	|S|	Wor[%]	Obj	Time[s]	Gap[%]
1	0	1.82	11	76.34	5700	382	0.00	1.82	11	76.34	5700	382	0.00
1	a	1.91	11	86.78	5700	318	0.00	1.73	11	82.45	5700	320	0.00
1	b	1.82	11	93.05	6180	338	0.00	1.58	12	86.56	6180	344	0.00
1	c	1.69	13	85.09	6660	3604	7.21	1.69	13	95.00	6660	342	0.00
2	0	1.91	11	80.48	5220	350	0.00	1.91	11	80.48	5220	350	0.00
2	a	1.64	11	81.00	5220	343	0.00	1.91	11	91.00	5700	605	0.00
2	b	1.36	11	81.69	5700	416	0.00	1.77	13	86.14	6180	3600	6.30
2	c	2.00	13	92.86	6180	430	0.00	1.86	14	93.06	6660	3601	5.93
3	0	1.94	16	97.82	10500	3601	4.02	1.94	16	97.82	10500	3601	4.02
3	a	2.00	18	99.31	11460	3602	7.44	1.83	18	100.00	11460	3601	3.72
3	b	1.79	19	96.31	11940	3601	3.59	1.60	20	97.07	12420	3601	3.46
3	c	1.59	22	97.52	13380	3601	9.31	1.43	21	96.38	12900	3600	8.79
4	0	1.83	12	92.52	5700	460	0.00	1.83	12	92.52	5700	460	0.00
4	a	1.83	12	97.85	5700	1932	0.00	1.92	13	96.15	6180	3603	6.30
4	b	1.69	13	99.30	6180	960	0.00	1.54	13	98.60	6180	3150	0.00
4	c	1.60	15	83.90	7140	3600	5.59	1.47	15	98.79	7140	3601	11.19
5	0	1.69	13	93.85	6180	3601	6.30	1.69	13	93.85	6180	3601	6.30
5	a	1.62	13	94.17	6180	1697	0.00	1.62	13	99.30	6180	1972	0.00
5	b	1.46	13	100.00	6180	2827	0.00	1.53	15	94.69	10020	3601	29.32
5	c	1.40	15	88.00	6660	2546	0.00	1.54	13	98.60	11460	3244	0.00
6	0	1.73	11	93.09	5700	2700	0.00	1.73	11	93.09	5700	2700	0.00
6	a	1.58	12	89.48	5700	2007	0.00	1.75	12	92.20	6180	1746	0.00
6	b	1.31	13	89.72	6180	1583	0.00	1.54	13	95.42	6180	1023	0.00
6	c	1.46	13	98.79	6180	2211	0.00	1.55	11	100.00	10500	1823	0.00
7	0	1.64	11	92.34	5220	326	0.00	1.64	11	92.34	5220	326	0.00
7	a	1.67	12	99.48	5700	3612	6.72	1.75	12	94.10	6180	423	0.00
7	b	1.69	13	99.36	6180	732	0.00	1.62	13	99.30	6660	1702	0.00
7	c	Infeasible						Infeasible					

References

1. Azadeh, A., Pashapour, S., Zadeh, S.A.: Designing a cellular manufacturing system considering decision style, skill and job security by NSGA-II and response surface methodology. Int. J. Prod. Res. **54**(22), 6825–6847 (2016). https://doi.org/10.1080/00207543.2016.1178407
2. Calzavara, M., Battini, D., Bogataj, D., Sgarbossa, F., Zennaro, I.: Ageing workforce management in manufacturing systems: state of the art and future research Agenda. Int. J. Prod. Res. **58**, 1–19 (2019). https://doi.org/10.1080/00207543.2019.1600759

3. Liu, R., Liu, M., Chu, F., Zheng, F., Chu, C.: Eco-friendly multi-skilled worker assignment and assembly line balancing problem. Comput. Ind. Eng. **151**(106944), 1–19 (2021). https://doi.org/10.1016/j.cie.2020.106944
4. McWilliams, D.L., Tetteh, E.G.: Managing lean DRC systems with demand uncertainty: an analytical approach. Int. J. Adv. Manuf. Technol. **45**(9–10), 1017–1032 (2009). https://doi.org/10.1007/s00170-009-2030-y
5. Moussavi, S.E., Mahdjoub, M., Grunder, O.: A multi-objective programming approach to develop an ergonomic job rotation in a manufacturing system. IFAC-PapersOnLine **51**(11), 850–855 (2018). https://doi.org/10.1016/j.ifacol.2018.08.445
6. Niakan, F., Baboli, A., Moyaux, T., Botta-Genoulaz, V.: A bi-objective model in sustainable dynamic cell formation problem with skill-based worker assignment. J. Manuf. Syst. **38**, 46–62 (2016). https://doi.org/10.1016/j.jmsy.2015.11.001
7. Polat, O., Kalayci, C.B., Mutlu, Ö., Gupta, S.M.: A two-phase variable neighbourhood search algorithm for assembly line worker assignment and balancing problem type-II: an industrial case study. Int. J. Prod. Res. **54**(3), 722–741 (2016). https://doi.org/10.1080/00207543.2015.1055344
8. Ritt, M., Costa, A.M., Miralles, C.: The assembly line worker assignment and balancing problem with stochastic worker availability. Int. J. Prod. Res. **54**(3), 907–922 (2016). https://doi.org/10.1080/00207543.2015.1108534
9. Tamke, F., Schiebold, N.: Multi-skilled worker assignment problem in multi-shift cell manufacturing. In: Buscher, U., Lasch, R., Schönberger, J. (eds.) Logistics Management. LNL, pp. 151–164. Springer, Cham (2021). https://doi.org/10.1007/978-3-030-85843-8_10
10. Zheng, X., Ning, S., Sun, H., Zhong, J., Tong, X.: Solving multi-objective two-sided assembly line balancing problems by harmony search algorithm based on pareto entropy. IEEE Access **9**, 121728–121742 (2021). https://doi.org/10.1109/access.2021.3108818

Author Index

The manufacturer's authorised representative in the EU is Springer Nature Customer Service Centre GmbH, Europaplatz 3, 69115 Heidelberg, Germany. If you have any concerns regarding our products, please contact ProductSafety@springernature.com

Printed and bound by CPI Group (UK) Ltd, Croydon, CR0 4YY
28/09/2026
02224064-0004